Lecture Notes in Computer Science 8553

Commenced Publication in 1973
Founding and Former Series Editors:
Gerhard Goos, Juris Hartmanis, and Jan van Leeuwen

Oscar H. Ibarra
Lila Kari
Steffen Kopecki (Eds.)

Unconventional Computation and Natural Computation

13th International Conference, UCNC 2014
London, ON, Canada, July 14-18, 2014
Proceedings

 Springer

Volume Editors

Oscar H. Ibarra
University of California
Department of Computer Science
Santa Barbara, CA 93106, USA
E-mail: ibarra@cs.ucsb.edu

Lila Kari
Steffen Kopecki
University of Western Ontario
Department of Computer Science
London, ON N6A 5B7, Canada
E-mail: {lila, steffen}@csd.uwo.ca

ISSN 0302-9743   e-ISSN 1611-3349
ISBN 978-3-319-08122-9   e-ISBN 978-3-319-08123-6
DOI 10.1007/978-3-319-08123-6
Springer Cham Heidelberg New York Dordrecht London

Library of Congress Control Number: 2014940804

LNCS Sublibrary: SL 1 – Theoretical Computer Science and General Issues

Typesetting: Camera-ready by author, data conversion by Scientific Publishing Services, Chennai, India

Printed on acid-free paper

Springer is part of Springer Science+Business Media (www.springer.com)

Preface

The International Conference on Unconventional Computation and Natural Computation, UCNC, is an interdisciplinary meeting where scientists with different backgrounds, yet sharing a common interest in novel forms of computation, human-designed computation inspired by nature, and the computational aspects of processes taking place in nature, present their latest theoretical or experimental results. The topics of the conference typically include:

Molecular computing	Cellular automata	Computational
Quantum computing	Neural computation	systems biology:
Optical computing	Evolutionary	○ genetic networks
Chaos computing	computation	○ protein–protein
Physarum computing	Swarm intelligence	networks
Hyperbolic space	Ant algorithms	○ transport networks
computation	Artificial immune	Computational
Collision-based	systems	neuroscience
computing	Artificial life	Synthetic biology
Super-Turing	Membrane computing	Cellular (in vivo)
computation	Amorphous computing	computing

The first edition of UCNC (formerly called Unconventional Models of Computation and Unconventional Computation) was held at the Centre for Discrete Mathematics and Theoretical Computer Science, Auckland, New Zealand, in 1998, and the conference logo became the logo of its first host. Subsequent sites of the conference were Brussels, Belgium, in 2000, Kobe, Japan, in 2002, Seville, Spain, in 2005, York, UK, in 2006, Kingston, Canada, in 2007, Vienna, Austria, in 2008, Ponta Delgada, Portugal, in 2009, Tokyo, Japan, in 2010, Turku, Finland, in 2011, Orléans, France, in 2012, and Milan, Italy, in 2013.

The 13th edition in this conference series, UCNC 2014, was organized in London, Ontario, Canada, in the Deparment of Computer Science of the University of Western Ontario, during the week of July 14–18, 2014.

The meeting was pleased to have four distinguished invited speakers who presented talks touching on several UCNC topics:

- Yaakov Benenson (ETH Zürich), "Molecular Computing Meets Synthetic Biology"
- Charles H. Bennett (IBM T. J. Watson Research Center), "From Quantum Dynamics to Physical Complexity"
- Hod Lipson (Cornell University), "The Robotic Scientist: Distilling Natural Laws from Experimental Data, from Cognitive Robotics to Computational Biology"
- Nadrian C. Seeman (New York University), "DNA: Not Merely the Secret of Life – Using the Information in DNA to Control Molecular Structure"

The meeting was also pleased to have three distinguished invited tutorial speakers:

- Anne Condon (University of British Columbia), "Programming with Chemical Reaction Networks and DNA Strand Displacement Systems"
- Ming Li (University of Waterloo), "Approximating Semantics"
- Tommaso Toffoli (Boston University), "Do We Compute to Live, or Live to Compute? Entropy Pumps, Evolution vs Emergence, and the Risks of Success"

This year, in response to the Call for Papers, there were 79 articles submitted by authors from 30 countries. Each paper was reviewed by at least three referees and discussed by the members of the Program Committee. Finally, 31 papers were selected for oral presentation at the conference and inclusion in these proceedings.

The conference has a long history of hosting workshops. The 2014 edition in London hosted three workshops:

- "DNA Computing by Self-assembly," organized by Matthew Patitz, with invited speakers Scott Summers and Damien Woods (Tuesday, July 15)
- "Computational Neuroscience," organized by Mark Daley, with invited speakers Randy McIntosh and William Cunningham (Thursday, July 17)
- "Unconventional Computation in Europe," organized by Martyn Amos and Susan Stepney, with invited speaker Ricard Solé (Friday, July 18)

We are grateful for the support of the FIELDS Institute for Research in Mathematical Sciences, the PERIMETER Institute for Theoretical Physics, the Department of Computer Science and the Faculty of Science of the University of Western Ontario, Research Western, IBM, and the Rotman Institute of Philosophy.

We thank all those who have contributed to this meeting. In particular, we thank the invited speakers, the contributing authors, the referees, the members of the Program Committee, the members of the Steering Committee, the local organizers and the Student Volunteer Team, all of whose efforts have contributed to the practical and scientific success of the meeting.

July 2014

Oscar H. Ibarra
Lila Kari
Steffen Kopecki

Organization

Program Committee

Andrew Adamatzky	University of the West of England, UK
Selim G. Akl	Queen's University, Canada
Eshel Ben-Jacob	Tel Aviv University, Israel
Cristian S. Calude	University of Auckland, New Zealand
José Félix Costa	IST University of Lisbon, Portugal
Erzsébet Csuhaj-Varjú	Eötvös Loránd University, Hungary
Alberto Dennunzio	University of Milano-Bicocca, Italy
Marco Dorigo	Université Libre de Bruxelles, Belgium
Jérôme Durand-Lose	University of Orléans, France
Masami Hagiya	University of Tokyo, Japan
Oscar H. Ibarra	University of California, Santa Barbara, USA (Co-chair)
Kazuo Iwama	Kyoto University, Japan
Jarkko Kari	University of Turku, Finland
Lila Kari	University of Western Ontario, Canada (Co-chair)
Viv Kendon	University of Leeds, UK
Kamala Krithivasan	IIT Madras, India
Giancarlo Mauri	University of Milano-Bicocca, Italy
Yongli Mi	Hong Kong University of Science and Technology, China
Mario J. Pérez-Jiménez	University of Seville, Spain
Kai Salomaa	Queen's University, Canada
Hava Siegelmann	University of Massachusetts Amherst, USA
Susan Stepney	University of York, UK
Damien Woods	California Institute of Technology, USA
Byoung-Tak Zhang	Seoul National University, Korea

Steering Committee

Thomas Bäck	Leiden University, The Netherlands
Cristian S. Calude	University of Auckland, New Zealand (Founding Chair)
Lov K. Grover	Bell Labs, USA
Nataša Jonoska	University of South Florida, USA (Co-chair)
Jarkko Kari	University of Turku, Finland (Co-chair)
Lila Kari	University of Western Ontario, Canada

Seth Lloyd   Massachusetts Institute of Technology, USA
Giancarlo Mauri   University of Milano-Bicocca, Italy
Gheorghe Păun   Institute of Mathematics of the Romanian
                            Academy, Romania
Grzegorz Rozenberg   Leiden University, The Netherlands
                            (Emeritus Chair)
Arto Salomaa   University of Turku, Finland
Tommaso Toffoli   Boston University, USA
Carme Torras   Institute of Robotics and Industrial
                            Informatics, Spain
Jan van Leeuwen   Utrecht University, The Netherlands

Organizing Committee

Mark Daley   University of Western Ontario, Canada
Helmut Jürgensen   University of Western Ontario, Canada
Lila Kari   University of Western Ontario, Canada (Chair)
Steffen Kopecki   University of Western Ontario, Canada
Stephen Watt   University of Western Ontario, Canada

Student Volunteer Team

Rallis Karamichalis   University of Western Ontario, Canada
Manasi Kulkarni   University of Western Ontario, Canada
Srujan Kumar Enaganti   University of Western Ontario, Canada
Amirhossein Simjour   University of Western Ontario, Canada
Tina Wu   University of Western Ontario, Canada

Additional Reviewers

Arrighi, Pablo   Dinneen, Michael   Gutiérrez-Naranjo,
Barr, Katie   Domaratzki, Mike   Miguel A.
Bazso, Fulop   Doty, David   Han, Yo-Sub
Becker, Florent   Elias, Susan   Harju, Tero
Beretta, Stefano   Eom, Hae-Sung   Hickinbotham, Simon
Besozzi, Daniela   Fates, Nazim   Hirvensalo, Mika
Bienvenu, Laurent   Fazekas, Szilard Zsolt Hunyadvári, László
Borello, Alex   Ferretti, Claudio   Imai, Katsunobu
Bown, James   Gajardo, Anahi   Jonoska, Nataša
Cabajal, Juan   Gopinath, Ashwin   Kaced, Tarik
Cabessa, Jeremie   Gorecki, Jerzy   Kanter, Ido
Capobianco, Silvio   Graça, Daniel   Kawamata, Ibuki
Castelli, Mauro   Guillon, Pierre   Ko, Sang-Ki

Kobayashi, Satoshi
Kolonits, Gábor
Kurka, Petr
Lakin, Matthew R.
Lázár, Katalin A.
Leporati, Alberto
Lu, Mingyang
Ma, Xiongfeng
Macías-Ramos,
   Luis Felipe
Manea, Florin
Manzoni, Luca
Marchetti, Luca
Marion, Jean-Yves
Mercaş, Robert
Metta, Padma
Meunier, Pierre-Étienne
Miller, Julian
Moisset De Espanes,
   Pablo
Murphy, Niall

Mutyam, Madhu
Nair, Achuthsankar
Neary, Turlough
Nobile, Marco
Palioudakis, Alexandros
Pescini, Dario
Polack, Fiona
Porreca, Antonio E.
Poulding, Simon
Poupet, Victor
Pradella, Matteo
Proctor, Timothy
Rahman, Afroza
Rama, Raghavan
Ramanujan, Ajeesh
Richard, Gaétan
Riscos-Núñez, Agustín
Romashchenko, Andrei
Romero-Campero,
   Francisco J.
Salo, Ville

Saubion, Frédéric
Schulman, Rebecca
Seki, Shinnosuke
Sobot, Robert
Song, Bosheng
Stannett, Mike
Stefanovic, Darko
Summers, Scott
Svozil, Karl
Szabados, Michal
Thachuk, Chris
Tichler, Krisztián
Timmis, Jon
Timperley, Chris
Unold, Olgierd
Winslow, Andrew
Yokomori, Takashi
Zandron, Claudio
Zizza, Rosalba

Sponsors

We deeply thank the sponsors that made UCNC 2014 possible.

Fields Institute for Research in Mathematical Sciences
http://www.fields.utoronto.ca/

Perimeter Institute for Theoretical Physics
http://www.perimeterinstitute.ca/

IBM
http://www.ibm.com/

University of Western Ontario
http://www.uwo.ca/
Department of Computer Science
Faculty of Science
Research Western
Rotman Institute of Philosophy

Invited Talks

Molecular Computing Meets Synthetic Biology

Yaakov Benenson

Synthetic Biology Group
Department of Biosystems Science and Engineering
ETH Zürich, Mattenstrasse 26, 4058 Basel, Switzerland

Abstract. One of the motivations behind computing with molecules is to "computerize" living systems, for example to prevent disease or control artificial tissues. Biology, however, is already very good at computing — the human brain being one example. Even on a single cell level information is constantly being processed, and the development of a functional organism from a single fertilized cell is controlled by an ingenious if only partially understood program encoded in DNA. Does this mean that the efforts to "write" new molecular programs are redundant? Not at all — natural programs have taken three billion years to evolve and, despite their beauty, are very difficult to alter in any way.

In my view the optimal approach is to balance the engineering principles inspired by computer science and engineering, such as universal models, reprogrammability, modularity, etc., with the harsh reality of cell and organismal biology. The simple fact is that we do not know yet, even at the theory level, whether it is possible to perform reliable information processing in actual living cells as opposed to idealized "well-mixed reactors". Despite these limitations, the field of molecular computing in cells, or biological computing, has made significant steps forward with new design principles, new architectures, and new exciting experimental results. These developments also inform basic biological research.

From Quantum Dynamics to Physical Complexity

Charles H. Bennett

IBM Research, Thomas J. Watson Research Center
Yorktown Heights, NY 10598, USA

Abstract. Quantum effects in information processing, aside from making possible feats like quantum cryptography and Shor's factoring algorithm, have led to more coherent and powerful ways of thinking about information, computation, and cosmology. We review this approach, especially the uniquely private form of correlation known as entanglement, whose very pervasiveness makes it hard to detect, allowing it to remain undiscovered until the 20th century. In combination with thermal disequilbrium, entanglement helps us understand why the future is more uncertain than the past, and how our world produces structures that are logically "deep", having internal evidence of a complicated history, an idea that can be made precise using the tools of algorithmic information and computational complexity. Finally we consider the Boltzmann brain problem afflicting many modern cosmologies, where similar structures are predicted to fluctuate into existence even at thermal equilibrium, bearing false evidence of a complicated history that never happened.

The Robotic Scientist
Distilling Natural Laws from Experimental Data, from Cognitive Robotics to Computational Biology

Hod Lipson

Sibley School of Mechanical and Aerospace Engineering, Cornell University
Ithaca, NY 14853-7501, USA

Abstract. Can machines discover scientific laws automatically? Despite the prevalence of computing power, the process of finding natural laws and their corresponding equations has resisted automation. We will outline a series of recent research projects, starting with self-reflecting robotic systems, and ending with machines that can formulate hypotheses, design experiments, and interpret the results, to discover new scientific laws. We will then present examples from psychology to cosmology, from classical physics to modern physics, from big science to small science.

Reference

1. Schmidt, M., Lipson, H.: Distilling free-form natural laws from experimental data. Science 324(5923), 81–85 (2009)

DNA: Not Merely the Secret of Life
Using the Information in DNA to Control Molecular Structure*

Nadrian C. Seeman

Chemistry Department, New York University
New York, NY 10003, USA

Abstract. Our laboratory is investigating unusual DNA molecules in model systems that use synthetic molecules. A major effort in our laboratory is devoted to DNA nanotechnology. The attachment of specific sticky ends to a DNA branched junction enables the construction of stick figures, whose edges are double-stranded DNA. This approach has already been used to assemble a cube, a truncated octahedron, nanomechanical devices and 2D crystals and 3D crystals from DNA. Ultimate goals for this approach include the assembly of a biochip computer, nanorobotics and nanofabrication and the exploitation of the rational synthesis of periodic matter.

Thus, we build branched DNA species that can be joined using Watson-Crick base pairing to produce N-connected objects and lattices. We have used ligation to construct DNA topological targets, such as knots, polyhedral catenanes, Borromean rings and a Solomon's knot. Branched junctions with up to 12 arms have been made.

Nanorobotics is a key area of application. We have made robust 2-state and 3-state sequence-dependent devices and bipedal walkers. We have constructed a molecular assembly line using a DNA origami layer and three 2-state devices, so that there are eight different states represented by their arrangements. We have demonstrated that all eight products can be built from this system.

A central goal of DNA nanotechnology is the self-assembly of periodic matter. We have constructed 2D DNA arrays with designed patterns from many different motifs. We have used DNA scaffolding to organize active DNA components. We have used pairs of 2-state devices to capture a variety of different DNA targets.

One of the key aims of DNA-based materials research is to construct complex material patterns that can be reproduced. We have built such a system from bent TX molecules, which can reach 2 generations of replication. This system represents a first step in self-reproducing materials. We are making progress towards selection of self-replicating materials.

* This research has been supported by the NIGMS, NSF, ARO, ONR, DOE and the Gordon and Betty Moore Foundation.

Recently, we have self-assembled a 3D crystalline array and have solved its crystal structure to 3Å resolution, using unbiased crystallographic methods. We can use crystals with two molecules in the crystallographic repeat to control the color of the crystals. Thus, structural DNA nanotechnology has fulfilled its initial goal of controlling the structure of DNA in three dimensions. A new era in nanoscale control and molecular programming awaits us.

Invited Tutorials

Programming with Chemical Reaction Networks and DNA Strand Displacement Systems

Anne Condon

Department of Computer Science, University of British Columbia
Vancouver, BC, V6T 1Z4, Canada

Abstract. Chemical reaction networks (CRNs) and DNA strand displacement systems (DSDs) are widely-studied and useful models of molecular programming. In this tutorial, we introduce the models, illustrating the expressive power of CRNs as a molecular programming language and how CRNs can be compiled into lower-level, physically realizable DNA strand displacement systems. We characterize the power of CRNs in terms of well known complexity classes, describe connections with reversible and distributed computing models, and discuss limits to computing with CRNs. Finally, we discuss directions for future research that could advance our understanding of these models and the possibilities for efficient molecular programs.

Bio-molecules do remarkable things in our cells, including information processing, communication and transportation. Recent technological advances have enabled scientists to design and program simple DNA molecular systems with a variety of computational and functional capabilities, many of which already exceed the roles of DNA in the cell. Bio-molecules are interesting to program because of their dynamic structural and material properties, because they enable us to organize matter at the nano-scale and because they can naturally interact with biological systems at the cellular level. It is hard to imagine a future in which programming molecules will not be central to understanding and mediating cellular and other nano-scale processes.

So, how can we program molecules? Researchers in the field of DNA computing and molecular programming have developed many creative approaches, along with experimental demonstrations of the viability of these approaches. In this tutorial I'll focus on two such approaches, namely Chemical Reaction Networks (CRNs) [3,9,8] and DNA Strand Displacement Systems (DSDs) [12,15].

CRNs are a distributed computing model in which, starting from an initial pool of molecules, consisting of duplicates from a finite set of species, reactions ensue that consume and produce species, thereby converging on an "outcome" pool that indicates the result of a computation. CRNs are interesting in part because they model chemical system kinetics - the basis for biological information processing - and in part because they provide a very natural level of abstraction in which to design and reason about molecular processes.

DSD programs model a lower level of abstraction than CRNs. At their core is a basic primitive whereby an initially unbound input DNA strand I binds to a template T, thereby displacing an output strand O that was initially bound to T

so that O becomes unbound. Strand O can in turn act as input for a subsequent displacement. DSDs are collections of strands that can change configurations, i.e., which strands are bound and which are unbound, via successive strand displacements in a pre-programmed fashion, ultimately producing unbound strands that encode the result of a computation. There have been successful experimental demonstrations of DSD designs that realize logic circuits and even artificial neurons [5, 6].

In this tutorial, we'll describe why CRNs and DSDs are interesting programming models, what we know about effective ways to write CRN and DSD programs, and what are important directions for further progress. For example, CRNs can be "compiled" into DSDs [1, 9, 10], CRNs and thus DSDs can in principle provide an energy efficient realization of CRNs [13, 7, 10, 14].

Several approaches for deterministicially computing with CRNs have been studied. In this context, resources such as time, volume (i.e., space needed to store species as a computation proceeds), and energy are important. In some models, quantities are represented by the number of copies, or count, of a molecule. A computation is considered to have completed when the count of designated output species is stable, i.e., will not change regardless of which applicable reactions ensue. Such models are typically uniform, in the sense that the number of species needed to specify an algorithm is independent of the input size. Connections with population protocols, a distributed computing model, has provided valuable insights on the resources needed to compute with such models. Variants of these uniform models, in which molecular polymers can represent a stack data structure, can simulate Turing-general models of computation [7, 4]. In other, non-uniform models, the presence or absence of molecular species represent bit values and thus, like (non-uniform) circuit models of computation, the number of species needed for a computation is a function of the input length. It is possible to design non-uniform DSDs that "recycle" molecules by running reversible reactions or displacements in both forwards and reverse directions, so that t steps of the system use just $O(\log t)$ molecules [2, 11] and thus have limited volume.

A limitation of some designed DSDs [4, 2] is that, in order for them to compute correctly, a single copy of some reactants should be present initially. It is currently impractical to obtain the exact numbers in a wet lab. When multiple copies of all initial molecules are present, correctness requires that the length of the shortest sequence of reactions needed to produce any given molecule is bounded by a polynomial function of the (appropriately measured) size of the CRN [2].

There are many interesting directions for future research. Techniques are needed for establishing the correctness of even quite simple CRNs. Better mechanisms are needed for translating CRNs to physically realizable DSDs that can be implemented robustly in the face of errors. More work is needed to understand what can be computed reversibly and with limited volume. Such research, grounded in an appreciation for and understanding of thermodynamics and kinetics, as well as the potential and limitations of experimental systems, can help lay the foundations of an exciting new discipline.

References

1. Chen, H.-L., Doty, D., Soloveichik, D.: Deterministic function computation with chemical reaction networks. In: Stefanovic, D., Turberfield, A. (eds.) DNA 18 2012. LNCS, vol. 7433, pp. 25–42. Springer, Heidelberg (2012)
2. Condon, A., Hu, A.J., Maňuch, J., Thachuk, C.: Less haste, less waste: On recycling and its limits in strand displacement systems. J. R. Soc. Interface (2012)
3. Cook, M., Soloveichik, D., Winfree, E., Bruck, J.: Programmability of chemical reaction networks. Algorithmic Bioprocesses 133, 543–584 (2009)
4. Qian, L., Soloveichik, D., Winfree, E.: Efficient Turing-universal computation with DNA polymers. In: Sakakibara, Y., Mi, Y. (eds.) DNA 16 2010. LNCS, vol. 6518, pp. 123–140. Springer, Heidelberg (2011)
5. Qian, L., Winfree, E.: Scaling up digital circuit computation with DNA strand displacement cascades. Science 332, 1196–1201 (2011)
6. Qian, L., Winfree, E., Bruck, J.: Neural network computation with DNA strand displacement cascades. Nature 475, 368–372 (2011)
7. Seelig, G., Soloveichik, D., Zhang, D.Y., Winfree, E.: Enzyme-free nucleic acid logic circuits. Science 314(5805), 1585–1588 (2006)
8. Soloveichik, D.: Robust stochastic chemical reaction networks and bounded tau-leaping. J. Comput. Biol. 16(3), 501–522 (2009)
9. Soloveichik, D., Cook, M., Winfree, E., Bruck, J.: Computation with finite stochastic chemical reaction networks. Nat. Comp. 7, 615–633 (2008)
10. Soloveichik, D., Seelig, G., Winfree, E.: DNA as a universal substrate for chemical kinetics. Proc. Nat. Acad. Sci. USA 107(12), 5393–5398 (2010)
11. Thachuk, C., Condon, A.: Space and energy efficient computation with DNA strand displacement systems. In: Stefanovic, D., Turberfield, A. (eds.) DNA 2012. LNCS, vol. 7433, pp. 135–149. Springer, Heidelberg (2012)
12. Yurke, B., Mills, A.P.: Using DNA to power nanostructures. Genet. Program Evolvable Mach. 4(2), 111–122 (2003)
13. Yurke, B., Turberfield, A.J., Mills, A.P., Simmel, F.C., Neumann, J.L.: A DNA-fuelled molecular machine made of DNA. Nature 406, 605–608 (2000)
14. Zhang, D.Y., Seelig, G.: Dynamic DNA nanotechnology using strand displacement reactions. Nature Chemistry 3, 103–113 (2011)
15. Zhang, D.Y., Turberfield, A.J., Yurke, B., Winfree, E.: Engineering entropy-driven reactions and networks catalyzed by DNA. Science 318, 1121–1125 (2007)

Approximating Semantics[*]

Ming Li

David R. Cheriton School of Computer Science, University of Waterloo
Waterloo, Ontario N2L 3G1, Canada

Abstract. Latent search engines and question-answering (QA) engines
fundamentally depend on our intuitive notion of semantics and semantic
distance. However, such a semantic distance is likely undefinable, certainly un-computable, and often blindly approximated. Can we develop
a theoretical framework for this area?

We will describe a theory, using the well-defined information distance,
to approximate the elusive semantic distance such that it is mathematically proven that our approximation is "better than" any computable
approximation of the intuitive concept of semantic distance. Although
information distance itself is obviously also not computable, it does allow
a natural approximation by compression, especially with the availability
of big data. We will then describe a natural language encoding system
to implement our theory followed by experiments on a QA system.

---

[*] This work is supported in part by NSERC Grant OGP0046506, OCRiT Grant
115354, IDRC Research Chair in Information Technology, Project Number:
104519-006, CFI ORF equipment grant, and the CRC Program.

Do We Compute to Live, or Live to Compute?
Entropy Pumps, Evolution vs Emergence,
and the Risks of Success

Tommaso Toffoli

Department of Electrical and Computer Engineering
Boston University, Boston, MA 02215, USA

Abstract. We shall show that, in a "multiuser" world, strict immortality in the long term is a *contradiction in terms*. Next best, then, what is a good strategy for *at least some part* of me to still be present in a large proportion of samples of the future? Perhaps long individual life, many identical clones, continual repair, sexual reproduction, uploading myself to the cloud, or what else?

Even if for sake of argument I grant that "survival of the fittest" is a mere tautology, so that 'fittest' just means "whoever survives" (a fatalistic *que sera sera*; cf. analogous tautological constructs such as "the invisible hand of the marketplace"), I am still left with the fundamental question: What kinds of structure have what it takes to survive *in my current environment*? In other words, for a given natural or artificial environment, what properties of a complex structure give it a chance to enjoy permanence in it? It is remarkable, but perhaps not too surprising, that this problem may have quite different solutions depending on the time scale one has in mind (as we shall see, there are "greedy" strategies that can promise short-term permanence but virtually guarantee long-term disappearance).

'Apparition' and 'permanence' are key features of all sorts of *emergent systems* — and these are found virtually whenever there is available an *entropy pump*. *Lifelike* systems are emergent systems that have been caught in a special kind of positive-feedback loop: a *runaway* (at least for a while) loop with *branching tracks*, so that from the same initial conditions different "historical developments" are potentially available.

Evolution may be seen as a special case of emergence, namely, the development and interplay of a *tangled hierarchy* of emergent systems some of which are lifelike. We shall be specially interested in the nature of the entropy pumps on which emergent systems are dependent, and in the hierarchy of entropy pumps — the "entropy cascade" — that drives evolution. In this context, we shall present a novel way to look at both entropy and computation.

Table of Contents

Five Nodes Are Sufficient for Hybrid Networks of Evolutionary Processors to Be Computationally Complete

Artiom Alhazov[1], Rudolf Freund[2], and Yurii Rogozhin[1]

[1] Institute of Mathematics and Computer Science, Academy of Sciences of Moldova
Academiei 5, MD-2028, Chişinău, Moldova
{artiom,rogozhin}@math.md
[2] Faculty of Informatics, Vienna University of Technology
Favoritenstr. 9, 1040 Vienna, Austria
rudi@emcc.at

Abstract. A hybrid network of evolutionary processors (HNEP) is a graph where each node is associated with a special rewriting system called an evolutionary processor, an input filter, and an output filter. Each evolutionary processor is given a finite set of one type of point mutations (insertion, deletion or a substitution of a symbol) which can be applied to certain positions in a string. An HNEP rewrites the strings in the nodes and then re-distributes them according to a filter-based communication protocol; the filters are defined by certain variants of random-context conditions. HNEPs can be considered both as languages generating devices (GHNEPs) and language accepting devices (AHNEPs); most previous approaches treated the accepting and generating cases separately. For both cases, in this paper we improve previous results by showing that five nodes are sufficient to accept (AHNEPs) or generate (GHNEPs) any recursively enumerable language by showing the more general result that any partial recursive relation can be computed by an HNEP with (at most) five nodes.

1 Introduction

Networks of Evolutionary Processors (NEPs) were introduced in [10] as a model of string processing distributed over a graph. The nodes of the graph contain the processors that carry out operations of insertion, deletion, and substitution, which reflect basic biological processes known as point mutations. Models based on these operations are of particular interest in formal language theory due to the simplicity of these operations. In NEPs, an evolutionary processor is located at every node of a graph and processes objects, for example (finite) sets of strings. The system functions by rewriting the collections of objects present in the nodes and then re-distributing the resulting objects according to a communication protocol defined by a filtering mechanism. The language determined by the network is defined as the set of objects which appear at some distinguished node in the course of the computation. NEPs are models inspired by cell biology,

O.H. Ibarra et al. (Eds.): UCNC 2014, LNCS 8553, pp. 1–13, 2014.
DOI: 10.1007/978-3-319-08123-6_1, © Springer International Publishing Switzerland 2014

since each processor represents a cell performing point mutations of DNA and controlling its passage inside and outside the cell through a filtering mechanism. The evolutionary processor corresponds to the cell, the generated string to a DNA strand, and the operations insertion, deletion, and substitution of a symbol to the point mutations. By using an appropriate filtering mechanism, NEPs with a very small number of nodes are very powerful computational devices: already with two nodes, they are as powerful as Turing machines, see [4].

Special variants of these devices are the so-called *hybrid networks of evolutionary processors* (HNEPs), where each language processor performs only one of the above operations on a certain position of the strings in that node. Furthermore, the filters are defined by some variants of random-context conditions, i.e., they check the presence and the absence of certain symbols in the strings. These constructs can be considered both as language generating and accepting devices, i.e., generating HNEPs (GHNEPs) and accepting HNEPS (AHNEPs). The notion of an HNEP, as a language generating device, was introduced in [19], and the concept of an AHNEP was defined in [18].

In [11] it was shown that, for an alphabet V, GHNEPs with $27 + 3 \cdot card(V)$ nodes are computationally complete. For specific variants of AHNEPs, in [16] it was shown that 31 nodes are sufficient for recognizing any recursively enumerable language (irrespectively of the size of the alphabet); the result was improved considerably in [17] where the number of necessary nodes was reduced to 24. In the following, the results were significantly improved: AHNEPs and GHNEPs of the specific types as defined above were shown to be computationally complete already with 10 nodes in [1] and only 7 nodes in [2,3]. Then, in [15] it was claimed that accepting can be done with 6 nodes.

In this paper, we prove that *HNEPs are already computationally complete with five nodes*, i.e., any recursively enumerable language can already be generated or accepted by an HNEP having at most 5 nodes. In fact, we even show that any partial recursive relation can be computed by an HNEP with at most five nodes. This upper bound of five nodes improves previous results, see [3] and [15]. As it is known that the families of *HNEPs with two nodes are not computationally complete* (see [8]), the gap for HNEPs between being computationally complete or not now has already become very small.

2   Definitions

We start by recalling some basic notions of formal language theory. An alphabet is a non-empty finite set. A finite sequence of symbols from an alphabet V is called a *string* over V. The set of all strings over V is denoted by V^*; the *empty string* is denoted by λ; moreover, we define $V^+ = V^* \setminus \{\lambda\}$. The *length* of a string x is denoted by $|x|$, and by $|x|_a$ we denote the number of occurrences of a letter a in a string x. For a string x, *alph(x)* denotes the smallest alphabet Σ such that $x \in \Sigma^*$. For more details of formal language theory the reader is referred to the monographs and handbooks in this area as [22] and [21].

Remark 1. In this paper, string rewriting systems as Turing machines, Post systems, etc. are called *computationally complete* if these systems are able to compute any partial recursive relation R on stings over any alphabet U, i.e., $R \subseteq (U^*)^m \times (U^*)^n$, for some $m, n \geq 0$. As input and output alphabet for these systems we assume to take $T = U \cup \{\$\}$, where $\$$ is a special delimiter separating the components of an input vector $(w_1, \ldots, w_m)$ and an output vector $(v_1, \ldots, v_n)$, $w_i \in U^*$, $1 \leq i \leq m$, $v_j \in U^*$, $1 \leq j \leq n$. In that sense, any relation $R \subseteq (U^*)^m \times (U^*)^n$ can also be considered as a special relation $R' \subseteq T^* \times T^*$.

Remark 2. Computational completeness in the usual sense with respect to acceptance and generation directly follows from this general kind of computational completeness, as any recursively enumerable language L can be viewed as partial recursive relation $L \times \{\lambda\}$ (acceptance) and $\{\lambda\} \times L$ (generation); λ can be replaced by any arbitrary string. For the accepting case, we can even take any relation R whose second component is L, which corresponds to take $\{u \in U^* \mid uRv, \ v \in U^*\}$ as the accepted language and also is the usual way how acceptance is defined in the previous papers on networks of evolutionary processors. The results proved in this paper, establishing acceptance even when restricting the second component, obviously also hold true for the case when taking the more relaxed original definitions.

2.1 Hybrid Networks of Evolutionary Processors

For introducing the notions concerning evolutionary processors and hybrid networks, we mainly follow [11] . These language processors use so-called *evolutionary operations*, simple rewriting rules which abstract local gene mutations.

For an alphabet V, let $a \to b$ be a rewriting rule with $a, b \in V \cup \{\lambda\}$; we call this rule a *substitution rule* if both a and b are different from λ; we call it a *deletion rule* if $a \neq \lambda$ and $b = \lambda$ and an *insertion rule* if $a = \lambda$ and $b \neq \lambda$. The set of all substitution rules, deletion rules, and insertion rules over an alphabet V is denoted by Sub_V, Del_V, and Ins_V, respectively. Given such rules $\pi \equiv a \to b \in Sub_V$, $\rho \equiv a \to \lambda \in Del_V$, and $\sigma \equiv \lambda \to a \in Ins_V$ as well as a string $w \in V^*$, we define the following *actions* of π, ρ, σ on w:

$$
\begin{aligned}
\pi^*(w) &= \{ubv \mid w = uav, \ u, v \in V^*\}, \\
\pi^l(w) &= \{bv \mid w = av\}, & \pi^r(w) &= \{ub \mid w = ua\}, \\
\rho^*(w) &= \{uv \mid w = uav, \ u, v \in V^*, \\
\rho^l(w) &= \{v \mid w = av\}, & \rho^r(w) &= \{u \mid w = ua\}, \\
\sigma^*(w) &= \{uav \mid w = uv, \ u, v \in V^*\}, \\
\sigma^l(w) &= \{aw\}, & \sigma^r(w) &= \{wa\},
\end{aligned}
$$

with the following exception: if some set, i.e., $\pi^*(w)$, $\pi^l(w)$, $\pi^r(w)$, $\rho^*(w)$, $\rho^l(w)$, $\rho^r(w)$, results to be empty (i.e., no strings u, or u and v, satisfy the indicated condition, because symbol a for substitution or deletion is not present in w, or it is not found in the expected position), the resulting set for the corresponding operation is defined to be its argument, i.e., w.

The symbol $\alpha \in \{*, l, r\}$ denotes the mode of applying a substitution, insertion or deletion rule to a string, namely, at any position ($\alpha = *$), on the left-hand end ($\alpha = l$), or on the right-hand end ($\alpha = r$) of the string, respectively. For any rule β, any mode $\alpha \in \{*, l, r\}$, and any $L \subseteq V^*$, we define the α-action of β on L by $\beta^\alpha(L) = \bigcup_{w \in L} \beta^\alpha(w)$. For a given finite set of rules M, we define the α-action of M on a string w and on a language L by $M^\alpha(w) = \bigcup_{\beta \in M} \beta^\alpha(w)$ and $M^\alpha(L) = \bigcup_{w \in L} M^\alpha(w)$, respectively.

We notice that, as in previous papers on HNEPs, substitutions in the following will only be used at arbitrary positions, i.e., with $\alpha = *$.

For two disjoint finite subsets P and F of an alphabet V and any string w over V, the two predicates $\varphi^{(1)}$ and $\varphi^{(2)}$ are defined as follows:

$$\varphi^{(1)}(w; P, F) \equiv P \subseteq alph(w) \wedge F \cap alph(w) = \emptyset,$$
$$\varphi^{(2)}(w; P, F) \equiv (P = \emptyset \vee alph(w) \cap P \neq \emptyset) \wedge (F \cap alph(w) = \emptyset).$$

The idea of these predicates is based on *random-context conditions* defined by sets P (*permitting contexts*) and F (*forbidding contexts*). Moreover, we define

$$\varphi^i(L, P, F) = \{w \in L \mid \varphi^i(w; P, F)\}, \ i \in \{1, 2\}, \text{ for any } L \subseteq V^*.$$

An evolutionary processor consists of a set of evolutionary operations (substitutions, insertions, deletions) and a filtering mechanism, i.e., we define an *evolutionary processor over* V as a 5-tuple (M, PI, FI, PO, FO) where

- either $M \subseteq Sub_V$ or $M \subseteq Del_V$ or $M \subseteq Ins_V$, i.e., the set M represents the set of evolutionary rules of the processor (notice that every processor is dedicated to only one type of the evolutionary operations);
- $PI, FI \subseteq V$ are the *input* permitting and forbidding contexts of the processor and $PO, FO \subseteq V$ are the *output* permitting and forbidding contexts of the processor.

The set of evolutionary processors over V is denoted by EP_V.

Definition 1. *A* hybrid network of evolutionary processors *(an HNEP for short) over* V *is a construct* $\Gamma = (V, T, H, \mathcal{N}, C_{\text{init}}, \alpha, \beta, C_{\text{input}}, i_0)$ *where*

- V *is the alphabet of the network;*
- T *is the input/output alphabet,* $T \subseteq V$;
- $H = (X_H, E_H)$ *is an undirected graph with set of vertices or nodes* X_H *and set of (undirected) edges* E_H; H *is called the underlying graph of the network;*
- $\mathcal{N} : X_H \longrightarrow EP_V$ *is a mapping which with each node* $x \in X_H$ *associates the evolutionary processor* $\mathcal{N}(x) = (M_x, PI_x, FI_x, PO_x, FO_x)$;
- $C_{\text{init}} : X_H \to 2^{V^*}$ *is a mapping which identifies the initial configuration of the network; it associates a finite set of words with each node of graph* H;
- $\alpha : X_H \longrightarrow \{*, l, r\}$; $\alpha(x)$ *defines the action mode of the rules performed on the strings occurring in node* x;
- $\beta : X_H \longrightarrow \{(1), (2)\}$ *defines the type of the input and output filters of a node; for every node* x, $x \in X_H$, *and for any language* L *we define* $\mu_x(L) = \varphi^{\beta(x)}(L; PI_x, FI_x)$ *and* $\tau_x(L) = \varphi^{\beta(x)}(L; PO_x, FO_x)$, *i.e.,* $\mu_x(L)$ *and* $\tau_x(L)$ *are the sets of strings of* L *that can pass the input and the output filter of* x, *respectively;*

- $C_{\text{input}} : X_H \longrightarrow 2^{V^*}$ defines a finite set of "initial strings for the input": for any $(x, w_0(x)) \in C_{\text{input}}$, the input string is concatenated to $w_0(x)$ and added to node x of the graph H, as described below;
- $i_0 \in X_H$ is the output node of Γ.

The *size* of Γ is defined to be the number of nodes in X_H. An HNEP is said to be a *complete HNEP* if its underlying graph is a complete graph.

Looking at HNEPs as devices computing partial recursive relations R on an alphabet U, i.e., $R \subseteq (U^*)^m \times (U^*)^n$, for some $m, n \geq 0$, we take $T = U \cup \{\$\}$, where \$ is a special delimiter separating the components of an input vector $(w_1, \ldots, w_m)$ and an output vector $(v_1, \ldots, v_n)$, $w_i \in U^*$, $1 \leq i \leq m$, $v_j \in U^*$, $1 \leq j \leq n$.

A configuration of an HNEP Γ, as defined above, is a mapping $C : X_H \longrightarrow 2^{V^*}$ which associates a set of strings over V with each node x of the graph. A component $C(x)$ of a configuration C is the set of strings that can be found in the node x in this configuration, hence, a configuration can be considered as a list of the sets of strings which are present in the nodes of the network at a given moment. For a given input vector $(w_1, \ldots, w_m)$, $w_i \in U^*$, $1 \leq i \leq m$, the initial configuration C_0 of the HNEP is obtained by adding to C_{init} the string $w_0(x)w_1\$ \ldots \$w_m$ in node x, for any $(x, w_0(x)) \in C_{\text{input}}$: $C_0(x) = C_{\text{init}}(x) \cup \{w_0(x)w_1\$ \ldots \$w_m \mid (x, w_0(x)) \in C_{\text{input}}\}$.

A configuration can change either by an evolutionary step or by a communication step. When it changes by an evolutionary step, then each component $C(x)$ of the configuration C is altered in accordance with the set of evolutionary rules M_x associated with the node x and the way of applying these rules, $\alpha(x)$. Formally, the configuration C' is obtained in one evolutionary step from the configuration C, written as $C \Longrightarrow C'$, if and only if $C'(x) = M_x^{\alpha(x)}(C(x))$ for all $x \in X_H$. When the configuration changes by a communication step, then each language processor $\mathcal{N}(x)$, where $x \in X_H$, sends a copy of each of its strings to every node y the node x is connected with, provided that this string is able to pass the output filter of x, and receives all the strings which are sent by the processor of any node y connected with x provided that these strings are able to pass the output filters of y and the input filter of x. Those strings which are not able to pass its output filter, remain at the node x. Formally, we say that configuration C' is obtained in one communication step from configuration C, written as $C \vdash C'$, if and only if

$$C'(x) = (C(x) - \tau_x(C(x))) \cup \bigcup_{(x,y) \in E_G} (\tau_y(C(y)) \cap \mu_x(C(y)))$$

holds for all $x \in X_H$. A *computation* in Γ is a sequence of configurations C_0, $C_1, C_2, \ldots$ where C_0 is the initial configuration of Γ, $C_{2i} \Longrightarrow C_{2i+1}$ and $C_{2i+1} \vdash C_{2i+2}$, for all $i \geq 0$. Note that each configuration C_{i+1} is uniquely determined by the configuration C_i, $i \geq 0$. The *result of a computation* in Γ for an input vector $(w_1, \ldots, w_m)$, $w_i \in U^*$, $1 \leq i \leq m$, i.e., for the initial configuration $\{(x, w_0(x)w_1\$ \ldots \$w_m) \mid x \in X_H\}$, is the set of all strings (of the form $v_1\$ \ldots \$v_n$,

$v_j \in U^*$, $1 \le j \le n$) arriving in the output node i_0 at any computation step of Γ, i.e.,

$$L(\Gamma)((w_1, \ldots, w_m)) = \{(v_1, \ldots, v_n) \mid v_j \in T, 1 \le j \le n,$$
$$v_1\$ \ldots \$v_n \in C_s(i_0), s \ge 0)\}.$$

Remark 3. Consider any input $w_{in} = w_1\$ \ldots \$w_m$. We first note that, since different strings do not influence each other, the strings in C_{init} do not affect the evolution of the strings in C_{input} concatenated with w_{in} and vice-versa. The results thus are the union of the strings obtained from C_{init}, which do not depend on the input, and the strings obtained from w_{in}, which do not depend on the strings in C_{init}. Therefore, for the results elaborated in this paper we may always assume C_{init} to be empty, and even exclude it from the tuple defining the network. Moreover, we may also assume that C_{input} only consists of one string in one node, i.e., $C_{\text{input}} = \{(x_0, w_0)\}$.

As special cases, HNEPs can be considered either as language generating devices (generating hybrid networks of evolutionary processors or *GHNEPs*) or language accepting devices (accepting hybrid networks of evolutionary processors or *AHNEPs*). In the case of GHNEPs, the relation to be computed is $\{\lambda\} \times L$, i.e., the initial configuration always equals $\{(x_0, w_0)\}$; the generated language is the set of all strings which appear in the output node at some step of the computation, i.e., the language generated by a generating hybrid network of evolutionary processors Γ is $L_{gen}(\Gamma) = \bigcup_{s \ge 0} C_s(i_0)$. In the case of AHNEPs, the relation to be computed is $L \times \{\lambda\}$, i.e., starting from the initial configuration $\{(x_0, w_0 w_1)\}$, we accept the input string w_1 if and only if at some moment of the computation the empty string appears in the output node, i.e., the language accepted by Γ is defined by $L_{acc}(\Gamma) = \{w_1 \in V^* \mid \exists s \ge 0(C_s(i_0) = \{\lambda\})\}$.

2.2   Post Systems and Circular Post Machines

The left and right insertion, deletion, and substitution rules defined in the preceding subsection are special cases of string rewriting rules only working at the ends of a string; they can be seen as restricted variants of Post rewriting rules as already introduced by Emil Post in [20]: for a *simple Post rewriting rule* $\Pi_s \equiv u\$x \to y\$v$ we define

$$\pi_s(w) = \{yzv \mid w = uzx, \ z \in V^*\}.$$

A *normal Post rewriting rule* $\pi_n \equiv \$x \to y\$$ is a special case of a simple Post rewriting rule $u\$x \to y\$v$ with $u = v = \lambda$; this normal Post rewriting rule $\$x \to y\$$ is the mirror version of the normal form rules $u\$ \to \$v$ as originally considered in [20] for Post canonical systems; yet this variant has already been used several times for proving specific results in the area of P systems, e.g., see [12]. A *Post system of type X* is a construct (V, T, A, P) where V is a (finite) set of *symbols*, $T \subseteq V$ is a set of *terminal symbols*, $A \in V^*$ is the *axiom*, and P is a finite set of *Post rewriting rules* of type X; for example, X can mean simple or normal Post rewriting rules. In both cases it is folklore that these Post systems of type X are computationally complete.

The basic idea of the computational completeness proofs for Post systems is the "rotate-and-simulate"-technique, i.e., the string is rotated until the string x to be rewritten appears on the right-hand side, where it can be erased and replaced by the string y on the left-hand side, which in total can be accomplished by the rule $\$x \to y\$$. By rules of the form $\$a \to a\$$ for each symbol a the string can be rotated. In order to indicate the beginning of the string in all its rotated versions, a special symbol B (different from all others) is used; B is to be erased at the end of a successful computation.

Circular Post machines are machine-like variants of Post systems using specific variants of simple Post rewriting rules; several variants named $CPMi$, $0 \le i \le 4$, were introduced in [6], and the variants of $CPM5$ we use in this paper were investigated in [5]. It was stated in [5] that CPM5 is an interesting model that deserves further attention; in the present paper we confirm that this is the case.

Definition 2. *A (non-deterministic) CPM5 is a construct*

$$M = (\Sigma, T, Q, q_1, q_0, R),$$

where Σ is a finite alphabet, $T \subseteq \Sigma$ is the set of terminal symbols, Q is the set of states, $q_1 \in Q$ is the initial state, $q_0 \in Q$ is the only terminal state, and R is a set of simple Post rewriting rules of the following types (we use the notation $Q' = Q \setminus \{q_0\}$):

- *$px\$ \to q\$$ (deletion rule) with $p \in Q'$, $q \in Q$, $x \in \Sigma$; we also write $px \to q$ and, for any $w \in \Sigma^*$, the corresponding computation step is $pxw \overset{px \to q}{\longrightarrow} qw$;*
- *$p\$ \to q\$y$ (insertion rule) with $p \in Q'$, $q \in Q$, $x \in \Sigma$; we also write $p \to yq$ and, for any $w \in \Sigma^*$, the corresponding computation step is $pw \overset{p \to yq}{\longrightarrow} qwy$.*

The CPM5 is called deterministic *if for any two deletion rules $px \to q_1$ and $px \to q_2$ we have $q_1 = q_2$ and for any two insertion rules $p \to q_1y_1$ and $p \to q_2y_2$ we have $q_1y_1 = q_2y_2$.*

The name circular Post machine comes up from the idea of interpreting the machines to work on circular strings where both deletion and insertion rules have local effects, as for circular strings the effect of the insertion rule $p\$ \to q\$y$ is the same as the effect of $p \to yq$ directly applied to a circular string, which also justifies writing $p\$ \to q\$y$ as $p \to yq$.

Definition 3. *A CPM5 $M = (\Sigma, T, Q, q_1, q_0, R)$ is said to be in* normal form *if*

- *$Q \setminus \{q_0\} = Q_1 \cup Q_2$ where $Q_1 \cap Q_2 = \emptyset$;*
- *for every $p \in Q_1$ and every $x \in \Sigma$, there is exactly one instruction of the form $px \to q$, i.e., Q_1 is the set of states for deletion rules;*
- *for every insertion rule $p \to yq$ we have $p \in Q_2$, i.e., Q_2 is the set of states for insertion rules, and moreover, if $p \to y_1q_1$ and $p \to y_2q_2$ are two different rules in R, then $y_1 = y_2$.*

In [5], CPM5 in normal form even obeying the constraint that for each $p \in Q_2$ there are at most two different rules $p \rightarrow yq_1$ and $p \rightarrow yq_2$ in R (and, again, M is called deterministic if $q_1 = q_2$) were shown to be computationally complete. The following result can be derived from the theorems proved in [5]:

Theorem 1. *(see [5]) Circular Post machines of type 5 (CPM5), even in normal form, are computationally complete.*

3   Computational Completeness of HNEPs with Five Nodes

HNEPs are defined as deterministic distributed string-processing devices where the evolution rules are simultaneously applied in all possible ways to (different copies of) all possible strings. However, since there is no interaction between the strings, it is sufficient to consider any possible behavior of an HNEP as a non-deterministic distributed device processing one string. Therefore, in the proof below, we consider configurations as $(\texttt{region}, \texttt{string})$, i.e., one string in one node, for any possible evolution.

Theorem 2. *Any (non-deterministic) CPM 5 M in normal form can be simulated by a complete HNEP Γ of size 5.*

Proof. Let $M = (\Sigma, T, Q, q_1, q_0, R)$ be a (non-deterministic) CPM5 in the normal form as defined in Definition 3, with symbols $\Sigma = \{a_j \mid 1 \le j \le m\}$ and states $Q = \{q_i \mid 0 \le i \le n\}$, where q_1 is the initial state and the only terminal state is $q_0 \in Q$. We now construct a complete HNEP $\Gamma = (V, T, H, \mathcal{N}, \alpha, \beta, C_0^0, 5)$ of size 5 which simulates the given CPM5 M. The following sets are used in its description:

$$
\begin{aligned}
J &= \{-1, 0, 1 \dots m\}, \; U = \{u_i \mid q_i \in Q_1\}, \; U' = \{u_i' \mid q_i \in Q_1\}, \\
P &= \{p_i \mid q_i \in Q\}, \; P' = \{p_i' \mid q_i \in Q\}, \; P'' = \{p_i'' \mid q_i \in Q\}, \\
A &= \Sigma \cup \{a_{-1}, a_0\}, \; A' = \{a_j' \mid a_j \in A\}, \; A'' = \{a_j'' \mid a_j \in A\}, \\
\bar{A} &= \{\bar{a}_{s,t} \mid q_s \in Q_1, \; t \in J\}, \; \hat{A} = \{\hat{a}_{s,t} \mid q_s \in Q_1, \; t \in J\}, \\
\tilde{Q} &= \{\tilde{q}_i \mid q_i \in Q_2\}, \; \bar{Q} = \{\bar{q}_i \mid q_i \in Q_1\}, \; \hat{Q} = \{\hat{q}_i \mid q_i \in Q_1\}, \\
Q' &= \{q_{s,t}' \mid q_s \in Q_2, \; t \in J\}, \; Q'' = \{q_{s,t}'' \mid q_s \in Q_2, \; t \in J\}, \\
V &= A \cup A' \cup A'' \cup \bar{A} \cup \hat{A} \\
&\quad \cup Q \cup P \cup P' \cup P'' \cup U \cup U' \cup Q' \cup Q'' \cup \tilde{Q} \cup \bar{Q} \cup \hat{Q} \cup \{\varepsilon\}.
\end{aligned}
$$

We take H to be a complete graph with 5 nodes; $C_0^0 = \{(1, q_1)\}$, i.e., for the input string w_1, the initial configuration is $\{(1, q_1 w_1)\}$; the output node of Γ for collecting the results of a computation is node 5. Moreover, we take $\beta(i) = 2$ for all $1 \le i \le 5$ as well as $\alpha(1) = \alpha(2) = \alpha(5) = *$, $\alpha(3) = r$, and $\alpha(4) = l$. The evolutionary processors $\mathcal{N}(i) = (M_i, PI_i, FI_i, PO_i, FO_i)$, $1 \le i \le 5$, are defined as follows (for the different kinds of rules, we use labels for identifying them later in the explanations given below).

$$M_1 = \{1.1 : q_i \to \tilde{q}_i \mid q_i \in Q_2\} \cup \{1.2 : q''_{s,t} \to q'_{s,t} \mid q''_{s,t} \in Q'', \ q'_{s,t} \in Q'\}$$
$$\cup \{1.3 : a''_l \to a'_l \mid l \in J\} \cup \{1.4 : a''_l \to a_l \mid a_l \in \Sigma\} \cup \{1.5 : q_0 \to \varepsilon\}$$
$$\cup \{1.6 : q_l \to p_l \mid q_l \in Q_1\} \cup \{1.7 : a_j \to \bar{a}_{0,j} \mid a_j \in \Sigma\}$$
$$\cup \{1.8 : \hat{q}_l \to \bar{q}_l \mid q_l \in Q, \ l > 0\} \cup \{1.9 : \hat{a}_{s,t} \to \bar{a}_{s,t} \mid \hat{a}_{s,t} \in \hat{A}, \ \bar{a}_{s,t} \in \bar{A}\}$$
$$\cup \{1.10 : p'_l \to p''_l \mid q_l \in Q\} \cup \{1.11 : u_p \to u'_p \mid q_p \in Q\},$$
$$PI_1 = Q \cup Q' \cup Q'' \cup P'' \cup \hat{Q} \cup P' \cup U, \ FI_1 = \tilde{Q} \cup A' \cup U' \cup \bar{Q} \cup \bar{A} \cup \{\varepsilon\},$$
$$PO_1 = \emptyset, \ FO_1 = \hat{A},$$
$$M_2 = \{2.1 : \tilde{q}_i \to q''_{k,j-1} \mid q_i \to a_j q_k \in R\}$$
$$\cup \{2.2 : q'_{s,t} \to q''_{s,t-1} \mid t > 0, \ q'_{s,t} \in Q', \ q''_{s,t} \in Q''\}$$
$$\cup \{2.3 : a'_l \to a''_{l+1} \mid a'_l \in A', \ a''_l \in A''\}$$
$$\cup \{2.4 : q'_{s,0} \to q_s \mid q'_{s,0} \in Q', \ q_s \in Q\}$$
$$\cup \{2.5 : \bar{q}_l \to \hat{q}_{l-1} \mid \bar{q}_l \in \bar{Q}, \ \hat{q}_{l-1} \in \hat{Q}, \ l > 0\}$$
$$\cup \{2.6 : \bar{a}_{s,t} \to \hat{a}_{s+1,t} \mid \bar{a}_{s,t} \in \bar{A}, \ \hat{a}_{s,t} \in \hat{A}\} \cup \{2.7 : \bar{q}_1 \to \varepsilon\}$$
$$\cup \{2.8 : \bar{a}_{s,t} \to u_p \mid q_{s+1} a_t \to q_p \in R, \ s > 0\} \cup \{2.9 : p_l \to p'_l \mid q_l \in Q\}$$
$$\cup \{2.10 : t'_p \to q_p \mid q_p \in Q\} \cup \{2.11 : p''_i \to \hat{q}_{i-1} \mid q_i \in Q, \ i > 2\}$$
$$\cup \{2.12 : p''_1 \to \varepsilon\},$$
$$PI_2 = A' \cup P \cup \bar{A} \cup U', \ FI_2 = Q \cup A'' \cup Q'' \cup P' \cup \hat{A} \cup \hat{Q} \cup \{\varepsilon\} \cup U,$$
$$PO_2 = \emptyset, \ FO_2 = P \cup \bar{Q} \cup \bar{A} \cup \tilde{Q} \cup P'' \cup Q' \cup A',$$
$$M_3 = \{3.1 : \lambda \to a'_{-1} \mid a'_{-1} \in A'\}, \ PI_3 = \tilde{Q},$$
$$FI_3 = A' \cup A'' \cup \bar{Q} \cup \{\varepsilon\} \cup \bar{A} \cup \hat{A} \cup \hat{Q} \cup U \cup U' \cup P \cup P' \cup P'' \cup Q \cup Q' \cup Q'',$$
$$PO_3 = \{a'_{-1}\}, \ FO_3 = \emptyset,$$
$$M_4 = \{4.1 : \varepsilon \to \lambda\}, \ PI_4 = \{\varepsilon\},$$
$$FI_4 = \bar{A} \cup \hat{A} \cup \hat{Q} \cup U' \cup P \cup P' \cup P'' \cup Q \cup Q' \cup Q'' \cup \tilde{Q} \cup A' \cup A'',$$
$$PO_4 = \emptyset, \ FO_4 = \{\varepsilon\},$$
$$M_5 = \emptyset, \ PI_5 = \emptyset, \ FI_5 = V \setminus T, \ PO_5 = \emptyset, \ FO_5 = \emptyset.$$

Let $q_1 w_1$, $w_1 \in T^*$, be the initial configuration of CPM5 M and $q_0 w_0$ the final configuration of M, i.e., M starts with $q_1 w_1$ and ends with $q_0 w_0$, $w_1 \in T^*$, $w_0 \in T^*$. Then the HNEP Γ starts the simulation with the initial configuration $C_0 = \{(1, q_1 w_1)\}$, and we show that the simulation in Γ only yields string w_0 in the output node 5 of Γ, and moreover, if M never stops when starting with $q_1 w_1$, then Γ generates nothing in the output node.

Without loss of generality, we assume that CPM5 M starts with a rule of type $q_1 \to a_j q_k$ with $q_k \in Q_2$ and halts after applying a rule of type $q_i a_j \to q_0$, and thus any sequence of consecutive rules $q_{i_1} \to a_{j_1} q_{i_2}$, $q_{i_2} \to a_{j_2} q_{i_3}, \cdots, q_{i_t} \to a_{j_t} q_{k_{t+1}}$ with $q_{k_{t+1}} \in Q_2$ from any halting computation ends with a rule $q_{k_{t+1}} a_s \to q_{k_{t+2}}$ with $q_{k_{t+2}} \in Q_1$.

Case 1. Consider any insertion rule $q_i \to a_j q_k \in R$, $q_i \in Q_2$, $q_k \in Q \setminus \{q_0\}$, $a_j \in \Sigma$, and let $q_i w \implies q_k w a_j$ be a computation step in M, i.e., rule $q_i \to a_j q_k$ is applied to the string $q_i w$ yielding $q_k w a_j$. Starting with the string $q_i w$ being situated in node 1 of Γ, we now describe the possible evolutions of this string $q_i w$ in Γ. If $(1, q_i w) \overset{1.1}{\implies} (1, \tilde{q}_i w) \vdash (3, \tilde{q}_i w) \overset{3.1}{\implies} (3, \tilde{q}_i w a'_{-1})$, then string $\tilde{q}_i w a'_{-1}$ can only go to node 2. Notice that if rule **1.7** is applied, i.e., $(1, q_i w = q_i w' a_s w'') \overset{1.7}{\implies} (1, q_i w' \bar{a}_{0,s} w'')$, then the string $q_i w' \bar{a}_{0,s} w''$ is lost as it cannot enter any node.

In node 2 only the two rules $\mathbf{2.1} : \tilde{q}_i \to q''_{k,j-1}$ and $\mathbf{2.3} : a'_l \to a''_{l+1}$ (for $l = -1$) can be applied, i.e.,

$$(3, \tilde{q}_i w a'_{-1}) \vdash (2, \tilde{q}_i w a'_{-1}) \overset{2.1,2.3}{\implies} (2, q''_{k,j-1} w a''_0) \vdash (1, q''_{k,j-1} w a''_0)$$

(if more than one evolution step is necessary in a node, we do not indicate the intermediate communication step leaving the string in the node). Again, if rule **1.7** is applied to $q''_{k,j-1} w a''_0$ in node 1, the resulting string $q''_{k,j-1} w' \bar{a}_{0,s} w'' a''_0$ is lost, and moreover, if rules **1.2**, **1.4**, and **1.7** are applied in any combination, then the developing strings are lost, too. Thus, only the rules **1.2** and **1.3** should be applied in node 1, i.e., $(1, q''_{k,j-1} w a''_0) \overset{1.2,1.3}{\implies} (1, q'_{k,j-1} w a''_0)$. Back in node 2, only the rules **2.2** and **2.3** are to be applied, i.e.,

$$(1, q'_{k,j-1} w a''_0) \vdash (2, q'_{k,j-1} w a''_0) \overset{2.2,2.3}{\implies} (2, q''_{k,j-2} w a''_1) \vdash (1, q''_{k,j-2} w a''_1).$$

The computation now can be continued in the same way as above, i.e., $(1, q''_{k,j-2} w a''_1) \overset{1.2,1.3}{\implies} (1, q'_{k,j-2} w a''_1)$ (recall that the application of rules **1.4** and **1.7** leads to strings that will not lead to any result); in sum, we obtain

$$(1, q''_{k,j-2} w a''_1) \overset{1.2,1.3}{\implies} \ldots \vdash (1, q'_{k,1} w a''_{j-2}) \vdash (2, q'_{k,1} w a''_{j-2}) \overset{2.2,2.3}{\implies}$$
$$(2, q''_{k,0} w a''_{j-1}) \vdash (1, q''_{k,0} w a''_{j-1}) \overset{1.2,1.3}{\implies} (1, q'_{k,0} w a''_{j-1}) \vdash (2, q'_{k,0} w a''_{j-1}).$$

The main idea of this construction is to decrease the index h for the state symbols $q''_{k,j-2}/q'_{k,j-2}$ while increasing the index g for the symbols a''_g/a'_g; by construction, h reaches 0 at the same moment when g reaches $j - 1$. At the end, in node 2, only the rules **2.3** and **2.4** are to be applied, and the resulting string $q_k w a''_j$ enters node 1, i.e., $(2, q'_{k,0} w a'_{j-1}) \overset{2.3,2.4}{\implies} (2, q_k w a''_j) \vdash (1, q_k w a''_j)$.

It is easy to see that in node 1, strings resulting from applying rules **1.3** $(q_k w a'_j)$, **1.1** $(\tilde{q}_k w a''_j)$, **1.6** $(p_k w a''_j)$, and **1.7** $(q_k w' \tilde{a}_{0,s} w'' a''_j)$ will be lost. Hence, only the application of rule $\mathbf{1.4} : a''_l \to a_l$ leads to the desired correct string $q_k w a_j$, i.e., $(1, q_k w a''_j) \overset{1.4}{\implies} (1, q_k w a_j)$. In sum, we conclude that Γ has correctly simulated the application of the insertion rule $q_i \to a_j q_k$ in M.

Case 2. Consider any deletion rule $q_i a_j \to q_k \in R$, $q_i \in Q_1$, $q_k \in Q$, $a_j \in \Sigma$, and let $q_i a_j w \implies q_k w$ be a computation step in M, i.e., rule $q_i a_j \to q_k$ is applied to the string $q_i a_j w$ yielding $q_k w$. Starting with the string $q_i a_j w$ being situated in node 1 of Γ, we now describe the possible evolutions of this string $q_i a_j w$ in Γ. At the beginning of the computation in Γ, the application of rule $\mathbf{1.7} : a_j \to \bar{a}_{0,j}$ leads to a string that will get lost; instead, we have to take $(1, q_i a_j w) \overset{1.6}{\implies} (1, p_i a_j w) \vdash (2, p_i a_j w) \overset{2.9}{\implies} (2, p'_i a_j w) \vdash (1, p'_i a_j w)$. Notice that now rule **1.7** may not only be applied to a symbol a_j at the second position in the developing string, but at any position, yet if we apply rule **1.7** at the correct second position in the developing string, we get the following computations:

$$(1, p'_i a_j w) \overset{1.10, 1.7}{\Longrightarrow} (1, p''_i \bar{a}_{0,j} w) \vdash (2, p''_i \bar{a}_{0,j} w) \overset{2.6, 2.11}{\Longrightarrow} (2, \hat{q}_{i-1} \hat{a}_{1,j} w) \vdash$$
$$(1, \hat{q}_{i-1} \hat{a}_{1,j} w) \overset{1.8, 1.9}{\Longrightarrow} (1, \bar{q}_{i-1} \bar{a}_{1,j} w) \vdash (2, \bar{q}_{i-1} \bar{a}_{1,j} w) \overset{2.5, 2.6}{\Longrightarrow} (2, \hat{q}_{i-2} \hat{a}_{2,j} w).$$

If during the computation instead of rule **2.6** : $\bar{a}_{s,t} \to \hat{a}_{s+1,t}$ we apply rule **2.8** : $\bar{a}_{s,t} \to u_p$, the resulting string $\hat{q}_s u_p w$ is lost: in node 1, there are only three possibilities for a rule to be applied to the string $\hat{q}_s u_p w$, namely rule **1.8** : $\hat{q}_l \to \bar{q}_l$, rule **1.11** : $u_p \to u'_p$, and rule **1.7** : $a_j \to \bar{a}_{0,j}$, but the resulting strings $\bar{q}_s u_p w$, $\hat{q}_s u'_p w$, and $\hat{q}_s u_p w_1 \bar{a}_{0,s} w_2$ (where $w = w_1 a_s w_2$, $\bar{a}_{0,s} \in \bar{A}$) are not able to enter another node.

The sequences of rules **1.8, 1.9** and **2.5, 2.6** then are iterated until we reach $\bar{q}_1 \bar{a}_{i-1,j} w$, i.e., for $h = i - 1, \ldots, 2$ we have the following computations:

$$(1, \hat{q}_h \hat{a}_{i-h,j} w) \overset{1.8, 1.9}{\Longrightarrow} (1, \bar{q}_h \bar{a}_{i-h,j} w) \vdash (2, \bar{q}_h \bar{a}_{i-h,j} w) \overset{2.5, 2.6}{\Longrightarrow} (2, \hat{q}_{h-1} \hat{a}_{i-h+1,j} w).$$

Finally, to $\bar{q}_1 \bar{a}_{i-1,j} w$ the rules **2.6** and **2.7** : $\bar{q}_1 \to \varepsilon$ might be applied, but then the obtained string $\varepsilon \hat{a}_{i,j} w$ is lost. Thus, only the sequence of rules **2.7** and **2.8** : $\bar{a}_{i-1,j} \to u_k$ is to be applied; the simulation of the derivation step $q_i a_j w \Longrightarrow q_k w$ in M correctly ends in node 1 with the string $q_k w$ after the following computation steps in Γ:

$$(2, \bar{q}_1 \bar{a}_{i-1,j} w) \overset{2.7, 2.8}{\Longrightarrow} (2, \varepsilon u_k w) \vdash (4, \varepsilon u_k w) \overset{4.1}{\Longrightarrow} (4, u_k w) \vdash$$
$$(1, u_k w) \overset{1.11}{\Longrightarrow} (1, u'_k w) \vdash (2, u'_k w) \overset{2.10}{\Longrightarrow} (2, q_k w) \vdash (1, q_k w).$$

If we apply rule **1.7** at a position $i > 2$, i.e., to the a_j in $q_i w' a_j w''$ with $|w'| > 0$, then, at the end of the simulation (carried out as described above) we have the string $w' q_k w''$ in node 1. First consider $q_k \in Q_1$; then $w' q_k w''$ has to be transformed into $w_1 \varepsilon w_2$, $w_1, w_2 \in V^*$, $|w_1| > 0$, and at the end the derived string is lost, as the rule $\varepsilon \to \lambda$ can only be applied at the left end of a string in node 4. Notice that the symbol ε may appear in string w_1 (in this case the developing string also will be rejected by node 4), but it is not possible that two symbols ε simultaneously appear in $w_1 \varepsilon w_2$, as immediately the developing string will be rejected in node 4 when moved there. If $q_k \in Q_2$, then in several circles of the computation the developing string will look as $w_1 q_t w_2$, $|w_1| > 0$, $q_t \in Q_1$, and we return to the case considered before. In sum, we conclude that Γ correctly simulates the application of rule $q_i a_j \to q_k$ in M.

Case 3. As soon as a string $q_0 w_0$ with the final node q_0 at its beginning (and $w_0 \in T^*$) appears in node 1, which in fact means that the circular Post machine M has stopped with having computed w_0, we can apply rule **1.5** : $q_0 \to \varepsilon$ and send the resulting string εw_0 to node 4 where ε is erased by rule **4.1** : $\varepsilon \to \lambda$; the resulting terminal string $w_0 \in T^*$ then can enter the terminal node 5, i.e., we get w_0 as the result of this computation in Γ:

$$(1, q_0 w_0) \overset{1.5}{\Longrightarrow} (1, \varepsilon w_0) \vdash (4, \varepsilon w_0) \overset{4.1}{\Longrightarrow} (4, w_0) \vdash (5, w_0).$$

In sum, we observe that every computation of the CPM5 in normal form M can be simulated correctly by the HNEP Γ, yielding exactly the same results;

any other computation paths in Γ not correctly simulating the computation steps of M do not yield any result, which observation completes the proof.   □

Corollary 1. *Complete hybrid networks of evolutionary processors with* 5 *nodes are computationally complete.*

Proof. As the circular Post machines of type 5 (CPM5) in normal form are computationally complete (see Theorem 1), the result directly follows from our main result, Theorem 2.   □

The following two results are immediate consequences of Corollary 1, as any recursively enumerable language L can be viewed as partial recursive relation $L \times \{\lambda\}$ (acceptance) and $\{\lambda\} \times L$ (generation), see Remark 2.

Corollary 2. *Any recursively enumerable language L can be accepted by a complete AHNEP of size* 5.

Corollary 3. *Any recursively enumerable language L can be generated by a complete GHNEP of size* 5.

4   Conclusions

We have improved previous results for hybrid networks of evolutionary processors (HNEPs) showing that computational completeness can already be obtained with only 5 nodes. Any partial recursive relation can be computed by a (complete) HNEP with 5 nodes, and any recursively enumerable language can be accepted by a complete AHNEP with 5 nodes or even generated by a complete GHNEP with only 5 nodes.

Acknowledgements. The first author and the third author acknowledge project STCU-5384 awarded by the Science and Technology Center in the Ukraine.

References

1. Alhazov, A., Csuhaj-Varjú, E., Martín-Vide, C., Rogozhin, Y.: About Universal Hybrid Networks of Evolutionary Processors of Small Size. In: LATA 2008. LNCS, vol. 5196, pp. 28–39. Springer, Heidelberg (2008)
2. Alhazov, A., Csuhaj-Varjú, E., Martín-Vide, C., Rogozhin, Y.: Computational Completeness of Hybrid Networks of Evolutionary Processors with Seven Nodes. In: Campeanu, C., Pighizzini, G. (eds.) Descriptional Complexity of Formal Systems, Proceedings DCFS 2008, Univ. Prince Edward Island, Charlottetown, pp. 38–47 (2008)
3. Alhazov, A., Csuhaj-Varjú, E., Martín-Vide, C., Rogozhin, Y.: On the Size of Computationally Complete Hybrid Networks of Evolutionary Processors. Theoretical Computer Science 410, 3188–3197 (2009)
4. Alhazov, A., Dassow, J., Martín-Vide, C., Rogozhin, Y., Truthe, B.: On Networks of Evolutionary Processors with Nodes of Two Types. Fundamenta Informaticae 91(1), 1–15 (2009)

5. Alhazov, A., Krassovitskiy, A., Rogozhin, Y.: Circular Post Mahines and P Systems with Exo-insertion and Deletion. In: Gheorghe, M., Păun, G., Rozenberg, G., Salomaa, A., Verlan, S. (eds.) CMC 2011. LNCS, vol. 7184, pp. 73–86. Springer, Heidelberg (2012)

6. Alhazov, A., Kudlek, M., Rogozhin, Y.: Nine Universal Circular Post Machines. Computer Science Journal of Moldova 10(3), 247–262 (2002)

7. Alhazov, A., Martín-Vide, C., Rogozhin, Y.: On the Number of Nodes in Universal Networks of Evolutionary Processors. Acta Inf. 43(5), 331–339 (2006)

8. Alhazov, A., Martín-Vide, C., Rogozhin, Y.: Networks of Evolutionary Processors with Two Nodes are Unpredictable. In: Pre-Proceedings of the 1st International Conference on Language and Automata Theory and Applications, LATA, GRLMC report 35/07, Rovira i Virgili University, Tarragona, 521–528 (2007)

9. Castellanos, J., Leupold, P., Mitrana, V.: On the Size Complexity of Hybrid Networks of Evolutionary Processors. Theoretical Computer Science 330(2), 205–220 (2005)

10. Castellanos, J., Martín-Vide, C., Mitrana, V., Sempere, J.M.: Solving NP-complete Problems with Networks of Evolutionary Processors. In: Mira, J., Prieto, A.G. (eds.) IWANN 2001. LNCS, vol. 2084, pp. 621–628. Springer, Heidelberg (2001)

11. Csuhaj-Varjú, E., Martín-Vide, C., Mitrana, V.: Hybrid Networks of Evolutionary Processors are Computationally Complete. Acta Inf. 41(4-5), 257–272 (2005)

12. Freund, R., Rogozhin, Y., Verlan, S.: Generating and Accepting P Systems with Minimal Left and Right Insertion and Deletion. Natural Computing. Springer (2014), doi:10.1007/s11047-013-9396-3

13. Kudlek, M., Rogozhin, Y.: Small Universal Circular Post Machines. Computer Science Journal of Moldova 9(1), 34–52 (2001)

14. Kudlek, M., Rogozhin, Y.: New Small Universal Circular Post Machines. In: Freivalds, R. (ed.) FCT 2001. LNCS, vol. 2138, pp. 217–227. Springer, Heidelberg (2001)

15. Loos, R., Manea, F., Mitrana, V.: Small Universal Accepting Hybrid Networks of Evolutionary Processors. Acta Informatica 47(2), 133–146 (2010)

16. Manea, F., Martín-Vide, C., Mitrana, V.: On the Size Complexity of Universal Accepting Hybrid Networks of Evolutionary Processors. Mathematical Structures in Computer Science 17(4), 753–771 (2007)

17. Manea, F., Martín-Vide, C., Mitrana, V.: All NP-problems can be Solved in Polynomial Time by Accepting Hybrid Networks of Evolutionary Processors of Constant Size. Information Processing Letters 103, 112–118 (2007)

18. Margenstern, M., Mitrana, V., Jesús Pérez-Jímenez, M.: Accepting Hybrid Networks of Evolutionary Processors. In: Ferretti, C., Mauri, G., Zandron, C. (eds.) DNA 2004. LNCS, vol. 3384, pp. 235–246. Springer, Heidelberg (2005)

19. Martín-Vide, C., Mitrana, V., Pérez-Jiménez, M.J., Sancho-Caparrini, F.: Hybrid Networks of Evolutionary Processors. In: Cantú-Paz, E., et al. (eds.) GECCO 2003. LNCS, vol. 2723, pp. 401–412. Springer, Heidelberg (2003)

20. Post, E.L.: Formal Reductions of the General Combinatorial Decision Problem. American Journal of Mathematics 65(2), 197–215 (1943)

21. Rozenberg, G., Salomaa, A. (eds.): Handbook of Formal Languages, vol. 3. Springer (1997)

22. Salomaa, A.: Formal Languages. Academic Press, New York (1973)

Learning Two-Input Linear and Nonlinear Analog Functions with a Simple Chemical System

Peter Banda[1] and Christof Teuscher[2]

[1] Department of Computer Science
Portland State University
banda@pdx.edu
[2] Department of Electrical and Computer Engineering
Portland State University
teuscher@pdx.edu

Abstract. The current biochemical information processing systems behave in a pre-determined manner because all features are defined during the design phase. To make such unconventional computing systems reusable and programmable for biomedical applications, adaptation, learning, and self-modification based on external stimuli would be highly desirable. However, so far, it has been too challenging to implement these in wet chemistries. In this paper we extend the chemical perceptron, a model previously proposed by the authors, to function as an analog instead of a binary system. The new analog asymmetric signal perceptron learns through feedback and supports Michaelis-Menten kinetics. The results show that our perceptron is able to learn linear and nonlinear (quadratic) functions of two inputs. To the best of our knowledge, it is the first simulated chemical system capable of doing so. The small number of species and reactions and their simplicity allows for a mapping to an actual wet implementation using DNA-strand displacement or deoxyribozymes. Our results are an important step toward actual biochemical systems that can learn and adapt.

Keywords: Chemical perceptron, analog perceptron, supervised learning, chemical computing, RNMSE, linear function, quadratic function.

1 Introduction

Biochemical information processing systems, which are crucial for emerging biomedical applications, cannot typically be programmed once built. After an *in vitro* or *in vivo* injection, the behavior, i.e., the program of such nano-scale chemical machines [1] cannot be changed. That limits their applicability and reusability. To address this limitation, future biochemical machinery should function not only in uniform, well-known lab settings but also in previously unknown environments. Such adaptive chemical systems would decide autonomously and learn new behaviors through reinforcements in response to external stimuli.

O.H. Ibarra et al. (Eds.): UCNC 2014, LNCS 8553, pp. 14–26, 2014.
DOI: 10.1007/978-3-319-08123-6_2, © Springer International Publishing Switzerland 2014

We could imagine that in the future millions of molecular agents would help our immune system fight viruses, deliver medications [2], or fix broken cells. Adaptive chemical systems may also simplify the manufacturing and design processes: instead of designing multiple systems with predefined functionality embedded in their species and reactions one could train and recycle a single adaptive machine for a desired functionality.

Neural network theory [3] inspired numerous chemical implementations [4–6], however, only the input-weight integration part of a single perceptron model [7] was successfully mapped to chemistry. Learning (i.e., weight adaptation) was either not addressed or delegated to an external non-chemical system [6, 8] that calculated new weights values (i.e., chemical concentrations) to achieve a desired system behavior.

Our previous work [9] introduced the first simulated artificial chemical system that can learn and adapt autonomously to feedback provided by a teacher. We coined the term *chemical perceptron* because the system qualitatively mimics a two-input binary perceptron. In a second step we aimed to simplify the model to make wet biochemical implementations feasible. We achieved that by employing the asymmetric representation of values and by using thresholding. The new *asymmetric signal perceptron* (ASP) model [10] requires less than a half of the reactions of its predecessors with comparable performance (i.e., $99.3 - 99.99\%$ success rates). The flip side of the more compact design is a reduced robustness to rate constant perturbations due to a lack of structural redundancy.

In real biomedical applications one is often required to distinguish subtle changes in concentrations with complex linear or nonlinear relations among species. Such behavior cannot easily be achieved with our previous binary perceptron models, thus, several improvements are necessary. In this paper we present a new *analog asymmetric signal perceptron* (AASP) with two inputs. We will refer to the original ASP as a binary ASP (BASP). The AASP model follows mass-action and Michaelis-Menten kinetics and learns through feedback from the environment. The design is modular and extensible to any number of inputs. We demonstrate that the AASP can learn various linear and nonlinear functions. For example, it is possible to learn to produce the average of two analog values. In combination with a chemical delay line [11], the AASP could also be used to predict time series.

2   Chemical Reaction Network

To model the AASP we employ the *chemical reaction network* (CRN) formalism. A CRN consists of a finite set of molecular species and reactions paired with rate constants [12]. CRN represents an unstructured macroscopic simulated chemistry, hence, the species labeled with symbols are not assigned a molecular structure yet. More importantly, since the reaction tank is assumed to be well-stirred, CRN lacks the notion of space. The state of the system does therefore not contain any spatial information and is effectively reduced to a vector of species concentrations. Without losing generality we treat a concentration as a dimensionless quantity. Depending on the required scale, a wet chemical implementation could use $mol \cdot L^{-1}$ (M) or $nmol \cdot L^{-1}$ (nM) with appropriate (scaled) rate constant units, such as $M \cdot s^{-1}$ or $M^{-1} \cdot s^{-1}$, depending on the order of a reaction.

The reaction rate defines the speed of a reaction application prescribed by kinetic laws. The mass-action law [12] states that the rate of a reaction is proportional to the product of the concentrations of the reactants. For an irreversible reaction $aS_1 + bS_2 \rightarrow P$, the rate is given by

$$r = \frac{d[P]}{dt} = -\frac{1}{a}\frac{d[S_1]}{dt} = -\frac{1}{b}\frac{d[S_2]}{dt} = k[S_1]^a[S_2]^b,$$

where $k \in \mathbb{R}^+$ is a reaction rate constant, a and b are stoichiometric constants, $[S_1]$ and $[S_2]$ are concentrations of reactants (substrates) S_1 and S_2, and $[P]$ is a concentration of product P.

Michaelis-Menten enzyme kinetics [13] describes the rate of a catalytic reaction $E + S \rightleftharpoons ES \rightarrow E + P$, where a substrate S transforms to a product P with a catalyst E, which increases the rate of a reaction without being altered. A species ES is an intermediate enzyme-substrate binding. By assuming quasi-steady-state approximation, the rate is given by

$$r = \frac{d[P]}{dt} = \frac{k_{cat}[E][S]}{K_m + [S]},$$

where $k_{cat}, K_m \in \mathbb{R}^+$ are rate constants. By combining kinetic expressions for all species, we obtain a system of ODEs that we simulate using a 4th order Runge-Kutta numerical integration with the temporal step 0.1.

3   Model

The AASP models a formal analog perceptron [7] with two inputs x_1 and x_2, similar to an early type of artificial neuron [3]. The perceptron is capable of simple learning and can be used as a building block of a feed-forward neural networks. Networks built from perceptrons have been shown to be universal approximators [14].

In a CRN we represent each formal variable with one or several species. While the previous BASP models a perceptron with two inputs and a binary output produced by external or internal thresholding, the new AASP is analog and does not use thresholding. Instead of a binary yes/no answer, its output is analog, which requires much finer control over the weight convergence. As a consequence, the AASP consists of more species, namely 17 vs. 13, and more reactions, namely 18 vs. 16.

3.1   Input-Weight Integration

A formal perceptron integrates the inputs $\mathbf{x}$ with the weights $\mathbf{w}$ linearly as $\Sigma_{i=0}^n w_i \cdot x_i$, where the weight w_0, a bias, always contributes to an output because

Table 1. (a) The AASP's species divided into groups according to their purpose and functional characteristics; (b) the AASP's reactions with the best rate constants found by the GA (see Section 3.3), rounded to four decimals. Groups $1-4$ implement the input-weight integrations, the rest implement learning. The catalytic reactions have two rates: k_{cat} and K_m

Group Name	Species
Inputs	X_1, X_2
Output	Y
Weights	W_0, W_1, W_2
Target output	$\hat{Y}$
Input (clock) signal	S_{in}
Learning signal	S_L
Input contributions	$X_1Y, X_2Y, S_{in}Y$
Weight changers	$W^\ominus, W^\oplus,$ $W_0^\ominus, W_1^\ominus, W_2^\ominus$
Total	17

Group	Reaction	Catalyst	Rates
1	$S_{in} + Y \rightarrow \lambda$		.1800
2	$S_{in} \rightarrow Y + S_{in}Y$	W_0	.5521, 2.5336
3	$X_1 + Y \rightarrow \lambda$		.3905
	$X_2 + Y \rightarrow \lambda$		
4	$X_1 \rightarrow Y + X_1Y$	W_1	.4358, 0.1227
	$X_2 \rightarrow Y + X_2Y$	W_2	
5	$\hat{Y} \rightarrow W^\oplus$		.1884
6	$Y \rightarrow W^\ominus$	S_L	.1155, 1.9613
7	$Y + \hat{Y} \rightarrow \lambda$		1.0000
8	$W^\ominus \rightarrow W_0\ominus$	$S_{in}Y$	0.600, 1.6697
9	$W_0 + W_0\ominus \rightarrow \lambda$		.2642
10	$W^\ominus \rightarrow W_0$	$S_{in}Y$	.5023, 2.9078
11	$W^\ominus \rightarrow W_1^\ominus$	X_1Y	.1889, 1.6788
	$W^\ominus \rightarrow W_2^\ominus$	X_2Y	
12	$W_1 + W_1^\ominus \rightarrow \lambda$		.2416
	$W_2 + W_2^\ominus \rightarrow \lambda$		
13	$W^\oplus \rightarrow W_1$	X_1Y	.2744, 5.0000
	$W^\oplus \rightarrow W_2$	X_2Y	
Total		18	

its associated input $x_0 = 1$. An activation function φ, such as a hyperbolic tangent or signum, then processes the dot product to produce the output y.

The reactions carrying out the chemical input-weight integration are structurally the same as in the BASP. The only difference is an addition of the partial input-weight contribution species, which are, however, required for learning only, and will be explained in Section 3.1. The AASP models a two-input perceptron where the output calculation is reduced to $y = \varphi(w_0 + w_1 x_1 + x_2 w_2)$. The concentration of input species X_1 and X_2 corresponds to the formal inputs x_1 and x_2, and the species Y to the output y. A clock (input) signal S_{in} is always provided along the regular input X_1 and X_2, since it serves as the constant-one coefficient (or the constant input $x_0 = 1$) of the bias weight w_0.

The AASP represents the weights by three species W_1, W_2, and W_0. As opposed to the formal model, the input-weight integration is nonlinear and based on an annihilatory version of the asymmetric representation of the values and the addition/subtraction operation as introduced in [10]. Since the concentration cannot be negative, we cannot map a signed real variable directly to the concentration of a single species. The weights require both positive and negative values, otherwise we could cover only functions that are strictly additive. The asymmetric representation uses a single species E that catalyzes a transformation of substrate S to a product P ($S \xrightarrow{E} P$) and competes against an annihilation of the substrate and the product $S + P \rightarrow \lambda$. For a given threshold concentration of the product we can determine the associated catalyst threshold, so all concentrations of catalyst $[E]_0$ to the left of this threshold represent negative numbers while all concentrations to the right represent positive numbers. The final product concentration $[P]_\infty$ is monotonically increasing and asymptotically reaches the initial concentration of the substrate $[S]_0$ for $[E]_0 \to \infty$.

Using the asymmetric comparison primitives, we map the AASP's weights to catalysts (E), the inputs to substrates (S), and the output to product (P) and obtain 6 reactions as shown in Figure 1(a) and Table 1(b), groups $1 - 4$. Each weight species races with its substrate's annihilation but also with other weights. Since the output Y is shared, this effectively implements a nonlinear input-weight integration. Note that by replacing annihilation with a decay of input species, we would end up having three independent races with additive contributions instead of one global race. An alternative symmetric representation embedded in the previously reported *weight-loop perceptron* and the *weight-race perceptron* [9] encodes the values by two complementary species, one for the positive and one for the negative domain. We opt for the asymmetric approach because it reduces the number of reactions by half compared to the symmetric one.

Because of the complexity of the underlying ODEs, no closed formula for the output concentration exists and theoretical conclusions are very limited. Although we cannot analyze the input-weight integration dynamics quantitatively, we can still describe the qualitative behavior and constraints. The weight concentration represents formally both positive and negative values, so the weights together with annihilatory reactions can act as both catalysts and inhibitors. More specifically a low weight concentration, which strengthens its input-specific annihilation, could impose a negative pressure on a different weight branch. Hence, we interpret a weight that contributes to the output less than its input consumes as negative. In an extreme case, when the weight concentration is zero, its branch would consume the same amount of output as its input injected. The relation between the concentration of weights and the final output $[Y]_\infty$ has a sigmoidal shape with the limit $[X_1]_0 + [X_2]_0 + [S_{in}]_0$ reaching for all weights $[W_i] \to \infty$. Clearly the output concentration cannot exceed all the inputs provided.

Figure 2 shows the relation between the concentration of weight W_1 and weight W_2 and the final output concentration. For simplicity the bias processing part is not considered ($[S_{in}] = 0$), so we keep only two branches of the input-weight integration triangle. Note that in the plots the concentration of weights span the interval 0 to 2 because in our simulations we draw the weights uniformly from the interval $(0.5, 1.5)$. On the z-axis we plotted the ratio of the output concentration $[Y]$ to $[X_1]_0 + [X_2]_0$. For learning to work we want the gradient of the output surface to be responsive to changes in the weight concentrations. Therefore, we restrict the range of possible outputs so it is neither too close to the maximal output, where the surface is effectively constant, nor too close to zero, where the surface is too steep and even a very small perturbation of the weight concentration would dramatically change the output. Note that we optimized the AASP's rate constants to obtain an optimal weight-output surface by genetic algorithms (discussed in Section 3.3).

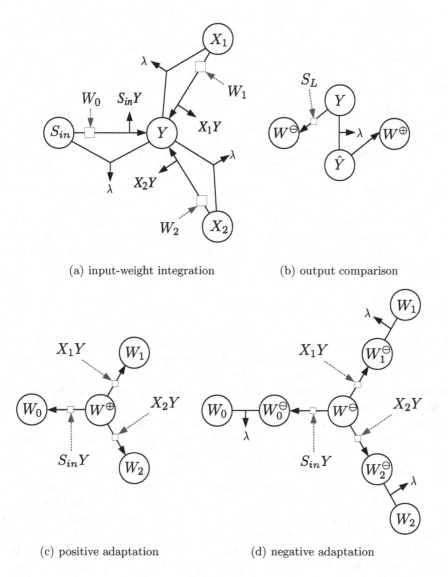

(a) input-weight integration   (b) output comparison

(c) positive adaptation   (d) negative adaptation

Fig. 1. (a) The AASP's reactions performing input-weight integration. Similarly to the BASP, cross-weight competition is achieved by the annihilation of the inputs S_{in}, X_1, X_2 with the output Y, an asymmetric strategy for representation of real values and subtraction. (b-d) the AASP's reactions responsible for learning. They are decomposed into three parts: (b) comparison of the output Y with the target-output $\hat{Y}$, determining whether weights should be incremented ($W^\oplus$ species) or decremented ($W^\ominus$ species), and (c-d) positive and negative adaptation of the weights W_0, W_1, and W_2, which is proportional to the part of the output they produced $S_{in}Y, X_1Y$, and X_2Y respectively. Nodes represent species, solid lines are reactions, dashed lines are catalysts, and λ stands for no or inert species.

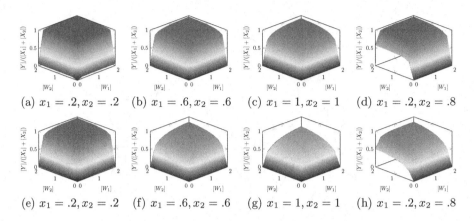

(a) $x_1 = .2, x_2 = .2$ (b) $x_1 = .6, x_2 = .6$ (c) $x_1 = 1, x_2 = 1$ (d) $x_1 = .2, x_2 = .8$

(e) $x_1 = .2, x_2 = .2$ (f) $x_1 = .6, x_2 = .6$ (g) $x_1 = 1, x_2 = 1$ (h) $x_1 = .2, x_2 = .8$

Fig. 2. The relation between the weight concentrations $[W_1]$ and $[W_2]$ and the final output concentration $[Y]_\infty$ normalized by $[X_1]_0 + [X_2]_0$ for the input-weight integration (excluding the bias W_0 part) showing various inputs. The rate constant of annihilatory reactions $X_i + Y \to \lambda, i \in \{1, 2\}$ is $k = 0.2$ in the top and $k = 1$ in the bottom row.

3.2   Learning

In the previous BASP model, learning reinforced the adaptation of weights by a penalty signal, whose presence indicated that the output was incorrect. Since the output is analog in the new AASP model, a simple penalty signal is not sufficient anymore. We therefore replaced the reinforcement learning by classical supervised learning [15]. Formally, the adaptation of a weight w_i for the training sample $(\mathbf{x}, \hat{y})$, where $\hat{y}$ is a target output, and $\mathbf{x}$ a input vector, is defined as $\triangle w_i = \alpha(\hat{y} - y(t))x_i$, where $\alpha \in (0, 1]$ is the learning rate. The AASP's, similarly to the BASP's input-weight integration, does not implement the formal $\triangle w_i$ adaptation precisely, rather, it follows the relation qualitatively.

The learning is triggered by an injection of the target output $\hat{Y}$ provided some time after the injection of the input species. The part presented in Figure 1(b) compares the output Y and the target output $\hat{Y}$ by annihilation. Intuitively a leftover of the regular output Y implies that the next time the AASP faces the same input, it must produce less output, and therefore it needs to decrease the weights by producing a negative weight changer $W^\ominus$ from Y. In the opposite case, the AASP needs to increase the weights, hence $\hat{Y}$ transforms to a positive weight changer $W^\oplus$. Since the AASP can produce output also without learning, just by the input-weight integration, we need to guard the reaction $Y \to W^\ominus$ by a learning signal S_L, which is injected with the target output and removed afterwards. To prevent creation of erroneous or premature weight changers, the annihilation $Y + \hat{Y} \to \lambda$ must be very rapid. Note that the difference between the actual output Y and the desired output $\hat{Y}$, materializing in the total concentration of weight changers $W^\oplus$ and $W^\ominus$, must not be greater that the required weight adaptation, otherwise the weights would diverge. The learning rate α is therefore effectively incorporated in the concentration of $W^\oplus$ and $W^\ominus$.

In the formal perceptron, the adaptation of a weight w_i is proportional to the current input x_i. Originally, the BASP distinguished which weights to adapt by a residual concentration of inputs X_1 and X_2. Because the inputs as well as an adaptation decision were binary, we cared only about whether some of the unprocessed input were still left, but not about its precise concentration. Thus, an injection of the penalty signal could not happen too soon, neither too late. Because the AASP's learning needs more information, the input-weight integration introduced three additional species, namely the partial input-weight contributions $X_1Y, X_2Y, S_{in}Y$, which are produced alongside the regular output Y. A decision which weights to update based on the input-weight contributions could be made even after the input-weight integration is finished. That allows to postpone an injection of the target output $\hat{Y}$ and the learning signal S_L.

Let us now cover a positive adaptation as shown in Figure 1(c), where the total amount of $W^\oplus$ is distributed among participating weights. The input contribution species $X_1Y, X_2Y, S_{in}Y$ race over the substrate $W^\oplus$ by catalyzing the reactions $W^\oplus \to W_i, i \in \{0, 1, 2\}$. Note that the traditional weight adaptation formula takes into count solely the input value, so here we depart further from the formal perceptron and have the combination of input and weights compete over $W^\oplus$. Since larger weights produce more output they get adapted more. In addition, once a weight reaches zero, it will not be recoverable.

The negative adaptation presented in Figure 1(d) is analogous to the positive one, but this time the input-weight contributions race over $W^\ominus$ and produce intermediates $W_0^\ominus, W_1^\ominus, W_2^\ominus$, which annihilate with the weights. Again, because the magnitude of a weight update depends on the weight itself, this feedback loop protects the weight from falling too low and reaching zero (i.e., a point of no return). This is beneficial because as opposed to the formal perceptron, a weight value (concentration) cannot be physically negative.

To implement the entire learning algorithm, the AASP requires 12 reactions as presented in Table 1(b), groups $5 - 13$.

3.3   Genetic Search

Since a manual trial-and-error setting of the rate constants would be very time-consuming, we optimize the rate constants by a standard genetic algorithm (GA). Possible solutions are encoded on chromosomes as vectors of rate constants, which undergo cross-over and mutation. We use elite selection with elite size 20, 100 chromosomes per generation, shuffle cross-over, per-bit mutation, and a generation limit of 50. The fitness of a chromosome defined as the RN-MSE reflects how well the AASP with the given rate constants (encoded in the chromosome) learns the target functions $k_1x_1 + k_2x_2 + k_0$, k_1x_1, and k_2x_2. The fitness of a single chromosome is then calculated as the average over 300 runs for each function. We included the k_1x_1 and k_2x_2 tasks to force the AASP to utilize and distinguish both inputs x_1 and x_2. Otherwise the GA would have a higher tendency to opt for a greedy statistical approach where only the weight W_0 (mean) might be utilized.

4   Performance

We demonstrate the learning capabilities of the AASP on 6 linear and nonlinear target functions as shown in Table 2. During each learning iteration we inject inputs X_1 and X_2 with concentrations drawn from the interval $(0.2, 1)$ and set the bias input S_{in} concentration to 0.5. We chose the target functions carefully, such that the output concentration is always in a safe region, i.e., far from the minimal (zero) and the maximal output concentration $[S_{in}]_0 + [X_1]_0 + [X_2]_0$. We then inject the target output $\hat{Y}$ with the learning signal S_L 50 steps after the input, which is sufficient to allow the input-weight integration to proceed.

For each function family we calculated the AASP's performance over $10,000$ simulation runs, where each run consists of 400 training iterations. We define performance as the root normalized mean square error (RNMSE)

$$\text{RNMSE} = \sqrt{\frac{\langle (y - \hat{y})^2 \rangle}{\sigma_{\hat{y}}^2}}.$$

A RNMSE of 1 means chance level. The AASP's RNMSE settles down to the range $(0.117, 0.0.388)$ (see Figure 3), which implies that it learns and generalizes all target functions sufficiently. When we include only the functions that utilize

Table 2. Target functions with uniform constant k_1, k_2, k_0 intervals

$\hat{y}$	k_1	k_2	k_0
$k_1 x_1 + k_2 x_2 + k_0$	$(0.2, 0.8)$	$(0.2, 0.8)$	$(0.1, 0.4)$
$k_1 x_1 - k_2 x_2 + k_0$	$(0.2, 0.8)$	$(0.0, 0.3)$	$(0.4, 0.7)$
$k_1 x_1$	$(0.2, 0.8)$	$-$	$-$
$k_2 x_2$	$-$	$(0.2, 0.8)$	$-$
$k_1 x_1 x_2 + k_0$	$(0.2, 0.8)$	$-$	0.25
k_0	$-$	$-$	$(0.1, 0.4)$

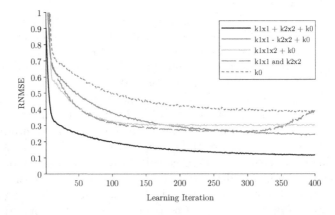

Fig. 3. RNMSE for 6 linear and nonlinear functions over 400 learning iterations

both inputs x_1 and x_2, as well as the bias, i.e., the scenario the AASP was primarily designed for, RNMSE drops to the range $(0.117, 0.298)$. Note that we do not distinguish between the training and testing set. During each iteration we draw the inputs with the target output for a given function independently.

Among all the functions, $k_1x_1 + k_2x_2 + k$ is the easiest (RNMSE of 0.117) and the constant function k_0 the most difficult (RNMSE of 0.388) one. The function k_0 is even more difficult than the nonlinear function $k_1x_1x_2 + k_0$ (RNMSE of 0.298). Compared to the formal perceptron, the constant function does not reach zero RNMSE because the AASP cannot fully eliminate the contribution (or

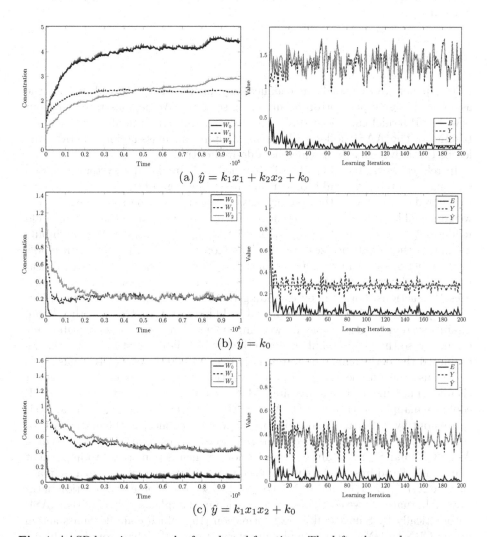

(a) $\hat{y} = k_1x_1 + k_2x_2 + k_0$

(b) $\hat{y} = k_0$

(c) $\hat{y} = k_1x_1x_2 + k_0$

Fig. 4. AASP learning examples for selected functions. The left column shows concentration traces of the weights, the right column the filtered output, the target output, and the absolute error.

consumption) of the X_1 and X_2 input-weight branches. The formal perceptron could simply discard both inputs and adjust only the bias weight, however, the AASP's weights W_1 and W_2 with zero concentration would effectively act as inhibitors, thus consuming a part of the output produced by the bias. On the other hand, a nonlinear $k_1 x_1 x_2 + k_0$ function with fairly low RNMSE would be impossible to calculate for the formal perceptron. Therefore it is an open question what function classes can be learned by the AASP. Note that for the nonlinear function we set $k_0 = 0.25$, which does not increase the variance, i.e., only the nonlinear part counts toward the error. Figure 4 shows the weight concentration traces as well as the output, the target output, and the absolute error for selected functions.

5   Conclusion

In this paper we extended our chemical asymmetric design introduced for the asymmetric signal perceptron to an analog scenario. We demonstrated that our new AASP model can successfully learn several linear and nonlinear two-input functions. The AASP follows Michaelis-Menten and mass-action kinetics, and learns through feedback provided as a desired output.

In related work, Lakin et al. [16] designed and simulated a system based on enzymatic chemistry, capable of learning linear functions of the form $k_1 x_1 + k_2 x_2$. Compared to the AASP, the system lacks cross-weight competition, meaning the weights could not formally represent negative numbers, and so the system could model only strictly additive functions with $k_1, k_2 \geq 0$. Besides regular inputs x_1 and x_2 the AASP utilizes also the bias (constant shift), hence it can model linear functions of a more general form $k_1 x_1 + k_2 x_2 + k_0$ as well as nonlinear (quadratic) functions of the form $k x_1 x_2 + k_0$, where $k_1, k_2, k_0 \in \mathbb{R}$. The AASP uses 18 reactions, however, by excluding the bias (k_0) part, it would need just 13 as opposed to 27 reactions employed in Lakin's system. On the other hand, Lakin's system targets a specific wet implementation based on deoxyribozyme chemistry, so the higher number of reactions is justifiable. Last but not least, we evaluated the performance more precisely over $10,000$ instead of 10 trials.

Because the number of species and reactions employed is fairly low, a wet chemical implementation is plausible. More precisely, we suggest that the AASP could be mapped to catalytic DNA chemistry [17, 18] by having each catalysis carried out by deoxyribozime-substrate cleavage. The most problematic part for this mapping would be the feedback reactions, where each of three enzymes, $X_1 Y, X_2 Y$, and $S_{in} Y$, catalyzes two reactions, which is non-trivial to implement in practice. To address that we would need to introduce two variants of a feedback enzyme $X_i Y^\oplus$ ($S_{in} Y^\oplus$) and $X_i Y^\ominus$ ($S_{in} Y^\ominus$) to separate these two reaction pathways. Alternatively we could obtain a wet chemical implementation of the AASP automatically by Soloveichik's transformation [19], which compiles mass-action driven CRN to DNA-strand displacement reactions [20]. That would produce a chemical circuit with around 80 different DNA strands, which is in the range of other state-of-the-art DNA circuits.

As opposed to our previous designs using simple binary signals, the AASP allows to adapt to precise concentration levels. By integrating the AASP with a chemical delay line as proposed in [11], we could also tackle time-series prediction. Consequently, chemical systems would be able monitor concentrations of selected molecular species and respond if a severe event, defined as a linear or nonlinear temporal concentration pattern, occurs. Such a system would be highly relevant where the quantity or type of the drug required could be adjusted in real-time with complex relations among species, e.g., produced by cancer cells.

Acknowledgment. This material is based upon work supported by the National Science Foundation under grant no. 1028120.

References

1. Wang, W., Li, S., Mair, L., Ahmed, S., Huang, T.J., Mallouk, T.E.: Acoustic Propulsion of Nanorod Motors Inside Living Cells. Angewandte Chemie International Edition 53(12), 3201–3204 (2014)
2. LaVan, D.A., McGuire, T., Langer, R.: Small-scale systems for in vivo drug delivery. Nature Biotechnology 21(10), 1184–1191 (2003)
3. Haykin, S.: Neural networks and learning machines, 3rd edn. Pearson, New Jersey (2009)
4. Bray, D.: Protein molecules as computational elements in living cells. Nature 376(6538), 307–312 (1995)
5. Mills, A.P., Yurke, B., Platzman, P.M.: Article for analog vector algebra computation. Biosystems 52(1-3), 175–180 (1999)
6. Kim, J., Hopfield, J.J., Winfree, E.: Neural network computation by in vitro transcriptional circuits. In: Saul, L.K., Weiss, Y., Bottou, L. (eds.) Advances in Neural Information Processing Systems, vol. 17, pp. 681–688. MIT Press (2004)
7. Rosenblatt, F.: The perceptron: A probabilistic model for information storage and organisation in the brain. Psychological Review 65, 368–408 (1958)
8. Qian, L., Winfree, E., Bruck, J.: Neural network computation with DNA strand displacement cascades. Nature 475(7356), 368–372 (2011)
9. Banda, P., Teuscher, C., Lakin, M.R.: Online learning in a chemical perceptron. Artificial Life 19(2), 195–219 (2013)
10. Banda, P., Teuscher, C., Stefanovic, D.: Training an asymmetric signal perceptron through reinforcement in an artificial chemistry. Journal of the Royal Society Interface 11(93) (2014)
11. Moles, J., Banda, P., Teuscher, C.: Delay line as a chemical reaction network (under review). Parallel Processing Letters (2014)
12. Espenson, J.: Chemical kinetics and reaction mechanisms. McGraw-Hill, Singapore (1995)
13. Copeland, R.A.: Enzymes: A practical introduction to structure, mechanism, and data analysis, 2nd edn. John Wiley & Sons, Inc., New York (2002)
14. Hornik, K., Stinchcombe, M., White, H.: Multilayer feedforward networks are universal approximators. Neural Networks 2(5), 359–366 (1989)
15. Rojas, R.: Neural networks: A systematic introduction. Springer, Berlin (1996)
16. Lakin, M.R., Minnich, A., Lane, T., Stefanovic, D.: Towards a biomolecular learning machine. In: Durand-Lose, J., Jonoska, N. (eds.) UCNC 2012. LNCS, vol. 7445, pp. 152–163. Springer, Heidelberg (2012)

17. Stojanovic, M.N., Stefanovic, D.: A deoxyribozyme-based molecular automaton. Nature Biotechnology 21(9), 1069–1074 (2003)
18. Liu, J., Cao, Z., Lu, Y.: Functional nucleic acid sensors. Chemical Reviews 109(5), 1948–1998 (2009); PMID: 19301873
19. Soloveichik, D., Seelig, G., Winfree, E.: DNA as a universal substrate for chemical kinetics. Proceedings of the National Academy of Sciences of the United States of America 107(12), 5393–5398 (2010)
20. Zhang, D.Y., Seelig, G.: Dynamic DNA nanotechnology using strand-displacement reactions. Nature Chemistry 3(2), 103–113 (2011)

Scaled Tree Fractals Do not Strictly Self-assemble

Kimberly Barth, David Furcy, Scott M. Summers, and Paul Totzke

Department of Computer Science, University of Wisconsin–Oshkosh,
Oshkosh, WI 54901, USA
{barthk63,furcyd,summerss,totzkp00}@uwosh.edu

Abstract. In this paper, we show that any scaled-up version of any
discrete self-similar *tree* fractal does not strictly self-assemble, at any
temperature, in Winfree's abstract Tile Assembly Model.

1 Introduction

The stunning, often mysterious complexities of the natural world, from nanoscale
crystalline structures to unthinkably massive galaxies, all arise from the same
elemental process known as *self-assembly*. In the absence of a mathematically
rigorous definition, self-assembly is colloquially thought of as the process through
which simple, unorganized components spontaneously combine, according to local interaction rules, to form some kind of organized final structure. A major
objective of nanotechnology is to harness the power of self-assembly, perhaps for
the purpose of engineering atomically precise medical, digital and mechanical
components at the nanoscale. One strategy for doing so, developed by Nadrian
Seeman, is *DNA tile self-assembly* [8, 9].

In DNA tile self-assembly, the fundamental components are "tiles", which are
comprised of interconnected DNA strands. Remarkably, these DNA tiles can be
"programmed", via the careful configuration of their constituent DNA strands,
to automatically coalesce into a desired target structure, the characteristics of
which are completely determined by the "programming" of the DNA tiles. In
order to fully realize the power of DNA tile self-assembly, we must study the
algorithmic and mathematical underpinnings of tile self-assembly.

Perhaps the simplest mathematical model of algorithmic tile self-assembly
is Erik Winfree's abstract Tile Assembly Model (aTAM) [11]. The aTAM is a
deliberately over-simplified, combinatorial model of nanoscale (DNA) tile self-
assembly that "effectivizes" classical Wang tiling [10] in the sense that the former
augments the latter with a mechanism for sequential "growth" of a tile assembly.
Very briefly, in the aTAM, the fundamental components are un-rotatable, trans-
latable square "tile types" whose sides are labeled with (alpha-numeric) glue
"colors" and (integer) "strengths". Two tiles that are placed next to each other
interact if the glue colors on their abutting sides match, and they *bind* if the

O.H. Ibarra et al. (Eds.): UCNC 2014, LNCS 8553, pp. 27–39, 2014.
DOI: 10.1007/978-3-319-08123-6_3, © Springer International Publishing Switzerland 2014

strengths on their abutting sides match and sum to at least a certain (integer) "temperature". Self-assembly starts from a "seed" tile type, typically assumed to be placed at the origin, and proceeds nondeterministically and asynchronously as tiles bind to the seed-containing assembly one at a time.

Despite its deliberate over-simplification, the aTAM is a computationally expressive model. For example, Winfree [11] proved that the model is Turing universal, which means that, in principle, the process of self-assembly can be directed by any algorithm. In this paper, we will specifically study the extent to which tile sets in the aTAM can be algorithmically directed to "strictly" self-assemble (place tiles at and only at locations that belong to) shapes that are discrete self-similar tree fractals.

There are examples of prior results related to the self-assembly of fractals in the aTAM, in general [1, 2, 6], as well as the strict self-assembly of tree fractals in the aTAM, specifically [3, 4]. In fact, a notable example of the latter is [3], Theorem 3.2 of which bounds from below the size of the smallest tile set in which an arbitrary shape X strictly self-assembles by the depth of X's largest finite sub-tree. Although not stated explicitly, an immediate corollary of Theorem 3.2 of [3] is that no tree fractals strictly self-assemble in the aTAM.

While the strict self-assembly of tree fractals in the aTAM is well-understood (via Theorem 3.2 of [3]), nothing is known about the strict self-assembly of "scaled-up" versions of tree fractals ("scaled-up" meaning each point in the original shape is replaced by a $c \times c$ block of points). After all, the scaled-up version of any shape – tree or otherwise – is *not* a tree in the sense of the "full connectivity graph" of the shape, i.e., each point in the shape is represented by one vertex and edges exist between vertices that represent adjacent points in the shape. This means that prior proof techniques, which exploit the intricate geometry of tree fractals (e.g., [3, 4]), simply cannot be applied to scaled-up versions of tree fractals. Thus, in this paper, we ask if it is possible for a scaled-up version of a tree fractal to strictly self-assemble in the aTAM.

The main contribution of this paper provides an answer to the previous question, perhaps not too surprisingly to readers familiar with the aTAM, in the negative: we prove that there is no tree fractal that strictly self-assembles in the aTAM – at any positive scale factor. Thus, our main result generalizes Theorem 3.4 of [3], which says that the Sierpinski triangle, perhaps the most famous, well-studied example of a tree fractal, does not strictly self-assemble at scale factor 1. Our proof makes crucial use of a recent technical lemma developed by Meunier, Patitz, Summers, Theyssier, Winslow and Woods [5], known as the "Window Movie Lemma" (WML), which gives a sufficient condition for taking any pair of tile assemblies, at any temperature, and "splicing" them together to create a new valid tile assembly. The WML is, in some sense, a pumping lemma for self-assembly that mitigates the need to use overly-complicated, convoluted case-analyses that typically arise when doing impossibility proofs in self-assembly.

What follows is a list of the main technical contributions presented in – and the general outline of – this paper:

- In Section 2.2, we exhibit a natural characterization of a tree fractal in terms of a few simple, easily checkable geometric properties of its generator. While perhaps well-known, this type of characterization, to the best of our knowledge, has yet to be explicitly documented or proved in the literature.
- In Section 2.3, we develop a modified version of the general WML. Our version of the WML, which we call the "Closed Window Movie Lemma", allows us to replace one portion of a tile assembly with another, assuming certain extra "containment" conditions are met. Moreover, unlike in the original WML that lacks the extra containment assumptions, the replacement of one tile assembly with another in our Closed WML only goes "one way", i.e., the part of the tile assembly being used to replace another part cannot itself be replaced by the part of the tile assembly it is replacing.
- In Section 3, we use our closed WML to prove that any scaled-up version of any tree fractal does not strictly self-assemble in the aTAM at any temperature. Our main result generalizes the claim that every tree fractal, at scale factor 1, does not strictly self-assemble in the aTAM (an implicit corollary to the main negative result of [3]).

2 Definitions

In this section, we give a formal definition of Erik Winfree's abstract Tile Assembly Model (aTAM), define and characterize tree fractals and develop a "Closed" Window Movie Lemma.

2.1 Formal Description of the Abstract Tile Assembly Model

This section gives a formal definition of the abstract Tile Assembly Model (aTAM) [11]. For readers unfamiliar with the aTAM, [7] gives an excellent introduction to the model.

Fix an alphabet Σ. Σ^* is the set of finite strings over Σ. Let $\mathbb{Z}$, $\mathbb{Z}^+$, and $\mathbb{N}$ denote the set of integers, positive integers, and nonnegative integers, respectively. Given $V \subseteq \mathbb{Z}^2$, the *full grid graph* of V is the undirected graph $G^f_V = (V, E)$, such that, for all $x, y \in V$, $\{x, y\} \in E \iff \|x - y\| = 1$, i.e., if and only if x and y are adjacent in the 2-dimensional integer Cartesian space.

A *tile type* is a tuple $t \in (\Sigma^* \times \mathbb{N})^4$, e.g., a unit square, with four sides, listed in some standardized order, and each side having a *glue* $g \in \Sigma^* \times \mathbb{N}$ consisting of a finite string *label* and a nonnegative integer *strength*.

We assume a finite set of tile types, but an infinite number of copies of each tile type, each copy referred to as a *tile*. A tile set is a set of tile types and is usually denoted as T.

A *configuration* is a (possibly empty) arrangement of tiles on the integer lattice $\mathbb{Z}^2$, i.e., a partial function $\alpha : \mathbb{Z}^2 \dashrightarrow T$. Two adjacent tiles in a configuration *interact*, or are *attached*, if the glues on their abutting sides are equal (in both label and strength) and have positive strength. Each configuration α induces a *binding graph* G_α^b, a grid graph whose vertices are positions occupied by tiles, according to α, with an edge between two vertices if the tiles at those vertices interact. An *assembly* is a connected, non-empty configuration, i.e., a partial function $\alpha : \mathbb{Z}^2 \dashrightarrow T$ such that $G_{\text{dom } \alpha}^f$ is connected and dom $\alpha \neq \varnothing$.

Given $\tau \in \mathbb{Z}^+$, α is τ-*stable* if every cut-set of G_α^b has weight at least τ, where the weight of an edge is the strength of the glue it represents.[1] When τ is clear from context, we say α is *stable*. Given two assemblies α, β, we say α is a *subassembly* of β, and we write $\alpha \sqsubseteq \beta$, if dom $\alpha \subseteq$ dom β and, for all points $p \in$ dom α, $\alpha(p) = \beta(p)$. For two non-overlapping assemblies α and β, $\alpha \cup \beta$ is defined as the unique assembly γ satisfying, for all $\boldsymbol{x} \in$ dom α, $\gamma(\boldsymbol{x}) = \alpha(\boldsymbol{x})$, for all $\boldsymbol{x} \in$ dom β, $\gamma(\boldsymbol{x}) = \beta(\boldsymbol{x})$, and $\gamma(\boldsymbol{x})$ is undefined at any point $\boldsymbol{x} \in \mathbb{Z}^2 \backslash (\text{dom } \alpha \cup \text{dom } \beta)$.

A *tile assembly system* (TAS) is a triple $\mathcal{T} = (T, \sigma, \tau)$, where T is a tile set, $\sigma : \mathbb{Z}^2 \dashrightarrow T$ is the finite, τ-stable, *seed assembly*, and $\tau \in \mathbb{Z}^+$ is the *temperature*.

Given two τ-stable assemblies α, β, we write $\alpha \to_1^{\mathcal{T}} \beta$ if $\alpha \sqsubseteq \beta$ and $|\text{dom } \beta \backslash \text{dom } \alpha| = 1$. In this case we say α $\mathcal{T}$-*produces* β *in one step*. If $\alpha \to_1^{\mathcal{T}} \beta$, dom $\beta \backslash \text{dom } \alpha = \{p\}$, and $t = \beta(p)$, we write $\beta = \alpha + (p \mapsto t)$. The $\mathcal{T}$-*frontier* of α is the set $\partial^{\mathcal{T}} \alpha = \bigcup_{\alpha \to_1^{\mathcal{T}} \beta}(\text{dom } \beta \backslash \text{dom } \alpha)$, the set of empty locations at which a tile could stably attach to α. The t-*frontier* $\partial_t^{\mathcal{T}} \alpha \subseteq \partial^{\mathcal{T}} \alpha$ of α is the set $\{ p \in \partial^{\mathcal{T}} \alpha \mid \alpha \to_1^{\mathcal{T}} \beta \text{ and } \beta(p) = t \}$.

Let $\mathcal{A}^T$ denote the set of all assemblies of tiles from T, and let $\mathcal{A}_{<\infty}^T$ denote the set of finite assemblies of tiles from T. A sequence of $k \in \mathbb{Z}^+ \cup \{\infty\}$ assemblies $\alpha_0, \alpha_1, \ldots$ over $\mathcal{A}^T$ is a $\mathcal{T}$-*assembly sequence* if, for all $1 \leq i < k$, $\alpha_{i-1} \to_1^{\mathcal{T}} \alpha_i$. The *result* of an assembly sequence $\boldsymbol{\alpha}$, denoted as res($\boldsymbol{\alpha}$), is the unique limiting assembly (for a finite sequence, this is the final assembly in the sequence).

We write $\alpha \to^{\mathcal{T}} \beta$, and we say α $\mathcal{T}$-*produces* β (in 0 or more steps) if there is a $\mathcal{T}$-assembly sequence $\alpha_0, \alpha_1, \ldots$ of length $k = |\text{dom } \beta \backslash \text{dom } \alpha| + 1$ such that (1) $\alpha = \alpha_0$, (2) dom $\beta = \bigcup_{0 \leq i < k} \text{dom } \alpha_i$, and (3) for all $0 \leq i < k$, $\alpha_i \sqsubseteq \beta$. If k is finite then it is routine to verify that $\beta = \alpha_{k-1}$.

We say α is $\mathcal{T}$-*producible* if $\sigma \to^{\mathcal{T}} \alpha$, and we write $\mathcal{A}[\mathcal{T}]$ to denote the set of $\mathcal{T}$-producible assemblies. The relation $\to^{\mathcal{T}}$ is a partial order on $\mathcal{A}[\mathcal{T}]$ [3, 7].

An assembly α is $\mathcal{T}$-*terminal* if α is τ-stable and $\partial^{\mathcal{T}} \alpha = \varnothing$. We write $\mathcal{A}_\square[\mathcal{T}] \subseteq \mathcal{A}[\mathcal{T}]$ to denote the set of $\mathcal{T}$-producible, $\mathcal{T}$-terminal assemblies. If $|\mathcal{A}_\square[\mathcal{T}]| = 1$ then $\mathcal{T}$ is said to be *directed*.

We say that a TAS $\mathcal{T}$ *strictly* (a.k.a. *uniquely*) *self-assembles* $X \subseteq \mathbb{Z}^2$ if, for all $\alpha \in \mathcal{A}_\square[\mathcal{T}]$, dom $\alpha = X$; i.e., if every terminal assembly produced by $\mathcal{T}$ places tiles on – and only on – points in the set X.

In this paper, we consider scaled-up versions of subsets of $\mathbb{Z}^2$. Formally, if X is a subset of $\mathbb{Z}^2$ and $c \in \mathbb{Z}^+$, then a c-*scaling* of X is defined as the set $X^c = \{(x,y) \in \mathbb{Z}^2 \mid (\lfloor \frac{x}{c} \rfloor, \lfloor \frac{y}{c} \rfloor) \in X\}$. Intuitively, X^c is the subset of $\mathbb{Z}^2$ obtained by

---

[1] A *cut-set* is a subset of edges in a graph which, when removed from the graph, produces two or more disconnected subgraphs. The *weight* of a cut-set is the sum of the weights of all of the edges in the cut-set.

replacing each point in X with a $c \times c$ block of points. We refer to the natural number c as the *scaling factor* or *resolution loss*.

2.2   Discrete Self-similar Tree Fractals

In this section, we introduce a new formal characterization of discrete self-similar tree fractals. The proof of Theorem 1 below is omitted from this version of the paper due to lack of space.

Notation 1. *We use $\mathbb{N}_g$ to denote the subset $\{0, \ldots, g-1\}$ of $\mathbb{N}$.*

Notation 2. *If A and B are subsets of $\mathbb{N}^2$ and $k \in \mathbb{N}$, then $A + kB = \{m + kn \mid m \in A \text{ and } n \in B\}$.*

The following definition is adapted from [6].

Definition 1. *Let $1 < g \in \mathbb{N}$ and $\mathbf{X} \subset \mathbb{N}^2$. We say that $\mathbf{X}$ is a g-discrete self-similar fractal (or g-dssf for short), if there is a set $\{(0,0)\} \subset G \subset \mathbb{N}_g^2$ with at least one point in every row and column, such that $\mathbf{X} = \bigcup_{i=1}^{\infty} X_i$, where X_i, the ith stage of $\mathbf{X}$, is defined by $X_1 = G$ and $X_{i+1} = X_i + g^i G$. We say that G is the generator of $\mathbf{X}$.*

Intuitively, a g-dssf is built as follows. Start by selecting points in $\mathbb{N}_g^2$ satisfying the constraints listed in Definition 1. This first stage of the fractal is the generator. Then, each subsequent stage of the fractal is obtained by adding a full copy of the previous stage for every point in the generator and translating these copies so that their relative positions are identical to the relative positions of the individual points in the gnerator.

In this paper, we focus on *tree* fractals, that is, fractals whose underlying graph is a tree. We introduce terminology and notation that will help us in formulating a complete characterization of tree fractals in terms of geometric properties of their generator.

Definition 2. *Let S be any finite subset of $\mathbb{Z}^2$. Let l, r, b, and t denote the following integers:*

$$l_S = \min_{(x,y)\in S} x \qquad r_S = \max_{(x,y)\in S} x \qquad b_S = \min_{(x,y)\in S} y \qquad t_S = \max_{(x,y)\in S} y$$

An h-bridge of S is any subset of S of the form $hb_S(y) = \{(l_S, y), (r_S, y)\}$. Similarly, a v-bridge of S is any subset of S of the form $vb_S(x) = \{(x, b_S), (x, t_S)\}$. We say that a bridge is connected if there is a simple path in S connecting the two bridge points.

Notation 3. *Let S be any finite subset of $\mathbb{Z}^2$. We will denote by nhb_S and nvb_S, respectively, the number of h-bridges and the number of v-bridges of S.*

The following theorem is a new characterization of tree fractals in terms of simple connectivity properties of their generator.

Theorem 1. $\mathbf{T} = \bigcup_{i=1}^{\infty} T_i$ *is a g-discrete self-similar tree fractal, for some $g > 1$, with generator G if and only if*

  a. G is a tree, and
  b. $nhb_G = nvb_G = 1$

Notation 4. *The directions $\mathcal{D} = \{N, E, S, W\}$ will be used as functions from $\mathbb{Z}^2$ to $\mathbb{Z}^2$ such that $N(x, y) = (x, y + 1)$, $E(x, y) = (x + 1, y)$, $S(x, y) = (x, y - 1)$ and $W(x, y) = (x - 1, y)$. Note that $N^{-1} = S$ and $W^{-1} = E$.*

Notation 5. *Let $X \subseteq \mathbb{Z}^2$. We say that a point $(x, y) \in X$ is D-free in X, for some direction D, if $D(x, y) \notin X$.*

Definition 3. *Let G be the generator of any g-discrete self-similar fractal. A* pier *is a point in G that is D-free for exactly three of the four directions in $\mathcal{D}$. We say that a pier (p, q) is D-pointing if $D^{-1}(p, q) \in G$. Note that a pier always points in exactly one direction*

Finally, the following observation follows from the fact that a tree with more than one vertex must contain at least two leaf nodes.

Observation 1. *If G is the generator of any discrete self-similar fractal and G is a tree, then it must contain at least two piers.*

2.3 The Closed Window Movie Lemma

In this subsection, we develop a more accommodating (modified) version of the general Window Movie Lemma (WML) [5]. Our version of the WML, which we call the "Closed Window Movie Lemma", allows us to replace one portion of a tile assembly with another, assuming certain extra "containment" conditions are met. Moreover, unlike in the original WML that lacks the extra containment assumptions, the replacement of one tile assembly with another in our Closed WML only goes "one way", i.e., the part of the tile assembly being used to replace another part cannot itself be replaced by the part of the tile assembly it is replacing. We must first define some notation that we will use in our closed Window Movie Lemma.

  A window w is a set of edges forming a cut-set of the full grid graph of $\mathbb{Z}^2$. For the purposes of this paper, we say that a *closed window* w induces a cut[2] of the full grid graph of $\mathbb{Z}^2$, written as $C_w = (C_{<\infty}, C_\infty)$, where C_∞ is infinite, $C_{<\infty}$ is finite and for all pairs of points $\boldsymbol{x}, \boldsymbol{y} \in C_{<\infty}$, every simple path connecting $\boldsymbol{x}$ and $\boldsymbol{y}$ in the full grid graph of $C_{<\infty}$ does not cross the cut C_w. We call the set of vertices that make up $C_{<\infty}$ the *inside* of the window w, and write $inside(w) = C_{<\infty}$ and $outside(w) = \mathbb{Z}^2 \setminus inside(w) = C_\infty$. We say that a window w is *enclosed* in another window w' if $inside(w) \subseteq inside(w')$.

---

[2] A *cut* is a partition of the vertices of a graph into two disjoint subsets that are joined by at least one edge.

Given a window w and an assembly α, a window that *intersects* α is a partitioning of α into two configurations (i.e., after being split into two parts, each part may or may not be disconnected). In this case we say that the window w cuts the assembly α into two configurations α_L and α_R, where $\alpha = \alpha_L \cup \alpha_R$. For notational convenience, if w is a closed window, we write α_I for the assembly inside w and α_O for the assembly outside w. Given a window w, its translation by a vector c, written $w + c$ is simply the translation of each of w's elements (edges) by c.

For a window w and an assembly sequence α, we define a window movie M to be the order of placement, position and glue type for each glue that appears along the window w in α. Given an assembly sequence α and a window w, the associated *window movie* is the maximal sequence $M_{\alpha,w} = (v_0, g_0), (v_1, g_1), (v_2, g_2), \ldots$ of pairs of grid graph vertices v_i and glues g_i, given by the order of the appearance of the glues along window w in the assembly sequence α. Furthermore, if k glues appear along w at the same instant (this happens upon placement of a tile that has multiple sides touching w) then these k glues appear contiguously and are listed in lexicographical order of the unit vectors describing their orientation in $M_{\alpha,w}$.

Let w be a window and α be an assembly sequence and $M = M_{\alpha,w}$. We use the notation $\mathcal{B}(M)$ to denote the *bond-forming submovie* of M, i.e., a restricted form of M that consists of only those steps of M that place glues that eventually form positive-strength bonds in the assembly $\alpha = \text{res}(\alpha)$. Note that every window movie has a unique bond-forming submovie.

Lemma 1 (Closed Window Movie Lemma). *Let $\alpha = (\alpha_i \mid 0 \le i < l)$, with $l \in \mathbb{Z}^+ \cup \{\infty\}$, be an assembly sequence in some TAS $\mathcal{T}$ with result α. Let w be a closed window that partitions α into α_I and α_O, and w' be a closed window that partitions α into α_I' and α_O'. If $\mathcal{B}(M_{\alpha,w}) + c = \mathcal{B}(M_{\alpha,w'})$ for some $c \neq (0,0)$ and the window $w + c$ is enclosed in w', then the assembly $\alpha_O' \cup (\alpha_I + c)$ is in $\mathcal{A}[\mathcal{T}]$.*

Proof. Before we proceed with the proof, the next paragraph introduces some notation taken directly from [5].

For an assembly sequence $\alpha = (\alpha_i \mid 0 \le i < l)$, we write $|\alpha| = l$ (note that if α is infinite, then $l = \infty$). We write $\alpha[i]$ to denote $x \mapsto t$, where x and t are such that $\alpha_{i+1} = \alpha_i + (x \mapsto t)$, i.e., $\alpha[i]$ is the placement of tile type t at position x, assuming that $x \in \partial_t \alpha_i$. We write $\alpha[i] + c$, for some vector c, to denote $(x + c) \mapsto t$. We define $\alpha = \alpha + (x \mapsto t) = (\alpha_i \mid 0 \le i < k + 1)$, where $\alpha_k = \alpha_{k-1} + (x \mapsto t)$ if $x \in \partial_t \alpha_{k-1}$ and undefined otherwise, assuming $|\alpha| > 0$. Otherwise, if $|\alpha| = 0$, then $\alpha = \alpha + (x \mapsto t) = (\alpha_0)$, where α_0 is the assembly such that $\alpha_0(x) = t$ and is undefined at all other positions. This is our notation for appending steps to the assembly sequence α: to do so, we must specify a tile type t to be placed at a given location $x \in \partial_t \alpha_i$. If $\alpha_{i+1} = \alpha_i + (x \mapsto t)$, then we write $Pos(\alpha[i]) = x$ and $Tile(\alpha[i]) = t$. For a window movie $M = (v_0, g_0), (v_1, g_1), \ldots$, we write $M[k]$ to be the pair (v_k, g_k) in the enumeration of M and $Pos(M[k]) = v_k$, where v_k is a vertex of a grid graph.

We now proceed with the proof, throughout which we will assume that $M = \mathcal{B}(M_{\alpha,w})$ and $M' = \mathcal{B}(M_{\alpha,w'})$. Since $M + c = M'$ for some $c \neq (0,0)$ and w and w' are both closed windows, it must be the case that the seed tile of α is in dom $\alpha_O \cap$ dom α'_O or in dom $\alpha_I \cap$ dom α'_I. In other words, the seed tile cannot be in dom $\alpha_I \setminus$ dom α'_I nor in dom $\alpha'_I \setminus$ dom α_I. Therefore, assume without loss of generality that the seed tile is in dom $\alpha_O \cap$ dom α'_O.

The algorithm in Figure 1 describes how to produce a new valid assembly sequence γ.

> Initialize $i, j = 0$ and γ to be empty
> **for** $k = 0$ **to** $|M| - 1$ **do**
>   **if** $Pos(M'[k]) \in$ dom α'_O **then**
>   **while** $Pos(\alpha[i]) \neq Pos(M'[k])$ **do**
>   **if** $Pos(\alpha[i]) \in$ dom α'_O **then**
> $\gamma = \gamma + \alpha[i]$
> $i = i + 1$
> $\gamma = \gamma + \alpha[i]$
> $i = i + 1$
>   **else**
>   **while** $Pos(\alpha[j]) \neq Pos(M[k])$ **do**
>   **if** $Pos(\alpha[j]) \in$ dom α_I **then**
> $\gamma = \gamma + (\alpha[j] + c)$
> $j = j + 1$
> $\gamma = \gamma + \alpha[j]$
> $j = j + 1$
> **while** $inside(w) \cap \partial res(\gamma) \neq \varnothing$ **do**
>   **if** $Pos(\alpha[j]) \in$ dom α_I **then**
> $\gamma = \gamma + (\alpha[j] + c)$
> $j = j + 1$
> **while** $i < |\alpha|$ **do**
>   **if** $Pos(\alpha[i]) \in$ dom α'_O **then**
> $\gamma = \gamma + \alpha[i]$
> $i = i + 1$
> **return** γ

Fig. 1. The algorithm to produce a valid assembly sequence γ

If we assume that the assembly sequence γ ultimately produced by the algorithm is valid, then the result of γ is indeed $\alpha'_O \cup (\alpha_I + c)$. Observe that α_I must be finite, which implies that M is finite. If $|\alpha| < \infty$, then all loops will terminate. If $|\alpha| = \infty$, then $|\alpha'_O| = \infty$ and the first two loops will terminate and the last loop will run forever. In either case, for every tile in α'_O and $\alpha_I + c$, the algorithm adds a step to the sequence γ involving the addition of this tile to the assembly. However, we need to prove that the assembly sequence γ is valid. It may be the case that either: 1. there is insufficient bond strength between the tile to be placed and the existing neighboring tiles, or 2. a tile is already present at this location.

Case 1: In this case, we claim the following: at each step of the algorithm, the current version of γ is a valid assembly sequence whose result is a producible subassembly of $\alpha'_O \cup (\alpha_I + \boldsymbol{c})$. Note that three loops in the algorithm iterate through all steps of $\boldsymbol{\alpha}$, such that at any time when adding $\boldsymbol{\alpha}[i]$ (or $\boldsymbol{\alpha}[j] + \boldsymbol{c}$) to γ, all steps of the window movie occurring before $\boldsymbol{\alpha}[i]$ (or $\boldsymbol{\alpha}[j]$) in $\boldsymbol{\alpha}$ have occurred. Similarly, all tiles in α'_O (or $\alpha_I + \boldsymbol{c}$) added to α before step i in the assembly sequence have occurred.

So, if the tile $Tile(\boldsymbol{\alpha}[i])$ that is added to the subassembly of α produced after $i - 1$ steps can bond at a location in α'_O to form a τ-stable assembly, then the same tile added to the producible assembly of γ must also bond to the same location in γ, as the neighboring glues consist of (i) an identical set of glues from tiles in the subassembly of α'_O and (ii) glues on the side of the window movie containing $\alpha_I + \boldsymbol{c}$. Similarly, the tiles of $\alpha_I + \boldsymbol{c}$ must also be able to bind.

Case 2: Since we only assume that $\mathcal{B}(M_{\boldsymbol{\alpha},w}) + \boldsymbol{c} = \mathcal{B}(M_{\boldsymbol{\alpha},w'})$, as opposed to the stronger condition $\mathcal{B}(M_{\boldsymbol{\alpha},w+\boldsymbol{c}}) = \mathcal{B}(M_{\boldsymbol{\alpha},w'})$, which is assumed in the original WML, we must show that dom $(\alpha_I + \boldsymbol{c}) \cap$ dom $\alpha'_O = \varnothing$. To see this, observe that, by assumption, $w + \boldsymbol{c}$ is enclosed in w', which, by definition, means that $inside(w + \boldsymbol{c}) \subseteq inside(w')$. Then we have $\boldsymbol{x} \in$ dom $\alpha'_O \Rightarrow \boldsymbol{x} \in outside(w') \Rightarrow \boldsymbol{x} \notin inside(w') \Rightarrow \boldsymbol{x} \notin inside(w + \boldsymbol{c}) \Rightarrow \boldsymbol{x} \notin$ dom $(\alpha_I + \boldsymbol{c})$. Thus, locations in $\alpha_I + \boldsymbol{c}$ only have tiles from α_I placed in them, and locations in α'_O only have tiles from α'_O placed in them.

So the assembly sequence of γ is valid, i.e., every addition to γ adds a tile to the assembly to form a new producible assembly. Since we have a valid assembly sequence, as argued above, the finished producible assembly is $\alpha'_O \cup (\alpha_I + \boldsymbol{c})$.   □

3   Main Result: Scaled Tree Fractals do not Strictly Self-assemble

In this section, we first define some notation and then prove our main result.

3.1   Notation

Recall that each stage X_s ($s > 1$) of a g-dssf (scaled by a factor c) is made up of copies of the previous stage X_{s-1}, each of which is a square of size cg^{s-1}. In the proof of our main result, we will need to refer to one of the squares of size cg^{s-2} inside the copies of stage X_{s-1}, leading to the following notation.

Notation 6. *Let* $c \in \mathbb{Z}^+$, $1 < s \in \mathbb{N}$ *and* $1 < g \in \mathbb{N}$. *Let* $e, f, p, q \in \mathbb{N}_g$. *We use* $S^c_s(e, f, p, q)$ *to denote* $\{0, 1, \ldots, cg^{s-2} - 1\}^2 + cg^{s-1}(e, f) + cg^{s-2}(p, q)$ *and* $W^c_s(e, f, p, q)$ *to denote the square-shaped, closed window whose inside is* $S^c_s(e, f, p, q)$.

In Figure 2 below, the small and large red windows are $W^1_2(0, 1, 3, 2)$ and $W^1_3(0, 1, 3, 2)$, respectively.

Next, we will need to translate a small window to a position inside a larger window. These two windows will correspond to squares at the same relative position in different stages i and j of a g-dssf.

Notation 7. *Let* $c \in \mathbb{Z}^+$, $i, j \in \mathbb{N} \setminus \{0, 1\}$, *with* $i < j$, *and* $e, f, p, q \in \mathbb{N}_g$. *We use* $t_{i \to j}^c(e, f, p, q)$ *to denote the vector joining the southwest corner of* $W_i^c(e, f, p, q)$ *to the southwest corner of* $W_j^c(e, f, p, q)$. *In other words,* $t_{i \to j}^c(e, f, p, q) = \left(c \left(g^{j-1} - g^{i-1} \right) e + c \left(g^{j-2} - g^{i-2} \right) p, c \left(g^{j-1} - g^{i-1} \right) f + c \left(g^{j-2} - g^{i-2} \right) q \right)$.

For example, in Figure 2 below, $t_{2 \to 3}^1(0, 1, 3, 2) = (9, 18)$.

Finally, to apply Lemma 1, we will need the bond-forming submovies to line up. Therefore, once the two square windows share their southwest corner after using the translation defined above, we will need to further translate the smallest one either up or to the right, or both, depending on which side of the windows contains the bond-forming glues, which, in the case of scaled tree fractals, always form a straight (vertical or horizontal) line of length c. We will compute the coordinates of this second translation in our main proof. For now, we establish an upper bound on these coordinates that will ensure that the translated window will remain enclosed in the larger window.

Lemma 2. *Let* $c \in \mathbb{Z}^+$, $i, j \in \mathbb{N} \setminus \{0, 1\}$, *with* $i < j$, $e, f, p, q \in \mathbb{N}_g$, *and* $x, y \in \mathbb{N}$. *Let* $m = c(g^{j-2} - g^{i-2})$. *If* $x \leq m$ *and* $y \leq m$, *then the window* $W_i^c(e, f, p, q) + t_{i \to j}^c(e, f, p, q) + (x, y)$ *is enclosed in the window* $W_j^c(e, f, p, q)$.

Finally, the following lemma establishes that any scaled tree fractal $\mathbf{T}^c$ contains an infinite number of closed windows that all cut the fractal along a single line of glues.

Lemma 3. *Let* $\mathbf{T}$ *be any tree fractal with generator* G. *If* $c \in \mathbb{Z}^+$, *then it is always possible to pick one pier* (p, q) *and one point* (e, f), *both in* G, *such that, for* $1 < s \in \mathbb{N}$, $W_s^c(e, f, p, q)$ *encloses a configuration that is connected to* $\mathbf{T}^c$ *via a single connected (horizontal or vertical) line of glues of length* c.

The proofs of the lemmas in this sub-section are omitted from this version of the paper due to lack of space.

3.2   Application to Scaled Tree Fractals

The main contribution of this paper is the following theorem.

Theorem 2. *Let* $\mathbf{T}$ *be any tree fractal. If* $c \in \mathbb{Z}^+$, *then* $\mathbf{T}^c$ *does not strictly self-assemble in the aTAM.*

Proof. Let $\mathbf{T}$ be any tree fractal with a $g \times g$ generator G, where $1 < g \in \mathbb{N}$. Let c be any positive integer. For the sake of obtaining a contradiction, assume that $\mathbf{T}^c$ does strictly self-assemble in some TAS $\mathcal{T} = (T, \sigma, \tau)$. Further assume that $\vec{\alpha}$ is some assembly sequence in $\mathcal{T}$ whose result is α, such that $\text{dom} \, \alpha = \mathbf{T}^c$.

According to Lemma 3, we can always pick one pier (p, q) and a point (e, f), both in G, such that, for $1 < s \in \mathbb{N}$, the window $W_s^c(e, f, p, q)$, which we will abbreviate w_s, encloses a configuration that is connected to $\mathbf{T}^c$ via a single

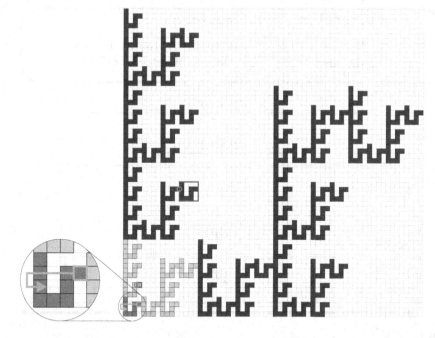

Fig. 2. First three stages ($s = 1, 2, 3$) of an unscaled ($c = 1$) 4-dssf tree fractal with an east-pointing pier at position $(3, 2)$ (the green square). The E-free point $(0, 1)$ is at the tip of the green arrow. In other words, $(p, q) = (3, 2)$, and $(e, f) = (0, 1)$.

line of glues of length c.[3] The maximum number of distinct combinations and orderings of glue positionings along this line of glues is finite.[4] By the generalized pigeonhole principle, since $|\{w_s \mid 1 < s \in \mathbb{N}\}|$ is infinite, there must be at least one bond-forming submovie such that an infinite number of windows generate this submovie (up to translation). Let us pick two such windows, say, w_i and w_j with $i < j$, such that $\mathcal{B}(M_{\alpha, w_i})$ and $\mathcal{B}(M_{\alpha, w_j})$ are equal (up to translation). We must pick these windows carefully, since as stated in the proof of Lemma 1, the seed of α must be either in both windows or in neither. This condition can always be satisfied. The only case where the seed is in more than one window is when it is at position $(0, 0)$ and $e = f = p = q = 0$, which implies that all windows include the origin. In all other cases, none of the windows overlap. So, if the seed belongs to one of them, say w_k, then we can pick any i greater than k (and $j > i$). Finally, if the seed does not belong to any windows, then any choice of i and $j > i$ will do.

---

[3] Without loss of generality, we will assume that this line of glues is positioned on the western side of the windows and is thus vertical (see the orange circles in Figure 2, where $s = 2$ and $s = 3$ for the small and large red windows, respectively, and $(p, q) = (3, 2)$ and $(e, f) = (0, 1)$), because the chosen pier in our example points east. A similar reasoning holds for piers pointing north, south or west.

[4] This number is $(T_{glue})^{2c} \cdot (2c)!$, where T_{glue} is the total number of distinct glue types in T.

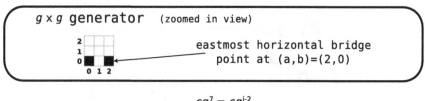

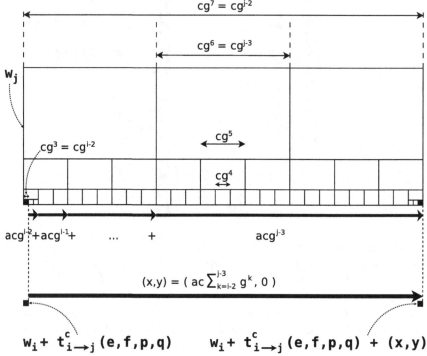

Fig. 3. (x, y) translation needed to align w_i and w_j on their east side once their southwest corners already match. Example with a west-pointing pier (not shown) and $g = 3$, $i = 5$, $j = 9$, $(a, b) = (2, 0)$.

We will now prove that w_i and w_j satisfy the two conditions of Lemma 1.

First, we compute c such that $\mathcal{B}(M_{\alpha, w_i}) + c = \mathcal{B}(M_{\alpha, w_j})$. We know that $w_i + t^c_{i \to j}(e, f, p, q)$ and w_j share their southwest corner. We need to perform one more translation to align the bond-forming glues of w_i and w_j. We use (a, b) to denote the position of the western point in the horizontal bridge of the generator. In our example (east-pointing pier), $a = 0$ and b is a variable with domain $\mathbb{N}_g$ ($b = 2$ in Figure 2). To align the bond-forming glues of w_i and w_j, we must translate $w_i + t^c_{i \to j}(e, f, p, q)$ by $(x, y) = \left(0, bc \sum_{k=i-2}^{j-3} g^k\right)$. The general computation for this translation is illustrated in Figure 3. Since $x \le m$ (as defined in Lemma 2) and $bc \sum_{k=i-2}^{j-3} g^k \le (g-1)c \sum_{k=i-2}^{j-3} g^k = c \left(\sum_{k=i-1}^{j-2} g^k - \sum_{k=i-2}^{j-3} g^k\right) = c \left(g^{j-2} - g^{i-2}\right) = m$, we can apply Lemma 2 to infer that, with $c = t^c_{i \to j}(e, f, p, q) + (x, y)$, $w_i + c$ is enclosed in w_j. Therefore, the second condition of Lemma 1 holds.

Second, by construction, $\mathcal{B}(M_{\alpha, w_i}) + c = \mathcal{B}(M_{\alpha, w_j})$. Therefore, the first condition of Lemma 1 holds.

In conclusion, the two conditions of Lemma 1 are satisfied, with α_I and α'_O defined as the intersection of $\mathbf{T}^c$ with the inside of w_i and the outside of w_j, respectively. We can thus conclude that the assembly $\alpha_I \cup (\alpha'_O - c)$ is producible in $\mathcal{T}$. Note that this assembly is identical (up to translation) to $\mathbf{T}^c$, except that the interior of the large window w_j is replaced by the interior of the small window w_i. Since the configurations in these two windows cannot be identical, we have proved that $\mathcal{T}$ does not strictly self-assemble $\mathbf{T}^c$, which is a contradiction.   □

4   Conclusion

In this paper, we made three contributions. First, we gave a new characterization of tree fractals in terms of simple geometric properties of their generator. Second, we proved a new variant of the Window Movie Lemma in [5], which we call the "Closed Window Movie Lemma." Third, we proved that no scaled-up version of any discrete self-similar tree fractal strictly self-assembles in the aTAM. In future work, we plan to extend this result to larger classes of non-tree fractals similar to the class of pinch-point fractals in [6].

References

1. Kautz, S.M., Lathrop, J.I.: Self-assembly of the discrete Sierpinski carpet and related fractals. In: Deaton, R., Suyama, A. (eds.) DNA 15. LNCS, vol. 5877, pp. 78–87. Springer, Heidelberg (2009)
2. Kautz, S.M., Shutters, B.: Self-assembling rulers for approximating generalized sierpinski carpets. Algorithmica 67(2), 207–233 (2013)
3. Lathrop, J.I., Lutz, J.H., Summers, S.M.: Strict self-assembly of discrete Sierpinski triangles. Theoretical Computer Science 410, 384–405 (2009)
4. Lutz, J.H., Shutters, B.: Approximate self-assembly of the sierpinski triangle. Theory Comput. Syst. 51(3), 372–400 (2012)
5. Meunier, P.-E., Patitz, M.J., Summers, S.M., Theyssier, G., Winslow, A., Woods, D.: Intrinsic universality in tile self-assembly requires cooperation. In: Proceedings of the 25th Annual ACM-SIAM Symposium on Discrete Algorithms (SODA), pp. 752–771 (2014)
6. Patitz, M.J., Summers, S.M.: Self-assembly of discrete self-similar fractals. Natural Computing 1, 135–172 (2010)
7. Rothemund, P.W.K.: Theory and experiments in algorithmic self-assembly, Ph.D. thesis, University of Southern California (December 2001)
8. Seeman, N.C.: Nucleic-acid junctions and lattices. Journal of Theoretical Biology 99, 237–247 (1982)
9. Seeman, N.C.: De novo design of sequences for nucleic acid structural engineering. Journal of Biomolecular Structural Dynamics 8, 573–581 (1990)
10. Wang, H.: Proving theorems by pattern recognition – II. The Bell System Technical Journal XL(1), 1–41 (1961)
11. Winfree, E.: Algorithmic self-assembly of DNA, Ph.D. thesis, California Institute of Technology (June 1998)

GUBS a Language for Synthetic Biology: Specification and Compilation

Adrien Basso-Blandin and Franck Delaplace

IBISC Lab, Evry University, IBGBI
23, boulevard de France, 91037 Evry, France
abasso@ibisc.fr, fdelaplace@ibisc.if

Abstract. The field of synthetic biology is looking forward principles and tools to make the biological devices inter-operable and programmable with, as long-term goal, the design of *de-novo* synthetic genome [14].

In this endeavour, computer-aided-design (CAD) environments play a central role by providing the required features to engineer systems: specification, analysis, and tuning [9,17,20,12]. Scaling up the complexity of devices necessitates to harness the development of CAD environments based on an automatic conversion of the design specification into DNA sequences, like compilers for programming languages.

Currently, domain specific languages for synthetic biology mainly address the design of structure, namely the biological component assembly, where programming relates to DNA sequence description. Although the structural description is an indispensable step in the design-to-manufacture chain and provide an accurate description of devices, the required size of program for sequence description likely makes the task error-prone and infeasible.

In this context, high level programming language for synthetic biology is announced as a key milestone for the second wave of synthetic biology to overcome the complexity of such large synthetic system design.

We have proposed a domain specific language, GUBS [5] (Genomic Unified Behaviour Specification), dedicated to the behavioural specification of synthetic biological devices, viewed as discrete open dynamical systems. GUBS is a rule-based declarative language. In contrast to a closed system, a program is always a partial description of the behaviour of the system. The semantics of the language accounts the existence of some hidden non-specified actions (trigged by the environment for example) that possibly alter the behaviour of the programmed devices.

Here we describe in detail the compilation framework, GGC(GUBS Genetic Compiler), an automated compiler translating a program into biological components usable in living cells. The compilation process assemble biological components from a database to behaviourally cover the behaviour described by a program.

Introduction

Synthetic biology is an emerging research field at the intersection of several fields ranging from biochemistry to computer science. Synthetic biology aims at

O.H. Ibarra et al. (Eds.): UCNC 2014, LNCS 8553, pp. 40–53, 2014.
DOI: 10.1007/978-3-319-08123-6_4, © Springer International Publishing Switzerland 2014

synthesizing large biological network based on assembly of biological components such as BioBricks[19]. Synthetic biology projects were first focusing on the design and the improvement of small genetic devices comparable to logical gates for electronic circuits [18,11]. Recently, projects have attempted to develop large biosystems integrating different devices with as a long-term goal, the design of *de-novo* synthetic genome [14]. To this end, synthetic biology is seeking to develop engineering methods for providing rational framework for design in biology.

Despite the technological progress made in the field of gene characterization and their interaction into networks, the complete understanding of an organism remains out of our knowledge, then limiting the scope of the control action on the organism. In addition, biological systems are open systems, which raise the question: how to define a model of a system where interactions with the environment are multiple and potentially unknowns ?

Development of such a tool is based on the definition of a language to describe the system and components as well as assembly and modelling tools dedicated to circuits. They are currently under development and used for synthetic biology[8]. The "manufacture" of the synthetic biological function could be carried on directly by "plugging" a synthesiser transforming the designed DNA sequence to a real one.

In this context, we propose a tool for automatically generating set of biological components which, once assembled, generates a behaviour previously defined in a specification language dedicated to synthetic biology. To this end we have previously introduced a DSL[1] specification language, called Gubs aiming at providing a framework for behavioural description of biological component, taking into account the openness of such a system by describing the behaviour as a trace of observable atomic behaviours.

In this article, we introduce Ggc, a compiler for Gubs that compiles a program into a set of biological components extracted from a database. The goal of Ggc is to provide tools lying at the core of the chain of biological assembly, indeed, it can translate a model into a set of biological components that can then be synthesized.

We begin by presenting the Gubs language, then in a second part we will present the challenges of compilation in synthetic biology, next, we introduce the Ggc compiler and finish on several compilation examples, finally we conclude on the opportunity offered by this tool as well as optimizations in order to match biological needs.

1   Gubs

In this section we briefly define Gubs language. The reader can refer to the following articles [5,6] for a complete description of the language. First we explain how the notion of variables and constant are interpreted in Gubs. Then we introduce concepts specific to this language for the description of biological systems.

---

[1] Domain Specific Language.

1.1   Programming Language Objects

GUBS uses variables and constants. Variables correspond to generic elements such as a gene whereas constants correspond to existing biological objects in a database. Variables and constants are defined as agents which can have qualitative attributes such as *low* or *high*. We differentiate them with an uppercase letter at the beginning of a constant. For instance, $gene1(low)$ is a variable with the attribute *low* where $TetR(high)$ is a constant with the attribute high.

Pieces of a program are enclosed in compartments and may depend on a context. Compartment describes a workspace with its own set of agents (constants and variables), these compartments being recursively included. They may model sub part of a cell, or two separate organisms for instance. A context meanwhile describes a set of behaviours that are triggered after a particular intervention on the external environment of the system such as the presence of a given enzyme in the cellular vector or the presence of light. For example, $cell\{[light]\{gene1, TetR(high)\}\}$ describe a compartment named *cell* with $gene1$ and $TetR(high)$ triggered when there is *light*.

1.2   Traces

A GUBS program describes a behaviour that can be observed in a trace. We focus on the notion of a *trace* that symbolically represents the evolution of some quantities related to the agents of interest by the evolution of these agent states. Formally, a trace, $(T_t)_{1 \leq t \leq m}$, is a finite sequence of agent state sets where each set contains all observed agent states at a given instant. For instance, the evolution of a concentration evolving from *Low* to *High* for G may be described by the following trace of 6 instants[2]: $(\{G(Low)\}_1, \{G(Low)\}_2, \{G(Mid)\}_3, \{G(Mid)\}_4, \{G(Mid)\}_5, \{G(High)\}_6)_7$. A trace can be obtained from experiments by establishing a correspondence between measurements of some quantities (*e.g.*, RNA transcript concentration) and attributes of agents. We define an *history* as a trace condensed to relevant element.

1.3   Causal Representation

In a GUBS program, instructions describing behaviours are causal relations. The description of open systems raise the question of taking into account the causality in the context of openness where some causes may be unknown. More precisely two notion should be accounted: the notion of pre-emption (an outer member system triggers inhibition behaviour induced by the system), and the principle of over-determination (events in the environment generate additional or already active behaviour in the system).

Proposition 1 (Over-determination Principle). *The over-determination case can be considered negligible considering that the behaviours described by the user are not naturally existing behaviours, and therefore cannot be triggered*

---

[2] Step 7 is inserted as an extra step to comply with the definition of the chronological division.

by the environment. The case of additional behaviour can for its part be checked to ensure that they are not harmful.

To provide an interpretation of causality accounting the pre-emption, we use the notion of reverse causation[16] defined as:

if the effect is observable, then the cause has occurred.

This representation allows us to ensure that in all cases, if we observe the expected behaviour, then the causal chain described by the program is executed and otherwise, one element of this chain has been locked by the environment preventing the occurrence of the behaviour that we want to observe.

For example, $gene1 \circ \rightarrow TetR(high)$ describe a behaviour where $gene1$ activate $TetR(high)$.

Three behavioural dependences are defined in GUBS: the *normal* denoted by $\circ \rightarrow$, *persistent* by $\odot \rightarrow$, and *residual* by $\oplus \rightarrow$. These dependences are primitive in the sense that they cannot be expressed by the others without weakening their properties. Informally, for normal dependence the cause precedes the effect providing the effect is observed; for persistent dependence the cause still precedes the effect but it is maintained while the effect is observed; and for residual dependence, the effect is maintained despite the cause has disappeared. These dependences symbolize common biological interactions. For instance, in genetic engineering, a recombination enables the emergence of a regulated gene or an hereditary trait permanently. Such a mechanism typifies the residual dependence in biology. The relations between gene expressions at steady state are symbolized by persistent dependence, finally the simple causation is a simplified representation of the principle of protein synthesis by a gene.

1.4   Remarks on Semantic

GUBS is a behavioural description formalization language based on modal logic. In order to effectively represent the notion of temporally ordered causal chain without owning a notion of unity of time, more, hybrid modal logic *HL* brings the concept of classical observation point during an experiment biological as described above. Each GUBS program can be translated into logic, and then in the form of a Kripke model.

The semantics formalizes the observed behaviour and used to: insure the correctness of the compilation process (Section 2.1), and to check the satisfiability of the program, interpreted here as the ability to observe a result.

2   Compilation

In this section, we describe the main features of GUBS. Informally, a GUBS program describes the expected observed behaviour of a biological component.

Usually, compilation consists in a translation of a programming language into computer's code using a compiler [1,2]. As explained previously, we introduces this scheme in order to adapt this principle to synthetic biology [7] where binary code is replaced DNA sequences.

In this endeavour, we define GGC compiling GUBS program [6] to an assembly of biological components insertable in a cellular vector. The result of the compilation is a set of components having at least the behaviour described by the program. This means that the final component assembly potentially has additional properties.

A central notion governing the compilation design is the notion of *behavioural inclusion*. Informally an assembly of components Q behaviourally including the behaviour of a program P.

Formally, by considering that the interpretation of P and Q ($[\![P]\!],[\![Q]\!]$) provides an hybrid logic formula and are modelled by a Kripke model [10], the behavioural inclusion denoted by $P \sqsubseteq Q$ is defined as a logical consequence (Definition 1).

Definition 1 (Behavioural inclusion). *A program Q behaviourally includes another program P, if and only if the interpretation of the latter is a logical consequence of the interpretation of the former:*

$$P \sqsubseteq Q \triangleq \forall \mathcal{M} : \mathcal{M} \Vdash [\![Q]\!] \implies \mathcal{M} \Vdash [\![P]\!].\text{where } \mathcal{M} \text{ is a model (Krypke structure)}$$

The behavioural inclusion is a pre-order[3] such that the empty program, denoted by ϵ, is a minimum, meaning that a program with no expected behaviour can be observed in all traces. A program whose interpretation equals $\bot$, is a maximum. Figure 1 illustrates the behavioural inclusion on a particular model P.

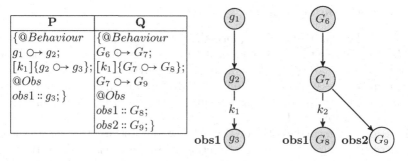

P	Q
{@*Behaviour*	{@*Behaviour*
$g_1 \circlearrowright g_2$;	$G_6 \circlearrowright G_7$;
$[k_1]\{g_2 \circlearrowright g_3\}$;	$[k_1]\{G_7 \circlearrowright G_8\}$;
@*Obs*	$G_7 \circlearrowright G_9$
*obs*1 :: g_3; }	@*Obs*
	*obs*1 :: G_8;
	*obs*2 :: G_9; }

Fig. 1. Behavioural inclusion example. In the figure, each node correspond to a Kripke world of the model. k stand for a context and we define observer as *obs* ::. Histories of P necessarily contains worlds coloured in grey. From the observation spots, the model corresponding to worlds in grey validate the original model. Hence, the behaviour of P is included in the model of Q represented by the entire graph.

---

[3] A reflexive and transitive relation.

Compilation will therefore be based on two principles, resulting in two questions:

1. Given a set of components Q, does it behaviourally include P?
2. Given a set of components Q, is it the smallest component satisfying 1?

To answer the first question, we define the functional synthesis principle, describing rewriting rules used in the compilation process.

2.1 Functional Synthesis

Functional synthesis is the operation whereby biological components of a library are selected and assembled to generate a device behaviourally including the designed function. The behaviour of each component is described by a GUBS program. At its simplest, the functional synthesis could be considered as a substitution of variables by constants. For example, in the following activation ($\xrightarrow{+}$) $\{G_1 \xrightarrow{+} g_2\}$, g_2 will be substituted by gene G_2, providing that component Q describes the activation $\{G_1 \xrightarrow{+} G_2\}$. However, more complex situations may arise during component selection. For example, if the activation $G_1 \xrightarrow{+} G_2$ occurs with another regulation only *i.e.*, $Q = \{G_1 \xrightarrow{+} G_2, G_3 \xrightarrow{+} G_4\}$ then the selection of Q adds a supplementary regulation.

Functional synthesis is defined by rules (Table 1) governing the component assembly. To ensure the correctness, each transform must preserve the behaviour. Hence, each program resulting from the application of a rule must behaviourally include the previous one. Formally, the functional synthesis is modelled by a relation on programs denoted by $\hookleftarrow$, *i.e.*, $Q \hookleftarrow_\sigma P$ where P is the initial program and Q the transformed one, such that each rule insures that: *$Q \hookleftarrow_\sigma P$ is correct in regard to a substitution σ, that is $P[\sigma] \sqsubseteq Q[\sigma]$ and $Q[\sigma]$ is observable.*

A finite substitution is a set of mappings, $\sigma = \{v_i/b_i\}_i$, on variables and constants such that a variable can be substituted by a variable or a constant, and a constant can only substituted by itself[4]. For instance, we have: $\{Obs::G(l) + b_2, b_1 \circlearrowright G(l)\}[\{b_1 \mapsto B_1, b_2 \mapsto B_2, l \mapsto Low\}] = \{Obs::G(Low) + B_2, B_1 \circlearrowright G(Low)\}$.

Also notice that the behavioural inclusion is preserved by substitution (Proposition 2 - proof in [5]).

Proposition 2. *For all substitutions σ, we have: $P \sqsubseteq Q \implies P[\sigma] \sqsubseteq Q[\sigma]$.*

Table 1 describes the functional synthesis rules[5]. Γ is a set of components representing the library. $P \subseteq_{Asm} Q$ denotes the fact that program Q corresponds to an assembly including P *i.e.*, $Q = (Q_1, P, Q_2)$ where Q_1 or Q_2 may be an empty program.

---

[4] $P\sigma$ or $P[\sigma]$ represents its application on program P and identity substitutions are omitted.

[5] Rules are of the form: . $\dfrac{\text{hypothesis}}{\text{conclusion}}$.

- INSTANTIATION -

$$\frac{P[\sigma] \subseteq_{\text{Asm}} Q[\sigma] \qquad \mathbf{obs}\,(Q[\sigma]) \qquad Q \in \Gamma}{Q \vdash_\sigma P} \text{ (Inst.)}$$

- COMMUTATIVITY, CONTRACTION -

$$\frac{Q \vdash_\sigma P, P'}{Q \vdash_\sigma P', P} \text{ (Com.)} \qquad\qquad\qquad \frac{Q \vdash_\sigma P}{Q \vdash_\sigma P, P} \text{ (Cont.)}$$

- ASSEMBLY -

$$\frac{Q \vdash_\sigma P \qquad Q' \vdash_{\sigma'} P' \qquad \sigma|_{\text{VA}(P) \cap \text{VA}(P')} = \sigma'|_{\text{VA}(P) \cap \text{VA}(P')} \qquad \mathbf{obs}\,(Q[\sigma], Q'[\sigma'])}{Q, Q' \vdash_{\sigma \cup \sigma'} P, P'} \text{ (Asm.)}$$

Table 1. Functional synthesis rules VA(P) stands for the set of variables of the program and $\sigma|_V$ is the restriction of the substitution on a set of variables V

Rule (Inst.) describes the fact that an observable instance of a part of a component in the library is functionally synthesized. Rule (Com.) expresses the commutativity of the assembly. Rule (Cont.) contracts the redundant formulation of programs. Finally, Rule (Asm.) details the conditions for an assembly of two components, each representing a functional synthesis of a part of the designed function.

- DEPENDENCES -

$$\frac{Q \vdash_\sigma S_1 \circlearrowleft\!\!\to S_2, S_2 \circlearrowleft\!\!\to S_3, \Delta}{Q \vdash_\sigma S_1 \circlearrowleft\!\!\to S_3, \Delta} \text{ (Trans.)} \quad \frac{Q \vdash_\sigma S_1 \circlearrowleft\!\!\to S_2, \Delta}{Q \vdash_\sigma S_1 \circlearrowleft\!\!\to S_2, \Delta} \text{ (N2P.)} \quad \frac{Q \vdash_\sigma S_1 \circ\!\!\to S_2, \Delta}{Q \vdash_\sigma S_1 \oplus\!\!\to S_2, \Delta} \text{ (R2N.)}$$

- AGENT STATES -

$$\frac{S_1 + S_2}{S_2 + S_1} \text{ (SCom.)} \qquad \frac{S + s}{S + s + s} \text{ (SCont.)} \qquad \frac{S + s}{S} \text{ (Incl.)}$$

Table 2. Rules for the dependences and the agent states. S_i stands for a collection, $s_1 + \ldots + s_n$, of agent states, including negation, and Δ stands for the rest of the program.

Another set of rules, more specifically devoted to dependences (Table 2), defines the alternate possibilities to express similar behaviours. The table also includes the rules for agent sets. Rule (Trans.) expands the chain of the persistent dependences ($S_1 \circlearrowleft\!\!\to S_3$) by adding intermediary dependence (S_2) to refine a pathway. Rule (N2P.) weakens a normal dependence ($S_1 \circ\!\!\to S_2$) to a *persistent* one ($S_1 \circlearrowleft\!\!\to S_2$) since the latter is a normal dependence with an additional property. And Rule (R2N.) weakens a *residual* dependence($S_1 \oplus\!\!\to S_2$) to a normal dependence ($S_1 \circ\!\!\to S_2$), since normal dependence is also residual dependence with a repetition of the effect restricted to one step. According to these rules, all the dependence chains can be implemented with persistent dependences. Final rules are devoted to agent states. Rule (SCom.) and (SCont.) describe the propriety of + operator. Finally (Incl.) specifies that a behaviour can be extended with another unless the original one still present.

Basically, the compilation consists in the iterated application of rule, until the behaviour of the assembled component cover the original program.

Technically, the algorithm of rule application corresponds to an unification [15] where the causal relation are assimilated to terms. The unification is an *ACI-unification* [4,3] : Associative (rule Asm.), Commutative (rules Com. and SCom.) and idempotent (rules Cont. and SCont.). ACI-unification is a NP-complete problem, so we will use some specific properties of the GUBS program to improve the algorithm efficiency.

2.2   Normal Form

For the compilation, we consider a normal form of the causal rules, $\aleph(P)$, with the following properties:

1. Unity: the normal form is unique
2. Idempotents: $\aleph \circ \aleph(P) = \aleph(P)$
3. Semantics correctiveness: $\forall P : \mathcal{M} \Vdash [\![P]\!] \Leftrightarrow \mathcal{M} \Vdash [\![\aleph(P)]\!]$
4. Normalization: $\forall P_1, P_2 : \aleph(P_1) = \aleph(P_2) \Leftrightarrow (\mathcal{M} \Vdash [\![P_1]\!] \Leftrightarrow \mathcal{M} \Vdash [\![P_2]\!]$

The transformation from a program P to its normal form relies on classical rules (distributivity, commutativity), that are not described here. In the normal form, the context is applied to each cause and there is only one compartment encapsulating all the causes.

$$[k_1, ... k_n]\{\sum_{i=1}^{m} C_i \circledast\!\!\to \sum_{j=1}^{l} E_j\}$$

For instance, the normal form of $[k]\{C\{a \circ\!\!\to b\}D\{c \circ\!\!\to d\}\}$ is
$[k]\{C.a \circ\!\!\to C.b\}, [k]\{D.c \circ\!\!\to D.d\}$

The normal form $[k_1, ... k_n]\{\sum_{i=1}^{m} C_i \circledast\!\!\to \sum_{j=1}^{l} E_j\}$ can be interpreted as term: $(\circledast\!\!\to)(\{K\}, \{C\}, \{E\})$, where $K = \{k_1, ... k_n\}$, $C = \{c_1, ... c_m\}$ and $E = \{e_1, ... e_l\}$ are agents sets of variables and constants in P and only constants for components Q of the database.

2.3   Getting the Smallest Component

In this section, we assume that we have an assembly of component covering the behaviour of a program, indeed, Q is a component potentially comprising several other components extracted from a database, so it can exists a multitude of assembled components covering P. Based on this premise, how to generate the smallest component Q unifying P ?

The problem actually depends on the size of the database. For small database, ACI-unification will compute the functional synthesis by identifying which components own causal rules unified with the program. For large database, the unification may be too time-consuming to be effective. In this case, the unification will operate on a part of database.

Finding the appropriate components for the unification appears crucial. Hence, we select the component insuring that they will not obviously cause the unification failure. Selection process operates heuristically by considering the following requirements.

1. A set of components must have a sufficient number of causes with the right type.
2. Each cause have a sufficient number of agent in the both sets.
3. they have at least constants present in the original program.

Amongst the set of components we select a sub-part using a *directed* evolution algorithm. By directed we mean that we proceed to a pre selection, checking that each individuals (subset of components) comply to the above mentioned requirement.

2.4   GGC(Gubs Genetic Compiler) Algorithm

The functional synthesis algorithm is structured in two stage: the ACI-unification algorithm and the directed evolutionary algorithm. Depending on the size of the database, the evolutionary algorithm will be used or not. In the case of a small database, the P program will be directly unified with the whole database, and for large database, several subsets of components will be selected for the unification. A genetic algorithm is used to select the best subsets of component with respect to a fitness function. An individual (subset of components) is viable if and only if it is observable (namely there exists a model satisfying the assembly). The fitness function accounts two characteristics:

– The number of components used for the unification in an individual.
– The number of unified rules in the original program.

The best individuals have the minimal number of unified components and maximize the number of unified rules in the program.

Minimizing the number of component is motivated by the fact that, in biology the stability and the understanding of pathway directly depends on the number of involved components. Notice that: for each individual of a population, the unification could be partial and some components of an individual may not be used during the unification process, in this case, they are removed in the compilation result. The compilation process may fail if all the rules of the original program are not unified by a best individual. To attempt to overcome the failure, two optimisations are applied: variant of some individuals are generated by combining the extension (Rule Trans. Table 2) and the weakening (Rules N2P. and R2N. Table 2) of their causal rules. Those variants are then included in the population.

Figure 2 describes the compilation process of a GUBS program. Although the use of evolutionary algorithm in GUBS differs, it supports the same objective and opens up the possibility of an integration based on the same optimization framework.

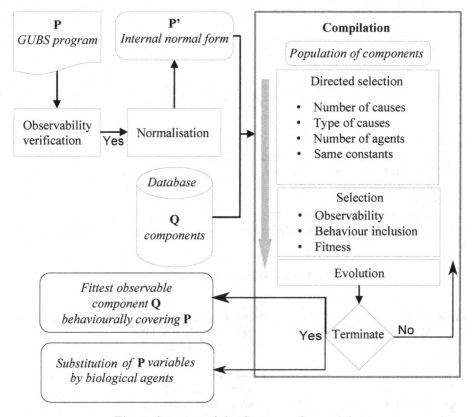

Fig. 2. Overview of the GGC compiler modules

3   Example

In this section we introduce the Repressilator [13] compilation with GGC For this example, we use the database described in the Appendix 5 defined as an XML document.

3.1   Repressilator

The Repressilator was designed to exhibit a stable oscillation which is reported via the expression of green fluorescent protein, and acts like an electrical oscillator system with fixed time periods. The network was implemented in *Escherichia coli* using standard molecular biology methods and observations were performed that verify that the engineered colonies do indeed exhibit the desired oscillatory behaviour. here we detailed the compilation of such a system, the first step consist in translating this model into GUBS as described in the first figure (figure 3).

We define two compartments each one describing one plasmid. The first one describes the behaviour of the inhibition loop with three causal relations and

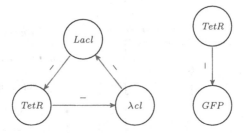

```
Repressilator{
    @Observer{obs1:TetR_lite; obs2:!TetR_lite;}
    @Behavior{g1 -> !g2;    g2 -> !TetR_lite;    TetR_lite -> !g1;}
};
Reporter{
    @Observer{obs1:GFP; obs2:!GFP;}
    @Behavior{TetR_lite -> !GFP;}
};
```

Fig. 3. Repressilator GUBS program

```
Parts list:                     Substitution:
   Q4, Q5, Q6, Q15, Q16             g1::> LambdaCL_lite
                                    g2::> Lacl_lite
Details:
   Q4: Lambda Cl                Added genes:
   Q5: Lacl_lite                   add1::> LambdaPr
   Q6: Tetr_lite                   add2::> PLlac01
   Q15: PLtet01                    add3::> PLtet01
   Q16: activation tetr            add4::> PLtet01
```

Fig. 4. Repressilator GGC output. notice that, in order to find a solution, the compiler uses the extension rule (Trans.) in order to add 4 genes.

two observation spots which are the presence or absence of $TetR_{lite}$. The second one simply describe the activation of GFP.

After compilation we obtain the result in figure 4.

4   Conclusion

GUBS language is a language dedicated to the design of synthetic biological systems. Hence, the proposed features were adapted to this domain. A program in GUBS describes the observation of a trace expressed by causal relations.

Actually, the semantics based on the observation instead of a model formalizing the behaviour appears to be the most suitable approach for addressing biodevice specification in synthetic biology by considering that a living organism is an open system where some rules governing its processes remain incomplete and even unknown. In GGC, we propose a new approach for synthetic biology design based on the compilation of a program describing the behaviour of biological functions to an assembly of biological components stored in a database.

```
<name>Q4</name><meta>Lambda Cl</meta>
<prog>@B{LambdaCL_lite -> LambdaPr; LambdaPr -> !Lacl_lite;}</prog>
//=================================================================
<name>Q5</name><meta>Lacl_lite</meta>
<prog>@B{Lacl_lite -> PLlacO1; PLlacO1 -> !TetR_lite;}</prog>
//=================================================================
<name>Q6</name><meta>TetR_lite</meta>
<prog>@B{TetR_lite -> PLtetO1; PLtetO1 -> !LambdaCL_lite;}</prog>
//=================================================================
<name>Q7</name><meta>sensor</meta>
<prog>@B{[Light]{Detect -> Tetr};}</prog>
//=================================================================
<name>Q8</name><meta>Tetr</meta>
<prog>@B{Tetr -> Luxl;}</prog>
//=================================================================
<name>Q9</name><meta>Luxl</meta>
<prog>@A{AHL:[][low != mid != high];}
@B{Luxl -> AHL(low); !Luxl -> !AHL(low); Luxl -> AHL(mid);
!Luxl -> !AHL(mid); Luxl -> AHL(high); !Luxl -> !AHL(high);}</prog>
//=================================================================
<name>Q10</name><meta>Ahl</meta>
<prog>@A{AHL:[][low != mid != high]; LuxR:[mid < high][low != mid];}
@B{AHL(mid) -> LuxR(mid);   AHL(high) -> LuxR(high);}</prog>
//=================================================================
<name>Q11</name><meta>luxr</meta>
<prog>@A{LuxR:[mid < high][low != mid];}
@B{LuxR(mid)->Cl,!LaclM1; LuxR(low)->!Cl; LuxR(high)->Cl,LaclM1;}</prog>
//=================================================================
<name>Q12</name><meta>Cl</meta>
<prog>@B{Cl -> !Lacl; !Cl -> Lacl;}</prog>
//=================================================================
<name>Q13</name><meta>laclm1</meta>
<prog>@B{LaclM1 -> !GFP; !LaclM1 -> GFP;}</prog>
//=================================================================
<name>Q14</name><meta>gfp inhibitor lacl</meta>
<prog>@B{Lacl -> !GFP; !Lacl -> GFP;}</prog>
//=================================================================
<name>Q15</name><meta>PLtetO1</meta>
<prog>@B{PLtetO1 -> !GFP;}</prog>
//=================================================================
<name>Q16</name><meta>activation tetr</meta>
<prog>@B{TetR_lite -> PLtetO1;}</prog>
```

Fig. 5. Components database. The XML code correspond to the description of a set of selected biological components in GUBS.

The compilation principle relies on the notion of behavioural covering of the initial program by the assembly. We define a compilation algorithm based on the ACI-unification algorithm adapted to the features of the GUBS language. We have developed a prototype of compiler (in Ocaml language) and demonstrate its feasibility on some examples coming from synthetic biology literature. The compiler combines the ACI-unification algorithm with a directed evolutionary algorithm in order to tackle with the complexity of the compilation for large biological databases. In dedicated domain specification language, the possibility to extend the language easily is required for refining some domain specific feature. The compilation principles of GGC enable the swift extension of the causal rules since they are considered as new terms treated in the same way than the other causal rules. However, specific algorithmic methods must be devised for their optimizations such as "causal rule weakening" because the optimizations are based on the semantics of the rules an not merely on their syntactic structure.

The perspectives is to improve the component selection by identifying relevant biological parameters. The parameters extend the notion of attributes of agents without replacing it, to quantitatively assess the adequacy of the selection of an agent to a variable. The issue is in twofold: finding some relevant biological parameters for the synthetic biology design, and appropriately accounting these parameters to improve the compilation process.

Acknowledgements. The funding for most of this work is granted by the Anr synbiotic (Anr blanc 0307 01) and we would like to thank the colleagues of this project for their fruitful discussions.

References

1. Aho, A., Lam, M., Ullman, J., Sethi, R.: Compilers: Principles, Techniques, and Tools. Pearson Education (1986)
2. Aho, A., Ullman, J.: Principles of Compiler Design. Addison-Wesley Series in Computer Science and Information Processing. Addison-Wesley Publ. (1977)
3. Baader, F., Snyder, W.: Unification Theory. In: Robinson, A., Voronkov, A. (eds.) Handbook of Automated Reasoning, ch. 8, pp. 441–523. The MIT Press (2001)
4. Baader, F., Büttner, W.: Unification in commutative idempotent monoids. Theoretical Computer Science 56, 345–352 (1988)
5. Basso-Blandin, A., Delaplace, F.: Gubs, a behavior-based language for open system dedicated to synthetic biology. CoRR abs/1206.6098 (2012)
6. Basso-Blandin, A., Delaplace, F.: Gubs, a behaviour-based language for design in synthetic biology. Sci. Ann. Comp. Sci. 23(1), 1–38 (2013)
7. Beal, J., Bachrach, J.: Cells Are Plausible Targets for High-Level Spatial Languages. In: 2008 Second IEEE International Conference on Self-Adaptive and Self-Organizing Systems Workshops, pp. 284–291 (October 2008)
8. Beal, J., Lu, T., Weiss, R.: Automatic Compilation from High-Level Biologically-Oriented Programming Language to Genetic Regulatory Networks. PLoS ONE 6(8), e22490 (2011)

9. Bilitchenko, L., Liu, A., Cheung, S., Weeding, E., Xia, B., Leguia, M., Anderson, J.C., Densmore, D.: Eugene–A Domain Specific Language for Specifying and Constraining Synthetic Biological Parts, Devices, and Systems. PloS One 6(4), e18882 (2011)
10. Cerrito, S., Cialdea Mayer, M.: A tableaux based decision procedure for a broad class of hybrid formulae with binders. In: Brünnler, K., Metcalfe, G. (eds.) TABLEAUX 2011. LNCS, vol. 6793, pp. 104–118. Springer, Heidelberg (2011)
11. Clancy, K., Voigt, C.A.: Programming Cells: Towards an Automated Genetic Compiler. Current Opinion in Biotechnology 21(4), 581–572 (2010)
12. Czar, M.J., Cai, Y., Peccoud, J.: Writing DNA with GenoCAD. Nucleic Acids Research 37(Web Server issue), W40–W47 (2009)
13. Elowitz, M.B., Leibler, S.: A synthetic oscillatory network of transcriptional regulators. Nature 403(6767), 335–338 (2000)
14. Gibson, D., Glass, J., Lartigue, C., Noskov, V., Chuang, R., Algire, M., Benders, G., Montague, M., Ma, L., Moodie, M., et al.: Creation of a Bacterial Cell Controlled by a Chemically Synthesized Genome. Science 329(5987), 52 (2010)
15. Knight, K.: Unification: a multidisciplinary survey. ACM Computing Surveys 21(1), 93–124 (1989)
16. Lewis, D.: Causation as Influence. The Journal of Philosophy 97(4), 182–197 (2000)
17. Pedersen, M.P.: Towards Programming Languages for Genetic Engineering of Living Cells. Journal of the Royal Society, Interface 6(suppl. 4), S437–S450 (2009)
18. Regot, S., Macia, J., Conde, N., Furukawa, K., Kjellén, J., Peeters, T., Hohmann, S., de Nadal, E., Posas, F., Solé, R.: Distributed Biological Computation with Multicellular Engineered Networks. Nature 469(7329), 207–211 (2011)
19. Shetty, R., Endy, D., Knight, T.: Engineering BioBrick vectors from BioBrick parts. Journal of Biological Engineering 2, 5+ (2008)
20. Umesh, P., Naveen, F., Rao, C., Nair, S.: Programming languages for synthetic biology. Systems and Synthetic Biology 4(4), 265–269 (2010)

Modeling Syntactic Complexity with P Systems: A Preview*

Gemma Bel Enguix[1] and Benedek Nagy[2,3]

[1] Laboratoire d'Informatique Fondamentelle, Aix-Marseille University
13288 Marseille, France
gemma.belenguix@gmail.com
[2] Department of Mathematics, Eastern Mediterranean University,
Famagusta, North Cyprus, via Mersin-10, Turkey
[3] Faculty of Informatics, University of Debrecen, Hungary
nbenedek.inf@gmail.com

Abstract. Membrane systems have been applied to several branches of linguistics, taking advantage of their possibilities when describing contexts and environments. However, not much research has been performed in the field of modeling syntax. The paper introduces a preliminary approach to syntactic complexity using the basic operations of membranes.

1 Introduction

As stated by Marcus in [10], language is at the crossroad of computation and biology. The two last disciplines were the pivotal sciences of the XXth century, whereas language is a universal paradigm like time, space, error, and others.

There are various traditional and unconventional models for natural languages [11–13]. Mathematics and computation provided the first formal models for natural language. Following Marcus [10] we can say that *computation became a cognitive model for natural languages with the pioneering word of Chomsky. Chomsky's hierarchy of formal grammars and languages was motivated by needs of the study of syntax of natural languages. Since each type of formal grammars in Chomsky's hierarchy is equivalent to a specific type of automata, which, in their turn, are specific types of a Turing machine, it follows that Chomsky's hierarchy leads to a hierarchy of computational models for natural languages.*

However, these models could never totally cover the phenomena of natural language. At the end of the century, with the increasing development of biology and bioinformatics, the issue of tackling natural language with biological models arose as a direct consequence of the scientific scenario.

From the XIXth Century it has been highlighted that both, natural languages and species, shared a key feature: evolution. In biology, the idea was developed by Darwin [8] in the work *The origin of the species*; in historical linguistics, August Schleicher [16] introduced the theory of the Stammbaum, with very similar parameters as that of Darwin. Roughly speaking, if species (DNA) and

---

* First author's research has been supported by a IEF Marie Curie Fellowship.

O.H. Ibarra et al. (Eds.): UCNC 2014, LNCS 8553, pp. 54–66, 2014.
DOI: 10.1007/978-3-319-08123-6_5, © Springer International Publishing Switzerland 2014

verbal languages are natural evolving entities, they should be approached with similar methods.

Nowadays, the theory of complex adaptive systems (CAS) [9] gives a new perspective to the problem. Several natural and artificial entities in the world seem to share the same features: emergency, evolution, self-organization and collective behavior. Natural language is certainly one of these structures, as well as the genetic code and the immune system. In this framework, the idea to tackle natural languages by means of formal models coming from biology, especially molecular biology becomes even more relevant.

From the works of Chomsky, the main goal of linguistics has been explaining the syntax of natural languages [7]. But in the last years, the incapability of formal models and the arising of statistic models has led to a different way to tackle linguistics, more centered in applications like automatic translation, data mining, summarization, etc. Natural computing in general, and membrane systems in particular, have followed the same tendencies when used for modeling a language. Indeed they have been applied mainly to semantics and pragmatics, as can be seen in [4].

Nonetheless, some attempts to model the structure of natural language by means of membranes have been performed. The first authors connecting P systems and syntax were Gramatovici & Bel-Enguix [6], who explored the way of parsing natural languages using P automata. Although this was a promising line of research, this possibility has not been developed in subsequent studies.

There are other branches of natural computing that have approached syntax. The best example is [5], that offers a general method to tackle complexity and sentence composition using only DNA recombination methods. The results obtained in this research clearly indicate that natural formalisms can be a very suitable model for natural language, encouraging the development of other natural approaches to syntax.

Some fields that can be related to syntax have been approached by P systems. Some attempts have been made to define logic gates and logic operations by means of SN P systems [1]. Other researchers [3] have introduced a rewriting logic framework for operational semantics of membrane systems. Even though modelization of logic environments and logic gates can be very useful for syntax, the perspective of these papers is still far from being able to deal with natural language structure.

This paper introduces a preliminary way to represent syntactic relations with general membrane operations. Our aim is to give some clues on how P systems can be a good support for approaching syntax with a simple and intuitive formalization. The work may have several benefits for linguistics and language production. On one hand, we show how there are alternative models to rewriting. On the other, we offer a system that can be analyzed and implemented more easily than current models. Finally, we pose the question of the boundaries and classification of complex syntactic structures, that could be revised according with the membrane operations that are needed to generate them.

In section 2 we explain the main features of Syn(tactic) P Systems, and give a definition. Section 3 deals with Syn P Systems that generate different types of complex sentences. Section 4 deals with P systems that are able to simulate non-context free structures in natural languages. Finally, in section 5 we give some final remarks and outline the future work.

2   Syntactic P Systems

We use the name *Syntactic P Systems* (Syn P Systems) for specific type of P systems with the following features:

- The objects of the system, O, belong to two different groups: a) sentences $s_1, \ldots, s_n$ predefined in a pool of sentences S; b) words from the set C, that corresponds to 'conjunctions'.
- In the final configuration, every membrane of the system can only have one sentence from S.
- The system uses basic membrane operations. Membrane rules do not belong to any membrane, but to the system.

First, we explain which basic membrane operations the Syntactic P Systems are using.

2.1   Basic Membrane Operations

P systems with active membranes were introduced by Păun [14], and membrane operations were clearly defined by Alhazov and Ishdorj [2]. Paun [15] takes into account four operations (actually seven, because for three of them reverse operation is also defined) with membranes:

- Creation / Dissolution: Creation is an operation that generates a new membrane that can contain objects inside. Dissolution is the reverse operation; by means of that a membrane can be deleted, generating the objects defined by the rule.
- Divide / Merge: By division a membrane is split in two new ones. The contrary operation is merging, that consists in joining two membranes in the new one generated. In both cases the membrane or membranes initially existing disappear.
- Endocytosis / Exocytosis: Endocytosis is a rule producing an elementary membrane i to enter an adjacent membrane j. The reverse operation is exocytosis, by means of which an elementary membrane j nested in i is sent out of i. The objects in the membranes can be modified during the process.
- Gemmation: By this operation a membrane i is created with some objects inside and later sent into an adjacent membrane j. The moving membrane i is dissolved inside j releasing its contents there. This is a way of transporting objects between membranes.

2.2   Formalization of Syntactic P Systems

A syntactic P system (Syn P System) can be formalized as follows:

$$\Pi = \{L, \mu, O, W, R\},$$

where

> L is the finite set of labels that can be used to label membranes;
> μ is the initial membrane structure;
> $O = S \cup C$, where $S = \{s_1, ..., s_n\}$, $C = \{c_1, ..., c_n\}$, $S \cap C = \emptyset$;
> W contains $w_i \in O^*$ for every $i \in L$ that is included in μ: it is the initial content of each membrane i;
> $R = \{r_1, ..., r_n\}$ is the set of rules of the system.

The basic idea of this paper is that some complexity phenomena in natural languages can be explained using the basic operations on membranes. The approach we are taking assumes some basic statements.

- In our representation, every elementary membrane stands for a simple sentence. Simple means that it has only one inflected verb.
- In two nested membranes we consider the main to be the outer.
- Skin membrane stands for the text or the oral speech production.

3   P Systems for Complex Sentences

In linguistics, complex sentences are defined as the ones including two or more simple sentences, that we will call *clauses* along the paper. Classical grammar assumes that complex sentences can only be created by joining two simple sentences, and generative grammar follows this idea. Therefore, this paper is not dealing with the generation of simple sentences in any language, but with how simple syntactic units combine in order to get a new complex item.

We define three types of complex structures that are being tackled in this piece of work:

- *Coordination.* Composition of sentences with no dependence relation between them. Clauses of a coordinate sentence are usually joined by logical relations, mainly $\wedge$, $\vee$, or express a contrast with what has been said, like *but*. Coordination is the co-referent of concatenation in formal languages. The conjunctions that are used in English to coordinate sentences are: *and, but, for, nor, or, so,* and *yet*.
- *Relative sentences.* Joining two sentences sharing a common element. Relative subordination is built with the particles *that, which, whom*.
- *Subordination.* One sentence is inside another one with a given syntactic function or one clause is dependent on another one. Examples of subordination conjunctions are: *after, although, as, as if, because, before, even if, even though, if, if only, rather than, since, that, though, unless, until, when, where, whereas, wherever, whether, which,* and *while*.

3.1 Coordination

In terms of membranes, to generate coordinate sentences the only thing we need is a creation rule. $[b]_s \rightarrow [[\ ]_i b]_s$. The rule can be applied recursively, in a sequential manner, producing systems like: $[[\ ]_i[\ ]_j[\ ]_k...[\ ]_n b]_s$.

It is also possible to obtain these results in a parallel manner. Since here we do not go inside the structure of a clause we use object-alphabet including the clauses and connectives that are intended to use in the sentence. The label alphabet should be $\{s\} \cup \{1, \ldots, n\}$ where n is the number of clauses that we want to use in our sentence.

To generate coordinate sentences we can use a 'pool' of simple statements, for example: $s_1 = $ *John went to the house*, $s_2 = $ *Mary plays tennis*, $s_3 = $ *They eat pizza*. The restriction can be established that every clause can be used only once.

A P system capable of generating coordinated sentences could be the following:

$$\Pi_c = (L, \mu, O, W, R)$$

where

- $L = \{s, 1, 2, 3\}$
- $\mu = [\ ]_s$
- $O = \{s_1, s_2, s_3\} \cup \{and, but\}$
- $w_s = s_1 s_2 s_3$
- $R = \{s_1 \rightarrow [s_1]_1, s_2 \rightarrow [\ and\ s_2]_2, s_3 \rightarrow [\ but\ s_3]_3\}$

This system generates the sentence *John went to the house and Mary plays tennis but they eat pizza*.

Note that assuming all the sentences of the pool given in the initial configuration, the sentence can be generated in one step applying every membrane creation rule in a parallel manner. These systems are uniform in the sense that they are entirely the same for every sentence based on n clauses, however the objects $s_1, \ldots, s_n$ and also the connectives *and, but*, etc. should be fixed 'by the input', and thus in this way the system can only be counted as a semi-uniform system.

3.2 Relative Clauses

Rules for generation of relative clauses can be simulated using the membrane operation of *endocytosis*. However, this can only be applied in restrictive contexts, so that it could be called 'selective' endocytosis. The rule can be triggered only if the two sentences have a common element, that has to be labelled with the same symbol. For example, given two sentences $s_1:abc$ and $s_2:cde$, the endocytosis can be applied only if the common element in both sentences, c, is labelled with the same symbol, in this case u. Therefore, a rule can be defined: $[abc_u]_j\ [c_u de]_k \rightarrow [abc[u_c de]_k]_j$, u_c being a trace of c. In natural language, the trace is always one of these pronouns: *that, which, who, whose*. In the paper, for the sake of simplicity, we always use *that*.

Relative clauses are generated in natural language when two different sentences have some common 'referent', i.e., they have the common element referring to the same object. Syntax deals with the process of generation of sentences and does not deal with 'referents'. In our examples, if two items are labelled we assume the operation can be performed and, for that example, we assume the object of reference is the same. Anyway, this fact is not relevant for syntax, but for other fields like pragmatics or semantics.

Given two sentences with labelled common elements, the endocytosis can work in both ways, so as, having the two sentences above, the process could also be defined as follows: $[abc_u]_j \ [c_ude]_k \rightarrow [cde[abu_c]_j]_k$.

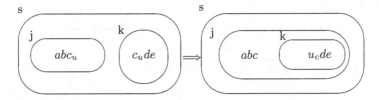

Fig. 1. Example for a configuration scheme for relative sentences

We establish the condition that, when an object has been used in a rule, it cannot be used again, even though the element is repeated. By these we avoid, at this stage, results with two relative clauses depending on the same word. Therefore, the element is used will not be labelled in the right part of the rule; instead the labelled trace is used.

First, a store of simple sentences is considered, containing the following elements: $s_1 = The \ boy_t \ eats \ an \ apple_u \ (a_tbc_u)$, $s_2 = The \ boy_t \ runs \ the \ marathon_w$ (a_tde_w), $s_3 = I \ bought \ an \ apple_u \ (fgc_w)$, $s_4 = The \ marathon_w \ was \ organized \ by$ $the \ City \ Hall \ (e_whi)$.

Then, a system can be defined, as follows:

$$\Pi_r = (L, \mu, O, W, R)$$

where

- $L = \{s, 1, 2\}$
- $\mu = [[\ ]_1 \ [\ ]_2]_s$
- $O = \{a, a_t, b, c, c_u, d, e, e_w, f, g, h, i\} \cup \{that_x \mid x \in \{a, c, e\}\}$
- $w_1 = s_1 = a_tbc_u, w_2 = s_2 = a_tde_w$
- $R = \{[a_tdc_u]_1 \ [a_tde_w]_2 \rightarrow [adc_u[that_a \ de_w]_2]_1\}$

The system generates the sentence: *The boy that runs the marathon eats an apple*.

But some systems can be defined in a bit more sophisticated way (where we allow subsequent use of these endocytosis rules):

$$\Pi'_r = (L, \mu, O, W, R)$$

where

- $L = \{s, 1, 2, 3\}$
- $\mu = [[\ ]_1 [\ ]_2 [\ ]_3]_s$
- $O = \{a, a_t, b, c, c_u, d, e, e_w, f, g, h, i\} \cup \{that_x \mid x \in \{a, c, e\}\}$
- $w_1 = s_1 = a_t b c_u, w_2 = s_2 = a_t d e_w, w_3 = s_3 = f g c_u$
- $R = \{[a_t dc_x]_1 [a_t de_y]_2 \rightarrow [adc_x[that_a \ de_y]_2]_1$, where $x \in \{u, \lambda\}, y \in \{w, \lambda\}$
  and $[a_z dc_u]_1 [f g c_u]_3 \rightarrow [a_z dc[that_c \ fg]_3]_1$, where $z \in \{t, \lambda\}\}$.

Applying both types of rules the system produces:
The boy that$_{boy}$ runs the marathon eats an apple that$_{apple}$ I bought.
The final P system configuration would be the one seen in Figure 2.

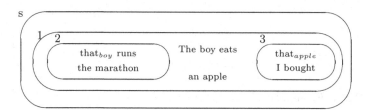

Fig. 2. Syntactic structure of a sentence with two relative clauses inserted by endocytosis at the same level

With some of the 'clauses' of the pool, many different sentences can be generated in a similar way, for instance:

- *The boy that runs the marathon eats an apple.*
- *The boy that eats an apple runs the marathon.*
- *The boy eats an apple I bought.*
- *The boy runs the marathon that was organized by the city hall.*
- *The marathon that the boy runs is organized by the city hall.*
- *The boy that runs the marathon that was organized by the city hall eats an apple that I bought.*
- *I bought an apple that the boy that runs the marathon that was organized by the city hall eats.*
- *...*

An easy way to generate some of these sentences is by defining *enchained rules*, that simply provide an order for the endocytosis. The rules can be applied only if there is a common element. We may also use endocytosis in a more general way allowing not only elementary membranes to enter into another one. Using these new features we can obtain more complex sentences in a similar way as we have shown in the previous examples, as we describe briefly (using only the abbreviation s_i for the sentences):

Let us have a P system with as many adjacent membranes inside the skin as 'clauses' in the pool. In our example we have four clauses, therefore the system has the structure $\mu = [[\ ]_1 [\ ]_2 [\ ]_3 [\ ]_4]_s$. Every one of the adjacent membranes contains one of the sentences: $w_1 = s_1, w_2 = s_2, w_3 = s_3, w_4 = s_4$. The set of objects includes every one of the classes plus the *trace-word*, *that*. Then, a chain of endocytosis can be described, in the following way: $R_\mu = \{s_3 \xrightarrow{\text{endo}} s_1 \xrightarrow{\text{endo}} s_2 \xrightarrow{\text{endo}} s_4\}$. The initial configuration of the system is seen in Figure 3.

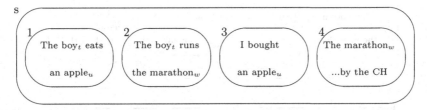

Fig. 3. Initial configuration of a system with several sentences that can start a process of recursive endocytosis

If the chain of endocytosis $s_3 \xrightarrow{\text{endo}} s_1 \xrightarrow{\text{endo}} s_2 \xrightarrow{\text{endo}} s_4$ is applied, we obtain, in the first step: *The boy eats an apple that I bought*, in the second step: *The boy that eats an apple that I bought runs the marathon.* The final outcome is: *The marathon that the boy that eats an apple that I bought runs was organized by the City Hall.* This is shown in Figure 4.

3.3 Subordination

Subordination means joining two sentences, in the case in which one is dependent on the other one. This definition is very general and rough, but it can be enough for a preliminary paper like this to show the main idea how this phenomenon can be modeled.

Subordination can be modeled by endocytosis, being the inner clause of the resultant sentence the subordinate one and the outer the main one. The relation main-subordinate is a dependence relation that places the sentences in different levels. Two main types of subordination are considered:

– *Noun and adverbial clauses.* The ones that have a function inside the main clause. Some examples: *I think [that you are clever]*, *He will come [when he wants]*.
– *Complex sentences.* The ones syntactically independent but with a logical subordination. Some examples *I will eat it [although I do not like]*, *If you go, [I don't]*.

Noun and adverbial clauses can allow recursive processes; they allow insertion of one clause into the other several times. An example could be: *I thought [that John liked [me to think [that the girl wanted [what we saw]]]]*.

Complex sentences have usually a binary structure. Conditional sentences belong to this type, as well as the ones with the particles: *although, as, as if,*

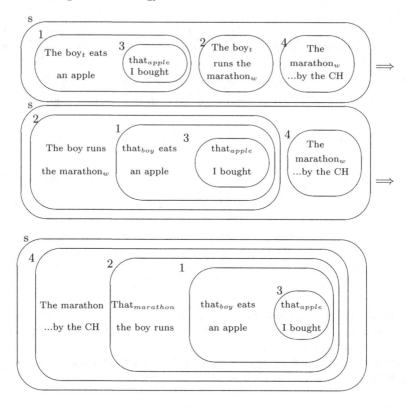

Fig. 4. Evolution of the system with several rules of endocytosis to reach the final structure of the sentence

because, even if, even though, if, if only, rather than, since, though, unless... As an example, we state that structures like IF (IF... THEN)... THEN are not possible in natural language. Actually by considering the logical structure of these sentences they are very close to the ones that we have seen at Subsection 3.1. This is the type of subordination that we are considering in this preliminary introduction. This could also be useful to built some type of logical rules with membranes.

The process can be very simply illustrated with only two sentences s_1: *Jane sold the apartment,* s_2: *The crisis is deep.*

$$\Pi_s = (L, \mu, O, W, R)$$

where

- $L = \{s, 1, 2\}$
- $\mu = [[\ ]_1\ [\ ]_2]_s$
- $O = \{s_1, s_2\} \cup \{although\}$
- $w_1 = s_1, w_2 = s_2,$
- $R = \{[s_1]_1[s_2]_2 \to [[althought\ s_1]_1 s_2]_2,\ [s_1]_1[s_2]_2 \to [[although\ s_2]_2 s_1]_1\}$

This system can generate two very different results when applying the first or the second rule. With the first, the sentence obtained is *Although Jane sold the apartment the crisis is deep*. The main clause in the outcome is *The crisis is deep*. However, applying the second one, the result is *Jane sold the apartment although the crisis is deep*, where the main clause is *Jane sold the apartment*. This difference can be seen in Figure 5.

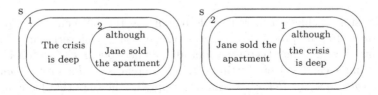

Fig. 5. Two different results obtained by the system

4   P Systems for Non Context-Free Structures

A challenging problem of the formalization of natural languages by formal languages, is the modeling of non context-free structures. P systems can provide a way to deal with such structures. The present work deals with the generation of syntactic complexity starting from simple clauses. Therefore, the question we pose is whether starting with elementary membranes each one of them containing a simple sentence a complex structure can be created with the form $s_1s_2s_3vp_1p_2p_3$, where s_1 is correlated with v and p_1, an so on.

To model a P system converting $n_1v_1p_1n_2v_2p_2n_3v_3p_3 \to n_1n_2n_3vp_1p_2p_3$, let us define a sentence pool with j elements: $s_1{:}n_1v_1p_1$, $s_2{:}n_2v_2p_2$, $s_3{:}n_3v_3p_3$, $\ldots$, $s_j{:}n_jv_jp_j$, where $v_1 = v_2 = v_3 = \ldots = v_j$.

A system generating such structure could be the following:

$$\Pi_n = (L, \mu, O, W, R)$$

where

- $L = \{s, n, p\} \cup \{k \mid k \in \mathbb{N}, 1 \leq k \leq j\}$
- $\mu = [\,[\,]_1[\,]_2[\,]_3 \cdots [\,]_j]_s$
- $O = \{n_i, p_i \mid i \in \mathbb{N}, 1 \leq i \leq j\} \cup \{v\}$
- $w_i = n_ivp_i$, for $1 \leq i \leq j$
- $R = \{\ r_1: [v]_i \to v, out$, for every $1 \leq i \leq j$
    $r_2: v^n \to v$
    $r_3: [p_i]_i \to p_i, out$
    $r_4: p_1, \ldots, p_j \to [p_1, \ldots, p_j]_p$
    $r_5: [n_1]_1, [n_2]_2 \ldots [n_j]_j, \to [n_1, n_2 \ldots n_j]_n\ \}$

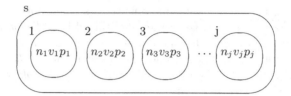

Fig. 6. Pool of sentences

The system includes a merging rule to put together elements form different membranes. In this process the indices of the nouns and verbs are also very important, because they keep the order and connections in the sentence.

An example can be given starting with the sentences s_1: *John eats a sandwich*, s_2: *Ann eats pizza*, s_3: *Peter eats chicken*. Applying the rules that have just been defined, we obtain: *John, Ann and Peter eat sandwich, pizza and chicken*. The process is shown in Figure 7.

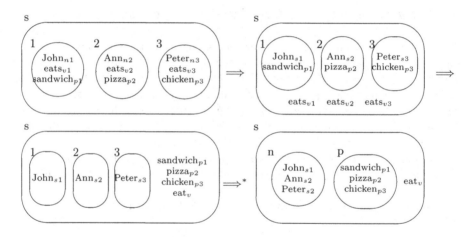

Fig. 7. Process of representation of non-CF sentence structures with membranes

5   Conclusions and Future Work

In this paper, we have shown that membrane systems are capable to mimic various complex syntactical forms of natural language.

When coordination is used to form a complex sentence we do not need to go into the structure of clauses. Moreover, depending on the logical relations between the clauses, free order can be used, so that there is a very suitable and easy way to model this type of linguistic supra-structures by membranes.

Using relative sentences we need a higher resolution. They present a phenomenon that is not very 'frequent' in membrane systems, two membranes sharing the same copy of an element. When this happens, a process of endocytosis is triggered, suggesting that one of the clauses must be inside the other in order to make possible to have a common object.

Concerning subordination, only some very simple cases have been tackled, and the topic should be more carefully approached if we want to enable P systems to describe the many types of relations between clauses/membranes that subordination implies.

Finally, to show non context-free nature of natural languages we need to use the verbs and nouns of the clauses and reorder them. In these sentences we needed to go inside the structure of the clauses.

The model we are offering, however, has several restrictions when approaching natural language. One of them is recursivity. Three of the clause structures that have been tackled in this paper allow recursivity: coordination, relatives and non context-free structures. However, human mind has a limit in the number of levels that a syntactic construction can have. At this stage, P systems present the same problems than formal languages have to model cognition and natural languages. Actually by the term of syntax a sentence can be well formed by allowing any depth of recursion. However in real life practice (and more strictly in the spoken language) it is not a valid assumption to require that a listener/reader can (easily) get the meaning of a sentence in which recursion of depth, let us say, 12 is used. This question can also be connected to the question whether there are infinitely many possible sentences in a natural language.

Membrane systems generally work with multisets, without ordering their elements. In one side, to describe languages, where the order takes matter, we need special indices that keep tracking this order, in other cases, if the word order is strict in a language there is only one way to form a sentence from the given words. On the other side, in some languages the word order is free, and this property can also be represented by the membrane systems: the order of the words of some regions can be written in any order to obtain a syntactically correct sentence. These are some phenomena that can also be used in the model later. Natural languages are very complex and therefore to have a better description of them we need much complex systems. Therefore the next steps could be to restrict ourself to some given languages (sharing some important features, e.g., they have free word order) and to some specific parts of the syntax and/or to specific domains.

The utility of the work like the one that has been presented in this paper is twofold. On one hand, if every type of complex structure of natural language can be 'simulated', then probably formal linguistics will be able to develop new syntactic theories based on the results that such systems can provide. The current distribution of complexity in natural languages does not seem very consistent when analyzed under the methods of natural computing. For example, the boundaries between coordination and subordination seem to be more semantical than structural. On the other hand, modeling clauses with molecular methods can help to built better syntactic analyzers in the future, capable to overcome the wall of shallow parsing.

References

1. Adl, A., Badr, A., Farag, I.: Towards a Spiking Neural P Systems OS, arxiv.org/pdf/1012.0326 (2010)
2. Alhazov, A., Ishdorj, T.-O.: Membrane Operations in P Systems with Active Membranes. In: RGNC report 2001/2004, pp. 37–44. University of Seville, Second Brainstorming Week on Membrane Computing, Sevilla (2004)
3. Andrei, A., Ciobanub, G., Lucanu, D.: A rewriting logic framework for operational semantics of membrane systems. Theor. Comp. Sci. 373, 163–181 (2007)
4. Bel-Enguix, G., Jiménez-López, M.D.: Linguistic membrane systems and applications. In: Ciobanu, G., Păun, G., Pérez-Jimńez, M.J. (eds.) Applications of Membrane Computing, pp. 347–388. Springer, Berlin (2005)
5. Bel-Enguix, G., Jiménez-López, M.D.: Biosyntax An overview. Fundamenta Informaticae 64(1-4), 17–28 (2005)
6. Bel-Enguix, G., Gramatovici, R.: Parsing with Active P Automata. In: Martín-Vide, C., Mauri, G., Păun, G., Rozenberg, G., Salomaa, A. (eds.) WMC 2003. LNCS, vol. 2933, pp. 31–42. Springer, Heidelberg (2004)
7. Chomsky, N.: Three models for the description of language. IEEE Transactions on Information Theory 2(3), 113–124 (1956)
8. Darwin, C.: The Origin of Species (1859), http://www.infidels.org/library/historical/charles_darwin/origin_of_species/
9. Holland, J.H.: Studying Complex Adaptive Systems. Journal of Systems Science and Complexity 19(1), 1–8 (2006)
10. Marcus, S.: Language at the crossroad of computation and biology. In: Păun, G. (ed.) Computing with Bio-Molecules, Singapore, pp. 1–35. Springer (1998)
11. Mitkov, R.: The Oxford Handbook of Computational Linguistics. Oxford University Press (2003)
12. Nagy, B., Kovács, L.: Linguistic Applications of Finite Automata with Translucent Letters. In: Proc. of ICAART 2013, Barcelona, vol. 1, pp. 461–469 (2013)
13. Nagy, B., Kovács, L.: Finite automata with translucent letters applied in natural and formal language theory. Transactions on Computational Collective Intelligence (LNCS journal) (to appear)
14. Păun, G.P.: systems with active membranes. Attacking NP complete problems, CDMTCS Report series - 102 (May 1999)
15. Păun, Gh.: Membrane Computing, An Introduction. Springer, Berlin (2002)
16. Schleicher, A.: Die ersten Spaltungen des indogermanischen Urvolkes. Allgemeine Zeitung fuer Wissenschaft und Literatur (1853)

Simulating Cancer Growth Using Cellular Automata to Detect Combination Drug Targets

Jenna Butler[1], Frances Mackay[2], Colin Denniston[2], and Mark Daley[1,3]

[1] Department of Computer Science
[2] Department of Applied Mathematics
[3] Department of Biology
University of Western Ontario
London, Ontario, Canada

Abstract. Cancer treatment is a fragmented and varied process, as "cancer" is really hundreds of different diseases. The "hallmarks of cancer" were proposed by Hanahan and Weinberg in 2000 and gave a framework for viewing cancer as a single disease - one where cells have acquired ten properties that are common to almost all cancers, allowing them to grow uncontrollably and ravage the body. We used a cellular automata model of tumour growth paired with lattice Boltzmann methods modelling oxygen flow to simulate combination drugs targeted at knocking out pairs of hallmarks. We found that knocking out some pairs of cancer-enabling hallmarks did not prevent tumour formation, while other pairs significantly prevent cancer from growing beyond a few cells ($p=0.0004$ using Wilcoxon signed-rank adjusted with Bonferroni for multiple comparisons). This is not what would be expected from models of knocking out the hallmarks individually, as many pairs did not have an additive effect but either had no effect or a multiplicative one. We propose that targeting certain pairs of cancer hallmarks, specifically cancer's ability to induce blood vessel development paired with another cancer hallmark, could prove an effective cancer treatment option.

1 Introduction and Previous Work

As of 2009, cancer was the leading cause of death in Canada [30]. While much time, money and research are dedicated to cancer the statics are grim, with little to no progress in some cancers - for example, there was no significant improvement in survival rates of pancreatic cancer for two decades (between the 80s and 90s) [27]. We have created a highly abstract cellular automaton model of early cancer growth and a lattice Boltzmann model of oxygen flow in blood that investigates the impact of knocking out pairs of "cancer hallmarks".

While the traditional reductionist approach to studying cancer has been successful in targeting some forms of the disease, new approaches are needed that can study cancer across scales [23]. *In silico* modelling of cancer is an nascent approach available to attack this problem. Multiscale modelling is a powerful tool for cancer simulation as it allows modelling at the cellular level, and at the

O.H. Ibarra et al. (Eds.): UCNC 2014, LNCS 8553, pp. 67–79, 2014.
DOI: 10.1007/978-3-319-08123-6_6, © Springer International Publishing Switzerland 2014

fluid level in order to accurately model oxygen flow. Since oxygen availability is critical for cancer progression, modelling both scales provides a more realistic model. Many cancer models currently exist, including: Anderson *et al.'s* multiscale mathematical model of 2-dimensional tumour growth [4]; Lloyd *et al.'s* computational framework for solid tumour growth, which comprised models at the tissue, cellular and subcellular levels [19]; and Ramis-Conde *et al.'s* hybrid-discrete model which looked at tissue invasion by cancer cells [22]. Models focus on different aspects of tumour growth (including the use of the glycolytic phenotype [11], evolution of cell motility [12] and confined environments [13]) and employ different modelling approaches (mathematical, [17], [22], hybrid, [25], and [10], agent-based [20], [31]). Readers who wish to know more are directed to the following review articles: [2], [3], [24].

Currently the state of the art in cancer modelling is spread across these different modelling techniques. A recent review paper looking at cancer invasion discusses the use of both hybrid discrete-continuous (HDC) and immersed boundary model of a cell (IBCell) models. HDC allows for cells to be modelled discretely but microenvironmental variables such as nutrients and oxygen to be modelling using reaction-diffusion equations. The IBCell model is beneficial for capturing the morphology of a tumour cell as the cells in this model are deformable [18]. In addition to these two types of agent based models, cellular automata models are also used frequently. Gerlee and Anderson [10] created an evolutionary hybrid cellular automata model where the cancer cells are modelled using cellular automata to capture the behaviour of the tissue as a whole, while using an artificial neural network for cell decisions. This type of hybrid cellular automata model has recently been built on by Shrestha *et al.* who used a similar model to look at large-scale growth of tumours [28]. Recently, cellular automata models have been used to look at the hallmarks of cancer [1], [5], [26] as proposed by Hanahana and Weinberg [14], [15].

Today survival rates and treatment options for cancers vary widely. Hanahan and Weinberg proposed that almost all cancers actually share eight phenotypic changes and two unique characteristics: SELF SUFFICIENCY IN GROWTH SIGNALS; IGNORING GROWTH INHIBITION; AVOIDANCE OF PROGRAMMED CELL DEATH (APOPTOSIS); LIMITLESS REPRODUCTIVE POTENTIAL; SUSTAINED ANGIOGENESIS; TISSUE INVASION AND METASTASIS; REREGULATED METABOLISM; EVADING THE IMMUNE SYSTEM; INFLAMMATION; and GENETIC INSTABILITY [14], [15]. The ubiquitous nature of these hallmarks in cancer suggests that treatments able to target them may be useful against multiple types of cancer.

Both Abbott *et al.* [1] and Santos *et al.* [26] have developed models looking at these hallmarks. Abbott *et al.* primarily focused on looking at the order in which hallmarks were acquired in the growing tumour. Abbott's results differed from the pathway to cancer proposed by Hanahan and Weinberg, as did the results of an ordinary differential equation model looking at the pathway [29]. Abbott's model was an agent based model that simulated the progression of cancer from a single healthy cell to a tumour with at least 90% cancer cells. They found that hallmarks that confer an advantage to all cells (such as SUSTAINED ANGIOGENE-

SIS which creates blood vessels carrying oxygen into the tumour which all nearby cells can benefit from), do not dominate a cancer clone, whereas hallmarks such as LIMITLESS REPLICATION appear early and dominate as they turn over very quickly.

Santos *et al.* built on the work of Abbott by using a similar modelling approach, but focused on the impact of removing different hallmarks on tumour growth. They investigated how critical to growth each hallmark was by removing it from the system and comparing the total number of cancerous and healthy cells present with and without the hallmark. They used a cellular automata model which determined cell division and apoptosis (programmed cell death) based on internal rules and acquired hallmarks. They found that with high mutation rates, the most critical hallmark is APOPTOSIS, while in tumours with little room to grow the IGNORE GROWTH INHIBITION hallmark proved most impactful on overall growth.

We have used similar model parameters and methods outlined in Abbott *et al.'s* work to build upon Santos *et al.'s* hallmark relevance study. We have implement five of the six original hallmarks as well as two of the newly introduced hallmarks and enabling characteristics (focusing on those relevant during initial tumour growth), and knocked them out in pairs to see which have the greatest combined effect.

Henderson [16] stated that "in the most general sense, combinations of therapies, whether drugs and/or other modalities, will always play an important role in the management of diseases for which there exists no single specific and totally effective treatment". Combination treatment involves pairing multiple drugs with the hope that two in combination will not just be an additive advantage but a multiplicative one. Targeted therapy involves identifying key pathways involved in cancer progression and creating drugs to target these pathways. This model simulates targeted combination therapy as we remove key cancer properties in pairs and compare cancer growth rates to tumours with all hallmarks active. We hypothesize that knocking out pairs of hallmarks will not necessarily have the additive effect of knocking the hallmarks out separately but rather will sometimes have an even greater, potentially multiplicative, combined impact.

2   Methods

We have chosen to model two dimensional cancer growth where the biological cells are represented by cellular automata and the oxygen in the environment is modelled as a two-phase fluid using the lattice Boltzman method. Most models in the literature currently restrict themselves to two dimensions as it is more computationally feasible and since cancer does not grow in a sphere but rather an oblate spheroid. In order to compare findings with both existing models and 2D biopsy slices we have done a 2D simulation. Here we will present a high level outline of the method, and each section will be covered in more detail below. The simulation begins with a single healthy cell at the center of a 2-dimensional grid. An event queue keeps track of cellular events, and initially a single mitotic event is placed on the queue for the healthy cell. Each event popped from the queue is another loop in the model and puts that cell through a life cycle. The cell is checked for whether it still has enough oxygen to survive, is in a location with growth factor, has access to blood, has space to grow, and has sufficiently long telomeres. If all of these checks are successful, or if mutations make the checks unnecessary, the cell enters a mitotic event. This creates a daughter cell and potentially introduces mutations into the daughter or parent. Both cells have events scheduled for some point in the future and are added to the event queue, then the next event is popped. Oxygen is consumed by cells when they divide or every 25 time steps if they are not actively dividing.

2.1   Modelling the Hallmarks

The "hallmarks of cancer" proposed by Hanahan and Weinberg [14], [15] are changes to cell phenotype (characteristics of the cell based on its genotype and the environment - in our model, the collection of hallmark mutations it has along with the parameter values) that seem to be consistent across a variety of cancers. These hallmarks give a structure and common signature to a disease that is actually a combination of hundreds of different types of diseases. The six hallmarks originally proposed were: sustained growth; evading growth suppressors; avoiding programmed cell death (apoptosis); enabling replicative immortality; inducing angiogenesis and activating tissue invasion and metastasis. In 2011, Hanahan and Weinberg added two characteristics that underlay these hallmarks: genetic instability and inflammation. They also added two "emerging hallmarks": reprogramming of energy metabolism and evading immune destruction. We have simulated 5 of the 6 original hallmarks and two of the recently added characteristics and hallmarks. This model is specifically interested in pre-metastatic growth, when a patient has the greatest chances of survival. Therefore, we have not modelled the sixth hallmark, tissue invasion and metastasis. To keep our results credibly comparable with previous work in this field, we have not included inflammation or energy metabolism in our model. Our model is inspired by work in artificial life [21], [8] where agent based and mathematical models are used to simulate cancer growth and angiogenesis. Here we will briefly describe the implementation of each hallmark. The parameters described can be found in Table 1.

Sustained Growth: SG. To model SG, healthy cells can only grow within a predefined boundary of growth factor (all cells can grow in the inner boundary, then three consecutive inner boundaries allow for growth with 50%, 30% and 10% chances of survival). Outside of this cells can not actively divide unless they have the SG mutation.

Ignoring Growth Inhibition: IGI. Cancer cells in our system can have the IGI hallmark activated, allowing cells to grow even without space around them on the grid. If a cell with the IGI hallmark attempts to grow and is out of space, it competes for growth, with a $1/c$ likelihood of success, with its neighbouring cells then takes over the space if successful.

Table 1. Parameters used in simulations

Description	Symbol	Value	Ref
Initial telomere length	t	100	[1]
Evade apoptosis factor	ev	10	[1]
Mutation rate	m	500	Chosen to lay between two used in [26]
Random death rate	d	10000	Simulation
Competition likelihood	c	10	Simulation
Angiogenesis immunity	ai	10	Simulation
Avoid immunity	aip	10	Simulation
Immunity death	i	1000	Simulation (equal to random cell death in [26])
Genetic instability factor	gif	10	Simulation

Avoiding Apoptosis: AA. In our simulation, apoptosis can occur to any cell that has a single mutation. Since apoptosis is initiated when aberrant activity is detected, the chances of a cancer cell dying via apoptosis increases with each subsequent mutation (m/a likelihood of death). Cells with AA mutation in this mechanism cannot die by apoptosis.

Enabling Replicative Immortality (by Ignoring Telomeres): IT. We have modelled telomeres as an integer in each cell that decreases by one after every division, and must be greater than zero for division to occur. Cells with the IT hallmark turned on will replicate regardless of telomere length.

Inducing Angiogenesis: A. Similar to growth factor, lattice sites have to be within a gradually reducing predefined boundary in order to access nutrients from the blood. Cells with the A mutation induce new vasculature, and these cells and any neighbouring cells can survive outside the blood boundary. A cells also have a higher ($(ai) * (1/i)$) chance of being killed by the immune system.

Genetically Unstable: GU. GU cells have an increased chance of mutation in each mitotic event by a factor of ($1/gif$) where gif is the genetic instability factor parameter.

Avoids Immune System: AI. AI cells have lowered chances of being killed by the immune system by a factor of aip, the avoids immune system parameter.

2.2   Event Queue

Mitotic events are the driving force in this model. An event queue keeps track of all events scheduled for the simulation. Initially, the cell has a mitotic event scheduled for 5-11 time steps in the future. When the event is popped the time is checked. If the time for the event is beyond the current time in the simulator the current time is updated. If the cell is to grow in a North, East, South or West direction, the time is scheduled 5-11 time points in the future (chosen by random number). If the cell is growing on a diagonal on the grid then the event is scheduled for 7-14 ($\sqrt{2}$ of the normal mitotic time) time points in the future as it takes longer to move on the diagonal.

Since the cells in the simulation (the biologic cells, not necessarily "cells" in the classical cellular automaton sense) are impacted by rules that use probability, this model deviates slightly from standard cellular automata. Also, at every time step only a handful of cells are actually updated (those that were scheduled for a mitotic event). As pointed out by Abbott *et al.*, the cells could instead have a counter that is updated each time through the life cycle, but since real biological cells are not updating that often it makes sense to schedule their events for some time in the future and save computation time [1].

2.3 Oxygen

Oxygen is modelled as a two phase fluid, oxygen molecules in blood, using lattice-Boltzmann algorithms. Every time a cell completes a division it consumes oxygen. Cells that are not actively dividing consume oxygen every 25 time steps. We have assumed that: biological cells consume a constant amount of oxygen regardless of phenotype, die if they ever fail an attempt to consume oxygen (because there isn't enough present at the lattice site), and that oxygen consumption by a healthy or cancerous cell removes that oxygen from the overall system.

3 Results

With all hallmarks active, every simulation run produced a tumour using parameters described in Table 1. A "tumour" is classified as a mass in which 99% or more of its alive cells have at least one mutation. The growth over time for a simulation with all hallmarks available can be seen in Figure 1.

Figure 1a shows total cell counts throughout growth. Initially healthy cells grow rapidly, however around event 8000 they sharply decline. Then, around event 10000 cancer cells rapidly start to increase. This corresponds to a sharp increase in angiogenic cells as well as cells that avoid apoptosis, and relatively stable numbers of healthy cells. Figure 1c through h shows the images produced from the same simulation. It can be seen in Figure 1c that initially healthy cells dominate the clone. Death is occurring, most likely due to random cell death or the initial fast killing of any cancerous cells by apoptosis and the immune system. By 1d we can already see the emergence of different cancer phenotypes. There are three major phenotypes present in the tumour from early on. The center of the tumour also begins to die at 1d. This is due to a lack of oxygen getting to the center of the tumour (called necrosis). At 1g the outside of the tumour is also dying, as regular cells can go no further as they are outside the growth factor and blood range. In 1h we see the tumour is almost entirely cancerous, with a few

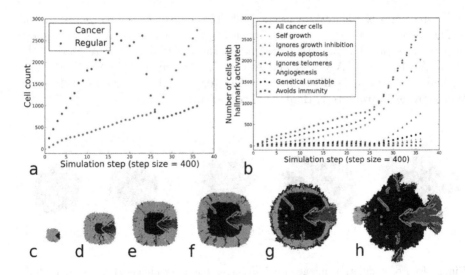

Fig. 1. a and b: Total cell count for cancerous, non cancerous, and each hallmark is shown for an entire simulation with all hallmarks available for activation. a) Regular vs cancerous cell growth b) Growth of cells with each individual hallmark and total cancer cell growth. c - h: Simulation of a colony of cells with all hallmarks available for activation at event steps 400 to 12800. Dead cells are black, healthy cells are blue, all other colours represent some kind of unique cancer phenotype. Event points: c) 400 events d) 2400 e) 4800 f) 7200 g) 9600 h) 12800.

different phenotypes protruding from the mass. This "fingering morphology", where the border is not smooth but rough, is consistent with other models [6], [4], [7]. It is believed that there are two forms of tumour invasion - either tumour cells outgrow normal tissue and expand as a bulk mass, or they form invasive contingents by intermingling with stromal cells. The fingering morphology is a consequence of this intermingling [18]. It was noted in [18] that this fingering morphology looks like a crab, from which the word cancer was derived. The fingering morphology is correlated with harsher microenvironments where only cells with particular phenotypes survive. This behaviour is evident in our model where certain subclones and phenotypes dominate the tumour.

Knocking out some hallmark pairs had very little effect on the growth of the tumour. In fact, knockout pairs SG & IGI, SG & AA, SG & IT, IGI & AA, IGI & GU, IGI & AI, AA & GU, AA & AI, IT & GU and GU & AI had no significant effect (all p values greater than 0.05 using Wilcoxon signed-rank test Bonferroni corrected for multiple comparisons) (see Figure 2 b and c for examples of final simulation image when cancer took over despite hallmark pair knockouts). Other pairs of hallmark knockouts had such a large effect that a cancerous tumour never took over and the simulation ended prematurely as not enough cells survived. The normal cells continued to grow to the edge of the growth factor barrier, and then eventually consumed all of the oxygen in the system and the healthy cells died off. This can be seen in Figure 2 d and e. The following hallmark pairs significantly (p=0.0004 using Wilcoxon signed-rank test, Bonferroni corrected) decreased cancer growth: SG & A, SG & GU, SG & AI, IGI & A, AA & A and A & GU. Other pairs, AA & IT and A & AI had a smaller but still significant effect (0.017 and 0.019 respectively using Wilcoxon signed-rank test, Bonferroni corrected).

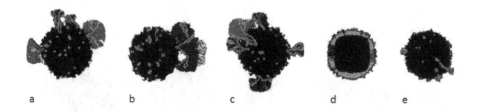

Fig. 2. End of simulation images for 5 different hallmark-knockout pairs. a) no hallmarks knocked out b) IGI & AA c) IGI & IT d) SG & A e) IGI & A.

The effect of various hallmark pairs can be seen in Figure 3a. This shows that some hallmark knockouts (A & GU, IGI & A, IT & A, SG & A, A & AI, SG & AI) do not result in a tumour. Cancer growth is fairly consistent across all of the simulations, regardless of knockout, until event 8000. Here, all cell populations take a dip however certain simulations show strong growth after this point. The knockout pairs listed above however die off at this point, and these simulations do not result in a cancerous tumour.

Figure 3b shows a histogram of phenotypes that were in the top 10 phenotypes by cell count during the last stage of simulation for 14 unique simulations (knockout pairs that still resulted in a tumour). While it is obvious that dead cells will be present in large numbers in all runs, it is interesting that phenotype A and D,A are also present in every run in large numbers - these are cells with the ANGIOGENESIS hallmark activated and no other hallmarks, both alive and dead. Also, by the end of simulation almost all tumours have a large population of dead SELF GROWTH cells and AVOIDS APOPTOSIS cells. It is interesting that the dominate ANGIOGENIC cells are alive, while the SELF GROWTH and APOPTOSIS dominant clones are dead. Also present in the majority of simulations in large numbers are dead cells with IGNORES GROWTH INHIBITION activated and IGNORES TELOMERES activated, as well as alive cells that are both ANGIOGENIC and AVOID APOPTOSIS.

4   Discussion

As expected, when all hallmarks are available for activation the tumour grows to the largest extent, presumably as these tumours can take advantage of all hallmarks and the different abilities each confers. It was also expected that knocking

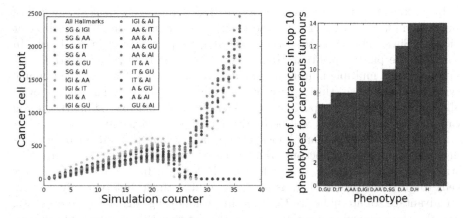

Fig. 3. a) Total alive cancer cell count every 400 simulation steps is shown. Each hallmark-knockout pair simulation was run 10 times. The average cell count from these runs was calculated and plotted. b) Each tumour at the end of the simulation had different phenotypes present. The top 10 phenotypes, by total number in the tumour, in each separate simulation were recorded at the end of simulation and totals were plotted. All hallmark abbreviations are these used in the text, with the addition of H for healthy cells and D for dead cells.

out 2 hallmarks would significantly lower the growth of cancer. We hypothesized that certain pairs would perform better than others, and that knocking out hallmarks in pairs could have more than just an additive effect.

Half of all tumours with SELF GROWTH knocked out did not result in a tumour. SG allows a tumour to extend beyond the normal boundary of growth. In areas of the body where growth factor is limited, this would be a very important hallmark. However if a tumour is growing where there is ample growth factor the hallmark may be less effective as a drug target.

All simulations with ANGIOGENESIS knocked out failed to result in a tumour. Similar to SG, ANGIOGENESIS allows a cell to live outside the predefined blood boundary. One reason the ANGIOGENESIS hallmark is more powerful is because it conveys benefit to not just the cell with the mutation, but surrounding cells, as all nearby cells benefit from the new vasculature.

The last hallmark that was knocked out in more than one pair that did not lead to a tumour is GENOME INSTABILITY. Since GENOME INSTABILITY can lead to all of the other mutations being activated more this is understandable.

As is evident in Figure 3a, there is a bifurcation in total cell count - either similar to when all hallmarks are active, or almost no growth. This is because cell populations which result in a tumour show almost exponential growth and are not limited by oxygen or space due to acquired mutations. Cell populations that do not result in a tumour are limited by both of these factors, and so eventually almost all cells die as this slight overpopulation cannot be sustained by the normal vasculature.

It is interesting that of the phenotypes that dominated clones at the end of simulation (shown in Figure 3b), those with a single mutation grew quickly but died off. Single mutation phenotypes were largely present, but in dead cells. In contrast, the phenotypes that dominated and were still alive had multiple mutations. While multiple mutations increase the chances of death by the immune system and apoptosis, this suggests it still conveys a very strong advantage overall. This supports the hypothesis that knocking out multiple hallmarks, if you can find the correct pairs, will be better than single treatments.

It is interesting that many knockouts did not prevent the tumour from forming. For example, all knockouts that included IGNORING GROWTH INHIBITION still resulted in a tumour, except for one (IGI & A). In our model IGI allows cells to grow even when there is no space around them, but this only conveys an advantage to internal cells. Cells on the proliferating edge always have space, and therefore removing it does not seem to hurt growth to a significant degree. This could be a limitation of the model as in reality the proliferating rim of a tumour may have space constraints from surrounding tissue.

Some limitations of the model are present, and include the fact that AN-GIOGENESIS only provides a benefit to itself or cells immediately around it. In addition, it only provides an advantage while the cell is living. In reality angiogenic cells start the creation of blood vessels and those remain even if the cells die.

5   Conclusions

We have modelled the impact of knocking out pairs of cancer hallmarks, as proposed by Hanahan and Weinberg [14], [15], on early tumour growth using a cellular automaton model of cancer cells and lattice Boltzmann methods for two phase fluids (oxygen in the blood). Our results show that knocking out pairs of hallmarks does not necessarily have an additive effect. Santos *et al.* found that AVOIDING APOPTOSIS and IGNORING GROWTH INHIBITION were the most critical hallmarks independently when cells had a high rate of mutation, and they also found that IGNORING TELOMERES and SELF GROWTH had a small impact [26]. Looking at the impact of knocking out both AVOIDING APOPTOSIS and IGNORING GROWTH INHIBITION, we did not see a significant decrease in tumour growth. This is interesting as it is not what would be expected from the findings of knocking out singular hallmarks.

We found that knocking out the ability for a cancer cell to SELF GROW and AVOID THE IMMUNE SYSTEM, as well as SELF GROW and be GENETICALLY UN-STABLE, prevents a tumour from growing. Neither SELF GROWTH nor GENETIC INSTABILITY had a great effect in the simulations done by Santos *et al.* (the immune system was not modelled in this work) however in combination they had a strong and significant effect. This supports our hypothesis that knowing the impact of individual hallmarks, which can be extended to individual drugs, does not necessarily give insight into the impact of combining those knockouts and drugs.

Lastly, we found that knocking out the ability for cells to INDUCE ANGIOGEN-ESIS combined with any other hallmark prevented tumour growth. Research has been done into anti-angiogenesis drugs however the conclusions were not always positive. Often patients still died from small tumours throughout the body as opposed to one large tumour, which was seen without the drugs [9]. It is hypothesized that without angiogenesis, other factors became important, such as metastasis and the glycolytic phenotype. Perhaps the key is preventing cells from inducing angiogenesis and limiting other cancerous abilities. Currently trials are under way to test pairing anti-angiogenesis drugs with current chemotherapy drugs (La Roche Limited onging trial).

We have found that the effect of knocking out cancer hallmarks in pairs can have varying levels of success. This suggests that clinical research should be done into combination drug treatment as not all drugs that are strong individually will necessarily be strong in combination. Since cancer treatments can be physically and emotionally challenging for patients, knowing in advance what combinations will not be successfully could greatly enhance the quality of life of people undergoing cancer treatment.

References

1. Abbott, R., Forrest, S., Pienta, K.: Simulating the hallmarks of cancer. Artificial Life 4(12), 34–617 (2006)
2. Anderson, A.R.A., Rejniak, K.A., Gerlee, P., Quaranta, V.: Modelling of Cancer Growth, Evolution and Invasion: Bridging Scales and Models. Mathematical Modelling of Natural Phenomena 2(3), 1–29 (2008),
   http://www.mmnp-journal.org/10.1051/mmnp:2007001
3. Anderson, A.R.A., Quaranta, V.: Integrative mathematical oncology. Nature Reviews Cancer 8(3), 227–234 (2008),
   http://www.ncbi.nlm.nih.gov/pubmed/18273038
4. Anderson, A.R.A., Weaver, A.M., Cummings, P.T., Quaranta, V.: Tumor morphology and phenotypic evolution driven by selective pressure from the microenvironment. Cell 127(5), 905–915 (2006),
   http://www.ncbi.nlm.nih.gov/pubmed/17129778
5. Basanta, D., Ribba, B., Watkin, E., You, B., Deutsch, A.: Computational analysis of the influence of the microenvironment on carcinogenesis. Mathematical Biosciences 229(1), 22–29 (2011),
   http://www.sciencedirect.com/science/article/pii/S0025556410001616
6. Bello, L., Lucini, V., Costa, F., Pluderi, M., Giussani, C., Acerbi, F., Carrabba, G., Pannacci, M., Caronzolo, D., Grosso, S., et al.: Combinatorial administration of molecules that simultaneously inhibit angiogenesis and invasion leads to increased therapeutic efficacy in mouse models of malignant glioma. Clinical Cancer Research 10(13), 4527–4537 (2004)
7. Bellomo, N., De Angelis, E.: Selected topics in cancer modeling: genesis, evolution, immune competition, and therapy. Springer (2008)
8. Bentley, K., Bates, P., Gerhardt, H.: Artificial life as cancer research: Embodied agent modelling of blood vessel growth in tumours. In: Proceedings of Artifical Life XI (2008)

9. Ebos, J.M.L., Lee, C.R., Cruz-Munoz, W., Bjarnason, G.A., Christensen, J.G., Kerbel, R.S.: Accelerated metastasis after short-term treatment with a potent inhibitor of tumor angiogenesis. Cancer Cell 15(3), 232–239 (2009), http://www.ncbi.nlm.nih.gov/pubmed/19249681

10. Gerlee, P., Anderson, A.R.A.: An evolutionary hybrid cellular automaton model of solid tumour growth. Journal of Theoretical Biology 246(4), 583–603 (2007)

11. Gerlee, P., Anderson, A.R.A.: A hybrid cellular automaton model of clonal evolution in cancer: The emergence of the glycolytic phenotype. Journal of Theoretical Biology 250, 705–722 (2008)

12. Gerlee, P., Anderson, A.R.A.: Evolution of cell motility in an individual-based model of tumour growth. Journal of Theoretical Biology 259(1), 67–83 (2009)

13. Gevertz, J.L., Gillies, G.T., Torquato, S.: Simulating tumor growth in confined heterogeneous environments. Physical Biology 5(3) (2008), http://www.ncbi.nlm.nih.gov/pubmed/18824788

14. Hanahan, D., Weinberg, R.: The hallmarks of cancer. Cell 100(1), 57–70 (2000)

15. Hanahan, D., Weinberg, R.: Hallmarks of cancer: the next generation. Cell 144(5), 646–674 (2011)

16. Henderson, E., Samaha, R.: Evidence that drugs in multiple combinations have materially advanced the treatment of human malignancies. Cancer Research 29(12), 2272–2280 (1969)

17. Hirata, Y., Bruchovsky, N., Aihara, K.: Development of a mathematical model that predicts the outcome of hormone therapy for prostate cancer. Journal of Theoretical Biology 264(2), 517–527 (2010), http://www.ncbi.nlm.nih.gov/pubmed/20176032

18. Kam, Y., Rejniak, K.A., Anderson, A.R.A.: Cellular modeling of cancer invasion: integration of in silico and in vitro approaches. Journal of Cellular Physiology 227(2), 431–438 (2012), http://www.ncbi.nlm.nih.gov/pubmed/21465465

19. Lloyd, B.A., Szczerba, D., Rudin, M., Székely, G.: A computational framework for modelling solid tumour growth. Philosophical transactions, Series A, Mathematical, physical, and engineering sciences 366(1879), 3301–3318 (2008), http://www.ncbi.nlm.nih.gov/pubmed/18593664

20. Macklin, P., Edgerton, M.E., Thompson, A., Cristini, V.: Patient-calibrated agent-based modelling of ductal carcinoma in situ (DCIS) I: Model formulation and analysis. Journal of Theoretical Biology 301, 122–140 (2011)

21. Maley, C.C., Forrest, S.: Modelling the role of neutral and selective mutations in cancer. In: Artificial Life VII: Proceedings of the Seventh International Conference on Artificial Life, pp. 395–404 (2000)

22. Ramis-Conde, I., Chaplain, M.A.J., Anderson, A.R.: Mathematical modelling of cancer cell invasion of tissue. Mathematical and Computer Modelling 47(5-6), 533–545 (2008), http://linkinghub.elsevier.com/retrieve/pii/S0895717707001823

23. Rejniak, K.A., Anderson, A.R.A.: State of the art in computational modelling of cancer. Mathematical Medicine and Biology 29(1), 1–2 (2012), http://www.ncbi.nlm.nih.gov/pubmed/22200587

24. Rejniak, K.A., Anderson, A.R.: Hybrid models of tumor growth. Wiley Interdisciplinary Reviews: Systems Biology and Medicine 3(1), 115–125 (2011)

25. Ribba, B., Alarcón, T., Marron, K., Maini, P.K., Agur, Z.: The use of hybrid cellular automaton models for improving cancer therapy. In: Sloot, P.M.A., Chopard, B., Hoekstra, A.G. (eds.) ACRI 2004. LNCS, vol. 3305, pp. 444–453. Springer, Heidelberg (2004)

26. Santos, J., Monteagudo, Á.: Study of cancer hallmarks relevance using a cellular automaton tumor growth model. In: Coello, C.A.C., Cutello, V., Deb, K., Forrest, S., Nicosia, G., Pavone, M. (eds.) PPSN 2012, Part I. LNCS, vol. 7491, pp. 489–499. Springer, Heidelberg (2012)
27. Sener, S., Fremgen, A., Menck, H., Winchester, D.: Pancreatic cancer: A report of treatment and survival trends for 100,313 patients diagnosed from 1985–1995, using the national cancer database. Journal of the American College of Surgeons 189(1), 1–7 (1999)
28. Shrestha, S., Joldes, G.R., Wittek, A., Miller, K.: Cellular automata coupled with steady-state nutrient solution permit simulation of large-scale growth of tumours. International Journal for Numerical Methods in Biomedical Engineering 29, 542–559 (2013)
29. Spencer, S., Berryman, M., Garcia, J., Abbott, D.: An ordinary differential equation model for the multistep transformation to cancer. Journal of Theoretical Biology 231, 515–524 (2004)
30. StatCan: Leading causes of death, by sex. Statistics Canada (2009)
31. Sun, X., Zhang, L., Tan, H., Bao, J., Strouthos, C., Zhou, X.: Multi-scale agent-based brain cancer modeling and prediction of TKI treatment response: Incorporating EGFR signaling pathway and angiogenesis. BMC Bioinformatics 13(1), 218 (2012),
http://www.biomedcentral.com/1471-2105/13/218

Towards an MP Model
for B Lymphocytes Maturation

Alberto Castellini[1], Giuditta Franco[1,*], Vincenzo Manca[1],
Riccardo Ortolani[2], and Antonio Vella[2]

[1]Department of Computer Science and [2]Department of Pathology and Diagnostics,
[1] Strada Le Grazie 15, and [2]Piazzale Antonio Scuro 10,
[1] Unversity and [2]Polyclinic Hospital of Verona, 37100 Verona, Italy
giuditta.franco@univr.it

Abstract. A first dynamical model is given to explain maturation steps
of B limphocytic cells in human body, based on Metabolic P systems with
genetic regression of regulation maps. In humans, B cell development constitutes the steps that lead to B cell commitment and to expression of
surface immunoglobulin, which is essential for B cell survival and function. Mature and fully functional B cells population (CD19+) include
phenotypically and functionally different subgroups which persist during
all stages of B-cell maturation. Quantities of eight different subgroups of
B cells, identified by presence or absence of given receptors, were measured in about six thousands patients of all ages. Here we present a long
work of preparation and analysis of (ex-vivo) data, and a preliminary
model to explain the eight statistically refined time series, which opened
up interesting questions about network inference and methodologies to
analyze cross sectional data.

Keywords: B lymphocytic cells maturation, cross sectional data, genetic algorithms, parameter regression, MP systems.

1 Introduction

Immunological system is one of the most complex and adaptive known systems
in nature, which is basically responsibile for our health, since most of the human
diseases are induced by some fall or misplay in our body defence system. Immune
system provides us with lots of complex and intriguing open problems of recognition and coordination, based on distributed signaling and phisycal cell interaction, that may be tackled by approaches typical of systems biology [4]. From
an experimental viewpoint, immunology is dominated by a stimulus-response
model, currently concealed by an interest in the mechanism of single regulatory
responses, induced by *ad hoc* in vitro experiments. Alternatively, important aims
of immunology could be a description of invariants of the global immune system organization, and a description of interfaces and interactions between the
immune system and the organism. A systems biology view of immune activity

---

* Corresponding author.

O.H. Ibarra et al. (Eds.): UCNC 2014, LNCS 8553, pp. 80–92, 2014.
DOI: 10.1007/978-3-319-08123-6_7, © Springer International Publishing Switzerland 2014

mainly focuses on modeling the dynamics of reciprocal interactions between the immune system and the physiology of the organism of which it is a component [19].

In this paper, we started a work aimed to understand the order of maturation steps through which B cells may pass, since when they enter circulation in human body until they die (usually by apoptosis). Cells in the spleen and lymphonodes, with the help of T cells forming the germinal-centre, proliferate rapidly, by undergoing on somatic hypermutation of their immunoglobulin variable gene segments and isotype-switching recombination of immunoglobulin genes, and are mainly responsible for generating humoral immune responses to protein antigens. At about day ten after immunization, the germinal-centre reaction reaches its peak (as also confirmed by our model, see curves in Figure 3 representing observed dynamics of B cell quantities). Mechanisms and factors that guide some germinal-centre B cells to become memory B cells and others to become plasma cells are not yet clear. Such a stepwise sort of differentiation has been first characterized in mice. For humans, it has been understood that in vitro these cells are capable of stepwise differentiation into mature-naïve-phenotype B cells, although their obligate precursor-progeny relationships in-vivo await confirmation.

During recent years, a tremendous effort has been devoted to characterization of phenotype and function of distinct lymphocyte subpopulations and B lymphocytes in humans, as well as to their pathway(s) of differentiation and role in immune responses. Despite the great results obtained with regard to the mechanisms involved in the maturation of B lymphocytes and the related phenotype these studies seem to have also generated more questions than definitive answers.

The immunological *self* as a structural cellular organization could provide new insight and/or tools in fields as autoimmunity and/or cancer immunology that within the classical immunological paradigm struggling to find definitive answers. For example, the cellular origin of Chronic Lymphocytic leukemia (CLL) is still debated, although some information about the adaption of cellular immunological network is critical to understanding its pathogenesis [17]. Un-mutated CLL (immunoglobulin variable region gene) are more aggressive than mutated CLL in clinical terms, and aggressive CLL derives from mature CD5+ B cells (naïve B cells) whereas mutated CLL derives from a distinct, previously unrecognized CD5+CD27+ post-germinal center B cell subset (memory B cells). Notably, both these CD5+ B cell populations include oligoclonal expansions that were also found in young healthy adults [17].

We here present an MP system to model a possible sequence of (ex-vivo observed) B cell maturation steps, which has found some confirm in experiments from the immunological literature. MP systems are discrete dynamical systems [12,13], arisen in the context of membrane computing [9,2], introducing a deterministic perspective where multiset rewriting rules are equipped with state functions that determine the quantities of transformed elements. They had successful applications in the analysis of biological phenomena. In particular, an algebraic formulation of their dynamics, combined with methods of statistical regression, provided systemetic solutions to complex Inverse Dynamical Problems of biological systems [14], by determining MP systems able to generate observed time series of given phenomena. When such a kind of inverse processes find some possible MP models, very often hidden mechanisms are made evident that reveal an internal logics. In [7] statistical methods were replaced by genetic algorithms, by obtaining, in many cases, the same level of accuracy in the solution of inverse problems. A great number of concepts and algorithms developed within MP theory were implemented in public software platforms equipped with examples and technical documentation[1].

In next section our current knowledge about the biological process under investigation is given, while in its subsections 2.1 and 2.2 data collection and analysis are described in details. In section 3 the model is presented, with a discussion in section 4.

2   The Biological Process

New B cells are generated throughout life in humans, first in the liver, during gestation, and thereafter in the bone marrow. Early B cell development constitutes the steps that lead to B cell commitment and the expression of surface immunoglobulin, which is essential for B cell survival and function. B cells undergo selection for self-tolerance and ability to survive in the peripheral lymphoid tissues. These events culminate in the production of *transitional* B cells, which leave the marrow and migrate to secondary lymphoid tissues, such as the lymph nodes, the spleen, and the Peyer's patches of the gut. Subsequent steps occur after B cells interact with exogenous antigen and/or T helper cells; these constitute the "antigen dependent phase" that results in the generation of plasma cells, antibodies and memory B cells. Newly formed B cells, after entering into the spleen first remain immature. They are referred to as transitional (T1 and T2), based on their phenotypes and ontogeny, and have been characterized primarily in the mouse.

All B-lymphocytes are characterized by the expression of CD19 surface antigen, which is present early on bone marrow progenitor cells and persists during all stages of B-cell maturation [15]. Mature and fully functional B cells population (CD19+) include phenotypically and functionally different subgroups. The largest subgroup is formed of B2 cells, or conventional B cells, which account for about 10% of peripheral blood lymphocytes in humans. Marginal-zone B cells and B1 cells are Thymus-independent (TI) antigens (Ag) and, by many microbial constituents are activated to antibody production in the absence of helper T-cells [11].

Marginal-zone B cells represent the 10% of mature splenic B cells and are strategically positioned at the bloodlymphoid tissue interface whereas B1 migrate preferentially in body cavities [16] and can be distinguished by the presence

---

[1] See some related links: `mptheory.scienze.univr.it/`, `mplab.sci.univr.it/`, `www.cbmc.it/software/Software.php`

of CD5 (B1-a cells) or absence (B1-b cells). In mice, B1 cells represent a unique cell population distinguished from follicular B cells (B-2 cells) by their surface marker expression, developmental origin, self-renewing capacity, and functions whereas the identity and existence of the human counterpart of murine B-1 cells have been in doubt for many years, mainly because of the absence of known cell surface markers to identify this population.

In humans, most of the mature B cells in fetal circulation express CD5, but they decrease to 11–49% in the adult circulation [1]. Recently, human transitional T1 B cells were shown to express CD5, although the murine counterpart does not express this molecule [18]. However, human transitional B cells account for only 1–2% of total circulating B cells, suggesting the existence of other CD5+ B cell subsets. To address this issue, some authors have identified a distinct pre-naïve B cell population in human peripheral blood, that exhibits an intermediate phenotype between transitional and naive B cells (having some B cell functions in common with naive B cells, including the capacity to differentiate into plasma cells and Ag presentation) [18]. Of interest, this pre-naïve B cell population accounted for the majority of circulating human CD5 B cells, and an increase of this population was found in peripheral blood of patients with systemic lupus erythematosus (SLE). It was also suggested that increased production or lack of further maturation of these pre-naïve B cells can occur in autoimmune diseases, and may contribute to the development of autoimmunity [18].

More than half of naïve-phenotype B cells express the molecules CD23 that is released by stimulated B cells as soluble CD23. Receptor CD23 is also involved in B-cell proliferation and apoptosis [3]. An additional receptor CD27 indicates the transition from naïve B cells to memory cells, even if some memory B cells do not express CD27 molecules. In addition, some *not conventional memory B cells* that reassemble marginal zone B cells express the molecules CD27 [8].

In this work we focused on the analysis of eighth specific B cell subsets:

Cell phenotype	Variable in MP model
CD19+ CD5- CD23+ CD27-	N2
CD19+CD5- CD23+ CD27+	C
CD19+ CD5- CD23- CD27-	F
CD19+ CD5- CD23- CD27+	M5-
CD19+ CD5+ CD23+ CD27-	N1
CD19+ CD5+ CD23+ CD27+	D
CD19+ CD5+ CD23- CD27-	E
CD19+ CD5+ CD23- CD27+	M5+

Quantities of above types of B cells in the blood of a population of patients of all ages have been collected (as a cross sectional dataset) at one specific point of time. By Flow-Cytometry we used antibodies panels to determinate lymphocytes subsets, and in order to define some B lymphocytes subsets gating strategies were established, resulting in diagrams such as that in Figure 1. We search for a possible time order of maturation of such phenotypes. The ultimate goal is to describe time relations among these eight different gruops of B cells.

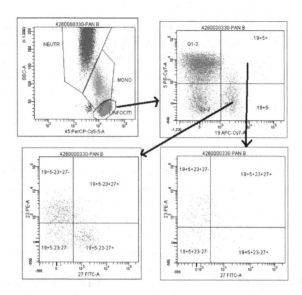

Fig. 1. Data recovery. Top-left: by means of heterogeneous gate (CD45/SS) all lymphocytes were recovered from other blood cells. Top-right: B lymphocytes expressing CD19 antigen were recovered. Bottom Left-Rigth: B-cells with expressed and down-modulate CD5 are partitionated respectively in four classes, depending on the expression or down-modulation of CD23 and CD 27.

2.1   Collection of Ex-vivo Data

Between January 2001 and December 2012, University Hospital of Verona, we assessed the cell surface expression of CD19, CD5, CD23 and CD27 on peripheral blood lymphocytes from 5,955 subjects of all ages undergoing peripheral blood immunophenotyping for a variety of reasons. The median age of the patients was 37 years (range: 0-95 years). There were 2,910 males and 3,045 females (male/female ratio: 0.95). Broadly speaking, the majority of infants were born from HIV-positive mothers; the children were affected by recurrent infections, allergies, autism and Down's syndrome; the young adults suffered from recurrent infections, allergies, fever, and autoimmune diseases; the middle-aged adults and elderly people were affected by autoimmune diseases and, to a lesser extent, by cancer. Subjects with known HIV infection, those with evidence or a history of haematological malignancies, and/or subjected to biological therapies with drugs that target B cells, were excluded from evaluation.

2.2   Data Processing

Data matrix from which we start our analysis has 8 columns (one for each type of B cell) and almost 6000 rows (corresponding to the number of patients). Our goal has been to find main relationships among these 8 types of B cells, starting from the assumption that patients can be sorted by age and a median cell value can be computed from patients having a similar age, so that the columns of our matrix could be seen as time series coming from a single macro-patient. In other words, for each type of B cell, we have a different chart, where the median of measured values is plotted for each age, according to a sliding window which defines the range of ages to be aggregated. Values have been computed by taking into account i) average and standard deviation of observed amounts of cells, ii) number of patients having those ages (for example, we have numerous babies and very few being 80-90 years old), iii) statistical distribution of patients.

After testing several window dimensions (i.e., 3 months, 6 months, 1 year, 2 years) and sliding window step (6 months and 1 year) we obtained good results by using a window of 1 year and a step of 6 months. Our time series have thus 185 points each, since the older patients are about 90 years old. Unfortunately these time evolutions were still quite noisy, as shown in the second chart of Figure 2, which represents the median time evolution of cells $M5+$. In order to smooth these curves we interpolated them with splines, obtaining the curves shown in Figure 3. Pearson correlations have been computed between couples of time series and also cross-correlations have been calculated to understand if some delays between these signals can be observed, with no significant results.

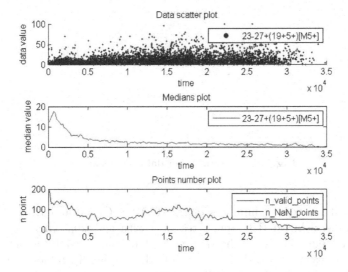

Fig. 2. On top: Original data for cells $M5+$, where patients are sorted by age (x axis). In the middle: median values computed from patients having a similar age, according to a sliding window which defines the range of ages to be aggregated. In this case a window of 1 year has been used and moved by 0.5 years at every step. In the bottom: number of valid and NaN (i.e., not a number) points in the sliding window. This chart enables to assess the quality of the time series for each age of patients. In this case, no NaN values are present, while it is clear that several patients are just one or two years old (beginning of x axis) and very few of them are 90 years old (right x axis).

After the necessary phase of data preparation [5], and a ponderate choice of the eight variables to analyze (as size of specific groups of B cells, characterized by having different receptors), a first problem has been encountered when applying a time-series based modeling tool as an MP system to simulate cross sectional data. In other terms, rather than variables observed in time (i.e., time series) here we have clinical data, collected by observing some variables in a population of patients at one specific point of time (the moment when individuals gave their blood for medical controls). In our case, we have numerous patients eventually affected by various diseases, as reported in section 2.1.

MP modeling framework requires time-series having fixed time intervals, and this is why we chose to fix the window size and the window temporal step during the generation of our time series. Another possibility which we considered was to fix the number of patients from which to compute the median. In this case, for instance, we would compute the median among the first 100 patients (in terms of age), then the median between the second 100 patients and so on. However, this methodology would have brought time series with different time intervals, because patients are not uniformly distributed with respect to age.

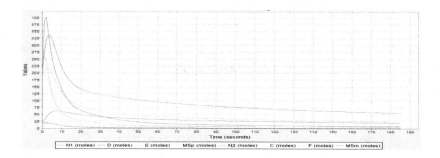

Fig. 3. Time series after data processing

As reported previously, numbers of B2 (CD19+ CD5-) and B1-a (CD19+ CD5+) peripheral blood B lymphocytes vary with age [20]. There is a sharp increase of B cells mainly in the first year of life, followed by a progressive decrease (as it results in the dynamics reported in Figure 3). In addition to the functional changes of B cell subsets due to antigen encounters, a decrease in the absolute number of B lymphocytes in elderly men has been reported, perhaps due to precursor depletion in the bone marrow and altered T-cell activity. The dynamics of the expression of CD23 and CD27 on peripheral blood B cells with ageing is similar when analyzed in the whole B-cell compartment or in the B2 and B1-a subsets separately, indicating a uniform pathway of maturation, and although CD23 and CD27 surface antigens are co-expressed in a small group of B cells, the majority of memory cells (CD27+) are CD23 negative [21].

The immune system as an organized determined structure is maintained throughout the life span and shared by all human [19]. Here we have defined an observational domain as the space represented by B lymphocytes subsets (cellular count) of numerous subjects of different age versus time (age of the subjects). Once we have found the curves in Figure 3, we consider them as time series of a "macro-patient", who is the human being.

3 An MP Model

An MP system is a dynamical system specified by a grammar $M = (X; R; \Phi, \delta)$, where X is a set of variables, R is a set of multiset rewriting rules over X, and Φ is a set of regulators, that is, functions assigned to the rules (each rule has its regulator). A state s is an assignment of values to variables, and in any state a regulator of a rule r specifies a quantity u_s, called *flux*, such that any left variables x of r is decreased of $p * u_s$ (where p denotes the multiplicity of x), while any right variable is increased of $q * u_s$ (if q is the multiplicity of y). Starting from an initial state, the dynamics δ of M, provides the next state by changing the values of every variable, according to the increase-decrease updating due to the values of fluxes (if a variable does not occur in a rule r, its multiplicity in r is zero). An MP grammar becomes an MP model when time/mass values are specified (step interval, measurement quantities) that provide physical intepretations of the discrete dynamics specified by the grammar (for more details, the reader may refer to chap 3 in [12]). In this case, the set of rewriting rules has been not given, while it actually being the goal of this modeling. We started from the simplest MP system simulating a given dynamics, that has the eight substances regulated by only input and output rules, as in Figure 4.

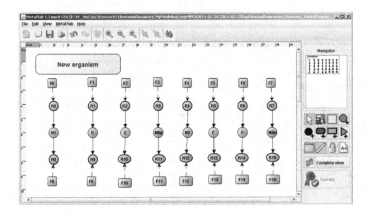

Fig. 4. MP model as an MP graph

We have tried several attempts to simplify the model , by reducing to only eight rewriting rules (rather than sixteen) with eventual negative fluxes, but simulation performances were not as good. A best model has been selected, by computing regulators by genetic regression, where polynomials of at most second degree have been choosen, as parsimonious (with few monomials) as possible, and with a relatively small fitting (quadratic) error [6]. The following set of regulators has been found, having simulation performances reported in Figure 5.

$$
\begin{aligned}
F_0 &= 4.48282 * F - 0.01102 * F^2 - 4.89806 * (M5-) \\
F_1 &= 0.06516 * D + 0.03127 * D^2 + 0.01317 * (M5+)^2 - 0.00213 * N1 * D \\
&\quad + 24.73 * 10^{-6} * N1^2 \\
F_2 &= 0.06707 * D * (M5-) - 0.01183 * E * (M5+) + 26.31 * 10^{-4} * F^2 \\
F_3 &= 18.71 * 10^{-4} * C * F + 1.458 * 10^{-4} * E^2 - 0.11809 * (M5+) \\
F_4 &= 0.68022 * E \\
F_5 &= 1.44946 + 0.42814 * (M5+) \\
F_6 &= 6.673 * 1 -{}^{-4} * N1 * E \\
F_7 &= 0.03146 * D^2 + 9.519 * 10^{-4} * (M5+) * F \\
F_8 &= 0.7723 * N1 \\
F_9 &= 0.01933 * D * C + 70.53 * 10^{-6} * N1 * (M5-) \\
F_{10} &= 0.01712 * (M5+) * N2 \\
F_{11} &= 0.02883 * (M5+)^2 \\
F_{12} &= 4.11056 * D + 79.27 * 10^{-4} * N1 * (M5+) \\
F_{13} &= 0.36253 * C + 8.616 * 10^{-4} * C * (M5-) \\
F_{14} &= 80.2 * 10^{-4} * N1 * (M5+) \\
F_{15} &= 0.01011 * D * (M5-) - 0.00369 * (M5-)
\end{aligned}
$$

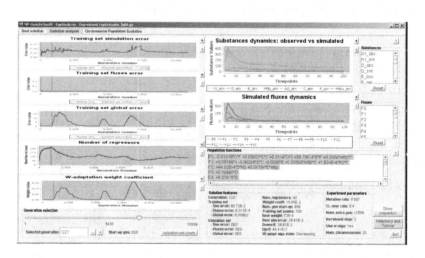

Fig. 5. Model simulation performances, evaluated by means of MP software [6]

Single regulators have been studied analytically, in order to select only the monomials (here called regressors) determinant for the variation of each substance, either as an input (in the increasing of the substance quantity) or as an output (in the descresing). This study opened up a problem of network inference, which has been here solved with a simple assumption: *any variable A such that its increment induces an increment of variable B is modeled as if cells A mature into cells B, and any variable A whose increment induces a decrement for B is modeled as A has a regulative role for B.* Indeed, it is known that cells mature into other phenotypes, while this process is slowed down by the presence of other cells (and signals). This is a first modeling attempt, which however gave some interesting preliminary results. Future extension (including interaction with other lymphocytes, such as T and NK cells) and refinements will be carried on to complete this study.

According to the assumptions above, we have inferenced the network reported in Figure 6 of maturation and regulation relations among different groups of B cells. Basic arrows represent cell maturation from one type of B cell to another, while dotted arrows represent regulations, where the increment in size of one type of B cells effects (positively or negatively) the increment of another one. An explanation of the this infered network is reported in more details.

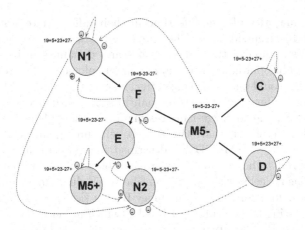

Fig. 6. B cellular immunological network

Maturation of cells N1. Cells N1=23+27- (19+ 5+) are the most naïve, maturing into F = 23 - 27 - (19+ 5-), that is, during their life they down modulate both receptors CD23 and CD5, along with a rate which is proportional to their quantity. Cells N1 are *self-ruled* (meaning that any increment of themselves slows down the next increment, and decrease by massive presence of (memory) cells M5-= 23- 27+ (19+ 5-). Their maturation into cells F is slowed down by the increasing of M5- and is alimented by the increment of cells F themselves.

Maturation of cells F. Cells F= 23 - 27 - (19+ 5-) may mature either into M5-=23 - 27 + (19+ 5-), that means they can express CD27, or into E=23-27-(19+5+), that means they can express CD5. Both the maturation ways are slowed down by the quantitity of M5- (which even slows down the immission N1=23+27- (19+ 5+) into the blood).

Maturation of cells E. Cells E=23- 27-(19+5+) may express CD27, and mature into M5+ =23-27+(19+5+), or, if they down modulate CD5, they mature into N2= 23+27- (19+ 5-). The last maturation way is self-regulated, that is, it is slowed down with the increasing of N2 (which in turn decreases with the increasing of D=23+27+ (19+ 5+) or both N1 with M5+). The expression of CD27, that is the maturation of E into M5+, is alimented by the increasing of both C= 23+ 27+ (19+ 5-) and F= 23 - 27 - (19+ 5-), both having CD19 expressed.

Maturation of Cells M5- and M5+. Cells M5-=23-27+(19+5-) mature into C= 23+ 27+ (19+ 5-) and D=23+27+ (19+ 5+), both self-ruled. In other terms, they tend to express CD23 (in one case together with CD5). Also cells M5+ are self-regulated, and when changing phenotype they express CD23 (in one case they down modulate CD5).

4 Discussion and Conclusions

Cells pass the majority of their life time in their differentiate state and their behavior, seen from outside, could be summarized in activation and proliferation. An understanding of the internal rules and dynamics inside the cellular network with additional information about immunological cells proliferation as seen from outside could be a new perspective, respect the traditional immunological way of seeing. Our model seems to confirm some maturation steps reported in literature [18,8], and to suggest interesting and reasonable new facts.

Our results have shown that, the first B cells undergoing cell maturation is N1 (CD19+CD5+ CD23+CD27-) described in literature as a pre-naïve B cell [18]. These cells, when isolated in vitro are able to differentiate into memory B cells and Plasma cells with specific antibody production. In our model N1 subset maturates into conventional memory B cells (M5-) [8,10,19], as reported in literature, passing by the subset of F cells (which are circulating "transient" not much studied B cells). In addition, memory B cells (M5-) mature versus subsets C and D, that share some markers with mutated CLL, whereas N1 share some markers present in un-mutated CLL. In our model N2 is the most regulated class of cells, which interestingly it is also the subset on which more fluctuations are observed in case of deseases. There were not found interactions which do not heppen in the physiology of the immune system, such as retro-differentiation (a reversible maturation), and it is perfectly logic (even if not known in literature) that memory cells M5- (which are highly mutated cells producing emoglobulines) may mature in small populations like C and D, the last one representing the phenotype of CLL. Indeed, during cellular proliferation the somatic accumulation of mutations can be seen as a natural process of the human life cycle and we think that this aspect and the determination of somatic accumulated mutation in ex-vivo isolated lymphocytes subsets could be an interesting tool and an effective investigation to validate oriented maturational steps found in our model [17].

Targeted immunological research approaches could help in the understanding mechanisms involved in the early phases preceded CLL origin. Our model is obviously only preliminary, it is to be considered in progress with early future up-grading. In traditional immunology, function and mechanisms of lymphocytes phenotype usually was described in association to cell function and/or diagnostics purpose. Lymphocyte phenotype analysis as determined by Flow-Cytometry has received improvements over time in both technological (the ability to stain more than one marker on the same cell) as well as in terms of mechanisms understanding (know what to look for). Our future intentions are oriented on define increasingly effective Flow-Cytometry protocols looking for unambiguous markers (cellular phenotype) with a well defined separation of lymphocyte subsets in their physical and differentiate state (structure) as observed in their existence domain [19]. In our model we have exclusively used observational data (structure) that mean not derived from functional experiments in the contest of stimulus/response model. By doing in this way we have obtained oriented maturation (structural relations) and cellular mechanism effects as seen by cellular count modulation (regulators, represented in the graph by dotted relations).

Materials and Methods. As blood specimens, peripheral blood samples were collected into EDTA Vacutainers (K2E) between 9 and 12 a.m. and processed within 4 h of being taken.

Flow cytometry protocols and samples preparation used in this study included one of a six-color protocol routinely applied in the Section of Immunology of University hospital of Verona for lymphocyte phenotyping, using the following fluorochrome-labeled monoclonal antibodies (mAbs): CD27-FITC, CD23-PE, CD45-PerCP, CD5-PECy7, CD3-APC, CD19-APCCy7 (Becton Dickinson Pharmingen, Franklin Lakes NJ, USA). Fifty microliters of each blood sample were incubated for 15 min in the dark at room temperature. Combination of mAbs 1 ml of lysing/fixative reagent was added to each tube before the flow-cytometry assay. The strategy used to determine the absolute lymphocyte count was referred to as a double-platform, and Lyse/No-Wash protocol was used to avoid potential cell loss during washing stages [21]. Flow analysis was performed using a 488/633 nm two-laser BD FACScanto Flow cytometer, an instrument that has a 10,000 events/s capability, six-color detection and 0.1% sample carryover. All combinations and gating regions as shown in Figure 1 were manually setup without applying automatic software features.

Software to compute genetic regression and estimation of best MP regulators according to several parameters may be downloaded on the MP Virtual laboratory website [6]: http://mplab.sci.univr.it/plugins/mpgs/index.html.

References

1. Berland, R., Wortis, H.H.: Origins and functions of B-1 cells with notes on the role of CD5. Annu. Rev. Immunol. 20, 253–300 (2002)
2. Bianco, L., Fontana, F., Franco, G., Manca, V.: P systems for biological dynamics. In: Ciobanu, G., Perez-Jimenez, M.J., Paun, G. (eds.) Applications of Membrane Computing, pp. 81–126. Springer (2006)

3. Campbell, K.A., Studer, E.J., Kilmon, M.A., et al.: Induction of B cell apoptosis by co-cross-linking CD23 and sIg involves aberrant regulation of c-myc and is inhibited by bcl-2. Int. Immunol. 9, 1131–1140 (1997)
4. Cao, H., Romero-Campero, F.J., Heeb, S., Cámara, M., Krasnogor, N.: Systems and synthetic biology. 4, 55–84 (2010)
5. Castellini, A., Franco, G., Pagliarini, R.: Data analysis pipeline from laboratory to MP models. Natural Computing 10(1), 55–76 (2011)
6. Castellini, A., Paltrinieri, D., Manca, V.: MP-GeneticSynth: Inferring Biological Network Regulations from Time Series (submitted)
7. Castellini, A., Zucchelli, M., Busato, M., Manca, V.: From time series to biological network regulations: An evolutionary approach. Molecular BioSystems 9(2), 225–233 (2013)
8. Fecteau, J.F., Côté, G., Néron, S.: A new memory CD27-IgG+ B cell population in peripheral blood expressing VH genes with low frequency of somatic mutation. J. Immunol. 177(6), 3728–3736 (2006)
9. Franco, G., Manca, V.: A Membrane System for the Leukocyte Selective Recruitment. In: Martín-Vide, C., Mauri, G., Păun, G., Rozenberg, G., Salomaa, A. (eds.) WMC 2003. LNCS, vol. 2933, pp. 181–190. Springer, Heidelberg (2004)
10. LeBien, T.W., Tedder, T.F.: B lymphocytes: how they develop and function. Blood 112(5), 1570–1580 (2008)
11. Loder, F., et al.: B cell development in the spleen takes place in discrete steps and is determined by the quality of B cell receptor derived signals. J. Exp. Med. 190, 75–89 (1999)
12. Manca, V.: Infobiotics: Information in biotic systems. Spinger (2013)
13. Manca, V., Castellini, A., Franco, G., Marchetti, L., Pagliarini, R.: Metabolic P Systems: A Discrete Model for Biological Dynamics. Chinese Journal of Electronics 22(CJE-4), 717–723 (2013)
14. Manca, V., Marchetti, L.: An algebraic formulation of inverse problems in MP dynamics. International Journal of Computer Mathematics 90(4), 845–856 (2013)
15. Nadler, L.M., Anderson, K.C., Marti, G., et al.: B4, a human B lymphocyte-associated antigen expressed on normal, mitogen-activated, and malignant B lymphocytes. J. Immunol. 131, 244–250 (1983)
16. Nisitani, S., Murakami, M., Akamizu, T., Okino, T., Ohmori, K., Mori, T., Imamura, M., Honjo, T.: Preferential localization of human CD5 B cells in the peritoneal cavity. Scand. J. Immunol. 46, 541–545 (1997)
17. Seifert, M., Sellmann, L., Bloehdorn, J., Wein, F., Stilgenbauer, S., Dürig, J., Küppers, R.: Cellular origin and pathophysiology of chronic lymphocytic leukemia. JEM 209(12), 2183–2198 (2012)
18. Sims, G., Ettinger, P.R., Shirota, Y., Yarboro, C.H., Illei, G.G., Lipsky, P.E.: Identification and characterization of circulating human transitional B cells. Blood 105, 4390–4398 (2005)
19. Urrestarazu, H.: Autopoietic Systems: A Generalized Explanatory Approach Part 1. Constructivist Foundation 6(3) (2011)
20. Veneri, D., Franchini, M., Vella, A., et al.: Changes of human B and B-1a peripheral blood lymphocytes with age. Hematology 12, 337–341 (2007)
21. Veneri, D., Ortolani, R., Franchini, M., Tridente, G., Pizzolo, G., Vella, A.: Expression of CD27 and CD23 on peripheral blood B lymphocytes in humans of different ages. Blood Transfus 7, 29–34 (2009)

Pseudo-inversion on Formal Languages

Da-Jung Cho[1], Yo-Sub Han[1], Shin-Dong Kang[1], Hwee Kim[1],
Sang-Ki Ko[1], and Kai Salomaa[2]

[1] Department of Computer Science, Yonsei University
50, Yonsei-Ro, Seodaemum-Gu, Seoul 120–749, Republic of Korea
{dajung,emmous,shindong1992,kimhwee,narame7}@cs.yonsei.ac.kr
[2] School of Computing, Queen's University
Kingston, Ontario K7L 3N6, Canada
ksalomaa@cs.queensu.ca

Abstract. We consider the pseudo-inversion operation inspired by a bi-ological event as a result of the partial inversion. We define the pseudo-inversion of a string $w = uxv$ to consist of all strings $v^R x u^R$, where $uv \neq \lambda$ and consider the operation from a formal language theoretic viewpoint. We show that regular languages are closed under the pseudo-inversion operation whereas context-free languages are not. Furthermore, we consider the iterated pseudo-inversion operation and establish the basic properties. Finally, we introduce the pseudo-inversion-freeness and examine closure properties and decidability problems for regular and context-free languages. We establish that pseudo-inversion-freeness is de-cidable in polynomial time for regular languages and undecidable for context-free languages.

1   Introduction

There have been many approaches that relate biological phenomena to formal languages. This makes it possible to study biological phenomena using tools of formal language theory [7, 8]. Several researchers investigated the algebraic and code-theoretic properties of DNA encoding based on formal language theory [11, 13, 14, 17]. Jonoska et al. [13] introduced involution codes based on the Watson-Crick complementarity, and Kari and Mahalingam [17] investigated the algebraic properties of DNA languages that avoid intermolecular cross hybridization. Kari et al. [16] also studied the DNA hairpin-free structure with respect to algebraic and decision properties.

A DNA sequence undergoes various transformations from the primitive se-quence through the biological operations such as insertions, deletions, substitu-tions, inversions, translocations and duplications. This motivates researchers to investigate the genetic operations for tracing the evolution process on a DNA sequence [1, 3–6, 18, 21, 23, 25]. For the DNA evolutionary analysis, an *inver-sion*—an operation to reverse an infix (substring) of a sequence—is one of the well-studied operations in both DNA computing and formal language theory. Yokomori and Kobayashi [25] showed that the inversion can be simulated by the

O.H. Ibarra et al. (Eds.): UCNC 2014, LNCS 8553, pp. 93–104, 2014.
DOI: 10.1007/978-3-319-08123-6_8, © Springer International Publishing Switzerland 2014

set of primitive operations and languages using GSM mapping. Dassow et al. [6] noticed that regular and context-free languages are closed under the inversion. They also proved that regular and context-free languages are not closed under the iterated inversion. Daley et al. [4, 5] investigated the closure and decidability properties of some language classes with respect to biological operations including the *hairpin inversion*, which is an extended variant of the inversion. Since the inversion is an important operation in biology, researchers investigated the string matching and alignment problems considering inversions [1, 18, 21, 23].

Here we define a new operation called a *pseudo-inversion* operation. While the inversion operation reverses an infix of an input sequence, a pseudo-inversion operation reverses only the outermost parts of the sequence and the middle part of the sequence is not reversed. See Fig. 1 for an example.

We notice that there are two possible situations where a pseudo-inversion occurs in practice. The first case is—an inversion operation itself is a mutational process—that the inversion process may not be completed in the sense that the sequence of the central part is not fully reversed in the process. The second case is that an inversion is carried out once and the central part of the reversed part is reversed once again; this makes the sequence of the central part where the inversion is applied twice the same as the original sequence. Given two strings of the same length, we design a linear-time algorithm that determines whether or not one string is a pseudo-inversion of the other string.

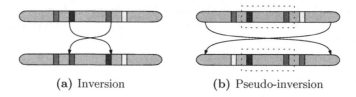

(a) Inversion   (b) Pseudo-inversion

Fig. 1. The left figure describes the inversion operation and the right figure describes the pseudo-inversion operation. Note that the sequence in the dotted box is not reversed in pseudo-inversion.

We also introduce an *iterated pseudo-inversion* operation based on the pseudo-inversion. We establish some closure properties of the pseudo-inversion and the iterated pseudo-inversion on regular languages and context-free languages. Moreover, we demonstrate that the iterated pseudo-inversion of a context-free language is recognized by a nondeterministic reversal-bounded multicounter machine. Furthermore, we investigate the decision problems regarding the proposed operations. In particular, we study the question whether a given language L is *pseudo-inversion-free*, that is, no string of L contains a pseudo-inversion of another string of L as a substring. Analogous properties have been studied in the theory of codes [15] and pseudo-inversion-free languages have potential applications in DNA encoding.

We give basic definitions and notations in Section 2. We define the pseudo-inversion operation and the iterated pseudo-inversion in Section 3. Some closure properties of the proposed operations are also studied in Section 3. Then, we consider the decision problems—whether or not a given language is pseudo-inversion-free—and the closure properties of pseudo-inversion-free languages in Section 4 and conclude the paper in Section 5.

2 Preliminaries

We briefly present definitions and notations. Let $\mathbb{N}$ be the set of positive integers and $\mathbb{N}_0$ be the set of non-negative integers. Let S be a set and k be a positive integer. We use $[S]^k$ to denote the set of all k-tuples $(s_1, s_2, \ldots, s_k)$, where $s_i \in S$.

Let Σ be a finite alphabet and Σ^* be the set of all strings over Σ. A language over Σ is any subset of Σ^*. The symbol $\emptyset$ denotes the empty language, the symbol λ denotes the null string and Σ^+ denotes $\Sigma^* \setminus \{\lambda\}$. Given a string w, we denote the reversal of w by w^R. Let $|w|$ be the length of w. For each $a \in \Sigma$, we denote the number of occurrences of a in w by $|w|_a$. Given a language $L \subseteq \Sigma^*$, $\bar{L}$ denotes the complement of L—$\Sigma^* \setminus L$. Given an alphabet $\Sigma = \{a_1, a_2, \ldots, a_k\}$, let $\Psi : \Sigma^* \to [\mathbb{N}_0]^k$ be a mapping defined by $\Psi(w) = (|w|_{a_1}, |w|_{a_2}, \ldots, |w|_{a_k})$. This function is called a *Parikh mapping* and $\Psi(w)$ is called the *Parikh vector* of w. We denote the symbol of the string w at position i by $w[i]$ and the substring $w[i]w[i+1]\cdots w[j]$ of w by $w[i \cdots j]$, where $1 \le i \le j \le |w|$. We say that languages L_1 and L_2 are *letter-equivalent* if $\{\Psi(w) \mid w \in L_1\} = \{\Psi(w) \mid w \in L_2\}$.

A *nondeterministic finite automaton with λ-transitions* (λ-NFA) is a five-tuple $A = (Q, \Sigma, \delta, Q_0, F)$ where Q is a finite set of states, Σ is a finite alphabet, δ is a multi-valued transition function from $Q \times (\Sigma \cup \lambda)$ into 2^Q, $Q_0 \subseteq Q$ is the set of initial states and $F \subseteq Q$ is the set of final states. By an NFA we mean a nondeterministic automaton without λ-transitions, that is, A is an NFA if δ is a function from $Q \times \Sigma$ into 2^Q. The automaton A is *deterministic* (a DFA) if Q_0 is a singleton set and δ is a (single-valued) function $Q \times \Sigma \to Q$. The language $L(A)$ recognized by A is the set of strings w such that some sequence of transitions spelling out w takes an initial state of A to a final state.

It is well known that λ-NFAs, NFAs and DFAs all recognize the regular languages [22, 24]. Note that any regular language recognized by a λ-NFA of size n can be also recognized by an NFA with the same number of states [24].

Proposition 1 (Wood [24]). *The language recognized by a λ-NFA A can be also recognized by an NFA (without λ-transitions) of the same number of states as A.*

A *context-free grammar* (CFG) G is a four-tuple $G = (V, \Sigma, R, S)$, where V is a set of variables, Σ is a set of terminals, $R \subseteq V \times (V \cup \Sigma)^*$ is a finite set of productions and $S \in V$ is the start variable. Let $\alpha A \beta$ be a string over $V \cup \Sigma$, where $A \in V$ and $A \to \gamma \in R$. Then, we say that A can be rewritten as γ and the corresponding derivation step is denoted by $\alpha A \beta \Rightarrow \alpha \gamma \beta$. The reflexive, transitive closure of $\Rightarrow$ is denoted by $\overset{*}{\Rightarrow}$ and the context-free language generated by G is $L(G) = \{w \in \Sigma^* \mid S \overset{*}{\Rightarrow} w\}$.

A *context-sensitive grammar* (CSG) G is a four-tuple $G = (V, \Sigma, R, S)$, where V is a set of variables, Σ is a set of terminals, $R \subseteq (V \cup \Sigma)^* V (V \cup \Sigma)^* \times (V \cup \Sigma)^*$ is a finite set of productions and $S \in V$ is the start variable.

A *nondeterministic reversal-bounded multicounter machine* (NCM) [2, 12] consists of a finite state control that reads input one-way from the input tape and a finite number of counters, that is a pushdown store over a one-letter alphabet. Furthermore, the counters are reversal-bounded, that is, the number of alternations between the non-decreasing and the non-increasing mode for each counter is bounded by a constant.[1] Thus, an NCM is a λ-NFA equipped with a finite number of reversal-bounded counters.

The reader may refer to the textbooks [10, 22, 24] for complete knowledge of formal language theory.

3   Pseudo-inversion

The pseudo-inversion reverses a given string, but the central part of the string may not be reversed. This is the reason why we call the operation the pseudo-inversion. Fig. 2 depicts an example of a pseudo-inversion of a string.

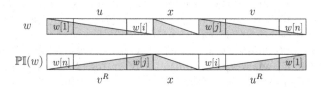

Fig. 2. Given a string $w = uxv$, the pseudo-inversion $\mathbb{PI}(w)$ of w is defined as $v^R x u^R$, where $vu \neq \lambda$

Formally, we define the pseudo-inversion as follows:

Definition 1. *For a string $w \in \Sigma^*$, we define the* pseudo-inversion *of w to be*

$$\mathbb{PI}(w) = \{v^R x u^R \mid u, x, v \in \Sigma^*, w = uxv, \text{ and } vu \neq \lambda\}.$$

As a special case, the pseudo-inversion of λ is λ. We can extend the *pseudo-inversion* of strings to languages. Given a language L, $\mathbb{PI}(L) = \bigcup_{w \in L} \mathbb{PI}(w)$. We also define an *iterated pseudo-inversion* operation, which is an iterated version of the pseudo-inversion. First, we set $\mathbb{PI}^1(w) = \mathbb{PI}(w)$. Given a string w, we define $\mathbb{PI}^{i+1}(w) = \mathbb{PI}(\mathbb{PI}^i(w))$ for a positive integer $i > 0$.

Definition 2. *Given a string w, we define the* iterated pseudo-inversion $\mathbb{PI}^*(w)$ *of w to be* $\mathbb{PI}^*(w) = \bigcup_{i=1}^{\infty} \mathbb{PI}^i(w).$

---

[1] Unrestricted two-counter machines accept all recursively enumerable languages [9].

Furthermore, given a language L, we define the iterated pseudo-inversion $\mathbb{PI}^*(L)$
of L to be $\mathbb{PI}^*(L) = \bigcup_{w \in L} \mathbb{PI}^*(w)$.

Next we define a *pseudo-inversion-free* language L (or code) where there is
no pair of strings in L such that a string is a pseudo-inversion substring of the
other string.

Definition 3. *Let $L \subseteq \Sigma^*$ be a language. We define L to be* pseudo-inversion-
free if no string in L is a pseudo-inversion substring of any other string in L.
In other words, L is pseudo-inversion-free if $\Sigma^* \cdot \mathbb{PI}(L) \cdot \Sigma^* \cap L = \emptyset$.

3.1   Closure Properties of Pseudo-inversion

It is well-known that regular languages are closed under the reversal operation.
Given an NFA recognizing a regular language L, we can easily obtain an NFA
of the same size for the reversal of L by flipping the transition directions and
exchanging the set of initial states and the final states [10, 24]. We may need
one more state if we do not allow the multiple initial states.

We show that regular languages are also closed under the pseudo-inversion
operation.

Theorem 1. *If L is a regular language, then $\mathbb{PI}(L)$ is also regular.*

Theorem 1 shows that regular languages are closed under the pseudo-inversion
operation. Based on the result, we have the following observation.

Observation 2. *Given a regular language L, $\mathbb{PI}^n(L)$ is regular for any integer $n \geq 1$.*

Notice that context-free languages are closed under reversal operation [10].
However, we demonstrate that context-free languages are not closed under the
pseudo-inversion operation.

Theorem 3. *Context-free languages are not closed under the pseudo-inversion.*

Proof. We prove the statement by the context-free pumping lemma [10, 24].
Consider the context-free language $L = \{a^i b^j c^j d^i \mid i, j \geq 1\}$.

We pick a string $w = d^{2n} c^{2n} a^n b^{2n} a^n \in \mathbb{PI}(L)$, where n is the pumping constant, see Fig. 3. According to the pumping lemma we can split w into five parts,
$w = uvxyz$, where the parts u, v, x, y and z satisfy the conditions of the pumping
lemma. By the pumping lemma $|vxy| \leq n$, and hence vxy cannot contain both
a's and d's and vxy cannot contain both b's and c's.

Remember that if a string w is in $\mathbb{PI}(L)$, then $|w|_a = |w|_d$ and $|w|_b = |w|_c$ should
hold. However, since $vy \neq \lambda$, the string $uv^2 xy^2 z$ does not satisfy this condition.
Therefore, $uv^2 xy^2 z \notin \mathbb{PI}(L)$ and we conclude that $\mathbb{PI}(L)$ is not context-free.   □

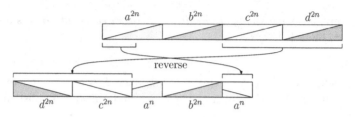

Fig. 3. For a language $L = \{a^i b^j c^j d^i \mid i, j \geq 1\}$, we pick a string $d^{2n} c^{2n} a^n b^{2n} a^n \in \mathbb{PI}(z)$, where $z = a^{2n} b^{2n} c^{2n} d^{2n} \in L$

3.2 Iterated Pseudo-inversion

We investigate the closure properties of the iterated pseudo-inversion operation. It turns out that the iterated pseudo-inversion is equivalent to the permutation operation. Given a string w, let $\pi(w)$ be the set of all permutations of w, that is, $\pi(w) = \{u \in \Sigma^* \mid (\forall a \in \Sigma)|u|_a = |w|_a\}$.

We establish the following result:

Theorem 4. *Given a string w over Σ, the iterated pseudo-inversion of w is the same as the set of all possible permutations of w; namely, $\mathbb{PI}^*(w) = \pi(w)$.*

Based on Theorem 4, we show that regular and context-free languages are not closed under the iterated pseudo-inversion.

Lemma 1. *Regular languages and context-free languages are not closed under the iterated pseudo-inversion operation. Furthermore, the iterated pseudo-inversion of a regular language need not be context-free.*

Proof. Consider a regular language $L = \{(abc)^*\}$. For L, the iterated pseudo-inversion $\mathbb{PI}^*(L)$ of L is

$$\mathbb{PI}^*(L) = \{w \in \{a, b, c\}^* \mid |w|_a = |w|_b = |w|_c\}.$$

We note that

$$\mathbb{PI}^*(L) \cap a^* b^* c^* = \{a^i b^i c^i \mid i \geq 0\}$$

is not context-free. Since the regular languages and the context-free languages are closed under intersection with regular languages, the claim follows. □

Below in Proposition 2 we see that the family of context-sensitive languages is closed under the iterated pseudo-inversion, and consequently it follows that the iterated pseudo-inversion of a regular or a context-free language is always context-sensitive.

In fact, as a consequence of Theorem 4 we see that the iterated pseudo-inversion of a context-free language can be recognized by a reversal-bounded multicounter machine NCM that defines a considerably more restricted language family than the context-sensitive languages. The Parikh set of any language recognized by an NCM is semi-linear and the emptiness problem for NCMs is decidable [12]. Furthermore, the NCMs cannot recognize, for example, the set of marked palindromes $\{w \# w^R \mid w \in \{0, 1\}^*\}$ [2].

Corollary 1. *If L is a context-free language over an alphabet Σ, $\mathbb{PI}^*(L)$ can be recognized by an NCM with $|\Sigma|$ counters that each makes only one reversal.*

Proof. There exists a regular language L' that is letter equivalent to L ([20], part I, Theorem 7.2) and let A be an NFA for L'. On an input w, the NCM stores the value $|w|_a$ for each $a \in \Sigma$ in the available counters. After that, using λ-transitions, the NCM simulates the NFA A for L'. For a transition of A on input $b \in \Sigma$, the counter corresponding to symbol b is decremented and at the end of the computation the NCM checks that all the counters are empty.

By Theorem 4, the NCM recognizes the language $\mathbb{PI}^*(L)$.   □

Corollary 1 uses only Theorem 4 and the observation that the Parikh set of a context-free language is semi-linear, which means that the corollary can be stated as:

Corollary 2. *If the Parikh set of L is semi-linear, then $\mathbb{PI}^*(L)$ can be recognized by a reversal-bounded multicounter machine.*

Corollary 2 implies, in particular, that the family of languages recognized by reversal-bounded multicounter machines is closed under iterated pseudo-inversion. To conclude this section we examine the closure properties for context-sensitive languages and establish the following result. A similar result for inversion of context-sensitive languages is known from Dassow et al. [6].

Proposition 2. *Given a context-sensitive language L, $\mathbb{PI}^*(L)$ is context-sensitive.*

4   Pseudo-inversion-Freeness

We investigate the decidability problem for pseudo-inversion-freeness and establish the closure properties of pseudo-inversion-free languages.

4.1   Decidability of Pseudo-inversion-freeness

We say that a language L is pseudo-inversion-free if no string in L is a pseudo-inversion substring of any other string in L. We consider the decidability problem of pseudo-inversion-freeness when L is regular or context-free.

We first consider a simple case when we are given two strings of the same length. We determine whether or not a string is not a pseudo-inversion of the other string. In other words, given two strings u and v, is u in $\mathbb{PI}(v)$? We present a linear-time algorithm in the size of u for the question. We rely on the following observation to simplify the presentation of the algorithm.

Observation 5. *Let u and v be two strings of the same length. Then, $u \in \mathbb{PI}(v)$ if and only if $u = wxy$ and $v^R = wx^Ry$, where $wy \neq \lambda$.*

The main idea of the linear-time algorithm is to scan two strings v^R and u from both end-sides until we find an index where two strings have different

---

Algorithm 1. A linear-time algorithm for deciding $v \in \mathbb{PI}(u)$

    Input: Two strings u and v of the same length n

1 $i \leftarrow 0$

2 $j \leftarrow n$

3 **while** $i \leq n \wedge u[i] = v^R[i]$ **do** $i \leftarrow i + 1$

4 **while** $1 \leq j \wedge u[j] = v^R[j]$ **do** $j \leftarrow j - 1$

5 **if** $i \geq j$ **then return false**

6 **else**

7   **for** $k = i$ **to** j **do**

8   **if** $u[k] \neq v^R[i + j - k]$ **then return false**

9   **return true**

---

characters. Let $\mathbb{M}_L$ denote the *left maximum matching index*, where the first discrepancy occurs and $\mathbb{M}_R$ denote the *right maximum matching index* where the last discrepancy occurs. Lastly, we check whether or not $u[\mathbb{M}_L \cdots \mathbb{M}_R]^R = v^R[\mathbb{M}_L \cdots \mathbb{M}_R]$. See Algorithm 1 for the whole procedure.

Theorem 6. *Given two strings u and v of length n, we can determine whether or not $v \in \mathbb{PI}(u)$ in $O(n)$ time.*

We can also determine if $v \in \mathbb{PI}^*(u)$ by checking whether or not the two Parikh vectors $\Psi(u)$ and $\Psi(v)$ are the same.

Corollary 3. *Given two strings u and v of length n, we can determine whether or not $v \in \mathbb{PI}^*(u)$ in $O(n)$ time.*

Next, we consider the regular language case. Recalling from Definition 3 the notion of pseudo-inversion-freeness, we can decide whether or not a regular language L is pseudo-inversion-free by checking whether or not $\Sigma^* \cdot \mathbb{PI}(L) \cdot \Sigma^* \cap L = \emptyset$.

Theorem 7. *Given an FA of size n recognizing a regular language L, we can determine whether or not L is pseudo-inversion-free in $O(n^4)$ time.*

Proof. Based on the NFA construction in Theorem 1, we can construct an NFA of size $O(n^3)$ recognizing $\mathbb{PI}(L)$. Since we can check the intersection emptiness of two NFAs of size m and n in $O(mn)$ time [24], we can determine whether or not L is pseudo-inversion-free in $O(n^3 \times n) = O(n^4)$ time.   □

Theorem 7 shows that it is decidable whether or not a given language L is pseudo-inversion-free in polynomial time when L is regular. We prove that pseudo-inversion-freeness is undecidable for context-free languages.

First we recall the following undecidability result. An instance of the *Post's Correspondence Problem* (PCP) [19] consists of $n \in \mathbb{N}$ and two ordered n-tuples of strings (U, V), where $U = (u_0, u_1, \ldots, u_{n-1})$ and $V = (v_0, v_1, \ldots, v_{n-1})$, $u_i, v_i \in \Sigma^*$, $0 \leq i \leq n - 1$. A solution for the PCP instance (U, V) is a sequence of integers $i_1, \ldots, i_k$, $0 \leq i_j \leq n - 1$, $j = 1, \ldots, k$, $k \geq 1$, such that

$$u_{i_1} u_{i_2} \cdots u_{i_k} = v_{i_1} v_{i_2} \cdots v_{i_k}.$$

Proposition 3 (E. Post [19]). *The decision problem of determining whether or not a given PCP instance has a solution is unsolvable.*

Now we can prove that deciding the pseudo-inversion-freeness of a given context-free language is undecidable by reducing PCP to this problem.

Theorem 8. *It is undecidable to determine whether or not a given context-free language L is pseudo-inversion-free.*

Proof. Let Σ be an alphabet and (U, V) be an instance of Post's Correspondence Problem, where $U = (u_0, u_1, \ldots, u_{n-1})$ and $V = (v_0, v_1, \ldots, v_{n-1})$. Assume that the symbols $0, 1, \#, \$, \%, \phi, \natural$ and $\flat$ are not in Σ. Let $\Sigma' = \Sigma \cup \{0, 1, \#, \$, \%, \phi, \natural, \flat\}$. For any nonnegative integer i, let β_i be the shortest binary representation of i.

We define a linear grammar $G = (N, \Sigma', R, S)$, where

- $N = \{S, T_U, T_V\}$ is a nonterminal alphabet,
- Σ' is a terminal alphabet,
- S is the sentence symbol, and
- R has the following rules:
  - $S \to \beta_i \phi T_U u_i \#\#\%\flat\natural\natural \mid \natural\natural\%\flat\#\# v_i^R T_V \phi \beta_i$,
  - $T_U \to \beta_i \phi T_U u_i \mid \beta_i \$ u_i$, and
  - $T_V \to v_i^R T_V \phi \beta_i \mid v_i^R \$ \beta_i$

  for $i \in \{0, 1, \ldots, n-1\}$.

Then $L(G)$ consists of the following strings:

$$\beta_{i_{n-1}} \phi \cdots \phi \beta_{i_0} \$ u_{i_0} \cdots u_{i_{n-2}} u_{i_{n-1}} \#\#\%\flat\natural\natural \tag{1}$$

and

$$\natural\natural\%\flat\#\# v_{i_{n-1}}^R v_{i_{n-2}}^R \cdots v_{i_0}^R \$ \beta_{i_0} \phi \cdots \phi \beta_{i_{n-1}}. \tag{2}$$

We now show that $L(G)$ is not pseudo-inversion-free if and only if the PCP instance (U, V) has a solution.

($\Longleftarrow$) We prove that $L(G)$ is not pseudo-inversion-free if the PCP instance (U, V) has a solution. Assume that the PCP instance (U, V) has a solution. Let $z = vwx$ and $z' = ux^R wv^R y$, where $xv \neq \lambda$. Then, L is not pseudo-inversion-free if both z' and z exist in L. Since the PCP instance has a solution by the assumption, there should be a sequence $i_0, i_1, \ldots, i_{n-2}, i_{n-1}$ satisfying

$$u_{i_0} \cdots u_{i_{n-2}} u_{i_{n-1}} = v_{i_0} \cdots v_{i_{n-2}} v_{i_{n-1}}.$$

Now we decompose (1) into $uvwxy$ such that

- $v = \beta_{i_{n-1}} \phi \cdots \phi \beta_{i_0} \$ u_{i_0} \cdots u_{i_{n-2}} u_{i_{n-1}} \#\#$,
- $w = \%\flat$,
- $x = \natural\natural$, and
- $u, y = \lambda$.

Then, $x^R w v^R = \natural\natural \% \flat \# \# u_{i_{n-1}} u_{i_{n-2}} \cdots u_{i_0} \$ \beta_{i_0} \phi \cdots \phi \beta_{i_{n-1}} \in L(G)$. Therefore, $L(G)$ is not pseudo-inversion-free.

($\Longrightarrow$) If $L(G)$ is not pseudo-inversion-free, then there exist two strings $z = vwx$ and $z' = ux^R w v^R y$ in $L(G)$, where $xv \neq \lambda$. Then, there are two possible decompositions as follows:

C1. $u = \lambda, v = \beta_{i_{n-1}} \phi \cdots \phi \beta_{i_0} \$ u_{i_0} \cdots u_{n_{i-1}} \# \#, w = \% \flat, x = \natural\natural$, and $y = \lambda$.

C2. $u = \lambda, v = \natural\natural, w = \% \flat, x = \# \# v_{i_{n-1}}^R v_{i_{n-2}}^R \cdots v_{i_0}^R \$ \beta_{i_0} \phi \cdots \phi \beta_{i_{n-1}}$, and $y = \lambda$.

It implies that the PCP instance (U, V) has a solution since

$$v = \beta_{i_{n-1}} \phi \cdots \phi \beta_{i_0} \$ u_{i_0} \cdots u_{n_{i-1}} \# \#$$

should be equal to

$$x^R = \beta_{i_{n-1}} \phi \cdots \phi \beta_{i_0} \$ v_{i_0} \cdots v_{n_{i-1}} \# \#.$$

Thus, $L(G)$ is not pseudo-inversion-free if and only if the PCP instance (U, V) has a solution. Since PCP is undecidable [19], it is also undecidable whether or not L is pseudo-inversion-free when L is context-free. $\square$

We summarize the results for decision properties of pseudo-inversion-freeness:

(i) It can be decided in polynomial time whether or not a given regular language is pseudo-inversion-free (Theorem 7).

(ii) It is undecidable whether or not a given linear context-free language is pseudo-inversion-free (Theorem 8).

4.2   Closure Properties of Pseudo-inversion-free Languages

We first consider closure properties of the pseudo-inversion-free languages under the basic operations.

Theorem 9. *Pseudo-inversion-free languages are closed under intersection but not under catenation or union.*

We note that the pseudo-inversion free languages are not closed under complementation nor Kleene star. Moreover, the complementation or the Kleene star of any pseudo-inversion-free language is not pseudo-inversion-free.

Theorem 10. *For any pseudo-inversion-free language $L \subseteq \Sigma^*$, $\bar{L}$ is not pseudo-inversion-free.*

Theorem 11. *For a nonempty language $L \subseteq \Sigma^* \setminus \{\lambda\}$, $L^m \cup L^n$ is not pseudo-inversion-free, for $1 \leq m < n$. Moreover, L^* is not pseudo-inversion-free, either.*

Proof. Let $w = au$ be a string in L, where $a \in \Sigma$ and $u \in \Sigma^*$. Then, we have $w^m \in L^m$ and $w^n \in L^n$. Then, $w^m = av$ and $w^n = avw^{n-m}$, where $v = uw^{m-1}$. Since $w = au$, $w^n = avauw^{n-m-1}$ in which va appears as a substring. Since $va \in \mathbb{PI}(w^m)$, $L^m \cup L^n$ is not pseudo-inversion-free. It is easy to see that L^* is not pseudo-inversion-free since $L^* = L^0 \cup L^1 \cup L^2 \cup \cdots$. $\square$

5   Conclusions

We have defined a biologically inspired operation called the pseudo-inversion. Informally, the pseudo-inversion incompletely reverses the order of strings while the inversion operation reverses the order of infix of strings. Given a string $w = uxv$, we define the pseudo-inversion of w to be the set of strings $v^R x u^R$, where $uv \neq \lambda$.

We have investigated the closure properties of the pseudo-inversion operation and the iterated pseudo-inversion operation. While regular languages are closed under the pseudo-inversion, context-free languages are not closed. Moreover, we have established that the iterated pseudo-inversion is equivalent to the permutation operation. We also have considered the problem of deciding whether or not a given language is pseudo-inversion-free. We have designed a polynomial-time algorithm for regular languages and established an undecidability result for linear context-free languages.

Acknowledgements. Cho, Han, Kang and Ko were supported by the Basic Science Research Program through NRF funded by MEST (2012R1A1A2044562), Kim was supported by NRF-2013-Global Ph.D. Fellowship Program and Salomaa was supported by the Natural Sciences and Engineering Research Council of Canada Grant OGP0147224.

References

1. Cantone, D., Cristofaro, S., Faro, S.: Efficient string-matching allowing for non-overlapping inversions. Theoretical Computer Science 483, 85–95 (2013)
2. Chiniforooshan, E., Daley, M., Ibarra, O.H., Kari, L., Seki, S.: One-reversal counter machines and multihead automata: Revisited. Theoretical Computer Science 454, 81–87 (2012)
3. Cho, D.-J., Han, Y.-S., Kim, H.: Alignment with non-overlapping inversions on two strings. In: Pal, S.P., Sadakane, K. (eds.) WALCOM 2014. LNCS, vol. 8344, pp. 261–272. Springer, Heidelberg (2014)
4. Daley, M., Ibarra, O.H., Kari, L.: Closure and decidability properties of some language classes with respect to ciliate bio-operations. Theoretical Computer Science 306(1-3), 19–38 (2003)
5. Daley, M., Kari, L., McQuillan, I.: Families of languages defined by ciliate bio-operations. Theoretical Computer Science 320(1), 51–69 (2004)
6. Dassow, J., Mitrana, V., Salomaa, A.: Operations and language generating devices suggested by the genome evolution. Theoretical Computer Science 270(1), 701–738 (2002)
7. Deaton, R., Garzon, M., Murphy, R.C., Rose, J.A., Franceschetti, D.R., Stevens Jr., S.E.: Genetic search of reliable encodings for DNA-based computation. In: First Conference on Genetic Programming, pp. 9–15 (1996)
8. Garzon, M., Deaton, R., Nino, L.F., Stevens, E., Wittner, M.: Encoding genomes for DNA computing. In: Proceedings of the Third Annual Conference on Genetic Programming 1998, pp. 684–690 (1998)

9. Ginsburg, S.: Algebraic and automata-theoretic properties of formal languages. North-Holland Publishing Company (1975)
10. Hopcroft, J., Ullman, J.: Introduction to Automata Theory, Languages, and Computation, 2nd edn. Addison-Wesley, Reading (1979)
11. Hussini, S., Kari, L., Konstantinidis, S.: Coding properties of DNA languages. Theoretical Computer Science 290(3), 1557–1579 (2003)
12. Ibarra, O.H.: Reversal bounded multicounter machines and their decision problems. Journal of the ACM 25, 116–133 (1978)
13. Jonoska, N., Kari, L., Mahalingam, K.: Involution solid and join codes. Fundamenta Informaticae 86(1-2), 127–142 (2008)
14. Jonoska, N., Mahalingam, K., Chen, J.: Involution codes: With application to DNA coded languages. Natural Computing 4(2), 141–162 (2005)
15. Jürgensen, H., Konstantinidis, S.: Codes. In: Handbook of Formal Languages. I, pp. 511–607. Springer (1997)
16. Kari, L., Losseva, E., Konstantinidis, S., Sosík, P., Thierrin, G.: A formal language analysis of DNA hairpin structures. Fundamenta Informaticae 71(4), 453–475 (2006)
17. Kari, L., Mahalingam, K.: DNA codes and their properties. In: Mao, C., Yokomori, T. (eds.) DNA12. LNCS, vol. 4287, pp. 127–142. Springer, Heidelberg (2006)
18. Kececioglu, J., Sankoff, D.: Exact and approximation algorithms for the inversion distance between two chromosomes. In: Apostolico, A., Crochemore, M., Galil, Z., Manber, U. (eds.) CPM 1993. LNCS, vol. 684, pp. 87–105. Springer, Heidelberg (1993)
19. Post, E.L.: A variant of a recursively unsolvable problem. Bulletin of the American Mathematical Society 52(4), 264–268 (1946)
20. Salomaa, A.: Formal Languages. Academic Press (1973)
21. Schniger, M., Waterman, M.S.: A local algorithm for DNA sequence alignment with inversions. Bulletin of Mathematical Biology 54(4), 521–536 (1992)
22. Shallit, J.: A Second Course in Formal Languages and Automata Theory. Cambridge University Press (2009)
23. Vellozo, A.F., Alves, C.E.R., do Lago, A.P.: Alignment with non-overlapping inversions in $O(n^3)$-time. In: Bücher, P., Moret, B.M.E. (eds.) WABI 2006. LNCS (LNBI), vol. 4175, pp. 186–196. Springer, Heidelberg (2006)
24. Wood, D.: Theory of Computation. Harper & Row (1986)
25. Yokomori, T., Kobayashi, S.: DNA evolutionary linguistics and RNA structure modeling: A computational approach. In: Proceedings of the 1st Intelligence in Neural and Biological Systems, pp. 38–45. IEEE Computer Society (1995)

Reverse-Engineering Nonlinear Analog Circuits with Evolutionary Computation

Theodore W. Cornforth[1] and Hod Lipson[2]

[1] Department of Biological Statistics and Computational Biology,
Cornell University, Ithaca, USA 14853
twc63@cornell.edu

[2] Department of Mechanical and Aerospace Engineering, Cornell University,
Ithaca, USA 14853
hl274@cornell.edu

Abstract. The design of analog circuits by hand is a difficult task, and many successful approaches to automating this design process based on evolutionary computation have been proposed. The fitness evaluations necessary to evolve linear analog circuits are relatively straightforward. However, this is not the case for nonlinear analog circuits, especially for the most general class of design tasks: reverse-engineering an arbitrary nonlinear 'black box' circuit. Here, we investigate different approaches to fitness evaluations in this setting. Results show that an incremental algorithm outperforms naive approaches, and that it is possible to evolve robust nonlinear analog circuits with time-domain output behavior that closely matches that of black box circuits for any time-domain input.

1   Introduction

Analog circuit design is a challenging task that typically requires a domain expert with years of experience [14]. As a result, the costs associated with developing circuits for new applications can be very high. Many studies reported in the literature have attempted to automate the circuit design process in an attempt to reduce the human effort required [4,5,7,13]. Approaches involving evolutionary computation have been particularly successful, and these generally allow both the topology and component sizes of a circuit to be optimized. Perhaps the earliest work in this area was by Koza and colleagues, who employed genetic programming and a developmental encoding [8]. Later work showed that simpler methods based on genetic algorithms could also obtain good results [1,9,10,19].

All approaches to the automation of analog circuit design involving evolutionary computation rely on fitness evaluations in which the behavior of a candidate circuit is simulated and compared with a design specification. For linear circuits, such as those comprised only of passive resistors, capacitors, and inductors, these fitness evaluations are relatively straightforward as the behavior of a linear circuit is fully characterized by its frequency and phase responses [16]. In a typical application, the AC frequency response of an evolved circuit can be compared with the desired frequency response using a measure such as the mean-squared

O.H. Ibarra et al. (Eds.): UCNC 2014, LNCS 8553, pp. 105–116, 2014.
DOI: 10.1007/978-3-319-08123-6_9, © Springer International Publishing Switzerland 2014

error [8]. This error then serves as the basis for assigning a fitness value to the evolved circuit (Fig. 1A.). For nonlinear circuits, such as those with transistors, diodes or other nonlinear components, fitness evaluations can be considerably more difficult, as it is generally not possible to fully characterize the behavior of a nonlinear circuit with a single measurement such as AC frequency or phase response.

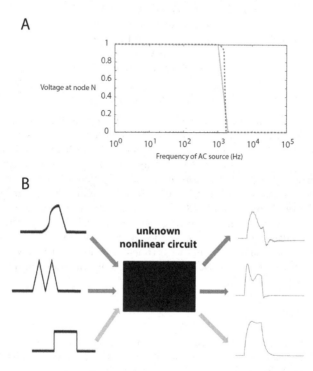

Fig. 1. Fitness evaluations for linear and non-linear circuits. **A.** The fitness of an evolved linear circuit can easily be assessed by comparing its frequency response (red) to a desired frequency response (blue). In this case the desired behavior is that of a low pass filter. **B.** To reverse-engineer an unknown 'black box' nonlinear circuit, time domain inputs (black) are used to probe the black box. The resulting outputs (red) are compared with the outputs of an evolved circuit in response to the same inputs as a means of assigning a fitness value to the evolved circuit.

Despite this complicating factor, some studies have successfully 'forward-engineered' nonlinear analog circuits with evolutionary computation [8, 15]. In these studies, a problem-specific design specification is developed and the task is to evolve a circuit that meets this design specification. Depending on the nature of the target design, Fourier analysis, DC sweeps, time-domain transient analysis, or other analyses are applied to an evolved circuit and used to compare its behavior to the design specification. Although time-domain analyses are the most computationally expensive, these are often considered necessary to evolve the most robust circuit designs [11, 15].

The forward-engineering tasks considered in previous studies of nonlinear analog circuit evolution are fundamentally different from a reverse-engineering task in which a nonlinear circuit must be evolved without a design specification. Instead, the circuit is evolved to match the behavior of an unknown 'black box' nonlinear circuit (Fig. 1B.). The black box circuit must be probed with different voltage or current inputs in order to obtain information used as the basis for evaluating the fitness of evolved circuits, yet the appropriate type of stimuli to use for these probes would generally not be known in advance. This is especially true if the goal is to evolve a circuit that generalizes well and reproduces the time-domain output behavior of a black box circuit for arbitrary time-domain inputs not used during evolution.

In this study, we investigate different algorithms for selecting the type of probe stimuli to use for the efficient evolutionary design of nonlinear analog circuits in the most general reverse-engineering setting. Many possibilities exist for such an algorithm, including the incremental approaches that have proven very powerful in other applications of evolutionary hardware [18]. Using randomly-generated nonlinear circuits in order to evaluate different approaches in as unbiased a manner as possible, our results show that incrementally presenting probe stimuli is a particularly efficient means of guiding nonlinear circuit evolution. Importantly, the evolved circuits generalize well and match target circuit behavior for arbitrary stimuli.

2   Methods

2.1   Genetic Algorithm

We use a genetic algorithm in which circuits are represented as variable-length linear chromosomes, where each gene contains four elements (Fig. 2). The circuits considered in this work were composed of five component types: resistors, capacitors, inductors, pnp bipolar transistors, and npn bipolar transistors. In the case of resistors, capacitors, and inductors, the elements in a gene specify the type, connection nodes, and parameter value of the component. To mimic the limitations of physical hardware, these components had one of 96 possible parameter values taken from a log10 scale with 12 values per decade. These values ranged from $1.0 - 8.2 \times 10^7$ pF, nH, and Ω for capacitors, inductors, and resistors respectively. In the case of bipolar transistors, NG-Spice default models are used and the four-element gene specifies transistor type (pnp or npn) and the connection nodes for emitter, base, and collector.

Each individual in the population of 64 circuits was initialized by concatenating 1-9 randomly chosen genes. The resulting circuit was checked for topological validity. This included checks for dangling nodes, disconnected subcircuits, inductor loops, the lack of capacitor paths to ground, and other common problems that would make the circuit unsimulatable in Spice.

...

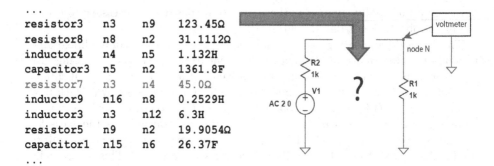

resistor3	n3	n9	123.45Ω
resistor8	n8	n2	31.1112Ω
inductor4	n4	n5	1.132H
capacitor3	n5	n2	1361.8F
resistor7	n3	n4	45.0Ω
inductor9	n16	n8	0.2529H
inductor3	n3	n12	6.3H
resistor5	n9	n2	19.9054Ω
capacitor1	n15	n6	26.37F

...

Fig. 2. Circuit representation. Circuits were represented as linear chromosomes, with each gene (such as the one highlighted in red) corresponding to one component. This list specifies the components in a variable portion of an otherwise invariant embryonic circuit. Note that the embryonic circuit contains both a voltage source and an output node at which voltage measurements are made.

As in standard genetic algorithms, crossover and mutation were used to create new members of the population. Parents were selected at random from the population of 64 and used to generate two offspring with a 90% chance of crossover. Instead of one point, two point, uniform or another standard type of crossover for linear chromosomes, we used the topology-aware crossover described in [3]. Regardless of whether the two offspring were generated by crossover, each gene in each offspring was mutated with a probability of 5%. A mutation consisted of the change from one type of element to another, a change of connections from one node to another, or a change in parameter values. We did not find it necessary to use mutations to add or delete genes as crossover in the variable-length chromosomes provided sufficient variation in offspring size. Offspring were created in this manner until 64 offspring were obtained. Both crossover and mutation ensured that topologically valid circuits resulted from the operation.

We used genotypic age to perform survival selection with the Age-fitness Pareto algorithm [17] for some experiments. Survival selection was performed by culling the combined population of parents and offspring using tournament selection with replacement and tournaments of size 2. This process was implemented with a Pareto tournament scheme in which two random members of the combined population were selected. If one of the pair had both lower fitness and higher age than the other, it was thrown out. The survivor was then returned to the pool. This continued until the population size was reduced back to 64. Age was defined as the number of generations in which an individual had been present in the population. Offspring inherited the age of the older parent in the case of crossover. One new, randomly generated individual with an age of 0 and created in the same way as members of the initial population was added to the population each generation.

When evaluating the fitness of a circuit, the linear chromosome was translated into a netlist recognizable by the NG-Spice circuit simulator [12]. This netlist specified the variable portion of an otherwise invariant embryonic circuit common to all evolved and target circuits (Fig. 2). Time-domain transient analysis was used to measure the voltage of the circuit at the output node in response to a voltage source with an arbitrary waveform as the input. The differences between evolved circuit outputs and target outputs were compared by calculating the sum of squared errors in the time domain. Random voltage source waveforms were specified by 20 parameters: 18 random parameters corresponding to the first nine coefficients of the Fourier series, one parameter controlling the scaling of the waveform with respect to time, and one parameter controlling the phase offset of the waveform.

2.2   Stimulus Selection

As the focus of this study was on comparing different methods of selecting probe stimuli for obtaining information about target circuits and evaluating the fitness of evolved circuits, we employed several methods for doing so. The simplest method ('fixed single') was to probe the target black box circuit with a single randomly generated voltage source waveform. The resulting voltage output was then used as the basis for assigning fitness values to evolved circuits. Each fitness evaluation consisted of applying the same input to the evolved circuit and comparing the resulting output in the time domain with that output originally obtained for the target circuit. Fitness was calculated as the sum of squared errors between target output and the output of the evolved circuit.

A second method for stimulus selection, 'fixed four', was inspired by the fact that voltage ramp and step functions are very common hand-designed waveforms used to probe circuits [11]. Two fixed but different voltage ramps and two fixed but different step functions were each used to probe the target and evolved circuits. Fitness was assigned as the sum of the errors on each of the four targets.

The third stimulus selection method, 'switching single', was the same as fixed single except that a new randomly generated target input/output pair was generated periodically. In other words, the stimulus switched at regular intervals during evolution. This method was used to determine whether overfitting to a fixed single input/output pair was a significant problem.

Finally, we also employed incremental stimulus selection. Inspired by work in digital circuit evolution [18] and other evolvable hardware domains, this method involved periodically generating a new random stimulus, applying it to the black box target circuit, and then adding this new input/output pair to the set of test cases used to evaluate fitness of an evolved circuit. The fitness of an evolved circuit was then defined simply as the sum of its fitnesses for each individual stimulus. The 'switching incremental' algorithm employed this approach without Age-fitness Pareto optimization whereas the 'age-fitness incremental' algorithm was identical except that Age-fitness Pareto optimization was used.

For all five algorithms, the time required to evolve circuits was almost entirely spent on the computationally expensive Spice simulations required for fitness evaluation. As there are significant differences in the number of fitness evaluations required for the five algorithms for a given number of evolutionary generations, all experiments below account for these differences and use the same total number of fitness evaluations (Spice simulations) for all algorithm comparisons. Given the computational expense of Spice simulations, we performed evolutionary runs for a predetermined number of fitness evaluations instead of following the standard practice of letting the genetic algorithm run until stagnation. However, we found that the number of fitness evaluations used was sufficient to draw preliminary conclusions about the performance of the various algorithms.

2.3   Target Circuits

We initially used a hand-designed RTL inverter circuit as a reverse-engineering target. A RTL inverter is a simple transistor switch that implements logical negation. Not counting the elements of the embryonic circuit, this circuit had three elements as shown in (Fig. 3). Each of 40 evolutionary trials used this same simple circuit as a target to obtain baseline information about the performance of the algorithms.

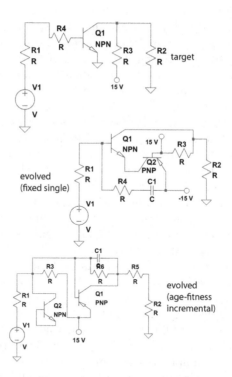

Fig. 3. RTL inverter target and evolved circuits. The target circuit is shown at the top. The other circuits are those evolved to match the behavior of this target circuit using a fixed single stimulus (middle) and the age-fitness incremental algorithm (bottom).

In order to evaluate different stimulus selection methods in as unbiased a manner as possible, we also used randomly-generated nonlinear circuits as the black box targets. An example of such a random circuit is shown in (Fig. 4). These random circuits were generated by creating random netlists with 3–11 elements and at least one nonlinear element (bipolar transistor). The elements specified by a netlist were inserted into the variable portion of the embryonic circuit and the resulting circuit was simulated. If the circuit was simulatable and for 25 randomly chosen input stimuli the outputs of the circuit were of sufficient variability, the circuit was included in the set of black box targets. Otherwise, it was discarded and a new random circuit was generated. This process continued until 40 random circuits with a variety of sizes were generated.

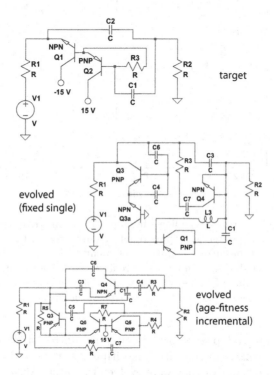

Fig. 4. Random target and evolved circuits. One randomly generated target circuit is shown at the top. The other circuits are those evolved to match the behavior of this target circuit using a fixed single stimulus (middle) and the age-fitness incremental algorithm (bottom).

3   Results

Each of the five stimulus selection algorithms were applied to the target circuits in 40 trials. The results summarizing evolutionary progress across all 40 trials for all five algorithms with the RTL inverter as the target are shown in Fig. 5. Similar results were obtained for random circuits as shown in Fig. 6. In both cases, presenting stimuli with the incremental algorithm was clearly the most effective method of evolving circuits that generalized well and that matched the performance of the target circuits for several random stimuli not used during evolution. In contrast, little benefit was gained by using different non-incremental approaches given a fixed computational budget.

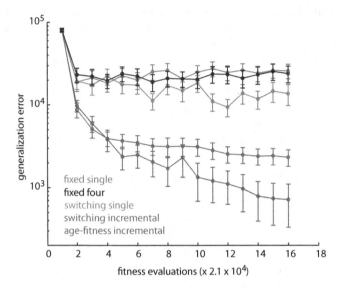

Fig. 5. Generalization error for the five stimulus selection methods with the RTL inverter target. At regular intervals (approximately once every 2.1×10^4 fitness evaluations), each member of the current population of circuits was evaluated on 25 randomly chosen stimuli not seen during training. The circuit with the lowest total error was then recorded. The mean value of this error across each of 40 trials is plotted, with error bars representing plus or minus the standard error of the mean.

Fig. 3 shows two examples of circuits obtained with a fixed single stimulus and with the age-fitness incremental algorithm, as well as the RTL inverter target circuit whose behavior they were evolved to match. Although the evolved circuits do not match the target circuit in size or structure, the circuit evolved using the age-fitness incremental algorithm closely matched the behavior of the target circuit for arbitrary stimuli (Fig. 7). A similar conclusion can be drawn from the results for random circuits as shown in Fig. 4 and Fig. 8.

4   Discussion and Conclusion

In this study, we compared different methods of fitness evaluation for reverse-engineering nonlinear analog circuits with a genetic algorithm. Stimulus presentation with an incremental algorithm proved to be a particularly effective means of performing these fitness evaluations. This method successfully produced circuits that closely matched the behavior of black box target circuits.

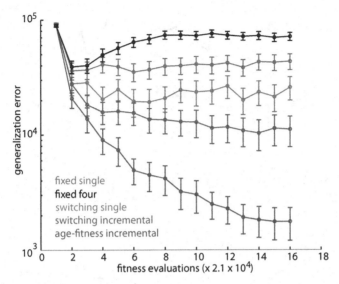

Fig. 6. Generalization error for the five stimulus selection methods with random targets. Axes and bars are the same as in Fig. 5.

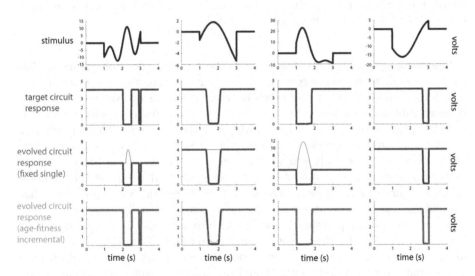

Fig. 7. RTL inverter target and evolved circuit behavior. Four randomly chosen stimuli not used during training (top row) were applied to the target circuit, which generated the responses shown in the second row. The response of the circuit evolved with a fixed single stimulus shown in Fig. 5 to those same four stimuli is shown in red in the third row. These red curves are plotted over the target responses for reference. The response of the circuit evolved with the age-fitness incremental algorithm shown in Fig. 5 to those four stimuli is shown in green in the bottom row plotted over the target responses.

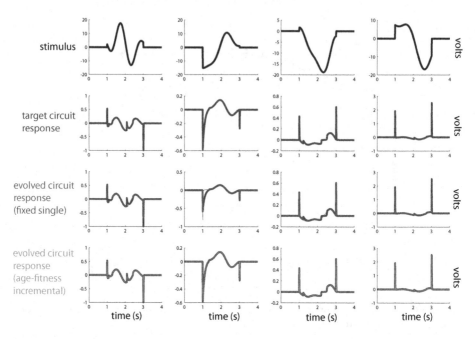

Fig. 8. Random target and evolved circuit behavior. Panels are the same as in Fig. 7 except that results are for circuits shown in Fig. 6.

One weakness of the approaches studied here is that the evolved circuits fail to match their respective target circuits in size and structure, even when they match them in behavior. It could then be argued that the evolved circuits are no more valuable as models of the target circuit than a neural network or other universal function approximator that can also reproduce the input/output behavior of the target circuit. However, we argue that using circuits as the function approximator confers two advantages. First, circuits are almost certainly the most useful function approximators for a reverse-engineered circuit if the function approximator is to be implemented in hardware. Second, we hypothesize that circuits and electrical components, although computationally expensive to simulate, are a natural representation with which to approximate the input/output functions embodied by the target nonlinear circuits and are therefore easier to identify than neural networks or other non-domain specific representations. We are currently testing this hypothesis and preliminary results are supportive.

For future work, we intend to extend the results here in several ways. First, we are studying random target circuits of larger sizes, as reverse engineering targets in real life applications tend to contain considerably more components than 3-11 as in the circuits considered here. Second, we will consider physical circuits implemented in hardware as targets as an important means of confirming the results obtained here with simulations. Third, we intend to investigate the prospect of coevolving stimuli instead of randomly generating them as in the current study. Such an approach has proven effective in other evolutionary computation problem domains such as symbolic regression [2]. Fourth, formally characterizing the complete input/output behavior of nonlinear dynamical systems such as the analog circuits in this work would be feasible with enough computational effort [6]. Such steps will be important to provide a firm theoretical basis for concluding that the evolved circuits are robust under real-life operating conditions, a conclusion that was only informally demonstrated with the experiments described in the present work. Finally, the approaches here will be applied to additional circuits with specific, known functions such as cube root circuits [8]. Although the results will not be as general as when the targets are random circuits, this will be useful as a baseline comparison of the approaches considered here to the more common evolutionary hardware methods oriented to forward-engineering tasks.

Acknowledgments. Support was provided by the Tri-Institutional Training Program in Computational Biology and Medicine, National Science Foundation grant ECCS 0941561 on Cyber-enabled Discovery and Innovation (CDI), National Institutes of Health NIDA grant RC2 DA028981, and the U.S. Defense Threat Reduction Agency (DTRA) grant HDTRA 1-09-1-0013.

References

1. Ando, S., Ishizuka, M., Iba, H.: Evolving Analog Circuits by Variable Length Chromosomes. In: Ghosh, A., Tsutsui, S. (eds.) Advances in Evolutionary Computing. Springer (2003)
2. Bongard, J., Lipson, H.: Automated Reverse Engineering of Nonlinear Dynamical Systems. PNAS 104, 9943–9948 (2007)
3. Das, A., Vemuri, R.: An Automated Passive Analog Circuit Synthesis Framework Using Genetic Algorithms. In: Proc. IEEE VLSI 2007, pp. 145–152 (2007)
4. El-Turky, F.M., Nordin, R.A.: BLADES: An Expert System for Analog Circuit Design. In: Proc. IEEE ISCAS, pp. 552–555 (1986)
5. Harjani, R., Rutenbar, R.A., Carley, L.R.: OASYS: A Framework for Analog Circuit Synthesis. Trans. Comp.-Aided Des. Integ. Cir. Sys. 8, 1247–1266 (2006)
6. Hedrich, L., Barke, E.: A Formal Approach to Nonlinear Analog Circuit Verification. In: Proc. IEEE ICCAD 1995, pp. 123–127 (1995)
7. Koh, H.Y., Sequin, C.H., Gray, P.R.: OPASYN: A Compiler for CMOS Operational Amplifiers. IEEE Trans. Comput.-Aided Des. 9, 113–125 (1990)
8. Koza, J.R., Bennett III, F.H., Andre, D., Keane, M.A., Dunlap, F.: Automated Synthesis of Analog Electrical Circuits by Means of Genetic Programming. IEEE Trans. Evol. Comp. 1, 109–128 (1997)
9. Kruiskamp, W., Leenaerts, D.: DARWIN: CMOS Opamp Synthesis by Means of a Genetic Algorithm. In: Proc. of the 32nd Design Automation Conference, pp. 433–438 (1995)
10. Lohn, J.D., Colombano, S.P.: Automated Analog Circuit Synthesis Using a Linear Representation. In: Sipper, M., Mange, D., Pérez-Uribe, A. (eds.) ICES 1998. LNCS, vol. 1478, pp. 125–133. Springer, Heidelberg (1998)
11. Mydlowec, W., Koza, J.: Use of Time-domain Simulations in Automatic Synthesis of Computational Circuits Using Genetic Programming. In: Proc. GECCO 2000, pp. 187–197 (2000)

12. NG-Spice, `http://sourceforge.net/projects/ngspice`
13. Rutenbar, R.A.: Analog Design Automation: Where Are We? Where Are We Going? In: Proc. 15th IEEE CICC, pp.13.1.1–13.1.8 (1993)
14. Rutenbar, R.A., Gielen, G.G.E., Antao, B.A.: Computer-Aided Design of Analog Integrated Circuits and Systems. Wiley-IEEE Press (2002)
15. Sapargaliyev, Y.A., Kalganova, T.G.: Open-Ended Evolution to Discover Analogue Circuits for Beyond Conventional Applications. Genet. Prog. Evol. Mach. 13, 411–443 (2012)
16. Schaumann, R., Van Valeknburg, M.E.: Design of Analog Filters. Oxford University Press, New York (2001)
17. Schmidt, M.D., Lipson, H.: Age-Fitness Pareto Optimization. Genetic Programming Theory and Practice 8, 129–146 (2010)
18. Torresen, J.: A Scalable Approach to Evolvable Hardware. Genet. Prog. Evol. Mach. 3, 259–282 (2002)
19. Zebulum, R.S., Pacheco, M.A., Vellasco, M.: Comparison of Different Evolutionary Methodologies Applied to Electronic Filter Design. In: Proc. IEEE WCCI, pp. 434–439 (1998)

Steps toward Developing an Artificial Cell Signaling Model Applied to Distributed Fault Detection

Dipankar Dasgupta and Guilherme Costa Silva

Department of of Computer Science, University of Memphis
120 Dunn Hall, 38152-3240, Memphis, TN
dasgupta@memphis.edu,guicosta@ufmg.br

Abstract. Cell signaling mechanism provides robust immune response and protects our body from a wide variety of pathogens. This work attempts to develop an artificial signaling model inspired by biological signaling process and derived abstractions. In this paper, we described various aspects of immune cell signaling and their integration towards a system-level response. Based on these abstractions, we synthesized a simple artificial cell signaling model in order to solve fault detection with the objective to provide early detection of faulty system components, as well as the overall analysis of the distributed system.

Keywords: Artificial Immune Systems, Bio inspired Models, Cell Signaling.

1 Introduction

Artificial Immune System (AIS) is a research field of Computational Intelligence which aims to provide more efficiency, robustness and accuracy in real-world problem solving. Applications of AIS include Anomaly Detection, Optimization, Clustering and Machine Learning, among others [7, 8]. Different computation models such as negative selection, clonal selection and immune networks have been developed, inspired by immunological features such as robustness, adaptability, memory, diversity and pattern recognition abilities. These algorithms were developed based on shape-space concepts [23], as the shape-space is a geometrical representation in which biological phenomena are described and simulated [22]. Other AIS approaches were developed from different perspectives such as the Conserved Self Pattern Recognition Algorithm [27], the Dendritic Cell Algorithm [11], and the T-Cell Receptor Density Algorithm [20] which are inspired on different immune models and have some immune signaling concepts applied to problem solving.

Inter and Intra-cellular signaling play a major role in the biological processes and in phenotypic behavior of cells. In AIS, cell signaling features were introduced but most aspects are yet to be exploited and successfully applied.

O.H. Ibarra et al. (Eds.): UCNC 2014, LNCS 8553, pp. 117–128, 2014.
DOI: 10.1007/978-3-319-08123-6_10, © Springer International Publishing Switzerland 2014

2   Biological Signaling Concepts

In biology, most cells communicate with their environment and with other cells, and this communication provides all basics mechanisms for cell survival, as well as its functions. These mechanisms are provided through electro-chemical signals, each signal is able to cause different effects on the cell and its phenotypic behavior. The process involving these signals and their effects on cells is called Cell Signaling.

Immune signaling occurs often by direct contact between cells which can provide distributed response throughout the immune system. For example, interferons (IFNs) are a large family of multifunctional secreted cytokines involved in antiviral defense, cell growth regulation and immune activation.

Basically, immune cell signaling processes have three phases: Reception, Transduction, and Response. Throughout these processes the converted signal changes actions in the cell. In the reception phase, the signal binds to the cell receptor and is associated to the cell membrane, assuming that the cell is intact. The transduction phase is a fundamental step in cell signaling, in which signals travel into the cell until they reach the final destination, where these cause changes to the cell. Finally, response phase involves the effects of a signal in the cell behavior; the interesting lessons to learn from these signals are:

- How these signals propagate, and;
- How signals cause or change actions in cells.

Among various signaling mechanisms in the immune system, the following provide an abstract view according to their functions, as mentioned [18]:

1. The presence of nonself antigens which provides specificity and memory of antigen;
2. Costimulatory signals providing magnitude, longevity and nature of response, and;
3. The expressed cytokines work in concert with others in the costimulation, differentiation and generation of memory cells.

For the immune response, signals 1 and signal 2 are required for Self-Nonself Discrimination by the T-helper cell where the antigen recognition is considered as primary function to identify the pathogen during an immune response. Signals from 3 have different effects on each cell, depending on their concentration. These signals can be described in Figure 1.

The second signal is also required for immune response [17], being associated with Antigen Presenting Cells (APCs) as a part of costimulation process which involves a family of receptors resulting from concentration of costimulatory and coinhibitory signals and is fundamental for regulation and maintenance of immunity [3].

The third signal considered is a family of cytokines, which are chemical messenger molecules that transmit information between cells. Essentially, these signals develop key roles in the immune system according to Borish et al. [2], by locally

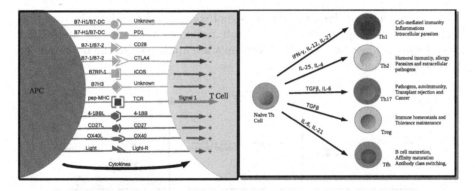

Fig. 1. Antigen and costimulatory signals [21] and cytokine roles, as described in [19]

controlling the amplitude, duration and determining nature of immune responses. They provide different functions such as the T-helper cell differentiation [16] or the inflammation control among others.

Nature-inspired computational systems are developed aiming to solve a particular problem by exploiting biological analogies and extrapolating their functionalities.

3   From Biological Signaling to Artificial Models

In biological systems, cell signals are responsible for the species survival. Based on this view, some abstractions were derived and incorporated in artificial models; in particular, the signaling mechanism provided a source of inspiration to develop abstract models for solving complex problems.

According to Goldstein et al. [10], mathematical or computational models of cell signaling may be developed by two ways: Simple models, where some features represent most important phenomena by one or more arbitrary transitions. In Detailed models, some realistic and detailed interactions between components are modeled. Some influence mechanisms are provided to assure that signals propagate and achieve their objective by providing cell actions and perform represent decision making mechanisms.

Scheider et al. [24] provided mathematical insights of intra-cellular signaling transduction where signals undergo various transformation in order to propagate and cause changes to cells:

1. Magnitude - the strength of a given signal in order to perform changes. A signal must be strong enough (exceeding a given threshold) to cause changes and efficacy in respect to its relevance and context.
2. Duration - only signals whose effects persist in long-term are able to perform changes to cells. A short-term signal, even if its strength is high, is unable to produce cellular changes. Duration of signals is related to how long the lifetime of a signal is and such signaling feature implies in robustness to noise, among other advantages.

The magnitude can be deducted by signal concentration, while the duration defines if a signal is good enough to activate responses during its lifetime within a cell. Figure 2 illustrates how both concepts are applicable to the development of an artificial model.

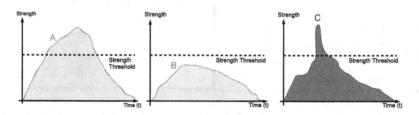

Fig. 2. Features of a signal in a given time and some examples: (A) The signal is strong enough to trigger some effects, as the signal is higher than a given threshold. (B) The signal cannot reach the given threshold and has no effect. (C) The signal is strong, but has a short duration and is unable to trigger its desirable effect within its lifetime.

4   The Artificial Signaling Model

The proposal of an artificial model is aimed to solve problems through biological inspiration provided by abstractions. The artificial model of cell signaling can be proposed after some definitions regarding how to use abstractions and the application environment in which the model will be applied. In order to provide a suitable model, some features are proposed for the signaling model as follows:

- Hierarchical - Signals are processed through the environment in a similar way to the one in Granular Computing [26];
- Distributed - Signals and responses are processed by different in cells in the same environment. Both features may provide cascading effects in cell behavior;
- Asynchronous - Signals collection processes are time-independent and there is no interdependence among processing units;
- Dynamic - where signals change with environmental conditions and internal states similar to the biological system.

The hierarchical model provides a processing environment that deals with signals analyzing them through a bottom-up leveling, where low level signals may lead to highly relevant signals in terms of information and representation as described in Figure 3. The highest(n^{th}) level of the signaling is the classification step. This strategy can provide continuous refinement and amalgamation of singals for decision-making and meaningful information processing.

Moreover, the distributed environment can provide collaborative environment for information spreading, where the hierarchical signaling may provide some cascading effects of signal analysis of different cells in each level, as illustrated in Figure 4.

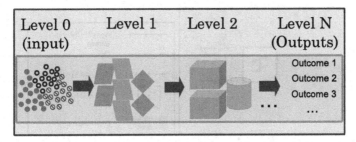

Fig. 3. The hierarchy of the artificial signaling model

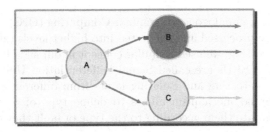

Fig. 4. Signals or messages are spreading in a distributed way

Different rules of signal spreading and propagation are defined in order to send information in a homogeneous (components have the same structure) or heterogeneous (components have different structures and treat information differently) way, according to the model so that information can be combined and also reinforced providing effectiveness and precision throughout the processing.

These abstractions also require the model to be asynchronous, which means that signals does not depend on time restrictions, however, in some cases, the order of signal arrival may be important while processing.

Each signal is subject to magnitude and duration conditions during its lifetime, these features aim to improve decision making tasks in the monitored system. Each signal is defined by the concentration of their stimuli through time and is tagged based on its intended destination.

For this purpose, two thresholds are calculated: Magnitude (ϕ) and Duration (ψ). Both thresholds define if a signal will produce its desirable effect in response variables.

In the first level, input signal is evaluated and then converted into numerical domain variables according to conditions, representing the information gathering based on the number of detected components. Another signal type to be considered is a categorical signal, analogous to costimulation, which acts as propagator of these responses through next levels of signal processing hierarchy.

In Figure 5, the main idea of the first Signal Processing Unit (SPU) is shown.

The number of SPUs in the first level may be dependent on the amount of evaluated data and can also be used for parallel processing. Hierarchical levels and the

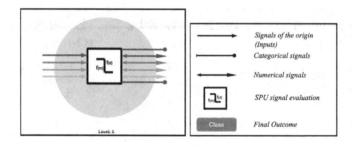

Fig. 5. Illustration of SPU from level 1 of signaling method

evolution of signals are analogous to Granular Computing (GrC), in which lower levels (granules) are processed and converted into higher levels (abstractions) in a feed-forward processing, we used a similar concept in our signaling model.

Intermediate level SPUs are called Signal Differentiation Unit (SDU) which are responsible for detecting and isolating faults from different system components. The distributed mechanism allows to define type of SDUs to analyze signals and differentiate them according to the type of fault they can identify in the system.

Responses from this level are modeled according to the signals from faulty components are reorganized and combined as a part of the decision making process; multiple levels may be involved during this processing. As presented in Figure 6. In addition, each signal may have more categories as needed and the strength of the resulting signals are calculated accordingly.

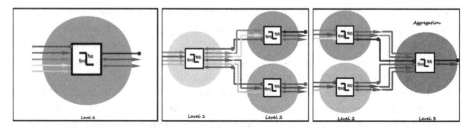

Fig. 6. Illustration of SDUs from intermediate levels of signaling method, in which fault isolation is properly processed. The relation between levels are also illustrated.

The upper level (highest) of the signaling component is called Signal Amalgamation Unit (SAU) which indicates the system status, as well as the type of fault. The SAUs identify faults according to all information processed through the environment as shown in Figure 7.

A feedback mechanism is considered, as in the biological system which is used to provide the system status. In the simple model, when all signals are discarded (as the normal), the second level SDU sends a feedback in order to inform the normal status of the monitored system.

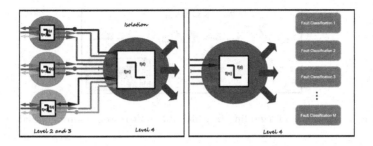

Fig. 7. Illustration of SAU features

Further details of this sigaling model and its different levels are discussed below.

4.1   Signaling Level 1

In this level, input signal is obtained and evaluated through the first SPU. Signals propagate according to Eq. 1, which stimulates the effects of signaling for each component monitored, where $f(X_{i(k)})$ is the transformation occurred to input signal X and integration in signal S, usually representing the quantitative variation $\bar{X}_i(k)$ of component $i \in X$ during the instant k, and θ represents the signaling decay rate. This equation is applied to all SPUs for collecting signals.

$$S_{i(k)}(1) = S_{i(k-1)}(1) * (1 - \theta) + f(X_{i(k)}) \tag{1}$$

After their calculation, signals are evaluated according to their magnitude and their duration of higher level of concentration. If a signal satisfies these conditions, it will propagate further.

The activation of responses is analogous to transcription factors in the biological system, and the equation is defined in (2) for N components where A_i is a boolean variable which defines the signaling activation conditions (3) for component i at duration $\bar{k}_i$ in the transcription factor F, which regulates the response.

$$Y_{o(k)} = \sum_{\forall i \in F_o} S_i * A_i \tag{2}$$

$$A_i = \begin{cases} 1, \text{ If } S_{i(k)} > \phi \text{ AND } \bar{k}_i \geqslant \psi \\ 0, \text{ Otherwise} \end{cases} \tag{3}$$

When a signal associated with input data (or a set of these) is activated, it generates a response of a one kind, but if integrated with another signal, this will generate a response of different kind. The example in Fig. 8 illustrates this model for two different signals but may apply applicabe to multiple levels.

In some cases, inactive factors in first level may be presented as a complementary response signal, which also propagates through other SPUs. Another signal

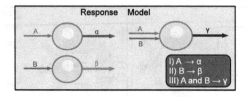

Fig. 8. Example of signaling in which different responses are generated

produced is the categorical signal, defined by positive and negative forms, based on the number of activated components, which allows the further propagation of a particular signal through the environment.

The co-stimulation signal which influences the response, allowing a signal transition through levels and reinforces further signals, is defined by the presence of faulty component evaluation and can assume positive or negative values, as defined in Eq. 4.

$$v(k) = \begin{cases} -1, \sum_{\forall i \in F_j}^{N} = 0 \\ +1, Otherwise \end{cases} \qquad (4)$$

Each output from this level is distributed through signaling environment, in order to produce a proper response within the system components.

4.2   Intermediate Levels

According to our signal hierarchy model, signals propagate and are processed by SPUs at different levels. When processing requires multiple cells in the same level, a distribution matrix κ_{co} should be provided Eq.(5), which defines the signal propagation Eq.(6) for each input i and output o, and the signaling rule applied to level $X(l)$ is defined in Eq. 7.

$$\kappa_{co}(l) = \begin{cases} 1, \text{If an output } o \text{ is destined to the cell } c \\ 0, \text{Otherwise} \end{cases} \qquad (5)$$

$$X_{ci}(l) = Y_o(l-1)\kappa_{co}(l) \qquad (6)$$
$$S_{i(k)}(l) = S_{i(k-1)}(l)(1-\theta) + f(X_{i(k)})(l) \qquad (7)$$

For propagation, the categorical signal may follow a binding rule $\Omega(c)$, as defined in Eq. 8, where $f(v)$ corresponds to a binding value, analogous to co-stimulation, which allows the propagation of these signals, once received by the SDU. The value of categorical signal is useful to define how signal will propagate within SDUs, as the 0 value implies that signal will not propagate.

$$\Omega(c) = \begin{cases} 1, \text{If } v_{l-1} = f(v) \\ 0, Otherwise \end{cases} \qquad (8)$$

Feedback of signaling is based on how successful was the propagation of signals once occurred. However, in this simple model, the feedback variable informs only if signals have propagated within the SPU, as a binary value. This scheme is applied to all levels of this proposed signaling model.

4.3   Upper Level of Signaling

The last level processes all signals collected from previous levels reorganized into a final outcome. The initial processing is similar to the previous levels, through the activation of signal conditions during the processing.

Once transcribed, all activated signal patterns take part in a decision process of the overall system fault detection. In SAU the signal integration plays an important role for determining the system state, fault identification, and classification depending primarily on activated signals during their processing, as shown in Fig. 9.

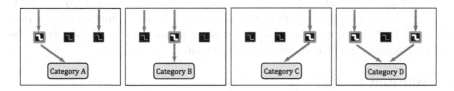

Fig. 9. Mechanism adopted in the Signal Amalgamation Unit (SAU) after activation of signal conditions

In simple systems, this processing is done at once, in a centralized way, based on the iterative processing of all hierarchies and the differentiation of cells provided by cytokines in the biological model. In more complex systems, various cells can process these information in order to provide a robust and distributed data evaluation, useful in communication-based systems.

The main ideas regarding the evaluation of components and combination of signals are the integration among signals, evaluation, and further decision about the classification of the anomaly considering the number of components and their collective behavior.

5   Possible Applications of the Model

The development of the cell signaling based approach aims to provide detection and classification tasks in distributed and complex systems, in which the component fault detection and analysis for a large-scale system are difficult.

In particular, the proposed model seems suitable for fault detection, specially in those systems whose components and its subcomponents are interlinked between each other. This application paradigm can be seen in some distributed system works [1, 6]. Some application examples include Power Systems [4, 25];

Smart Grid Systems [12, 14]; Distributed File Systems, as fault tolerance systems [5]; Cloud Computing Systems [9, 15] among others.

A typical description of Fault Detection problems is given in [13]. According to the study, some services may provide useful abstractions for building distributed systems, whose faults can be easily isolated and repaired. Some aspects such as the detection of arbitrary faults are discussed and most of these aspects have features in common with the signaling model.

These problems require the detection and isolation of faulty components, once noticed in different sections of a large scale system. Such a detection of component failure is very important before a critical fault occurs which may lead to a catastropic system failure.

This also implies in a Modularity-based strategy, in which the number of extreme signals are higher than mid-level ones, as well as a Divide-and-conquer strategy, in which distributed environment and signal combination provide more robustness.

The final outcome of the model is the detection flag or the fault category in which the processed information are associated to. Another expected feature is regarding some signaling metrics, which may also help on diagnosis by a possibility of level decomposition. The diagnosis depends on the complexity of the system and their monitored components as well.

6   Summary

In the immune system, signaling plays a major role in sharing and transmitting information during an immune response and is essential to the effectiveness of the immune defense. In immune diffusion, the message is passed from one immuno-component to others without any feedback. Another mechanism called immune dialogue exhibits continuous exchange of molecular signals with its counter parts. The immune reactivity is determined by context, where self and foreign agents play upon each other. Signaling also allows a cell to transfer information about its internal state to the outside, where it can be recognized by cells in the Immune system. Furthermore, signaling results in changes to the cell, allowing it to appropriately respond to a stimulus.

The proposed approach may provide a robust scheme of signaling, able to detect different types of faults with increase reliability. The method aims to gather relevant components statu signals from the monitored system and then use these signals in order to perform detection and/or fault classification.The main goal of the signaling method is to provide a distributed detection in which most components are coupled and the early detection of a fault is important.The practical effects of the novel approach may be seen in further evaluation in large and distributed systems. In summary, this signaling model will be able to discover the unknown Fault, and can also be applied in the monitoring state or health of the monitored system so to diagnose fault earlier.

Acknowledgements. The second author has received support from the Brazilian funding agency CAPES during the development of this work.

References

1. Aghasaryan, A., Fabre, E., Benveniste, A., Boubour, R., Jard, C.: Fault detection and diagnosis in distributed systems: An approach by partially stochastic petri nets. Discrete Event Dynamic Systems 8(2), 203–231 (1998)
2. Borish, L.C., Steinke, J.W.: 2. cytokines and chemokines. Journal of Allergy and Clinical Immunology 111(suppl. 2), 460–475 (2003)
3. Bour-Jordan, H., Bluestone, J.A.: Cd28 function: A balance of costimulatory and regulatory signals. Journal of Clinical Immunology 22(1), 1–7 (2002)
4. Bunnoon, P.: Fault detection approaches to power system: Stateoftheart article reviews for searching a new approach in the future. International Journal of Electrical and Computer Engineering (IJECE) 3(4), 553–560 (2013)
5. Calderón, A., García-Carballeira, F., Sánchez, L., García, J., Fernandez, J.: Fault tolerant file models for parallel file systems: Introducing distribution patterns for every file. The Journal of Supercomputing 47(3), 312–334 (2009)
6. Chen, H., Jiang, G., Yoshihira, K.: Fault detection in distributed systems by representative subspace mapping. In: 18th International Conference on Pattern Recognition, ICPR 2006, vol. 4, pp. 912–915 (2006)
7. Dasgupta, D., Niño, L.: Immunological Computation: Theory and Applications, 1st edn. Auerbach Publications, Boston (2008)
8. De Castro, L.N., Timmis, J.: Artificial Immune Systems: A New Computational Intelligence Approach. Springer (2002)
9. Fan, G., Yu, H., Chen, L., Liu, D.: Model based byzantine fault detection technique for cloud computing. In: 2012 IEEE Asia-Pacific Services Computing Conference (APSCC), pp. 249–256 (December 2012)
10. Goldstein, B., Faeder, J.R., Hlavacek, W.S.: Mathematical and computational models of immune-receptor signalling. Nat. Rev. Immunol. 4(6), 445–456 (2004)
11. Greensmith, J., Aickelin, U., Cayzer, S.: Introducing dendritic cells as a novel immune-inspired algorithm for anomaly detection. In: Jacob, C., Pilat, M.L., Bentley, P.J., Timmis, J.I. (eds.) ICARIS 2005. LNCS, vol. 3627, pp. 153–167. Springer, Heidelberg (2005)
12. Gudzius, S., Markevicius, L.A., Morkvenas, A.: Characteristics of fault detection system for smart grid distribution network. Electronics and Electrical Engineering 112(6) (2011)
13. Haeberlen, A., Kuznetsov, P.: The fault detection problem. In: Abdelzaher, T., Raynal, M., Santoro, N. (eds.) OPODIS 2009. LNCS, vol. 5923, pp. 99–114. Springer, Heidelberg (2009)
14. He, Q., Blum, R.: Smart grid monitoring for intrusion and fault detection with new locally optimum testing procedures. In: 2011 IEEE International Conference on Acoustics, Speech and Signal Processing (ICASSP), pp. 3852–3855 (May 2011)
15. Jhawar, R., Piuri, V., Santambrogio, M.: A comprehensive conceptual system-level approach to fault tolerance in cloud computing. In: 2012 IEEE International on Systems Conference (SysCon), pp. 1–5 (March 2012)
16. King, C.: New insights into the differentiation and function of t follicular helper cells. Nat. Rev. Immunol. 9(11), 757–766 (2009)
17. Lafferty, K.J., Cunningham, A.J.: A new analysis of allogeneic interactions. Aust. J. Exp. Biol. Med. Sci. 53(1), 27–42 (1975)
18. Noble, A.: Do we have memory of danger as well as antigen? Trends in Immunology 30(4), 150–156 (2009)

19. Nurieva, R.I., Chung, Y.: Understanding the development and function of t follicular helper cells. Cell Mol. Immunol. 7(3), 190–197 (2010)
20. Owens, N.D.L., Greensted, A., Timmis, J., Tyrrell, A.: T cell receptor signalling inspired kernel density estimation and anomaly detection. In: Andrews, P.S., Timmis, J., Owens, N.D.L., Aickelin, U., Hart, E., Hone, A., Tyrrell, A.M. (eds.) ICARIS 2009. LNCS, vol. 5666, pp. 122–135. Springer, Heidelberg (2009)
21. Pardoll, D.M.: Spinning molecular immunology into successful immunotherapy. Nat. Rev. Immunol. 2(4), 227–238 (2002)
22. Percus, J.K., Percus, O.E., Perelson, A.S.: Predicting the size of the t-cell receptor and antibody combining region from consideration of efficient self-nonself discrimination. Proceedings of the National Academy of Sciences 90(5), 1691–1695 (1993)
23. Perelson, A.S., Oster, G.F.: Theoretical studies of clonal selection: Minimal antibody repertoire size and reliability of self-non-self discrimination. Journal of Theoretical Biology 81(4), 645–670 (1979)
24. Schneider, A., Klingmüller, U., Schilling, M.: Short-term information processing, long-term responses: Insights by mathematical modeling of signal transduction. BioEssays 34(7), 542–550 (2012)
25. Shames, I., Teixeira, A., Sandberg, H., Johansson, K.H.: Distributed fault detection for interconnected second-order systems with applications to power networks. In: First Workshop on Secure Control Systems (2010)
26. Yao, J.: A ten-year review of granular computing. In: IEEE International Conference on Granular Computing, GRC 2007, pp. 734–734 (2007)
27. Yu, S., Dasgupta, D.: Conserved Self Pattern Recognition Algorithm. In: Bentley, P.J., Lee, D., Jung, S. (eds.) ICARIS 2008. LNCS, vol. 5132, pp. 279–290. Springer, Heidelberg (2008)

Dynamic Adaptive Neural Network Array

Mark E. Dean, Catherine D. Schuman, and J. Douglas Birdwell

Department of Electrical Engineering and Computer Science, University of Tennessee, Knoxville, TN, 37996-2250. United States of America

Abstract. We present the design-scheme and physical implementation for a Dynamic Adaptive Neural Network Array (DANNA) based upon the work by Schuman and Birdwell [1,2] and using a programmable array of elements constructed with a Field Programmable Gate Array (FPGA). The aim of this paper is to demonstrate how a single programmable neuromorphic element can be designed to support the primary components of a dynamic and adaptive neural network, e.g. a neuron and a synapse, and be replicated across a FPGA to yield a reasonably large programmable DANNA of up to 10,000 neurons and synapses. We describe element programmability, how the dynamic components of a neuron and synapse are supported, and the structure used to support the monitoring and control interface. Finally, we present initial results from simulations of the hardware, the projected performance of the array elements and the physical implementation of a DANNA on a Xilinx FPGA.

Introduction

Artificial Neural Networks (ANNs) constitute a powerful computational methodology that can outperform von Neumann schemes in numerous data-processing applications [11, 12, 13]. They have been shown effective in tasks such as pattern recognition, sensory reconstruction, image processing, streaming data analytics and deep learning applications, but they do not exhibit emergent dynamic behaviors. Rather, dynamic elements are typically incorporated with ANNs in architectures pre-defined by developers (using, for example, unit delay elements), and the ANNs are subsequently trained using machine learning (ML) methods. In contrast, biological neural systems are parallel and distributed information processing systems that incorporate state information (memory) and dynamics (enabling behaviors that depend upon past stimuli) in a distributed fashion using the charge states of individual neurons and propagation delays along axons. Spiking ANNs, which are event-based or event-driven networks, are the subject of continuing research and overcome some of these issues but appear to suffer from the need for large interconnection networks [14]. We use spiking behavior, and we believe our approach requires fewer interconnections between network components due to state information captured within the interconnections, as described in [1,2].

ANNs have been implemented in both software (modeling and simulation) and hardware (analog or digital circuit) constructs. ANNs implemented in software typically leverage a model of the target network components and structures, and simulate

O.H. Ibarra et al. (Eds.): UCNC 2014, LNCS 8553, pp. 129–141, 2014.
DOI: 10.1007/978-3-319-08123-6_11, © Springer International Publishing Switzerland 2014

the operation of the network on general-purpose sequential computers. This approach allows emulation of a wide range of environments and applications. The constraints of software simulated ANNs cause them to require large computing systems for performance or large run-times to complete a specific analysis. Specific-purpose fixed hardware implementations have also been used to implement ANNs for real-time, mission critical and/or streaming data environments. Many implementation examples using analog or digital circuits, and continuous, spiking, pulse-mode and/or discrete-event operation exist. But most hardware implementations for ANNs have static, or non-adaptive, structures, and are application specific. Many hardware implementations are also constrained by the use of components and structures commonly used in von Neumann based systems (such as RAM, buses, processors, and sequential instruction processing). There is still much room for improvement before artificial constructs approach the capabilities and efficiencies realized by the brain.

We have created a viable model for the components, connectivity, and adaptability of a dynamic neural network (implementing both distributed memory elements and distributed dynamic components): a neuron, a synapse, their associative operating characteristics, and a connection matrix. The goal is to enable not only a dynamic but also an adaptive network structure using these characteristic components. The structure and simplicity of this Dynamic Adaptive Neural Network model enable an efficient digital representation to be created and implemented in a single digital element that can be programmed to represent either a neuron or a synapse in a network. This digital element can then be replicated across a logic chip to enable an adaptive and programmable array of elements. This array of programmable elements creates a Dynamic Adaptive Neural Network Array, DANNA, which enables the creation of any neural network sized to fit within the capacity provided by the array. This provides one of the first physical implementations of a programmable adaptive and dynamic array of neuromophic elements not using traditional digital processing mechanisms.

There have been previous efforts in implementing neural networks with spiking neurons in VLSI. Examples of analog VLSI implementations include [15,16]. There have also been digital VLSI implementations of neural networks using FPGAs that provide a baseline comparison for our approach. These range from their use as an acceleration engine [17], to a multiplexing SIMD architecture [18], to a spiking neural array with a Leaky-Integrate and Fire (LIF) neuron model with variable synapse weights and delays [19]. We will show that the programmability, adaptive behavior, flexibility and scalability provided by DANNA enable support for more complex and larger target applications.

This paper explores how to implement an array of programmable adaptive neuromorphic elements using a FPGA and the DANNA component models. The capacity, logic structures, functions and layout of Xilinx Virtex-7 FPGAs provide the potential to support useful array sizes, up to 10,000 programmable elements. Programming, control and I/O interfaces are described to enable the creation of a target neural network and the monitoring of its operation. Finally, we provide a perspective on the potential performance of the FPGA-based DANNA and project what we believe will be feasible with a VLSI-based DANNA implementation.

An Artificial Neural Network

The concept of ANNs emerged from knowledge of the principle constructs of the brain. The design of our dynamic adaptive neural networks draws inspiration from biological neural networks [5,6] and traditional ANNs [7,8] from machine learning. Our goal is not to directly implement or simulate a biological network or to represent what occurs in the brain. Our network model and the elements used within the network are highly simplified compared to higher fidelity models of the biological components. Our model of a neuron merely accumulates a quantity analogous to (and we call it this) charge, and the spiking output is an event, occurring in the hardware synchronously with a clock. Connections between neurons have limited fan-out and fan-in capabilities, and there are thus typically many fewer synaptic connections than are observed in biological networks. We believe, however, that the simple implementation used to represent neurons, synapses and their communications with each other is still sufficient to support complex behavior and applications environments.

In most ANN simulations or implementations the component elements, neurons and synapses, are unique and have specific designs and operating parameters. These components and their placement in a network often must be predetermined and constructed to support a specific task or problem. These networks, while effective for their targeted intent, lack the flexibility to adjust to changing conditions, problem space and/or the information input to the network. The networks we construct are "designed" using evolutionary optimization tools, which train both component (neuron and synapse) placement and interconnections, and the parameters of the components. This dynamic adaptability and configuration flexibility is one of the key attributes of our element design and array structure.

Communication paradigms for ANNs vary from continuous to discrete, spiking to pulse-mode excitation signaling for the networks' inputs/outputs or for signaling between elements. We implement a "spiking neural array" using a discrete event-driven signaling model where each communication between elements carries a "fire" signal and a "weight" signifying the strength or impact the communicated event must have on the receiving network components. Signal weights are most important as inputs to a neuron where they are used as input values to its excitation function.

Most ANNs have a physical implementation or "layout" driven by the specific characteristics of the networks function and the physical characteristics and constraints of the devices being used to construct the network. In most cases a von Neumann computer is used to create a virtual representation of the network and its components. In some cases special hardware is constructed to implement the network's components and function (e.g. analog and/or digital devices). In contrast, we build a 2-dimensional array or grid of identical "elements" where each element has input and output connections to its eight nearest neighbors (left, right, top, bottom and diagonal neighbor elements). Each element in the array can be programmed to be a neuron or a synapse.

We use a model of a neuron inspired by the Hodgkin-Huxley model [3]. Key operating components like neuron charge accumulators, thresholds and refractory periods, and synaptic propagation delays and weights all introduce dynamic behaviors in the network, serving as memory and influencing system dynamics. Unlike most proposed ANN architectures, but similar to natural neural processes, these dynamic effects are distributed throughout the network, and are directly influenced in our ANNs by the evolutionary programming methods we utilize to construct and adapt the ANNs for specific purposes [1,2].

A Neuron

The primary function of a DANNA neuron is to accumulate "charge" by adding the "weights" of firing inputs (synapses) to its existing charge level until that level reaches a programmable threshold level. Each neuron has an independently programmable threshold. When the threshold is reached, if the neuron is not in its refractory period, the neuron fires, and the neuron's charge is reset to a bias level, dependent on the design parameters for the network. If the neuron is within its refractory period, then the neuron maintains its charge but does not fire. Thus, a neuron can accumulate charge during its refractory period, but it cannot fire during this period. As soon as a neuron fires, it enters its refractory period. The refractory period for all neurons is a constant value set for a given application or operational characteristic.

We have chosen a weighted-sum threshold activation function for the neuron charge given its implementation simplicity and functionality, but other activation functions could be implemented (e.g. linear, sigmoid or Gaussian).

The neuron charge function $H_{kj}(t)$ can be expressed as:

$$H_{kj}(t) = \sum_{i=1}^{N} w_i(t) x_i(t) + H_{kj}(t-1)$$

where kj is the location address in the 2-dimensional array, N is the number of neuron inputs, w_i is the weight of input x_i and t is the discrete sample time for network sequencing. Weights can be negative or positive discrete values with minimum and maximum limits set by the functional requirements of the target applications. For this implementation we chose to use signed 8-bit weights (-128 to +127) and a 9-bit charge accumulator.

The neuron activation function $a_{kj}(t)$ (the point at which a neuron will fire its output) can be expressed as:

$$a_{kj}(t) = f\left(H_{kj}(t)\right) = \begin{cases} 1 & if \ H_{kj}(t) \geq \theta(t) \\ 0 & if \ H_{kj}(t) < \theta(t) \end{cases}$$

where θ is the neuron's programmable threshold. When the neuron's charge reaches its threshold level the charge of the neuron is reset to a predetermined bias level before starting a new accumulation cycle. The bias value is the same for all neurons in the network in the current design. For this implementation the thresholds are limited to binary values from 0 to +127. This neuron model follows the computational model for a neuron proposed by Rosenblatt [4].

Additional key features of our neuron model are the number of inputs/outputs and its firing refractory period. Our present implementations support 8 input/output (I/O) ports connecting to nearest neighbor elements. Note that each port can be programmed as an input and/or an output, and each port that is enabled must connect to an element programmed as a synapse. Input port sampling is done sequentially and must be randomized to avoid having a single synapse dominate the interactions with the neuron. This is done by having the first port address sampled in a network cycle be random and each subsequent port address be in a binary ordered sequence from the first address.

The neuron refractory period is the amount of time, measured in network cycles, which a neuron must hold off firing from a previous firing condition. We have set the neuron refractory period to one network cycle, meaning if the input firing rate and weights are sufficiently high, a neuron can fire on every network cycle. With further testing if we find the firing rate for neurons needs to be programmable, we have a design which implements a programmable firing refractory period.

Our model for neurons allows them to be either input neurons or internal neurons. Input neurons are placed along specified edges of an array to facilitate routing. Neurons are connected to other neurons via synapses. These synapses are directed, so each neuron has a set of synapses to other neurons and a set of synapses from other neurons.

A Synapse

Synapses are defined by the neurons they connect; each synapse goes from one neuron to another neuron. Each synapse represents the distance between two neurons and the weight (or strength) of the synaptic connection. The distance between the two neurons is represented as a delay, implemented using a first-in/first-out (FIFO) shift register clocked at the network cycle rate, and affects how long it takes for charge to travel along the synapse. The weight of the synaptic connection determines how much charge arrives at the second neuron after the first neuron fires. Our network model does not currently include the concept of myelination; if two synapses are each of length d, then it takes the same amount of time (delay) for charge to travel from one end of each synapse to the other. Synapses capture selected features of both axons and synapses found in biological neural networks.

The primary function of a DANNA synapse is to adapt and transmit a weighted firing signal based on: 1) the firing rate of its input neuron, 2) the firing conditions of its output neuron and 3) its programmable distance which represents the effective length of the synapse. Two of the unique characteristics of our synapse model are: 1) the weight value held by the synapse can automatically potentiate (long-term potentiation, or LTP) or depress (long-term depression, or LTD) depending on the firing condition of its output neuron and 2) the ability to store a string of firing events in its "distance FIFO" to simulate a synapse transmitting a set of firing events down its length. Note we are translating a synapse's length into a representative number of discrete time periods through a programmable shift register.

A synapse can have one (out of eight) I/O ports enabled as an input and one (out of eight) I/O ports enabled as an output. When a synapse receives a firing event from an input neuron it places this event on its distance FIFO. The distance FIFO is a programmable shift register that can store from 1 to 256 firing events (one per network cycle programmed as the "distance" of the synapse). When each firing event reaches the output of the distance FIFO the present weight value stored in the synapse is transmitted as a firing event on its output port.

As mentioned, the synapse weight will automatically adapt based on its firing condition and the firing response of its output neuron. LTP and LTD occur in biological brains; it is speculated that they play a major role in learning [9]. The adaptive synapse weight function, $w_{kj}(t)$, can be expressed as follows:

$$if\ S_{kj}(t) = 1,\ then\ w_{kj}(t+1) =$$

$$\begin{cases} w_{kj}(t) + LTD\ if\ a_{neuron}(t_s) = 1 \\ w_{kj}(t) + LTP\ if\ a_{neuron}(t_s) = 0\ and\ a_{neuron}(t_s + 1) = 1 \\ w_{kj}(t)\ if\ a_{neuron}(t_s) = 0\ and\ a_{neuron}(t_s + 1) = 0 \end{cases}$$

where $S_{kj}(t)$ is the synapse output firing condition, $a_{neuron}(t_s)$ is the activation function or firing condition of the neuron connected to the synapse's output at the time during the network cycle it samples the synapse output, *LTD* is the "long term depression" value for the synapse, and *LTP* is the "long term potentiation" value for the synapse. Note that $(t_s + 1)$ is the next input sample cycle after the neuron has sampled the synapse output; given eight inputs, the network cycle is divided into eight input sample cycles.

For our implementation the LTP and LTD values are set at +1 and -1, respectively. Therefore, a synapse's weight is increased by one if it causes its output neuron to fire and is decreased by one if it fires when its output neuron is already firing. It is unchanged in all other conditions.

Finally, a synapse has a programmable LTP/LTD refractory period. This programmable value (ranging from 0 to 15) represents the number of network cycles a synapse must wait from its last weight potentiation or depression before it can adjust its weight again. This function limits the rate of potentiation/depression of a synapse's weight. All potentiation and/or depression conditions experienced during the LTP/LTD refractory period are ignored; they have no effect on the synapse weight.

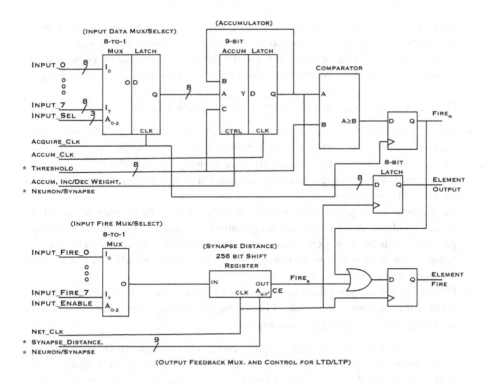

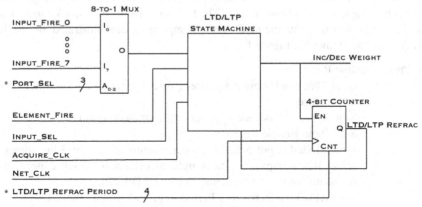

* Signals provided from programmable registers implemented in each element.

Note: All signals shown are connections to other elements or global clocks in the array except for: Inc/Dec Weight, LTD/LTP Refrac, Fire and signals from the elements programmable registers.

Fig. 1. Element block diagram

An Element

An array element implements all the functions necessary to support its operation as a neuron or a synapse. To minimize the physical implementation size of the array element, as many functional components as possible are used to support portions of each neuromorphic function. To maximize performance and minimize size we use a very simple state-machine design and avoid the use of digital signal processors, floating-point units, arithmetic-logic units, memory arrays and other common microprocessor units.

The states used to sequence the array element are defined as follows:

- Select an input port (1 of 8) and acquire input fire condition (Note: all 8 ports of an element are sampled during a single network cycle). Check the fire condition of the element assigned to the output port (used to determine LTD/LTP if the element is configured as a synapse). Load the synapse FIFO with the input fire condition if the element is a synapse.
- Accumulate the acquired input weight with the current charge state and compare the accumulated charge with the programmed threshold if the element is configured as a neuron. The accumulator holds the LTD/LTP weight if the element is a synapse. Depress or potentiate synapse the weight based on the firing condition of the element assigned to the output port.
- Fire the output and reset the accumulator to the bias value if the charge $\geq$ the threshold if the element is a neuron. Fire the output if a fire event is at the output of the synapse FIFO if the element is a synapse.

We overlap the "Fire Output" and "Acquire Input" states, reducing the state machine to two states. A network cycle consists of eight element cycles, and the element samples all eight inputs during a single network cycle. Therefore, it takes eight element cycles to complete one network cycle. The following list of functional components is implemented in the array element; these components are illustrated in the block diagram of the element in Figure 1.

- Programmable Registers:
    - o   8-bit Threshold/Weight Register (stores threshold for neuron, or weight for synapse).
    - o   8-bit Synapse Distance Register (synapse mode only)
    - o   8-bit Input Enable Register
    - o   4-bit Mode/Output Select Register (Neuron/Synapse; 3-bit output port select if a synapse, which is used to determine which connected elements output should be monitored for LTD/LTP).
    - o   4-bit LTD/LTP Refractory Period Register (synapse mode only)
- 8x9-bit I/O port. Each port includes an 8-bit uni-directional I/O data interface to communicate "weights" and a "fire" signal. An I/O can communicate a "fire event" from a neuron to a synapse or a "weight" from a synapse to a neuron.
- 8-to-1 input port multiplexer and latch. Each input port is 9-bits wide (1-bit "fire" and 8-bit "weight" signals). The network provides global input select signals to support sequencing through all connected inputs. A pseudo-random number generator is used to randomize the input sampling sequence during each network cycle.
- 9-bit accumulator (adder, comparator and latch). This holds and calculates "charge" for a neuron or "weight" for a synapse. It also compares "charge" to "threshold" for a neuron. The accumulator accumulates input firings from all

enabled inputs to the neuron. The weight of each input firing event is stored and added to the "charge" in the order it is sampled. Each weight is an 8-bit signed integer. When an element is a synapse, its weight will be depressed or potentiated, by adding -1 or +1 respectively, depending on the effect the synapse firing event has on its connected neuron.

- 8-bit output register to hold output communications to connected array elements (the "threshold" when configured as a neuron and the "weight" when configured as a synapse). The output register value is driven onto the output port during a "firing event" and held active for one network cycle. At all other times the output is zero.
- A Synapse Distance FIFO stores input firing events to a synapse and maintains the firing delays between those events. This is implemented via a 1-bit wide x 256 entry shift register. The Synapse Distance Register selects the appropriate "tap" off the event shift register to implement the "distance" (a delay) associated with the configured synapse.
- 4-bit counter and register (or 16-bit shift register) with programmable length. This holds and implements the LTP/LTD refractory period for a synapse. A global programmable refractory period register is used to drive a 4-bit refractory period "length" to all elements.
- Clock inputs (created by a network clocking circuit and distributed to manage fanout and minimize clock skew), including a Global Network Clock (Net_Clk), an Acquire/Fire Clock (Acquire_Clk), and an Accumulate Clock (Accum_Clk). The Global Network Clock sets the network cycle time. Acquire/Fire Clock controls the element cycle time and Accumulate Clock enables the accumulator to perform two operations every element cycle (load and accumulate).
- Programing/monitoring interface to enable register reads/writes from/to the external interface. In the current implementation, each element in the array is directly addressed via a multiplexed 8-bit address/data port (which supports a 16-bit global element address and an 8-bit data port), a 3-bit element register select, a read/write signal, a strobe, a clock, a Run/Halt signal and Reset (16 signals total).

An Element Array

Figure 2 provides a high-level block diagram of the array of elements and the programmatic and control functional elements. This may be modified in future implementations to provide additional control and monitoring functions. The element array is structured as a 2-dimensional array that is k elements wide by j elements high. Each element connects to eight of its nearest neighbor elements (directly above, below, to the right and left, and diagonal), except for elements on the edge of the array, which have a limited number of connections. Some of the edge elements are used as inputs/outputs to external signals and devices. We have also placed static "pass-thru" elements throughout the array. These pass-thru elements provide a static connection between corresponding horizontally, vertically and diagonally connected ports. The pass-thru element provides additional flexibility to the network configuration software, allowing it to avoid creating chains of connected elements that block access to other parts of the array.

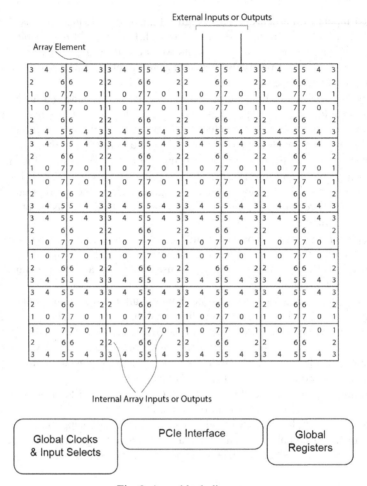

Fig. 2. Array block diagram

The FPGA connects to a PCIe interface that is used for external programming and adaptive "learning" algorithms that monitor and control the configuration and characteristics of the network. Each element must sample all eight of its input ports within a network cycle. This is accomplished using a global input select function. A 63-bit linear-feedback shift register (LFSR) is used with a loadable 3-bit counter to generate random starting address sequences for the input selects which guarantee that the first element selected during each network cycle is randomly chosen with roughly uniform probability. All eight element-inputs are sequentially sampled beginning with the randomly chosen one within a single network cycle. Randomization of input sampling is important to prevent the domination by one input of the behavior of a neuron.

A key design feature of the element array is the numbering scheme used for the I/O ports. Connected I/O ports on adjacent network elements must have the same port number to facilitate implementation of the synapse's LTD/LTP function. The element I/O port number scheme used is shown in Figure 2.

Results

The Xilinx Vivado™ Design Suite was used for the design, implementation, simulation and layout of the DANNA element array. VHDL was used as the description language for all designed components. We targeted the Virtex-7 series of Xilinx FPGAs. The main logic resource used on the Xilinx 7-series FPGAs is the "configuration logic block" or CLB. Each CLB contains two Slices, which each have four 6-input "look-up tables" (LUTs), eight flip-flops and arithmetic carry logic. There is also logic to implement wide multiplexers and long shift registers.

The element implementation required 84 LUTs and 64 flip-flops. We were able to fit the element in a tightly arranged 28 Slices or 14 CLBs using the Vivado floor planning and placement tools. Note that none of the on-chip DSPs or Distributed Ram Blocks was used in the element design.

Our element simulations verified full functionality for both neuron and synapse modes. Our target clock rate for the network was 1MHz and 8MHz for the element (sample rate for the inputs). Further timing simulations showed we could clock the network at 8MHz and the element at 64MHz. We believe we can achieve a 10MHz network clock and 80MHz element clock rate. The higher clock rates are important because evolutionary optimization (EO) is typically used to design a DANNA for a specific implementation. EO requires the configuration of multiple DANNAs, simulation or execution of them against the application (for example, for signal detection or classification, or to control a (possibly simulated) physical object's behavior, and the limiting factor in the optimization is usually execution and evaluation of the performance of individual DANNAs. Higher clock rates translate directly to more rapid convergence of the EO design steps.

The global functions were implemented and tested using the same design tools and simulation models as the element. This included the Clocks, Input Select, PCIe, programming interface, and programmable registers for network control and LTD/LTP refractory period. The PCIe and programming interface took the most logic to implement. By reducing the PCIe interface to a single lane (1x) this significantly reduced the logic required to interface the array to an external computer.

The final design was then configured, loaded and tested on two different Xilinx evaluation boards: the VC709 evaluation board featuring the XC7VX690T FPGA and the VC707 evaluation board featuring the XC7VX485T. The 485T FPGA has 75,900 Slices, and the 690T FPGA has 108,300 Slices. We were able to place an array of approximately 2500 elements on the 485T FPGA and approximate 3500 elements on the 690T FPGA. We believe using Xilinx's largest Virtex-7 FPGA, the XC7V2000T, we will be able to build an element array of approximately 10,000 elements. With the array sizes achieved, many solutions needing a neural network array can be supported.

Conclusion

We have developed and constructed a dynamic and adaptive neural network array (DANNA) using the neural network model proposed by Schuman/Birdwell [1,2], a programmable element design that can be configured to be a neuron or a synapse, and a 2-dimensional array structure and interface to allow neural networks to be created and dynamically modified. Synapse distance and LTP/LTD functions were also implemented. We have demonstrated the functionality, capacity and performance of this DANNA structure on Xilinx Virtex-7 FPGAs and project the maximum performance and capacity expected on Xilinx's largest FPGA. By moving the design to a custom VLSI design in the same CMOS process as the Xilinx FPGAs (28nm), we believe we can increase capacities by two orders of magnitude (1 million elements) and network clocking rates by at least one order of magnitude (100 MHz). Our next effort will be to interface the array to the physical world (sensors, actuators, imaging devices, etc.) via ADCs and DACs on its input and output elements, and configure the array to perform selected tasks (detection, classification, pattern recognition, control, and image and video processing such as edge and feature detection, classification, and tracking). This will help to evaluate and establish the effectiveness, adaptability and flexibility of the DANNA structure. We will also continue work on learning/programming schemes and tools to optimize configuring and routing of elements and their connections. It may, for example, be the case that a programmable "pass-thru" function for the element will be required to route larger network configurations. We have proven that a programmable neural network can be constructed using a simple array of elements built on an FPGA. More work is required to apply this concept to real world problems.

Acknowledgments. "This material is based upon work supported by the National Science Foundation Graduate Research Fellowship Program under Grant No. DGE-0929298. Any opinions, findings, and conclusions or recommendations expressed in this material are those of the author(s) and do not necessarily reflect the views of the National Science Foundation."

References

1. Schuman, C.D., Birdwell, J.D.: Variable structure dynamic artificial neural networks. Biologically Inspired Cognitive Architectures 6, 126–130 (2013)
2. Schuman, C.D., Birdwell, J.D.: Dynamic artificial neural networks with affective systems. PLOS One 8(11) (November 2013)
3. Hodgkin, A.L., Huxley, A.F.: Propagation of electrical signals along giant nerve fibers. Proceedings of the Royal Society of London, Series B, Biological Sciences, 177–183 (1952)
4. Rosenblatt, F.: Principles of Neurodynamics. Spartan, Washington, DC (1961)
5. Dayan, P., Abbott, I.: Theoretical Neuroscience: Computational and Mathematical Modeling of Neural Systems. The MIT Press, Cambridge (2001)
6. Trappenberg, T.P.: Fundamentals of Computational Neuroscience, 2nd edn. Oxford University Press, New York (2010)
7. Haykin, S.: Neural Networks: A Comprehensive Foundation. Macmillan College Publishing Company (1994)
8. Lau, C. (ed.): Neural Networks: Theoretical Foundations and Analysis. IEEE Press (1992)
9. Kandel, E., Schwartz, J., Jesell, T.: Principles of Neural Science, 4th edn. McGraw-Hill Medical (2000)

10. Perez-Uribe, A.: Artificial Neural Networks: Algorithms and Hardware Implementation. In: Bio-Inspired Computing Machines: Toward Novel Computational Architectures, pp. 289–316. PPUR Press (1998)
11. Leiner, B.J., Lorena, V.Q., Cesar, T.M., Lorenzo, M.V.: Hardware architecture for FPGA implementation of a neural network and its application in images processing. In: Proceedings of the 5th Meeting of the Electronics, Robotics and Automotive Mechanics Conference, pp. 405–410 (October 2008)
12. Saif, S., Abbas, H.M., Nassar, S.M., Wahdan, A.A.: An FPGA implementation of a neural optimization of block truncation coding for image/video compression. Microprocessors and Microsystems 31(8), 477–486 (2007)
13. Stepanova, M., Lin, F.: A Hopfield Neural Classifier and its FPGA implementation for identification of symmetrically structured DNA Motifs. In: Proceedings of the International Joint Conference on Neural Networks, Orlando, FL (August 2007)
14. Moradi, S., Imam, N., Manohar, R., Indiveri, G.: A memory-efficient routing method for large-scale spiking neural networks. In: 2013 European Conference on Circuit Theory and Design (ECCTD), pp. 1–4 (September 2013)
15. Vogelstein, R., Mallik, U., Vogelstein, J., Cauwenberghs, G.: Dynamically recongifurable silicon array of spiking neurons with conductance-based synapses. IEEE Transactionas of Neural Networks 18(1), 253 (2007)
16. Indiveri, B., Chicca, E., Douglas, R.: A VLSI reconfigurable network of integrate-and-fire neurons with spike-based learning synapses. In: ESAN 2004, pp. 405–410 (2004)
17. Graas, E., Brown, E., Lee, R.: An FPGA-based approach to high-speed simulation of conductance-based neuron models. NeuroInformatics 2(4), 417–435 (2004)
18. Pearson, M., Gilhespy, I., Gurney, K., Melhuish, C., Mitchinson, B., Nibouche, M., Pipe, A.: A real-time, FPGA based, biologically plausible neural network processor. In: Duch, W., Kacprzyk, J., Oja, E., Zadrożny, S. (eds.) ICANN 2005. LNCS, vol. 3697, pp. 1021–1026. Springer, Heidelberg (2005)
19. Cassidy, A., Denham, S., Kanold, P., Andreou, A.: FPGA based silicon spiking neural array. In: Proceedings of the Biomedical Circuits and Systems Conference, Montreal, Que, pp. 75–78 (2007)

Producibility in Hierarchical Self-assembly

David Doty*

California Institute of Technology, Pasadena, CA, USA
ddoty@caltech.edu

Abstract. Three results are shown on producibility in the hierarchical model of tile self-assembly. It is shown that a simple greedy polynomial-time strategy decides whether an assembly α is producible. The algorithm can be optimized to use $O(|\alpha| \log^2 |\alpha|)$ time. Cannon, Demaine, Demaine, Eisenstat, Patitz, Schweller, Summers, and Winslow [4] showed that the problem of deciding if an assembly α is the unique producible terminal assembly of a tile system $\mathcal{T}$ can be solved in $O(|\alpha|^2|\mathcal{T}|+|\alpha||\mathcal{T}|^2)$ time for the special case of noncooperative "temperature 1" systems. It is shown that this can be improved to $O(|\alpha||\mathcal{T}| \log |\mathcal{T}|)$ time. Finally, it is shown that if two assemblies are producible, and if they can be overlapped consistently – i.e., if the positions that they share have the same tile type in each assembly – then their union is also producible.

1 Introduction

1.1 Background of the Field

Winfree's abstract Tile Assembly Model (aTAM) [16] is a model of crystal growth through cooperative binding of square-like monomers called *tiles*, implemented experimentally (for the current time) by DNA [3,18]. In particular, it models the potentially algorithmic capabilities of tiles that can be designed to bind if and only if the total strength of attachment (summed over all binding sites, called *glues* on the tile) is at least a parameter τ, sometimes called the *temperature*. In particular, when the glue strengths are integers and $\tau = 2$, this implies that two strength 1 glues must cooperate to bind the tile to a growing assembly. Two assumptions are key: 1) growth starts from a single specially designated *seed* tile type, and 2) only individual tiles bind to an assembly, never larger assemblies consisting of more than one tile type. We will refer to this model as the *seeded aTAM*. While violations of these assumptions are often viewed as errors in implementation of the seeded aTAM [14,15], relaxing them results in a different model with its own programmable abilities. In the *hierarchical* (a.k.a. *multiple tile* [2], *polyomino* [12,17], *two-handed* [4,7,10]) *aTAM*, there is no seed tile, and an assembly is considered producible so long as two producible assemblies are able to attach to each other with strength at least τ, with all

---
* The author was supported by NSF grants CCF-1219274 and CCF-1162589 and the Molecular Programming Project under NSF grants 0832824 and 1317694 and by a Computing Innovation Fellowship under NSF grant 1019343.

O.H. Ibarra et al. (Eds.): UCNC 2014, LNCS 8553, pp. 142–154, 2014.
DOI: 10.1007/978-3-319-08123-6_12, © Springer International Publishing Switzerland 2014

individual tiles being considered as "base case" producible assemblies. In either model, an assembly is considered *terminal* if nothing can attach to it; viewing self-assembly as a computation, terminal assembly(ies) are often interpreted to be the output. See [8,13] for an introduction to recent work in these models.

The hierarchical aTAM has attracted considerable recent attention. It is coNP-complete to decide whether an assembly is the unique terminal assembly produced by a hierarchical tile system [4]. There are infinite shapes that can be assembled in the hierarchical aTAM but not the seeded aTAM, and vice versa, and there are finite shapes requiring strictly more tile types to assemble in the seeded aTAM than the hierarchical aTAM, and vice versa [4]. Despite this incomparability between the models for exact assembly of shapes, with a small blowup in scale, any seeded tile system can be simulated by a hierarchical tile system [4], improving upon an earlier scheme that worked for restricted classes of seeded tile systems [12]. However, the hierarchical aTAM is not able to simulate itself from a single set of tile types, i.e., it is not *intrinsically universal* [7], unlike the seeded aTAM [9]. It is possible to assemble an $n \times n$ square in a hierarchical tile system with $O(\log n)$ tile types that exhibits a very strong form of fault-tolerance in the face of spurious growth via strength 1 bonds [10]. The parallelism of the hierarchical aTAM suggests the possibility that it can assemble shapes faster than the seeded aTAM, but it cannot for a wide class of tile systems [5].

1.2   Contributions of This Paper

We show three results on producibility in the hierarchical aTAM.

1. In the seeded aTAM, there is an obvious linear-time algorithm to test whether assembly α is producible by a tile system: starting from the seed, try to attach tiles until α is complete or no more attachments are possible. We show that in the hierarchical aTAM, a similar greedy strategy correctly identifies whether a given assembly is producible, though it is more involved to prove that it is correct. The idea is to start with all tiles in place as they appear in α, but with no bonds, and then to greedily bind attachable assemblies until α is assembled. It is not obvious that this works, since it is conceivable that assemblies must attach in a certain order for α to form, but the greedy strategy may pick another order and hit a dead-end in which no assemblies can attach. The algorithm can be optimized to use $O(|\alpha| \log^2 |\alpha|)$ time. This is shown in Section 3.

2. The temperature 1 Unique Production Verification (UPV) problem studied by Cannon, Demaine, Demaine, Eisenstat, Patitz, Schweller, Summers, and Winslow [4] is the problem of determining whether assembly α is the unique producible terminal assembly of tile system $\mathcal{T}$, where $\mathcal{T}$ has temperature 1, meaning that all positive strength glues are sufficiently strong to attach any two assemblies. They give an algorithm that runs in $O(|\alpha|^2|\mathcal{T}| + |\alpha||\mathcal{T}|^2)$ time. Cannon et al. proved their result by using an $O(|\alpha|^2 + |\alpha||\mathcal{T}|)$ time algorithm for UPV that works in the seeded aTAM [1], and then reduced the

hierarchical temperature-1 UPV problem to $|\mathcal{T}|$ instances of the seeded UPV problem. We improve this result by showing that a faster $O(|\alpha| \log |\mathcal{T}|)$ time algorithm for the seeded UPV problem exists for the special case of temperature 1, and then we apply the technique of Cannon et al. relating the hierarchical problem to the seeded problem to improve the running time of the hierarchical algorithm to $O(|\alpha||\mathcal{T}| \log |\mathcal{T}|)$. This is shown in Section 4. Part of the conceptual significance of this algorithm lies in the details of the proof. In particular, we show a relationship between deterministic seeded assembly at temperature 1 and biconnected decomposition of the binding graph of an assembly using the Hopcroft-Tarjan algorithm [11]. This relationship makes more precise the intuitive notion that determinism in temperature 1 systems with glue mismatches is enforced by "blocking." In particular, the tile that does the blocking must be a cut vertex of the binding graph and must be an ancestor of the blocked tile in the Hopcroft-Tarjan tree decomposition.

3. We show that if two assemblies α and β are producible in the hierarchical model, and if they can be overlapped consistently (i.e., if the positions that they share have the same tile type in each assembly), then their union $\alpha \cup \beta$ is producible. This is trivially true in the seeded model, but it requires more care to prove in the hierarchical model. It is conceivable *a priori* that although β is producible, β must assemble $\alpha \cap \beta$ in some order that is inconsistent with how α assembles $\alpha \cap \beta$. This is shown in Section 5.

This result is most interesting for the open question it raises: what happens if a tile system produces an assembly that overlaps consistently with a translation of *itself*? We conjecture, via a "pumping" argument, that this results in infinite producible assemblies, which would resolve an open question on lower bounds on the assembly time of hierarchical systems [5].

2   Informal Definition of the Abstract Tile Assembly Model

We give an informal sketch of the seeded and hierarchical variants of the abstract Tile Assembly Model (aTAM).

A *tile type* is a unit square with four sides, each consisting of a *glue label* (often represented as a finite string) and a nonnegative integer *strength*. We assume a finite set T of tile types, but an infinite number of copies of each tile type, each copy referred to as a *tile*. If a glue has strength 0, we say it is *null*, and if a positive-strength glue facing some direction does not appear on some tile type in the opposite direction, we say it is *functionally null*. We assume that all tile sets in this paper contain no functionally null glues. An *assembly* is a positioning of tiles on the integer lattice $\mathbb{Z}^2$; i.e., a partial function $\alpha : \mathbb{Z}^2 \dashrightarrow T$. We write $|\alpha|$ to denote $|\text{dom } \alpha|$. Write $\alpha \sqsubseteq \beta$ to denote that α is a *subassembly* of β, which means that dom $\alpha \subseteq$ dom β and $\alpha(p) = \beta(p)$ for all points $p \in$ dom α. In this case, say that β is a *superassembly* of α. We abuse notation and take a tile type t to be equivalent to the single-tile assembly containing only t (at the origin if not otherwise specified). Two adjacent tiles in an assembly *interact* if the glue labels on their abutting sides are equal and have positive strength. Each assembly induces a *binding graph*, a grid graph whose vertices are tiles, with an edge between two tiles if they interact. The assembly is τ-*stable* if every cut of its binding graph has strength at least τ, where the weight of an edge is the strength of the glue it represents.

A *seeded tile assembly system* (seeded TAS) is a triple $\mathcal{T} = (T, \sigma, \tau)$, where T is a finite set of tile types, $\sigma : \mathbb{Z}^2 \dashrightarrow T$ is a finite, τ-stable *seed assembly*, and τ is the *temperature*. If $\mathcal{T}$ has a single seed tile $s \in T$ (i.e., $\sigma(0, 0) = s$ for some $s \in T$ and is undefined elsewhere), then we write $\mathcal{T} = (T, s, \tau)$. Let $|\mathcal{T}|$ denote $|T|$. An assembly α is *producible* if either $\alpha = \sigma$ or if β is a producible assembly and α can be obtained from β by the stable binding of a single tile. In this case write $\beta \rightarrow_1 \alpha$ (α is producible from β by the attachment of one tile), and write $\beta \rightarrow \alpha$ if $\beta \rightarrow_1^* \alpha$ (α is producible from β by the attachment of zero or more tiles). An assembly is *terminal* if no tile can be τ-stably attached to it.

A *hierarchical tile assembly system* (hierarchical TAS) is a pair $\mathcal{T} = (T, \tau)$, where T is a finite set of tile types and $\tau \in \mathbb{N}$ is the temperature. An assembly is *producible* if either it is a single tile from T, or it is the τ-stable result of translating two producible assemblies without overlap. Therefore, if an assembly α is producible, then it is produced via an *assembly tree*, a full binary tree whose root is labeled with α, whose $|\alpha|$ leaves are labeled with tile types, and each internal node is a producible assembly formed by the stable attachment of its two child assemblies. An assembly α is *terminal* if for every producible assembly β, α and β cannot be τ-stably attached. If α can grow into β by the attachment of zero or more assemblies, then we write $\alpha \rightarrow \beta$.

Our definitions imply only finite assemblies are producible. In either model, let $\mathcal{A}[\mathcal{T}]$ be the set of producible assemblies of $\mathcal{T}$, and let $\mathcal{A}_\square[\mathcal{T}] \subseteq \mathcal{A}[\mathcal{T}]$ be the set of producible, terminal assemblies of $\mathcal{T}$. A TAS $\mathcal{T}$ is *directed* (a.k.a., *deterministic, confluent*) if $|\mathcal{A}_\square[\mathcal{T}]| = 1$. If $\mathcal{T}$ is directed with unique producible terminal assembly α, we say that $\mathcal{T}$ *uniquely produces* α.

3   Efficient Verification of Production

Let S be a finite set. A *partition* of S is a collection $\mathcal{C} = \{C_1, \ldots, C_k\} \subseteq \mathcal{P}(S)$ such that $\bigcup_{i=1}^{k} C_i = S$ and for all $i \neq j$, $C_i \cap C_j = \varnothing$. A *hierarchical division* of S is a full binary tree Υ (a tree in which every internal node has exactly two children) whose nodes represent subsets of S, such that the root of Υ represents S, the $|S|$ leaves of Υ represent the singleton sets $\{x\}$ for each $x \in S$, and each internal node has the property that its set is the (disjoint) union of its two childrens' sets. The following lemma is proven in the full version of this paper.

Lemma 3.1. *Let S be a finite set with $|S| \geq 2$. Let Υ be any hierarchical division of S, and let $\mathcal{C}$ be any partition of S other than $\{S\}$. Then there exist $C_1, C_2 \in \mathcal{C}$ with $C_1 \neq C_2$, and there exist $C_1' \subseteq C_1$ and $C_2' \subseteq C_2$, such that C_1' and C_2' are siblings in Υ.*

Lemma 3.1 will be useful when we view Υ as an assembly tree for some producible assembly α, and we view $\mathcal{C}$ as a partially completed attempt to construct another assembly tree for α, where each element of $\mathcal{C}$ is a subassembly that has been produced so far.

When we say "by monotonicity", this refers to the fact that glue strengths are nonnegative, which implies that if two assemblies α and β can attach, the addition of more tiles to either α or β cannot *prevent* this binding, so long as the additional tiles do not overlap the other assembly.

We want to solve the following problem: given an assembly α and temperature τ, is α producible in the hierarchical aTAM at temperature τ?[1] The algorithm IS-PRODUCIBLE-ASSEMBLY (Algorithm 1) solves this problem.

Algorithm 1. IS-PRODUCIBLE-ASSEMBLY(α, τ)

---

1. **input:** assembly α and temperature τ
2. $\mathcal{C} \leftarrow \{ \{v\} \mid v \in \text{dom } \alpha \}$ // *(positions defining) subassemblies of α*
3. **while** $|\mathcal{C}| > 1$ **do**
4.   **if** there exist $C_i, C_j \in \mathcal{C}$ with glues between C_i and C_j of total strength at least τ **then**
5. $\mathcal{C} \leftarrow (\mathcal{C} \setminus \{C_i, C_j\}) \cup \{C_i \cup C_j\}$
6.   **else**
7.   **print** "α is not producible" and **exit**
8.   **end if**
9. **end while**
10. **print** "α is producible"

Theorem 3.1. *There is an $O(|\alpha| \log^2 |\alpha|)$ time algorithm deciding whether an assembly α is producible at temperature τ in the hierarchical aTAM.*

Proof. **Correctness:** IS-PRODUCIBLE-ASSEMBLY works by building up the initially edge-free graph with the tiles of α as its nodes (the algorithm stores the nodes as points in $\mathbb{Z}^2$, but α would be used in step 4 to get the glues and strengths between tiles at adjacent positions), stopping when the graph becomes connected. The order in which connected components (implicitly representing assemblies) are removed from and added to $\mathcal{C}$ implicitly defines a particular assembly tree with α at the root (for every C_1, C_2 processed in line 5, the assembly $\alpha \upharpoonright (C_1 \cup C_2)$ is a parent of $\alpha \upharpoonright C_1$ and $\alpha \upharpoonright C_2$ in the assembly tree). Therefore, if the algorithm reports that α is producible, then it is. Conversely, suppose that α is producible via assembly tree Υ. Let $\mathcal{C} = \{C_1, \dots, C_k\}$ be the set of assemblies at some iteration of the loop at line 3. It suffices to show that some pair of assemblies C_i and C_j are connected by glues with strength at least τ. By Lemma 3.1, there exist C_i and C_j with subsets $C_i' \subseteq C_i$ and $C_j' \subseteq C_j$ such that C_i' and C_j' are sibling nodes in Υ. Because they are siblings, the glues between

---

[1] We do not need to give the tile set T as input because the tiles in α implicitly define a tile set, and the presence of extra tile types in T that do not appear in α cannot affect its producibility.

C_i' and C_j' have strength at least τ. By monotonicity these glues suffice to bind C_i to C_j, so IS-PRODUCIBLE-ASSEMBLY is correct.

Running Time: Let $n = |\alpha|$. The running time of the IS-PRODUCIBLE-ASSEMBLY (Algorithm 1) is polynomial in n, but the algorithm can be optimized to improve the running time to $O(n \log^2 n)$ by careful choice of data structures. IS-PRODUCIBLE-ASSEMBLY-FAST (Algorithm 2) shows pseudo-code for this optimized implementation, which we now describe. Let $n = |\alpha|$. Instead of searching over all pairs of assemblies, only search those pairs of assemblies that are adjacent. This number is $O(n)$ since a grid graph has degree at most 4 (hence $O(n)$ edges) and the number of edges in the full grid graph of α is an upper bound on the number of adjacent assemblies at any time. This can be encoded in a dynamically changing graph G_c whose nodes are the current set of assemblies and whose edges connect those assemblies that are adjacent.

Each edge of G_c stores the total glue strength between the assemblies. Whenever two assemblies C_1 and C_2, with $|C_1| \geq |C_2|$ without loss of generality, are combined to form a new assembly, G_c is updated by removing C_2, merging its edges with those of C_1, and for any edges they already share (i.e., the neighbor on the other end of the edge is the same), summing the strengths on the edges. Each update of an edge (adding it to C_1, or finding it in C_1 to update its strength) can be done in $O(\log n)$ time using a tree set data structure to store neighbors for each assembly.

We claim that the total number of such updates of all edges is $O(n \log n)$ over all time, or amortized $O(\log n)$ updates per iteration of the outer loop. To see why, observe that the number of edges an assembly has is at most linear in its size, so the number of new edges that must be added to C_1, or existing edges in C_1 whose strengths must be updated, is at most (within a constant) the size of the smaller component C_2. The total number of edge updates is then, if Υ is the assembly tree discovered by the algorithm, $\sum_{\text{nodes } u \in \Upsilon} \min\{|\text{left}(u)|, |\text{right}(u)|\}$, where $|\text{left}(u)|$ and $|\text{right}(u)|$ respectively refer to the number of leaves of u's left and right subtrees. For a given number n of leaves, this sum is maximized with a balanced tree, and in that case (summing over all levels of the tree) is $\sum_{i=0}^{\log n} 2^i(n/2^i) = O(n \log n)$. So the total time to update all edges is $O(n \log^2 n)$.

As for actually finding C_1 and C_2, each iteration of the outer loop, we can look at *any* pair of adjacent assemblies with sufficient connection strength. So in addition to storing the edges in a tree-backed set data structure, store them also in one of two linked lists: H and L in the algorithm, for "high" (strength $\geq \tau$) and "low" (strength $< \tau$), with each edge storing a pointer to its node in the linked list for $O(1)$ time removal (and also to its node in the tree-backed set for $O(\log n)$ time removal). We can simply choose an arbitrary edge from H to be the next pair of connected components to attach. We update the keys containing C_1 whose connection strength changed and removing those containing C_2 but not C_1. The edges whose connection strength changed correspond to precisely those neighbors that C_1 and C_2 shared before being merged. Therefore $|C_2|$ is an upper bound on the number of edge updates required. Thus the amortized number of linked list updates is $O(\log n)$ per iteration of the outer loop by the same argument as above. Since we can have each edge $\{C_1, C_2\}$ store a pointer to its node in the linked list to which it belongs, each list update can be done in $O(1)$ time. Thus each iteration takes amortized time $O(\log n)$.

Algorithm 2. Is-Producible-Assembly-Fast(α, τ)

---

1. **input:** assembly α and temperature τ
2. $V_c \leftarrow \{\ \{v\}\ |\ v \in \mathrm{dom}\ \alpha\ \}$ // *(positions defining) subassemblies of α*
3. $E_c \leftarrow \{\{\{u\}, \{v\}\}\ |\ \{u\} \in V_c$ and $\{v\} \in V_c$ and u and v interact$\}$
4. $H \leftarrow$ empty linked list   // *pairs of subassemblies binding with strength $\geq \tau$*
5. $L \leftarrow$ empty linked list   // *pairs of subassemblies binding with strength $< \tau$*
6. **for all** $\{\{u\}, \{v\}\} \in E_c$ **do**
7. $w(\{u\}, \{v\}) \leftarrow$ strength of glue binding $\alpha(u)$ and $\alpha(v)$
8.   append $\{\{u\}, \{v\}\}$ to L if $w(\{u\}, \{v\}) < \tau$, and append to H otherwise
9. **end for**
10. **while** $|V_c| > 1$ **do**
11.   **if** H is empty **then**
12.   **print** "α is not producible" and **exit**
13.   **end if**
14. $\{C_1, C_2\} \leftarrow$ first element of H // *assume $|C_1| \geq |C_2|$ W.L.O.G.*
15.   remove $\{C_1, C_2\}$ from H
16.   remove C_2 from V_c
17.   **for all** neighbors C of C_2 **do**
18.   remove $\{C_2, C\}$ from E_c and H or L
19.   **if** $\{C_1, C\} \in E_c$ **then**
20. $w(C_1, C) \leftarrow w(C_1, C) + w(C_2, C)$
21.   **if** $w(C_1, C) \geq \tau$ and $\{C_1, C\} \in L$ **then**
22.   remove $\{C_1, C\}$ from L and add it to H
23.   **end if**
24.   **else**
25. $w(C_1, C) \leftarrow w(C_2, C)$
26.   add $\{C_1, C\}$ to E_c and to H if $w(C_1, C) \geq \tau$ and to L otherwise
27.   **end if**
28.   **end for**
29. **end while**
30. **print** "α is producible"

The algorithm Is-Producible-Assembly-Fast (Algorithm 2) implements this optimized idea. The terminology for data structure operations is taken from [6]. Note that the way we remove C_1 and C_2 and add their union is to simply delete C_2 and then update C_1 to contain C_2's edges. The graph G_c discussed above is $G_c = (V_c, E_c)$ where V_c and E_c are variables in Is-Producible-Assembly-Fast.

Summarizing the analysis, each data structure operation takes time $O(\log n)$ with appropriate choice of a backing data structure. The two outer loops (lines 6 and 10) take $O(n)$ iterations. The inner loop (line 17) runs for amortized $O(\log n)$ iterations, and its body executes a constant number of $O(\log n)$ and $O(1)$ time operations. Therefore the total running time is $O(n \log^2 n)$.   □

4 Efficient Verification of Temperature 1 Unique Production

This section shows that there is an algorithm, faster than the previous known algorithm [4], that solves the temperature 1 *unique producibility verification* (UPV) problem: given an assembly α and a temperature-1 hierarchical tile system $\mathcal{T}$, decide if α is the unique producible, terminal assembly of $\mathcal{T}$. This is done by showing an algorithm for the temperature 1 UPV problem in the seeded model (which is faster than the general-temperature algorithm of [1]), and then applying the technique of [4] relating producibility and terminality in the temperature 1 seeded and hierarchical models.

Let the decision problems sUPV$_1$ and hUPV$_1$ be represented by the language $\{(\mathcal{T}, \alpha) | \mathcal{A}_\square[\mathcal{T}] = \{\alpha\}\}$, where $\mathcal{T}$ is a temperature 1 seeded TAS in the former case and a temperature 1 hierarchical TAS in the latter case. To simplify the time analysis we assume $|\mathcal{T}| = O(|\alpha|)$. The following is the only result in this paper on the seeded aTAM.

Theorem 4.1. *There is an algorithm that solves the* sUPV$_1$ *problem in time* $O(|\alpha| \log |\mathcal{T}|)$.

Proof. Let $\mathcal{T} = (T, s, 1)$ and α be a instance of the sUPV$_1$ problem. We first check that every tile in α appears in T, which can be done in time $O(|\alpha| \log |T|)$ by storing elements of T in a data structure supporting $O(\log n)$ time access. In the seeded aTAM at temperature 1, α is producible if and only if it contains the seed s and its binding graph is connected, which can be checked in time $O(|\alpha|)$. We must also verify that α is terminal, which is true if and only if all glues on unbound sides are null, checkable in time $O(|\alpha|)$.

Once we have verified that α is producible and terminal, it remains to verify that $\mathcal{T}$ uniquely produces α. Adleman, Cheng, Goel, Huang, Kempe, Moisset de Espanés, and Rothemund [1] showed that this is true (at any temperature) if and only if, for every position $p \in \text{dom } \alpha$, if $\alpha_p \sqsubset \alpha$ is the maximal producible subassembly of α such that $p \notin \text{dom } \alpha_p$, then $\alpha(p)$ is the only tile type attachable to α_p at position p. They solve the problem by producing each such α_p and checking whether there is more than one tile type attachable to α_p at p. We use a similar approach, but we avoid the cost of producing each α_p by exploiting special properties of temperature 1 producibility.

Given $p, q \in \text{dom } \alpha$ such that $p \neq q$, write $p \prec q$ if, for every producible assembly β, $q \in \text{dom } \beta \implies p \in \text{dom } \beta$, i.e., the tile at position p must be present before the tile at position q can be attached. We must check each $p \in \text{dom } \alpha$ and each position $q \in \text{dom } \alpha$ adjacent to p such that $p \not\prec q$ to see whether a tile type $t \neq \alpha(p)$ shares a positive-strength glue with $\alpha(q)$ in direction $q - p$ (i.e., whether, if $\alpha(p)$ were not present, t could attach at p instead). If we know which positions q adjacent to p satisfy $p \not\prec q$, this check can be done in time $O(\log |T|)$ with appropriate choice of data structure, implying total time $O(|\alpha| \log |T|)$ over all positions $p \in \text{dom } \alpha$. It remains to show how to determine which adjacent positions $p, q \in \text{dom } \alpha$ satisfy $p \prec q$.

Recall that a *cut vertex* of a connected graph is a vertex whose removal disconnects the graph, and a subgraph is *biconnected* if the removal of any single vertex from the subgraph leaves it connected. Every graph can be decomposed into a tree of biconnected components, with cut vertices connecting different biconnected components (and belonging to all biconnected components that they connect). If p is not a cut vertex of the binding graph of α, then dom α_p is simply dom $\alpha \setminus \{p\}$ (i.e., it is possible to produce the entire assembly α except for position p) because, for all $q \in$ dom $\alpha \setminus \{p\}$, $p \not\prec q$. If p is a cut vertex, then $p \prec q$ if and only if removing p from the binding graph of α places q and the seed position in two different connected components, since the connected component containing the seed after removing p corresponds precisely to α_p.

Run the linear time Hopcroft-Tarjan algorithm [11] for decomposing the binding graph of α into a tree of its biconnected components, which also identifies which vertices in the graph are cut vertices and which biconnected components they connect. Recall that the Hopcroft-Tarjan algorithm is an augmented depth-first search. Root the tree with s's biconnected component (i.e., start the depth-first search there), so that each component has a parent component and child components. In particular, each cut vertex p has a "parent" biconnected component and $k \geq 1$ "child" biconnected components. Removing p will separate the graph into $k + 1$ connected components: the k subtrees and the remaining nodes connected to the parent biconnected component of p. Thus $p \prec q$ if and only if p is a cut vertex and q is contained in the subtree rooted at p.

This check can be done for all positions p and their ≤ 4 adjacent positions q in linear time by "weaving" the checks into the Hopcroft-Tarjan algorithm. As the depth-first search executes, each vertex p is marked as either *unvisited, visiting* (meaning the search is currently in a subtree rooted at p), or *visited* (meaning the search has visited and exited the subtree rooted at p). If p is marked as visited or unvisited when q is processed, then q is not in the subtree under p. If p is marked as visiting when q is processed, then q is in p's subtree.

At the time q is visited during the Hopcroft-Tarjan algorithm, it may not yet be known whether p is a cut vertex. To account for this, simply run the Hopcroft-Tarjan algorithm first to label all cut vertices, then run a second depth-first search (visiting the nodes in the same order as the first depth-first search), doing the checks described previously and using the cut vertex information obtained from the Hopcroft-Tarjan algorithm.   □

Theorem 4.2. *There is an algorithm that solves the* hUPV$_1$ *problem in time* $O(|\alpha||\mathcal{T}| \log |\mathcal{T}|)$.

Proof. Cannon, Demaine, Demaine, Eisenstat, Patitz, Schweller, Summers, and Winslow [4] showed that a temperature 1 hierarchical TAS $\mathcal{T} = (T, 1)$ uniquely produces α if and only if, for each $s \in T$, the seeded TAS $\mathcal{T}_s = (T, s, 1)$ uniquely produces α. Therefore, the hUPV$_1$ problem can be solved by calling the algorithm of Theorem 4.1 $|\mathcal{T}|$ times, resulting in a running time of $O(|\alpha||\mathcal{T}| \log |\mathcal{T}|)$.   □

5   Consistent Unions of Producible Assemblies Are Producible

Throughout this section, fix a hierarchical TAS $\mathcal{T} = (T, \tau)$. Let α, β be assemblies. We say α and β are *consistent* if $\alpha(p) = \beta(p)$ for all points $p \in \operatorname{dom} \alpha \cap \operatorname{dom} \beta$. If α and β are consistent, let $\alpha \cup \beta$ be defined as the assembly $(\alpha \cup \beta)(p) = \alpha(p)$ if α is defined, and $(\alpha \cup \beta)(p) = \beta(p)$ if $\alpha(p)$ is undefined. If α and β are not consistent, let $\alpha \cup \beta$ be undefined.

Theorem 5.1. *If α, β are producible assemblies that are consistent and* $\operatorname{dom} \alpha \cap \operatorname{dom} \beta \neq \varnothing$, *then $\alpha \cup \beta$ is producible. Furthermore, $\alpha \to \alpha \cup \beta$, i.e., it is possible to assemble exactly α, then to assemble the missing portions of β.*

Proof. If α and β are consistent and have non-empty overlap, then $\alpha \cup \beta$ is necessarily stable, since every cut of $\alpha \cup \beta$ is a superset of some cut of either α or β, which are themselves stable.

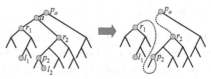

(a) First operation to combine the assembly trees for α and β. l_1 and l_2 are two leaves representing the same position in $\operatorname{dom} \alpha \cap \operatorname{dom} \beta$.

(b) Operation to eliminate one of two leaves l_1 and l_2 representing the same tile in the tree while preserving that all attachments are stable.

Fig. 1. Constructing assembly tree for $\alpha \cup \beta$ from assembly trees for α and β

Let Υ_α and Υ_β be assembly trees for α and β, respectively. Define an assembly tree Υ for $\alpha \cup \beta$ by the following construction. Let l_1 be a leaf in Υ_α and let l_2 be a leaf in Υ_β representing the same position $x \in \operatorname{dom} \alpha \cap \operatorname{dom} \beta$, as shown in Figure 1(a). Remove l_2 and replace it with the entire tree Υ_α. Call the resulting tree Υ'. At this point, Υ' is not an assembly tree if α and β overlapped on more than one point, because every position in $\operatorname{dom} \alpha \cap \operatorname{dom} \beta \setminus \{x\}$ has duplicated leaves. Therefore the tree Υ' is not a hierarchical division of the set $\operatorname{dom} \alpha \cup \operatorname{dom} \beta$, since not all unions represented by each internal node are disjoint unions. However, each node does represent a stable assembly that is the union of the (possibly overlapping) assemblies represented by its two child nodes. We will show how to modify Υ' to eliminate each of these duplicates – at which point all unions represented by internal nodes will again be disjoint – while maintaining the invariant that each internal node represents a stable assembly, proving there is an assembly tree Υ for $\alpha \cup \beta$. Furthermore, the subtree Υ_α that was placed under p_2 will not change as a result of these modifications, which implies $\alpha \to \alpha \cup \beta$.

The process to eliminate one pair of duplicate leaves is shown in Figure 1(b). Let l_1 and l_2 be two leaves representing the same point in $\operatorname{dom} \alpha \cap \operatorname{dom} \beta$, and let a be their least common ancestor in Υ, noting that a is not contained in Υ_α since l_2 is not contained in Υ_α. Let p_a be the parent of a. Let r_1 be the root of the subtree under a containing l_1. Let r_2 be the root of the subtree under a containing l_2. Let p_2 be the parent of l_2. Remove the leaf l_2 and the node a. Set the parent of r_1 to be p_2. Set the parent of r_2 to be p_a.

Since we have replaced the leaf l_2 with a subtree containing the leaf l_1, the subtree rooted at r_1 is an assembly containing the tile represented by l_2, in the same position. Since the original attachment of l_2 to its sibling was stable, by monotonicity, the attachment represented by p_2 is still legal. The removal of a is simply to maintain that Υ is a full binary tree; leaving it would mean that it represents a superfluous "attachment" of the assembly r_2 to $\varnothing$. However, it is now legal for r_2 to be a direct child of p_a, since r_2 (due to the insertion of the entire r_1 subtree beneath a descendant of r_2, again by monotonicity) now has all the tiles necessary for its attachment to the old sibling of a to be stable. Since a was not contained in Υ_α, the subtree Υ_α has not been altered.

This process is iterated for all duplicate leaves. When all duplicates have been removed, Υ is a valid assembly tree with root $\alpha \cup \beta$. Since Υ contains Υ_α as a subtree, $\alpha \to \alpha \cup \beta$. □

It is worthwhile to observe that Theorem 5.1 does not immediately follow from Theorem 3.1. Theorem 3.1 implies that *if $\alpha \cup \beta$ is producible*, then this can be verified simply by attaching subassemblies until $\alpha \cup \beta$ is produced. Furthermore, since the hypothesis of Theorem 5.1 implies that α is producible, the greedy algorithm of Theorem 3.1 could potentially assemble α along the way to assembling $\alpha \cup \beta$, which implies that *if $\alpha \cup \beta$ is producible*, then it is producible from α. However, nothing in Theorem 3.1 guarantees that $\alpha \cup \beta$ is producible in the first place. There may be some additional details that could be added to the proof of Theorem 3.1 that would cause it to imply Theorem 5.1, but those details are likely to resemble the existing proof of Theorem 5.1, and it is conceptually cleaner to keep the two proofs separate.

6   Open Question

Theorem 5.1 shows that if assemblies α and β overlap consistently, then $\alpha \cup \beta$ is producible. What if $\alpha = \beta$? Suppose we have three copies of α, and label them each uniquely as $\alpha_1, \alpha_2, \alpha_3$. (See Figure 2 for an example.) Suppose further than α_2 overlaps consistently with α_1 when translated by some non-zero vector $\boldsymbol{v}$. Then we know that $\alpha_1 \cup \alpha_2$ is producible. Suppose that α_3 is α_2 translated by $\boldsymbol{v}$, or equivalently it is α_1 translated by $2\boldsymbol{v}$. Then $\alpha_2 \cup \alpha_3$ is producible, since this is merely a translated copy of $\alpha_1 \cup \alpha_2$. It seems intuitively that $\alpha_1 \cup \alpha_2 \cup \alpha_3$ should be producible as well. However, while α_1 overlaps consistently with α_2, and α_2 overlaps consistently with α_3, it could be the case that α_3 intersects α_1 inconsistently, i.e., they share a position but put a different tile type at that position. In this case $\alpha_1 \cup \alpha_2 \cup \alpha_3$ is undefined.

In the example of Figure 2, although $\alpha_1 \cup \alpha_2 \cup \alpha_3$ is not producible (in fact, not even defined), "enough" of α_3 (say, $\alpha_3' \sqsubseteq \alpha_3$) can grow off of $\alpha_1 \cup \alpha_2$ to

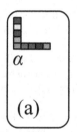 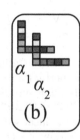 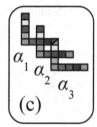 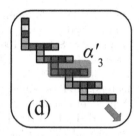

Fig. 2. (a) A producible assembly α. Gray tiles are all distinct types from each other, but red, green, and blue each represent one of three different tile types, so the two blue tiles are the same type. (b) By Theorem 5.1, $\alpha_1 \cup \alpha_2$ is producible, where $\alpha_1 = \alpha$ and $\alpha_2 = \alpha_1 + (2, -2)$, because they overlap in only one position, and they both have the blue tile type there. (c) α_1 and α_3 both have a tile at the same position, but the types are different (red in the case of α_1 and green in the case of α_3). (d) However, a subassembly α_i' of each new α_i can grow, enough to allow the translated equivalent subassembly α_{i+1}' of α_{i+1} to grow from α_i', so an infinite structure is producible.

allow a fourth copy α_4' to begin to grow to an assembly to which a fifth copy α_5' can attach, etc., so that an infinite assembly can grow by "pumping" additional copies of α_3'. Is this always possible? In other words, is it the case that if α is a producible assembly of a hierarchical TAS $\mathcal{T}$, and α overlaps consistently with some non-zero translation of itself, then $\mathcal{T}$ necessarily produces arbitrarily large assemblies? If true, this would imply that no hierarchical TAS producing such an assembly could be uniquely produce a finite assembly. This would settle an open question posed by Chen and Doty [5], who showed that as long as a hierarchical TAS does not produce assemblies that consistently overlap any translation of themselves, then the TAS cannot uniquely produce any shape in time sublinear in its diameter.

Acknowledgements. The author is very grateful to Ho-Lin Chen, David Solove-ichik, Damien Woods, Matt Patitz, Scott Summers, Robbie Schweller, Ján Maňuch, Ladislav Stacho, Andrew Winslow for many insightful discussions, and to anony-mous reviewers for their detailed and useful comments.

References

[1] Adleman, L.M., Cheng, Q., Goel, A., Huang, M.-D.A., Kempe, D., de Espanés, P.M., Rothemund, P.W.K.: Combinatorial optimization problems in self-assembly. In: Proceedings of the Thirty-Fourth Annual ACM Symposium on Theory of Computing, STOC 2002, pp. 23–32 (2002)

[2] Aggarwal, G., Cheng, Q., Goldwasser, M.H., Kao, M.-Y., de Espanés, P.M., Schweller, R.T.: Complexities for generalized models of self-assembly. SIAM Journal on Computing 34, 1493–1515 (2004); Preliminary version appeared in SODA 2004

[3] Barish, R.D., Schulman, R., Rothemund, P.W.K., Winfree, E.: An information-bearing seed for nucleating algorithmic self-assembly. Proceedings of the National Academy of Sciences 106(15), 6054–6059 (2009)

[4] Cannon, S., Demaine, E.D., Demaine, M.L., Eisenstat, S., Patitz, M.J., Schweller, R.T., Summers, S.M., Winslow, A.: Two hands are better than one (up to constant factors). In: Proceedings of the Thirtieth International Symposium on Theoretical Aspects of Computer Science, STACS 2013, pp. 172–184 (2013)

[5] Chen, H.-L., Doty, D.: Parallelism and time in hierarchical self-assembly. In: Proceedings of the 23rd Annual ACM-SIAM Symposium on Discrete Algorithms, SODA 2012, pp. 1163–1182 (2012)

[6] Thomas, H., Cormen, C.E., Leiserson, R.L.: Rivest, and Clifford Stein. In: Introduction to Algorithms. MIT Press (2001)

[7] Demaine, E.D., Patitz, M.J., Rogers, T.A., Schweller, R.T., Summers, S.M., Woods, D.: The two-handed tile assembly model is not intrinsically universal. In: Fomin, F.V., Freivalds, R., Kwiatkowska, M., Peleg, D. (eds.) ICALP 2013, Part I. LNCS, vol. 7965, pp. 400–412. Springer, Heidelberg (2013)

[8] Doty, D.: Theory of algorithmic self-assembly. Communications of the ACM 55(12), 78–88 (2012)

[9] Doty, D., Lutz, J.H., Patitz, M.J., Schweller, R.T., Summers, S.M., Woods, D.: The tile assembly model is intrinsically universal. In: Proceedings of the 53rd Annual IEEE Symposium on Foundations of Computer Science, FOCS 2012, pp. 302–310. IEEE (2012)

[10] Doty, D., Patitz, M.J., Reishus, D., Schweller, R.T., Summers, S.M.: Strong fault-tolerance for self-assembly with fuzzy temperature. In: Proceedings of the 51st Annual IEEE Symposium on Foundations of Computer Science, FOCS 2010, pp. 417–426. IEEE (2010)

[11] Hopcroft, J., Tarjan, R.: Algorithm 447: Efficient algorithms for graph manipulation. Communications of the ACM 16(6), 372–378 (1973)

[12] Luhrs, C.: Polyomino-safe DNA self-assembly via block replacement. Natural Computing 9(1), 97–109 (2008), Preliminary version appeared in DNA 2008

[13] Patitz, M.J.: An introduction to tile-based self-assembly. In: Durand-Lose, J., Jonoska, N. (eds.) UCNC 2012. LNCS, vol. 7445, pp. 34–62. Springer, Heidelberg (2012)

[14] Schulman, R., Winfree, E.: Synthesis of crystals with a programmable kinetic barrier to nucleation. Proceedings of the National Academy of Sciences 104(39), 15236–15241 (2007)

[15] Schulman, R., Winfree, E.: Programmable control of nucleation for algorithmic self-assembly. SIAM Journal on Computing 39(4), 1581–1616 (2009), Preliminary version appeared in DNA 2004

[16] Winfree, E.: Simulations of computing by self-assembly. Technical Report CaltechCSTR:1998.22. Institute of Technology, California (1998)

[17] Winfree, E.: Self-healing tile sets. In: Chen, J., Jonoska, N., Rozenberg, G. (eds.) Nanotechnology: Science and Computation. Natural Computing Series, pp. 55–78. Springer (2006)

[18] Winfree, E., Liu, F., Wenzler, L.A., Seeman, N.C.: Design and self-assembly of two-dimensional DNA crystals. Nature 394(6693), 539–544 (1998)

Unconventional Arithmetic: A System for Computation Using Action Potentials

Jonathan Edwards[1], Simon O'Keefe[2], and William D. Henderson[1]

[1] Thoughtful Technology, Newcastle, UK
jonny@thoughtfultech.co.uk
[2] YCCSA, University of York, York, UK
simon.okeefe@york.ac.uk

Abstract. This paper examines a scheme to perform arithmetic and logic computation using time delays inspired by neuronal Action Potentials. The method is reliant on a simple abstraction which utilises very little logical infrastructure, in fact, the only requirements necessary to carry out computation are a binary channel, a clock, and a rudimentary instruction look-up table.

The conclusions are that the method is viable for all forms of arithmetic and logical computation including comparison, however one practical aspect that hinders a full move to a time delay based architecture is the inability to perform random memory access without waiting for the data to recirculate.

1   Introduction

It is not an overstatement to say we are fixated with digital processing. Since Shannon's initial exposition of methods to perform digital operations [1] a Herculean effort has been applied both academically and commercially to construct ever more sophisticated methods for performing digital arithmetic and logical operations. This paper takes a step back from that research, and addresses the problem from a fundamentally different starting point, that of using *time* to represent data rather than the manipulation of transistors which expose themselves as states within a processing unit. The theme of the work is that time is a free resource and is only limited in resolution by the accuracy of the clock one is using, unlike electronics which require matter (atomic states) to be manipulated. We demonstrate surprisingly simple methods to perform all major arithmetic and logical operations using a single general processing unit which can be easily replicated.

The paper is structured as follows: Initially the action potential method is described in detail, this is demonstrated in the context of computation with examples for each of the arithmetic and logic operations. The paper then presents a more complex example which demonstrates the chaining of operations. Following this, we examine practical considerations, most notably the crucial issue of clock synchronisation. The paper concludes with a summary, which revisits the deep-rooted debate comparing analogue (often biological) systems with our predominant implementation of computation via digital methods.

O.H. Ibarra et al. (Eds.): UCNC 2014, LNCS 8553, pp. 155–163, 2014.
DOI: 10.1007/978-3-319-08123-6_13, © Springer International Publishing Switzerland 2014

2   Time Delay Processing

Models of neuronal activation are central to the description of function in the brain, they are broadly split between statistical measures of firing rates called **Rate Codes** or codes that are related to the delay between two spikes, often referred to as **Pulse Codes** ([2] chapter 1).

The Action Potential model proposed by [3] is a pulse code. In the Action Potential model the signal is transferred via spikes along a channel, and the information is contained in the time *between* spikes. In this work we describe an abstract model which is inspired by this "delay timing" value representation. The model consists of a processing unit with a binary channel, which has the capacity to carry unit impulses, and a clock with a variable speed, relative to an underlying synchronising, system wide, clock. The processing unit sends operand values as a time delay *between* pulses, so two unit impulses act as the "head" and "tail" of a time based value. The resultant signal is analogue in time. Figure 1 explains this visually, the value `two` is represented by passing an impulse de-limited signal across the channel, with the clock scaled to the value 1. This has similarity with Pulse Width Modulation (PWM) [2], but with only the "head" and "tail" impulses.

Importantly, a continuous stream of these values can exist on one processing unit. Using this as our model for processing, all arithmetic and logical operators can be derived.

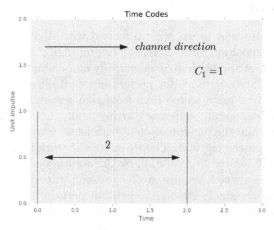

Fig. 1. A Time Delay Unit representing the value 2 as a delay between two impulses

3   Requirements for a Realisable Computing Architecture

At the lowest level, the major functions of a processing unit are to move data within memory and to perform simple mathematical computation ([4] page 11).

Typically an operation requires a specific hardware part, so for instance addition is performed using the half and full adder circuitry ([4] page 90).

Different architectural approaches have been explored. The simplest is the Minimal Instruction Set Architecture (MISC), similar to the Java Virtual Machine (JVM)[1]. This sets a minimum level for the infrastructure necessary to perform computation, and again reduces down to simple arithmetic and memory manipulation. The following section describes the architecture necessary for all the arithmetic operations including comparison, it demonstrates that these can be built with relative ease on a general simple binary channel and clock architecture. The channel forms a flow from left to right, hence in the figures below the result is calculated at the right hand side.

3.1 Addition

Addition is the simplest operation to perform with the processing unit, simply "forgetting" the "tail" of the first operand and the "head" of the second operand. The signal then becomes the conglomeration of the two values, and hence addition is performed. Figure 2 gives an example of this for the sum $1+1$:

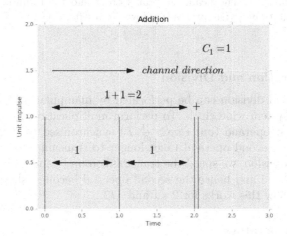

Fig. 2. Addition: 1+1, two values are added by ignoring the middle impulses, the full concatenation forms the addition. The flow of the processing is the signal moving from left to right.

3.2 Subtraction

Subtraction relies on the processing unit sending two signals starting with the same "head", so both the signals are sent at the same time. Absolute subtraction then becomes the time between the two "tails", whilst performing true subtraction requires attaching a "tag" pattern of impulses, to ascertain order. This tag

---

[1] http://docs.oracle.com/javase/specs/jvms/se7/html/

is in effect a known pattern in the look-up table that is indicative of the order of presentation of the operands. Figure 3 visualises $2 - 1$, the two signals are overlaid and subtraction becomes their difference:

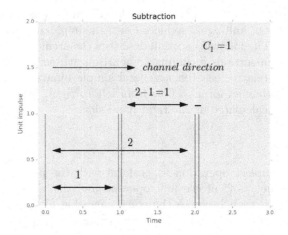

Fig. 3. Subtraction: 2-1. The header indicates order and the resultant difference be calculated through timing. The processing flows from left to right.

3.3   Multiplication and Division

Multiplication and division can be performed by manipulating the clock speed relative to the system wide clock. To perform multiplication we slow the clock down by the first operand ($op1 * op2$: $\frac{1}{op1}T$) synchronised to the System wide clock so that the second operand takes longer to transmit across the channel. Conversely, for division, we speed the transmission up by increasing clock speed by the first operand and hence the second operand becomes shorter. Figures 4 and 5 visualise how this works for $2 * 1$ and $4/2$:

3.4   Logical Operators

Once arithmetic operators are implemented it is trivial to implement the AND (addition) and OR (multiplication). The NOT operator is performed by look-up, with a send/don't send switch in the operator look-up table.

3.5   Comparison Operators

The implementation of the minus operator gives rise to a natural method of comparing operands. A similar operation to negation occurs but the arrival of the tag impulse is recorded, if it arrives before the second impulse the first operand is the greatest, if it arrives after then the first operand is smaller and if they arrive at the same time then there is equality. Figure 6 demonstrates this with a comparison between the values 2 and 1:

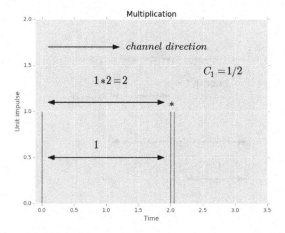

Fig. 4. Multiplication: 2*1. Changing the clock speeds relative to a central clock allows the signal to be scaled and hence multiplied. Processing is again performed from the left to the right.

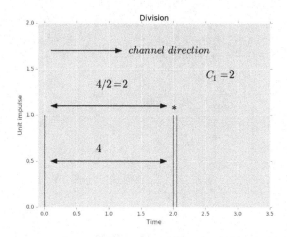

Fig. 5. Division: 4/2. Using the relative clock speed, clock scaling can perform division as well as multiplication.

3.6 Multiple Operations

To build more complex statements, the operations can be arranged into the traditional Reverse Polish queue. The whole calculation then becomes a procession through a *general* processing unit. Figure 7 shows how this queue might work, implicit in this is a method to deliver the multiplication and division operand to the clock. The figure presents an example for the expression $(3+1)/2$:

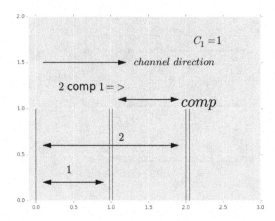

Fig. 6. A comparison operator, here we compare the values 2 and 1. Given that subtraction can be performed natively it is easy to implement comparison using a similar method.

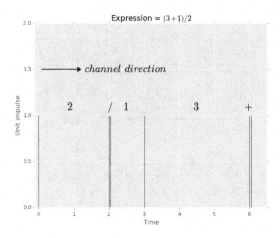

Fig. 7. A more complex arithmetical operation. However processing is still performed on one channel proceeding from left to right with the right acting as a receiver.

4   Time Delay Storage

Time delay storage through the re-circulation of a signal is not a new idea - in fact it was the pre-eminent storage method before transistors and integrated circuitry [5]. Several implementation methods exist [6]. The main disadvantage of this approach is that re-circulation slows down read/write access, and electrical circuitry requires fast op-amps[2]. Additionally, and more recently, alternative

---

[2] http://electronicdesign.com/analog/accurate-analog-delay-circuit

work with memory enabled resisitors, so-called *memristors*, has also focused on strategies for non-transistor based computation [7].

5   Practical Considerations

5.1   Large Values

Large values present a problem for processing as they are formed from long delays, this is akin to large amounts of infrastructure to store large values in traditional processors. One way to mitigate against this is to use more channels to represent large numerical values, so effectively have an analogue equivalent of a bit-width, which we will refer to as the *resolution*.

As a trivial example we could arbitrarily set the resolution of a time-delay channel to one thousand, so a channel will have a time interval of a thousand clock cycles, and hence any number up to a thousand can be represented. Two channels could be used to encode all values up to one million by representing the upper and lower 3 digits (0-999) by individual time-delay channels. Addition and subtraction will function with a carry operation, and only a slight modification of interleaving the multiplication/division operands, for example $12 * 12$ will equal $10 * 10 + 2 * 10 + 10 * 2 + 2 * 2$.

5.2   Clock Drift

It may be necessary in this system to use more than one clock, and the limits on the precision of the transmitter and receiver clocks are readily computed. N is limited as follows:

- Rx clock is faster than Tx clock:

$$N < \frac{1}{2(\frac{\rho_{Tx}}{\rho_{Rx}} - 1)} \qquad (1)$$

Table 1. Table of maximum usable values against clock tolerances

Tolerance ppm	Rx faster than Tx	Tx faster than Rx
10	25000	25000
20	12500	12500
30	8333	8334
40	6250	6250
50	5000	5000
60	4166	4167
70	3571	3572
80	3125	3125
90	2778	2778
100	2500	2500

– Rx Clock is slower than Tx clock:

$$N < \frac{1}{2(1 - \frac{\rho_{Tx}}{\rho_{Rx}})} \tag{2}$$

Surprisingly, the limits on N are independent of δT, the time quantum or the nominal clock frequency and depend only on the relative clock drift rate (ρ_{Tx}/ρ_{Rx}). Table 1 records the calculated limiting values against clock tolerances:

6   Conclusions and Further Work

The high level architecture described above represents a strong deviation from current Von-Neumann implementations, however it has several advantages. The above method blurs the lines between storage and processing. The circuitry required to process *and* store data is essentially homogeneous as memory units are similar to computation units (apart from the concept of re-circulation). Furthermore, there is also no need to implement specialist hardware for individual processing operations (e.g. multiplicative circuitry). However, there are still strong disadvantages. Speed of processing is relative to data value size (even with multiple channels for numerical encoding) and conditional on clock resolution. Storage requires amplification and is limited to re-circulation time.

In the short term, our next avenue for investigation is to implement the methods described in this paper as a virtual MISC processor. It is hoped that this will enable direct comparison with alternative architectures, and illuminate the selection of a medium for hardware implementation.

Longer term aims are to assess in more detail, and on a more practical level, the comparative advantages of this approach compared to the established norm. There are clearly areas of computation [3] that lend themselves to analogue interpretation and the authors are interested in developing systems that model these in greater detail. Many biological system perform tasks that are presently proving difficult for digital technology. Perhaps moving to a fundamentally different representation as offered by encoding in *time* will make these problems more amenable and we will arrive at the best of both worlds - analogue and digital processing where best suited.

References

1. Shannon, C.E.: A symbolic analysis of relay and switching circuits. Electrical Engineering 57(12), 713–723 (1938)
2. Maass, W., Bishop, C.M. (eds.): Pulsed Neural Networks. MIT Press, Cambridge (1999)
3. Hopfield, J.J., Brody, C.D., Roweis, S.: Computing with action potentials. In: Adv. Neural Inf. Processing 10, pp. 166–172. MIT Press (1998)
4. Burrell, M.: Fundamentals of Computer Architecture. Palgrave (2003)
5. Wilkes, M.V.: Computers then and now. J. ACM 15(1), 1–7 (1968)

6. Buckwalter, J., Hajimiri, A.: An active analog delay and the delay reference loop. In: Proc. of IEEE RFIC Symposium, pp. 17–20 (2004)
7. Gale, E., de Lacy Costello, B., Adamatzky, A.: Boolean logic gates from a single memristor via low-level sequential logic. CoRR - Computing Research Repository abs/1402.4046 (2014)

Reservoir Computing Approach to Robust Computation Using Unreliable Nanoscale Networks

Alireza Goudarzi[1], Matthew R. Lakin[1], and Darko Stefanovic[1,2]

[1] Department of Computer Science
University of New Mexico
[2] Center for Biomedical Engineering
University of New Mexico
alirezag@cs.unm.edu

Abstract. As we approach the physical limits of CMOS technology, advances in materials science and nanotechnology are making available a variety of unconventional computing substrates that can potentially replace top-down-designed silicon-based computing devices. Inherent stochasticity in the fabrication process and nanometer scale of these substrates inevitably lead to design variations, defects, faults, and noise in the resulting devices. A key challenge is how to harness such devices to perform robust computation. We propose reservoir computing as a solution. In reservoir computing, computation takes place by translating the dynamics of an excited medium, called a reservoir, into a desired output. This approach eliminates the need for external control and redundancy, and the programming is done using a closed-form regression problem on the output, which also allows concurrent programming using a single device. Using a theoretical model, we show that both regular and irregular reservoirs are intrinsically robust to structural noise as they perform computation.

1 Introduction

The approaching physical limits of silicon-based semiconductor technology are making conventional top-down designed computer architecture prohibitive [1]. Recent advances in materials science and nanotechnology suggest that unconventional computer architectures could be a viable technological and economical alternative. Some proposed alternative architectures are based on molecular switches and memristive crossbars [2, 3] that possess highly regular structure. Another emerging approach is self-assembly of nanowires and memristive networks [4, 5], which results in irregular structure. Major obstacles to using such architectures are design variations, defects, faults, and susceptibility to environmental factors such as thermal noise and radiation [6]. How should one *program* an unreliable system with unknown structure to perform reliable computation? Here we use a novel implementation of reservoir computing with sparse input and output connections to model self-assembled nanoscale systems and analyze their robustness to structural noise in the system.

Most approaches assume knowledge of the underlying architecture and rely on reconfiguration and redundancy to achieve programming and fault tolerance [7–10]. There

O.H. Ibarra et al. (Eds.): UCNC 2014, LNCS 8553, pp. 164–176, 2014.
DOI: 10.1007/978-3-319-08123-6_14, © Springer International Publishing Switzerland 2014

have been two recent proposals on how to program such devices to perform classification and logic operation using a "black-box" approach [11, 12]. Both approaches are based on a theoretical model, called a randomly assembled computer (RAC), realized by a network of interacting nodes with sparse and irregular connectivity. All nodes are initialized to zero and update their state according to a global clock, and each node calculates its next state using its transfer function and connections to other nodes. Three types of external signals are connected to randomly chosen nodes: inputs, outputs, and controls. The task is to program the device to compute the desired output for a given input using a proper control signal. The optimal control signal will modify the propagation of input across the network so that input is processed as required and the desired result is presented at the output. The optimal control signals are computed using simulated annealing. The key property of this model is sparse random external interfaces, i.e., input, output, and controls. The model's only fundamental and reasonable assumption is that there is enough connectivity that the input and control signals can propagate through the network and reach the output. This model has shown impressive performance and inherent robustness to noise [11]. In RAC, the computation takes place by initializing the network with a fixed state and presenting the input signal to the network, and then the network runs until the output is produced. This cycle is repeated for each new input pattern. The computation is therefore sensitive to the initial state of the network and the control signals must be calculated based on the desired computation, the structure, and the initial state of the network.

We propose the reservoir computing (RC) paradigm [13] as an alternative programming approach to unconventional and irregular architectures. RC lets the network dynamics be perturbed by the input signal and maps the network states to the desired output using closed-form linear regression. In addition to the connectedness assumption from RAC, we require the network to have a slowly converging dynamics. RC provides several advantages over RAC. In RC, the computation is not sensitive to the initial state of the system and there is no need for control signals, which leads to simpler design and implementation. Also, the training is done in a closed-form regression and does not need an iterative process. Moreover, nonlinear computation is inherently enabled by the network dynamics acting as a recursive kernel and extracting nonlinear features of the input signal [14]. Noise in the input, the network states, and the interactions between the nodes can be treated using a regularization term and can be scaled to achieve the best performance. This is particularly attractive, because RC depends on the dynamics to compute, and structural change may have adverse effects on the dynamical regime of the system, which would normally require retraining the network. In addition, the programming is performed on the output instead of the task-specific control of the network, and therefore we can compute multiple functions simultaneously using the same device. In contrast to existing RC implementations [15, 16], the novelty of our work is the consideration of sparse input and output to model unconventional computer architectures, and the analysis of robustness in the presence of structural noise in the network, possibly due to thermal noise and radiation that change the electrical properties of the network. In classical implementations of RC, the input and output are connected to all the internal nodes and the system is assumed to operate in a noise-free environment. We demonstrate the performance and robustness of RC using regular and irregular networks and analyze the memory capacity and nonlinear computational performance of the system subject to structural noise. Our results show that RC can be a viable approach to using self-assembled and nanoscale substrates to implement robust, special-purpose signal processing devices.

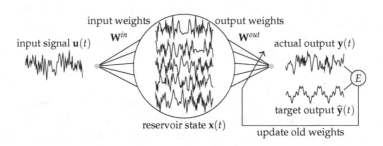

Fig. 1. Computation in a reservoir computer. The reservoir is an excitable dynamical system with N readable output states represented by the vector $\mathbf{X}(t)$. The input signal $\mathbf{u}(t)$ is fed into one or more points i in the reservoir with a corresponding weight w_i^{in} denoted with weight column vector $\mathbf{W}^{in} = [w_i^{in}]$.

2   Background

Reservoir computing was independently introduced by Maass, Natschläger, and Markram [17] and by Jaeger [18]. Echo state networks (ESN) are one of the most popular RC paradigms, and have shown promising results in time series computing and prediction [19, 20], voice recognition [21], nonlinear system identification [22], and robot control [23]. An ESN [16, 22, 24, 25] consists of an input-driven recurrent neural network, which acts as the reservoir, and a readout layer that reads the reservoir states and produces the output. Unlike a classical recurrent neural network, where all the nodes are interconnected and their weights are determined during a training process, in an ESN the nodes are interconnected using random weights and random sparse connectivity between the nodes. The input and reservoir connections are initialized and fixed, usually with no further adaptation.

Figure 2 shows a schematic of an ESN. The readout layer is usually a linear combination of the reservoir states. The readout weights are determined using supervised learning techniques, where the network is driven by a teacher input and its output is compared with a corresponding teacher output to estimate the error. Then, the weights can be calculated using any closed-form regression technique [25] in offline training contexts, or using adaptive techniques if online training is needed [22]. Mathematically, the input-driven reservoir is defined as follows. Let N be the size of the reservoir. We represent the time-dependent inputs as a column vector $\mathbf{u}(t)$, the reservoir state as a column vector $\mathbf{x}(t)$, and the output as a column vector $\mathbf{y}(t)$. The input connectivity

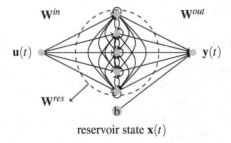

reservoir state $\mathbf{x}(t)$

Fig. 2. Schematic of an ESN. A dynamical core called a reservoir is driven by input signal $\mathbf{u}(t)$. The states of the reservoir $\mathbf{x}(t)$ extended by a constant 1 and combined linearly to produce the output $\mathbf{y}(t)$. The reservoir consists of N nodes interconnected with a random weight matrix $\mathbf{W}^{res}$. The connectivity between the input and the reservoir nodes is represented with a randomly generated weight matrix $\mathbf{W}^{in}$. The reservoir states and the constant are connected to the readout layer using the weight matrix $\mathbf{W}^{out}$. The reservoir and the input weights are fixed after initialization, while the output weights are learned using a regression technique.

is represented by the matrix $\mathbf{W}^{in}$ and the reservoir connectivity is represented by an $N \times N$ weight matrix $\mathbf{W}^{res}$. For simplicity, we assume one input signal and one output, but the notation can be extended to multiple inputs and outputs. The time evolution of the reservoir is given by:

$$\mathbf{x}(t+1) = f(\mathbf{W}^{res} \cdot \mathbf{x}(t) + \mathbf{W}^{in} \cdot \mathbf{u}(t)), \qquad (1)$$

where f is the transfer function of the reservoir nodes that is applied element-wise to its operand. This is usually the hyperbolic tangent, but sigmoidal or linear functions can be used instead. The output is generated by the multiplication of an output weight matrix $\mathbf{W}^{out}$ of length $N+1$ and the reservoir state vector $x(t)$ extended by a constant 1 represented by $\mathbf{x}'(t)$:

$$\mathbf{y}(t) = \mathbf{W}^{out} \cdot \mathbf{x}'(t). \qquad (2)$$

The output weights $\mathbf{W}^{out}$ must be trained using a teacher input-output pair using regression [16, 26, 27]. This regression can be performed in closed form and therefore ESN training is very efficient compared with classical recurrent neural network training, which requires a time-consuming iterative process [28].

In ESN, the reservoir acts as a recursive kernel which creates an expressive spatiotemporal code for the input signal [14]. In ESNs, to create the required spatiotemporal feature space, the reservoir must enjoy the so-called echo state property [24] (ESP): over time the asymptotic state of the reservoir depends only on the history of the input signal $\mathbf{u}(t)$, i.e., the dynamics is independent of the initial state of the network. Jaeger [24] showed that to satisfy this condition, the reservoir weight matrix $\mathbf{W}^{res}$ must have the spectral radius $\lambda^{max} < 1$ and the largest singular values $\sigma^{max} < 1$.

3   Experimental Setup

3.1   Reservoir Generation and Inducing Noise

Similar to [27], we use RC with a simple cycle reservoir (SCR) and ESNs with sparse randomly generated reservoirs for our experiments. We specify the number of reservoir nodes by N. We use the hyperbolic tangent transfer function in both models. In SCR, the reservoir nodes are connected in a cycle and have identical weights r, $0 < r < 1$. It has been shown [27] that despite the simplicity of this model its performance is comparable to

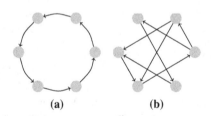

Fig. 3. Schematic for structure of a SCR reservoir (a) and a random sparse reservoir (b)

sparse random reservoirs. In an ESN, a fraction l of all possible connections are chosen to have non-zero weights and the rest of the connections are assigned zero; half of the non-zero weights are assigned -0.47 and the other half are assigned $+0.47$. The choice of ±0.47 ensures ESP, which otherwise can be achieved by scaling the reservoir weight matrix as $\mathbf{W}^{res} \leftarrow \lambda \mathbf{W}^{res}/\lambda^{max}$, where λ^{max} is the spectral radius of $\mathbf{W}^{res}$ and λ is the desired spectral radius $0 < \lambda < 1$. The non-zero weights are chosen independently and randomly, which results in an Erdös-Rényi network structure [29]. Figure 3 illustrates the structure of SCR and random sparse reservoirs. For both models, the input signal is connected to half of the nodes that are picked randomly and the input weights are chosen from the set $\{-v, +v\}$ according to Bernoulli distribution, where v is the input coefficient. For our experiments, we use sets of input coefficients V, SCR reservoir weights R, and ESN spectral radii Λ varying in the range $[0.1, 0.9]$ with 0.1 increments.

To study the effect of structural noise on RC performance, we add a white noise term, with standard deviation σ, to n randomly chosen non-zero entries of $\mathbf{W}^{res}$ at each time step t. This will cause the non-zero entries of $\mathbf{W}^{res}$ to vary around their initial value according to a normal distribution. Our motivation for this is to model short term temporal variations in the structural properties of nanoscale networks. These variations are known to follow a normal distribution [30]. We choose n for each experiment to make sure the fraction of noisy weights is constant across all reservoirs.

3.2   Simulation, Training, and Evaluation

To evaluate the performance of each model, we generate 50 streams of random numbers picked uniformly from the interval $[-1, +1]$. For each stream a new ESN or SCR was instantiated with randomized states uniformly picked from the interval $[-1, +1]$. The system was then driven for $T + 2,000$ time steps. The first T steps were then discarded to account for the transient period, where T is chosen to be half of the reservoir size N. We randomly chose half the reservoir nodes to read reservoir states; the states of these nodes were then collected and augmented with a constant 1 as inductive bias and arranged row-wise into a matrix $\mathbf{X}$, which was used for calculating the output weights $\mathbf{W}^{out}$ given by:

$$\mathbf{W}^{out} = \mathbf{M} \cdot \widehat{\mathbf{y}}, \tag{3}$$

where $\widehat{\mathbf{y}}$ is the expected output. The matrix $\mathbf{M}$ is usually calculated using either an ordinary linear regression technique as $(\mathbf{X}^T \cdot \mathbf{X})^{-1} \cdot \mathbf{X}^T$, or a ridge regression technique as $(\mathbf{X}^T \cdot \mathbf{X} + \gamma^2 \mathbf{I})^{-1} \cdot \mathbf{X}^T$, where γ is the regularization factor, and $\mathbf{I}$ is the identity matrix of order $N + 1$. In general the spectra of $\mathbf{X}^T \mathbf{X}$ should be studied to choose an appropriate inversion technique. We found that using the Penrose-Moore pseudo-inverse of $\mathbf{X}$ for $\mathbf{M}$, which minimizes its norm, produces the most stable results. We calculated this using MATLAB's *pinv* function. To test performance, we drove the system for another $T + 2000$ time steps of each stream, created the matrix $\mathbf{X}$ as before, and calculated the output as in Equation 2. We evaluate the robustness of SCR and ESN as percent change in their performance for two different tasks described below.

Memory Capacity (MC). Jaeger [24] defined the memory capacity task to quantify the short-term memory of the reservoir in ESN by measuring how well the network can reconstruct the input after τ number of time steps. The coefficient of determination between the input and a τ-delayed version of the input as output of ESN is:

$$MC_\tau = \frac{\text{cov}^2(u(t-\tau), y(t))}{\text{var}(u(t)) \text{var}(y(t))}. \tag{4}$$

The total memory capacity of a network is then given by:

$$MC = \sum_{\tau=1}^{\infty} MC_\tau. \tag{5}$$

Assuming a zero-centered uniformly random stream as input, the memory capacity for ESN is bounded by the size of the reservoir $MC < N$ [24] , and $N - 1 < MC < N$ for SCR [27]. However, the empirical values vary based on experimental conditions. We derive the networks with the input streams as described previously in this section and we measure the MC for both ESN and SCR of size $N = 50$, using a finite sum of MC_τ up to $\tau = 200$. We can then measure memory robustness as the ratio of memory capacity of noisy systems MC to the noise-free systems MC^* for ESN and SCR as follows:

$$\Gamma_{MC}^{ESN}(v, \lambda) = \frac{MC(v, \lambda)}{MC^*(v, \lambda)} \text{ and } \Gamma_{MC}^{SCR}(v, r) = \frac{MC(v, r)}{MC^*(v, r)} \tag{6}$$

where k is the fraction of noise-induced connections and σ is the standard deviation of the noise. We let $MC(v, \lambda)$ and $MC(v, r)$ denote the memory capacity of ESN with parameters v and λ, and memory capacity of SCR with parameters v and r, respectively.

Nonlinear Autoregressive Moving Average (NARMA). NARMA is a nonlinear task with long time lag designed to measure neural network capability to compute nonlinear functions of previous inputs and outputs. The 10-th order NARMA system NARMA10 is defined as follows:

$$y(t) = 0.3y(t-1) + 0.05y(t-1) \sum_{i=1}^{10} y(t-i) + 1.5u(t-10)u(t-1) + 0.1. \quad (7)$$

The input u_t is drawn from a uniform distribution in the interval $[0,0.5]$. To generate the input for this task, we shift our input streams by 2 and divide them by 4 to ensure the values are in the internal $[0,0.5]$. We calculate the performance of ESN and SCR on this task by the test error measured by the normalized mean squared error (NMSE) given by:

$$NMSE = \frac{\langle (y(t) - \widehat{y}(t))^2 \rangle}{\mathrm{var}(\widehat{y}(t))}. \quad (8)$$

If the mean squared error of the output is larger than the variance of the target output then $NMSE > 1$, in which case we consider the $NMSE = 1$ to simplify our analysis. Once again we measure robustness with respect to the error as the ratio between the error of a noisy system $NMSE$ to the error of a noise free-system $NMSE^*$ as follows:

$$\Gamma_{NMSE}^{ESN}(v,\lambda) = \frac{NMSE^*(v,\lambda)}{NMSE(v,\lambda)} \text{ and } \Gamma_{NMSE}^{SCR}(v,r) = \frac{NMSE^*(v,r)}{NMSE(v,r)}, \quad (9)$$

using $NMSE(v,\lambda)$ and $NMSE(v,r)$ as shorthand for the performance of ESN with parameters v and λ, and the performance of SCR with parameters v and r, respectively.

4   Results

First we analyze the memory capacity in SCR and ESN under structural noise. All the results in this section are the average value over 60 runs as described in Section 3. Figure 4a shows the memory capacity of SCR for reservoirs of size $N = 50$ without any structural noise. The MC shows a nonlinear increase for increasing r and decreasing v up to $r = 0.8$ and $v = 0.1$, where the MC reaches its maximum $MC = 17.15$. Figure 4b shows the memory capacity of SCR under noisy conditions where at each time step a single randomly chosen node is perturbed with a white noise with standard deviation $\sigma = 0.01$. For suboptimal r and v, the noise distorts the memory of the system, resulting in lower memory capacity, whereas for optimal parameters, the memory capacity increases due to the regularization effect of noise terms on the regression; in fact, at its peak memory capacity is $MC = 19.74$. According to the ratio Γ_{MC}^{SCR}, shown in Figure 4c, for $r > 0.6$ and $v \geq 0.1$ the noise improves the memory capacity. Figure 4d shows the memory capacity of ESNs of size $N = 50$ and connection fraction $l = 0.2$. Due to the variation inside the reservoir, the memory capacity surface for ESNs is not as smooth as the MC surface for SCRs. In ESNs, the memory capacity increases nonlinearly with increasing λ and decreasing v and reaches its maximum $MC = 17.15$ at $\lambda = 0.8$ and $v = 0.1$. Figure 4e shows the memory capacity of ESNs under noisy conditions. At each step $n = 10$ connections are perturbed using a white noise of standard deviation $\sigma = 0.01$ to achieve the same noise level as for SCR. The effect of noise in ESN is

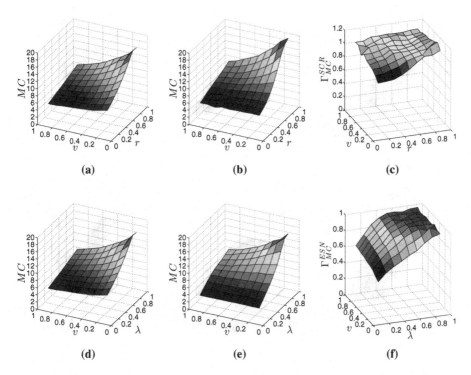

Fig. 4. Memory capacity (MC) in noise-free SCR (a) and SCR with structural noise (b). The ratio $\Gamma_{MC}^{SCR}(v, r)$ showing the overall variation of the *MC* between noisy and noise-free conditions (c). MC in noise-free ESN (d) and ESN with structural noise (e). The ratio $\Gamma_{MC}^{ESN}(v, \lambda)$ showing the overall variation of the *MC* between noisy and noise-free conditions (f). SCR memory is robust to noise for $r > 0.6$ and $v \geq 0.1$ and ESN memory is robust to noise for $\lambda > 0.8$ and $v \geq 0.1$.

slightly higher. The memory capacity changes slowly from $MC = 3.40$ to its maximum $MC = 16.72$ for $\lambda = 0.9$. According to Figure 4f for all v and $\lambda > 0.8$ the MC is not decreased significantly in noisy conditions. In summary, both SCR and ESN are highly robust to structural noise.

For the nonlinear computation NARMA10, we used SCRs of size $N = 100$ and plotted the testing error as a function of v and r (Figure 5a). The best observed SCR performance ($NMSE = 0.16$) occurs for $r = 0.9$ and $v = 0.1$. Figure 5b shows the performance of noisy SCRs for which at every time step $n = 2$ connections are perturbed with a white noise with standard deviation $\sigma = 0.01$. For low r and any v the system performs poorly with $NMSE \approx 0.8$. For $r > 0.4$, there is a sharp drop in $NMSE$ and the system achieves an average optimal error of $NMSE = 0.16$ for $r = 0.9$ and $v = 0.1$. Figure 5c shows the general effect of noise on SCR performance using the ratio Γ_{NMES}^{SCR}. We observe that for all $v = 0.1$ and for $r = 0.4$ this significantly reduces the performance to below 50% of the original values while for $r > 0.8$ the performance is virtually unaffected. Figure 5d shows the performance result of NARMA10 task for noise-free ESNs of size

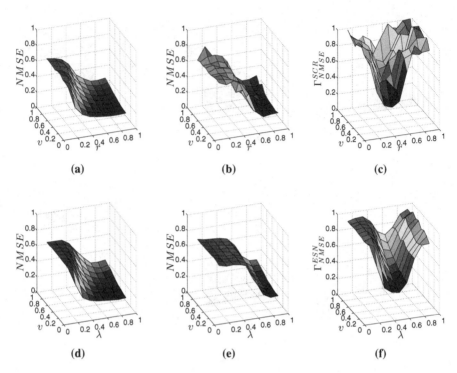

Fig. 5. Performance of ESN and SCR in solving the NARMA10 task measured using $NMSE$. The $NMSE$ in noise-free SCR (a) and SCR with structural noise (b). The ratio $\Gamma_{NMSE}^{SCR}(v,r)$ showing the overall variation of the performance between noisy and noise-free conditions (c). $NMSE$ in noise-free ESN (d) and ESN with structural noise (e). The ratio $\Gamma_{NMSE}^{ESN}(v,\lambda)$ showing the overall variation of the performance between noisy and noise-free conditions (f). For $r > 0.8$, the SCR nonlinear task solving performance is completely robust to structural noise. ESN performance is also robust to noise for a critical spectral radius $\lambda > 0.8$.

$N = 100$ and connection fraction $l = 0.2$. Similar to SCRs, the optimal performance is in the region $\lambda = 0.9$ and $v = 0.1$ with an average error of $NMSE = 0.16$. To test the performance of noisy ESNs when computing the NARMA10 task, $n = 40$ reservoir connections are perturbed at each time step using identical white noise as before to achieve the same noise level. Figure 5e shows the result of this experiment. The optimal spectral radius for noisy ESN does not change ($\lambda = 0.9$ with average error $NMSE = 0.19$). However, performance is very sensitive to spectral radius and for $\lambda < 0.8$ shows a sharp increase in error. The effect of noise on the ESNs is summarized in Figure 5f. Networks with spectral radius $\lambda = 0.5$ are affected the most and networks with $\lambda = 0.9$ are robust. Compared with SCR, ESN is more sensitive to noise. We can summarize the comparison between SCRs and ESNs using the following aggregate measures:

$$\widehat{NMSE}^{SCR} = \sum_{v \in V} \sum_{r \in R} NMSE(v,r), \widehat{NMSE}^{ESN} = \sum_{v \in V} \sum_{\lambda \in \Lambda} NMSE(v,\lambda), \qquad (10)$$

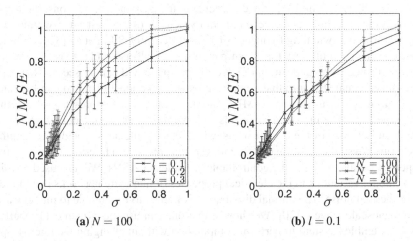

Fig. 6. Performance on the NARMA10 task as a function of standard deviation of noise σ. Under fixed size $N = 100$, networks with higher connection fraction l lose their performance more quickly than sparser networks (a). Under fixed connection fraction $l = 0.1$, the performance does not show significant sensitivity to network size as the noise level increases.

and aggregate measures:

$$\widehat{\Gamma}_{NMSE}^{SCR} = \sum_{v \in V} \sum_{r \in R} \log(\Gamma_{NMSE}^{SCR}(v,r)), \ \widehat{\Gamma}_{NMSE}^{ESN} = \sum_{v \in V} \sum_{\lambda \in \Lambda} \log(\Gamma_{NMSE}^{ESN}(v,\lambda)). \quad (11)$$

For noise-free systems $\widehat{NMSE}^{SCR} = 28.71$ and $\widehat{NMSE}^{ESN} = 32.02$, showing that SCR outperforms ESN by 10.3%. For noisy systems, $\widehat{NMSE}^{SCR} = 36.10$ and $\widehat{NMSE}^{ESN} = 42.62$ which suggests the simple structure of SCR makes it perform 15% better than ESN in noisy environment. Finally, $\widehat{\Gamma}_{NMSE}^{SCR} = -17.40$ and $\widehat{\Gamma}_{NMSE}^{ESN} = -25.74$, indicating that SCRs are 1.47 times more robust than ESNs for nonlinear task solving over the parameter space that we studied.

Finally, we studied the sensitivity of ESN performance in the NARMA10 task under different noise levels σ, different network size N, and reservoir sparsity l (Figure 6). For fixed network size, as we increase the connection fraction, the error increases more quickly as a function of noise (Figure 6a). This is expected since in denser networks, variations in the state of one node propagate to many downstream nodes. We hypothesize that if we control for node out-degree, we can contain this effect. We did not find any significant variation in the performance of networks with different sizes as a function of changing noise σ (Figure 6b).

5 Discussion

We used theoretical models to investigate robustness of reservoir computing as an approach to computation in emerging nanoscale and self-assembled devices. An example of such networks is *Atomic switch networks* (ASN). These were based on a technology developed by Terabe et al. [31] aimed at reducing the cost and energy consumption of electronic devices. They can achieve a memory density of $2.5\,\mathrm{Gbit\,cm^{-2}}$ without any optimization, and a switching frequency of 1 GHz. Recently, Sillin et al. [32] combined bottom-up self-assembly and top-down patterning to self-assemble ASN. These networks are formed using deposition of silver on pre-patterned copper seeds. They have a three-dimensional structure that contains cross-bar-like junctions, and can be transformed into metal-insulator-metal (MIM) atomic switches in the presence of external bias voltage [32]. The morphology of this self-assembled network can be directed by the pitch and the size of the copper seeds, which control the density and wire lengths, respectively. We studied ESN and SCR with varying connection fraction, input weights, and spectral radius to model the controllable variables in ASNs. We also used a white noise to model variations in the electrical properties of nanowire networks due to radiation or thermal noise. The normal distribution is known to be suitable to model variations in nanoscale devices [30]. We showed that one can use the dynamical properties of a self-assembled system to perform computation without changing the microscopic structure of the system itself. The only modification to the structure of ESN and SCR is to adjust the spectral radius and therefore dynamical regime of the system, which is independent of the specific computation and can be done using external control signals [33].

6   Conclusions

We presented reservoir computing as an alternative approach to randomly assembled computers for implementing computation on top of emerging nanoscale computing substrates. Using RC, we can compute with such devices assuming only enough connectivity in the system to propagate signals from the input to the output. This approach eliminates the need for control signals and redundancy for programming and fault-tolerance in emerging architectures, which simplifies its implementation and makes the training more efficient. In addition, because the programming takes place in the output layer, the same device can be used to compute multiple functions simultaneously. We showed that the system resists noise in the interaction between nodes. This is a surprising feature because structural change in the system affects the long-term dynamics of the network. In RC with full input-output connectivity, the performance of SCR is similar to ESN. However, with sparse input-output connectivity the readout layer only has limited observation of the reservoir dynamics, therefore the dynamics of different nodes in the reservoir have to be as independent as possible to represent independent spatiotemporal features of the input signal. In ESN, the reservoir nodes have more interactions and therefore their dynamics are more correlated resulting in a lower performance. In addition, with higher interactions between nodes, noise in a single connection can propagate to several other nodes, which distorts the dynamics of the ESN. In SCR, on the other hand, each node is only connected to one downstream node which limits the propagation of noise to only one other node. This result in higher robustness to noise in SCR. In future work, we will study this hypothesis by controlling the out-degree of ESN reservoir nodes. This is the first time RC has been used to solve nonlinear tasks with sparse readout and structural noise. Exact characterization of performance and robustness under varying sparsity and weight distribution conditions is left for future work.

Another future direction is implementation of a "detect-and-recompute" schema as a fault-tolerance mechanism against one or more permanently failed nodes or connections.

Acknowledgments. This material is based upon work supported by the National Science Foundation under grant 1028238. M.R.L. gratefully acknowledges support from the New Mexico Cancer Nanoscience and Microsystems Training Center (NIH/NCI grant 5R25CA153825). We thank the anonymous reviewers for their constructive comments.

References

1. Haselman, M., Hauck, S.: The future of integrated circuits: A survey of nanoelectronics. Proceedings of the IEEE 98(1), 11–38 (2010)
2. Chen, Y., Jung, G.Y., Ohlberg, D.A.A., Li, X., Stewart, D.R., Jeppesen, J.O., Nielsen, K.A., Stoddart, J.F., Williams, R.S.: Nanoscale molecular-switch crossbar circuits. Nanotechnology 14(4), 462 (2003)
3. Snider, G.: Computing with hysteretic resistor crossbars. Appl. Phys. A 80, 1165–1172 (2005)
4. Xu, P., Jeon, S.H., Chen, H.T., Luo, H., Zou, G., Jia, Q., Marian, T.C., Williams, D.J., Zhang, B., Han, X., Wang, H.L.: Facile synthesis and electrical properties of silver wires through chemical reduction by polyaniline. The Journal of Physical Chemistry C 114(50), 22147–22154 (2010)
5. Stieg, A.Z., Avizienis, A.V., Sillin, H.O., Martin-Olmos, C., Aono, M., Gimzewski, J.K.: Emergent criticality in complex Turing B-type atomic switch networks. Advanced Materials 24(2), 286–293 (2012)
6. Semiconductor Industry Association: International technology roadmap for semiconductors, ITRS (2011), http://www.itrs.net/Links/2011ITRS/
7. Schmid, A., Leblebici, Y.: A modular approach for reliable nanoelectronic and very-deep submicron circuit design based on analog neural network principles. In: Proc. IEEE-NANO, pp. 647–650 (2003)
8. Žaloudek, L., Sekanina, L.: Cellular automata-based systems with fault-tolerance. Natural Computing 11(4), 673–685 (2012)
9. Tran, A.H., Yanushkevich, S., Lyshevski, S., Shmerko, V.: Design of neuromorphic logic networks and fault-tolerant computing. In: Proc. IEEE-NANO, pp. 457–462 (2011)
10. Zhang, W., Wu, N.J.: CMOL-based cellular neural networks and parallel processor for future image processing. In: Proc. IEEE-NANO, pp. 737–740 (2008)
11. Lawson, J.W., Wolpert, D.H.: Adaptive programming of unconventional nano-architectures. Journal of Computational and Theoretical Nanoscience 3(2), 272–279 (2006)
12. Anghel, M., Teuscher, C., Wang, H.L.: Adaptive learning in random linear nanoscale networks. In: Proc. IEEE-NANO, pp. 445–450 (2011)
13. Lukoševičius, M., Jaeger, H., Schrauwen, B.: Reservoir computing trends. KI - Künstliche Intelligenz 26(4), 365–371 (2012)
14. Hermans, M., Schrauwen, B.: Recurrent kernel machines: Computing with infinite echo state networks. Neural Computation 24(1), 104–133 (2011)
15. Lukoševičius, M., Jaeger, H.: Reservoir computing approaches to recurrent neural network training. Computer Science Review 3(3), 127–149 (2009)

16. Verstraeten, D., Schrauwen, B., D'Haene, M., Stroobandt, D.: An experimental unification of reservoir computing methods. Neural Networks 20(3), 391–403 (2007)
17. Maass, W., Natschläger, T., Markram, H.: Real-time computing without stable states: a new framework for neural computation based on perturbations. Neural computation 14(11), 2531–2560 (2002)
18. Jaeger, H.: The "echo state" approach to analysing and training recurrent neural networks. Technical Report GMD Rep. 148, St. Augustin. German National Research Center for Information Technology (2001)
19. Wyffels, F., Schrauwen, B.: A comparative study of reservoir computing strategies for ly time series prediction. Neurocomputing 73(10-12), 1958–1964 (2010)
20. Jaeger, H., Haas, H.: Harnessing nonlinearity: Predicting chaotic systems and saving energy in wireless communication. Science 304(5667), 78–80 (2004)
21. Paquot, Y., Duport, F., Smerieri, A., Dambre, J., Schrauwen, B., Haelterman, M., Massar, S.: Optoelectronic reservoir computing. Scientific Reports 2 (2012)
22. Jaeger, H.: Adaptive nonlinear system identification with echo state networks. In: NIPS, pp. 593–600 (2002)
23. Dasgupta, S., Wörgötter, F., Manoonpong, P.: Information theoretic self-organised adaptation in reservoirs for temporal memory tasks. In: Jayne, C., Yue, S., Iliadis, L. (eds.) EANN 2012. CCIS, vol. 311, pp. 31–40. Springer, Heidelberg (2012)
24. Jaeger, H.: Short term memory in echo state networks. Technical Report GMD Report 152. GMD-Forschungszentrum Informationstechnik (2002)
25. Jaeger, H.: Tutorial on training recurrent neural networks, covering BPPT, RTRL, EKF and the "echo state network" approach. Technical Report GMD Report 159. German National Research Center for Information Technology, St. Augustin-Germany (2002)
26. Penrose, R.: A generalized inverse for matrices. Mathematical Proceedings of the Cambridge Philosophical Society 51, 406–413 (1955)
27. Rodan, A., Tiňo, P.: Minimum complexity echo state network. IEEE Transactions on Neural Networks 22, 131–144 (2011)
28. Atiya, A., Parlos, A.: New results on recurrent network training: Unifying the algorithms and accelerating convergence. IEEE Transactions on Neural Networks 11, 697–709 (2000)
29. Erdös, P., Rényi, A.: On random graphs. Publ. Math. Debrecen 6, 290–297 (1959)
30. Sarangi, S., Greskamp, B., Teodorescu, R., Nakano, J., Tiwari, A., Torrellas, J.: VARIUS: A model of process variation and resulting timing errors for microarchitects. IEEE Transactions on Semiconductor Manufacturing 21(1), 3–13 (2008)
31. Terabe, K., Hasegawa, T., Nakayama, T., Aono, M.: Quantized conductance atomic switch. Nature 433(7021), 47–50 (2005)
32. Sillin, H.O., Aguilera, R., Shieh, H.H., Avizienis, A.V., Aono, M., Stieg, A.Z., Gimzewski, J.K.: A theoretical and experimental study of neuromorphic atomic switch networks for reservoir computing. Nanotechnology 24(38), 384004 (2013)
33. Ozturk, M.C., Xu, D., Príncipe, J.C.: Analysis and design of echo state networks. Neural Computation 19(1), 111–138 (2007)

On DNA-Based Gellular Automata

Masami Hagiya[1], Shaoyu Wang[1], Ibuki Kawamata[2], Satoshi Murata[2],
Teijiro Isokawa[3], Ferdinand Peper[4], and Katsunobu Imai[5]

[1] The University of Tokyo, Tokyo, Japan
[2] Tohoku University, Sendai, Japan
[3] University of Hyogo, Himeji, Japan
[4] National Institute of Information and Communications Technology, Kobe, Japan
[5] Hiroshima University, Higashihiroshima, Japan

Abstract. We propose the notion of gellular automata and their possible implementations using DNA-based gels. Gellular automata are a
kind of cellular automaton in which cells in space are separated by gel
materials. Each cell contains a solution with designed chemical reactions
whose products dissolve or construct gel walls separating the cells. We
first introduce the notion of gellular automata and their computational
models. We then give examples of gellular automata and show that computational universality is achieved through the implementation of rotary
elements by gellular automata. We finally examine general strategies for
implementing gellular automata using DNA-based gels and report results
of preliminary experiments.

Keywords: DNA computing, molecular computing, molecular robotics,
cellular automata, gel, DNA gel, soft matter.

1 Introduction

Since the innovative founding of DNA computing, a great deal of effort has
been devoted to building molecular computing systems in a test tube. It has
been increasingly recognized that the realization of more sophisticated molecular
systems with information processing capabilities, such as molecular robots [1],
will necessitate the organization of molecular devices in two- or three-dimensional
structures.

In order to organize and coordinate molecular devices in space, it is necessary
to control communication among devices in terms of signaling molecules that
diffuse in space. Although principles of reaction-diffusion kinetics have been ex-
tensively investigated in the theory of complex systems, it is still not easy to
design and control reaction-diffusion systems as intended for applications like
molecular robots. In contrast, their discrete counterparts, i.e., cellular automata,
have also been investigated and are relatively easy to design and control.

Soft materials, including various kinds of gels, have been well-studied in chemistry, and such materials can be controlled by products of reactions that are active inside the materials. Some of such gel materials are based on DNA molecules

O.H. Ibarra et al. (Eds.): UCNC 2014, LNCS 8553, pp. 177–189, 2014.
DOI: 10.1007/978-3-319-08123-6_15, © Springer International Publishing Switzerland 2014

and can be controlled by reactions involving DNA, e.g., DNA computations [2–6]. In particular, gelation and solation of polyacrylamide gels cross-linked by double strands of DNA can be controlled by DNA reactions [3, 5].

Another recent technological progress related to this research is that of three-dimensional printers, among which so-called gel printers can build three-dimensional structures out of various gel materials and solutions [7].

Against the background described above, we propose the concept of gellular automaton in this paper and examine its possible implementations. *Gellular automata* are cellular automata in which cells in space are separated by gel materials. Each cell contains a solution with designed chemical reactions whose products dissolve or form gel walls separating the cells. We expect that gellular automata can actually be constructed by next generation gel printers.

Recently, artificial membranes made of lipid and artificial channels penetrating such membranes have been investigated, and artificial channels made of DNA origami have been implemented [8]. Based on these results, vesicles enclosed by artificial membranes can in principle communicate with one another via artificial channels. It will also become possible to control the activity of channels by reactions inside vesicles. However, it is still difficult to implement such controllable artificial membrane channels. We therefore assume that gels are currently the most promising materials that can implement artificial cellular systems as proposed in this paper.

In the rest of this paper, we first introduce the notion of gellular automata and their mathematical models followed by related work on P systems. In Section 3, we give examples of gellular automata in which a signal is propagated in a controlled manner, and a rotary element is implemented. Universality is not the main issue of the paper, but we touch upon computational universality as a consequence of the examples. We then give general strategies for implementing gellular automata using DNA-based gels in Section 4, and report results of preliminary experiments in Section 5. We conclude the paper in Section 6 by giving some future perspectives.

2   Gellular Automata

2.1   Intuitive Idea

Gellular automata consist of cells that are separated by walls made of gels. Each cell is filled with a liquid solution containing molecular species that obey certain chemical reactions. Each wall is associated with two molecular species. One of the two species dissolves the wall or makes a hole through it. After a wall is dissolved or a hole is made, the cells separated by the wall are merged and their solutions are mixed, possibly triggering new reactions. The other species constructs the wall or fills the hole. The merged cells are separated again when the wall is reconstructed or the hole is filled.

As a very simple example, consider the following one-dimensional cellular space.

A	X	X	X	X	X	X	X

Each cell consists of a solution filled with molecular species A and/or X. All the walls are assumed to be dissolved by A. The following reaction is also assumed.

$$A, X \rightarrow A, A$$

Firstly, the solution in the leftmost cell dissolves its right wall and merges the two cells.

A, X	X	X	X	X	X	X

Since the merged cells still contain A, while the concentration of A increases due to the reaction, the next wall is also dissolved.

A, X	X	X	X	X	X

Eventually, all the walls are dissolved and the resulting large cell contains only A.

A

2.2   Mathematical Models

Various mathematical models are derived from the intuitive idea presented in the previous subsection, and they can be categorized with respect to the following aspects.

A solution in a cell can be modeled either as a tuple of continuous real-valued concentrations of molecular species, or as a multiset of molecular species. In more abstract models, a solution might be regarded simply as a set of molecular species that exist in it.

Reaction rules reflect chemical reactions in a solution. They are modeled based on how solutions are formalized. If molecular species have continuous concentrations, it is natural to adopt mass action kinetics for reaction rules, where a reaction rate is assigned to each rule. Concentrations are then continuously changed over time in accordance with differential equations derived from the rules and their reaction rates.

On the other hand, if a solution is regarded as a multiset of molecular species, reaction rules are considered *rewrite rules* of multisets. The result of applying a reaction rule to a multiset is obtained by subtracting the left hand side of the rule from the multiset and adding the right hand side to it. There are a few strategies to apply rewrite rules to a multiset. In the *maximally parallel strategy,* (possibly duplicated) rewrite rules are applied to a multiset in parallel in such a way that no more application of a rewrite rule is possible. In the *sequential strategy*, rewrite rules are applied to a multiset one by one sequentially, possibly stopping application at any time. In both strategies, rewriting is instantaneous and nondeterministic. One can also introduce a probability for applying a rewrite rule to a multiset, resulting in stochastic simulation such as Gillespie's [9].

Each wall separating cells has two states, the closed and open states, and is associated with two molecular species, the *decomposer* and *composer* of the wall. In the closed state the wall separates two adjacent cells and their solutions are not mixed. If the decomposer exists in one or both cells, the wall is dissolved and changed to the open state. The cells are then merged and their solutions are mixed. In the open state, if the composer exists in the merged cells, the wall is constructed and changed to the closed state.

The time required for a state change of a wall depends on how solutions and reaction rules are modeled. In a continuous model, it is natural to assume that the time is proportional to the temporal integral of the concentration of the decomposer or composer. When the integral exceeds a certain limit, a state change occurs and the adjacent solutions are mixed or separated instantaneously. (If both the decomposer and the composer exist, they may compete with each other in contributing to the integral.) While contributing to the integral, the decomposer or composer may be consumed to a certain degree, as a result of which its concentration will decrease.

In a discrete model, a state change of a wall should be instantaneous just as an application of a rewrite rule to a cell. State changes of walls and applications of rewrite rules are interleaved and coordinated under a certain strategy.

The number of times each wall can be dissolved or constructed strongly depends on the implementation of walls and is also crucial to the computational power of gellular automata. One can classify gellular automata according to this parameter. In the extreme case, a wall is dissolved at most once and never reconstructed in the course of a computation.

The topology of cells depends on how gellular automata are used. It is natural to imagine a regular mesh structure of one-, two- or three-dimensional cellular space. The initial solutions in cells are defined according to some regular pattern over the space. The walls separating cells are also defined according to some pattern. It is natural to assume a block of cells and walls that is repeated and fills the cellular space. For example, in Fig.1, four kinds of walls are repeated in two-dimensional cellular lattice space. In this space, each cell is enclosed by four kinds of walls, so the solution in the cell can determine which wall to dissolve.

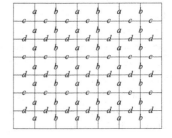

Fig. 1. Two-dimensional cellular lattice

2.3   Related Work

Tissue P systems consist of cells connected by synapses [10]. Rewrite rules for a cell transform a multiset of symbols in the cell. They can also specify symbols that are sent to adjacent cells through synapses. Although synapses do not have states, cells have states that can control application of rewrite rules. Therefore, discrete models of gellular automata introduced in the previous subsection can in principle be simulated by tissue P systems. Since molecules in each cell are represented by symbols in a multiset and they can be *counted*, it is usually the case that a small number of cells suffices to gain computational power.

It is possible to compare continuous models of gellular automata and tissue P systems with a set of symbols (not a multiset of symbols) in each cell. Alhazov showed that even if multiplicity of symbols is ignored, it is possible to achieve computational universality by allowing one to create and dissolve arbitrarily many membranes [11]. Giavitto, et al. studied Cayley P systems where cells are organized on a Cayley graph [12]. They also care only about existence or non-existence of a symbol in a cell, and characterize the final configuration of symbols under rewrite rules that are restricted to moving symbols between cells. Our work in the next section can be placed in this line of research because we only care which molecular species exist in a cell (though we adopt a continuous model).

3   Continuous Model and Signal Propagation

3.1   Continuous Model

In this section, we assume a continuous model of gellular automata, where each molecular species within a cell has a (possibly zero) real-valued concentration which changes in accordance with mass action kinetics defined by the reaction rules and their rates. As we pointed out in the previous section, we also think that being able to count the number of molecules is unrealistic and underlying mathematical models should be based on continuous kinetics for real-world applications. (But of course theoretical studies on various mathematical models are important.)

In the following, we allow a set of reaction rules that does not necessarily satisfy conservation of energy or mass as a whole. This means that some hidden molecules are supplied to or discharged from the entire system. For example, we assume that small molecules, such as ATP, can freely diffuse though gel walls. In this way, we can supply energy to the system.

Although behaviors of continuous models depend on concrete parameters such as reaction rates, they often allow qualitative reasoning based on big differences between parameters. For example, we sometimes assume that certain reactions are sufficiently fast compared with other reactions so that their reactants are consumed up almost instantaneously.

As we wrote in Section 2.2, the time to dissolve or construct a wall depends on the temporal integral of the concentration of the decomposer or composer of the wall with an appropriate coefficient. We assume that even while the decomposer or the composer contribute to the integral, their concentrations are not affected. We also assume that when a wall is dissolved, the adjacent solutions are mixed instantaneously.

3.2 Unidirectionally Propagating Signal

We consider a one-dimensional cellular space separated by gel walls. The i-th cell in the space is filled with a solution containing molecular species X_i. The concentrations of all X_i's are assumed to be identical. For example, they are initialized with 1.0. The i-th and $i+1$-th cell is separated by wall w_i.

	w_i	w_{i+1}	
X_i	X_{i+1}	X_{i+2}	

We prepare another molecular species that dissolves wall w_i and constructs wall w_{i-1} if w_{i-1} is absent, i.e., A_i is the decomposer of w_i as well as the composer of w_{i-1}. Now, assume that the solution of the i-th cell has been replaced with a solution containing A_i (of the same concentration 1.0), which dissolves wall w_i so that the i-th and $i+1$-th cells are merged.

A_i	X_{i+1}	X_{i+2}	

A_i, X_{i+1}	X_{i+2}	

We then assume two reaction rules: $A_i, X_{i+1} \to A_{i+1}, A_{i+1}$ and $A_{i+1} \to X_i$. The first reaction is assumed to be fast, so the solution will soon consist of only A_{i+1} and X_i. It is further assumed that A_{i+1} reconstructs w_i faster than it dissolves w_{i+1}. So, the i-th and $i+1$-th cells are separated again.

A_{i+1}, X_i	X_{i+2}	

A_{i+1}, X_i	A_{i+1}, X_i	X_{i+2}

The $i+1$-th cell will then be merged with the $i+2$-th cell because wall w_{i+2} will be dissolved by A_{i+1}.

	A_{i+1}, X_i	A_{i+1}, X_i, X_{i+2}	

We expect that the contents of the i+2-th cell will become A_{i+2}, X_{i+1}, and the above process will repeat. The i-th cell will eventually consist of only X_i due to the reaction $A_{i+1} \rightarrow X_i$.

We therefore assume the following three rules for each index i.

$$A_i, X_{i+1} \rightarrow A_{i+1}, A_{i+1} \quad X_{i-1}, X_{i+1} \rightarrow A_{i+1}, A_{i+1} \quad A_{i+1} \rightarrow X_i$$

The first two rules are assumed to be fast. For example, in our tentative numerical simulation, we assigned 0.1, 0.2, and 0.01 as reaction rates to the three rules, respectively.

For each wall, we assign a variable, say w, that ranges from 0 to 1. In the closed state, w is initialized as 1 and decreases by the temporal coefficient $0.03d$, i.e., $dw/dt = -0.03d$, where d is the average of the concentrations of the decomposer in the adjacent cells. When w reaches 0, the wall changes to the open state, and it increases with the temporal coefficient $0.03c$, i.e., $dw/dt = 0.03c$, where c is the concentration of the composer. When it reaches 1, the wall changes to the closed state.

In order to repeat the above process, we need at least five kinds of X_i, A_i and w_i for avoiding unintended interactions because X_{i+2} can interact with X_i and X_{i+4}. In other words, X_{i+5}, A_{i+5} and w_{i+5} can be identical to X_i, A_i and w_i, respectively.

3.3   Rotary Element

The construction in the previous subsection can be extended to implement a *rotary element*, which was introduced by Morita et al. for achieving computational universality in reversible computing [13]. As in Fig.2, a rotary element has four inputs and four outputs. The state of the rotary element, which is either 0 or 1, determines how the inputs are propagated to the outputs as shown in Fig.2. It is assumed that at most one of the four inputs is 1 and the others are 0. The input 1 can therefore be interpreted as a particle or a token. In the following, we use a propagating signal in the previous subsection to implement it.

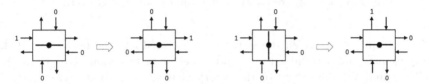

Fig. 2. A rotary element and its input/output

We assume two-dimensional cellular space. Our implementation of a rotary element consists of the central cell that is adjacent to four input cells and four output cells (Fig.3). A signal is propagated through the element as in the one-dimensional cellular space in the previous subsection. Let us regard one of the input cells as the i-th cell in the previous subsection, the central cell as the $i+1$-th cell, and one

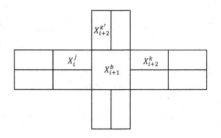

Fig. 3. Implementation of a rotary element

of the output cells as the $i+2$-th cell. Since the rotary element has two states 0 and 1, we prepare two molecular species X^0_{i+1} and X^1_{i+1}, respectively. For four input cells, we use superscript j ($1 \leq j \leq 4$) to identify the corresponding molecular species.

When a signal comes from the j-th input cell, it should consist of A^j_i and X^j_{i-1} and the central cell undergoes the following reaction rules.

$$A^j_i, X^b_{i+1} \rightarrow A^{bj}_{i+1}, A^{bj}_{i+1} \quad X^j_{i-1}, X^b_{i+1} \rightarrow A^{bj}_{i+1}, A^{bj}_{i+1} \quad A^{bj}_{i+1} \rightarrow X^{bj}_i$$

Molecular species A^{bj}_{i+1} and X^{bj}_i are prepared for each b and j. (Since the old state b of the rotary element is kept in X^{bj}_i, we should have introduced two versions of X^j_i. They behave identically when a signal comes from the $i-1$-th cell and produce A^j_i and X^j_{i-1}.)

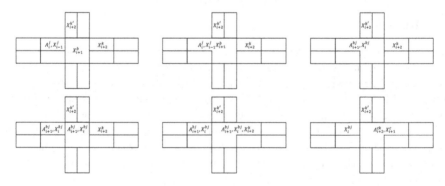

Fig. 4. Signal propagation through a rotary element (left to right)

The output cell to which the signal is propagated and the next state of the rotary element are determined by b and j. Let us assume that the k-th output is chosen and the next state of the rotary element is c. In this case, A^{bj}_{i+1} is assumed to reconstruct the wall from the j-th input cell and dissolves the wall to the k-th output cell, so the following reaction rules are prepared.

$$A^{bj}_{i+1}, X^k_{i+2} \rightarrow A^{ck}_{i+2}, A^{ck}_{i+2} \quad X^{bj}_i, X^k_{i+2} \rightarrow A^{ck}_{i+2}, A^{ck}_{i+2} \quad A^{ck}_{i+2} \rightarrow X^c_{i+1}$$

Note that the new state c of the rotary element is kept in A^{ck}_{i+2} for determining the next state of the rotary element in X^{c}_{i+1}. In this way (Fig.4), the signal is propagated according to the definition of the rotary element, and the element changes its state properly.

3.4   Computational Universality

Computational universality is not a major goal of the research on gellular automata, but it is a milestone to examine the computational power of various models of gellular automata.

As shown in the previous subsection, rotary elements can be implemented in a continuous model of gellular automata. Since it is possible to implement a universal (reversible) Turing machine by rotary elements, computational universality is achieved [13]. Note that in order to achieve universality, it should be possible to dissolve and reconstruct walls repeatedly, i.e., for an undetermined number of times.

4   DNA-Based Implementations

4.1   DNA-Based gels

Acrylamide gels can be constructed by cross links made of DNA strands that are tethered with polyacrylamide via acrydite modification [2, 3]. It is possible to control such a gel by displacing strands of DNA as in Fig.5. A cross link in a gel is made of a double strand, and a single strand that is complementary to

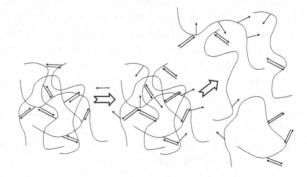

Fig. 5. Displacement of cross links in a DNA-based gel

one of the strands in a cross link displaces the other and breaks the link. Consequently, the gel is transformed to a sol and diluted in the surrounding solution. Conversely, if two sols containing complementary single strands tethered with polyacrylamide are mixed, they form a gel cross-linked by the double strands.

Another kind of acrylamide gel can be made of two kinds of cross links. One is by double strands of DNA as above, and the other is by bis-acrylamide as in ordinary acrylamide gels used for electrophoresis. This kind of gel can be swollen by destroying cross links by DNA because it absorbs water when it partially loses cross links [5].

On the other hand, shrinkable gels are not so easy to implement. Murakami and Maeda report a gel with single strands of DNA as cross links can be shrunk with complementary single strands that make links doubly stranded [6]. However, the gel cannot be swollen, and it is in general difficult to implement both shrinkable and swellable DNA-based gels.

4.2   Implementation of Walls

Using DNA-based gels as explained above, one can propose several approaches to
dissolve or construct walls by
DNA molecules. Decompos-
able walls are easy to implement. Acrylamide gels cross-
linked by double strands of
DNA can be dissolved by single strands of DNA that break
the cross links.

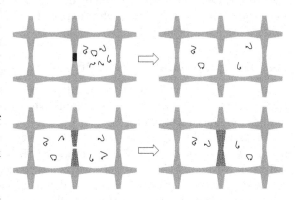

Fig. 6. Decomposable and composable walls

On the other hand, com-
posable walls are not so easy
to implement. One possible
approach is to use a swellable
gel that has a small hole. When the gel is swollen, the hole disappears and the
gel becomes a wall [14].

Walls that are both decomposable and composable (and
even repeatedly) are more difficult to implement. It is easy
to combine a decomposable and composable gels to make
a single wall, which can be decomposed once and composed once. By further combining such gels as in Fig.7, it
is possible to implement a wall that can be decomposed n
times and composed n times (but with different decom-
posers and composers). However, since both shrinkable
and swellable gels are not easy to implement, it remains
to design a wall that can be decomposed and composed
for an undetermined number of times.

Fig. 7. Combination
of walls

5   Preliminary Experiments

5.1   Dissolution of a Wall

A preliminary experiment was conducted to confirm that a DNA-based gel can
be used as a decomposable wall.

Materials and Methods. A PVC tube (Tygon® tube from Saint-Gobain
in Japan) with 3mm inside diameter and 5mm outside diameter (the thick tube)
and another tube with 1mm inside diameter and 3mm outside diameter (the
thin tube) were connected as in Fig.8. Two complementary DNA strands (F and
LB from [15]) with acrydite at their 5′-end were mixed at concentration about
300μM in a TAE solution of 10μL containing 12.5mM Mg^{2+}, 5% acrylamide,
0.21% TEMED and 0.42% APS. The solution was annealed (before APS was
put) from 95°C to the room temperature in about 70 minutes. The solution
(after APS was put) was injected at the junction of the two tubes as in Fig.8.

Another TAE solution of $40\mu L$ containing 12.5mM Mg^{2+} with or without $300\mu M$ of the displacing DNA strand (complementary to LB and denoted by Comp-LB) was then placed inside the thick tube. In addition, a 6x loading buffer of $8\mu L$ was placed in the thin tube.

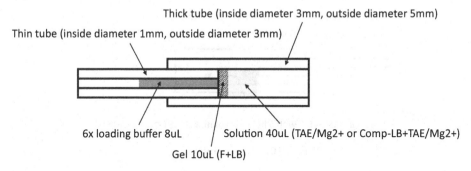

Thick tube (inside diameter 3mm, outside diameter 5mm)

Thin tube (inside diameter 1mm, outside diameter 3mm)

6x loading buffer 8uL   Solution 40uL (TAE/Mg2+ or Comp-LB+TAE/Mg2+)

Gel 10uL (F+LB)

Fig. 8. Decomposable wall

Result. After 115 minutes, the gel was dissolved only by the solution containing Comp-LB, and the loading buffer diffused to the side of the thick tube. In the case of the solution without Comp-LB, the gel remained even after a few days.

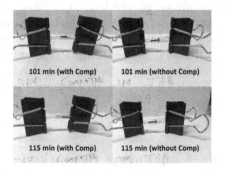

Fig. 9. The wall dissolved only by the solution with Comp-LB (left)

5.2   Construction of a Wall

A preliminary experiment was conducted to confirm that a swellable DNA-based gel can be used for making a composable wall.

Materials and Methods. Two complementary DNA strands (S and B8 from [5]) with acrydite at their 5′-end were mixed at concentration 4.42mM in a TAE solution of $20\mu L$ containing 12.5mM Mg^{2+}, 10% acrylamide, 1.4% (9mM) bis-acrylamide, 0.2% TEMED and 0.2% APS. The solution was annealed (before APS was put) from 95°C to the room temperature in about 70 minutes. The solution (after APS was put) was injected into a thick tube and a tiny tip (from Watson® used for gel loading) was inserted into the solution. After the gel was formed in one hour, the tip was removed and a small hole was made in the gel. A TAE solution of $30\mu L$ containing 12.5mM Mg^{2+} was placed in the tube and the gel was incubated in the solution for 3 hours. The solution was then removed. Two thin tubes, one is long and the other is short, were put inside the thick tube with narrow gaps between the gel and the thin tubes as in Fig.10. A TAE solution of 30µL containing 12.5mM Mg^{2+} and 4.42mM of the displacing DNA strand (P18 from [5]) was then placed inside the tubes. At this point, it was checked that the two thin tubes were connected via the gaps and the hole in the gel. After about 15 hours, a 6x loading buffer of 5µL was placed in the thick tube at the side of the short thin tube.

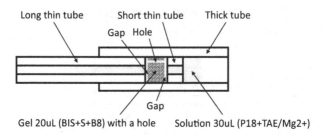

Long thin tube   Short thin tube   Thick tube

Gap Hole

Gap

Gel 20uL (BIS+S+B8) with a hole   Solution 30uL (P18+TAE/Mg2+)

Fig. 10. Composable wall

Result. As in Fig.11, the loading buffer could not diffuse to the long thin tube. This indicated that the gel was swollen and the gaps disappeared so that the two thin tubes were separated. The hole in the gel made by the tip was not filled (as checked with eyes). Although we put the loading buffer after about 15 hours, the gaps seemed to be filled in less than five hours.

Fig. 11. The gaps filled

6   Concluding Remarks

With the future progress of gel materials and gel printers, it will be possible to make more and more complex cellular space, and with the progress of DNA computing, it will also be possible to implement more and more sophisticated reaction rules. Alt-hough we used PVC tubes in our preliminary experiments, in the future it should be possible to construct the entire cellular space out of merely gels of various kinds. If walls in the cellular space shrink and swell, they not only control the flow of solutions but also lead to conformational changes of the entire structure. We therefore think that gellular automata are a good candidate for a chassis of a molecular robot.

We also think that gellular automata can be easily combined with electronics (cf. the fourth generation of molecular robots [1]) because circuits can be distributed over cellular space, and small chips can be embedded inside cells [16].

Acknowledgements. This research is supported by Grant-in-Aid for Scientific Research on Innovative Areas "Molecular Robotic" from MEXT, Japan.

References

1. Murata, S., Konagaya, A., Kobayashi, S., Saito, H., Hagiya, M.: Molecular Robotics: A New Paradigm for Artifacts. New Generation Computing 31, 27–45 (2013)
2. Liu, J.: Oligonucleotide-functionalized hydrogels as stimuli responsive materials and biosensors. Soft Matter 7, 6757–6767 (2011)
3. Lin, D.C., Yurke, B., Langrana, N.A.: Mechanical Properties of a Reversible, DNA-Crosslinked Polyacrylamide Hydrogel. J. Biomech. Eng. 126, 104–110 (2004)
4. Lee, J.B., Peng, S., Yang, D., Roh, Y.H., Funabashi, H., Park, N., Rice, E.J., Chen, L., Long, R., Wu, M., Luo, D.: A mechanical metamaterial made from a DNA hydrogel. Nature Nanotech. 7, 816–820 (2012)
5. Gao, M., Gawel, K., Stokke, B.T.: Toehold of dsDNA exchange affects the hydrogel swelling kinetics of a polymerdsDNA hybrid hydrogel. Soft Matter 7, 1741 (2011)
6. Murakami, Y., Maeda, M.: DNA-Responsive Hydrogels That Can Shrink or Swell. Biomacromolecules 6, 2927–2929 (2005)
7. Villar, G., Graham, A.D., Bayley, H.: A Tissue-Like Printed Material. Science 340, 48–52 (2013)
8. Langecker, M., Arnaut, V., Martin, T.G., List, J., Renner, S., Mayer, M., Dietz, H., Simmel, F.C.: Synthetic Lipid Membrane Channels Formed by Designed DNA Nanostructures. Science 338, 932–936 (2012)
9. Gillespie, D.T.: Exact stochastic simulation of coupled chemical reactions. J. Phys. Chem. 81(25), 2340–2361 (1977)
10. Martn-Vide, C., Pun, G., Pazos, J., Rodrguez-Patn, A.: Tissue P systems. Theoretical Computer Science 296, 295–326 (2003)
11. Alhazov, A.: P systems without multiplicities of symbol-objects. Information Processing Letters 100(3), 124–129 (2006)
12. Giavitto, J.-L., Michel, O., Cohen, J.: Accretive Rules in Cayley P Systems. In: Păun, G., Rozenberg, G., Salomaa, A., Zandron, C. (eds.) WMC-CdeA. LNCS, vol. 2597, pp. 319–338. Springer, Heidelberg (2003)
13. Morita, K.: A simple universal logic element and cellular automata for reversible computing. In: Margenstern, M., Rogozhin, Y. (eds.) MCU 2001. LNCS, vol. 2055, pp. 102–113. Springer, Heidelberg (2001)
14. Beebe, D.J., Moore, J.S., Bauer, J.M., Yu, Q., Liu, R.H., Devadoss, C., Jo, B.-H.: Functional hydrogel structures for autonomous flow control inside microfluidic channels. Nature 404, 588–590 (2000)
15. Zhang, D.Y., Turberfield, A.J., Yurke, B., Winfree, E.: Engineering Entropy-Driven Reactions and Networks Catalyzed by DNA. Science 318, 1121–1125 (2007)
16. McCaskill, J.S., et al.: Microscale chemically reactive electronic agents. International Journal of Unconventional Computing 8, 289–299 (2012)

Doubles and Negatives are Positive
(in Self-assembly)

Jacob Hendricks*, Matthew J. Patitz**, and Trent A. Rogers***

Abstract. In the abstract Tile Assembly Model (aTAM), the phenomenon of cooperation occurs when the attachment of a new tile to a growing assembly requires it to bind to more than one tile already in the assembly. Often referred to as "temperature-2" systems, those which employ cooperation are known to be quite powerful (i.e. they are computationally universal and can build an enormous variety of shapes and structures). Conversely, aTAM systems which do not enforce cooperative behavior, a.k.a. "temperature-1" systems, are conjectured to be relatively very weak, likely to be unable to perform complex computations or algorithmically direct the process of self-assembly. Nonetheless, a variety of models based on slight modifications to the aTAM have been developed in which temperature-1 systems are in fact capable of Turing universal computation through a restricted notion of cooperation. Despite that power, though, several of those models have previously been proven to be unable to perform or simulate the stronger form of cooperation exhibited by temperature-2 aTAM systems.

In this paper, we first prove that another model in which temperature-1 systems are computationally universal, namely the restricted glue TAM (rgTAM) in which tiles are allowed to have edges which exhibit repulsive forces, is also unable to simulate the strongly cooperative behavior of the temperature-2 aTAM. We then show that by combining the properties of two such models, the Dupled Tile Assembly Model (DTAM) and the rgTAM into the DrgTAM, we derive a model which is actually more powerful at temperature-1 than the aTAM at temperature-2. Specifically, the DrgTAM, at temperature-1, can simulate any aTAM system of any temperature, and it also contains systems which cannot be simulated by any system in the aTAM.

1 Introduction

Composed of large collections of relatively simple components which autonomously combine to form predetermined structures, self-assembling systems provide a framework in which structures can grow from the bottom up, with precise placement of individual molecules. Natural self-assembling systems, the results of which

* Department of Computer Science and Computer Engineering, University of Arkansas, `jhendric@uark.edu` Supported in part by National Science Foundation Grant CCF-1117672.

** Department of Computer Science and Computer Engineering, University of Arkansas, `patitz@uark.edu` Supported in part by National Science Foundation Grant CCF-1117672.

*** Department of Mathematical Sciences, University of Arkansas, `tar003@uark.edu` Supported in part by National Science Foundation Grant CCF-1117672.

O.H. Ibarra et al. (Eds.): UCNC 2014, LNCS 8553, pp. 190–202, 2014.
DOI: 10.1007/978-3-319-08123-6_16, © Springer International Publishing Switzerland 2014

include structures ranging from crystalline snowflakes to cellular membranes and viruses, have inspired a large body of research focused on both studying their properties and creating artificial self-assembling systems to mimic them. As experimental and theoretical research into self-assembly has increased in sophistication, particular attention has been focused upon the domain of *algorithmic self-assembly*, which is self-assembly intrinsically directed by algorithms, or step-by-step procedures used to perform computations. An example of a model supporting algorithmic self-assembly is the abstract Tile Assembly Model (aTAM) [16], which has spawned much research investigating its powers and limitations, and even more fundamentally those of algorithmic self-assembly in general.

In the aTAM, the fundamental components are square *tiles* which have sticky *glues* on the edges which allow them to bind with other tiles along edges sharing matching glues. Self-assembly begins from special *seed* assemblies, and progresses as tiles attach one at a time to the growing assembly. As simple as the aTAM sounds, when initially introducing it in 1998 [16], Winfree showed it be to capable of Turing universal computation, i.e. it can perform any computation possible by any computer. It was soon also shown that the algorithmic nature of the aTAM can be harnessed to build squares [14] and general shapes [15] with (information theoretically) optimal efficiency in terms of the number of unique kinds of tiles used in the assemblies. The rich set of results displaying the power of the aTAM (e.g. [4, 9, 13] to name just a few), however, have appeared to be contingent upon a minimal value of 2 for a system parameter known as the *temperature*. The temperature of an aTAM system is the threshold which, informally stated, determines how many glues a tile must bind to a growing assembly with in order to remain attached. Temperature-2 systems have the property that they can enforce *cooperation* in which the attachment of a tile requires it to correctly bind to at least two tiles already in the assembly (thus, those two tiles *cooperate* to allow the new tile to attach). This cooperation allows for each tile to effectively perform a primitive logical operation (e.g. **and**, **or**, **xor**, etc.) on the "input" values supplied by the tiles they bind to, and careful combination of these operations, just as with the gates in a modern electronic processor, allow for complex computations to occur. In contrast, the requirement for cooperation cannot be enforced in temperature-1 systems which only require one binding side, and it has thus been conjectured that temperature-1 aTAM systems are "weak" in the sense that they cannot perform universal computation or be guided algorithmically [5]. While this long-standing conjecture remains unproven in the general case of the aTAM, a growing body of work has focused on attempts to circumvent the limitations of temperature-1 self-assembly by making small variations to the aTAM. For instance, it has been shown that the following models are computationally universal at temperature-1: the 3-D aTAM [1], aTAM systems which compute probabilistically [1], the restricted glues TAM (rgTAM) which allow glues with repulsive (rather than just attractive) forces [12], the Dupled aTAM which allows tiles shaped like 2×1 rectangles [8], and the Signal-passing Tile Assembly Model [11] which contains dynamically reconfigurable tiles.

While such results may seem to indicate that those computationally universal models are as powerful as the temperature-2 aTAM, in [10] it was shown that 3-D temperature-1 aTAM systems cannot possibly simulate very basic "glue cooperation" exhibited in the temperature-2 aTAM where a new tile actually binds to two already placed tiles. Essentially, the weaker form of cooperation exploited by the 3-D temperature-1 aTAM to perform computation does allow for the restriction of tile placements based on the prior placement of two other tiles, but that form of cooperation seems to be fundamentally restrictive and "non-additive", meaning that the previously placed tiles can only prevent certain future tile bindings, but not cooperate to support new binding possibilities. In fact, that lesser form of cooperation now appears to be the limit for those temperature-1 models which can compute (with perhaps the exception of the active signal-passing tiles), as it was shown in [8] that the DaTAM also cannot simulate glue cooperation. It appears that the landscape modeling the relative powers of models across various parameters is more subtle and complicated than originally recognized, with the original notion of cooperative behavior being more refined.

The contributions of this paper are threefold. First, we show that the rgTAM is also not capable of simulating glue cooperation. Second, we introduce the Dupled restricted glue TAM (DrgTAM) which allows for both square tiles and "duple" tiles, which are simply pre-formed pairs of 2 tiles joined along one edge before assembly begins, and it allows for glues with negative strength (i.e. those which exert repulsive force). However, it is restricted similar to the rgTAM in that the magnitude of glue strengths cannot exceed 1 (i.e. only strengths 1 and −1 are allowed). Third, we show that by creating the DrgTAM by combining two models (the rgTAM and the Dupled aTAM) which are computationally universal at temperature 1 but which cannot independently simulate glue cooperation, the result is a model which in some measures is greater than the sum of its parts. That is, the resulting DrgTAM is capable of both universal computation *and* the simulation of glue cooperation. This is the first such result for passive (i.e. non-active) tile assembly systems. In fact, we show the stronger result that there is a single tile set in the DrgTAM which can be configured to, in a temperature-1 system, simulate any arbitrary aTAM system, making it intrinsically universal for the aTAM. Coupled with the result in [8] which proves that there are temperature-1 systems in the DTAM, which are thus also in the DrgTAM, that cannot be simulated by the aTAM at temperature-2, this actually implies that the DrgTAM is more powerful than the temperature-2 aTAM.

The paper is organized as follows. In Section 2 we give high-level sketches of the definitions of the models and of the concepts of simulation used throughout the paper. In Section 3 we prove that rgTAM systems cannot simulate the glue cooperation of temperature-2 aTAM systems, and in Section 4 we present the proof that the DrgTAM can simulate the temperature-2 aTAM and in fact contains a tile set which is intrinsically universal for it. Due to printing constraints, the formal definitions, color images, and proofs can be found in [7].

2   Preliminaries

Throughout this paper, we use three tile assembly models: 1. the aTAM, 2. the restricted glue TAM (rgTAM), and 3. the dupled rgTAM (DrgTAM). We now informally describe these models. Due to space limitations, the formal definitions can be found [7].

Informal Description of the Abstract Tile Assembly Model. A *tile type* is a unit square with four sides, each consisting of a *glue label*, often represented as a finite string, and a nonnegative integer *strength*. A glue g that appears on multiple tiles (or sides) always has the same strength s_g. There are a finite set T of tile types, but an infinite number of copies of each tile type, with each copy being referred to as a *tile*. An *assembly* is a positioning of tiles on the integer lattice $\mathbb{Z}^2$, described formally as a partial function $\alpha : \mathbb{Z}^2 \dashrightarrow T$. Let $\mathcal{A}^T$ denote the set of all assemblies of tiles from T, and let $\mathcal{A}^T_{<\infty}$ denote the set of finite assemblies of tiles from T. We write $\alpha \sqsubseteq \beta$ to denote that α is a *subassembly* of β, which means that $\operatorname{dom} \alpha \subseteq \operatorname{dom} \beta$ and $\alpha(p) = \beta(p)$ for all points $p \in \operatorname{dom} \alpha$. Two adjacent tiles in an assembly *interact*, or are *attached*, if the glue labels on their abutting sides are equal and have positive strength. Each assembly induces a *binding graph*, a grid graph whose vertices are tiles, with an edge between two tiles if they interact. The assembly is τ-*stable* if every cut of its binding graph has strength at least τ, where the strength of a cut is the sum of all of the individual glue strengths in the cut. When τ is clear from context, we simply say that a τ-stable assembly is stable.

A *tile assembly system* (TAS) is a triple $\mathcal{T} = (T, \sigma, \tau)$, where T is a finite set of tile types, $\sigma : \mathbb{Z}^2 \dashrightarrow T$ is a finite, τ-stable *seed assembly*, and τ is the *temperature*. An assembly α is *producible* if either $\alpha = \sigma$ or if β is a producible assembly and α can be obtained from β by the stable binding of a single tile. In this case we write $\beta \to_1^{\mathcal{T}} \alpha$ (to mean α is producible from β by the attachment of one tile), and we write $\beta \to^{\mathcal{T}} \alpha$ if $\beta \to_1^{\mathcal{T}*} \alpha$ (to mean α is producible from β by the attachment of zero or more tiles). When $\mathcal{T}$ is clear from context, we may write $\to_1$ and $\to$ instead. We let $\mathcal{A}[\mathcal{T}]$ denote the set of producible assemblies of $\mathcal{T}$. An assembly is *terminal* if no tile can be τ-stably attached to it. We let $\mathcal{A}_\square[\mathcal{T}] \subseteq \mathcal{A}[\mathcal{T}]$ denote the set of producible, terminal assemblies of $\mathcal{T}$. A TAS $\mathcal{T}$ is *directed* if $|\mathcal{A}_\square[\mathcal{T}]| = 1$. Hence, although a directed system may be nondeterministic in terms of the order of tile placements, it is deterministic in the sense that exactly one terminal assembly is producible (this is analogous to the notion of *confluence* in rewriting systems).

Since the behavior of a TAS $\mathcal{T} = (T, \sigma, \tau)$ is unchanged if every glue with strength greater than τ is changed to have strength exactly τ, we assume that all glue strengths are in the set $\{0, 1, \ldots, \tau\}$.

Informal Description of the Restricted Glue Tile Assembly Model. The rgTAM was introduced in [12] where it was shown that the rgTAM is computationally universal even in the case where only a single glue has strength -1. The definition used in [12] and the definition given here are similar to the irreversible negative glue tile assembly model given in [3].

The restricted glue Tile Assembly Model (rgTAM) can be thought of as the aTAM where the temperature is restricted to 1 and glues may have strengths $-1, 0$, or 1. A system in the rgTAM is an ordered pair (T, σ) where T is the *tile set*, and σ is a stable *seed assembly*. We call an rgTAM system an rgTAS. *Producible* assemblies in an rgTAS can be defined recursively as follows. Let $\mathcal{T} = (T, \sigma)$ be an rgTAS. Then, an assembly α is producible in $\mathcal{T}$ if 1. $\alpha = \sigma$, 2. α is the result of a stable attachment of a single tile to a producible assembly, or 3. α is one side of a cut of strength ≤ 0 of a producible assembly.

In [3], Doty et al. give a list of the choices that can be made when defining a model with negative glues. These choices are (1) seeded/unseeded, (2) single-tile addition/two-handed assembly, (3) irreversible/reversible, (4) detachment precedes attachment/detachment and attachment in arbitrary order, (5) finite tile counts/infinite tile counts, and (6) tagged result/tagged junk. Here we have chosen the rgTAM to be a seeded, single-tile addition, irreversible model that uses infinite tiles. We also assume that attachment and detachment in the model occur in arbitrary order, however the results presented here also hold in the case where detachment precedes attachment. Finally, the definition of simulation (see Section 2.1) implicitly enforces a notion of tagged result and tagged junk. In particular, if detachment occurs in a simulating system, of the two resulting assemblies one contains the seed and represents some assembly in the simulated system, while the other resulting assembly must map to the empty tile.

Informal Description of the Dupled Restricted Glue Tile Assembly Model. The DrgTAM is an extension of the rgTAM which allows for systems with square tiles as well as rectangular tiles. The rectangular tiles are 2×1 or 1×2 rectangles which can logically be thought of as two square tiles which begin pre-attached to each other along an edge, hence the name *duples*. A *DrgTAM system* (DrgTAS) is an ordered 4-tuple (T, S, D, σ) where, as in a TAS, T is a tile set and σ is a seed assembly. S is the set of singleton (i.e. square) tiles which are available for assembly, and D is the set of duple tiles. The tile types making up S and D all belong to T, with those in D each being a combination of two tile types from T.

It should be noted that the glue binding two tiles that form a duple must have strength 1, and the glues exposed by a duple may have strength -1, 0, or 1. Also notice that for an assembly α in a DrgTAS, a cut of strength ≤ 0 may separate two nodes of the grid graph that correspond to two tiles of a duple. Then, the two producible assemblies on each side of this cut each contain one tile from the duple.

2.1   Informal Definitions of Simulation

In this section, we present a high-level sketch of what we mean when saying that one system *simulates* another. Please see [7] for complete, technical definitions, which are based on those of [10].

For one system $\mathcal{S}$ to simulate another system $\mathcal{T}$, we allow $\mathcal{S}$ to use square (or rectangular when simulating duples) blocks of tiles called *macrotiles* to represent the simulated tiles from $\mathcal{T}$. The simulator must provide a scaling factor c

which specifies how large each macrotile is, and it must provide a *representation function*, which is a function mapping each macrotile assembled in S to a tile in T. Since a macrotile may have to grow to some critical size (e.g. when gathering information from adjacent macrotiles about the simulated glues adjacent to its location) before being able to compute its identity (i.e. which tile from T it represents), it's possible for non-empty macrotile locations in S to map to empty locations in T, and we call such growth *fuzz*. We follow the standard simulation definitions (see [2,4,6,10]), and restrict fuzz to being laterally or vertically adjacent to macrotile positions in S which map to non-empty tiles in T.

Given the notion of block representations, we say that S simulates T if and only if (1) for every producible assembly in T, there is an equivalent producible assembly in S when the representation function is applied, and vice versa (thus we say the systems have *equivalent productions*), and (2) for every assembly sequence in T, the exactly equivalent assembly sequence can be followed in S (modulo the application of the representation function), and vice versa (thus we say the systems have *equivalent dynamics*). Thus, equivalent production and equivalent dynamics yield a valid simulation.

We say that a tile set U is *intrinsically universal* for a class $\mathfrak{C}$ of tile assembly systems if, for every system $T \in \mathfrak{C}$ a system $\mathcal{U}_T$ can be created for which: 1. U is the tile set, 2. there is some initial seed assembly consisting of tiles in U which is constructed to encode information about the system T being simulated, 3. there exists a representation function R which maps macrotiles in the simulator $\mathcal{U}_T$ to tiles in the simulated system, and 4. under R, $\mathcal{U}_T$ has equivalent productions and equivalent dynamics to T. Essentially, there is one tile set which can be used to simulate any system in the class, using only custom configured input seed assemblies. For formal definitions of intrinsic universality in tile assembly, see [4,6,10].

3   A Temperature-2 aTAM System That Cannot Be Simulated by Any rgTAS

In this section we show that there exists a temperature-2 aTAM system that cannot be simulated by any rgTAM system. Here we give an overview of the TAS, T, that we show cannot be simulated by any rgTAS, and an overview of the proof. For sake of brevity, more rigorous details of the following proof can be found in [7].

Theorem 1. *There exists a temperature-2 aTAM system $T = (T, \sigma, 2)$ such that T cannot be simulated by any rgTAS.*

Let $T = (T, \sigma, 2)$ denote the system with T and σ given in Figure 1. The glues in the various tiles are all unique with the exception of the common east-west glue type used within each arm to induce non-deterministic and independent arm lengths. Glues are shown in part (b) of Figure 1. Note that cooperative binding happens at most once during growth, when attaching the keystone tile

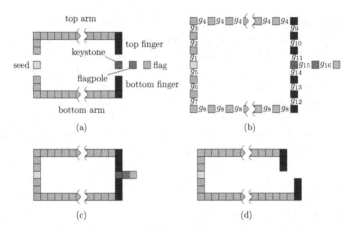

Fig. 1. (Figure taken from [10]) (a) An overview of the tile assembly system $\mathcal{T} = (T, \sigma, 2)$. $\mathcal{T}$ runs at temperature 2 and its tile set T consists of 18 tiles. (b) The glues used in the tileset T. Glues g_{11} and g_{14} are strength 1, all other glues are strength 2. Thus the keystone tile binds with two "cooperative" strength 1 glues. Growth begins from the pink seed tile σ: the top and bottom arms are one tile wide and grow to arbitrary, nondeterministically chosen, lengths. Two blue figures grow as shown. (c) If the fingers happen to meet then the keystone, flagpole and flag tiles are placed, (d) if the fingers do not meet then growth terminates at the finger "tips".

to two arms of identical length. All other binding events are noncooperative and all glues are strength 2 except for g_{11}, g_{14} which are strength 1.

The TAS $\mathcal{T}$ was used in [10] to show that there is a temperature-2 aTAM system that cannot be simulated by a temperature-1 aTAM system. To prove that there is no rgTAS that simulates $\mathcal{T}$, we use a similar proof to the proof for aTAM systems, however, we must take special care to show that allowing for a single negative glue does not give enough strength to the model to allow for simulation of cooperative glue binding.

The proof is by contradiction. Suppose that $\mathcal{S} = (S, \sigma_S)$ is an rgTAS that simulates $\mathcal{T}$. We call an assembly sequence $\boldsymbol{\alpha} = (\alpha_0, \alpha_1, \dots)$ in an rgTAS *detachment free* if for all $i \geq 0$, α_{i+1} is obtained from α_i by the stable attachment of a single tile. The following lemma gives sufficient conditions for the existence of a detachment free assembly sequence.

Lemma 1. *Let* $\mathcal{S} = (S, \sigma_S)$ *be an rgTAS and let* $\alpha \in \mathcal{A}[\mathcal{S}]$ *be a finite stable assembly. Furthermore, let* β *be a stable subassembly of* α. *Then there exists a detachment free assembly sequence* $\boldsymbol{\alpha} = (\alpha_1, \alpha_2, \dots, \alpha_n)$ *such that* $\alpha_1 = \beta$, *and* $\alpha_n = \alpha$.

A corollary of this lemma is that if an rgTAS gives a valid simulation of $\mathcal{T}$, it can do so using detachment free assembly sequences. Using detachment free assembly sequences, it is possible to use a technique for "splicing" subassemblies of producible assemblies of $\mathcal{S}$. This technique uses a lemma referred to as the "window movie lemma". For aTAM systems, this lemma is shown in [10]

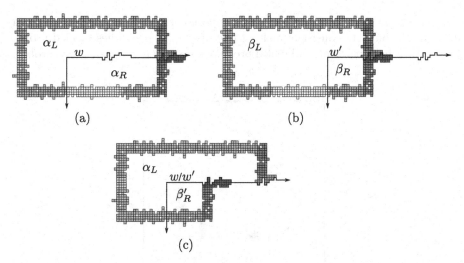

Fig. 2. An example assembly formed by S simulating $\mathcal{T}$ – (a) and (b), and the resulting producible assembly (c) constructed via a "splicing" technique that uses the window movie lemma. The assembly in (c) shows that S is incapable of valid simulation of $\mathcal{T}$.

(Lemma 3.1). We give a version of the window movie lemma that holds for detachment free assembly sequences. See [7] for the formal definitions of windows and window movies, and for a formal statement of the window movie lemma that we use. Figure 2 gives a depiction of this splicing technique. Here we use this lemma for detachment free assembly in the rgTAM. Then, using this splicing technique, we show that if S can simulate $\mathcal{T}$, it can also produce assemblies that violate the definition of simulation. In other words, we arrive at our contradiction and conclude that there is no rgTAS that can simulate $\mathcal{T}$.

4   Simulation of the aTAM with the DrgTAM

In this section, given an aTAM system $\mathcal{T} = (T, \sigma, 2)$, we describe how to simulate $\mathcal{T}$ with a DrgTAS at temperature 1 with $O(1)$ scale factor and tile complexity $O(|T|)$. It will then follow from [4] that there exists a tile set in the DrgTAM at $\tau = 1$ which is intrinsically universal for the aTAM at any temperature, i.e. it can be used to simulate any aTAM system of any temperature.

Theorem 2. *For every aTAM system* $\mathcal{T} = (T, \sigma, 2)$, *there exists a DrgTAS* $\mathcal{D} = (T_{\mathcal{D}}, S, D, \sigma', 1)$ *such that* $\mathcal{D}$ *simulates* $\mathcal{T}$ *with* $O(1)$ *scale factor and* $|S \cup D| = O(|T|)$.

We now provide a high-level overview of the construction. For the remainder of this section, $\mathcal{T} = (T, \sigma, 2)$ will denote an arbitrary TAS being simulated, $\mathcal{D} = (T_{\mathcal{D}}, S, D, \sigma', 1)$ the simulating DrgTAS, and R the representation function which maps blocks of tiles in $\mathcal{D}$ to tiles in $\mathcal{T}$. The system $\mathcal{T}$ is simulated by a DrgTAS through the use of macrotiles which consist of the components shown in Figure 3.

Note that macrotiles are not necessarily composed of all of the components shown in Figure 3, but will consist of at least one of the subassemblies labeled probe. Informally, the subassemblies labeled probe, which we will now refer to as probes,

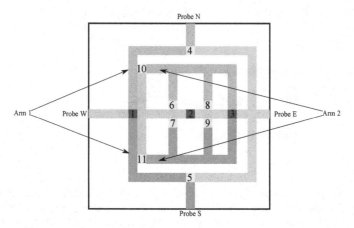

Fig. 3. Macrotile probes, points of cooperation, and points of competition

"simulate" the glues of the tiles in T. If a probe is simulating a glue which is of strength 2, then it does not require the assistance of any other probes in order to complete the macrotile containing it. On the other hand, if the glue which the probe is simulating is of strength 1, then the probe cannot assemble a new macrotile until another probe arrives which simulates a glue with which the other glue can cooperate and place a new tile in T. Before probes can begin the growth of a new macrotile, they must claim (i.e. place a tile in) one of the *points of competition* (shown as red in Figure 3) depending on the configuration of the macrotile. Once a special tile is placed in one of the points of competition, the representation function R maps the macrotile to the corresponding tile in T, and the growth of the macrotile can begin.

We use the following conventions for our figures. All duples are shown in darker colors (even after they are broken apart) and singletons are shown in lighter colors. Negative glues are represented by red squares protruding from tiles, and positive glues are represented by all other colored squares protruding from tiles. We represent glue mismatches (a glue mismatch occurs when two different glues are adjacent or a glue is adjacent to a tile side that does not have a glue) by showing the mismatching glues receded into the tiles from which they would normally protrude. A red box enclosing a subassembly indicates that subassembly has total binding strength 0.

The cooperator gadget is the underlying mechanism that allows for the DrgTAM to simulate the cooperative placement of a tile in a $\tau \geq 2$ TAS. We consider two cases of cooperative tile placement: 1) the tiles that cooperatively contribute to the placement of a tile have adjacent corners (e.g. one is north of the location to be cooperatively tiled while the other is to the east or west), and 2) the tiles that

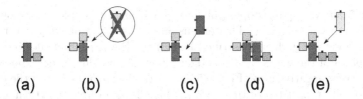

Fig. 4. An assembly sequence of an adjacent cooperator gadget

cooperatively contribute to the placement of a tile are non-adjacent, that is there is a tile wide gap between the two tiles. We create a cooperator gadget for each of these two cases. Not surprisingly, we call the cooperator gadget that mimics the former case the *adjacent cooperator gadget* and the cooperator gadget that mimics the latter case the *gap cooperator gadget*. Each of these two gadgets is asymmetric in nature and consists of two parts: 1) a finger and 2) a resistor. The function of the resistor is to cause a duple that is attached to the finger gadget to break apart and expose the internal glue of the duple which can then be used for binding of another tile.

An adjacent cooperator gadget is shown in Figure 4. Part (a) of this figure depicts the finger part of the gadget, and the subassembly labeled (b) is the resistor. Note that the only tiles which have the ability to bind to the exposed glues are duples with a negative glue that is aligned with the negative glue that is adjacent to the exposed glues. This means that neither subassembly can grow any further until its counterpart arrives. In Figure 4 parts (c) - (e) we see the assembly sequence showing the interaction between the two parts of the cooperator gadget. In this particular assembly sequence we have assumed that the resistor piece of the gadget has arrived first. In part (c), we see the arrival of a tile (presumably from a probe) which allows for the duple that is a part of the finger gadget to bind with total strength 1. The 0 strength cut that is induced by this binding event is shown by the red box in part (d) of the figure. Since the tile encapsulated in the red box is bound with total strength 0, it eventually detaches which leads us to part (e) of the figure. Notice that the dissociation event has caused a new glue to be exposed. This glue now allows for the binding of a duple as shown in part (e) of Figure 4.

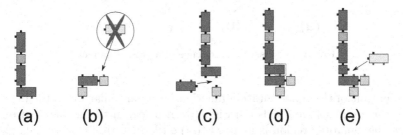

Fig. 5. An assembly sequence of a gap cooperator gadget

Figure 5 shows a gap cooperator gadget which is a simple extension of the adjacent cooperator gadget. This extension of the adjacent cooperator gadget allows for a crosser gadget (described below) to grow a path of tiles in between the two parts of the gadget. This gadget allows a new glue to be exposed upon the arrival of a negative glue (Figure 5 part (c)) which causes half of the duple to detach (shown in part (d) of the figure). This allows a duple to attach as shown in Figure 5(e) which depends on both of the glues exposed by the two parts of the gadget. Notice that the binding of this tile cannot occur unless both parts of the gadget are present.

The previous gadgets showed that in order for two probes to cooperate, they must be connected by a path of tiles. In order for other probes to cross in between these connected probes we utilize what we call a "crosser gadget". The assembly sequence for a crosser is shown in Figure 6. Growth of the gadget begins with the placement of a singleton which is prevented from growing further. This singleton exposes glues which allow for duples to bind (Figure 6(b) and (c)) that cause the path of tiles blocking the singleton's growth to detach (Figure 6(d)). Note that the attachment of these duples cannot occur before the singleton arrives since they would only have total binding strength zero. [7] offers a more in-depth description of the gadgets described above.

We can now use these gadgets to give a more complete description of the probes which are shown in Figure 3. All of the numbered regions represent gadgets. Gadgets labeled 1-3 in the figure represent gap cooperator gadgets which allow for cooperation between the probes to which they are attached. The gadgets labeled 5-9 denote adjacent cooperator gadgets which allow for the potential of cooperation between the probes to which they are attached. Finally, the gadgets labeled 10 and 11 are cooperator gadgets which allow for Probe W to trigger the growth of the second arms of Probe N and Probe S. See [7] for more details about the structure of probes and their accompanying gadgets.

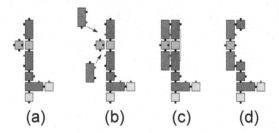

Fig. 6. An assembly sequence of a crosser gadget

The output of the representation function for a particular macrotile depends on the three regions labeled 1-3 in Figure 3. If a special tile is placed in region 1, then the macrotile region is mapped to the tile in T that corresponds to the special tile regardless of the tiles in the other regions. Similarly, region 3 takes precedence over region 2. Finally, if a special tile has not been placed in either region 1 or 3, then the output of the representation function depends on the tile placed in region 2.

The seed of our simulator is formed from a set of tiles in $S \cup D$ which have been hardcoded. For a more detailed explanation of the representation function and regions 1-3 see, a case analysis of how our construction handles all possible binding scenarios, and a more detailed explanation about the construction of the seed in the simulator, see [7].

Corollary 1. *There exists a DrgTAM tile set U which, at temperature-1, is intrinsically universal for the aTAM. Furthermore, the sets of singletons and duples, S and D, created from U are constant across all simulations.*

As mentioned above this result follows from [4]. See [7] for more details.

References

1. Cook, M., Fu, Y., Schweller, R.T.: Temperature 1 self-assembly: Deterministic assembly in 3D and probabilistic assembly in 2D. In: Proceedings of the 22nd Annual ACM-SIAM Symposium on Discrete Algorithms, SODA 2011. SIAM (2011)
2. Demaine, E.D., Patitz, M.J., Rogers, T.A., Schweller, R.T., Summers, S.M., Woods, D.: The two-handed assembly model is not intrinsically universal. In: Fomin, F.V., Freivalds, R., Kwiatkowska, M., Peleg, D. (eds.) ICALP 2013, Part I. LNCS, vol. 7965, pp. 400–412. Springer, Heidelberg (2013)
3. Doty, D., Kari, L., Masson, B.: Negative interactions in irreversible self-assembly. Algorithmica 66(1), 153–172 (2013)
4. Doty, D., Lutz, J.H., Patitz, M.J., Schweller, R.T., Summers, S.M., Woods, D.: The tile assembly model is intrinsically universal. In: Proceedings of the 53rd Annual IEEE Symposium on Foundations of Computer Science, FOCS 2012, pp. 302–310 (2012)
5. Doty, D., Patitz, M.J., Summers, S.M.: Limitations of self-assembly at temperature 1. Theoretical Computer Science 412, 145–158 (2011)
6. Hendricks, J., Padilla, J.E., Patitz, M.J., Rogers, T.A.: Signal transmission across tile assemblies: 3d static tiles simulate active self-assembly by 2d signal-passing tiles. In: Soloveichik, D., Yurke, B. (eds.) DNA 2013. LNCS, vol. 8141, pp. 90–104. Springer, Heidelberg (2013)
7. Hendricks, J., Patitz, M.J., Rogers, T.A.: Doubles and negatives are positive (in self-assembly). CoRR, abs/1403.3841 (2014)
8. Hendricks, J., Patitz, M.J., Rogers, T.A., Summers, S.M.: The power of duples (in self-assembly): It's not so hip to be square. In: Proceedings of 20th International Computing and Combinatorics Conference (COCOON 2014), Atlanta, Georgia, USA, August 4-6 (to appear, 2014)
9. Lathrop, J.I., Lutz, J.H., Patitz, M.J., Summers, S.M.: Computability and complexity in self-assembly. Theory Comput. Syst. 48(3), 617–647 (2011)
10. Meunier, P.-E., Patitz, M.J., Summers, S.M., Theyssier, G., Winslow, A., Woods, D.: Intrinsic universality in tile self-assembly requires cooperation. In: Proceedings of the ACM-SIAM Symposium on Discrete Algorithms (SODA 2014), Portland, OR, USA, January 5-7, pp. 752–771 (2014)

11. Padilla, J.E., Patitz, M.J., Pena, R., Schweller, R.T., Seeman, N.C., Sheline, R., Summers, S.M., Zhong, X.: Asynchronous signal passing for tile self-assembly: Fuel efficient computation and efficient assembly of shapes. In: Mauri, G., Dennunzio, A., Manzoni, L., Porreca, A.E. (eds.) UCNC 2013. LNCS, vol. 7956, pp. 174–185. Springer, Heidelberg (2013)
12. Patitz, M.J., Schweller, R.T., Summers, S.M.: Exact shapes and turing universality at temperature 1 with a single negative glue. In: Cardelli, L., Shih, W. (eds.) DNA 17. LNCS, vol. 6937, pp. 175–189. Springer, Heidelberg (2011)
13. Patitz, M.J., Summers, S.M.: Self-assembly of decidable sets. Natural Computing 10(2), 853–877 (2011)
14. Paul, W.K.: Rothemund and Erik Winfree. The program-size complexity of self-assembled squares (extended abstract). In: Proceedings of the Thirty-Second Annual ACM Symposium on Theory of Computing, STOC 200, Portland, Oregon, United States, pp. 459–468. ACM (2000)
15. Soloveichik, D., Winfree, E.: Complexity of self-assembled shapes. SIAM Journal on Computing 36(6), 1544–1569 (2007)
16. E. Winfree.: Algorithmic Self-Assembly of DNA. PhD thesis. California Institute of Technology (June 1998)

On String Languages Generated by Sequential Spiking Neural P Systems Based on Maximum Spike Number

Keqin Jiang[1,2], Yuzhou Zhang[2], and Linqiang Pan[1,⋆]

[1] Key Laboratory of Image Information Processing and Intelligent Control,
School of Automation, Huazhong University of Science and Technology,
Wuhan 430074, Hubei, China
jiangkq0519@163.com, lqpan@mail.hust.edu.cn
[2] School of Computer and Information, Anqing Normal University,
Anqing 246133, Anhui, China
zhangyuzhou@aqtc.edu.cn

Abstract. Spiking neural P systems (SN P systems, for short) are a class of distributed parallel computing devices inspired from the way neurons communicate by means of spikes. In this work, we consider SN P systems with the restriction: at each step the neuron with the maximum number of spikes among the neurons that can spike will fire (if there is a tie for the maximum number of spikes stored in the active neurons, only one of the neurons containing the maximum is chosen non-deterministically). We investigate the computational power of such sequential SN P systems that are used as language generators. We prove that recursively enumerable languages can be characterized as projections of inverse-morphic images of languages generated by that sequential SN P systems. The relationships of the languages generated by these sequential SN P systems with finite and regular languages are also investigated.

Keywords: Membrane computing, Spiking neural P system, Sequentiality, Maximum spike number.

1 Introduction

Spiking neural P systems were introduced in [4] as a class of distributed parallel computing models which were abstracted from the way neurons process information and communicate to each other by sending spikes along synapses. Since then, many computational properties of SN P systems have been studied. SN P systems were proved to be computationally complete as number generating or accepting devices [3,4,12,13], language generators [1,2,14], and function computing devices [8,9,15]. SN P systems can be also used to (theoretically) solve computationally hard problems in a feasible time [5,7]. Readers can refer to the

---

⋆ Corresponding author.

O.H. Ibarra et al. (Eds.): UCNC 2014, LNCS 8553, pp. 203–215, 2014.
DOI: 10.1007/978-3-319-08123-6_17, © Springer International Publishing Switzerland 2014

handbook [10] for the details of SN P systems, and the up-to-date information is available at the membrane computing website http://ppage.psystems.eu.

Briefly, an SN P system consists of a set of *neurons*, which are placed in the nodes of a directed graph whose arcs represent the *synapses*. Each neuron can contain a number of copies of a single object type, called the *spike*, *spiking* rules and *forgetting* rules. Using its rules, a neuron can send information (in the form of spikes) to all neurons connected by an outgoing synapse from it. The applicability of a rule is determined by checking the total number of spikes contained in the neuron against a regular expression associated with the rule. One of the neurons is the output neuron and its spikes are sent to the environment. The moments of time when a spike is emitted by the output neuron are marked with 1, the other moments are marked with 0. This binary sequence is called the *spike train* of the system. A result can be associated with a computation in various ways: for example, as the number of spikes sent to the environment or as the time elapsed between the first two consecutive spikes sent to the environment by the system. An SN P system can be used as a computing device in various ways, for example, as an acceptor, a transducer or as a language generator.

In [3], SN P systems were used as number generating devices and as number accepting devices with the restriction: at each step the neuron with the maximum number of spikes among the neurons that can spike will fire; if there is a tie for the maximum number of spikes stored in the active neurons, only one of the neurons containing the maximum is chosen non-deterministically. Such restriction under which SN P systems work is called "max-sequentiality". The computational power of SN P systems working in the max-sequentiality manner used as number generating devices and as number accepting devices was already investigated [3].

In this work, we investigate the computational power of SN P systems working in the max-sequentiality manner used as language generators. We prove that recursively enumerable languages can be characterized as projections of inverse-morphic images of languages generated by sequential SN P systems. The relationships of the languages generated by sequential SN P systems with finite and regular languages are also investigated.

2   SN P Systems Working in Max-sequentiality Manner

We recall the definition of SN P systems working in max-sequentiality manner. In the definition of the systems, the notion of regular expression is used, readers can refer to [11] for the details.

An SN P system working in max-sequentiality manner, of degree $m \geq 1$, is a construct of the form

$$\Pi = (O, \sigma_1, \sigma_2, \ldots, \sigma_m, syn, out), \text{ where:}$$

- $O = \{a\}$ is a singleton alphabet (a is called *spike*);
- $\sigma_1, \sigma_2, \ldots, \sigma_m$ are *neurons*, of the form $\sigma_i = (n_i, R_i)$ with $1 \leq i \leq m$, where
  a) $n_i \geq 0$ is the *initial number of spikes* contained in σ_i;

  b) R_i is a finite set of *rules* of the following two forms:
    (1) *firing* (or *spiking*) *rules*: $E/a^c \rightarrow a; d$, where E is a regular expression
        over O and $c \geq 1$, $d \geq 0$;
    (2) *forgetting rules*: $a^s \rightarrow \lambda$, for some $s \geq 1$, with the restriction that
        $a^s \notin L(E)$ for any rule $E/a^c \rightarrow a; d$ from R_i;
  • $syn \subseteq \{1, 2, \ldots, m\} \times \{1, 2, \ldots, m\}$ with $(i, i) \notin syn$ for $1 \leq i \leq m$ (*synapses*
    between neurons);
  • $out \in \{1, 2, \ldots, m\}$ indicates the *output* neuron of the system.

Firing rules are applied as follows. If the neuron σ_i contains k spikes, and $a^k \in L(E)$, $k \geq c$, then the rule $E/a^c \rightarrow a; d \in R_i$ can be applied. This means consuming c spikes (thus only $k - c$ spikes remain in neuron σ_i), the neuron is fired, and it produces one spike after d time units (as usual in membrane computing, a global clock is assumed, marking the time for the whole system). If $d = 0$, then the spike is emitted immediately, if $d = 1$, then the spike is emitted in the next step, etc. If the rule is used in step t and $d \geq 1$, then in steps $t, t+1$, $\ldots, t+d-1$ the neuron is closed (this corresponds to the refractory period from neurobiology), so that it cannot receive new spikes (if a neuron has a synapse to a closed neuron and tries to send some spikes along it, then these particular spikes are lost). In the step $t + d$, the neuron spikes and becomes again open, so that it can receive spikes (which can be used starting with the step $t + d + 1$, when the neuron can again apply rules).

If neuron σ_i contains exactly s spikes, then the forgetting rule $a^s \rightarrow \lambda$ from R_i can be used, meaning that all s spikes are removed from neuron σ_i. Note that, by definition, if a firing rule is applicable, then no forgetting rule is applicable, and vice versa.

Since two firing rules, $E_1/a^{c_1} \rightarrow a; d_1$ and $E_2/a^{c_2} \rightarrow a; d_2$, can have $L(E_1) \cap L(E_2) \neq \emptyset$, it is possible that two or more spiking rules can be applied in a neuron, and in that case only one of them is chosen non-deterministically.

A system works in *max-sequentiality* manner if, at each step, the neuron with the maximum number of spikes among the neurons that can spike will fire; if there is a tie for the maximum number of spikes stored in the active neurons, only one of the neurons containing the maximum is chosen non-deterministically.

The *configuration* of the system is described by both the number of spikes present in each neuron and by the number of steps to wait until the neuron becomes open (this number is zero if the neuron is already open). Thus, the *initial configuration* is $\langle n_1/0, n_2/0, \ldots, n_m/0 \rangle$. Using the rules as described above, we can define *transitions* from one configuration to another. Any sequence of transitions starting from the initial configuration is called a *computation*. A computation halts if it reaches a configuration where all neurons are open and no rule can be used. With any computation, halting or not, we associate a spike train, the sequence of symbols 0 and 1 describing the behavior of the output neuron: if the output neuron spikes, then we write 1, otherwise we write 0. The result of a halting computation is defined as the spike train associated with the computation. Note that, in order to associate a language of finite strings with an SN P system, we take into consideration only halting computations.

We denote by $L(\Pi)$ the language generated by system Π, and by $LSN_{mseq}P_m$ $(rule_k, cons_p, forg_q)$ the family of all languages generated by SN P systems working in the max-sequentiality manner, with at most $m \geq 1$ neurons, using at most $k \geq 1$ rules in each neuron, with all spiking rules $E/a^c \rightarrow a; d$ having $c \leq p$ and all forgetting rules $a^s \rightarrow \lambda$ having $s \leq q$ (the subscript $mseq$ stands for the max-sequentiality manner). When any of the parameters m, k, p, q is not bounded, then it is replaced by $*$.

3   The Computational Power of SN P Systems as Language Generators

In this section, we investigate the computational power of SN P systems working in the max-sequentiality manner as language generators.

3.1   Relationships with Finite Languages

It is known that the finite languages $\{0^k, 10^j\}$, $k \geq 1$, $j \geq 0$, cannot be generated by any standard SN P system [1]. However, in the next theorem, we will prove that such finite languages can be generated by SN P systems working in the max-sequentiality manner.

Theorem 1. *If $L_{k,j} = \{0^k, 10^j\}$, for $k \geq 1$, $j \geq 0$, then $L_{k,j} \in LSN_{mseq}P_4$ $(rule_1, cons_1, forg_0)$.*

Proof. For any $k \geq 2$ and $j \geq 1$, the finite language $L_{k,j} = \{0^k, 10^j\}$ can be generated by the SN P system shown in Fig. 1, working in the max-sequentiality manner.

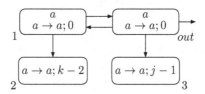

Fig. 1. A system generating the language $\{0^k, 10^j\}$, $k \geq 2$, $j \geq 1$

The system works as follows. Initially, each of neurons σ_1 and σ_{out} contains one spike. Both of them can fire, and both of them have the maximum number of spikes among the active neurons, so one of neurons σ_1 and σ_{out} must fire at the first step, which is non-deterministically chosen.

- If neuron σ_1 fires, it sends a spike to each of neurons σ_2 and σ_{out}, then neuron σ_{out} becomes inactive after receiving this spike and neuron σ_2 is enabled to fire at the next step. Because neuron σ_2 has a delay of size $k - 2$ associated

with its rule, neuron σ_2 fires, but its spike is lost, the system halts after step k. During this computation, the system sends no spike into the environment, so the system generates the string 0^k.
- If neuron σ_{out} fires at the first step, it sends one spike into the environment and one spike to each of neurons σ_1 and σ_3. At the next step, neuron σ_1 becomes inactive, and neuron σ_3 fires, with a delay of size $j-1$ associated with its rule, so the system halts after step $j+1$. During this computation, the system sends only one spike into the environment at the first step. So, the system generates the string 10^j.

If we remove neuron σ_2 and synapse $(1,2)$ from the system given in Fig. 1, then we can check that the obtained system generates $L_{1,j} = \{0, 10^j\}$, $j \geq 1$.

If we remove neuron σ_3 and synapse $(out, 3)$ from the system given in Fig. 1, then we can check that the obtained system generates $L_{k,0} = \{0^k, 1\}$, $k \geq 2$. If we remove neurons σ_2 and σ_3, and their related synapses from the system given in Fig. 1, then we can check that the obtained system generates $L_{1,0} = \{0, 1\}$.

Theorem 2. *If* $L = \{x\}$, $x \in \{0,1\}^+$, $|x|_1 = r$, $r \geq 0$, *then* $L \in LSN_{mseq}P_2$ $(rule_{max\{1,r\}}, cons_1, forg_0)$.

Proof. The string $x = 0^{n_1}10^{n_2}\ldots0^{n_r}10^{n_{r+1}}$, $n_j \geq 0$, $1 \leq j \leq r+1$, $r \geq 1$, and $n_{r+1} \geq 1$ can be generated by the SN P system given in Fig. 2, working in the max-sequentiality manner. The output neuron σ_{out} initially contains r spikes. At the first step, the rule $a^r/a \to a; n_1$ is applied consuming one spike, and at step $n_1 + 1$ one spike is sent to both the environment and neuron σ_1. Neuron σ_{out} continues firing until the rule $a/a \to a; n_r$ is applied, i.e., until all spikes in neuron σ_{out} are consumed. At step $n_1+n_2+\ldots+n_r+r$, the last spike is sent into the environment. At this moment, neuron σ_1 accumulates r spikes and becomes active. Neuron σ_1 fires, which makes the computation last for n_{r+1} more steps without any spikes sent into the environment. That is, the system halts after having generated n_{r+1} more occurrences of 0.

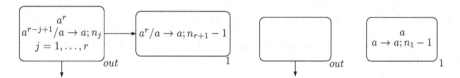

Fig. 2. A system generating a singleton language

Fig. 3. A system generating the language $\{0^{n_1}\}$

If we remove neuron σ_1 and synapse $(out, 1)$ from the system given in Fig. 2, then we can check that the obtained system generates the string $x = 0^{n_1}10^{n_2}\ldots$ $0^{n_r}1$, $n_j \geq 0$, $1 \leq j \leq r$, $r \geq 1$ (i.e., for the case $n_{r+1} = 0$).

The string $x = 0^{n_1}$ (i.e., for the case $r = 0$) can be generated by the system given in Fig. 3.

Theorem 3. *If $L \in FIN$, $L \subseteq \{0,1\}^+$, then $L\{1\} \in LSN_{mseq}P_1(rule_*, cons_*, forg_0)$.*

Proof. Let us assume that $L = \{x_1, x_2, \ldots, x_m\}$, with $|x_j 1| = n_j \geq 2, 1 \leq j \leq m$; denote $\alpha_j = \sum_{i=1}^{j} n_i$, for $1 \leq j \leq m$. We write $x_j 1 = 0^{s_{j,1}} 10^{s_{j,2}} 1 \ldots 10^{s_{j,r_j}} 1$, for $r_j \geq 1$, $s_{j,k} \geq 0$, $1 \leq k \leq r_j$.

The finite language $L\{1\}$ can be generated by the SN P system shown in Fig. 4, working in the max-sequentiality manner. The output neuron σ_{out} initially contains $\alpha_m + 1$ spikes. At the first step, only a rule $a^{\alpha_m+1}/a^{\alpha_m+1-\alpha_j} \to a; s_{j,1}$ can be used, and in this way we non-deterministically choose the string x_j we want to generate. After $s_{j,1}$ steps, for some $1 \leq j \leq m$, the system outputs a spike, hence, in this way the prefix $0^{s_{j,1}} 1$ of the string x_j is generated. Because α_j spikes remain in the neuron σ_{out}, we have to continue with rules $a^{\alpha_j - t + 2}/a \to a; s_{j,t}$, for $t = 2$, and then for the respective $t = 3, 4, \ldots, r_j - 1$; in this way, we introduce the substrings $0^{s_{j,t}} 1$ of x_j, for all $t = 2, 3, \ldots, r_j - 1$. The last substring, $0^{s_{j,r_j}} 1$, is introduced by the rule $a^{\alpha_j - r_j + 2} \to a; s_{j,r_j}$, which concludes the computation.

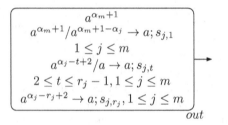

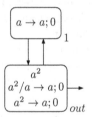

Fig. 4. A system generating the language $L\{1\}$

Fig. 5. A system generating an infinite language

Theorem 4. $LSN_{mseq}P_2(rule_2, cons_2, forg_0) - FIN \neq \emptyset$.

Proof. We can check that the system given in Fig. 5 generates the infinite language $(10)^+$.

3.2 Relationships with Regular Languages

As shown in Theorem 4, SN P systems with two neurons working in max-sequentiality manner can generate an infinite language. Similar with Lemma 7.1 from [2], we can also prove that an SN P system with two neurons working in the max-sequentiality manner can never generate a language which goes beyond regular languages; that is, we have $LSN_{mseq}P_2(rule_*, cons_*, forg_*) \subseteq REG$.

Theorem 5. $LSN_{mseq}P_3(rule_2, cons_2, forg_0) - REG \neq \emptyset$.

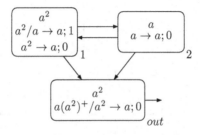

Fig. 6. A system generating a non-regular language

Proof. We can check that the SN P system given in Fig. 6 working in the max-sequentiality manner can generate the language $\{0^{2n-1}1^n \mid n \geq 1\}$, which is non-regular.

Theorem 6. *For every alphabet $V = \{a_1, a_2, \ldots, a_s\}$, there is a morphism $h : V^* \to \{0, 1\}^*$ such that for each language $L \subseteq V^*$, $L \in REG$, there is an SN P system Π working in the max-sequentiality manner such that $L = h^{-1}(L(\Pi))$.*

Proof. Let $V = \{a_1, a_2, \ldots, a_s\}$ and $L \subseteq V^*$, $L \in REG$. Consider a regular grammar $G = (N, V, S, P)$ such that $L(G) = L$ with $N = \{A_1, A_2, \ldots, A_n\}$, $n \geq 1$, $S = A_n$, and the productions in P are of the forms $A_i \to a_k A_j$ or $A_i \to a_k$, $1 \leq i, j \leq n$, $1 \leq k \leq s$. Then we consider the morphism $h : V^* \to \{0, 1\}^*$ defined by $h(a_k) = 0^k 10^{n+1}$, $1 \leq k \leq s$. The language $h(L)$ is regular. We modify the regular grammar G to obtain a regular grammar $G' = (N, \{0, 1\}, S, P')$ such that $L(G') = h(L)$, where the productions in P' are of the forms $A_i \to 0^k 10^{n+1} A_j$ or $A_i \to 0^k 10^{n+1}$, $1 \leq i, j \leq n$, $1 \leq k \leq s$. In what follows, we prove that $L(G')$ can be generated by the SN P system Π given in Fig. 7 working in the max-sequentiality manner.

The system Π works as follows. Initially, neuron σ_2 contains $n - 1$ spikes, neuron σ_3 contains $n - 2$ spikes, $\ldots$, neuron σ_n contains 1 spike and neuron σ_{out} contains $2n$ spikes. At the first step, only the output neuron σ_{out} can use its rule $a^{2n}/a^{2n-j} \to a; k$ or $a^{2n} \to a; k$, non-deterministically chosen, which are associated with the production $A_n \to 0^k 10^{n+1} A_j$ or $A_n \to 0^k 10^{n+1}$, respectively.

If the rule $a^{2n}/a^{2n-j} \to a; k$ is used, then one spike is produced and sent to neuron σ_1 and the environment in step $k + 1$, $2n - j$ spikes are consumed, and j spikes remain in neuron σ_{out}. At the next step, neuron σ_1 fires sending a spike to each of neurons $\sigma_2, \sigma_3, \ldots, \sigma_{n+1}$, then all of these neurons are active. Due to the max-sequentiality strategy, neurons $\sigma_2, \sigma_3, \ldots, \sigma_{n+1}$ fire in order one by one. Because these neurons have a delay of different size associated with their rules, n spikes from neurons $\sigma_2, \sigma_3, \ldots, \sigma_{n+1}$ will arrive at the same time in σ_{out}. Thus σ_{out} accumulates $n + j$ spikes, and a rule for $A_j \to 0^k 10^{n+1} A_{j'}$ or $A_j \to 0^k 10^{n+1}$ can be used. In this way, the simulation of rules in G' continues.

When a rule $a^{n+j} \to a; k$ (initially, $j = n$) is applied, i.e., $A_j \to 0^k 10^{n+1}$ is simulated, the output neuron σ_{out} will receive n spikes eventually from neurons

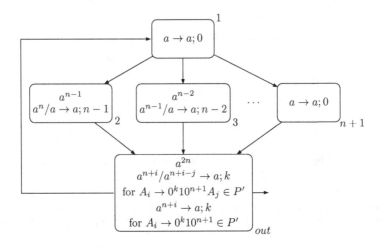

Fig. 7. The SN P system from the proof of Theorem 6

$\sigma_2, \sigma_3, \ldots, \sigma_{n+1}$ and no rule can be used, which means that the computation halts. The generated string is one from $h(L)$. Therefore, we have $L = h^{-1}(L(\Pi))$.

3.3   A Characterization of Recursively Enumerable Languages

Theorem 7. *For every alphabet $V = \{a_1, a_2, \ldots, a_s\}$, there are a morphism $h_1 : (V \cup \{b, c\})^* \to \{0, 1\}^*$ and a projection $h_2 : (V \cup \{b, c\})^* \to V^*$ such that for each language $L \subseteq V^*$, $L \in RE$, there is an SN P system Π' working in the max-sequentiality manner such that $L = h_2(h_1^{-1}(L(\Pi')))$.*

Proof. The two morphisms are defined as follows:

$$h_1(a_i) = 10^{3i+1}1, i = 1, 2, \ldots, s, \ h_1(b) = 0, \ h_1(c) = 01,$$
$$h_2(a_i) = a_i, i = 1, 2, \ldots, s, \ h_2(b) = h_2(c) = \lambda.$$

For a string $x = a_{i_1} a_{i_2} \ldots a_{i_k} \in V^*$, $1 \leq i_l \leq s$, $1 \leq l \leq k$, we denote $val_s(x) = i_1(s+1)^{k-1} + i_2(s+1)^{k-2} + \cdots + i_k$. We can extend this notation in the natural way to sets of strings, i.e., denote $val_s(L) = \{val_s(x) | x \in L\}$. For any language $L \subseteq V^*$, obviously $L \in RE$ if and only if $val_s(L) \in NRE$ [6]. In turn, a set of numbers is recursively enumerable if and only if it can be accepted by a deterministic register machine of the form $M = (m, H, l_0, l_h, I)$, where m is the number of registers, H is the set of instruction labels, l_0 is the start label, l_h is the halt label, and I is the set of instructions labeled in a one-to-one manner by the labels from H. The instructions are of the following forms:

- $l_i : (\text{ADD}(r), l_j)$ (add 1 to register r, then go to the instruction with label l_j),
- $l_i : (\text{SUB}(r), l_j, l_k)$ (if register r is non-empty, then subtract 1 from it and go to the instruction with label l_j, otherwise go to the instruction l_k),
- $l_h : \text{HALT}$ (the halt instruction).

In what follows, we give a specific SN P system Π' working in the max-sequentiality manner to generate the language L, which is given in Fig. 8.

The subsystem M in Fig. 8 corresponds to a deterministic register machine such that $N(M) = val_s(L)$. The subsystem M_0 corresponds to another register machine M_0. The role of register machine M_0 is to produce the number $val_s(x)$ and put it in the common register c_1, for each $x \in L$. Once the register machine M is triggered, the system passes to the phase of checking whether the number $val_s(x)$ stored in register c_1 is accepted. We assume that the register machines $M_0 = (m_0, H_0, l_{0,0}, l_{h,0}, I_0)$ and $M = (m, H, l_0, l_h, I)$ have $H_0 \cap H = \emptyset$.

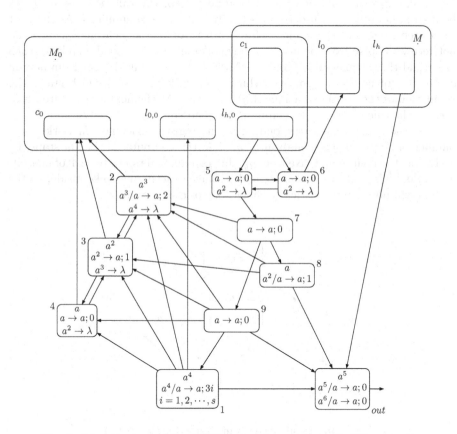

Fig. 8. The structure of the SN P system from the proof of Theorem 7

For each register r of the register machines M_0 and M, a neuron σ_r is associated in Π' whose contents correspond to the contents of the register. Specifically, if the register r holds the number $n \geq 0$, then neuron σ_r will contain $3n+3$ spikes; thus, the number zero (corresponding to the fact that the register is empty) is represented by a neuron with 3 spikes inside. Therefore, in the initial configuration, each of neurons σ_{c_0} and σ_{c_1} associated with registers c_0 and c_1 have three spikes. In order to produce the number $val_s(x)$ in the common neuron σ_{c_1}, the subsystem corresponding to register machine M_0 needs to perform the following operations: multiply the number stored in neuron σ_{c_1} by $s + 1$, then add the number from neuron σ_{c_0} (initially, having 3 spikes). Specifically, if neuron σ_{c_0} holds $3t + 3$ spikes and neuron σ_{c_1} holds $3n + 3$ spikes, for some $t \geq 0$, $n \geq 0$, then we end this step with $(3n + 3)(s + 1) + 3t + 3$ spikes in neuron σ_{c_1} and 3 spikes in neuron σ_{c_0}. In all cases below, $i \in \{1, 2, \ldots, s\}$.

The system Π' works as follows. Initially, neurons $\sigma_1, \sigma_2, \sigma_3, \sigma_4$ and σ_{out} contain 4, 3, 2, 1, 5 spikes, respectively. All of these neurons are active; due to the max-sequentiality manner, neuron σ_{out} fires by the rule $a^5/a \to a; 0$ sending the first spike into the environment. At the next step, the rule $a^4/a \to a; 3i$ can be used in neuron σ_1, non-deterministically choosing the number i. At the next three steps, neurons σ_2, σ_3 and σ_4 fire in turn. As long as neurons $\sigma_2, \sigma_3, \sigma_4$ do not receive a spike from neuron σ_1, they spike in turn and send a spike to each other and three spikes to neuron σ_{c_0}. After $3i$ steps a spike is sent from neuron σ_1 to each of neurons $\sigma_2, \sigma_3, \sigma_4$ (which stop working), $\sigma_{l_{0,0}}$ (which starts the simulation of the register machine M_0), and σ_{out}. At the next step, neuron σ_{out} fires by the rule $a^5/a \to a; 0$ sending the second spike into the environment.

Now, the subsystem corresponding to the register machine M_0 works for a number of steps (at least one); after a while the computation in M_0 stops, by activating the neuron $\sigma_{l_{h,0}}$. Neuron $\sigma_{l_{h,0}}$ fires sending one spike to each of neurons σ_5 and σ_6. Then both neurons σ_5 and σ_6 have exactly one spike inside, so the system will non-deterministically choose one of them to fire.

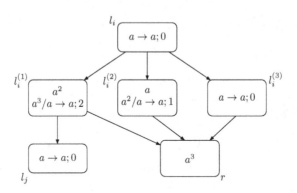

Fig. 9. Module ADD (simulating $l_i : (\text{ADD}(r), l_j)$)

If neuron σ_5 fires at the next step, then it sends one spike to each of neurons σ_6 and σ_7, making the forgetting rule in neuron σ_6 applicable, and making neuron σ_7 active. At the next step, neuron σ_7 fires sending one spike to each of neurons σ_2, σ_8 and σ_9. Then, neurons σ_8 and σ_9 fire in order, the two spikes from σ_8 and σ_9 arrive at the same time in the neurons σ_2, σ_3 and σ_{out}, because of the delay. Now, neurons $\sigma_1, \sigma_2, \sigma_3, \sigma_4$ and σ_{out} contain 4, 3, 2, 1, 6 spikes, respectively. Due to the max-sequentiality manner, neuron σ_{out} fires by the rule $a^6/a \to a; 0$

sending a spike into the environment. At the next step, neuron σ_{out} fires again by the rule $a^5/a \to a; 0$ sending a spike outside, and the system returns neurons $\sigma_1, \sigma_2, \sigma_3, \sigma_4$ to the initial state. This means that a sequence of two spikes is sent out, and the process continues by introducing another substring $0^{3i+1}10^j$ in the string produced by the system.

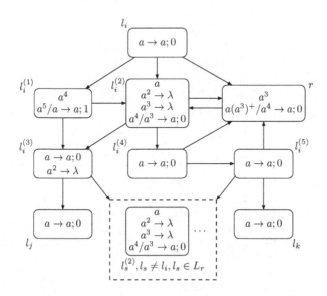

Fig. 10. Module SUB (simulating $l_i : (\text{SUB}(r), l_j, l_k)$) for the register machine M_0, where $L_r = \{l \mid l$ is a label of a SUB instruction acting on the register $r\}$

If neuron σ_6 fires, then it sends one spike to neuron σ_5, making the forgetting rule in σ_5 applicable, and another spike to neuron σ_{l_0} that is associated with the initial label of the register machine M. Thus we have got the number $val_s(x)$ stored in neuron σ_{c_1} for a string $x \in V^*$ such that the string produced by Π' up to now is of the form $z = 10^{3i_1+1}10^{j_1}110^{3i_2+1}10^{j_2}11 \ldots 110^{3i_k+1}10^{j_k}$, for $1 \le i_l \le s$, $j_l \ge 1$, $1 \le l \le k$, whereas, $h_1(x) = 10^{3i_1+1}110^{3i_2+1}1 \ldots 10^{3i_k+1}1$. The system starts to simulate the work of the machine M in recognizing the number $val_s(x)$. The subsystem M works for a number of steps (at least one), and the computation in M stops if and only if the number $val_s(x)$ is accepted, which means that $x \in L$. After receiving a spike from neuron σ_{l_h}, the output neuron σ_{out} fires and then the system halts. Therefore, the previous string z is continued with a suffix of the form 0^p1 for $p \ge 1$. In this way, a string of the form $y = 10^{3i_1+1}10^{j_1}110^{3i_2+1}10^{j_2}11 \ldots 110^{3i_k+1}10^{j_k}0^p1$ is produced by Π' if and only if $x \in L$. Moreover, it is obvious that $x = h_2(h_1^{-1}(y)) \in L$: we have $h_1^{-1}(y) = a_{i_1}b^{j_1-1}ca_{i_2}b^{j_2-1}c \ldots a_{i_k}b^{j_k+p-1}c$; the projection h_2 simply removes the auxiliary symbols b, c.

In order to complete the proof we have to show how the two register machines M_0 and M are simulated, using the common neuron σ_{c_1} but without mixing the

computations. To this aim, we consider the modules ADD and SUB from Figs.
9, 10 and 11. Because the constructions are similar to those used in the proof of
Theorem 1 from [9], we do not enter into details here.

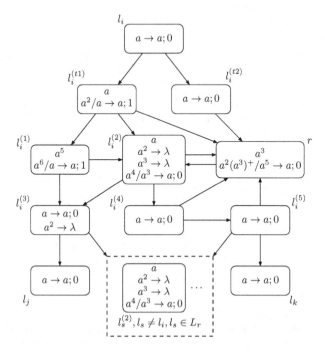

Fig. 11. Module SUB (simulating $l_i : (\mathtt{SUB}(r), l_j, l_k)$) for the register machine M, where
$L_r = \{l \mid l$ is a label of a SUB instruction acting on the register $r\}$

4   Conclusions and Remarks

In this work, we investigated the computational power of SN P systems working
in a max-sequentiality manner. We gave a characterization of recursively enumerable languages, and the relationships of the languages generated by such SN
P systems with finite and regular languages. It still remains open how we can
give a characterization of regular languages by that sequential SN P systems.

The sequentiality considered in this work is induced by the maximum number
of spikes among the active neurons. In [3], another way of sequentiality was considered, which is induced by the minimum number of spikes among the active
neurons, and it was shown that there is a difference in the universality results
of SN P systems working in these two kinds of sequentiality. Used as language
generators, it is still of interest to give a characterization of recursively enumerable languages by SN P systems working in the sequentiality induced by the
minimum number of spikes among the active neurons.

Acknowledgments. This work was supported by National Natural Science Foundation of China (61370105, 61033003, 91130034 and 61320106005), Ph.D. Programs Foundation of Ministry of Education of China (20120142130008), Anhui Provincial Natural Science Foundation (1408085MF131), Natural Science Research Project for Higher Education Institutions of Anhui Province(KJ2014A140).

References

1. Chen, H., Freund, R., Ionescu, M., Păun, G., Pérez-Jiménez, M.J.: On string languages generated by spikng neural P systems. Fund. Inform. 75, 141–162 (2007)
2. Chen, H., Ionescu, M., Ishdorj, T.-O., Păun, A., Păun, G., Pérez-Jiménez, M.J.: Spiking neural P systems with extended rules: universality and languages. Nat. Comput. 7(2), 147–166 (2008)
3. Ibarra, O.H., Păun, A., Rodríguez-Patón, A.: Sequential SNP systems based on min/max spike number. Theor. Comput. Sci. 410(30-32), 2982–2991 (2009)
4. Ionescu, M., Păun, G., Yokomori, T.: Spiking neural P systems. Fund. Inform. 71(2-3), 279–308 (2006)
5. Ishdorj, T.-O., Leporati, A., Pan, L., Zeng, X., Zhang, X.: Deterministic solutions to QSAT and Q3SAT by spiking neural P systems with pre-computed resources. Theor. Comput. Sci. 411(25), 2345–2358 (2010)
6. Minsky, M.: Computation – Finite and Infinite Machines. Prentice Hall, Englewood Cliffs, New Jersey (1967)
7. Pan, L., Păun, G., Pérez-Jiménez, M.J.: Spiking neural P systems with neuron division and budding. Sci. China Inform. Sci. 54(8), 1596–1607 (2011)
8. Păun, A., Păun, G.: Small universal spiking neural P systems. BioSystems 90(1), 48–60 (2007)
9. Păun, A., Sidoroff, M.: Sequentiality induced by spike number in SNP systems: Small universal machines. In: Gheorghe, M., Păun, G., Rozenberg, G., Salomaa, A., Verlan, S. (eds.) CMC 2011. LNCS, vol. 7184, pp. 333–345. Springer, Heidelberg (2012)
10. Păun, G., Rozenberg, G., Salomaa, A. (eds.): Handbook of Membrane Computing. Oxford University Press, Cambridge (2010)
11. Rozenberg, G., Salomaa, A. (eds.): Handbook of Formal Languages, vol. 3. Springer, Berlin (1997)
12. Song, T., Pan, L., Păun, G.: Asynchronous spiking neural P systems with local synchronization. Inform. Sciences 219, 197–207 (2013)
13. Wang, J., Hoogeboom, H.J., Pan, L., Păun, G., Pérez-Jiménez, M.J.: Spiking neural P systems with weights. Neural Comput. 22(10), 2615–2646 (2010)
14. Zhang, X., Zeng, X., Pan, L.: On languages generated by asynchronous spiking neural P systems. Theor. Comput. Sci. 410(26), 2478–2488 (2009)
15. Zhang, X., Zeng, X., Pan, L.: Smaller universal spiking neural P systems. Fund. Inform. 87(1), 117–136 (2008)

Languages Associated
with Crystallographic Symmetry

Nataša Jonoska, Mile Krajcevski, and Gregory McColm

Department of Mathematics and Statistics
University of South Florida, Tampa FL, 33620 USA
jonoska,mile@mail.usf.edu, mccolm@usf.edu

Abstract. We establish a relationship between periodic graphs representing crystallographic structures and an infinite hierarchy of intersection languages $\mathcal{DCL}_d$, $d = 0, 1, 2, \ldots$, within the intersection classes of deterministic context-free languages. We introduce a class of counter machines that accept these languages, where the machines with d counters recognize the class $\mathcal{DCL}_d$. Each language in $\mathcal{DCL}_d$ is an intersection of d languages in $\mathcal{DCL}_1$. We prove that there is a one-to-one correspondence between sets of walks starting and ending in the same unit of a d-dimensional periodic (di)graph and the class of languages in $\mathcal{DCL}_d$.

1 Introduction

We consider periodic digraphs that are often associated with periodic (or crystallographic) nano structures such that vertices of the graph correspond to the molecular (or atomic) arrangement in the structure and the edges, or arcs, represent their bonds. Often these structures are obtained by different building blocks (tiles) periodically arranged on a lattice with possibly different interconnecting bonds. Figure 1 depicts an example where the vertices of a two-dimensional lattice could be populated with hexagonal components which bond with other hexagonal tiles in one direction but requires another building block (star-shaped tiles) to connect in the other direction. Although the development of X-ray diffraction analysis of crystals [9,21] enabled physicists and chemists to develop graphical representations of crystals ("crystal nets") found in nature, or in the lab, the "de novo" generation of crystal nets appear to have begun in earnest in the 1970s and 1980s, especially with the cataloguing work of A. Wells [25] (see also [22]). A variety of crystallographic structures have been obtained by allowing self-assembly of chemical building blocks varying from DNA [26] to metal-organic frameworks [24]. However, a systematic theoretical study and analysis of self-assembled nanostructures seems to be lagging behind. Even the notion of a periodic structure seems to have different meanings in different contexts (see for example [6,8,17]). With this paper we suggest an approach to study periodic structures through formal language theory.

O.H. Ibarra et al. (Eds.): UCNC 2014, LNCS 8553, pp. 216–228, 2014.
DOI: 10.1007/978-3-319-08123-6_18, © Springer International Publishing Switzerland 2014

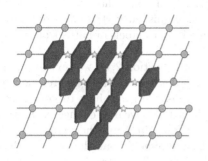

Fig. 1. Red irregular hexagonal tiles and orange pentagram-shaped tiles in a 2-periodic array. Edges mark bonds or ligands between hexagonal molecular building blocks.

What languages can describe walks in a given (crystallographic) nano structure? One way to answer this question is by considering walks in the underlying (periodic) (di)graphs. We label the edges of the graphs with appropriate labels indicating the distinct bonds within the structure. The set of labels of all such walks represents a language over the alphabet of bonds. In [14,15], the computational power of molecular bondings without the geometric constraints imposed by their spacial imbedding was considered, and it was shown that there is a hierarchy of complexity classes that can be associated with these constructions. In this paper we address periodic nano structures only, and examine the set of languages associated with cyclic walks in periodic digraphs, thereby considering also the spacial embedding of the structures. We show that these languages are closely related to nested families of deterministic context-free languages.

We introduce a new class of languages, a proper subclass of the Deterministic Context Free Languages ($\mathcal{DCFL}$), recognized by machines with counters. Ibarra et al ([11,12]) introduced PDA-like *multi-counter machines* with counters instead of stacks. As it is known that a two-counter machine has computational power equivalent to a universal Turing machine, the authors in [11] restricted the number of permitted "reversals" in the counters for each computation (i.e., the number of counter changes from incremental to decremental and vice versa was restricted). In this paper, we bar communication between the counters, there are no ϵ-moves, and the machine accepts only if all counters are at zero at the termination of the computation. Denote $\mathcal{DCL}_d$ as the class of languages accepted by such deterministic counter machines with d counters. We find that $\mathcal{DCL}_d$ is the intersection of d languages in $\mathcal{DCL}_1$.

Intuitively, a periodic (di)graph is a graph that is, or can be, embedded in a Euclidean space so that it is periodic in the requisite number of axial directions. As mentioned above, we suppose that the vertices of such embedding can be populated with chemical building blocks. The space that a Euclidean graph is embedded in can be regarded as being partitioned into *unit cells*, with the subgraph of each unit cell isomorphic to the subgraph of any other unit cell. The vertices in each unit cell could represent distinct chemical building block, such that vertices in each unit belonging to the same orbit represent the same chemical building block. Periodic digraphs capture the DCL hierarchy in the following way (Theorem 2): For any language $L \subseteq \Sigma^*$ in $\mathcal{DCL}_d$, there is a periodic digraph that can be embedded in d-dimensional Euclidean space, with a distinguished vertex v and arcs periodically labeled by letters in Σ, such that the words of L correspond precisely to labels of paths from v back to an appropriate vertex in

v's unit cell. Conversely, for any labeled periodic digraph that can be embedded in d-dimensional Eucledean space with a distinguished vertex v, there exists a $\mathcal{DCL}_d$ language whose words correspond precisely to labels of paths from v back to v's unit cell.

After notational and algebraic preliminaries (Section 2.1), we review the notion of a periodic graph (Section 2.2). In order to establish the relationship between counter machines and periodic graphs, we show how to construct a periodic graph that has as a quotient a given finite weakly connected digraph (Section 3.1). We define deterministic counter machines and their languages denoted DCLs (Section 3.2). Because of the requirement that the counters have no ϵ-moves and the computation terminates with all counters at value 0, it follows that DCLs form a proper subset of DCFLs (Proposition 3). We consider the DCL intersection hierarchy: we verify that it is of the same "height" if not the same "width," as the DCFL and CFL hierarchies. Section 3.3 contains the main theorem verifying that the cyclic walks in (appropriately labeled) periodic digraphs capture the DCL hierarchy.

2   Periodic Digraphs

2.1   Preliminaries and Nomenclature

A function $f\colon X \to Y$ is *partial* if its domain is a proper subset of X; it is *total* if X is its domain. A *digraph structure* is a tuple $\Gamma = \langle V, A, \tau, \iota \rangle$, where V is the set of *vertices*, A is the set of *arcs*, $\iota\colon A \to V$ is a (possibly partial) function assigning *initial vertices* to arcs and $\tau\colon A \to V$ is a (possibly partial) function assigning *terminal vertices* to arcs. We write a^{-1} for an arc $a \in A$ to indicate an arc with opposite orientation of a, that is, $\tau(a) = \iota(a^{-1})$ and $\iota(a) = \tau(a^{-1})$. Call Γ a *digraph* if ι and τ are total.

Let $\Gamma = \langle V, A, \tau, \iota \rangle$ be a digraph structure. A *digraph substructure* of Γ is a structure $\langle V', A', \iota', \tau' \rangle$, where $V' \subseteq V$, $A' \subseteq A$, and for each arc $a \in A'$ if $\iota(a) \in V' \implies \iota'(a) = \iota(a)$ and $\tau(a) \in V' \implies \tau'(a) = \tau(a)$. Notice that a digraph substructure of a digraph need not have total initial and terminal functions, hence a digraph substructure need not be a digraph.

Given a digraph $\Gamma = \langle V, A, \tau, \iota \rangle$, a *walk* in Γ is a string of arcs $a_1 a_2 \cdots a_n$ such that for each i, $\tau(a_i) = \iota(a_{i+1})$; $\iota(a_1)$ is the *initial vertex* of the walk while $\tau(a_n)$ is the *terminal vertex* of the walk. The number of arcs, n, is the length of the walk $a_1 a_2 \cdots a_n$. The walk is *trivial* if it's length is zero, meaning, it starts and ends at the same vertex and has no edges. There is one trivial walk for each vertex v. We say that a walk is a walk *from* its initial vertex *to* its terminal vertex. A walk in which the initial and terminal vertices are the same is *cyclic*.

A *semi-walk* in Γ is a string of arcs $a_1 a_2 \cdots a_n$ such that there is a subsequence $a_{i_1} \cdots a_{i_k}$ and a walk $a_1^{\epsilon_1} \cdots a_n^{\epsilon_n}$ where $\epsilon_j = \begin{cases} 1 & \text{if } j \neq i_s \text{ for all } s = 1, \ldots, k \\ -1 & \text{if } j = i_s \text{ for some } s = 1, \ldots, k \end{cases}$ for each $j = 1, \ldots, n$. Below we write $a_1^{\epsilon_1} a_2^{\epsilon_2} \cdots a_n^{\epsilon_n}$ for the semi-walk where the negative exponent for an arc indicates walking across the arc in an opposite direction. A semi-walk is *from* u *to* v if $u = \iota(a_1^{\epsilon_1})$ and $v = \tau(a_n^{\epsilon_n})$. A digraph structure Γ is *weakly connected* if, for any vertices u, v, there is a semi-walk from u to v.

An *automorphism* of Γ is a bijection $f\colon V \to V : A \to A$ such that for any $a \in A$, $f(\iota(a)) = \iota(f(a))$ and $f(\tau(a)) = \tau(f(a))$. Given any group G of automorphisms, and any $v \in V$, the *G-orbit of v* is the set of vertices $G(v) = \{g(v)\colon g \in G\}$; similarly, given any arc $a \in A$, the *G-orbit of a* is the set of arcs $G(a) = \{g(a)\colon g \in G\}$. If $V' \subseteq V$, let $G(V') = \bigcup_{v \in V'} G(v)$, and similarly if $A' \subseteq A$, let $G(A') = \bigcup_{a \in A'} G(a)$. Say that a group G of automorphisms of a digraph $\Gamma = \langle V, A, \tau, \iota \rangle$ *acts freely* on Γ if, for every $g \in G$ besides the identity, every $v \in V$ satisfies $g(v) \neq v$.

Given an alphabet Σ, the set of all words over Σ is denoted Σ^*, and the set of all words of positive length is Σ^+. For a word $w = a_1 \cdots a_k \in \Sigma^*$, $k = |w|$ is the length of w, and $(w)_j = a_j$ so that the last symbol a_k is $(w)_{|w|}$. Similarly, if S is a set, $|S|$ is the cardinality of S.

2.2   Periodic Digraphs and Units

There are several definitions of "periodic graphs" in literature, but we focus on one which turns out to be equivalent to a widely spread intuition. Given a digraph Γ with vertices V and arcs A, an injective map $\pi\colon V \to \mathbb{R}^d$ is *uniformly discrete* if there exist $\delta > 0$ such that for any $\mathbf{u}, \mathbf{v} \in \pi[V]$, $\|\mathbf{v} - \mathbf{u}\| > \delta$. The following definition seems to have emerged from a thread including [2] and [5]; see [7].

Definition 1. *A digraph $\langle V, A, \iota, \tau \rangle$ is d-periodic if there exists an injection $\pi\colon V \to \mathbb{R}^d$ and a basis $\{\mathbf{v}_1, \ldots, \mathbf{v}_d\}$ of $\mathbb{R}^d$ such that the image $\pi[V]$ is uniformly discrete, and the translations corresponding to the basis map the digraph onto itself.*

This notion of periodicity includes nets like those called rods and layers in the chemical literature (see, e.g., [7]): these are 1-periodic and 2-periodic nets, respectively, that do not lie in any plane in $\mathbb{R}^3$.

Proposition 1. *A digraph Γ is d-periodic if and only if there is a group G of automorphisms that is isomorphic to the free abelian group $\mathbb{Z}^d$ and satisfies the following two conditions: (a) G acts freely on V and (b) there are finitely many orbits of vertices and edges under G.*

The equivalence in Proposition 1 appears to be lore, although we do not know of any place that it has appeared in print. We will use both characterizations of periodic graphs as needed.

Given a d-periodic digraph $\Gamma = \langle V, A, \iota, \tau \rangle$, a *unit* is a weakly connected digraph substructure of Γ, $\Gamma_0 = \langle V_0, A_0, \iota_0, \tau_0 \rangle$, that intersects every $\mathbb{Z}^d$-orbit exactly once.

Proposition 2. *[20] For every weakly connected d-periodic digraph Γ and automorphism group $G \cong \mathbb{Z}^d$ such that there are finitely many G-orbits, there exists a unit for Γ.*

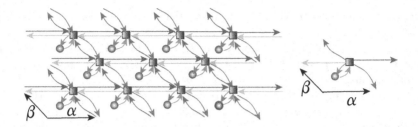

Fig. 2. (*left*) A digraph with two orbits of vertices, squares and spheres, (*right*) an isolated unit

Example 1. A 2-periodic digraph Γ is depicted in Figure 2 to the left. Its group of automorphisms contains a group isomorphic to $\mathbb{Z}^2$ generated by vectors α and β. There is no translation in Aut Γ sending square vertices to spherical vertices, or vice versa. One can consider the spherical vertices as being above the plane fixed by the square vertices. Similarly, there are six orbits of arcs: there is no translation sending arcs of one color onto arcs of another.

Units of periodic graphs and digraphs are not unique, as one can see from Figure 3. To the left, in Figure 3, an undirected 2-periodic graph is depicted with four types of units shown in red, blue, yellow, and green.

Lemma 1. *The vertices and arcs of a d-periodic digraph can be partitioned into units.*

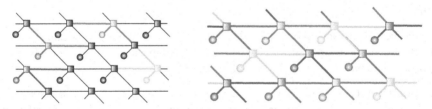

Fig. 3. (*left*) Units in a 2-periodic graph, (*right*) the periodic graph being partitioned by units

3 Walks in a Periodic Digraph

In this section we construct a machinery for navigating through periodic digraphs. We first demonstrate that every periodic digraph can be expressed as a "product" of a finite digraph and a copy of $\mathbb{Z}^d$ for some d. We define a counter machine that uses the finite digraph as a transition diagram and show one-to-one correspondence between sets of cyclic walks in a d-periodic graphs and languages recognized by d-counter machines.

3.1 Building a Periodic Digraph of a Given Quotient

Let Γ be a periodic graph with G being an abelian group of automorphisms acting freely on Γ, with finitely many orbits. A *labeled digraph* is a pair (Γ, ξ) where $\Gamma = \langle V, A, \iota, \tau \rangle$ is a digraph and $\xi \colon A \to G$ is a *labeling function*. We extend arc labels to labels on semi-walks $p = a_1^{\epsilon_1} a_2^{\epsilon_2} \cdots a_n^{\epsilon_n}$ with $\xi(p) = \sum_{k=1}^{n} \epsilon_k \xi(a_k)$.

Definition 2. *Let Γ be a periodic graph with G being an abelian group of automorphisms acting freely on Γ, with finitely many orbits. A G-labeling ξ of Γ is consistent with G (or G-consistent) if, for every pair of vertices v and v' such that $v' \in G(v)$, if p is a semi-walk from v to v', then $\xi(p)(v) = v'$.*

Here is one consequence of consistency.

Lemma 2. *Let Γ be a periodic graph with G being an abelian group of automorphisms acting freely on Γ, with finitely many orbits. Let ξ be a G-consistent labeling of Γ. If $a' \in G(a)$, then $\xi(a') = \xi(a)$.*

Proof. Assuming consistency and G acting freely on Γ, if $a' \in G(a)$ and p a semi-walk from $\iota(a)$ to $\iota(a')$, $\xi(p)$ is the only group element mapping $\iota(a)$ to $\iota'(a)$. It follows that $\xi(p)$ is the only map sending a to a', so $\xi(p)(\tau(a)) = \tau(a')$. Similarly, if q is a semi-walk from $\tau(a)$ to $\tau(a')$, $\xi(q)(\iota(a)) = \iota(a')$, and again as G acts freely on Γ, $\xi(q) = \xi(p)$. By consistency, $\xi(p) + \xi(a') = \xi(pa') = \xi(aq) = \xi(a) + \xi(q)$, so $\xi(a) = \xi(a')$. $\square$

Definition 3. *Let $\Gamma = \langle V, A, \iota, \tau \rangle$ be a digraph and let $G \subseteq \mathrm{Aut}\, \Gamma$. The quotient digraph Γ/G is the digraph $\langle V/G, A/G, \iota/G, \tau/G \rangle$ defined as follows.*

- *The vertices and edges of Γ/G are the sets of orbits $V/G = \{G(v) \colon v \in V\}$ and $A/G = \{G(a) \colon a \in A\}$.*
- *For each $a \in A$, let $(\iota/G)(G(a)) = G(\iota(a))$ and $(\tau/G)(G(a)) = G(\tau(a))$.*

Definition 4. *Let ξ be a G-consistent labeling of Γ and $\xi_{\Gamma/G} \colon A/G \to G$ be a G-labeling for Γ/G. We say that ξ honors $\xi_{\Gamma/G}$ if for each $a' \in G(a)$, we have $\xi(a') = \xi_{\Gamma/G}(G(a))$.*

For a semi-walk $p = a_1^{\epsilon_1} \cdots a_n^{\epsilon_n}$ in Γ, the semi-walk $G(a_1^{\epsilon_1}) \cdots G(a_n^{\epsilon_n})$ in Γ/G is denoted $G(p)$.

Example 2. Let Γ be the digraph depicted in Figure 2, where G is the group generated by the translations α and β, then the quotient graph Γ/G is the one shown to the right in Figure 4. Notice that as G acts freely on Γ, ξ is well-defined, and by construction, ξ is G-consistent. The labeling $\xi_{\Gamma/G}$ is also honored by ξ.

The theorem below is stated for abelian groups only (and as such was announced in [4]), although the statement holds for all groups [13].

Theorem 1. *Let G be an abelian group, and let (Δ, ξ_Δ) be a G-labeled weakly connected digraph. There exists a unique (up to isomorphism) digraph Γ with G-consistent labeling ξ such that G acts freely on Γ, and there is an isomorphism $\lambda \colon \Gamma/G \to \Delta$ with G-labeling $\xi_{\Gamma/G} = \xi_\Delta \lambda$ such that ξ honors $\xi_{\Gamma/G}$.*

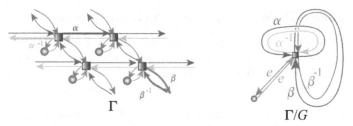

Fig. 4. (*left*) The graph Γ of Figure 2, (*right*) the quotient graph $\Gamma/\mathbb{Z}^2$

Proof. (Idea) Given $\Delta = \langle V_\Delta, A_\Delta, \iota_\Delta, \tau_\Delta \rangle$, abelian group G, and G-labeling $\xi_\Delta \colon A_\Delta \to G$, the desired graph Γ is obtained as follows. Let $V = V_\Delta \times G$ and $A = A_\Delta \times G$ and for each $(a, g) \in A$, let $\iota(a, g) = (\iota_\Delta, g)$ and $\tau(a, g) = (\tau_\Delta(a), g + \xi_\Delta(a))$. Then define $\xi(a, g) = \xi_\Delta(a)$. Let $\gamma \colon V \to V_\Delta, A \to A_\Delta$, and observe that by construction, γ is a homomorphism of Γ onto Δ. □

Example 3. Consider the digraph depicted to the left in Figure 5 containing $\mathbb{Z}$-labeling. The construction in Theorem 1 gives a graph Γ (to the right) where each vertex in Δ appears in $\mathbb{Z}$ copies, as labeled. The arcs are obtained such that each arc a from vertex v to vertex v' in Δ corresponds to an orbit of the set of arcs in Γ consisting of arcs that start at vertices (v, z) ($z \in \mathbb{Z}$) and terminate at vertices $(v', \xi(a) + z)$. The labels of the arcs are indicated in red. Clearly, Γ is 1-periodic.

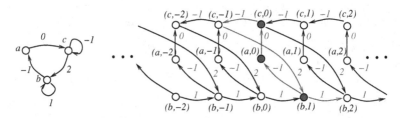

Fig. 5. A weakly connected digraph Δ with $\mathbb{Z}$-labeling to the left and the graph Γ obtained from the construction in Theorem 1. A unit in Γ is indicated in red.

We observe that every periodic digraph may be obtained by the above construction. Let $\Gamma = \langle V, A, \iota, \tau \rangle$ be a periodic digraph and let G be the group of translations preserving Γ. Let $\Gamma_0 = \langle V_0, A_0, \iota_0, \tau_0 \rangle$ be a unit of Γ, and by Lemma 1, $\{g(\Gamma_0) \colon g \in G\}$ partitions Γ into units isomorphic to Γ_0. For each $a \in A$, if $\iota(a) \in g(V_0)$ and $\tau(a) \in h(V_0)$, let $\xi(a) = hg^{-1}$. Then we can let $\Delta = \Gamma/G$ and $\xi_\Delta(G(a)) = \xi(a)$ for each a; by construction, ξ_Δ is well-defined. We obtain $\Gamma \cong \Delta \times G$, with ξ being the labeling derived from ξ_Δ.

3.2   Counter Machines and an Intersection Hierarchy

We presume familiarity with the notion of a regular language - a language accepted by some deterministic finite automaton (DFA) - and the notion of a context-free language (CFL) - a language accepted by some (nondeterministic) pushdown automaton (PDA). For background on these notions we refer the reader to [1,10]. We introduce a variant of the standard counter machines [11,12] with the following.

Definition 5. *A Deterministic d-Counter Machine (d-DCM) is a tuple*

$$M = (Q, \Sigma, \delta, q_0, F)$$

where Q is a finite set of states, Σ is a finite set of symbols, called the alphabet, $\delta: Q \times \Sigma \to Q \times \mathbb{Z}^d$ is a transition function, $q_0 \in Q$ is an initial state, while $F \subseteq Q$ is a set of accepting states.

We follow the standard approach of defining computations as a sequence of configurations of the machine. The computation is analogous to that of a pushdown automaton except there are d counters instead of a stack, the content of the counters is not consulted for making a transition, and the counters must all be zero in order to accept.

Definition 6. *Let $M = (Q, \Sigma, \delta, q_0, F)$ be a d-DCM. A configuration for a given state $q \in Q$ and word w is a triple*

$$(q, w, \mathbf{z}) \in Q \times \Sigma^* \times \mathbb{Z}^d.$$

A configuration $(q_0, w, (0, \ldots, 0))$ is initial on input w, while a configuration $(q, \epsilon, \mathbf{z})$ for some $\mathbf{z} \in \mathbb{Z}^d$, where ϵ is the empty word, is terminal. A terminal configuration $(q, \epsilon, \mathbf{z})$ is accepting if $q \in F$ and $\mathbf{z} = (0, \ldots, 0)$.

For two configurations $C = (q, aw, \mathbf{z})$ and $C' = (q', w, \mathbf{z}')$, we say C' *succeeds* C if $\delta(q, a) = (q', \mathbf{z}' - \mathbf{z})$. A *computation* of a d-DCM on an input $w = s_1 s_2 \cdots s_n$ is a sequence of configurations $C_0, \ldots, C_n$ such that C_0 is initial on input w, C_{i+1} succeeds C_i for $i = 0, \ldots, n - 1$, and C_n is terminal. The computation is *accepting* if C_n is accepting; it is *rejecting* otherwise.

A word w is accepted by a d-DCM if there is an accepting computation on input w. The set of all words accepted by a d-DCM M is called the language recognized by M, and is denoted $L(M)$. The class of languages recognized by d-DCMs is called the class of *deterministic d-counter languages* and it is denoted $\mathcal{DCL}_d$.

Our first observation is that languages recognized by 1-DCMs are deterministic context-free.

Proposition 3. *All languages in $\mathcal{DCL}_1$ are deterministic context-free.*

Given a class of languages $\mathcal{L}$, an *intersection hierarchy for $\mathcal{L}$* is the set of classes

$$\mathcal{L}_d = \left\{ \bigcap_{k=1}^{d} L_k : L_k \in \mathcal{L}, k = 1, \ldots, d \right\}.$$

This hierarchy *collapses* if, for some N, $\mathcal{L}_{N+1} = \mathcal{L}_N$; otherwise $\mathcal{L}_1 \subsetneq \mathcal{L}_2 \subsetneq \cdots$. By definition, $\mathcal{L}_1 = \mathcal{L}$, and frequently one adds some natural subclass $\mathcal{L}_0$ of $\mathcal{L}$. If $\mathcal{L}$ is closed under intersection, then the hierarchy collapses at $N = 1$.

One of the non-collapsing intersection hierarchies is the context-free language hierarchy. For each $d > 0$, let $\mathcal{CFL}_d$ be the class of intersections of d context free languages, and let $\mathcal{DCFL}_d$ be the class of intersections of d deterministic context free languages. Let $\mathcal{CFL}_0 = \mathcal{DCFL}_0$ be the class of regular languages. Then Liu and Weiner ([18], see also [16]) proved that for each $d > 0$, the language

$$L_d = \{a_1^{k_1} a_2^{k_2} \cdots a_d^{k_d} b_1^{k_1} b_2^{k_2} \cdots b_d^{k_d} : k_1, k_2, \ldots, k_d \geq 0\}$$
$$\subseteq \{a_1, a_2, \ldots, a_d, b_1, b_2, \ldots, b_d\}^*$$

satisfies $L_{d+1} \notin \mathcal{CFL}_d$. But as $L_d = \bigcap_{i=1}^d L_{d,i}$ where

$$L_{d,i} = \{a_1^{k_1} a_2^{k_2} \cdots a_d^{k_d} b_1^{l_1} b_2^{l_2} \cdots b_d^{l_d} : k_1, k_2, \ldots, k_d, l_1, l_2, \ldots, l_d \geq 0 \ \& \ k_i = l_i\},$$

and $L_{d,i}$ is a DCFL for each i, we have $L_{d+1} \in \mathcal{DCFL}_{d+1} - \mathcal{CFL}_d$ for each d. As $\mathcal{DCFL}_d \subseteq \mathcal{CFL}_d$ (we do not know if it has been determined whether this inclusion is strict for each d), we have a non-collapsing DCFL intersection hierarchy within a non-collapsing CFL intersection hierarchy.

In this subsection, we consider the intersection hierarchy of deterministic d-counter languages for $d = 0, 1, \ldots$.

Proposition 4. *For each d, $\mathcal{DCL}_d$ is the set of languages that are intersections of d languages in $\mathcal{DCL}_1$.*

Proposition 5. *The language L_d is in $\mathcal{DCL}_d$*

Proof. Because $L_d = \bigcap_{i=1}^d L_{d,i}$, the statement follows from Proposition 4 and the following observation that $L_{d,i} \in \mathcal{DCL}_1$. For each i there is a deterministic one-counter machine M that recognizes $L_{d,i}$ with $2d$ states. The first d states are used to read the a-symbols and the next d states are used to read the b-symbols such that the first encounter of symbol a_j $(j = 1, \ldots, d)$ changes the state of the machine to q_j where it remains until a different symbol is read. Similarly the first encounter of b_j changes the machine to state q_{d+j} where it remains until a different symbol is read. If a_j (or b_j) is followed by a_k (resp. b_k) with $k < j$, then machine rejects. Also, if any a's are encountered after a b (states $q_{d+1}, \ldots, q_{2d}$) then the machine rejects. If a symbol read is not a_i nor b_i, the counter is left unchanged. With each reading of a symbol a_i (moving to, or remaining at a state q_i) the counter is increased by 1, and with each reading of symbol b_i (moving to, or remaining at a state q_{d+i}) the counter is decreased by 1. Then a word w in $\{a_1, \ldots, a_d, b_1, \ldots, b_d\}^*$ is accepted if and only if the indexes of the a-symbols and the indexes of the b-symbols in w appear in ascending order and also $w = a_1^{k_1} a_2^{k_2} \cdots a_d^{k_d} b_1^{l_1} b_2^{l_2} \cdots b_d^{l_d}$ where $k_j, l_j \geq 0$ and $k_i = l_i$. $\square$

By Proposition 3, $\mathcal{DCL}_1 \subseteq \mathcal{DCFL}$, from which it follows that for each d, $\mathcal{DCL}_d \subseteq \mathcal{DCFL}_d$. Liu and Weiner's languages L_d show that for each d, $\mathcal{DCL}_{d+1} - \mathcal{CFL}_d$ is nonempty. We conclude the section with another observation. Let $\mathcal{DCL}_\infty = \bigcup_{k=0}^{\infty} \mathcal{DCL}_k$.

Proposition 6. *There exists a language in $\mathcal{DCFL}_1$ but not in $\mathcal{DCL}_\infty$.*

Seki [23], show that an n-DCM can be simulated by a nondeterministic 1-reversal counter machine as in [11] with $2n$ counters. Hence, the construction in [3] showing existence of a language in $\mathcal{DCFL}_1$ that cannot be accepted by any nondeterministic 1-reversal counter machine can be also used to show Proposition 6.

3.3 Cyclic Walks in Periodic Graphs and Counter Machines

In the following, Σ is a set of symbols.

Definition 7. *Given a d-DCM $M = (Q, \Sigma, \delta, q_0, F)$, its transition diagram is a pair (Δ_M, ζ) where $\Delta_M = \langle Q, A, \iota, \tau \rangle$ is a digraph having arcs $A = Q \times \Sigma$ with $\iota(q, s) = q$, $\tau(q, s) = q'$ if $\delta(q, s) = (q', \mathbf{z})$ for some $\mathbf{z}$, and $\zeta : A \to \Sigma$ an arc-labeling $\zeta(q, s) = s$.*

Notice that in such a transition diagram, due to determinism of M, for each $q \in Q$ and $s \in \Sigma$, there exists at most one $a \in A$ such that $\iota(a) = q$ and $\zeta(a) = s$.

Let $\Gamma = \langle V, A, \iota, \tau \rangle$ be d-periodic and let $G \leq \mathrm{Aut}\, \Gamma$ be isomorphic to $\mathbb{Z}^d$. A labeling $\zeta \colon A \to \Sigma$ is *G-invariant* if, for each $a_1, a_2 \in A$, $a_1 \in G(a_2)$ implies $\zeta(a_1) = \zeta(a_2)$. In addition, a set $F \subseteq V$ is *G-invariant* if it is a union of G-orbits of vertices.

If $F_\Gamma \subseteq V$ is a set of vertices in Γ with a G-invariant labeling ζ, the language that consists of labels of walks in Γ that start at a vertex v_0 and terminate in F_Γ is denoted with $L(\Gamma, F_\Gamma, \zeta, v_0)$. We state the main theorem connecting $\mathcal{DCL}_d$ with d-periodic graphs.

Theorem 2. *A language L is in $\mathcal{DCL}_d$ if and only if there exists a d-periodic digraph Γ with a translation group $\mathbb{Z}^d$, $\mathbb{Z}^d$-invariant labeling ζ and a set of vertices F_0 in a $\mathbb{Z}^d$-unit containing a vertex v_0 such that $L = L(\Gamma, F_0, \zeta, v_0)$.*

Proof. (Sketch) Suppose that L is in $\mathcal{DCL}_d$ and let $M = \langle Q, \Sigma, \delta, q_0, F \rangle$ be a d-counter machine with $L(M) = L$. Consider the transition diagram (Δ_M, ζ_M) of M. Let $\xi_\Delta \colon Q \times \Sigma \to \mathbb{Z}^d$ be defined by $\xi_\Delta(q, s) = \mathbf{z}$ for $\delta(q, s) = (q', \mathbf{z})$, where vector $\mathbf{z}$ changes the counters. By Theorem 1, there exists a digraph $\Gamma = \langle Q \times \mathbb{Z}^d, Q \times \Sigma \times \mathbb{Z}^d, \iota, \tau \rangle$ with $\Gamma / \mathbb{Z}^d$ isomorphic to Δ_M and labeling $\xi : Q \times \Sigma \times \mathbb{Z}^d \to \mathbb{Z}^d$ honoring ξ_Δ. As $A = Q \times \Sigma \times \mathbb{Z}^d$ is the set of arcs of Γ, we define $\zeta((a, \mathbf{z})) = \zeta_M(a) = s$ for each arc $a = (q, s)$ in Δ_M. Then $\zeta : Q \times \Sigma \times \mathbb{Z}^d \to \Sigma$ is $\mathbb{Z}^d$-invariant by definition. The natural homomorphism $\Gamma \to \Gamma / \mathbb{Z}^d \cong \Delta_M$ preserves the labels. Furthermore, $F \times \mathbb{Z}^d$ is a union of $\mathbb{Z}^d$-orbits. Consider the $\mathbb{Z}^d$-unit Γ_0 with vertices $V_0 = Q \times \{\mathbf{0}\}$, arcs $A_0 = Q \times \Sigma \times \{\mathbf{0}\}$ and $v_0 = (q_0, \mathbf{0}) \in V_0$. We set $F_0 = F \times \{\mathbf{0}\}$.

Conversely, suppose $L = L(\Gamma, F_0, \zeta, v_0)$ as stated in the theorem. Let $\Gamma_0 = \langle V_0, A_0, \iota_0, \tau_0 \rangle$ be the $\mathbb{Z}^d$-unit containing v_0 and F_0.

Consider $\Gamma/\mathbb{Z}^d$. Let $Q = V/\mathbb{Z}^d$ and we set $q_0 = \mathbb{Z}^d(v_0)$. Since ζ is a $\mathbb{Z}^d$-invariant labeling on the arcs of Γ, all arcs in the same orbit have the same label, hence we set $\zeta_\Delta : A/\mathbb{Z}^d \to \Sigma$ with $\zeta_\Delta(\mathbb{Z}^d(a)) = \zeta(a)$. For each $a \in A_0$, let

$$\xi(\mathbb{Z}^d(a)) = \begin{cases} (0, \ldots, 0) & \text{if } \iota(a), \tau(a) \in V_0 \\ \mathbf{z} = (i_1, \ldots, i_d) & \text{if for some } v \in V_0, \tau(a) = \mathbf{z}(v) \\ -\mathbf{z} = -(i_1, \ldots, i_d) & \text{if for some } v \in V_0, \iota(a) = \mathbf{z}(v). \end{cases}$$

Observe that by Lemma 1, ξ is well-defined. If $a \in A_0$, let $\delta(\mathbb{Z}^d(\iota_0(a)), \zeta(a)) = (\tau(a), \xi(\mathbb{Z}^d(a)))$. We set $F = \{\mathbb{Z}^d(v) : v \in F_0\}$. We claim that $M = (Q, \Sigma, \delta, q_0, F)$ is the desired DCM.   □

Corollary 1. *Given a d-periodic digraph $\Gamma = \langle V, A, \iota, \tau \rangle$ and automorphism group $G \cong \mathbb{Z}^d$, and given $v \in V$, the corresponding d-DCM $\langle V/G, A/G, \delta, G(v), \{G(v)\} \rangle$ accepts precisely those strings of arcs from Γ/G corresponding to cyclic walks starting and ending at v.*

Example 4. Observe that in Figure 5, the digraph Δ to the left is the transition diagram of a 1-counter DCM corresponding to the 1-periodic digraph at right. Conversely, given the periodic digraph to the right with the indicated unit with red arrows and vertices, the construction in Theorem 2 produces the 1-counter DCM to the left. In both cases the ζ-labelings are omitted.

4   Concluding Remarks

By showing how periodic structures represented by periodic digraphs may be described with types of cyclic walks that appear in these structures, we initiate a study of discrete geometric objects using formal language theory. These families of walks are associated with languages from the context free language intersection hierarchy and are recognized by a special class of devices, called here deterministic d-counter machines. This hierarchy of deterministic counter languages does not collapse, and it would be interesting to know how distinct this hierarchy is from the hierarchy of deterministic context-free languages.

We expect that the study of languages associated with (periodic) structures would give insight into the structures they are associated with. In particular, we expect that in certain cases equality of languages associated with the structures (digraphs) may imply the digraphs are isomorphic. We point out that several properties, such as Theorem 1, hold for arbitrary groups (groups that are not necessarily free abelian) [13], while we do not know what types of languages could be associated with more general structures including finite, or aperiodic structures. These studies may facilitate the implementation of the resulting theory in software for nanostructure design (results in this report are used in the "crystal turtlebug" program described in [19]).

Acknowledgement. This work has been supported in part by the NSF grants CCF-1117254 and DMS-0900671 and NIH grant R01GM109459-01.

References

1. Autebert, J.-M., Berstel, J., Boasson, L.: Context-free languages and pushdown automata. In: Rozenberg, G., Salomaa, A. (eds.) Handbook of Formal Languages. Word, Language, Grammar, vol. 1, pp. 111–174. Springer (1997)
2. Beukemann, A., Klee, W.E.: Minimal nets. Z. tür Kristallographie 201(1-2), 37–51 (1992)
3. Chiniforooshan, E., Daley, M., Ibarra, O.H., Kari, L., Seki, S.: One-reversal counter machines and multihead automata: Revisited. Theoretical Computer Science 454, 81–87 (2012)
4. Chung, S.J., Hahn, T., Klee, W.E.: Nomenclature and Generation of Three-Periodic Nets: the Vector Method. Acta Crys. A40, 42–50 (1984)
5. Cohen, E., Megiddo, N.: Recognizing properties of periodic graphs. J. Applied Geometry and Discrete Mathematics 4, 135–146 (1991)
6. Delgado-Friedrichs, O.: Equilibrium placement of periodic graphs and convexity of plane tilings. Discrete Comput. Geom. 33, 67–81 (2005)
7. Delgado-Friedrichs, O., O'Keeffe, M., Yaghi, O.M.: Taxonomy of periodic nets and the design of materials. Phys. Chem. Chem. Phys. 9, 1035–1043 (2007)
8. Eon, J.-G.: Graph-theoretical characterization of periodicity in crystallographic nets and other infinite graphs. Acta Crys. A 61, 501–511 (2005)
9. Glusker, J.P.: Brief history of chemical crystallography. ii: Organic compounds. In: Lima-De-Faria, J. (ed.) Historical Atlas of Crystallography, pp. 91–107. Kluwer (1990)
10. Hopcroft, J.E., Ullman, J.: Introduction to Automata Theory, Languages, and Computation. Addison-Wesley (1979)
11. Ibarra, O.: Reversal-bounded multicounter machines and their decision problems. J. Assoc. Comput. Mach. 25, 116–133 (1978)
12. Ibarra, O.H., Yen, H.-C.: On two-way transducers. In: Mauri, G., Leporati, A. (eds.) DLT 2011. LNCS, vol. 6795, pp. 300–311. Springer, Heidelberg (2011)
13. Jonoska, N., Krajcevski, M., McColm, G.: Counter machines and crystalographic structures (in preparation)
14. Jonoska, N., McColm, G.L.: Flexible versus rigid tile assembly. In: Calude, C.S., Dinneen, M.J., Păun, G., Rozenberg, G., Stepney, S. (eds.) UC 2006. LNCS, vol. 4135, pp. 139–151. Springer, Heidelberg (2006)
15. Jonoska, N., McColm, G.: Complexity classes for self-assembling flexible tiles. Theoretical Computer Science 410(4-5), 332–346 (2009)
16. Kintala, C.M.: Refining nondeterminism in context-free languages. Mathematical Systems Theory 12(1), 1–8 (1978)
17. Klee, W.E.: Crystallographic nets and their quotient graphs. Cryst. Res. Technol. 39(11), 959–968 (2004)
18. Liu, L.Y., Weiner, P.: An infinite hierarchy of intersections of context-free languages. Mathematical Systems Theory 7(2), 185–192 (1973)
19. McColm, G., Clark, W.E., Eddaoudi, M., Wojtas, L., Zaworotko, M.: Crystal engineering using a "turtlebug" algorithm: A de novo approach to the design of binodal metal organic frameworks. Crystal Growth & Design 19(9), 3686–3693 (2011)

20. Meier, J.: Groups, Graphs and Trees: An Introduction to the Geometry of Infinite Groups. Cambridge U. Pr. (2008)
21. Moore, P.B.: Brief history of chemical crystallography. i: Inorganic compounds. In: Lima-De-Faria, J. (ed.) Historical Atlas of Crystallography, pp. 77–90. Kluwer (1990)
22. O'Keeffe, M., Hyde, B.G.: Crystal Structures I. Patterns and Symmetry. Mineralogical Society of America (1996)
23. Seki, S.: N-dimensional crystallography. Private Communication (2013)
24. Wang, C., Liu, D., Lin, W.: Metal-organic frameworks as a tunable platform for designing functional molecular materials. J. American Chemical Society 135(36), 13222–13234 (2013)
25. Wells, A.F.: Three-dimensional Nets and Polyhedra. Wiley (1977)
26. Zheng, J., Birktoft, J., Chen, Y., Wang, T., Sha, R., Constantinou, P., Ginell, S., Mao, C., Seeman, N.: From molecular to macroscopic via the rational design of a self-assembled 3D DNA crystal. Nature 461(7260), 74–77 (2009)

An Energy-Efficient Computing Approach by Filling the Connectome Gap

Yasunao Katayama, Toshiyuki Yamane, and Daiju Nakano

IBM Research - Tokyo,
NANOBIC, 7-7 Shinkawasaki, Saiwai-ku, Kawasaki, 2120032 Kanagawa, Japan
{yasunaok,tyamane,dnakano}@jp.ibm.com
http://www.research.ibm.com/labs/tokyo/

Abstract. This paper presents an energy-efficient neuromorphic computing approach by filling the connectome gap between algorithm, brain, and VLSI. The gap exists in structural features such as the average number of synaptic connections per neural node as well as in dimensional features. We argue that the energy dissipation in complex computing tasks is more predominantly bounded by the control processes that synchronize and redirect both computing processes and data rather than the computing processes themselves. Therefore, it is crucial to fill the connectome gap and to avoid excessive interactions of the computing process and data with the control processes when achieving energy-efficient computing for large-scale cognitive computing tasks. The use of freespace optics is proposed as a means to efficiently handle sparse but still heavily entangled connections.

Keywords: Neuromorphic computing, low power, freespace optics.

1 Introduction

There have been a number of profound theoretical discussions on the ultimate lower bounds of the energy dissipation in computing systems. Landauer's principle [1] deals with the lower theoretical limit of energy consumption associated with bit erasure as $kT\ln 2$ [1]. Bennett claims that as long as no information is erased, computation may in principle be achieved in a thermodynamically reversible manner, and thus not even requires any release of heat [2]. The Margolus Levitin theorem [3] gives a fundamental limit on the performance of quantum computation for a quantum system of energy E. Quantum computations as well as inherently classical ones, need at least a time of $h/4E$ to go from one state to an orthogonal state.

In discussing a practical energy dissipation bound, the energy per computation is an important metric. The metric itself can change, as requirements for computing shift from conventional computation-centric tasks to cognitive ones. The metric in conventional computing has been often evaluated in closed and noninteractive environments, while cognitive tasks will more frequently deal with streamed unstructured data sets in open and interactive environments. As the

O.H. Ibarra et al. (Eds.): UCNC 2014, LNCS 8553, pp. 229–241, 2014.
DOI: 10.1007/978-3-319-08123-6_19, © Springer International Publishing Switzerland 2014

size of the working set increases, entropic aspects associated with appropriate control and selections of processing information [4] will require more significant attention in comparison to the computing counterpart in discussing the computational complexity and the associated power consumption. We are already facing this situation even in conventional computing tasks [5]. Here, we can consider a simple example: When calculating

$$C = A + B, \quad D = A - B$$

the complexity and energy consumption is not determined by how much energy is required in manipulating the two numbers, but by how much energy is required in selecting and transferring the data of interest out of an often unstructured sea of data encoded with physical degrees of freedom in Minkowski spacetime. Moving the computations to the data does not always help, since the computations often still require multiple data inputs that are entangled and that lack space-time locality. However, even though the performance and the power-efficiency bound can be more relevant to the entropic aspects as the scale increases, many existing neuromorphic device research activities (for example, refer to [6, 7]) focused on how to design limited size neural systems rather than how to interconnect a large number of neurons in a scalable manner until recently [8]. As CMOS scaling is approaching to its fundamental limits [9], we cannot expect that the orders of magnitude energy-efficiency gap between humans and computers in handling cognitive tasks can be filled only by further technology miniaturization.

Here we present an energy-efficient neuromorphic computing approach by filling the connectome gap between algorithm, brain, and VLSI. We argue that the practical energy dissipation bound is more relevant to the external control processes that synchronize and redirect both computing processes and data. Thus, in order to realize energy-efficient computing for large-scale cognitive computing tasks, it is quite important to fill the connectome gap between algorithm, brain, and VLSI such that we can minimize the excessive interactions of computing processes and data with controls. The use of a freespace crossconnect is proposed as a means to handle sparse but still heavily entangled connections efficiently. We also explore unconventional neural node implementation concepts.

2   Connectome Gap between Algorithm, Brain, and VLSI

Fig. 1 illustrates the interconnect scaling as a function of the number of unit nodes such as neurons or gates for algorithm, brain, and VLSI. In discussing the connectome gap (here we mean various, i.e., statistical, topological, dimensional etc., gaps in the interconnect diagrams), we should note that the brain connection matrix actually consists of structural and functional aspects [10]. For the neurosynaptic structural connections inside brains, the connectome projects is in progress [13, 14], and some statistical universal scaling laws that govern the interconnections of brains have been discovered. For example, it was found that there is a scaling law between the volumes of gray matter and white matter of the brains for various animal species [15]. Gray matter is composed of cell

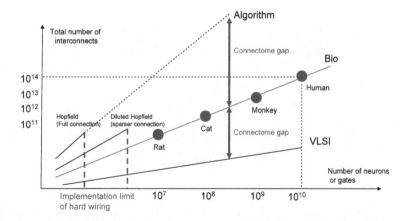

Fig. 1. Interconnect scaling for algorithm, brain, and VLSI as a function of the number of unit nodes such as neurons or gates. Note that many learning algorithms have prerequisites of fully-connected mesh topologies, while the interconnect capabilities in VLSIs are relatively limited.

bodies, dendrites, and short axons for information processing and white matter is consists of long axons for long-range communications between cortical areas. The strikingly simple relationship indicates that there exists a scaling law similar to Rent's rule [11] for brain interconnections as discussed in [12].

The dilution factor, D, is an appropriate statistical metric to analyze the gap as an indicator for the sparseness in the network [16, 17]. It is defined as

$$D = N_S/N_N^2,$$

where N_S is the total number of synapses (or switches) and N_N is the total number of neurons (or nodes). As N_N increases, the required N_S increases quadratically as $O(N_N^2)$ if D is kept at 1 for full mesh connectivity. If the number of connected synapses per neuron is low and constant, then D has to be reduced significantly as N_N increases, and signals typically need to make multiple hops to reach an arbitrarily selected neuron. When $N_N = 10^{10}$ and $N_S = 10^{14}$, each neuron contains 10^4 synapses on average and $D = 10^{-6}$. Thus, the connections are significantly diluted compared to a fully-connected situation. In contrast, in the present CMOS VLSI viewpoint, it is still a very-densely-connected network system, even when the redundancy and modularity aspects of the brain connectome are considered.

Many neural network algorithms, such as Hebbian rule [18, 19] and Hopfield network [20], are often based fully-connected nodes in the algorithm formulation, even though functionally significant paths tend to be more sparsely distributed. These algorithms, when implemented in real hardware, work efficiently with fully-connected nodes, but in reality, this is rarely possible since the number of required interconnect resources can increase rapidly as $O(N_N^2)$. Thus, the gap between algorithm, brain, and VLSI has to be filled in implementing scalable

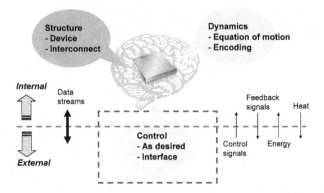

Fig. 2. Three key aspects in computing tasks: Structure, dynamics, and control. The structure defines the paths for information processing flow. There is no theoretical lower bound in energy dissipation in dynamics as long as the dynamics is thermodynamically reversible. The energy dissipation in computing is bounded by the control, particularly in open and interactive settings.

and efficient neuromorphic computing systems. The VLSI hardware will need to be flexible so that it can efficiently handle communications in unstructured and entangled connections.

In addition to the gap in the average number of connections per node, there exist gaps in the structural and dimensional arrangements as well. At an algorithmic level, every node is often treated in an isotropic manner without much considering the wiring constraints, while at the VLSI level, the regular and hierarchical structures are typically used to deal with a large number of node connectivities in a finite spatial dimension. The brain network is not likely to have precisely defined regular structures as those found in VLSIs, but is arranged in a more unstructured way to flexibly route within a given volume of space. Since there are many unknowns in the fine-grain structural and functional features in the brain and the exact connectome and underlying rules are still under investigation, a detailed argument needs to wait until the complete connectome of the brain is identified. The VLSI hardware needs to be flexible in emulating brain structure and functionalities.

3   Energy Dissipation for Control

We consider the role of control on the lower bound of energy dissipation by focusing on a computing framework interacting openly with external environments, which is increasingly the case for neuromorphic computing systems.

Let us start by representing the essence of the computing systems in three high-level aspects, as depicted in Fig. 2. First, the structure defines the static part of the computer systems by describing both the device and interconnect physical arrangements in space. The device structure defines primitive building

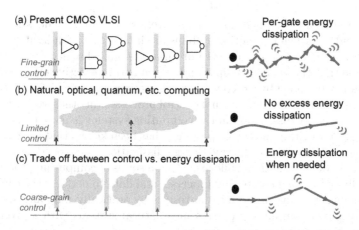

Fig. 3. Power saving strategy at function block level. (a) Present CMOS VLSI consumes power at every gate but allows for fine-grain control at an arbitrary location; (b) Natural or quantum computing does not require per-gate dissipation but offers very limited control options; (c) Trade off between control vs. energy dissipation by allowing control on a coarse-grain scale.

blocks as functional components such as switches, while the interconnect structure defines the system architecture by appropriately arranging and connecting a set of the building blocks. Second, the dynamics takes care of performing the actual computing tasks with an appropriate set of initial conditions and equations of motions as well as with encoding strategies for information and functions. A set of equations of motion determine the time evolution of the system. Theoretically, a system is known to work in a reversible manner as long as the operations under given structures and dynamics can support both the logical and physical reversibility.

When computing is performed in closed systems, the control functions remain internal and the external controls are rather irrelevant as long as the spatial and temporal separations of information encoding states are maintained to isolate the influences arising from noise and other disturbances. The system can evolve by itself to compute with an appropriately-configured set of initial conditions and the equations of motion. Quantum computing or natural computing often performs computational tasks in this manner. [1] On the other hand, in more practical computing systems, the computing is performed in open and interacting environments with a set of appropriate external control and feedback interfaces. The computing actions are expected to be appropriately controlled and fedback by dynamically-changing external IO signals. The performance bounds in quantum information processing with time-dependent Hamiltonian control were discussed recently [22]. Though it is argued that the external control system can be redefined as a part of the system for computing so now the whole system can

---

[1] Retaining the required precision of the system without appropriate control is not easy. An interesting analogy can be found in [21] on making a rocket to the moon.

be considered as a closed system without explicit control, this does not always work particularly when computing systems are interacting with living creatures, unless the whole system is considered at an astronomical scale.

We argue that the energy dissipation in open and interactive environments is predominantly bounded by the control processes since the reversible arrangement is limited particularly for the external control processes. In other words, the lower bound of the energy dissipation in the computing systems is more caused by the control part, not by the computing part, as it has been known that the computing will not necessarily dissipate energy. Energy dissipation has to occur as a result of changing the course of action while executing a series of computing processes, by dynamically redirecting computing processes and data to perform the computing as desired rather than computing the results by statically mapping specific or entire portions of computer processes into natural systems with a given set of initial conditions and equations of motions.

Fig. 3 compares various strategies for how the control paths can interact with the computing paths for optimum energy efficiency. Conventional computing such as that done with CMOS VLSI logic gates requires energy dissipation at every gate but this is a very controllable system both logically and physically by inserting the control points almost everywhere. In contrast, many approaches in natural as well as quantum computing cannot rely on per-gate energy-dissipative control and thus it is often limited to arrange the control paths. It is not easy to change the course of computing in the middle of action as desired by using initially unpredicted external controls. The approach with coarse-grain control options for modular blocks can trade off the two extreme cases by arranging that energy dissipation occurs only when necessary [23].

The control paths inherently require crossconnect between modular blocks. The overhead associated with the crossconnect can be considered using two extreme cases. One extreme is a completely serial approach where the crossconnect is realized with time-multiplexed bus connections only requiring $O(N_N)$ resources. Here, though the resources are relatively more efficiently used, the shared serialized connection can become a performance bottleneck. If the resources at the two sides are processing units and memory units, this is viewed as the von-Neumann bottleneck. The other extreme is a completely parallel approach where both sides are connected in a parallel and fully meshed topology. This can perform at high performance without blocking though it requires $O(N_N^2)$ resources. In reality, something in between such as a fat tree, butterfly, multi-dimensional torus, or hypercube, is often chosen [24].

As N_N increases, the entropic aspects in the crossconnect become more dominant than the computational aspects. Figure 4 compares the connection matrix and its modular implementation using crosspoint elements of size N_C, In this connection matrix, "0" means no connection and "1" means connection (with whatever weight). When the connection matrix can be arranged in a block diagonal form with using a size smaller than N_C, the breakdown of the connection matrix into fine-grain crosspoint elements is a straight forward task. However, the implementation of the connection matrix will become inefficient if the

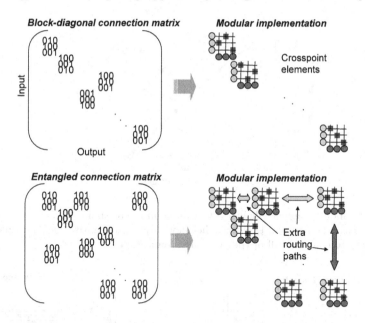

Fig. 4. Comparing connection matrices and their crosspoint element implementations. When the connection matrix can be arranged in a block diagonal form of a size smaller than N_C, the breakdown of the connection matrix into fine-grain crosspoint elements is a straight forward task. However, the implementation of the connection matrix will become inefficient if the connection matrix is heavily entangled and no block diagonal representation of a size smaller than N_C exists.

connection matrix is heavily entangled and no block diagonal representation of a size smaller than N_C exists. In that case, additional communication paths will be needed between crosspoint elements. Heavily entangled situations can occur even when the locality exists in the problem. For example, when there exists the dimensional gap between algorithmic requirements and implementation constraints, the locality in the algorithm will not be effectively mapped into that in the implementation. Fig. 5 shows the implementation efficiency of the connection matrix as a function of N_C. As N_C increases, the efficiency start to drop when $N_C > 1/D$, since multiple cycles are required to perform all of the required connections digitally.

The above argument is a good example to show that the efficiency of the large-scale neuromorphic computing is significantly affected by the connectome gap between algorithm requirements for fully-connected mesh topology and VLSI implementation constraints for the wiring. Though this gap needs to be filled using innovations in both algorithms and implementation techniques, we will propose freespace crossconnect to fill the gap mainly from the implementation perspective in section 4.

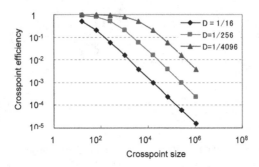

Fig. 5. Crosspoint element efficiency as a function of crosspoint element size, N_C. As N_C increases and crossovers $1/D$, the efficiency drops significantly, since multiple cycles are required to complete all of the necessary connections.

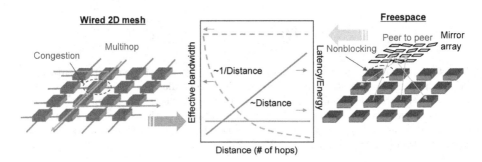

Fig. 6. Wired mesh vs freespace crossconnect network: Effective bandwidth, latency, and energy consumption comparisons. Note that the congestion due to shared multi-hop paths is a serious performance bottleneck since now the nodes, each consisting of a crosspoint element, are arranged in 2D, while the neurons within the crosspoint element are arranged in 1D in Fig. 4.

4   Energy-Efficient Neuromorphic Computing with Freespace Crossconnect

Freespace interconnect has been studied for several decades, and its advantages are known [25–27], but to the present authors' knowledge, it has never been considered in a neuromorphic computing context. The bandwidth, latency, and energy consumption advantages in freespace networking are illustrated in Fig. 6. In a wired network, the effective bandwidth decreases and the latency and energy consumption increases as the distance (the number of hops) increases unless the nodes are fully connected. The average distance increases as the neural network scale increases and as the dilution factor decreases. However, the bandwidth, latency, and energy consumption in freespace networks can remain almost

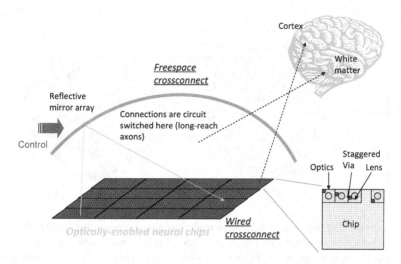

Fig. 7. Hybrid architecture option for general cognitive computing devices. Freespace connection can efficiently and flexibly remap brain connection matrix and also provide nonblocking reach for neuromorphic signals.

constant as long as nonblocking crossconnect can allow peer-to-peer connections effectively when needed. VLSI implementations of neuromorphic computing devices should satisfy both synapse-dendrite fan-in/fan-out conditions and axon reach requirements of the actual neurons and should flexibly support not very regular connectome connections. This results in limited scalability with conventional wired crossconnect, while freespace crossconnect can realize nonblocking crossconnect for large numbers of nodes, as long as the interference can be managed appropriately.

Fig. 7 shows a hybrid architecture considered for neuromorphic systems. Here, freespace is suitable for efficiently realizing sparsely connected network without prior knowledge of where each link will be connected. Another example, in which the freespace interconnect is used for deep belief neural networks [28], is illustrated in Fig. 8. In this example, three hidden layers are sandwiched by input and output layers. The freespace interconnect can be used between the modules as well as between the boards, racks, etc. Assuming each chip contains arithmetic components for processing each layer of the deep belief network, then reconfigurable module-to-module freespace interconnect can optimize connections and bandwidth between the layers according to the probabilistic message passing requirements between the nodes in peer to peer. In particular, freespace interconnect can reduce the in-plane traffic by appropriately connecting the interlayer nodes in peer to peer to significantly improve performance and power consumption at the same time. The performance of multilayer neural network implementations using wired connections significantly depends on the networking optimization [29].

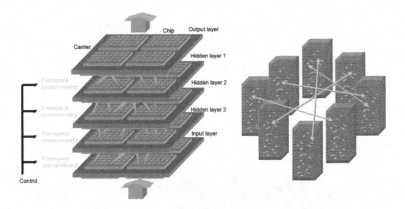

Fig. 8. A deep belief network architecture with freespace interconnect in inter-layer networking. Freespace interconnect can avoid excessive in-plane traffic by appropriately connecting the interlayer nodes in peer to peer, thus significantly improving performance and power consumption at the same time. The freespace interconnect can be used between the modules as well as between the boards, racks, etc.

Freespace connection efficiently remap brain connection matrices with reconfigurable extensions. Table 1 shows dimensional comparison of the interconnects between brain, wired, freespace, and hybrid. The hybrid architecture shown here takes advantage of the wired and freespace interconnect. Note that the straightforward parallel approach for wired crossconnect with 2D inputs and corresponding 2D outputs is not possible since it requires peer-to-peer wiring connections in 4D.

Table 1. Dimensional comparison

	Neuron node dimension	Utilization	Integration
Brain	3D	High	Good
Wired crossconnect	1D	Low	Good
Freespace crossconnect	2D	Medium	Challenging
Hybrid crossconnect	3D	High	Good

Fig. 9 compares the normalized bandwidth of the structure shown in Fig. 8 and that of a conventional chip stack as a function of the number of neurons in each plane. For chip stacks in which chips are connected using TSVs (Through Silicon Vias), the normalized bandwidth decreases sharply as the number of neurons in each plane increases because of the average number of required in-plane hops increases with the square root of the number of neurons in each plane. With freespace optical interconnect, the in-plane hopping does not matter much, so the normalized bandwidth can stay constant. Peer to peer transmission of freespace interconnect should also have latency and energy consumption advantages.

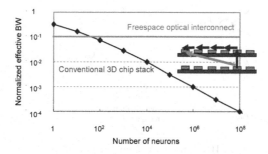

Fig. 9. Normalized bandwidth of the structure shown in Fig. 8 and that of a chip stack as a function of the number of neurons in each plane. Inter-plane bandwidths per node for conventional 3D chip stack and freespace interconnect are 1/3 and 1/10 of the in-plane nearest-neighbor hopping bandwidth. As the number of neurons increases, the normalized bandwidth of the freespace interconnect becomes higher by directly connecting two communicating nodes, rather than by using multiple hops. Note that peer to peer transmission of freespace interconnect should also have latency and energy consumption advantages, as already seen in Fig. 6.

Once the connectome aspects are appropriately handled, the node implementation has various options. Fig. 10 explores what we think is an unconventional way of implementing a neural node. First, we assume that neuromorphic systems mainly deal with statistical information processing of P_{IN}'s and P_{OUT}'s (they could be either p or $\bar{p} = 1 - p$) over a wide dynamic range.

$$P_{OUT} \simeq \prod_{i=0}^{n-1} P_{INj}^{W_j}$$

Then hardware deals with LLR(Log likelihood Ratio) [30] of such operations with time-dependent spike signals as 1-bit digital rate coding as the population coding [31]. Our brain can deal with wide dynamic range inputs [32] so log scale conversion is consistent with this feature.

$$\log P_{OUT} \simeq \sum_{j=0}^{n-1} W_j \log P_{INj}$$

Multiplicative gates can constitute universal logic gates as long as signals are represented in a dual rail as p and $1 - p$, which may correspond to excitatory and inhibitory neural connections. Since the output signal is the weighted sum of the input signals if the shaping function for signal regeneration can be ignored, a series of this kind of arithmetic operations can be implemented as an efficient combinational arithmetic. S/N degradation as a result of large fanout can be compensated for using an appropriate integrate and fire averaging mechanism with a large number of fanin signals.

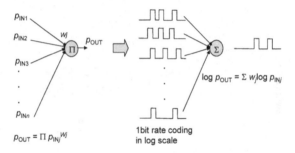

Fig. 10. A node implementation idea

5 Conclusion

In this paper, an energy-efficient neuromorphic computing approach by filling the connectome gap between algorithm, brain, and VLSI is presented. We argued that the energy dissipation in complex computing tasks is more predominantly bounded by the control processes that synchronize and redirect both computing processes and data rather than the computing processes themselves. Therefore, it is crucial to fill the connectome gap and to avoid excessive interactions of the computing process and data with the control processes when achieving energy-efficient computing for large-scale cognitive computing tasks. The use of freespace optics was proposed as a means to efficiently handle sparse but still heavily entangled connections. We acknowledge profs. T. Chikayama, G. Tanaka, R. Nakane, K. Aihara, M. Hagiya, and A. Hirose of the University of Tokyo for discussions.

References

1. Landauer, R.: Irreversibility and heat generation in the computing process. IBM Journal of Research and Development 5, 183–191 (1961)
2. Bennett, C.H.: Logical Reversibility of Computation. IBM Journal of Research and Development 17, 525–532 (1973)
3. Margolus, N., Levitin, L.B.: The maximum speed of dynamical evolution. Physica D 120, 188–195 (1998)
4. Katayama, Y.: On Entropic Aspects of VLSI Designs. In: IEEE International Midwest Symposium on Circuits and Systems (2004)
5. Kestor, G., Gioiosa, R., Kerbyson, D.J., Hoisie, A.: Quantifying the energy cost of data movement in scientific applications. In: IEEE International Symposium on Workload Characterization, IISWC (2013)
6. Jo, S.H., Chang, T., Ebong, I., Bhadviya, B.B., Mazumder, P., Lu, W.: Nanoscale Memristor Device as Synapse in Neuromorphic Systems. Nano Letters 10 (2010)
7. Sharad, M., Augustine, C., Panagopolous, G., Roy, K.: Proposal for Neuromorphic Hardware using Spin Devices, arXiv:1206.3227 (2012)
8. Esser, S.K., et al.: Cognitive Computing Systems: Algorithms and Applications for Networks of Neurosynaptic Cores. In: Proceedings of the International Joint Conference on Neural Networks in Dallas, TX (August 2013)

9. Chang, L., Frank, D.J., Montoye, R.K., Koester, S.J., Ji, B.L., Coteus, P.W., Dennard, R.H., Haensch, W.: Practical strategies for power-efficient computing technologies. In: IEEE Proc., vol. 98 (2010)
10. Kaiser, M.: A Tutorial in Connectome Analysis: Topological and Spatial Features of Brain Networks. Neuroimage 57(3), 892–907 (2011)
11. Bakoglu, H.B., Meindl, J.D.: A system-level circuit model for multi- and single-chip CPUs. In: ISSCC, pp. 308–309 (1987)
12. Beiu, V., et al.: On Two-layer Brain-inspired Hierarchical Topologies - A Rent's Rule Approach - Transactions on High-Performance Embedded Architectures and Compilers IV, pp. 311–333 (2011)
13. Sporns, O., Tononi, G., Kötter, R.: The Human Connectome: A Structural Description of the Human Brain. PLOD Computational Biology, 245-251 (2005)
14. http://www.humanconnectomeproject.org/
15. Zhang, K., Sejnowski, T.J.: A universal scaling law between gray matter and white matter of cerebral cortex. PNAS 97(10), 5621–5626 (2000)
16. Arenzon, J.J., Lemke, L.: Simulating highly diluted neural networks. J. Phys. A: Math. Gen. 27, 5161–5165 (1994)
17. Gripon, V., Berrou, C.: Sparse Neural Networks With Large Learning Diversity. IEEE Trans. Neural Networks 22, 1087–1096 (2011)
18. Hebb, D.O.: The Organization of Behavior. Wiley & Sons, New York (1949)
19. Caporale, N., Dan, Y.: Spike timing-dependent plasticity: A Hebbian learning rule. Annual Review of Neuroscience 31, 25–46 (2008)
20. Hopfield, J.J.: Neural network and physical systems with emergent collective computational abilities. Proceedings of the National Academy of Sciences of the United States of America 79, 2554–2558 (1982)
21. Kalman, R.E.:
http://www.inamori-f.or.jp/laureates/k01_a_rudolf/img/lct_e.pdf
22. Russell, B., Stepney, S.: Geometric Methods for Analysing Quantum Speed Limits: Time-Dependent Controlled Quantum Systems with Constrained Control Functions. In: Mauri, G., Dennunzio, A., Manzoni, L., Porreca, A.E. (eds.) UCNC 2013. LNCS, vol. 7956, pp. 198–208. Springer, Heidelberg (2013)
23. Katayama, Y.: New complementary logic circuits using coupled open quantum systems. IEEE Trans. Nanotechnology 4, 527–532 (2005)
24. Parhami, B.: Introduction to Parallel Processing: Algorithms and Architectures. Plenum Press, New York (1999)
25. Xue, J., et al.: An intra-chip free-space optical interconnect. ISCA (2010)
26. Wang, K., et al.: Experimental demonstration of high-speed freespace reconfigurable card-to-card optical interconnects. Optics Express (2013)
27. Katayama, Y., Okazaki, O., Ohba, N.: Software-defined massive multicore networking via freespace optical interconnect. In: ACM Conf. Computing Frontiers (2013)
28. Hinton, G.E., Osindero, S., Teh, Y.-W.: A fast learning algorithm for deep belief nets. Neuro Computation, 1527-1554 (2006)
29. Rast, A.D., Welbourne, S., Jin, X., Furber, S.B.: Optimal Connectivity in Hardware-Targetted MLP Networks. In: International Joint Conference on Neural Networks (2009)
30. Cover, T.M., Thomas, J.A.: Elements of Information Theory. John Wiley & Sons, Hoboken (2006)
31. Averbeck, B.B., Latham, P.E., Pouget, A.: Neural correlations, population coding and computation. Nature Reviews Neuroscience 7, 358–366 (2006)
32. Dehaene, S.: The neural basis of the Weber-Fechner law: A logarithmic mental number line. TRENDS in Cognitive Science 7(4) (2003)

Fast Arithmetic in Algorithmic Self-assembly

Alexandra Keenan*, Robert Schweller*, Michael Sherman*, and Xingsi Zhong*

Department of Computer Science
University of Texas - Pan American
{abkeenan,rtschweller,mjsherman,zhongx}@utpa.edu

Abstract. In this paper we consider the time complexity of adding two n-bit numbers together within the tile self-assembly model. The (abstract) tile assembly model is a mathematical model of self-assembly in which system components are square tiles with different glue types assigned to tile edges. Assembly is driven by the attachment of singleton tiles to a growing seed assembly when the net force of glue attraction for a tile exceeds some fixed threshold. Within this frame work, we examine the time complexity of computing the sum of 2 n-bit numbers, where the input numbers are encoded in an initial seed assembly, and the output sum is encoded in the final, terminal assembly of the system. We show that this problem, along with multiplication, has a worst case lower bound of $\Omega(\sqrt{n})$ in 2D assembly, and $\Omega(\sqrt[3]{n})$ in 3D assembly. We further design algorithms for both 2D and 3D that meet this bound with worst case run times of $O(\sqrt{n})$ and $O(\sqrt[3]{n})$ respectively, which beats the previous best known upper bound of $O(n)$. Finally, we consider average case complexity of addition over uniformly distributed n-bit strings and show how we can achieve $O(\log n)$ average case time with a simultaneous $O(\sqrt{n})$ worst case run time in 2D. As additional evidence for the speed of our algorithms, we implement our algorithms, along with the simpler $O(n)$ time algorithm, into a probabilistic run-time simulator and compare the timing results.

1 Introduction

Self-assembly is the process by which systems of simple objects autonomously organize themselves through local interactions into larger, more complex objects. Self-assembly processes are abundant in nature and serve as the basis for biological growth and replication. Understanding how to design and efficiently program molecular self-assembly systems to harness this power promises to be fundamental for the future of nanotechnology. One particular direction of interest is the design of molecular computing systems for efficient solution of fundamental computational problems. In this paper we study the complexity of computing arithmetic primitives within a well studied model of algorithmic self-assembly, the abstract tile assembly model.

* This author's research was supported in part by National Science Foundation Grant CCF-1117672.

O.H. Ibarra et al. (Eds.): UCNC 2014, LNCS 8553, pp. 242–253, 2014.
DOI: 10.1007/978-3-319-08123-6_20, © Springer International Publishing Switzerland 2014

Table 1. Summary of results

	Time Complexity	Average Case
Addition(2D)	$\Theta(\sqrt{n})$ (Thm. 1,Thm. 4)	$O(\log n)$ (Thm.4)
Addition(3D)	$\Theta(\sqrt[3]{n})$ (Thm. 1,Thm. 6)	$O(\log n)$ (Thm.6)
Previous Best(2D)	$O(n)$ [5]	-
Multiplication(d-D)	$\Omega(\sqrt[d]{n})$ (Thm. 2)	-

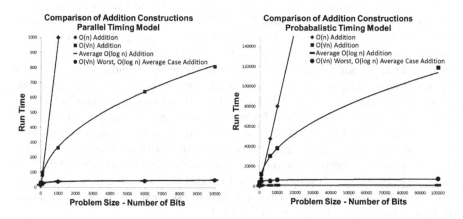

Fig. 1.

The abstract tile assembly model (aTAM) models system monomers with four sided Wang tiles with glue types assigned to each edge. Assembly proceeds by tiles attaching, one by one, to a growing initial seed assembly whenever the net glue strength of attachment exceeds some fixed temperature threshold (Figure 2). The aTAM has been shown to be capable of universal computation [21], and has promising computational potential with a DNA implementation [19]. Research leveraging this computational power has lead to efficient assembly of complex geometric shapes and patterns with a number of recent results in FOCS, SODA, and ICALP [1, 6, 7, 10–17, 20]. This universality also allows the model to serve directly as a model for computation in which an input bit string is encoded into an initial assembly. The process of self-assembly and the final produced terminal assembly represent the computation of a function on the given input. Given this framework, it is natural to ask how fast a given function can be computed in this model. Tile assembly systems can be designed to take advantage of massive parallelism when multiple tiles attach at distinct positions in parallel, opening the possibility for faster algorithms than what can be achieved in more traditional computational models. On the other hand, tile assembly algorithms must use up geometric space to perform computation, and must pay substantial time costs when communicating information between two physically distant bits. This creates a host of challenges unique to this physically motivated computational model that warrant careful study.

In this paper we consider the time complexity of adding two n-bit numbers within the abstract tile assembly model. We show that this problem, along with multiplication, has a worst-case lower bound of $\Omega(\sqrt{n})$ time in 2D and $\Omega(\sqrt[3]{n})$ time in 3D. These lower bounds are derived by a reduction from a simple problem we term the *communication* problem in which two distant bits must compute the AND function between themselves. This general reduction technique can likely be applied to a number of problems and yields key insights into how one might design a sub-linear time solution to such problems. We in turn show how these lower bounds, in the case of 2D and 3D addition, are matched by corresponding worst case $O(\sqrt{n})$ and $O(\sqrt[3]{n})$ run time algorithms, respectively, which improves upon the previous best known result of $O(n)$ [5]. We then consider the average case complexity of addition given two uniformly generated random n-bit numbers and construct a $O(\log n)$ average case time algorithm that achieves simultaneous worst case run time $O(\sqrt{n})$ in 2D. To the best of our knowledge this is the first tile assembly algorithm proposed for efficient average case adding. Our results are summarized in Table 1. Also, tile self-assembly software simulations were conducted to visualize the diverse approaches to fast arithmetic presented in this paper, as well as to compare them to previous work. The adder tile constructions described in Sections 4, 5 and 6, and the previous best known algorithm from [5] were simulated using the two timing models described in Section 2.4. These results can be seen in the graphs of Figure 1.

2   Definitions

2.1   Basic Notation

Let $\mathbb{N}_n$ denote the set $\{1, \ldots, n\}$ and let $\mathbb{Z}_n$ denote the set $\{0, \ldots, n-1\}$. Consider two points $p, q \in \mathbb{Z}^d$, $p = (p_1, \ldots p_d)$, $q = (q_1, \ldots, q_d)$. Define the *maximum norm* to be $\|p - q\|_\infty \triangleq \max_{1 \leq i \leq d}\{|p_i - q_i|\}$.

2.2   Abstract Tile Assembly Model

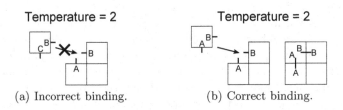

(a) Incorrect binding.   (b) Correct binding.

Fig. 2. Cooperative tile binding in the aTAM

Tiles. Consider some alphabet of symbols Π called the *glue types*. A tile is a finite edge polygon (polyhedron in the case of a 3D generalization) with some finite subset of border points each assigned some glue type from Π. Further, each glue type $g \in \Pi$ has some non-negative integer strength $str(g)$. For each tile t we also associate a finite string *label* (typically "0", or "1", or the empty label in this paper), denoted by label(t), which allows the classification of tiles by their labels. In this paper we consider a special class of tiles that are unit squares (or unit cubes in 3D) of the same orientation with at most one glue type per face, with each glue being placed exactly in the center of the tile's face. We denote the *location* of a tile to be the point at the center of the square or cube tile. In this paper we focus on tiles at integer locations.

Assemblies. An assembly is a finite set of tiles whose interiors do not overlap. Further, to simplify formalization in this paper, we further require the center of each tile in an assembly to be an integer coordinate (or integer triplet in 3D). If each tile in A is a translation of some tile in a set of tiles T, we say that A is an assembly over tile set T. For a given assembly Υ, define the *bond graph* G_Υ to be the weighted graph in which each element of Υ is a vertex, and the weight of an edge between two tiles is the strength of the overlapping matching glue points between the two tiles. Note that only overlapping glues that are the same type contribute a non-zero weight, whereas overlapping, non-equal glues always contribute zero weight to the bond graph. The property that only equal glue types interact with each other is referred to as the *diagonal glue function* property and is perhaps more feasible than more general glue functions for experimental implementation (see [8] for the theoretical impact of relaxing this constraint). An assembly Υ is said to be τ-*stable* for an integer τ if the min-cut of G_Υ is at least τ.

Tile Attachment. Given a tile t, an integer τ, and a τ-stable assembly A, we say that t may attach to A at temperature τ to form A' if there exists a translation t' of t such that $A' = A \bigcup \{t'\}$, and A' is τ-stable. For a tile set T we use notation $A \rightarrow_{T,\tau} A'$ to denote that there exists some $t \in T$ that may attach to A to form A' at temperature τ. When T and τ are implied, we simply say $A \rightarrow A'$. Further, we say that $A \rightarrow^* A'$ if either $A = A'$, or there exists a finite sequence of assemblies $\langle A_1 \ldots A_k \rangle$ such that $A \rightarrow A_1 \rightarrow \ldots \rightarrow A_k \rightarrow A'$.

Tile Systems. A tile system $\Gamma = (T, S, \tau)$ is an ordered triplet consisting of a set of tiles T referred to as the system's *tile set*, a τ-stable assembly S referred to as the system's *seed* assembly, and a positive integer τ referred to as the system's *temperature*. A tile system $\Gamma = (T, S, \tau)$ has an associated set of *producible* assemblies, PROD$_\Gamma$, which define what assemblies can grow from the initial seed S by any sequence of temperature τ tile attachments from T. Formally, $S \in$ PROD$_\Gamma$ is a base case producible assembly. Further, for any $A \in$ PROD$_\Gamma$, if $A \rightarrow_{T,\tau} A'$, then $A' \in$ PROD$_\Gamma$. That is, assembly S is producible, and for any producible assembly A, if A can grow into A', then A' is also producible. We further denote a producible assembly A to be *terminal* if A has no attachable tile from T at temperature τ. We say a system $\Gamma = (T, S, \tau)$ *uniquely produces* an assembly A if all producible assemblies can grow into A through some sequence of tile attachments. More formally, Γ *uniquely produces* assembly $A \in \text{PROD}_\Gamma$ if for any $A' \in \text{PROD}_\Gamma$ it is the case that $A' \rightarrow^* A$. Systems that uniquely produce one assembly are said to be *deterministic*. In this paper, we focus exclusively on deterministic systems, and our general goal will be to design systems whose uniquely produced assembly specifies the solution to a computational problem. For recent consideration of non-determinism in tile self-assembly see [6, 7, 10, 13, 17].

2.3   Problem Description

We now formalize what we mean for a tile self-assembly system to compute a function. To do this we present the concept of a *tile assembly computer* (TAC) which consists of a tile set and temperature parameter, along with input and output *templates*. The input template serves as a seed structure with a sequence of *wildcard positions* for which tiles of label "0" and "1" may be placed to construct an initial seed assembly. An output template is a sequence of points denoting locations for which the TAC, when grown from a filled in template, will place tiles with "0" and "1" labels that denote the output bit string. A TAC then is said to compute a function f if for any seed assembly derived by plugging in a bitstring b, the terminal assembly of the system with tile set T and temperature τ will be such that the value of $f(b)$ is encoded in the sequence of tiles placed according to the locations of the output template. We now develop the formal definition of the TAC concept. We note that the formality in the input template is of substantial importance. Simpler definitions which map seeds to input bit strings, and terminal assemblies to output bitstrings, are problematic in that they allow for the possibility of encoding the computation of function f in the seed structure. Even something as innocuous sounding as allowing more than a single type of "0" or "1" tile as an input bit has the subtle issue of allowing pre-computing of f[1].

Input Template. Consider a tile set T containing exactly one tile t_0 with label "0", and one tile t_1 with label "1". An n-bit input template over tile set T is an ordered pair $U = (R, B(i))$, where R is an assembly over $T - \{t_0, t_1\}$, $B : \mathbb{N}_n \rightarrow \mathbb{Z}^2$, and $B(i)$ is not the position of any tile in R for any i from 1 to n. The sequence of n coordinates denoted by B conceptually denotes "wildcard" tile positions for which copies of t_0 and t_1 will be filled in for any instance of the template. For notation we define assembly U_b over T, for bit string $b = b_1, \ldots b_n$, to be the assembly consisting of assembly R unioned with a set of n tiles t^i for i from 1 to n, where t^i is equal a translation of tile $t_{b(i)}$ to position $B(i)$. That is, U_b is the assembly R with each position $B(i)$ tiled with either t_0 or t_1 according to the value of b_i.

---

[1] This subtle issue seems to exist with some previous formulations of tile assembly computation.

Output Template. A k-bit output template is simply a sequence of k coordinates denoted by function $C : N_k \to \mathbb{Z}^2$. For an output template V, an assembly A over T is said to represent binary string $c = c_1, \ldots, c_k$ over template V if the tile at position $C(i)$ in A has label c_i for all i from 1 to k. Note that output template solutions are much looser than input templates in that there may be multiple tiles with labels "1" and "0", and there are no restrictions on the assembly outside of the k specified wildcard positions. The strictness for the input template stems from the fact that the input must "look the same" in all ways except for the explicit input bit patterns. If this were not the case, it would likely be possible to encode the solution to the computational problem into the input template, resulting is a trivial solution.

Function Computing Problem. A *tile assembly computer* (TAC) is an ordered quadruple $\mathfrak{S} = (T, U, V, \tau)$ where T is a tile set, U is an n-bit input template, and V is a k-bit output template. A TAC is said to compute function $f : \mathbb{Z}_2^n \to \mathbb{Z}_2^k$ if for any $b \in \mathbb{Z}_2^n$ and $c \in \mathbb{Z}_2^k$ such that $f(b) = c$, then the tile system $\Gamma_{\mathfrak{S},b} = (T, U_b, \tau)$ uniquely assembles an assembly A which represents c over template V. For a TAC $\mathfrak{S}$ that computes the function $f : Z_2^{2n} \to Z_2^{n+1}$ where $f(r_1 \ldots r_{2n}) = r_1 \ldots r_n + r_{n+1} \ldots r_{2n}$, we say that $\mathfrak{S}$ is an n-bit *adder* TAC with inputs $a = r_1 \ldots r_n$ and $b = r_{n+1} \ldots r_{2n}$. An n-bit *multiplier* TAC is defined similarly.

2.4   Run Time Models

We analyze the complexity of self-assembly arithmetic under two established run time models for tile self-assembly: the *parallel* time model [4, 5] and the *continuous* time model [2–4, 9]. Informally, the parallel time model simply adds, in parallel, all singleton tiles that are attachable to a given assembly within a single time step. The continuous time model, in contrast, models the time taken for a single tile to attach as an exponentially distributed random variable. The parallelism of the continuous time model stems from the fact that if an assembly has a large number of attachable positions, then the *first* tile to attach will be an exponentially distributed random variable with rate proportional to the number of attachment sites, implying that a larger number of attachable positions will speed up the expected time for the next attachment. Technical definitions for each run time model can be found in [18], along with an analysis for how different the two models might be. When not otherwise specified, we use the term *run time* to refer to parallel run time by default. The stated asymptotic worst case and average case run times for each of our algorithms hold within both run time models.

3   Lower Bound for Long Distance Communication

In this section we formulate a class of problems we term the *communication* problems in which the goal is to compute a simple AND function on a 2-bit input function given that the input template separates the 2 input bits some specified distance Δ. We formulate this problem for the purposes of providing lower bounds on the worst-case time complexity for this problem. We then reduce this problem to addition and multiplication problems in 2D and 3D to provide worst case lower bounds for addition and multiplication. In this extended abstract we provide a sketch of the lower bound arguments and refer the reader to [18] for a detailed proof.

3.1   High-Level Sketch of Lower Bound Proofs

To prove lower bounds for addition and multiplication in 2D and 3D, we do the following. First, we consider two identical tile systems with the exception of their respective seed assemblies which differ in exactly one tile location. It can be shown that after Δ time steps, all positions more than Δ distance from the point of initial difference of the assemblies must be identical among the two systems. We then consider the *communication* problem in which we compute the AND function of two input bits under the assumption that the input template for the problem separates the two bits by distance Δ. For such a problem, we know that the output position of the solution bit must be at least distance $\frac{1}{2}\Delta$ from one of the two input bits. As the correct output for the AND function must be a function of both bits, we get that at least $\frac{1}{2}\Delta$ steps are required to guarantee a correct solution to the distance Δ communication problem.

With the lower bound of $\frac{1}{2}\Delta$ established for the communication problem, we move on to the problems of addition and multiplication of n-bit numbers. We show how the communication problem can be reduced to these problems, thereby yielding corresponding lower bounds. In particular, consider the addition problem in 2D. As the input template must contain positions for $2n$ bits, in 2D it must be the case that some pair of bits are separated by at least $\Omega(\sqrt{n})$ distance. Focussing on this pair of bit positions in the addition template, we can create a corresponding communication problem template with the same two positions as input. To guarantee the correct output, we hard code the remaining bit positions of the addition template such that the addition algorithm is guaranteed to place the AND of the desired bit pair in a specific position in the output template, thereby constituting a solution to the $\Delta = \Omega(\sqrt{n})$ communication problem, which implies the addition solution cannot finish faster than $\Omega(\sqrt{n})$ in the worst case. A similar reduction can be applied to multiplication. The theorem statements for these lower bounds are provided below.

Theorem 1. *Any d-dimension n-bit adder TAC has worst case run-time $\Omega(\sqrt[d]{n})$.*

Theorem 2. *Any d-dimension n-bit multiplier TAC has worst case run-time $\Omega(\sqrt[d]{n})$.*

4   Addition in Average Case Logarithmic Time

Our first upper bound result is an adder TAC that achieves an $O(\log n)$ average case run-time. Our construction resembles an electronic carry-skip adder in that

a)   MSB of A 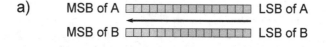 LSB of A

MSB of B  LSB of B

b)   MSB LSB

Fig. 3. Arrows represent carry origination and propagation direction. a) Represents previously described $O(n)$ worst case addition for addends A and B [5]. b) Average case $O(\log n)$ construction where addends A and B populate the linear assembly with bit A_i immediatly adjacent to B_i. Carry propagation is done in parallel.

the carry-out bit for addend pairs where each addend in the pair has the same bit value is generated in a constant number of steps and immediately propagated (Figure 3). When each addend in a pair of addends does not have the same bit value, a carry-out cannot be deduced until the value of the carry-in to the pair of addends is known. When such addend combinations occur in a contiguous sequence, the carry must ripple through the sequence from right-to-left, one step at a time as each position is evaluated. Within these worst-case sequences, our construction resembles an electronic ripple-carry adder. We show that using this approach it is possible to construct an n-bit adder TAC that can perform addition with an average runtime of $O(\log n)$ and a worst-case runtime of $O(n)$.

Theorem 3. *For any positive integer n, there exists an n-bit adder TAC (tile assembly computer) that has worst case run time $O(n)$ and an average case run time of $O(\log n)$.*

5   Optimal 2*D* Addition

Our next result is an adder TAC that achieves a run time of $O(\sqrt{n})$, which matches the lower bound from Theorem 1. This adder TAC closely resembles an electronic carry-select adder in that the addends are divided into sections of size $\sqrt{n}$ and the sum of the addends comprising each is computed for both possible carry-in values (Figure 5(b)). The correct result for the subsection is then selected after a carry-out has been propagated from the previous subsection. Within each subsection, the addition scheme resembles a ripple-carry adder.

The input and output templates for our construction are shown in Figures 4(a)and 4(b) with the input bit strings interleaved as green and orange tiles, and the output sum denoted with blue tiles. In parallel, each row of the input assembly computes the sum of a size $\sqrt{n}$ portion of the input strings to grow one additional layer for each row of the initial assembly in $O(\sqrt{n})$ time. A second layer for each row is then assembled which computes the previous value incremented by 1. Finally, a vertical chain of tiles grows from the bottom of the assembly up to the top which selects from each row either the original sum for the given row, or its increment, dependent on whether the previous row passed

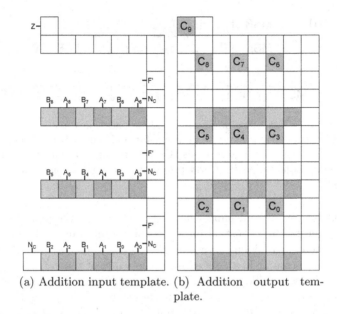

(a) Addition input template. (b) Addition output template.

Fig. 4. These are example I/O templates for the worst case $O(\sqrt{n})$ time addition introduced in Section 5.

on a carry bit. The details of this construction along with a proof of correctness and run time analysis can be found in [18]. The final result is the following theorem.

Theorem 4. *There exists an n-bit adder TAC with a worst case run-time of* $O(\sqrt[2]{n})$.

6   Towards Faster Addition

Our next result combines the approaches described in Sections 4 and 5 in order to achieve both $O(\log n)$ average case addition and $O(\sqrt{n})$ worst case addition with the same algorithm (Figure 5(a)). This construction resembles the construction described in Section 5 in that the numbers to be added are divided into sections and values are computed for both possible carry-in bit values. Additionally, the construction described here lowers the average case run time by utilizing the carry-skip mechanism described in Section 4 within each section and between sections.

Theorem 5. *There exists a 2-dimensional n-bit adder TAC with an average run-time of* $O(\log n)$ *and a worst case run-time of* $O(\sqrt{n})$.

Given this 2D construction, it is possible to stack multiple linked instances of this construction into the third dimension to achieve an analogous optimal result for 3D addition. A high-level sketch of the stacking is shown in Figure 6.

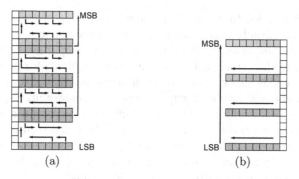

Fig. 5. Arrows represent carry origination and direction of propagation for a) $O(\log n)$ average case, $O(\sqrt{n})$ worst case combined construction and b) $O(\sqrt{n})$ worst case construction

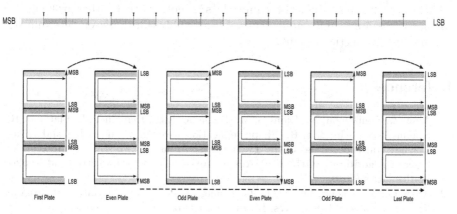

Fig. 6. An overview of the process to add two number in optimal time in $3D$

Theorem 6. *There exists a 3-dimensional n-bit adder TAC with an average run-time of $O(\log n)$ and a worst case run-time of $O(\sqrt[3]{n})$.*

For a detailed presentation of these results please see [18].

7   Future Work

The results of this paper are just a jumping off point and provide numerous directions for future work. One promising direction is further exploration of the complexity of multiplication. Can $O(n^{1/3})$ or $O(n^{1/2})$ be achieved in 3D or 2D, or can a better lower bound be found? In [18] we show how to achieve $O(n^{5/6})$ time multiplication in 3D. Can this bound be improved? Is sublinear multiplication possible in 2D, or is there a $\Omega(n)$ lower bound? What is the average case complexity of multiplication? What about other computational problems such as sorting?

Another direction for future work is the consideration of metrics other than run time. One potentially important metric is the geometric space taken up by the computation. Our intent is that fast function computing systems such as those presented in this paper will be used as building blocks for larger and more complex self-assembly algorithms. For such applications, the area and volume taken up by the computation is clearly an important constraint. Exploring trade-offs between run time and imposed space limitations for computation may be a promising direction with connections to resource bounded computation theory. Along these lines, another important direction is the general development of design methodologies for creating black box self-assembly algorithms that can be plugged into larger systems with little or no "tweaking".

A final direction focusses on the consideration of non-deterministic tile assembly systems to improve expected run times even for maniacally designed worst case input strings. Is it possible to achieve $O(\log n)$ expected run time for the addition problem regardless of the input bits? If not, are there other problems for which there is a provable gap in achievable assembly time between deterministic and non-deterministic systems?

References

1. Abel, Z., Benbernou, N., Damian, M., Demaine, E.D., Demaine, M., Flatland, R., Kominers, S., Schweller, R.: Shape replication through self-assembly and RNase enzymes. In: Proceedings of the Twenty-First Annual ACM-SIAM Symposium on Discrete Algorithms, SODA 2010, Austin, Texas, Society for Industrial and Applied Mathematics (2010)
2. Adleman, L., Cheng, Q., Goel, A., Huang, M.-D.: Running time and program size for self-assembled squares. In: Proceedings of the Thirty-Third Annual ACM Symposium on Theory of Computing, pp. 740–748. ACM, New York (2001)
3. Adleman, L.M., Cheng, Q., Goel, A., Huang, M.-D.A., Kempe, D., de Espanés, P.M., Rothemund, P.W.K.: Combinatorial optimization problems in self-assembly. In: Proceedings of the Thirty-Fourth Annual ACM Symposium on Theory of Computing, pp. 23–32 (2002)
4. Becker, F., Rapaport, I., Rémila, É.: Self-assembling classes of shapes with a minimum number of tiles, and in optimal time. In: Arun-Kumar, S., Garg, N. (eds.) FSTTCS 2006. LNCS, vol. 4337, pp. 45–56. Springer, Heidelberg (2006)
5. Brun, Y.: Arithmetic computation in the tile assembly model: Addition and multiplication. Theoretical Computer Science 378, 17–31 (2007)
6. Bryans, N., Chiniforooshan, E., Doty, D., Kari, L., Seki, S.: The power of nondeterminism in self-assembly. In: Proceedings of the 22nd Annual ACM-SIAM Symposium on Discrete Algorithms, SODA 2011, pp. 590–602. SIAM (2011)
7. Chandran, H., Gopalkrishnan, N., Reif, J.: The tile complexity of linear assemblies. In: Albers, S., Marchetti-Spaccamela, A., Matias, Y., Nikoletseas, S., Thomas, W. (eds.) ICALP 2009, Part I. LNCS, vol. 5555, pp. 235–253. Springer, Heidelberg (2009)
8. Cheng, Q., Aggarwal, G., Goldwasser, M.H., Kao, M.-Y., Schweller, R.T., de Espanés, P.M.: Complexities for generalized models of self-assembly. SIAM Journal on Computing 34, 1493–1515 (2005)

9. Cheng, Q., Goel, A., de Espanés, P.M.: Optimal self-assembly of counters at temperature two. In: Proceedings of the First Conference on Foundations of Nanoscience: Self-assembled Architectures and Devices (2004)
10. Cook, M., Fu, Y., Schweller, R.T.: Temperature 1 self-assembly: Deterministic assembly in 3d and probabilistic assembly in 2d. In: Randall, D. (ed.) Proceedings of the Twenty-Second Annual ACM-SIAM Symposium on Discrete Algorithms, SODA 2011, pp. 570–589. SIAM (2011)
11. Demaine, E.D., Patitz, M.J., Rogers, T.A., Schweller, R.T., Summers, S.M., Woods, D.: The two-handed tile assembly model is not intrinsically universal. In: Fomin, F.V., Freivalds, R., Kwiatkowska, M., Peleg, D. (eds.) ICALP 2013, Part I. LNCS, vol. 7965, pp. 400–412. Springer, Heidelberg (2013)
12. Demaine, E.D., Demaine, M.L., Fekete, S.P., Patitz, M.J., Schweller, R.T., Winslow, A., Woods, D.: One tile to rule them all: Simulating any tile assembly system with a single universal tile. In: Proceedings of the 41st International Colloquium on Automata, Languages and Programming, ICALP (2014)
13. Doty, D.: Randomized self-assembly for exact shapes. SIAM Journal on Computing 39(8), 3521–3552 (2010)
14. Doty, D., Lutz, J.H., Patitz, M.J., Schweller, R., Summers, S.M., Woods, D.: The tile assembly model is intrinsically universal. In: Proceedings of the 53rd IEEE Conference on Foundations of Computer Science, FOCS (2012)
15. Doty, D., Patitz, M.J., Reishus, D., Schweller, R.T., Summers, S.M.: Strong fault-tolerance for self-assembly with fuzzy temperature. In: Proceedings of the 51st Annual IEEE Symposium on Foundations of Computer Science (FOCS 2010), pp. 417–426 (2010)
16. Fu, B., Patitz, M.J., Schweller, R.T., Sheline, R.: Self-assembly with geometric tiles. In: Czumaj, A., Mehlhorn, K., Pitts, A., Wattenhofer, R. (eds.) ICALP 2012, Part I. LNCS, vol. 7391, pp. 714–725. Springer, Heidelberg (2012)
17. Kao, M.-Y., Schweller, R.T.: Randomized self-assembly for approximate shapes. In: Aceto, L., Damgård, I., Goldberg, L.A., Halldórsson, M.M., Ingólfsdóttir, A., Walukiewicz, I. (eds.) ICALP 2008, Part I. LNCS, vol. 5125, pp. 370–384. Springer, Heidelberg (2008)
18. Keenan, A., Schweller, R.T., Sherman, M., Zhong, X.: Fast arithmetic in algorithmic self-assembly, CoRR abs/1303.2416 (2013)
19. Mao, C., LaBean, T.H., Reif, J.H., Seeman, N.C.: Logical computation using algorithmic self-assembly of DNA triple-crossover molecules. Nature 407(6803), 493–496 (2000)
20. Schweller, R., Sherman, M.: Fuel efficient computation in passive self-assembly. In: Proceedings of the 24th Annual ACM-SIAM Symposium on Discrete Algorithms, SODA 2013, pp. 1513–1525. SIAM (2013)
21. Winfree, E.: Algorithmic self-assembly of DNA, Ph.D. thesis. California Institute of Technology (June 1998)

Pattern Formation by Spatially Organized Approximate Majority Reactions

Matthew R. Lakin[1] and Darko Stefanovic[1,2]

[1] Department of Computer Science, University of New Mexico, Albuquerque, NM, USA
[2] Center for Biomedical Engineering, University of New Mexico, Albuquerque, NM, USA
{mlakin,darko}@cs.unm.edu

Abstract. Pattern formation is a topic of great interest in biology and nanotechnology. In this paper we investigate a system of spatially-organized reactions inspired by a well-known distributed algorithm for approximate majority voting, and demonstrate that this system can lead to pattern formation from a randomly initialized starting state. We also show that the approximate majority reaction scheme can preserve an existing pattern in the face of noise, and that exerting control over reaction rates can influence the generated pattern. This work has potential applications in the rational design of pattern-forming systems in DNA nanotechnology and synthetic biology.

1 Introduction

Pattern formation is a fundamental topic in many areas of developmental biology. Turing [1] showed that certain systems of reaction-diffusion equations may give rise to spatiotemporal patterns, which can account for certain features of plant morphogenesis. Since nature has repeatedly found programmed pattern formation to be a robust means of directing the development of biological structures, the implementation of synthetic biochemical systems with similar spatial behavior has been a key goal of molecular programming [2,3].

Spatiotemporal patterning systems such as those discovered by Turing depend on a balance between diffusion timescales: short-range inhibition and long-range activation are required for pattern formation. This fact has made it challenging to engineer synthetic biological systems for programmed pattern formation, because suitable diffusible molecules must be chosen to set up the morphogen gradients. In this paper we investigate the formation and preservation of spatial patterns by purely local reaction rules, which could form the basis of simplified synthetic patterning systems. The reaction rules in question are the approximate majority reaction scheme of Angluin *et al.* [4], which were originally developed as a distributed voting algorithm but which we employ as a set of spatial reaction rules to enable pattern formation.

The remainder of this paper is structured as follows. We introduce the approximate majority reaction scheme in Section 2 and use it as the basis for a spatial reaction system in Section 3. We present the results of simulations of the spatial approximate majority system in Section 4 and conclude with a discussion in Section 5.

O.H. Ibarra et al. (Eds.): UCNC 2014, LNCS 8553, pp. 254–266, 2014.
DOI: 10.1007/978-3-319-08123-6_21, © Springer International Publishing Switzerland 2014

2   The Approximate Majority System

The approximate majority (AM) system was introduced by Angluin *et al.* [4] as a leaderless algorithm for rapidly converging to a consensus between distributed agents with limited computing power. In its simplest form, the AM system is a chemical reaction network comprising three species (A, B, and X) and three reactions:

$$A + B \rightarrow X + X \tag{1}$$

$$A + X \rightarrow A + A \tag{2}$$

$$B + X \rightarrow B + B \tag{3}$$

From an initial state consisting of just species A and B, the intent of the AM reaction system is to convert all of the individuals into whichever species was initially present in the majority. When an A and a B meet, they are each converted into an X by reaction (1). When an X subsequently encounters an A or a B, the X is converted into another copy of the species it encountered, by either reaction (2) or reaction (3). The original formulation of the AM system assumes that the system is dilute and well-mixed, and therefore obeys the laws of mass action chemical kinetics. In this situation, the intuition behind the AM algorithm is that when an X species is created, it will be more likely to subsequently encounter whichever of A and B is present in the majority. Hence it is more likely for the initial majority species to catalyze the conversion of the minority species into the majority than for the initial minority species to catalyze the conversion of the majority species into the minority.

Implementations of the AM system using DNA strand displacement reactions have been studied both theoretically [5,6] and in the laboratory [7], and networks with similar dynamic behavior have been observed in the regulatory systems that govern the cell cycle [8]. Hence this system of chemical reactions is of theoretical and practical interest as an object of study.

3   Spatially-organized Approximate Majority Reactions

In this paper we consider the AM reactions in the context of a spatially-organized reaction system. To our knowledge, this is the first paper to consider the approximate majority system in a spatial context. As shown in Figure 1, we consider a grid of hexagonal cells in which every cell is labeled with a species: either A, B, or X. If two neighbouring cells are labeled with species that are *reactants* for one of the AM reactions from Section 2, then those cells can be relabeled with the *products* from the corresponding reaction, as shown in Figure 1. Our scheme is essentially a hexagonal cellular automaton—we choose to work in a hexagonal structure to avoid the potentially thorny issue of whether a given cell should be able to interact with a diagonally adjacent cell. In the interest of simplicity, we do not consider diffusion, which is required for alternative models of pattern formation, such as Turing patterning.

The rationale behind the use of AM reactions for spatial pattern formation is as follows. When species A and B occur in proximity, reaction (1) converts them both into X. Then, depending on whether A or B is predominant in that part of the grid, the occurrences of X will be preferentially converted to either A or B by reaction (2) or (3).

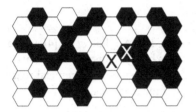 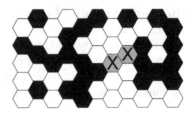

(a) A grid with two cells selected to interact (identified by an "X").

(b) The grid after relabeling the selected cells according to reaction (1).

Fig. 1. Hexagonal reaction grids with AM species and reactions. Here and henceforth, white cells represent species A, black cells represent species B, and light grey cells represent species X.

By this mechanism, patterning in the occurrence of species A and B should be, roughly, preserved by the AM reactions. The AM reactions may also provide a means to generate a stable, spatially heterogeneous pattern from a uniformly-distributed, random starting state. Furthermore, if there is a possibility of noise that causes species A and B spontaneously to interconvert, the AM reactions may enable us to prevent a heterogeneous pattern from degenerating towards a uniform species distribution due to the effects of noise. Below we present the results of simulations designed to investigate these properties of the spatial AM reaction system.

4   Results

4.1   Pattern Formation

We investigated the pattern formation capabilities of spatially organized AM reactions by running stochastic simulations starting from randomly-initialized, non-periodic grids, using a Gillespie-style algorithm [9]. In all simulations we used grids that are 40 cells wide and 40 rows tall. Each cell was initialized to either species A or B with equal probability—we did not include any cells of the intermediate species X in the initial grids. In these initial simulations, we fixed a uniform rate constant of 1.0 for all three AM reactions, throughout the grid. We ran all simulations for 100,000 time units, as this was empirically found to be a suitable timescale to observe the phenomena under study.

The simulation algorithm can be summarized as follows. At the beginning of the simulation, the set of all possible reactions between cells in the initial grid was enumerated. The next reaction to occur was selected at random, with the probability of selecting a given reaction proportional to its rate constant. Simulation time was advanced by the time until the next reaction, which was drawn from an exponential distribution with mean $1/\rho$, with ρ being the rate constant of the selected reaction. The grid was transformed by applying the selected reaction, the select of possible reactions was updated to reflect the changes in the grid. The simulation loop was iterated until either the time limit was reached or the grid reached a state from which no further reactions were possible.

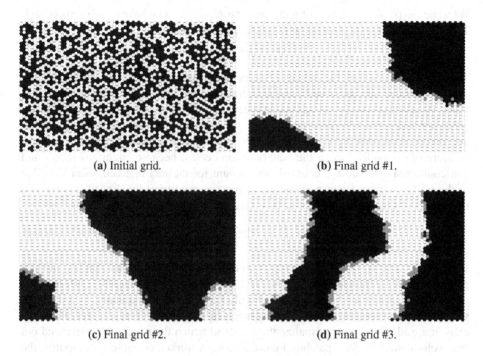

(a) Initial grid.   (b) Final grid #1.

(c) Final grid #2.   (d) Final grid #3.

Fig. 2. An initial grid and three example final grids generated from the initial grid via stochastic simulations.

Figure 2 shows a randomly-initialized grid together with three example grids derived from the initial grid by stochastic simulations using the AM reactions. In each case, we observe that the grid pattern evolves towards a state in which cells of a particular species accumulate into uniform patches, with the only subsequent reactions occurring at the borders between patches. These examples demonstrate that spatially-organized AM reactions can introduce long-distance order into a grid via purely localized reactions. This happens because the AM reactions allow the species that is dominant in a particular area of the grid to convert neighbouring cells of the other species to the dominant species, leading to the development of uniform patches.

To quantify this pattern-forming effect, we define a metric to measure the uniformity of the pattern around a given cell in a grid. We assume that each cell in the grid is labelled with a unique index i, and write $G(i)$ for the species of the cell in G that is labeled with i. We say that a *path*, p, is a finite list $[i_1, \ldots, i_n]$ of indices such that the grid cell labeled with i_{k+1} is a direct neighbour of the grid cell labeled with i_k and write $paths_G(i_1, i_2)$ for the set of paths that start from cell i_1 and end at cell i_2 in grid G. The *length*, $len(p)$, of a path p is the number of steps in the path, i.e., $len([i_1, \ldots, i_n]) = n - 1$. For two indices $i_1 \neq i_2$ in the grid G, we write $dist_G(i_1, i_2)$ for the length of the shortest path from i_1 to i_2 in grid G, i.e.:

$$dist_G(i_1, i_2) = \min(\{len(p) \mid p \in paths_G(i_1, i_2)\})$$

We write $sp_G(i_1, i_2)$ for the set of paths from $paths_G(i_1, i_2)$ that have length $dist_G(i_1, i_2)$. Then, we can define the n-neighbour metric, $\mu_{n,G}$, as follows:

$$\mu_{n,G}(i) = \{i' \mid dist_G(i, i') = n \wedge \exists p \in sp_G(i, i'). \, \forall i'' \in p. \, G(i'') = G(i)\}$$

The set $\mu_{n,G}(i)$ contains the indices of all cells at distance n from i in the grid G that contain the same species as cell i and are connected to i by a path of length n that *only* traverses cells that also contain the same species as cell i. This set excludes cells that are either not part of the same contiguous patch as i or are in the same contiguous patch but not directly connected by a minimal-length path within the patch. This gives a robust measure of the uniformity of the pattern around cell i, because circuitous routes and non-connected cells are not counted. To account for the fact that cells near the edge of the grid may have fewer neighbours, in practice we report the size of $\mu_{n,G}(i)$ as a percentage of the total number of cells at distance n from i, i.e.:

$$\pi_{n,G}(i) = \left(\frac{|\mu_{n,G}(i)|}{|\{i' \mid dist_G(i, i') = n\}|} \right) \times 100$$

If $\pi_{n,G}(i)$ is close to 100% then the region of radius n around cell i has a highly uniform pattern containing the same species as i. If $\pi_{n,G}(i)$ is close to 0% then the pattern in the region of radius n around cell i is either highly fragmented or dominated by a different species than the species in i. The distribution of the values of $\pi_{n,G}(i)$ for all of the cells in a grid allows us to visualize the extent to which the pattern has separated out into well-defined, uniform patches. Figure 3 shows a worked example of computing the value of this metric for an example grid.

To measure the changes between grids G_1 and G_2 of the same size and shape, we use the Hamming distance, $H(G_1, G_2)$, which is the number of cells that have different species in G_1 and G_2. Since the grids have the same size, this can be straightforwardly expressed as a percentage of the total number of cells in the grid, which we write as $H_p(G_1, G_2)$.

We ran simulations starting from 200 randomly-initialized grids, with 50 stochastic runs from each initial grid. Figure 4a plots the percentage Hamming distance between the grid states at time t and 1,000 time units earlier, i.e., $H_p(G(t), G(t-1000))$. The mean value of this metric decreases towards zero over time, showing that the rate of change of the pattern slows over time. Figure 4b quantifies the change in structure of the grid patterns by plotting the aggregated values of the $\pi_{3,G}$ metric for each cell in the initial and final grids from all 10,000 grid simulations. Here and henceforth, we report the values of neighbour metrics for $n = 3$ because the metric computation masks features of size less than n, so for larger values of n we may fail to detect some pattern features. Conversely, for smaller values of n the metric may be overly sensitive to small-scale pattern features in the computation. The initial grids show a broad distribution of $\pi_{3,G}$ values between 0% and 40%, which corresponds to a chaotic initial pattern. Conversely, the vast majority of the final grid cells have $\pi_{3,G}$ values between 95% and 100%, which means that almost all cells are surrounded by a highly homogeneous patch with a radius of at least 3 cells. Together, these results demonstrate that the grids tend to evolve towards a pattern consisting of homogeneous patches, where further interactions can only occur at patch boundaries, which causes the rate of change of the pattern to slow over time.

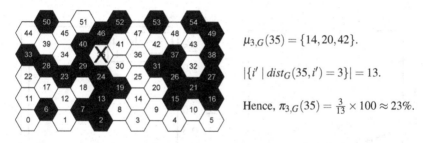

$\mu_{3,G}(35) = \{14, 20, 42\}.$

$|\{i' \mid dist_G(35, i') = 3\}| = 13.$

Hence, $\pi_{3,G}(35) = \frac{3}{13} \times 100 \approx 23\%.$

Fig. 3. Computing the value of the $\pi_{3,G}$ metric for cell 35 (identified by an "X") in an example grid. Note that $12, 17, 39 \notin \mu_{3,G}(35)$ because those cells are not connected to cell 35 by any path of cells with the same species as cell 35, i.e., species A. Furthermore, note that $8 \notin \mu_{3,G}(35)$ because it is not connected to cell 35 by a path of A cells with length 3 (the shortest such path is $[8, 14, 25, 30, 35]$, which has length 4).

4.2 Pattern Preservation in the Face of Noise

The ability of the spatial AM reaction scheme to generate patterns from randomized starting conditions should also make it well suited to preserve an existing pattern in the face of noise. To test this hypothesis, we augmented the standard AM reactions with two "noise" reactions that enable cells to unilaterally switch between species A and B with a noise rate v, as follows:

$$A \xrightarrow{v} B \qquad\qquad B \xrightarrow{v} A.$$

Instead of starting from a grid with uniformly-distributed species, we generated a uniform grid of A cells and added a number of hexagonal patches of B cells at random positions and with random sizes. We fixed the rates of the standard AM reactions at 1.0, and ran a total of $1,000$ simulations (50 repetitions from 20 initial grids) to observe how well the spatial AM reactions preserved the initial pattern over $100,000$ time units in the face of noise reactions with rate $v = 0.1$. Example initial and final grids from these simulations are presented in Figure 5, where we see that noise reactions alone completely obliterate the initial pattern. However, the inclusion of AM reactions preserves the pattern as well (or better) than in the noise-free case where only AM reactions may occur. This may be explained by the observation that, when noise reactions are included, some time is spent suppressing noise instead of altering the overall grid pattern, meaning that the overall pattern may be modified less in a given period of simulation time.

Figure 6a plots the percentage Hamming distance between the grid state at time t and the initial grid state, i.e., $H_p(G(t), G(0))$. With just noise reactions, the mean value of this metric converges to 50%, which is to be expected because the end result in this case will be a grid in which species A and B are uniformly distributed across the grid, so each cell has a 50% chance of being in a different species than in the initial grid. With both noise and AM reactions, however, the mean value rises more slowly. With just AM reactions, the mean value is in between the two, but with a larger variance due to the wide range of possible final states of the AM system. Figure 6b plots the

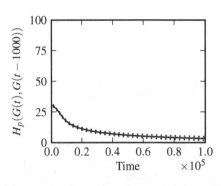
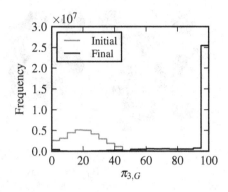

(a) Percentage Hamming distance between grid at time t and grid at time $t - 1000$.

(b) Histograms of values of $\pi_{3,G}$ for all cells in all initial and final grids.

Fig. 4. Statistics from simulations with randomly-initialized grids. (a) Solid line is the mean from 10,000 simulations, and dotted lines are one standard deviation above and below the mean. (b) Values of $\pi_{3,G}$ were computed for all cells in the initial and final grids of 10,000 simulations and combined into two histograms.

distribution of $\pi_{3,G}$ values across all initial grids and final grids. In the initial grids, we see that almost all cells have $\pi_{3,G}$ values close to 100%, representing the highly ordered initial grid states. With just AM reactions, the final grid state is even more ordered, with an even higher percentage of cells whose $\pi_{3,G}$ values are close to 100%. With just noise reactions, the distribution in the final states is shifted significantly, such that almost all $\pi_{3,G}$ values are between 0% and 50%, which represents the expected highly fragmented pattern. With the inclusion of AM reactions, however, the final states retain a significant proportion of cells with $\pi_{3,G}$ values between 50% and 100%, with the highest frequency between 90% and 95%. There is an additional peak between 0% and 5% which we interpret as cells whose species have been flipped by noise but which have not yet been flipped back by the AM reactions. These results demonstrate that the AM reactions significantly slow pattern degradation by noise and help to preserve regions of homogeneity in the initial pattern. As simulation time tends to infinity, we expect that the combination of noise and AM reactions would eventually disrupt the initial pattern, but this process should be slowed by the AM reactions.

4.3   Controlling Pattern Formation

In the reactions studied in Section 4.1, we observed pattern formation but without a means of controlling or predicting the resulting pattern. To demonstrate some control over the resulting pattern, we ran simulations starting from randomized initial grids with non-uniform reaction rates across the grid. We set the rate of the reaction $B + X \rightarrow B + B$ to $\rho < 1.0$ when one or both reactants are on the left-hand side of the grid (defined by a vertical line between the 20th and 21st columns of cells, which splits the grid into halves) and 1.0 when both reactants are on the right-hand side. The positions of the two

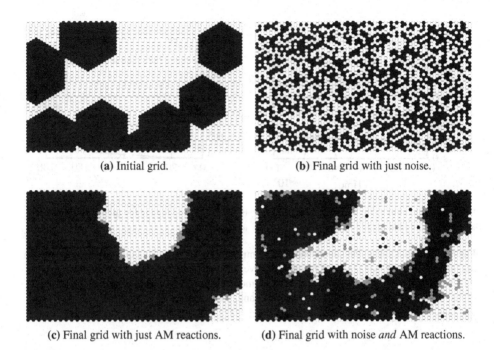

(a) Initial grid.   (b) Final grid with just noise.

(c) Final grid with just AM reactions.   (d) Final grid with noise *and* AM reactions.

Fig. 5. An initial grid and final grids generated under different reaction schemes from the initial grid via stochastic simulations. The noise rate was $v = 0.1$ in all cases.

reactants relative to each other were not used when computing these rates, only their absolute position on the grid. Similarly, we set the rate of the reaction $A + X \rightarrow A + A$ to be 1.0 when one or both reactants are on the left-hand side of the grid and $\rho < 1.0$ when both reactants are on the right-hand side. The rate of the reaction $A + B \rightarrow X + X$ was fixed at 1.0 across the whole grid. Since the reaction to replace X with B will be slower than the other reactions on the left-hand side of the grid, and the reaction to replace X with A will be slower than the other reactions on the right-hand side of the grid, the expected result of the simulations would be to generate a pattern in which the left-hand side of the grid is dominated by species A and the right-hand side of the grid is dominated by species B.

We ran a total of 1,000 simulations (50 repetitions from 20 initial grids, initialized with a uniform distribution of A and B) with non-uniform reaction rates as described above, using $\rho = 0.9$ as the slower reaction rate. Figure 7 shows an initial grid and example grids derived from it by a single stochastic simulation, at various time points. We observe that the grid pattern gradually moves from the chaotic initial grid towards a state in which the grid is split in half, with the left-hand side dominated by species A and the right-hand side dominated by species B. This supports our hypothesis that modifying the reaction rates as described above would produce a pattern of this kind.

Figure 8a plots the percentage Hamming distance between the grid state at time t and the expected grid G_{AB} (split exactly in half with the left-hand side containing only

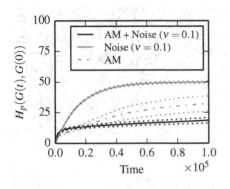 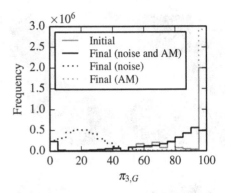

(a) Percentage Hamming distance between grid at time t and initial grid.

(b) Histograms of $\pi_{3,G}$ for all cells in all initial and final grids.

Fig. 6. Statistics from noise simulations. (a) Central lines are the mean from $1,000$ simulations, and dotted lines are one standard deviation above and below the mean. (b) Combined values of $\pi_{3,G}$ for all cells in the initial grids for $1,000$ simulations, and for the final grids in the presence of just AM reactions, just noise, and both noise and AM reactions. The noise rate was $v = 0.1$ in all cases.

species A and the right-hand side containing only species B), i.e., $H_p(G(t), G_{AB})$. The mean value of this metric is initially around 50% due to the uniform initial distribution of species in the grid, rises as cells are initially converted to the intermediate X species, and subsequently decreases towards zero, indicating that the simulations are tending to converge towards the expected pattern. Figure 8b plots the distribution of $\pi_{3,G}$ values across all initial grids and final grids. As discussed above, the distributions are indicative of a chaotic initial state and a well-ordered final state with well-defined patches. These results show that increasing the relative rate of the reaction that converts X into a given species in one part of the grid biases the pattern towards that species in that area, demonstrating that we can control pattern formation by controlling reaction rates.

5   Discussion

To summarize, we have demonstrated that the AM reaction scheme of Angluin *et al.* [4] provides a simple means for large-scale pattern generation via local interaction rules. The reactions enable the emergence of long-range order from random initial conditions and can preserve an established pattern in the face of noise. Manipulating reaction rates provides a possible means of controlling the generated pattern. This work has potential applications in morphogenetic engineering for synthetic biology [10], and in autonomous generation of patterned surfaces for DNA-templated nanofabrication [11].

Pattern formation is a well-developed field of study in many areas of science [12]. In statistical physics, a particular emphasis is placed on Ising spin models [13], which are capable of pattern generation [14]. In biology, reaction-diffusion systems were proposed

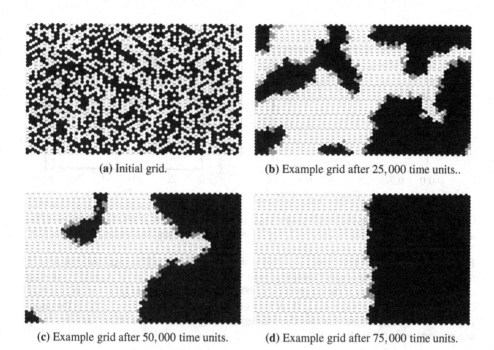

(a) Initial grid.   (b) Example grid after 25,000 time units..

(c) Example grid after 50,000 time units.   (d) Example grid after 75,000 time units.

Fig. 7. An initial grid and example grids generated by a stochastic simulation using non-uniform reaction rates to control pattern formation, with $\rho = 0.9$. The choice of reaction rates causes the chaotic initial pattern to move towards a pattern in which the left and right sides of the grid are dominated by species A and B, respectively.

by Turing [1] as the basis for various naturally-occurring patterns [15], and were first observed by Castets *et al.* [16]. Spatiotemporal patterns of predator and prey species are well-known in ecology, most famously predicted by the Lotka-Volterra model [17,18]. Pattern formation in chemistry is known to occur in a number of systems, in particular the Belousov-Zhabotinsky reaction [19,20], which can exhibit non-trivial spatiotemporal behaviour [21,22]. In DNA nanotechnology, similar spatiotemporal waves have been observed in synthetic genetic oscillators [3]. To our knowledge, the pattern formation scheme proposed in this paper is novel in that it specifically exploits the properties of the AM reactions as a rationally designed method to impose spatial order via local communication, as opposed to long-range coordination. Our work has clear links to recent attempts to understand the role of the AM reaction scheme in cell biology [8] and to implement the AM reactions in mass action chemistry using two-domain DNA strand displacement [7].

For future work, it will be important to investigate the robustness of the pattern formation process to changes in the experimental conditions. Our results from Section 4.3 suggest that variations in reaction rates can have dramatic effects on the generated pattern, which may be challenging for a practical implementation. It will also be interesting to investigate other methods of exerting control over the resulting pattern, and the

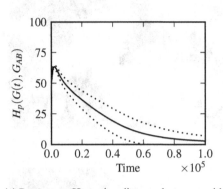
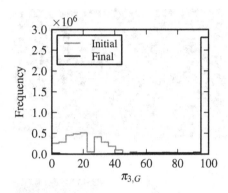

(a) Percentage Hamming distance between grid at time t and expected grid.

(b) Histograms of $\pi_{3,G}$ for all cells in all initial and final grids.

Fig. 8. Statistics from simulations to control pattern formation. (a) The expected grid is split in half, with the left-hand side containing only species A and the right-hand side containing only species B. Solid line is the mean from $1,000$ simulations and dotted lines are one standard deviation above and below the mean. (b) Values of $\pi_{3,G}$ were computed for all cells in the initial grids for $1,000$ simulations, and for the final grids obtained via stochastic simulations, using non-uniform reactions with $\rho = 0.9$.

classes of patterns that can be formed or preserved by this mechanism, e.g., patterns with complicated shapes such as mazes with thin walls of species A overlaid on a background of species B. As an alternative to modulating reaction rates, it may be possible to augment the basic AM reaction set with additional reactions to favour certain kinds of pattern. A detailed theoretical study of this pattern formation mechanism, e.g., to prove properties of the way the patterns evolve over time, may shed light on these issues. In particular, incorporating a temperature parameter and expressing reaction rates as functions of temperature may reveal non-linear, temperature-dependent effects in the pattern formation process. It may also be enlightening to simulate spatial AM reactions on larger grids, and in a toroidal cellular automaton framework with periodic boundary conditions. These would reduce any edge effects, as discussed in Section 4.1.

From a practical perspective, spatial reaction grids such as those described in this paper could be constructed in the laboratory using hexagonal DNA origami assembled on a pre-formed scaffold [23] or on tethered microspheres [24,25]. The pattern-generating interactions could be implemented using DNA strand displacement reactions [26,7]. Alternatively, spatial AM reaction systems could be constructed within networks of communicating bacteria [27,28,29,30], providing a means for rationally designed pattern generation [31,32] via local interactions, without a reliance on long-range diffusion.

Acknowledgments. This material is based upon work supported by the National Science Foundation under grants 1028238 and 1318833. M.R.L. gratefully acknowledges support from the New Mexico Cancer Nanoscience and Microsystems Training Center.

References

1. Turing, A.M.: The chemical basis of morphogenesis. Philosophical Transactions of the Royal Society B 237(641), 37–72 (1952)
2. Chirieleison, S.M., Allen, P.B., Simpson, Z.B., Ellington, A.D., Chen, X.: Pattern transformation with DNA circuits. Nature Chemistry 5, 1000–1005 (2013)
3. Padirac, A., Fujii, T., Estévez-Torres, A., Rondelez, Y.: Spatial waves in synthetic biochemical networks. Journal of the American Chemical Society 135(39), 14586–14592 (2013)
4. Angluin, D., Aspnes, J., Eisenstat, D.: A simple population protocol for fast robust approximate majority. Distributed Computing 21(2), 87–102 (2008)
5. Lakin, M.R., Parker, D., Cardelli, L., Kwiatkowska, M., Phillips, A.: Design and analysis of DNA strand displacement devices using probabilistic model checking. Journal of the Royal Society Interface 9(72), 1470–1485 (2012)
6. Lakin, M.R., Phillips, A., Stefanovic, D.: Modular verification of DNA strand displacement networks via serializability analysis. In: Soloveichik, D., Yurke, B. (eds.) DNA 2013. LNCS, vol. 8141, pp. 133–146. Springer, Heidelberg (2013)
7. Chen, Y.-J., Dalchau, N., Srinivas, N., Phillips, A., Cardelli, L., Soloveichik, D., Seelig, G.: Programmable chemical controllers made from DNA. Nature Nanotechnology 8, 755–762 (2013)
8. Cardelli, L., Csikász-Nagy, A.: The cell cycle switch computes approximate majority. Scientific Reports 2, 656 (2012)
9. Gillespie, D.T.: Exact stochastic simulation of coupled chemical reactions. Journal of Physical Chemistry 81(25), 2340–2361 (1977)
10. Doursat, R., Sayama, H., Michel, O.: A review of morphogenetic engineering. Natural Computing 12(4), 517–535 (2013)
11. Li, H., Carter, J.D., LaBean, T.H.: Nanofabrication by DNA self-assembly. Materials Today 12(5), 24–32 (2009)
12. Cross, M.C., Hohenberg, P.C.: Pattern formation outside of equilibrium. Reviews of Modern Physics 65(3), 851–1112 (1993)
13. Ising, E.: Beitrag zur Theorie des Ferromagnetismus. Zeitschrift für Physik 31(1), 253–258 (1925)
14. Antal, T., Droz, M., Magnin, J., Pekalski, A., Rácz, Z.: Formation of Liesegang patterns: Simulations using a kinetic Ising model. Journal of Chemical Physics 114(8), 3770–3775 (2001)
15. Murray, J.D.: A pre-pattern formation mechanism for animal coat markings. Journal of Theoretical Biology 88, 161–199 (1981)
16. Castets, V., Dulos, E., Boissonade, J., De Kepper, P.: Experimental evidence of a sustained standing Turing-type nonequilibrium chemical pattern. Physical Review Letters 64, 2953–2956 (1990)
17. Lotka, A.J.: Undamped oscillations derived from the law of mass action. Journal of the American Chemical Society 42, 1595–1599 (1920)
18. Volterra, V.: Fluctuations in the abundance of a species considered mathematically. Nature 118, 558–560 (1926)
19. Degn, H.: Oscillating chemical reactions in homogeneous phase. Journal of Chemical Education 49, 302–307 (1972)
20. Winfree, A.T.: Spiral waves of chemical activity. Science 175, 634–635 (1972)
21. Field, R.J., Noyes, R.M.: Explanation of spatial band propagation in the Belousov reaction. Nature (London) 237, 390–392 (1972)
22. Winfree, A.T.: Varieties of spiral wave behaviour: an experimentalist's approach to the theory of excitable media. Chaos 1, 303–334 (1991)

23. Zhao, Z., Liu, Y., Yan, H.: Organizing DNA origami tiles into larger structures using pre-formed scaffold frames. Nano Letters 11, 2997–3002 (2011)

24. Frezza, B.M., Cockroft, S.L., Ghadiri, M.R.: Modular multi-level circuits from immobilized DNA-based logic gates. Journal of the American Chemical Society 129, 14875–14879 (2007)

25. Yashin, R., Rudchenko, S., Stojanovic, M.: Networking particles over distance using oligonucleotide-based devices. Journal of the American Chemical Society 129, 15581–15584 (2007)

26. Zhang, D.Y., Seelig, G.: Dynamic DNA nanotechnology using strand-displacement reactions. Nature Chemistry 3(2), 103–113 (2011)

27. Weitz, M., Mückl, A., Kapsner, K., Berg, R., Meyer, A., Simmel, F.C.: Communication and computation by bacteria compartmentalized within microemulsion droplets. Journal of the American Chemical Society 136(1), 72–75 (2014)

28. Silva-Rocha, R., de Lorenzo, V.: Engineering multicellular logic in bacteria with metabolic wires. ACS Synthetic Biology 3(4), 204–209 (2014)

29. Bacchus, W., Lang, M., El-Baba, M.D., Weber, W., Stelling, J., Fussenegger, M.: Synthetic two-way communication between mammalian cells. Nature Biotechnology 30(10), 991–998 (2012)

30. Danino, T., Mondragón-Palomino, O., Tsimring, L., Hasty, J.: A synchronized quorum of genetic clocks. Nature 463, 326–330 (2010)

31. Rudge, T.J., Steiner, P.J., Phillips, A., Haseloff, J.: Computational modeling of synthetic microbial biofilms. ACS Synthetic Biology 1, 345–352 (2012)

32. Dalchau, N., Smith, M.J., Martin, S., Brown, J.R., Emmott, S., Phillips, A.: Towards the rational design of synthetic cells with prescribed population dynamics. Journal of the Royal Society Interface 9(76), 2883–2898 (2012)

Mecobo: A Hardware and Software Platform for In Materio Evolution

Odd Rune Lykkebø[1], Simon Harding[2], Gunnar Tufte[1], and Julian F. Miller[2]

[1] The Norwegian University of Science and Technology
Department of Computer and Information Science
Sem Selandsvei 7-9, 7491 Trondheim, Norway
{odd.lykkebo,gunnar.tufte}@idi.ntnu.no
[2] Department of Electronics
University of York
Heslington, York, UK. YO10 5DD
slh@evolutioninmaterio.com, julian.miller@york.ac.uk

Abstract. Evolution in Materio (EIM) exploits properties of physical systems for computation. "Designs" are evolved instead of a traditional top down design approach. Computation is a product of the state(s) of the material and input data. Evolution manipulates physical processes by stimulating materials assessed in situ. A hardware-software platform designed for EIM experimentation is presented. The platform, with features designed especially for EIM, is described together with demonstration experiments using carbon nanotubes in a thick film placed on micro-electrode arrays.

1 Introduction

Unconventional computation and unconventional machines try to move beyond the Turing/von Neumann [7,11] concept of computing and computer architecture [9]. Evolution in Materio (EIM) [5,3,6] is such an unconventional approach where the underlying physical properties of bulk materials are explored and exploited for computation. In contrast to a traditional approach where a substrate, e.g. silicon, is meticulously designed, produced and programmed, the essence of EIM is neatly phrased as "bulk processes" producing "logic by the pound" by Stewart [8] when introducing his experimental electrochemical system.

Figure 1 illustrates a possible scenario for an EIM experimental set-up. The configurable material can be seen as a black box. Incident data are applied, the response is measured and evaluated against a predefined function. The search algorithm can manipulate physical properties of the material by applying configuration data vectors.

The format of input data, response and configuration data are material specific. As such, any experimental EIM set-up must be capable to produce configurations with properties capable of manipulating physical properties in the material. Incident data properties must be of a type capable of produce an observable response, i.e. output data.

O.H. Ibarra et al. (Eds.): UCNC 2014, LNCS 8553, pp. 267–279, 2014.
DOI: 10.1007/978-3-319-08123-6_22, © Springer International Publishing Switzerland 2014

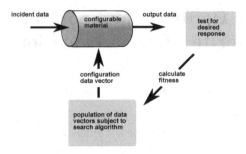

Fig. 1. Principle of evolution in materio

In Thompson's work [10] unconstrained evolution of configuration data for a Field Programmable Gate Array (FPGA) was used to evolve a tone discriminator. The FPGA may be considered as the material. The input signal to this digital circuit was analogue, the response was digital sampling of a captured analogue measurement. The configuration data for the chip was a digital bit stream. Even though Thompson exploited the physical properties of the chip, the configuration vector itself was digital. Harding and Miller [2] did a similar experiment with liquid crystal as material. In contrast to Thompson's experiment the configuration data signal property for the liquid crystal was evolved, the configuration data was unconstrained with regards to signal type, e.g. analogue, digital and time dependent.

In most EIM work an intrinsic approach has been taken, i.e. evaluation is performed on the physical material. An intrinsic approach allow access to all inherent physical properties of the material [6]. Intrinsic evolution requires an interface that can bridge the gap between the analogue physical world of materials and the digital world of EAs. We propose and demonstrate a flexible platform, Mecobo, designed to interface a large variety of materials. Flexible hardware allows for the possibility to map input, output and configuration terminals, signal properties and output monitoring capabilities in arbitrary ways. The platform's digital side, i.e. EA and software stack, is as important as the hardware. A flexible software platform including hardware drivers, support of multiple programming languages and a possibility to connect to hardware over the internet makes Mecobo a highly flexible platform for EIM experimentation.

Mecobo is part of a the NASCENCE project [1] targeting engineering of nano-scale units for computation. The demonstration experiments presented use single-walled carbon nanotubes mixed with poly(methyl methacrylate) (PMMA) dissolved in anisole (methoxy-benzene) as computational material.

The article is laid out as follows: Section 2 presents the nanoscale material and the physical electrical terminals. In Section 3 the architecture of the hardware of the interface is presented. Section 4 presents the software of Mecobo. Experiments demonstrating the platform are presented in Section 5. Discussion and conclusions are given in Section 6.

2   Nano Material as Computational Resource

The demonstration experiments in Section 5 show computation in carbon nanotubes. The material samples used are all part of the ongoing NASCENCE project. At present time micro electrode arrays are used to connect electrically to a thick film containing nanotube structures.

Figure 2 show two different glass slides. In Figure 2(a) a slide with 64 electrodes is shown. Left; the glass slide with contacts on the rim. On the right a microscope image of the array covered with the thick film. A second micro electrode array is shown in Figure 2(b) the glass slide include a 12 electrode array. The micro electrode array slides was produced by Kieran Massey at the University of Durham by depositing a solution of carbon nanotubes onto a slide and letting the solvent dry out, leaving a random distribution of nanotubes across the probes in the micro electrode array.

In the demonstration of the interface in Section 5 the sample used was of the type shown in Figure 2(b). As the main topic here is hardware and software properties to interface a variety of materials, details regarding the physical properties are not presented in detail.

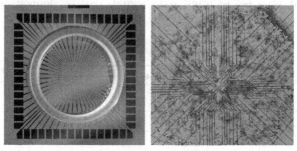

(a) Left: 64 electrode glass slide with contacts on the rim and electrode array in center. Right: close-up of the electrode array covered with a carbon nanotube thick film

(b) Left: 12 electrode glass slide with contacts on one side. Right: close-up of the electrode array covered with a carbon nanotube thick film

Fig. 2. Samples of materials placed on micro electrode arrays

3   Hardware: Interfacing the Black Box

Evolutionary exploration of computation by manipulation of physical systems is an intrinsic [10] approach. If the system is considered as a lump of matter, as illustrated in Figure 1, the selection of signal types, i.e. inputs, outputs and configuration data, assignment to I/O ports may not relate to material specific properties. As such, any I/O port can be assigned any signal type. Further, the signal properties, e.g. voltage/current levels, AC, DC, pulse or frequency, needed to unveil potential computational properties of different materials are unknown. To be able to explore and exploit a material's physical properties an experimental platform must have access to explore in as unconstrained a way as possible. However, in an evolutionary search the representation of genetic information, e.g. available voltage levels, will constrain the available search space.

3.1   Interface

The interface is designed to handle all the physical/electrical properties as mentioned above. To be able to ease the process of providing input data to any computational problem the interface also provides the possibility to provide input data. That is, a set of input data signals can be defined as part of the experimental set up to simulate external signals.

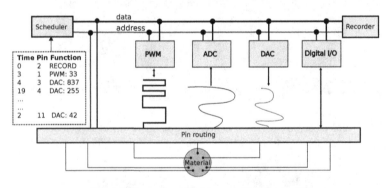

Fig. 3. Overview of the complete system

Figure 3 shows an overview of the hardware interface. In the figure an example set up is shown in the dotted box. The example genome defines pin 2 to be the output terminal, pin 1 to be the data input and pin 3 - 12 to be configuration signals. The architecture is controlled by a scheduler controlling the following modules: Digital I/O can output digital signals and sample responses. Analogue output signals can be produced by the DAC module. The DAC can be configured to output static voltages or any arbitrary time dependent waveform. Sampling of analogue waveforms from the material is performed by the ADC. Pulse Width Modulated (PWM) signals are produced by the PWM module.

The system's scheduler can set up the system to apply and sample signals statically or produce time scheduled configurations of stimuli/response. The recorder stores samples, digital discrete values, time dependent bit strings, sampled analogue discrete values or time dependent analogue waveforms. Note that the recorder can include any combination of these signals.

As stated, in a bulk materials there is no specific defined input and output locations, e.g. in the carbon nanotube PMMA samples is just distributed over the micro-electrode array. Thus it is desirable that the choice of data I/O and configuration terminals should be put under evolutionary control. In the interface all signals passes a crossbar, i.e. pin routing. Pin routing is placed between the signal generator modules and the sampling buffer (PWM, ADC, DAC, Digital I/O and Recorder) making it possible to configure any terminal of a material to be input, output or configuration.

The presented material signal interface in Figure 3 supports all our objectives. It is possible to evolve the I/O terminal placement. A large variety of configuration signals are available to support materials with different sensitivity, from static signals to time dependent analogue functions. The response from materials can be sampled as purely static digital signals, digital pulse trains or analogue signals. Further the scheduler can schedule time slots for different stimuli when time dependent functions are targeted or to compensate for configuration delay, i.e. when materials needs time to settle before a reliable computation can be observed.

3.2   Interface Physical Realization

The described system shown in Figure 3 is implemented as an autonomous interface hardware platform. The platform can communicate with a host computer over USB. The host can run an EA or stand as a bridge (server) connected to the internet.

The hardware implementation of the interface, which we call 'Mecobo', is shown as a block diagram in figure 4(a). Mecobo is designed as a PCB with an FPGA as the main component. The system shown in Figure 3 is part of the FPGA design together with communication modules interfacing a micro controller and shared memory. As shown in Figure 4(a) the digital and analogue designs are split into two. All analogue components are placed on a daughter board; such as crossbar switches and analogue-digital converters. This split enables redesign of the analogue part of the system without changing the digital part of the motherboard. The system shown in Figure 4(a) is an example of the current system, the Mecobo and an analogue daughter board. However, it is possible to include other extension boards to the Mecobo. The FPGA offers a possibility to include new modules adapted to any extension that can be connected to the digital I/O pin headers. The micro controller stands as a communication interface between the FPGA and the external USB port. The SRAM is available for the FPGA through the micro controller.

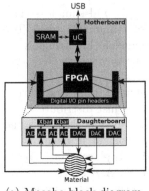

(a) Mecobo block diagram.   (b) Picture of Mecobo.

Fig. 4. Hardware interface implementation overview

Figure 4(b) show the motherboard with the Xilinx LX45 FPGA, Silicon Labs ARM based EFM32GG990 micro controller connected to a 12 terminal material sample.

The motherboard is capable of controlling 80 digital I/O signals, which can be connected directly to a material sample or used for controlling resources on a daughter board. The FPGA drives the I/O pins at LVCMOS33 level, giving a minimum input voltage level for switching to digital 'high' at 2.0V, and maximum 0.8 corresponding to 'low'.

The software interface sends commands to the scheduling unit (implemented in the micro controller). The scheduler takes care of controlling the various pin controllers. A pin controller is the abstract term we use to describe a unit that drives or sources a physical I/O pin. Each pin controller has a slice of the global address space of this bus and can be programmed individually by the scheduling unit by outputting the command and data on the bus.

The scheduler accepts a sequence of commands from the user software. Each sequence item consists of parameters that describe the state of the pin at a given point in time. In Figure 3 for example, pin 2 is set as a 'recording' pin from time 0 (it also has a duration, and sampling frequency attached that is not shown here). Pin 1 is set to output a pulse width modulated version of the value 33, and pin 3 is set to output the analogue voltage level corresponding to 837, which could for instance map to analogue voltage level -2.3V relative to the daughter board analogue ground. In this case the scheduler would issue commands to one of the DAC controllers and to two of the PWM controllers.

4   Software

As there is no known, and hence no standard programming model for in-materio computation, we developed a system inspired by the track based model of music or video editing applications. An example of this is shown in Figure 5. Each

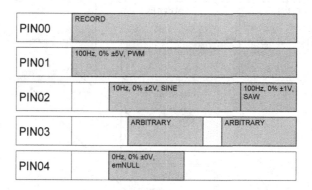

PIN00	RECORD		
PIN01	100Hz, 0% ±5V, PWM		
PIN02	10Hz, 0% ±2V, SINE		100Hz, 0% ±1V, SAW
PIN03	ARBITRARY		ARBITRARY
PIN04	0Hz, 0% ±0V, emNULL		

Fig. 5. Illustration of a genotype described in the 'track based' programming model. Each row is an output from the FPGA (and hence an input to the material). The horizontal axis is time. The model aligns closely with the hardware architecture, and also hints at a possible genotype representation.

track corresponds to an output pin of the FPGA, and on each track an action (or set of actions) are scheduled. Once the tracks are configured onto the FPGA, the sequence is 'played' back. As can be seen in the illustration, 'recordings' can also be scheduled. A recording in this case is the data captured from an input of the FPGA.

From this model, an Application Programming Interface (API) was developed that allows users to interact with the hardware. The main purpose of the API is to expose the functionality of the EM in a consistent and easy to use manner. Additional APIs provide support for data collection and for processing the data itself.

Client applications (i.e. software for performing the evolutionary algorithm), connects to a the EM via control software running on a PC. The control software is responsible for communicating at a low level to the EM, and translating the track based model into the FPGA's internal model.

The control software implements the API as a Thrift Server. Thrift[1] is a technology maintained by Apache that is designed to allow applications running on different operating systems, written in different languages and running on different computers to communicate with each other. Thrift provides a language that is used to define the functionality exposed by the server. This language is then compiled by the Thrift compiler into skeleton code that contains all the functionality needed to act as a server and accept connections, but is missing the functional components. These are then added to complete the server implementation.

On the client side, the interface can be compiled by Thrift into a library that exposes all the methods in the API. Thrift is able to generate the client and server code for many languages including C++, C#and Java. The client library

---

[1] http://thrift.apache.org/

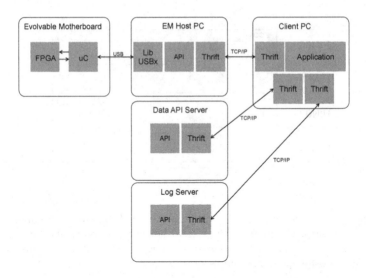

Fig. 6. Overview of the complete software architecture. Here the EA (user application) is run on a client PC. Communicating over TCP/IP to the EM host PC. The Mecobo platform is connected to and communicates with the host PC over USB. The log servers communicate with the client PC.

is then connected via TCP (or shared memory if the client/server are both on the same PC) to the server. Client applications then only need to implement their functionality, and no knowledge of the underlying protocols or workings of the EM or server software is required.

As the communication between Thrift Server and Client applications is based on TCP, there is no necessity for all components to run on the same computer. We have successfully tested the API over the internet, and have found that it is feasible for one institute to run the evolutionary algorithm, and another to host the EM.

Figure 6 shows the complete software architecture for the system. On the left we see the hardware (i.e. Mecobo), on the right is the client application. In the middle we see the main API components. Although only one EM is shown, it is possible to add more. Client applications can connect to multiple servers (and hence Mecobos), and hence can control a number of systems in parallel. We envisage this as being useful for robustness testing, investigating repeatability, and allowing multiple Mecobos to work together on a single problem.

5   Initial Experiments

To demonstrate the Mecobo platform, two experiments are presented. The experiments are executed on the presented hardware/software platform using a 12 electrode array similar to the shown example in Figure 2. The presented experiments only demonstrate a fraction of the capabilities of our hardware and software platform, and those that we expect the material to have. In the experiments an exhaustive search and a Genetic Algorithm (GA) was used. The exhaustive search was chosen to explore the potential functionality of the material at a coarse level. The GA approach is an example of how a search method can exploit the properties of materials toward achieving useful computation. However, other search/learning methods can also be used.

5.1   Exhaustive Sweep

If only digital time-independent logic is considered, then it is possible to run an exhaustive search mapping all possible configurations to the 12 pin sample. To take this into a more "computational" relevance, and to show the effect of interpreting the results when "programming" the material, we interpret two pins as input to a logic gates, the recording pin as gate output and the remaining 9 pins as configuration. This approach will leave 9 pins for configuration data. To represent functions a *gate output sum* can be constructed. The gate sum is the output of the truth table as shown in in table 1.

Table 1. Gate sum mapping. XOR. The gate sum is the decimal representation of the output column. 0110 binary give the gate sum 6.

Input	Config	Output
0,0	1,0,1,1,0,1,0,1,1	0
0,1	1,0,1,1,0,1,0,1,1	1
1,0	1,0,1,1,0,1,0,1,1	1
1,1	1,0,1,1,0,1,0,1,1	0

A '1' represents 3.3V and '0' represents 0V. All possible pin combinations for input, configuration and output are tested and mapped to a functionality plot. If a gate is found it is plotted as a gate output sum, e.g. XOR: 0110 (6). An example of such a plot is presented in Figure 7(a). The plot show all found two input logical functions for all possible input output mappings.

The gate output sums are represented in decimal on the vertical axis. The configuration vector is given (decimal) on the horizontal axis. Interesting cases include XOR (gate sum 6 (0110)) and NAND (gate sum 8) are present together with all other possible 2 input logic function. Figure 7(b) show one of the possible I/O configuration. Here all possible gate configurations are shown for one particular I/O mapping, i.e. pin 1 output and pin 3 and 11 as input.

5.2   Genetic Search for Logic Functions

In Section 5.1 it was shown that the nanotube sample was capable of producing logic gates. However, to be able to evolve a desired functionality the EA must be able to exploit and explore the genetic representation and the search space, i.e. evolvability [4] must be present.

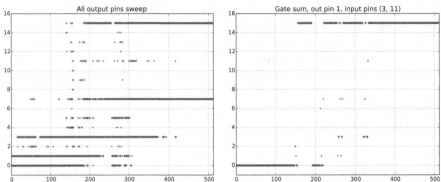

(a) Sweep all I/O combinations. The plot show all possible logical gates available in the material for all possible combinations of configuration and I/O pin mappings.

(b) Sweep fixed I/O combination. The plot show all possible logical gates available in the material if the configuration and I/O pin mapping is fixed.

Fig. 7. Example of logic gates found using exhaustive sweep. The x-axis uses a decimal representation of the 9 configuration bits. The resulting gate sum for each configuration is plotted. The decimal gate sum is given on the y-axis.

To explore evolvability, a Genetic Algorithm was used to search for stable XOR gates. The GA was quite standard; 25 individuals, two crossover points and tournament selection with 5 individuals as elite. Two different material samples was tested.

To demonstrate the platform's possibility to generate time dependent signals a genotype that allows dynamic PWM signals was chosen. The GA can adjust each configuration pin within a frequency range of 400Hz - 25MHz. The mapping of which material terminal to use as input, output or configuration was placed under genetic control. Figure 8(a) illustrates the representation. The first two genes assign the input signals, e.g. pin 0 and 2. The third gene gives the output, e.g. pin 11 is sampled by the recorder. The remaining 9 pins are mapped to configuration genes specifying frequency values. A restriction must be added to ensure that the same pin is not used for both input and output. To ensure "legal" gates, offspring with "illegal" pin mapping are not put back in the population. I/O and configuration genes were crossed over separately; hence the need for two point crossover.

The GA was set up to search for a stable 2-input XOR logic gate. The response is measured by setting up the gate input pins (i.e. the two first fields of the genome) to constant voltage levels at 0V or 3.3V. The configuration genes are frequencies of square waves, remaining fixed over the 2^2 possible inputs. The response is sampled from the GA-chosen output pin for 100ms at 10KHz. Referring to table1, the number of correct samples in each sample period for each row is further multiplied by a constant, indicating how hard this case is to find: (0,0): 0.3, (1,0): 0.5, (0,1): 0.5, (1,1): 1.15. Particularly promising cases are

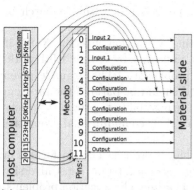
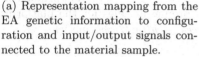
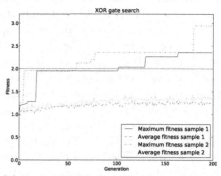

(a) Representation mapping from the EA genetic information to configuration and input/output signals connected to the material sample.

(b) Evolved XOR function in two different material samples.

Fig. 8. Experimental set-up. EA representation with unconstrained pin mapping and dynamic configuration signals are shown (left) with results for two different material samples (right).

further given a 0.5 bonus, giving a total possible fitness of 2.95 for a 'perfect' gate, and 1.95 for a functioning gate.

Figure 8(b) shows the evolution of fitness for these experiments. The horizontal line at 1.95 indicate the threshold for a functioning XOR gate where the majority of the samples in a sample buffer is over 55%. Note that a functioning XOR was found in both material samples, and in material sample 1 a near-perfect gate was discovered after 150 generations. The difference between the elite best and the average case is quite large. This can be explained by the relatively few XOR gates in the material, which can also be observed in figure 7(a).

6   Discussion and Conclusions

The presented hardware and software platform for EIM experimentation, known as Mecobo, is a tool enabling exploration and exploitation of materials for computation purposes. The flexibility in signal levels and types together with the possibility to put the mapping of input, output and configuration terminals under evolutionary control offers a possibility of relatively unconstrained material evolution.

The presented results demonstrate how the platform can be used. There are several interesting aspects worthy of note. In the exhaustive sweeps presented in Section 5.1 the gate sum plots are a course mapping of possible computational properties of the material. The plot in Figure 7 show that this sample is capable of solving problems beyond simple threshold functions. As such, results for such exhaustive sweeps can be used to coarsely classify a material and be used to measure the closeness/distance between materials samples within a batch or batches with different physical properties.

Even if a material is capable of implementing a function, like the XOR, it is not necessarily easy to evolve. Further, as indicated by earlier EIM work, the stability of discovered solutions may be problematic. The example given shows two important factors. Stability can (and should be part) of the problem definition. The change of representation shows the possibility to provide a variety of signal types. The material used in the example show computational properties for static and dynamic configuration data.

As stated in Section 1 this work is part of a bigger project. The platform is in use by several researchers in the NASCENCE project consortium, e.g. University of York for function optimization and machine Learning classification problems.

Software, HDL code, schematics and PCB production files for the platform can be downloaded from the *download resources* at: *http://www.nascence.eu*.

Acknowledgements. The research leading to these results has received funding from the [European Community's] Seventh Framework Programme ([FP7/2007-2013] [FP7/2007-2011]) under grant agreement no [317662]. We are grateful to Kieran Massey and Mike Petty for the preparation of materials and the micro-electrode array.

References

1. Broersma, H., Gomez, F., Miller, J.F., Petty, M., Tufte, G.: Nascence project: Nanoscale engineering for novel computation using evolution. International Journal of Unconventional Computing 8(4), 313–317 (2012)
2. Harding, S.L., Miller, J.F.: A tone discriminator in liquid crystal. In: Congress on Evolutionary Computation(CEC2004), pp. 1800–1807. IEEE (2004)
3. Harding, S.L., Miller, J.F., Rietman, E.: Evolution in materio: Exploiting the physics of materials for computing. Journal of Unconventional Computing 3, 155–194 (2008)
4. Kirschner, M., Gerhart, J.: Evolvability. Proceedings of the National Academy of Sciences of the United States of America 95(15), 8420–8427 (1998)
5. Miller, J.F., Downing, K.: Evolution in materio: Looking beyond the silicon box. In: 2002 NASA/DOD Conference on Evolvable Hardware, pp. 167–176. IEEE Computer Society Press (2002)
6. Miller, J.F., Harding, S.L., Tufte, G.: Evolution-in-materio: Evolving computation in materials. Evolutionary Intelligence 7(1), 49–67 (2014), http://dx.doi.org/10.1007/s12065-014-0106-6
7. von Neumann, J.: First draft of a report on the EDVAC. M. D. Godfrey (ed.) (1992), Technical report. Moore School of Electrical Engineering University of Pennsylvania (1945)
8. Stewart, R.M.: Electrochemically active field-trainable pattern recognition systems. IEEE Transactions on Systems Science and Cybernetics 5(3), 230–237 (1969)
9. Teuscher, C., Adamatzky, A.: Unconventional Computing 2005: From Cellular Automata to Wetware. Luniver Press (2005)

10. Thompson, A.: An evolved circuit, intrinsic in silicon, entwined with physics. In: Higuchi, T., Iwata, M., Weixin, L. (eds.) ICES 1996. LNCS, vol. 1259, pp. 390–405. Springer, Heidelberg (1997)
11. Turing, A.M.: On computable numbers, with an application to the Entscheidungsproblem. In: Proceedings of the London Mathematical Society 1936-1937. ser. 2, vol. 42, pp. 230–265. Mathematical Society, London (1937)

Compact Realization of Reversible Turing Machines by 2-State Reversible Logic Elements

Kenichi Morita and Rei Suyama

Hiroshima University, Higashi-Hiroshima, 739-8527, Japan
km@hiroshima-u.ac.jp

Abstract. A reversible logic element with memory (RLEM) is a primitive by which reversible computing systems can be constructed. Different from a reversible logic gate, it has a finite memory, and thus is defined as a kind of reversible sequential machine (RSM). It is known that any reversible Turing machine (RTM) can be built in a simple way using a rotary element (RE), a typical 2-state RLEM (i.e., having 1-bit memory) with four input/output lines. In this paper, we show another compact realization of an RTM using a 2-state RLEM No. 4-31 with four input/output lines. Since RLEM 4-31 can be simulated by a circuit composed of only two copies of 2-state RLEM 3-7, we also obtain another compact realization by an RLEM with three input/output lines.

1 Introduction

A reversible computing system is a backward deterministic one, and has a close relation to physical reversibility. It is also one of the bases of quantum computing since evolution of a quantum system is reversible. So far, many kinds of reversible computing models have been proposed and investigated. There are several levels of models ranging from a microscopic one to a macroscopic one. In the bottom level, there is a physically reversible model like the billiard ball model (BBM) of computing [2]. In the next level, there are reversible logic elements, from which reversible logic circuits are built, such as Fredkin gate [2], Toffoli gate [13,14], and reversible logic elements with memory [4]. In the still higher level, there are reversible logic circuits that are used as building modules for reversible computers. In the top level, there are models of reversible computers such as reversible Turing machines, reversible cellular automata, and others.

Here, we investigate a problem how reversible Turing machines can be built compactly using reversible logic elements with memory (RLEM). In the conventional design theory of logic circuits, logic gates are used as primitives for composing logic circuits. On the other hand, in the case of reversible computing, RLEMs are also known to be useful. The main reason is that if we use an appropriate RLEM, we can construct various kinds of reversible computing models in a simple manner. In particular, if we use a rotary element (RE), a typical 2-state RLEM (i.e., having 1-bit memory) with four input/output lines, we can construct reversible Turing machines (RTMs), and reversible sequential machines (RSMs) very easily [4,5,7]. It has also been proved that RE can be

O.H. Ibarra et al. (Eds.): UCNC 2014, LNCS 8553, pp. 280–292, 2014.
DOI: 10.1007/978-3-319-08123-6_23, © Springer International Publishing Switzerland 2014

simulated by a circuit composed of "any" one of non-degenerate 2-state RLEMs except only four RLEMs with two input/output lines [9]. Therefore, we can build RTMs using any of such RLEMs. However, besides RE, it is not known which RLEMs are useful for realizing RTMs simply.

In this paper, we show that a compact realization of an RTMs is possible if we use a 2-state RLEM No. 4-31 with four input/output lines. The total number of elements is comparable with the case of using RE. In addition, since RLEM 4-31 can be simulated by a circuit composed of only two copies of 2-state RLEM 3-7, we can obtain another compact realization for the case of RLEM with three input/output lines.

2   Reversible Logic Element with Memory (RLEM)

Definition 1. *A* sequential machine *(SM) is defined by* $M = (Q, \Sigma, \Gamma, \delta)$. *Here,* Q *is a finite set of internal states,* Σ *and* Γ *are finite sets of input and output symbols, and* $\delta : Q \times \Sigma \to Q \times \Gamma$ *is a move function. If* δ *is injective,* M *is called a* reversible sequential machine *(RSM). Note that, if* M *is reversible,* $|\Sigma| \leq |\Gamma|$ *must hold. A* reversible logic element with memory *(RLEM) is an RSM such that* $|\Sigma| = |\Gamma|$, *and it is also called a* $|Q|$-*state* $|\Sigma|$-*symbol RLEM.*

The move function δ determines the behavior of M as follows: if the present state is p, the input symbol is a_i, and $\delta(p, a_i) = (q, s_j)$, then the next state is q, and the output is s_j (Fig. 1 (a)). To use an SM as a primitive for logic circuit, we interpret the SM as a machine having "decoded" input and output ports as in Fig. 1 (b). Namely, for each input symbol, there corresponds a unique input port, to which a signal (or particle) can be given. Likewise, for each output symbol, there corresponds a unique output port, from which a signal can appear. Note that, in a logic circuit composed of such SMs, fan-out of an output of each SM is not allowed. Therefore, each output port of an SM can be connected to only one input port of another (maybe the same) SM.

Here, we investigate 2-state RLEMs. We give two examples of 2-state 4-symbol RLEMs with ID numbers 4-31 and 4-289 (the numbering method will be explained later). They are $M_{4\text{-}31} = (\{0, 1\}, \{a, b, c, d\}, \{s, t, u, v\}, \delta_{4\text{-}31})$ and $M_{4\text{-}289} = (\{0, 1\}, \{a, b, c, d\}, \{s, t, u, v\}, \delta_{4\text{-}289})$. The move functions $\delta_{4\text{-}31}$ and $\delta_{4\text{-}289}$ are given in Table 1. It is easy to see that $\delta_{4\text{-}31}$ and $\delta_{4\text{-}289}$ are injective. In the following, we describe the move functions of 2-state RLEMs by pictorial notations as shown in Fig. 2 instead of tables as in Table 1. Each of two states is represented by a rectangle having input ports and output ports. The relation between input and output is indicated by solid and dotted lines. We assume a signal is given to at most one input port at a time. If a signal is given to some input port, it travels along the line connected to the port. In the case that a signal goes through a dotted line, the state does not change (Fig. 3 (a)). On the other hand, if it goes through a solid line, the state changes to the other (Fig. 3 (b)).

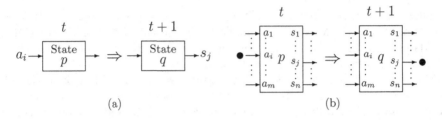

Fig. 1. (a) A sequential machine $M = (Q, \{a_1, \ldots, a_m\}, \{s_1, \ldots, s_n\}, \delta)$ such that $\delta(p, a_i) = (q, s_j)$, and (b) an interpretation of a sequential machine as a system having decoded input ports and output ports

Table 1. The move functions $\delta_{4\text{-}31}$ and $\delta_{4\text{-}289}$ of the 2-state RLEMs 4-31 and 4-289

Present state	Input				Present state	Input			
	a	b	c	d		a	b	c	d
State 0	$0\,s$	$0\,t$	$0\,u$	$1\,s$	State 0	$0\,s$	$0\,t$	$1\,s$	$1\,t$
State 1	$1\,t$	$0\,v$	$1\,v$	$1\,u$	State 1	$0\,u$	$0\,v$	$1\,v$	$1\,u$

$\delta_{4\text{-}31}$ of RLEM 4-31 $\delta_{4\text{-}289}$ of RLEM 4-289

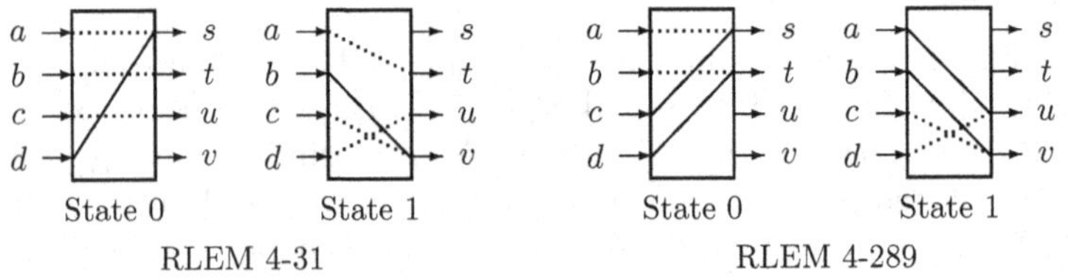

Fig. 2. A pictorial representation of the 2-state RLEMs 4-31 and 4-289

We now classify 2-state RLEMs. Since the move function δ of a 2-state k-symbol RLEM $M = (\{0, 1\}, \Sigma, \Gamma, \delta)$ is identified by a permutation of $\{0, 1\} \times \Gamma$, the total number of 2-state k-symbol RLEMs is $(2k)!$. They are numbered from 0 to $(2k)! - 1$ in the lexicographic order of permutations [10]. To indicate it is a k-symbol RLEM, the prefix "k-" is attached to its serial number like RLEM 4-31. We say that two RLEMs are *equivalent* if one can be obtained by renaming the states and/or the input/output symbols of the other [6,10]. It has been shown that the numbers of equivalence classes of 2-state 2-, 3-, and 4-symbol RLEMs are 8, 24, and 82, respectively [10].

Among RLEMs, there are *degenerate* ones, each of which is either equivalent to simple connecting wires, or equivalent to an RLEM with fewer symbols. The precise definition is in [9]. Thus, *non-degenerate* k-symbol RLEMs are the main concern of the study. It is known that the numbers of non-degenerate 2- 3- and 4-symbol RLEMs are 4, 14, and 55, respectively.

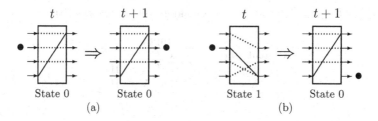

Fig. 3. Examples of operations of the 2-state RLEM 4-31. (a) If a signal passes a dotted line, then the state remains to be the same. (b) If a signal passes a solid line, then the state changes to the other.

A *rotary element* (RE) [4] is a 2-state 4-symbol RLEM defined by $M_{RE} = (\{H, V\}, \{n, e, s, w\}, \{n', e', s', w'\}, \delta_{RE})$, where δ_{RE} is given in Table 2. RE is equivalent to RLEM 4-289, since the latter is obtained by the following renaming of states and input/output symbols: $H \mapsto 0, V \mapsto 1, n \mapsto c, s \mapsto d, e \mapsto a, w \mapsto b, n' \mapsto u, s' \mapsto v, e' \mapsto t, w' \mapsto s$. Its behavior can be very easily understood, since it has the following interpretation on its operation. RE is depicted by a box that contains a rotatable bar inside (Fig. 4). Two states of an RE are distinguished by the direction of the bar corresponding to states H and V. There are four input lines and four output lines corresponding to the sets of input symbols $\{n, e, s, w\}$ and output symbols $\{n', e', s', w'\}$. The rotatable bar is used to control the move direction of an input signal (or particle). When no particle exists, nothing happens on the RE. If a particle comes from the direction parallel to the rotatable bar, then it goes out from the output line of the opposite side without affecting the direction of the bar (Fig. 4 (a)). If a particle comes from the direction orthogonal to the bar, then it makes a right turn, and rotates the bar by 90 degrees (Fig. 4 (b)).

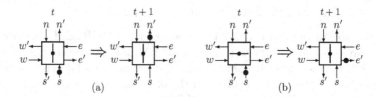

Fig. 4. Operations of rotary element (RE): (a) the parallel case, and (b) the orthogonal case

We now give a remark how RLEMs are related to reversible physical systems. The billiard ball model (BBM) proposed by Fredkin and Toffoli [2] is an idealized model of Newtonian mechanics in which reversible logic gates can be embedded. In [6,8], it is shown that RE can be directly and simply simulated in BBM without using reversible logic gates. It is also proved that any m-state k-symbol RLEM can be realized in BBM in a systematic way if $k \leq 4$ [11].

Table 2. The move function δ_{RE} of rotary element (RE)

Present state	Input			
	n	e	s	w
H	$V\,w'$	$H\,w'$	$V\,e'$	$H\,e'$
V	$V\,s'$	$H\,n'$	$V\,n'$	$H\,s'$

3   Universality of 2-state RLEMs

In this section, we give known results on universality of 2-state RLEMs. First, we define the notion of universality as follows.

Definition 2. *An RLEM is called* universal *if any RSM is realized by a circuit composed only of copies of the RLEM.*

Note that universal RLEMs can simulate each other, since RLEMs are RSMs. In [5], it is shown that for any given RSM we can construct a circuit out of REs that simulates the RSM. Hence, we have the following theorem.

Theorem 1. [5] *RE is universal.*

In [9], it is proved that for each non-degenerate 2-state k-symbol RLEM there is a circuit composed of it that simulates RE if $k > 2$. Hence, the following theorem is derived.

Theorem 2. [9] *Every non-degenerate 2-state k-symbol RLEM is universal if $k > 2$.*

On the other hand, it is proved that among four non-degenerate 2-state 2-symbol RLEMs, three of them are not universal [12] (see Fig. 5). However, it is an open problem whether RLEM 2-17 is universal or not.

Theorem 3. [12] *RLEMs 2-2, 2-3, and 2-4 are not universal.*

It is also shown that RLEM 2-2 is the weakest 2-state RLEM, i.e., it cannot simulate any other non-degenerate 2-state RLEM, but can be simulated by any of them [12]. Furthermore, RLEMs 2-3 and 2-4 cannot simulate each other [12]. Fig. 5 summarizes the above results. On the other hand, if we extend the notion of universality for an RLEM to a set of RLEMs, we obtain the following theorem.

Theorem 4. [3,12] *Any combination of two among RLEMs 2-3, 2-4 and 2-17 is universal.*

4   Constructing Reversible Turing Machines by RLEM 4-31

In this section we show a new compact realization method of a reversible Turing machine (RTM) by RLEM 4-31. First, we give a definition on RTM.

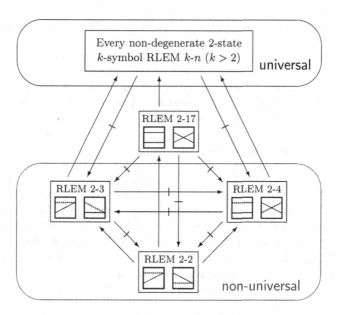

Fig. 5. A hierarchy among non-degenerate 2-state RLEMs. Here, $A \to B$ $(A \not\to B$, respectively) indicates that A can (cannot) be simulated by B

Definition 3. *A one-tape Turing machine (TM) is defined by* $T = (Q, S, q_0, F, s_0, \delta)$. *Here,* Q *is a set of states of the finite control,* S *is a set of tape symbols,* $q_0 \in Q$ *is an initial state,* $F \subset Q$ *is a set of final states, and* $s_0 \in S$ *is a blank symbol.* δ *is a move relation, which is a subset of* $(Q \times S \times S \times \{L, N, R\} \times Q)$, *where* L, N, *and* R *stand for left-shift, no-shift, and right-shift of the head.*

Each element of δ is a quintuple of the form $[p, s, s', d, q]$. It means if T reads the symbol s in the state p, then write s', shift the head to the direction d, and go to the state q. Here, we assume there is no quintuple of the form $[p, s, s', d, q_0]$ in δ. Let $\alpha, \beta \in S^*$ and $q \in Q$. Then, $\alpha q \beta$ is called a *computational configuration* (or *total state*) of T, which means that the contents of the tape is $\alpha\beta$, and T is reading the leftmost symbol of β (or s_0 in the case β is empty) in the state q.

T is called *deterministic* iff the following holds for any pair of distinct quintuples $[p_1, s_1, s'_1, d_1, q_1]$ and $[p_2, s_2, s'_2, d_2, q_2]$ in δ: if $p_1 = p_2$, then $s_1 \neq s_2$.

T is called *reversible* iff the following holds for any pair of distinct quintuples $[p_1, s_1, s'_1, d_1, q_1]$ and $[p_2, s_2, s'_2, d_2, q_2]$ in δ: if $q_1 = q_2$, then $s'_1 \neq s'_2 \wedge d_1 = d_2$. Hereafter, by RTM we mean a deterministic and reversible TM.

In [1] RTM was defined in the quadruple form, since an "inverse" RTM is easily obtained from a given RTM of this form. Here we define RTM in the quintuple form, because it makes a description of RTM shorter. It should be noted that if we use the quadruple form, determinism and reversibility can be defined in a symmetric way, and thus they are dual notions. Even in the case of the quintuple form as above, we can see they are symmetrically defined except the head shift operation. As for capability of an RTM, it has been shown that any irreversible TM can be converted into an equivalent RTM that leaves no garbage information. Thus RTMs are computationally universal [1].

Example 1. Let T_{parity} be an RTM defined by $T_{\text{parity}} = (Q, \{0, 1\}, q_0, \{q_a\}, 0, \delta)$, where $Q = \{q_0, q_1, q_2, q_a, q_r\}$, and $\delta = \{[\, q_0, 0, 1, R, q_1\,], [\, q_1, 0, 1, L, q_a\,], [\, q_1, 1, 0, R, q_2\,], [\, q_2, 0, 1, L, q_r\,], [\, q_2, 1, 0, R, q_1\,]\}$. T_{parity} checks if a given unary number n is even or odd. If it is even, T_{parity} halts in the accepting state q_a, otherwise halts in q_r. All the symbols read by T_{parity} are complemented. For example, if T starts from the configuration q_0011, then it eventually halts in $10q_a01$. It is easily verified that T_{parity} satisfies the reversibility condition.

In [4,7], it is shown that any reversible Turing machine (RTM) can be realized as a circuit composed of RE. A circuit for RTM T_{parity} is shown in Fig. 6. At the left end of the circuit, there is a circuit module that simulates a finite-state control of T_{parity}. To the right of it, an infinite number of copies of a circuit module for a memory cell, which simulates one square of the tape, are attached.

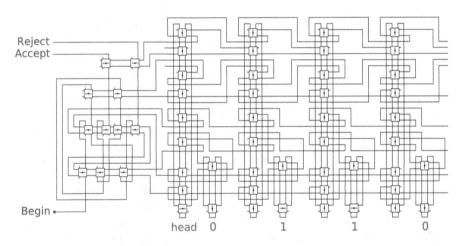

Fig. 6. A circuit made of RE that simulates RTM T_{parity} in Example 1. The state of the above circuit corresponds to the computational configuration q_0011 of T_{parity}. An example of its whole computing process is shown in 4406 figures in [7].

Since *any* universal RLEM can simulate RE, we can construct a circuit from the RLEM that simulates an RTM. This is done by replacing each occurrence of RE in a circuit that realizes an RTM (like the one shown in Fig. 6) by a circuit that simulates RE. However, if we use the systematic construction method of RE given in the proof of Theorem 2 [9], we need many copies of the RLEM. For example, 16 copies of RLEM 4-31 are required to simulate one RE. So far, besides RE, it is not known which RLEMs are useful for constructing RTMs compactly. Here, we give a new direct method of realizing 2-symbol RTMs by

RLEM 4-31. The numbers of elements for making a finite-state control and a memory cell by RLEM 4-31 are comparable with those numbers by RE.

We first prepare a circuit module called an *RLEM-column* made of n copies of RLEM 4-31 that are used both in a memory cell and a finite-state control to keep a head position or an internal state, and to control an incoming signal. Fig. 7 (a) shows an RLEM-column with $n = 3$. Though it has 2^n states in total, we consider only two "macroscopic" states **0** and **1**. Here, **0** (**1**, respectively) is the state such that all the elements are in state 0 (1). Then, the behavior of the RLEM-column in Fig. 7 (a) is described by a 6-symbol RLEM as shown in Fig. 7 (b).

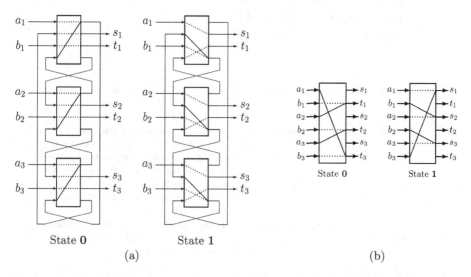

Fig. 7. (a) An RLEM-column with $n = 3$. (b) A 6-symbol RLEM that describes a macroscopic behavior of the RLEM-column.

A *memory cell* (MC) is a module that simulates one square of the tape. Here, we design an MC for 2-symbol RTM. It keeps a tape symbol $s \in \{0, 1\}$, and the information h whether the head of the RTM is on this cell ($h = 1$) or not ($h = 0$). Hence, its state set is $\{(h, s) \mid h, s \in \{0, 1\}\}$. It has ten kinds of input symbols listed in Table 3, which are the same as the case of constructing MC by RE [7]. For each input symbol x, there is an output symbol x', e.g., for the input symbol W0, there corresponds an output symbol W0'. These input/output symbols are interpreted as instruction signals to the tape unit or response signals to the finite-state control. From Table 3, MC is formalized as the following RSM M_{MC}.

$$M_{\text{MC}} = (Q_{\text{MC}}, \Sigma_{\text{MC}}, \Gamma_{\text{MC}}, \delta_{\text{MC}})$$

$$Q_{\text{MC}} = \{(h, s) \mid h, s \in \{0, 1\}\}$$

$$\Sigma_{\text{MC}} = \{ \text{ W0, W1, R0, R1, SL, SLI, SLc, SR, SRI, SRc } \}$$

$$\Gamma_{\text{MC}} = \{x' \mid x \in \Sigma_{\text{MC}}\}$$

$$\delta_{\text{MC}}((0, s), y) = ((0, s), y') \quad (y \in \Sigma_{\text{MC}} - \{\text{SLI, SRI}\})$$

$$\delta_{\text{MC}}((0, s), \text{SLI}) = ((1, s), \text{SLc}')$$

$$\delta_{\text{MC}}((0, s), \text{SRI}) = ((1, s), \text{SRc}')$$

$$\delta_{\text{MC}}((1, 0), \text{W0}) = ((1, 0), \text{R0}')$$

$$\delta_{\text{MC}}((1, 1), \text{W0}) = ((1, 0), \text{R1}')$$

$$\delta_{\text{MC}}((1, 0), \text{W1}) = ((1, 1), \text{R0}')$$

$$\delta_{\text{MC}}((1, 1), \text{W1}) = ((1, 1), \text{R1}')$$

$$\delta_{\text{MC}}((1, s), \text{SL}) = ((0, s), \text{SLI}')$$

$$\delta_{\text{MC}}((1, s), \text{SR}) = ((0, s), \text{SRI}')$$

Table 3. Ten kinds of input symbols of a memory cell, and their meanings

Symbol	Instruction/Response	Meaning
W0	Write 0	Instruction of writing the symbol 0 at the head position. By this instruction, read operation is also performed.
W1	Write 1	Instruction of writing the symbol 1 at the head position. By this instruction, read operation is also performed.
R0	Read 0	Response signal telling the read symbol at the head is 0.
R1	Read 1	Response signal telling the read symbol at the head is 1.
SL	Shift-left	Instruction of shift-left operation.
SLI	Shift-left immediate	Instruction of placing the head on this cell by shifting left.
SLc	Shift-left completed	Response (completion) signal of shift-left operation.
SR	Shift-right	Instruction of shift-right operation.
SRI	Shift-right immediate	Instruction of placing the head on this cell by shifting right.
SRc	Shift-right completed	Response (completion) signal of shift-right operation.

The RSM M_{MC} is implemented by a circuit composed of RLEM 4-31 shown in Fig. 8 (a). Here, the top RLEM keeps a tape symbol s, i.e., if $s = 0$ ($s = 1$, respectively), then the state of the top RLEM is set to 0 (1). The remaining eight RLEMs form an RLEM-column. If the head is absent (present, respectively) at this MC, then the state of the RLEM-column is set to **0** (**1**).

To construct a *finite-state control* (FSC) of RTM M, we prepare a q_i-*module* for each state q_i of M as shown in Fig. 8 (b). It has two RLEM-columns labeled by q_i and $\hat{q}_i$. The RLEM-column labeled by $\hat{q}_i$ is used to read the tape symbol and branch the program of the RTM, i.e., it determines which quintuple $[q_i, 0, t, d, q_j]$ or $[q_i, 1, t', d', q_{j'}]$ should be applied. The RLEM-column labeled by q_i is used to write a symbol, shift the head, and enter the state q_i.

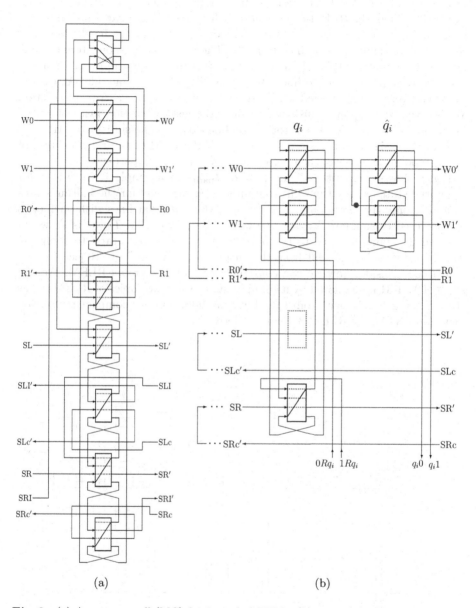

(a)   (b)

Fig. 8. (a) A memory cell (MC) for 2-symbol RTMs. (b) q_i-module. Here, we assume q_i is a right-shift state. If it is a left-shift state, then the bottom RLEM of the left RLEM-column should be placed at the position of the dotted rectangle.

Assume M is in state q_i. Then a signal should be given to the first input line of the second RLEM of the right column of the q_i-module as shown by • in Fig. 8 (b). Then, the RLEM-column enters the state **1**, and gives a signal on the command line W0′. By this, the tape symbol $s \in \{0, 1\}$ at the head position is read, and its response is obtained from Rs. Then, a signal goes out from the line labelled by $q_i s$ setting this column to state **0**. If there is a quintuple $[q_i, s, t, d, q_j]$, this line is connected to the line labelled by tdq_j of the q_j-module. At the q_j-module, after setting the left RLEM-column to the state **1**, write instruction Wt is given. Its response must be R0, since the last instruction just before the instruction Wt was W0. Then, the q_j module executes the shift instruction Sd, and finally a signal is transferred to the second RLEM of the right column of the q_j-module. By above, the operation of $[q_i, s, t, d, q_j]$ is performed.

Fig. 9 shows a circuit realizing FSC of T_{parity} in Example 1. Note that for the initial state q_0 only the right column is necessary, and for the halting states q_a and q_r only the left column is necessary. Also note that lines with open ends are not used to simulate T_{parity}. The whole circuit for RTM T_{parity} is shown in Fig. 10. By giving a signal to the port "Begin," the circuit starts to compute. Finally the signal comes out from the output port "Accept" or "Reject."

We now consider how we can construct RTMs by 3-symbol RLEM. We can see RLEM 4-31 is simulated by a circuit composed of two copies of RLEM 3-7 as shown in Fig. 11. Hence, from the above method, another compact realization method of RTMs by RLEM 3-7 can be derived.

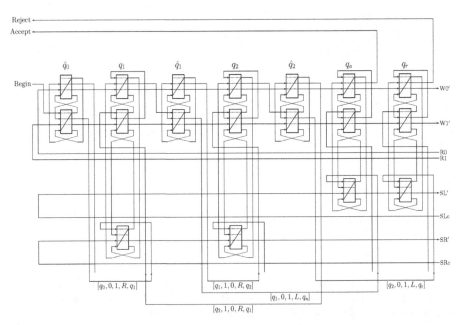

Fig. 9. A finite-state control of RTM T_{parity} in Example 1 realized by RLEM 4-31

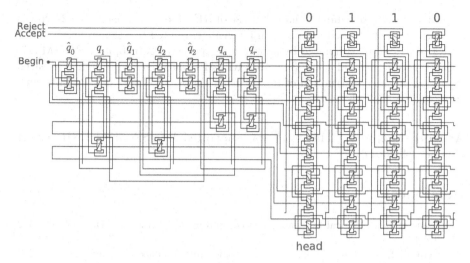

Fig. 10. A circuit made of RLEM 4-31 that simulates RTM T_{parity} in Example 1

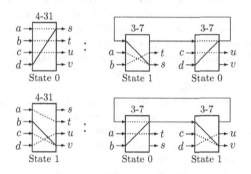

Fig. 11. A circuit composed of RLEM 3-7 that simulates RLEM 4-31

Table 4. Number of elements needed for composing a memory cell and a finite-state control of m-state 2-symbol RTM

RLEM	Memory cell	Finite-state control
4-289 (RE)	11	$\leq 3m$
4-31	9	$\leq 5m$
3-7	18	$\leq 10m$

5   Concluding Remarks

In this paper, we gave a method of realizing RTMs by RLEM 4-31. The number of RLEM 4-31 needed for composing RTMs is comparable with the case of using RE. As shown in Table 4, a memory cell composed of RLEM 4-31 is less complex than that of RE. On the other hand, a finite-state control composed of

RLEM 4-31 is more complex than the case of RE. Here, we constructed 2-symbol RTMs, but the proposed method can be easily extended to a general case. Since RLEM 4-31 can be simulated by a circuit composed of two copies of RLEM 3-7, a construction method using 3-symbol RLEM is also derived. Further research is needed on the construction of RTMs using simpler RLEMs, i.e., RLEMs with three or two symbols.

Acknowledgement. This work was supported by JSPS KAKENHI Grant Number 24500017.

References

1. Bennett, C.H.: Logical reversibility of computation. IBM J. Res. Dev. 17, 525–532 (1973)
2. Fredkin, E., Toffoli, T.: Conservative logic. Int. J. Theoret. Phys. 21, 219–253 (1982)
3. Lee, J., Peper, F., Adachi, S., Morita, K.: An asynchronous cellular automaton implementing 2-state 2-input 2-output reversed-twin reversible elements. In: Umeo, H., Morishita, S., Nishinari, K., Komatsuzaki, T., Bandini, S. (eds.) ACRI 2008. LNCS, vol. 5191, pp. 67–76. Springer, Heidelberg (2008)
4. Morita, K.: A simple universal logic element and cellular automata for reversible computing. In: Margenstern, M., Rogozhin, Y. (eds.) MCU 2001. LNCS, vol. 2055, pp. 102–113. Springer, Heidelberg (2001)
5. Morita, K.: A new universal logic element for reversible computing. In: Martin-Vide, C., Mitrana, V. (eds.) Grammars and Automata for String Processing, pp. 285–294. Taylor & Francis, London (2003)
6. Morita, K.: Reversible computing and cellular automata — A survey. Theoret. Comput. Sci. 395, 101–131 (2008)
7. Morita, K.: Constructing a reversible Turing machine by a rotary element, a reversible logic element with memory. Hiroshima University Institutional Repository (2010), http://ir.lib.hiroshima-u.ac.jp/00029224
8. Morita, K.: Reversible Computing. Kindai Kagaku-sha Co., Ltd., Tokyo (2012) (in Japanese) ISBN 978-4-7649-0422-4
9. Morita, K., Ogiro, T., Alhazov, A., Tanizawa, T.: Non-degenerate 2-state reversible logic elements with three or more symbols are all universal. J. Multiple-Valued Logic and Soft Computing 18, 37–54 (2012)
10. Morita, K., Ogiro, T., Tanaka, K., Kato, H.: Classification and universality of reversible logic elements with one-bit memory. In: Margenstern, M. (ed.) MCU 2004. LNCS, vol. 3354, pp. 245–256. Springer, Heidelberg (2005)
11. Mukai, Y., Morita, K.: Realizing reversible logic elements with memory in the billiard ball model. Int. J. of Unconventional Computing 8(1), 47–59 (2012)
12. Mukai, Y., Ogiro, T., Morita, K.: Universality problems on reversible logic elements with 1-bit memory. Int. J. Unconventional Computing (to appear)
13. Toffoli, T.: Reversible computing. In: de Bakker, J.W., van Leeuwen, J. (eds.) ICALP 1980. LNCS, vol. 85, pp. 632–644. Springer, Heidelberg (1980)
14. Toffoli, T.: Bicontinuous extensions of invertible combinatorial functions. Math. Syst. Theory 14, 12–23 (1981)

Universal Computation in the Prisoner's Dilemma Game

Brian Nakayama[1] and David Bahr[2]

[1] Department of Mathematics, Regis University, Denver, CO 80221, USA
[2] Department of Physics and Computational Science, Regis University, Denver, CO 80221, USA

Abstract. Previous studies of the Iterated Prisoner's Dilemma Game (IPDG) focus on the optimal strategies for accumulating points against another player or the evolution of cooperation. Instead, this paper expands upon the possible complexity in interactions by using a Cellular Automaton (CA) model to simulate large numbers of players competing within a limited space. Unlike previous works, we introduce a method for creating a wide variety of deterministic rules by mapping each possible interaction to a binary number. We then prove the computational universality of the resulting IPDG CA. An analysis of the number of interactions leads to the discovery of interesting properties when allowing only enough iterations for a strategy to use its "transient" instructions. The implications of universal computation (UC) are also discussed.

Keywords: Cellular Automata, Iterated Prisoner's Dilemma Game, Universal Computation, Universal Turing Machine.

1 Introduction

Studies about cooperation and optimal strategies abound for the Prisoner's Dilemma Game (PDG). As an approximation of interactions found in nature these studies impact our understanding of biology; however, to date few studies focus on the computational potential for the PDG when implemented in a cellular automaton (CA). Furthermore, none of the studies known presently provide a proof of universal computation in the aggregate interactions of players when situated in a lattice. In this paper, we introduce a memory based labeling scheme for strategies that allows 2^{15} different strategies to compete with each other. We report on the surprising effect of iterations on interactions and strategy. We then show interesting examples of self organization and a proof for Turing Universality in the iterated PDG CA.

The PDG [1] gets its name from the following scenario: Players A and B recently robbed a store, but the police do not quite have enough evidence to prove it. Players A and B know that they will both receive minor sentences of two months if they do not confess. Aware of this, the police put A and B in separate interrogation rooms and offer them each a deal. If A (or B) gives evidence on the other to the interrogators, A (or B) will get to leave without

O.H. Ibarra et al. (Eds.): UCNC 2014, LNCS 8553, pp. 293–304, 2014.
DOI: 10.1007/978-3-319-08123-6_24, © Springer International Publishing Switzerland 2014

receiving any charges, but the person who does not confess will receive a harsher sentence of five months. If both provide evidence on each other, both will spend at least four months in prison. This scenario creates the rewards in Table 1.

Table 1. The Prisoner's Dilemma Game

		Player B	
		cooperate	defect
Player A	cooperate	$R = 3/R = 3$	$S = 0/T = 5$
	defect	$T = 5/S = 0$	$P = 1/P = 1$

In addition to the basic scenario, the PDG includes any interactions between two players creating Table 1 with the rewards T, R, P, and $S \in \mathbb{R}$ having the properties $T > R > P > S$ and $R > (S + T)/2$ [2].

Previous works have implemented multiple iteration PDG (IPDG) simulations in CA. CA allow for the study of simple nearest neighbor interactions in a lattice on a discrete set of states [3]. Studies of the IPDG CA use strategies for playing the game as states, while the choice to cooperate or defect, along with a replacement rule, allows the states to interact.

Axelrod [2] was the first to use CA to study the IPDG, finding that a strategy called Tit for Tat did not perform as well as other strategies in CA despite Tit for Tat's dominance in other computer tournaments he designed. Nowak et al. [4] have studied simulations with and without memory, where the agents either always defected or cooperated. Nakamaru et al. [5], Brauchli et al. [6],and Szabó et al. [7] performed similar experiments on IPDG CA. Newth and Cornforth [8] extended the work of Nowak et al. on an asynchronous grid. Tanimoto and Sagara [9] studied alternating reciprocity in infinite length simulations on 2×2 grids. Gelimson et al. [10] investigated the effects of mobility on the evolution of cooperation. Alonso-Sanz [11][12], implemented an IPDG with memory of each player's points on a Moore lattice; however, though he found gliders, he did not find universal computation in his simulations. Finally, Pereira and Martinez [13] studied the IPDG on a 1D lattice. They also found emergent complexity in their random simulations with objects such as gliders [14] and "fingers".

In Sect. 2 we introduce a scheme for memory and interaction in the IPDG CA, while Sect. 3 reveals interesting results of our scheme. The paper concludes with a proof of Turing Universality in Sect. 4 and a short discussion in Sect. 5.

2   Implementation of the Prisoner's Dilemma Game

For a detailed explanation of the CA, one can refer to the original thesis [15].

The IPDG CA used in this paper creates strategies that can remember the past three iterations of an opponent. A strategy is described using binary by assigning cooperation the value 1, and defection 0. Using binary, we can define a unique history of three iterations from least recent (left bit) to most recent

Table 2. 3 memory transient strategy for Tit for Tat

Opponent's History	111	110	101	100	011	010	001	000
Cooperate / Defect	1	0	1	0	1	0	1	0

(right bit). Table 2 uses a robust strategy called Tit for Tat [2] to demonstrate the numbering scheme.

Table 2 will work when it has played at least three iterations of the PDG with an opponent. Tit for Tat only considers the most recent move (the rightmost bit), copying it, but it ignores the previous two moves. This strategy lacks information for what to do for its first, second, and third iteration. After a strategy has played three or more iterations, it can use the past three moves of the opponent to determine what to do. Thus Table 2 describes the long term, *asymptotic* behavior. In order to define the initial behavior we need something that describes the *transient*. Table 3 includes the missing information.

Table 3 contains both the asymptotic, and the transient instructions. The leftmost 1's position defines to which iteration a strategy responds. The column with "0001", represents the first iteration. Two columns have "001x_1" to represent the second iteration, because the opponent will have one of two optional histories, $x_1 = 0$ or $x_1 = 1$. Similarly four columns have "01x_1x_2" for the third iteration (x_2 is the opponent's most recent move), and eight columns have "1$x_1x_2x_3$" for the eight possible histories for iterations four and beyond (x_3 is the most recent). The column with "0000" is always a "0" and isn't used. Rather, it lets us think of the strategies as 2^{n+1} bit numbers, where n is the longest sequence of iterations a player can remember.

Table 3. Complete 3 memory strategy 10818

Opponent's History	1111	1110	1101	1100	1011	1010	1001	1000	0111	0110	0101	0100	0011	0010	0001	0000
Cooperate / Defect	0	0	1	0	1	0	1	0	0	1	0	0	0	0	1	0

To get the strategy number, or *10818* in this example, we convert the bottom row of Table 3 from binary to base 10. We order our bits to get 0010101001000 010$_2$ = 10818$_{10}$. Using this method we represent each possible strategy with its own unique number. For graphic simulations we assign each strategy a unique 24 bit-color by using the strategy bits for the green and blue hue while giving initial defecting strategies a red hue. Using this method, the IPDG CA has a total of 32,768 different strategies.

The IPDG CA simulations implement a Moore neighborhood on a 2D lattice. Each cell, representing a player, must interact with the eight cells closest to it (the northwest cell, the north, the northeast, east, etc.). In addition to choosing a lattice, we must also have a simple rule that determines how a cell changes states between rounds. For this research, cells use a "Darwinian" rule [7][13], picking the next state/strategy by changing a cell's current state to that of the neighbor with the highest points. If a neighbor does not have a higher point value, then the cell will not change states. Therefore, in the case of a tie between a cell and its neighbor, a cell will keep its own strategy. In order to keep our simulations deterministic and symmetrical around the square, the rule ignores all other ties. Ties do not arise often in simulations and have no noticeable effects.

In order to run the IPDG CA we need to define T, R, P, and S (Table 1) as well as the number of iterations. All simulations here will use the generic values $T = 5$, $R = 3$, $P = 1$, and $S = 0$ [4]. Further in this section we will determine the number of iterations.

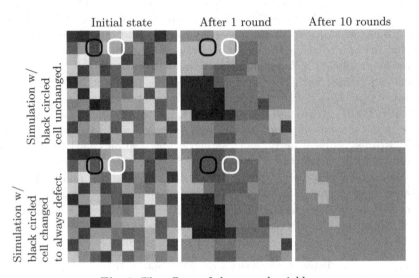

Fig. 1. The effects of the second neighbor

The Darwinian rule has the non-intuitive effect of creating second neighbor interactions. In a *round*, a cell plays the game with its eight neighbors for n iterations and sums up the points it receives. At the end of a round, it looks at all of its neighbors, and it picks the one with the most points and copies its strategy. Multiple rounds comprise a *simulation*. Suppose we have rules A (Fig. 1 circled in white), B, and C (Fig. 1 circled in black) where A is B's neighbor, B is C's neighbor, but A is not C's neighbor. C always defects, which brings down B's score. When A compares scores surrounding it, it will see that B has a lower score, and A will pick a different strategy for its next state. Thus, even though A is not C's neighbor, C affects whether or not A takes on B's strategy. Thus, *the neighbors of the neighbors of a cell, also known as a cell's second neighbors, affect its next state and strategy.* Figure 1 demonstrates this case example.

Both of the initial configurations for this simulation are the same except for the cell circled in black. Both start with a 10×10 lattice, and each cell plays 10 iterations with its neighbors each round. In the bottom simulation, the cell circled in black has the strategy *0* instead of strategy *18078*. The cell with strategy *0* always defects, bringing down the score of the cells next to it. This affects the next state of the cell circled in white. In the first simulation, the cell circled in white takes on the strategy of its neighbor to the left, strategy *36020*. Strategy *36020* goes on to take over the whole lattice after just 10 rounds. In the second simulation, strategy *0* brings down the score of strategy *36020*, which leads our cell circled in white to take on the strategy *9268* instead. After ten rounds, strategy *17540* takes over the lattice instead.

3 Initial Results

Data on the Hamming distance and strategy populations was gathered on random initial states (Fig. 2a) over the 2^{15} different strategies.

Fig. 2. a. A 800x600 random initial config, b. 4 iteration simulation after 750 rounds

The number of iterations for a simulation affected the outcome of the simulations by controlling how much a cell relied on either its asymptotic or transient memory. For a strategy with a memory of 3, a simulation must require the cells to do at least 4 iterations to take advantage of all of the transients: 1 iteration for the first move followed by 3 iterations to use the transient memory. After 4 iterations, the cell relies on its asymptotic memory for the past three moves. Thus, when we set the number of iterations, we inadvertently affect the ratio of transient to asymptotic iterations.

First, examine the Hamming distance (HD) in Fig. 3, which measures how many cells switch strategies each round. The following graphs show the HD for different simulations run on an 800 × 600 random initial state (where each cell contains a randomly chosen strategy). The x-axis and the y-axis represent the time step and number of cells that have changed strategy, respectively.

We observe that the HD for playing the game with only 4 iterations converges at a much higher number of cells than the simulation with 9 iterations. After 750 rounds, the six simulations sampled for 4 iterations averaged a HD of 2538

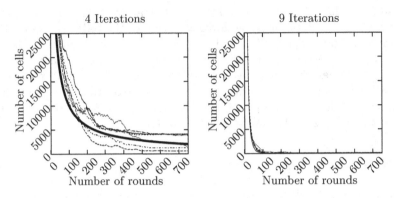

Fig. 3. The Hamming distance with a log-log plot approximation (the thick line)

or .0053% of the total number of cells. From 5 to 9 iterations, the simulations averaged a HD of 211, 295, 89, 63, and 77 after 750 rounds.

In all of the 4 iteration simulations, a log-log plot of the HD suggested that one can approximate the HD over rounds with the function, $f(x) = 393560 \cdot x^{-0.79645}$. When the HD decreases, one can interpret this as an increase of static neighborhoods in the system. Accordingly, we hypothesize that *if the IPDG CA contains a model of computation then the optimal number of iterations for finding UC in a random initial configuration exploits only the transient and none of the asymptotic.* Simulations with a high HD might represent more dynamic groups. Figure 2b shows a 4 iteration simulation converging to a steady state that coincidentally contains a glider gun [14]. The simulations that follow all use only 4 iterations unless specified otherwise.

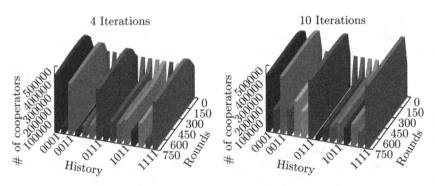

Fig. 4. Cooperating instructions over rounds

We next consider the number of strategies that cooperate or defect on a particular opponent's history. Figure 4 shows two graphs that trace the number of cells that cooperate for a particular history over time (rounds) on a 800 × 600 lattice. The vertical axis represents the number of cells cooperating for a certain history (the maximum is 480,000). The horizontal axis represents the history as defined in Sect. 2 earlier. The depth represents rounds, with the most recent round in front.

This method of gathering data on simulations provides insight into an ideal composite strategy made up of the most popular instructions for a lattice of cells. In both the 4 iteration and 10 iteration simulations *successful strategies almost always cooperate initially as well as whenever the strategy remembers that the opponent has always cooperated*; furthermore in both simulations, we should *always defect when the opponent has defected three times in a row.*

Contrasting the transient (4 iter.) to the more asymptotic (10 iter.) simulation reveals a difference in strategy. As the number of iterations increases, a strategy needs to cooperate more in the transient stage in order to survive; however, it should also cooperate less when the opponent has not cooperated historically for the past three moves in the asymptotic memory. Using this information, we can create a potentially optimal (for points) *ad hoc* strategy that cooperates more initially, but still defects as long as it remembers an opponent defecting.

Looking at Fig. 2b, one can see that *simulations eventually reach a stable state where many different groups of strategies persist side by side.* In order to understand how groups form we must look carefully at the borders between two competing strategies. Figure 5a shows a stabilized group of strategies, and the points that they attain in grey-scale (b). The lighter the area is, the more points cells received.

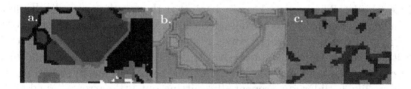

Fig. 5. a. A border, b. Point view of border, c. A natural "gun"

The cells with the lighter blue color in the middle of the trapezoidal shape use the strategy *38538* (A). The green colored cells have the strategy *41058* (B), and the darker blue color on the right border of that has strategy *33418* (C). The line of B cells attains less points than most of the A or C cells. However, the B cells drag down the points of surrounding A and C cells, preventing A or C from invading. *The inability of cells to invade results in many groups, despite high points between similar cells.*

When running random simulations, strategies sometimes self-organize into useful structures for computation. In Fig. 2 towards the bottom there is an interesting patch of red and navy blue dots on a teal background. Figure 5c zooms in on the patch to reveal a glider gun [14] and an arrow shaped glider. With enough space, interesting patterns emerge, similar to Conway's Game of Life [14].

Isolating certain strategies together increases the chances for formations like the glider gun. By combining strategies *11196*, *36866*, and *1088* in a specific initial configuration one can make a "program" that recursively builds the Sierpinski triangle. Figure 6 shows the initial setup on the left, and different time steps of the simulation as the triangle forms itself.

Fig. 6. An emergent Sierpinski triangle

Another example comes from the two-memory strategies *8748* (in red), *34954* (in blue), and *8746* (in black). This versatile set of strategies can make many patterns, the first of which can produce little "bullet" and "wave" like objects. Figure 7 shows these three strategies competing with only three iterations in order to avoid asymptotic behavior.

In both these simulations, the black-colored strategy separates the red and the blue creating borders and movement based on how one strategically places the cells. Figure 7a relies on making small walls of blue and black in order to produce a bullet. The borders keep in a spiral at the top that periodically shoots out a bullet, whose width the borders determine. Upon leaving the borders, they spread in all directions forming a wave. Figure 7b uses the same three strategies, but with a slightly different approach. Using the blue strategy (*34954*) for the background instead of the red one (*8748*), one can easily make something that looks more like a glider gun, repeatedly spitting out little arrow shaped gliders.

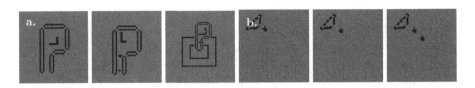

Fig. 7. Two different "guns" made with different config. of the same strategies.

4 Proof of Universal Computation

The glider guns observed while running random simulations prompted a search for a set of strategies capable of UC. We eventually found one set, strategies *10818*, *5218*, *3464*, and *33002*. The following proof of UC uses glider guns to create a NAND gate and memory in a similar style to the proof of UC in Conway's Game of Life [14].

Figure 8 shows the basic configurations capable of UC. The setup of strategies in Fig. 8a to make a glider follows. Using strategy *10818* as a background, the slightly lighter *5218* forms a head that replaces *10818* each round. The pink strategy *3464* replaces *5218*, preventing it from traveling diagonally in both directions. Figure 8b shows the point view (lighter gray = more points). The head of the glider moves by lowering the points of the background strategy in front of it, while giving the lower-right most cell of the head just slightly more points than the other cells around it.

Fig. 8. *a*. A glider, b. Glider's point view, c. A pin, d. Pin's point view

The pin in Fig. 8c is made up of strategy *33002* which cooperates with itself. The center of the pin achieves a high number of points each round. Figure 8c shows a basic 3×3 square of *33002*. The point view of the same object (d) shows the high points of the center cell.

If a glider runs into two pins placed carefully, the background strategy *10818* will replace the glider due to a border of high points the background attains from strategy *33002*. Figure 9a shows a glider eater[14] in action. If two gliders collide as in Fig. 9b, they destroy each other. Finally, Fig. 9c shows a glider colliding with the edge of a pin. The pin pulls the glider around itself, making the glider swerve around the edges of the pin. The glider swerving around the pin then starts to produce another glider on every corner of the pin. This creates a glider gun, and with some strategic placing of more pins we can control its output.

Now that we know how the gliders interact and how to make a glider gun, we can start making logic gates. *In order to prove UC we only need to show one kind of logic gate, the NAND*[14]. Figure 10 shows the before (a) and after (b) of a NAND gate simulation. (The lines help in understanding the data streams and their direction, but are not part of the simulation.) The absence of a glider also conveys information. We assign a glider the binary value 1, and the absence of a glider a 0. Figure 10a feeds in a stream 0, 1, 0, 1 starting from right to left. The bottom row will feed in 1, 1, 0, 0.

The first glider gun creates gliders that will collide with the incoming streams. If only one glider enters, the glider gun will block it, making the output a 0. Similarly if no gliders enter, none will come out. In the special case when two gliders try to enter at the same time, the glider gun will only block one of them, letting the other slip through. Thus we must have two 1's entering to get a 1 out. This is an AND gate. The second glider gun creates a NOT gate. The gliders

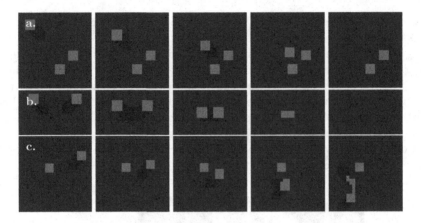

Fig. 9. a. A glider eater, b. A collision, c. A glider hooked on a pin

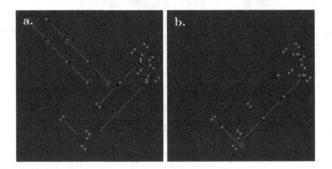

Fig. 10. A NAND gate made out of IPDG players

from this gun not only block the gliders input into it, but also create the output. If a glider enters, it will destroy a glider from the gun. Thus, a 1 will create a 0, and if nothing enters it outputs a 1. After going through the AND and the NOT gate, we have in Fig. 10b 1, 0, 1, 1.

Now we need to show that we can also store memory in this simulation. Figure 11 shows a D latch in CA form. One can create a register holding a unit of memory by placing two D latches together back to back. A register forms a safe way to store and retrieve bits with consistent results. However, half a register (a D latch) suffices for proving that the IPDG can hold memory.

The major gates and streams are labeled. The clock and the input each get split into two paths, with XOR gates crossing them. At the bottom we NOT the inputs and then AND them with the clock input. The clock has a cycle of 11 gliders "on" then 11 gliders "off". At the top, the input and the clock get ANDed together as well. This guarantees that the leftover latch will receive only one signal at a time. If it receives a signal from the top, the latch ORs it and then NOTs it, saving the value 1 in a loop. The same happens when a signal

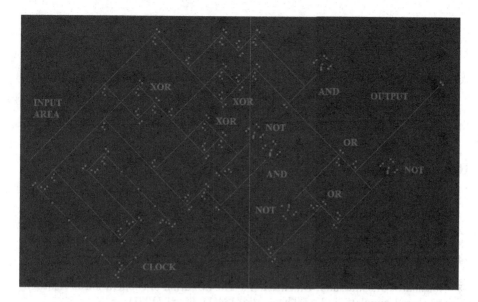

Fig. 11. D latch with a "0"

gets fed from the bottom, except that the opposite side of the loop will turn on. Figure 11 shows the D latch in its initial configuration. Eventually, since it has no input going into it, this latch will save a 0. To store a 1, instead put a stream of gliders on the input path. *Now that we have found a way to construct memory, we have proved that the IPDG CA has UC.*

5 Discussion

This proof shows the existence of UC in a subset of the strategies for playing the IPDG by the construction of a NAND gate and a D latch. The proof does not show all the possible ways to create a Universal Turing Machine (UC), as several sets of strategies seem to create similar gliders or other ways of transmitting information.

Furthermore, the IPDG CA introduced here contains persistent groupings of strategies that defect rather than cooperate in their interactions with each other and their surroundings. This model may help explain diversity in strategies present in nature. These defections were important for organizing larger structures within the CA, but perhaps most interesting is that this CA may also simulate a potential social interaction evident in human interactions [2]. Where other studies have focused on simpler strategies and the evolution of cooperation, this paper shows that complex players with history not only propagate themselves but also organize themselves through the adoption of strategies with higher points and through the imitation of more successful cells in a self-interested manner. Similar to Axelrod [2] which explains the "Evolution of

Cooperation", universal computation in IPDG cellular automata suggests the evolution of complexity and organization.

Acknowledgments. We thank James Seibert for advising the original thesis, Robyn Lutz for patiently editing, and Jack Lutz for advice on publishing. This work was supported by Regis University's Math-Science Scholarship, by RU's Math and Computer Science Departments, and by NSF grant 1247051.

References

1. Dresher, M.: Games of Strategy: Theory and Applications. Pren Hal. Appl. Math. Pren. Hal. (1961)
2. Axelrod, R.: The Evolution of Cooperation. Basic Books (1984)
3. Wolfram, S.: A New Kind of Science. Wolfram Media (2002)
4. Nowak, M.A., May, R.M., Sigmund, K.: The arithmetics of mutual help. Sci. Am. 272(6), 76 (1995)
5. Nakamaru, M., Matsuda, H., Iwasa, Y.: The evolution of cooperation in a lattice-structured population. J. of Theor. Bio. 184(1), 65–81 (1997)
6. Brauchli, K., Killingback, T., Doebeli, M.: Evolution of cooperation in spatially structured populations. J. Theor. Bio. 200(4), 405–417 (1999)
7. Szabó, G., Antal, T., Szabó, P., Droz, M.: Spatial evolutionary prisoners dilemma game with three strategies and external constraints. Phys. Rev. E 62(1), 1095 (2000)
8. Newth, D., Cornforth, D.: Asynchronous spatial evolutionary games. Biosystems 95(2), 120–129 (2009)
9. Tanimoto, J., Sagara, H.: A study on emergence of alternating reciprocity in a 2×2 game with 2-length memory strategy. Biosystems 90(3), 728–737 (2007)
10. Gelimson, A., Cremer, J., Frey, E.: Mobility, fitness collection, and the breakdown of cooperation. Phys. Rev. E 87(4), 042711 (2013)
11. Alonso-Sanz, R.: The historic prisoner's dilemma. Int. J. Bifurcat. Chaos 9(06), 1197–1210 (1999)
12. Alonso-Sanz, R.: Memory versus spatial disorder in the support of cooperation. Biosystems 97(2), 90–102 (2009)
13. Pereira, M.A., Martinez, A.S.: Pavlovian prisoner's dilemma-analytical results, the quasi-regular phase and spatio-temporal patterns. J. Theor. Biol. 265(3), 346–358 (2010)
14. Berlekamp, E., Conway, J., Guy, R.: Winning Ways for Your Mathematical Plays, vol. 4. A.K. Peters (2004)
15. Nakayama, B.: Universal computation in the prisoner's dilemma game. Undergraduate honors thesis, Regis U (2013)

Exact Simulation of One-Dimensional Chaotic Dynamical Systems Using Algebraic Numbers

Asaki Saito[1,*] and Shunji Ito[2]

[1] Faculty of Systems Information Science,
Future University Hakodate, Hakodate, Japan
saito@fun.ac.jp
[2] Faculty of Science, Toho University, Funabashi, Japan
shunjiito@gmail.com

Abstract. We introduce a method of true orbit generation that allowed us to perform, with digital computers, exact simulations of discrete-time dynamical systems defined by one-dimensional piecewise linear and linear fractional maps with integer coefficients by generalizing the method proposed by Saito and Ito (Physica D 268, 100-105 (2014)). The salient features of the new method are that it can use algebraic numbers of an arbitrarily high odd degree to represent numbers, and that it only involves integer arithmetic to compute true orbits. We demonstrated that it succeeded in generating true chaotic and intermittent orbits, respectively, by applying the method to a tent map and a map associated with a mediant convergents algorithm, in contrast with conventional methods of simulation. We particularly demonstrated through simulations regarding invariant measures that the statistical properties of the generated true orbits agreed well with those of the typical orbits of the two maps.

Keywords: Dynamical system, Exact simulation, True orbit, Chaos, Algebraic number, Integer arithmetic, Piecewise linear fractional map, Typical behavior.

1 Introduction

Dynamical systems, especially chaotic dynamical systems, have attracted attention as devices to achieve real or analog computation, and also as objects to be simulated with super-Turing models (e.g., see Refs. [1, 2]). However, as digital computers can, at most, perform computation that can be done by Turing machines, it is thus natural to expect difficulties in simulating a dynamical system that achieves super-Turing computation with such computers. This raises an interesting question of: To what extent can dynamical systems be simulated with digital computers? In fact, it has been well known that simulations of chaotic dynamical systems are very hard to deal with at various levels.

1. For example, it has been difficult thus far to reproduce the chaotic behavior of maps by using digital computers even for tent and Bernoulli maps,

---

* Corresponding author.

O.H. Ibarra et al. (Eds.): UCNC 2014, LNCS 8553, pp. 305–315, 2014.
DOI: 10.1007/978-3-319-08123-6_25, © Springer International Publishing Switzerland 2014

i.e., even for one of the best known maps in chaotic dynamics [3, 4]. (Actually, the cause of this is the fact that conventional simulation methods use finite binary numbers and rational numbers as numbers. We will later show that we can generate chaotic orbits of these maps by using the method proposed in this paper even with digital computers.)

2. Also, if we use a number representation with fixed precision, such as double-precision floating-point numbers usually used in computer simulations, then we cannot perform exact simulations of dynamical systems due to inevitable numerical errors. This especially becomes a serious problem when we deal with chaotic dynamical systems, which have sensitive dependence on initial conditions as a hallmark of chaos. Indeed, issues concerning the validity of such computer-generated pseudo-orbits have been constantly discussed since the early years of simulation studies on chaotic dynamics [5–11].

Based on this background, we recently proposed a method of true orbit generation that allowed us to perform exact simulations of discrete-time dynamical systems defined by one-dimensional piecewise linear fractional maps with integer coefficients with digital computers [12]. The most salient feature of the method was that it used cubic irrationals to represent numbers and it only involved integer arithmetic to compute true orbits. We have generalized that method in this study by using algebraic numbers of an arbitrarily high odd degree, where algebraic numbers are probably among the most basic computable real numbers [13].

This paper is organized as follows. Section 2 introduces a method of true orbit generation that can be applied to one-dimensional piecewise linear fractional maps with integer coefficients, which was extended to treat algebraic numbers of an arbitrarily high odd degree. Section 3 reports the results obtained with the method by performing exact simulations of two maps: a tent map and a map associated with a mediant convergents algorithm. We particularly demonstrated that it was possible for our method to generate typical orbits of the two maps, in contrast with conventional methods of simulation. Section 4 is devoted to the conclusion.

Before we proceed to the main subject, we need to remark on the following: We require simulations of a dynamical system to be able to compute (long) typical orbits of the dynamical system because simulations usually need to reproduce typical behaviors of target systems. Thus, we do not consider that simulations are properly carried out in cases where only atypical orbits can be generated or in cases where only the first several tens of time steps of orbits can be generated, possibly due to high computational cost. (As it is difficult to discuss the statistical properties of generated orbits in the latter cases, we cannot argue whether they are typical or not. It is well known that high computational cost is required to generate true orbits of general rational maps whose coefficients are algebraic numbers [14, 15].)

2   Our Method

We focused on discrete-time dynamical systems in the present study that were defined by a one-dimensional piecewise linear fractional map [16]:

$$M(x) = M_i(x) = \frac{a_i x + b_i}{c_i x + d_i} \quad \text{if } x \in (e_i, e_{i+1}), \ i = 0, 1, \cdots, N - 1, \quad (1)$$

where M_i is the linear fractional map on the ith subinterval (e_i, e_{i+1}) where a_i, b_i, c_i, and d_i are integers satisfying $a_i d_i - b_i c_i \neq 0$ (i.e., each M_i is invertible). For simplicity, we consider the case where the number N of subintervals partitioning the interval (e_0, e_N) is finite. We also consider all the endpoints of the subintervals to be rational numbers satisfying $e_0 < e_1 < \cdots < e_N$ to simplify the domain determination that will be explained later.

It should be noted that the eventually periodic points of M are usually rational numbers and quadratic irrationals (i.e., the roots of irreducible quadratic polynomials with integer coefficients). Thus, if one uses algebraic numbers whose degree is greater than two for computing true orbits of M, then one can usually guarantee the aperiodicity of the obtained true orbits.

Let us consider an algebraic equation

$$p_0 x^m + p_1 x^{m-1} + \cdots + p_m = 0, \quad (2)$$

where degree m is an odd number greater than one, coefficients $p_0 \ (\neq 0)$, p_1, $\cdots$, p_m are integers, and polynomial $p_0 x^m + p_1 x^{m-1} + \cdots + p_m$ is irreducible. We assume that Eq. (2) has a unique real root α. That is, α is a real algebraic number of degree m, all of whose conjugates, other than α itself, are non-real complex numbers. Let S_m be the set of such real algebraic numbers. Number $\alpha \in S_m$ satisfying Eq. (2) can be represented by a vector $(p_0, p_1, \cdots, p_m) \in \mathbb{Z}^{m+1}$. Note that such a representation of α is not unique: For example, $(p_0, p_1, \cdots, p_m) = (-p_0, -p_1, \cdots, -p_m)$.

We can easily see that M becomes a map from $S_m \cap (e_0, e_N)$ to S_m.[1] Furthermore, we can easily obtain a representation of $M(\alpha)$ with $\alpha \in S_m \cap (e_0, e_N)$ by using a matrix operation: Suppose that $\alpha \in S_m \cap (e_i, e_{i+1})$ has a representation $(p_0, p_1, \cdots, p_m)$. Then, $\alpha' = M(\alpha) = M_i(\alpha)$ has a representation $(p_0', p_1', \cdots, p_m')$ with

$$(p_0', p_1', \cdots, p_m')^{\mathrm{T}} = A_{mi} (p_0, p_1, \cdots, p_m)^{\mathrm{T}}, \quad (3)$$

---

[1] Let $\alpha \in S_m \cap (e_0, e_N)$ and let $\alpha' = M(\alpha) = M_i(\alpha)$. It is obvious that $\alpha' \in \mathbb{Q}(\alpha)$, where $\mathbb{Q}(\alpha)$ denotes the algebraic number field obtained by adjoining α to the rational number field $\mathbb{Q}$. On the other hand, since M_i is invertible, we have $\alpha = (d_i \alpha' - b_i)/(-c_i \alpha' + a_i)$, so that $\alpha \in \mathbb{Q}(\alpha')$. Thus, we have $\mathbb{Q}(\alpha) = \mathbb{Q}(\alpha')$, which implies that the degree of α' is equal to m. Now, let us consider the conjugates of α'. We can express a conjugate of α (denoted by α^{σ}) as $\alpha^{\sigma} = (d_i \alpha'^{\sigma} - b_i)/(-c_i \alpha'^{\sigma} + a_i)$, by using the corresponding conjugate of α' (denoted by α'^{σ}). From the fact that $\alpha'^{\sigma} \in \mathbb{R}$ implies $\alpha^{\sigma} \in \mathbb{R}$, it follows that all the conjugates of α', other than α' itself, must be non-real complex numbers. Therefore, we see $\alpha' \in S_m$. Note that, since $\alpha' \in S_m$, the polynomial $p_0' x^m + p_1' x^{m-1} + \cdots + p_m'$ with coefficients given by Eq. (3) has a unique real root α'.

where the superscript T denotes the transpose and A_{mi} is the matrix corresponding to M_i. We can obtain Eq. (3) and the explicit form of A_{mi} by substituting $\alpha = (d_i\alpha' - b_i)/(-c_i\alpha' + a_i)$ into Eq. (2). For example, the form of A_{3i} is given as

$$A_{3i} = \begin{pmatrix} d_i^3 & -c_i d_i^2 & c_i^2 d_i & -c_i^3 \\ -3b_i d_i^2 & a_i d_i^2 + 2b_i c_i d_i & -2a_i c_i d_i - b_i c_i^2 & 3a_i c_i^2 \\ 3b_i^2 d_i & -2a_i b_i d_i - b_i^2 c_i & a_i^2 d_i + 2a_i b_i c_i & -3a_i^2 c_i \\ -b_i^3 & a_i b_i^2 & -a_i^2 b_i & a_i^3 \end{pmatrix}. \tag{4}$$

Thus, if we can determine that $\alpha \in S_m$ represented by $(p_0, p_1, \cdots, p_m)$ is included in the ith subinterval (e_i, e_{i+1}), then we can obtain $A_{mi}(p_0, p_1, \cdots, p_m)^{\mathrm{T}}$ as a representation of $M(\alpha)$ from Eq. (3). Therefore, we need to errorlessly perform such domain determination to generate a true orbit of M (Eq. (1)). We can exactly determine the subinterval including α, and thus the matrix that should be applied to $(p_0, p_1, \cdots, p_m)$ as follows: Because $\alpha \in S_m$ is the only real root of $p_0 x^m + p_1 x^{m-1} + \cdots + p_m$, we see that $\alpha \in (e_i, e_{i+1})$ if and only if the signs of $p_0 e_i^m + p_1 e_i^{m-1} + \cdots + p_m$ and $p_0 e_{i+1}^m + p_1 e_{i+1}^{m-1} + \cdots + p_m$ are different. Thus, we only need to evaluate the sign of the polynomial at the endpoints of each subinterval sequentially, until we find a unique subinterval where the polynomial has different signs at its endpoints to determine the matrix to be applied to a given $(p_0, p_1, \cdots, p_m)$. Note that such determination can be errorlessly performed only by using integer arithmetic because the endpoints of the subintervals are taken from rational numbers, and that the subinterval including α can be found in finite time because the number N of subintervals is finite.

3   Simulation Results

This section presents the results from applying the method of true orbit generation to two maps on the unit interval $[0, 1]$: a tent map and a map associated with a mediant convergents algorithm [17]. We particularly report the results from generating true orbits of these maps by using cubic and quintic irrationals, as the simplest cases. We also describe why conventional methods of simulation have great difficulties in generating orbits of the two maps.

3.1   Tent Map

The tent map,

$$x(n+1) = \begin{cases} 2x(n) & \text{if } x(n) \in [0, 1/2] \\ -2x(n) + 2 & \text{if } x(n) \in [1/2, 1] \end{cases},$$

where $x(n)$ is a state at discrete times $n = 0, 1, 2, \cdots$, is a piecewise linear map often considered in the field of chaotic dynamics, but it is also a piecewise linear fractional map, which is obvious by considering the denominator to be one. The map is illustrated in Fig. 1. As was previously described, this tent map is well known to be a difficult map to simulate. We can cite two characteristics of the tent map as reasons for that.

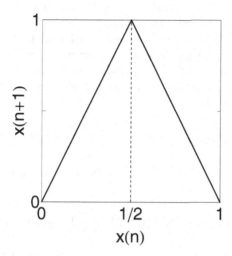

Fig. 1. Tent map

The first characteristic of the tent map is that the set of eventually fixed points of $x = 0$ (i.e., the set of initial points from which the orbit eventually maps directly onto the fixed point at $x = 0$) is identical with the set of finite binary numbers on $[0, 1]$. Therefore, if one uses the double-precision binary floating-point numbers usually used in the simulations of dynamical systems, then, even without numerical errors, one can only generate those orbits that eventually reach the unstable fixed point, and one cannot generate chaotic orbits typical for the tent map.

The second characteristic of the tent map is that the set of eventually periodic points (i.e., the set of initial points from which the orbit eventually maps directly onto a periodic orbit) is identical with the set of rational numbers on $[0, 1]$. The fractional representation of numbers can be cited as the next standard number representation other than fixed-precision ones, but we can only generate atypical orbits that eventually become periodic, even if we improve the number representation to the fractional representation.

Now let us explain the concrete application of the method of true orbit generation to the tent map. First, we will explain a case where we use cubic irrationals, i.e., algebraic numbers of degree $m = 3$. From Eq. (4), the matrices A_{30} and A_{31} that correspond to the left and right branches of the tent map, i.e., $M_0(x) = 2x/1$ and $M_1(x) = (-2x + 2)/1$, are given as

$$A_{30} = \begin{pmatrix} 1 & 0 & 0 & 0 \\ 0 & 2 & 0 & 0 \\ 0 & 0 & 4 & 0 \\ 0 & 0 & 0 & 8 \end{pmatrix}, \quad A_{31} = \begin{pmatrix} 1 & 0 & 0 & 0 \\ -6 & -2 & 0 & 0 \\ 12 & 8 & 4 & 0 \\ -8 & -8 & -8 & -8 \end{pmatrix}.$$

We choose $x(0) = \alpha \in S_3$ satisfying $x(0)^3 + 3x(0)^2 + 3x(0) - 1 = 0$ as an initial point. That is, we take $(p_0(0), p_1(0), p_2(0), p_3(0)) = (1, 3, 3, -1)$ as an initial condition. The following is the specific procedure for true orbit generation: Suppose that $(p_0(n), p_1(n), p_2(n), p_3(n))$ is a representation of $x(n)$. The signs of the polynomial $p_0(n)x^3 + p_1(n)x^2 + p_2(n)x + p_3(n)$ are evaluated at $x = 0$ and $x = 1/2$. If the two signs are different (and therefore $x(n) \in (0, 1/2)$), we obtain a representation of $x(n+1)$ as

$$(p_0(n+1), p_1(n+1), p_2(n+1), p_3(n+1))^{\mathrm{T}} = A_{30} \, (p_0(n), p_1(n), p_2(n), p_3(n))^{\mathrm{T}}.$$

Otherwise (and therefore $x(n) \in (1/2, 1)$), we obtain a representation of $x(n+1)$ by

$$(p_0(n+1), p_1(n+1), p_2(n+1), p_3(n+1))^{\mathrm{T}} = A_{31} \, (p_0(n), p_1(n), p_2(n), p_3(n))^{\mathrm{T}}.$$

By repeating this procedure, we can generate the true orbit $(p_0(n), p_1(n), p_2(n), p_3(n))$ $(n = 0, 1, 2, \cdots)$. Note that it is easy to obtain the value of $x(n)$ from $(p_0(n), p_1(n), p_2(n), p_3(n))$; Because the equation $p_0(n)x^3 + p_1(n)x^2 + p_2(n)x + p_3(n) = 0$ has the single real root $x(n)$, we can obtain its value with arbitrary precision, e.g., by using the bisection method.

When we use quintic irrationals, i.e., algebraic numbers of degree $m = 5$, the matrices A_{50} and A_{51} corresponding to M_0 and M_1 of the tent map are given as

$$A_{50} = \begin{pmatrix} 1 & 0 & 0 & 0 & 0 & 0 \\ 0 & 2 & 0 & 0 & 0 & 0 \\ 0 & 0 & 4 & 0 & 0 & 0 \\ 0 & 0 & 0 & 8 & 0 & 0 \\ 0 & 0 & 0 & 0 & 16 & 0 \\ 0 & 0 & 0 & 0 & 0 & 32 \end{pmatrix}, \quad A_{51} = \begin{pmatrix} 1 & 0 & 0 & 0 & 0 & 0 \\ -10 & -2 & 0 & 0 & 0 & 0 \\ 40 & 16 & 4 & 0 & 0 & 0 \\ -80 & -48 & -24 & -8 & 0 & 0 \\ 80 & 64 & 48 & 32 & 16 & 0 \\ -32 & -32 & -32 & -32 & -32 & -32 \end{pmatrix}.$$

In this case, we choose $x(0) = \alpha \in S_5$ satisfying $x(0)^5 + 5x(0)^4 + 10x(0)^3 + 10x(0)^2 + 5x(0) - 1 = 0$ as an initial point. The specific procedure for true orbit generation for $m = 5$ is almost the same as that explained for $m = 3$.

Figures 2(a) and (b) show the true orbits of the tent map, generated by using cubic irrationals for the former and quintic irrationals for the latter. These figures clearly indicate chaotic behavior, which implies that our method successfully generates true chaotic orbits of the tent map, in strong contrast with conventional methods of simulation.

Next, we demonstrate the statistical properties of the generated true orbits by estimating the invariant density of the tent map. The tent map has an invariant measure with the density $\rho(x) = 1$ for $x \in [0, 1]$. Figure 3 plots the results obtained from estimating the invariant density by using the true orbits treated in Figs. 2(a) and (b), where the length of each true orbit is taken to be equal to 10^6. As a result, the estimated densities take values very close to one, which agree well with the density of the tent map.

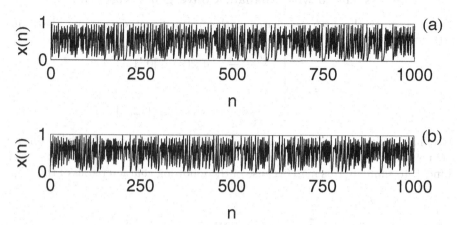

Fig. 2. True orbits of tent map. (a) $x(n)$ versus n of true orbit, generated by using cubic irrationals, starting from $(p_0(0), p_1(0), p_2(0), p_3(0)) = (1, 3, 3, -1)$. (b) $x(n)$ versus n of true orbit, generated by using quintic irrationals, starting from $(p_0(0), p_1(0), p_2(0), p_3(0), p_4(0), p_5(0)) = (1, 5, 10, 10, 5, -1)$.

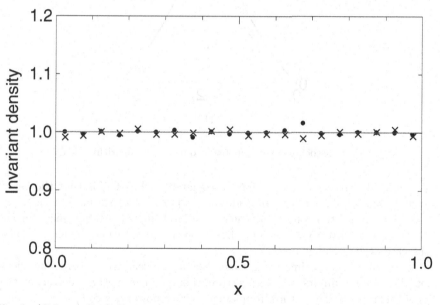

Fig. 3. (Color online) Estimation of invariant density of tent map by using true orbits with length 10^6. Dots represent estimated density obtained from true orbit generated by using cubic irrationals, starting from $(p_0(0), p_1(0), p_2(0), p_3(0)) = (1, 3, 3, -1)$. Crosses represent that by using quintic irrationals, starting from $(p_0(0), p_1(0), p_2(0), p_3(0), p_4(0), p_5(0)) = (1, 5, 10, 10, 5, -1)$. Line represents density $\rho(x) = 1$.

3.2   Map Associated with Mediant Convergents Algorithm

Next, we treat the map associated with the mediant convergents algorithm
(MCA) [17]:

$$
x(n+1) =
\begin{cases}
\dfrac{x(n)}{1-x(n)} & \text{if } x(n) \in [0,\, 1/2] \\[2ex]
\dfrac{1-x(n)}{x(n)} & \text{if } x(n) \in [1/2,\, 1]
\end{cases}
.
$$

The map is illustrated in Fig. 4, which exhibits intermittent behavior due to
the neutral (indifferent) fixed point at $x = 0$. Similar to the tent map, it is very
difficult to simulate this map because of the following characteristics of the map.

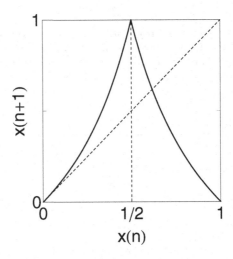

Fig. 4. Map associated with mediant convergents algorithm (MCA)

The first characteristic of the map associated with MCA is that the set of
eventually fixed points of $x = 0$ is identical to the set of rational numbers on
$[0, 1]$. This implies that one cannot generate intermittent orbits typical for the
map associated with MCA by using fractional representation, which is similar
to the case of the tent map.

Another difficulty in simulating this map can be seen from a different viewpoint. This map exhibits a $1/f$ spectrum. That is, the power spectral density
$S(f)$ of this map diverges at low frequencies with a power law $S(f) \propto 1/f$, where
f denotes frequency. This property stems from the local structure around the
fixed point at $x = 0$. The use of fixed-precision number representations, however,
breaks the property, since unavoidable round-off errors break the local structure,
at least theoretically.

Matrices necessary to generate true orbits of the map associated with MCA
can be obtained similarly to the case of the tent map. In fact, the matrices A_{30}

and A_{31}, that are necessary to generate true orbits by using cubic irrationals, that correspond to the left and right branches of the map associated with MCA are given as

$$A_{30} = \begin{pmatrix} 1 & 1 & 1 & 1 \\ 0 & 1 & 2 & 3 \\ 0 & 0 & 1 & 3 \\ 0 & 0 & 0 & 1 \end{pmatrix}, \quad A_{31} = \begin{pmatrix} 0 & 0 & 0 & -1 \\ 0 & 0 & -1 & -3 \\ 0 & -1 & -2 & -3 \\ -1 & -1 & -1 & -1 \end{pmatrix}.$$

Similarly, when generating true orbits by using quintic irrationals, we use matrices A_{50} and A_{51}:

$$A_{50} = \begin{pmatrix} 1 & 1 & 1 & 1 & 1 & 1 \\ 0 & 1 & 2 & 3 & 4 & 5 \\ 0 & 0 & 1 & 3 & 6 & 10 \\ 0 & 0 & 0 & 1 & 4 & 10 \\ 0 & 0 & 0 & 0 & 1 & 5 \\ 0 & 0 & 0 & 0 & 0 & 1 \end{pmatrix}, \quad A_{51} = \begin{pmatrix} 0 & 0 & 0 & 0 & 0 & -1 \\ 0 & 0 & 0 & 0 & -1 & -5 \\ 0 & 0 & 0 & -1 & -4 & -10 \\ 0 & 0 & -1 & -3 & -6 & -10 \\ 0 & -1 & -2 & -3 & -4 & -5 \\ -1 & -1 & -1 & -1 & -1 & -1 \end{pmatrix}.$$

We can use the same initial condition and procedure that were used before for true orbit generation.

Figures 5(a) and (b) show the true orbits of the map associated with MCA generated by using cubic irrationals for the former and quintic irrationals for the latter. We can see clear intermittent behavior from these figures, and that our method succeeded in generating true intermittent orbits of the map associated with MCA, in contrast to conventional methods of simulation.

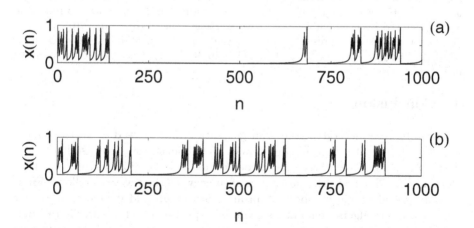

Fig. 5. True orbits of map associated with MCA. (a) $x(n)$ versus n of true orbit, generated by using cubic irrationals, starting from $(p_0(0), p_1(0), p_2(0), p_3(0)) = (1, 3, 3, -1)$. (b) $x(n)$ versus n of true orbit, generated by using quintic irrationals, starting from $(p_0(0), p_1(0), p_2(0), p_3(0), p_4(0), p_5(0)) = (1, 5, 10, 10, 5, -1)$.

Now, we will again consider whether the statistical properties of the generated true orbits are good. The map associated with MCA has a σ-finite but infinite invariant measure with the density $\rho(x) = 1/x$ for $x \in [0, 1]$ [17]. Figure 6 plots the estimated densities obtained from the true orbits treated in Figs. 5(a) and (b), where the length of each true orbit is taken to equal 10^6. As a result, the estimated densities coincide well with that of the map associated with MCA.

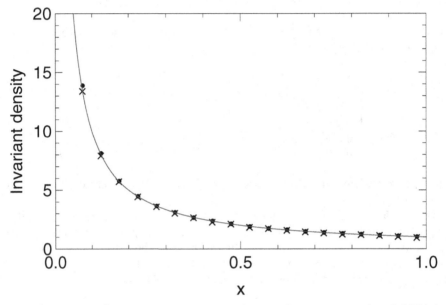

Fig. 6. (Color online) Estimation of invariant density of map associated with MCA by using true orbits with length 10^6. Dots represent estimated density obtained from true orbit generated by using cubic irrationals, starting from $(p_0(0), p_1(0), p_2(0), p_3(0)) = (1, 3, 3, -1)$. Crosses represent that by using quintic irrationals, starting from $(p_0(0), p_1(0), p_2(0), p_3(0), p_4(0), p_5(0)) = (1, 5, 10, 10, 5, -1)$. Curve represents density $\rho(x) = 1/x$.

4   Conclusion

We introduced a method of true orbit generation that allowed us to perform exact simulations with digital computers of one-dimensional piecewise linear and linear fractional maps with integer coefficients by generalizing Saito and Ito's method [12]. The main characteristics of the new method were as follows. First, it could use algebraic numbers of an arbitrarily high odd degree to represent numbers, where algebraic numbers could be expressed exactly with digital computers. Second, the method only involved integer arithmetic to compute true orbits, where integer arithmetic could also be precisely calculated with digital computers. We found that it could successfully generate true chaotic orbits by applying the method to a tent map and that it could successfully generate intermittent orbits by applying it to a map associated with the mediant convergents algorithm, in contrast to conventional methods of simulation. We have demonstrated through simulations concerning invariant measures that the statistical properties of the generated true orbits agreed well with those of typical orbits of the two maps.

Acknowledgements. We thank P. Ruthven-Stuart, J. Tamura, and S. Yasutomi for their suggestions. This research was supported by the JST PRESTO program and by a Grant-in-Aid for Young Scientists (B) 21700256 from the Ministry of Education, Culture, Sports, Science, and Technology (MEXT) in Japan.

References

1. Blum, L., Cucker, F., Shub, M., Smale, S.: Complexity and Real Computation. Springer, New York (1998)
2. Siegelmann, H.T.: Neural Networks and Analog Computation: Beyond the Turing Limit. Birkhäuser, Boston (1999)
3. Atlee Jackson, E.: Perspectives of Nonlinear Dynamics. Cambridge University Press, Cambridge (1991)
4. Saito, A.: Computational Aspects of a Modified Bernoulli Map. Prog. Theor. Phys. Supplement 161, 328–331 (2006)
5. Rannou, F.: Numerical Study of Discrete Plane Area-Preserving Mappings. Astron. Astrophys. 31, 289–301 (1974)
6. Binder, P.M., Jensen, R.V.: Simulating Chaotic Behavior with Finite-State Machines. Phys. Rev. A 34, 4460–4463 (1986)
7. Beck, C., Roepstorff, G.: Effects of Phase Space Discretization on the Long-Time Behavior of Dynamical Systems. Physica D 25, 173–180 (1987)
8. Grebogi, C., Hammel, S.M., Yorke, J.A., Sauer, T.: Shadowing of Physical Trajectories in Chaotic Dynamics: Containment and Refinement. Phys. Rev. Lett. 65, 1527–1530 (1990)
9. Earn, D.J.D., Tremaine, S.: Exact Numerical Studies of Hamiltonian Maps: Iterating without Roundoff Error. Physica D 56, 1–22 (1992)
10. Dawson, S., Grebogi, C., Sauer, T., Yorke, J.A.: Obstructions to Shadowing when a Lyapunov Exponent Fluctuates about Zero. Phys. Rev. Lett. 73, 1927–1930 (1994)
11. Sauer, T., Grebogi, C., Yorke, J.A.: How Long Do Numerical Chaotic Solutions Remain Valid? Phys. Rev. Lett. 79, 59–62 (1997)
12. Saito, A., Ito, S.: Computation of True Chaotic Orbits Using Cubic Irrationals. Physica D 268, 100–105 (2014)
13. Pour-El, M.B., Richards, J.I.: Computability in Analysis and Physics. Springer, Berlin (1989)
14. Vivaldi, F.: Dynamics over Irreducible Polynomials. Nonlinearity 5, 941–960 (1992)
15. Silverman, J.H.: The Arithmetic of Dynamical Systems. Springer, New York (2007)
16. Schweiger, F.: Ergodic Theory of Fibred Systems and Metric Number Theory. Clarendon Press, Oxford (1995)
17. Ito, S.: Algorithms with Mediant Convergents and Their Metrical Theory. Osaka J. Math. 26, 557–578 (1989)

Artificial Astrocyte Networks, as Components in Artificial Neural Networks

Zahra Sajedinia

Department of Computer Science
Memorial University of Newfoundland, St. John's, Canada
z.sajedinia@mun.ca

Abstract. Recent findings in neurophysiology provided evidence that not only neurons but also networks of glia-astrocytes are responsible for processing information in the human brain. Based on these new findings, information processing in the brain is defined as communication between neurons-neurons, neurons-astrocytes and astrocytes-astrocytes. Artificial neural networks (ANNs) model the neuron-neuron communications. Artificial neuron-glia networks (ANGN), in addition to neuron-neuron communications, model neuron-astrocyte connections. This research introduces a new model of ANGN that captures these three possible communications. In this model, random networks of artificial glia astrocytes are implemented on top of a typical neural network. The networks are tested on two classification problems, and the results show that on certain combinations of parameter values specifying astrocyte connections, the new networks outperform typical neural networks. This research opens a range of possibilities for future work on designing more powerful architectures of artificial neural networks that provide more realistic models of the human brain.

1 Introduction

The human brain consists of neurons and glia cells. It is estimated that there are 10 to 50 times more glia cells than there are neurons in the brain [6]. Until two decades ago, it was widely believed that glia cells only performed passive functions and they did not interfere with processing information [20]. New evidence supports the conception that glia-astrocytes affect learning by modulating synapses. This led to a new concept in neurophysiology, the tripartite synapse, which consists of three parts: presynaptic elements, post-synaptic elements, and surrounded astrocytes (Figure 1). While neurons communicate by electrical signals, astrocytes use chemicals for propagating information; therefore, astrocytes are slower than neurons in processing information [14,3,2,15,16,19,17,18,4,25,7].

Inspired by the manner in which glia astrocytes communicate, researchers developed a novel type of neural network termed "artificial neuron-glia network" (ANGN) [23,1]. In ANGNs, each neuron is connected to an astrocyte cell, and activation (inactivation) of the neuron for a specific period of time will make the connected astrocyte active; as a result, the connected weights will be increased

O.H. Ibarra et al. (Eds.): UCNC 2014, LNCS 8553, pp. 316–326, 2014.
DOI: 10.1007/978-3-319-08123-6_26, © Springer International Publishing Switzerland 2014

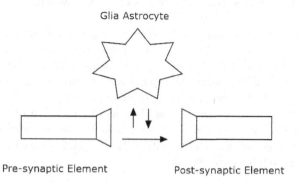

Fig. 1. A representation of a tripartite synapse (The figure is drawn based on the definition of tripartite synapse in [27]). The astrocyte (star-shaped cell) is able to modulate the synapse by releasing transmitters.

(or decreased) by a pre-defined factor [1]. Section 2 provides greater details on the architecture and algorithms of ANGNs.

From a physiological perspective, single astrocytes do not capture the whole story. Recent studies suggest that not only neurons, but also astrocytes are connected into networks. While neurons exchange information through synapses, gap junctions are the path of communication for astrocytes [5,20,13,21,12]. Some other studies have taken a further step and assigned the conscious processing to astrocyte networks [20,24]. Pereira, Jr. and Furlan in their 2010 paper stated that "the division of work in the brain is such that the astrocyte network conveys the feeling, while neural networks carry information about what happens". They believed consciousness is the result of integration of data by means of wavelike computing in the astrocytic networks [20].

In continuation of the research on neuron-glia networks, we designed a new type of ANGN in which artificial astrocyte networks (AANs) are connected to neurons rather than single astrocytes. The networks of astrocytes are implemented on top of a multi-layer back propagation ANN, and the resulting network is tested for classifying breast cancer cells and ionosphere data sets. The results show that having an attached network of astrocytes on top of a typical neural network improves the performance. The exact structure and algorithms of AANs and the results will be discussed in section 3 and section 4.

This paper is organized into the following sections: section 2 provides some background information on ANGNs; section 3 introduces the new network of glia astrocytes and how it can be connected to neurons; section 4 presents the implementations of the network and the results; section 5 summarizes the conclusions of the study, and the possible future work.

2   Previous Work on Neuron-Glia Networks

The concept of artificial neuron-glia networks was initially introduced by Porto in 2004 [22]; later, it was implemented in different ANN architectures [26,11,1,8], and was successfully tested on real world problems [11,23]. The results showed that adding artificial astrocytes to typical ANNs improves performance of the network, but it is highly dependent on the complexity of the problem [23]. The architecture of an ANGN can be described as an extension of a typical ANN. ANGN includes a novel type of processing element, the artificial glia astrocyte. Each neuron is associated with one astrocyte. Figure 2 shows how an astrocyte can modify the weights of a neuron.

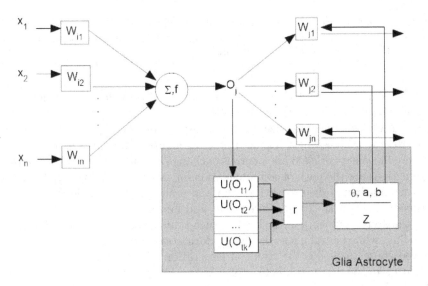

Fig. 2. The figure above illustrates the main idea described in [1], and it displays a neuron and its associated artificial astrocyte

The exact biological interactions between neurons and astrocytes have not been completely elucidated; therefore, different algorithms for describing the behavior of artificial astrocyte have been proposed. However, the key concept of all of the algorithms is the same: the lower processing speed in glia astrocytes in comparison to neurons leads to the decay of astrocyte activation [23,1,9,8]. In this paper, we have used a modified version of the most common model of artificial glia astrocytes. In this model, astrocytes are defined as a set of functions and parameters. The parameters are $k \in \mathbb{N}\backslash 0$, $\theta \in [1, k]$, $ft \in \mathbb{R}$ and $a, b \in [0, 1]$. The training data will be executed on the network for k times; if the corresponding neuron to astrocyte fired (output $> ft$, where ft represents firing threshold) for θ times in this k cycles, the astrocyte will be turned on and increase the connected weights of its associated neuron by a percentage. The inactivation of the neuron in θ iterations will result in the decrease of the associative weights by b percentage [1]. The artificial astrocyte does not affect the ANN algorithm. The astrocyte model is only executed once in every k cycles and based on the recorded activity of the associative neuron, decreases, increases or does not affect the weights.

3   Artificial Astrocytes Networks(AAN)

Inspired by the recent physiological findings, which claims activation of one glia-astrocyte propagate to other astrocytes through gap junctions [5,20,13,21,5,12], we designed a novel neural network architecture that benefits from a network of artificial astrocytes on top of a neuron-glia network. The remainder of this section introduces the architecture and the algorithms of this new network.

3.1   Structure of Artificial Astrocytes Networks

The structure of the astrocyte networks is founded on the neuron-glia networks; each neuron is associated with one astrocyte and the sufficient activity of the corresponding neuron turns the astrocyte on or off. This structure mimics the release of transmitter by glia astrocytes in the brain [21,3,23]. In this research, in addition to the components of neuron-glia networks, there are connections between astrocytes that comprise the astrocyte networks. An active astrocyte results in the activation of all other astrocytes in the same network. This behavior is inspired by the propagation of calcium wave through gap junctions in the brain [20].

The exact connection between biological astrocytes is not yet clear. The model we suggest for astrocyte networks is based on connecting random astrocytes. A set, which is composed of n randomly chosen astrocytes, will be determined. Then, each pair of astrocytes in the set will be connected by an edge. The result will be a complete (where there is an edge between all nodes) astrocyte

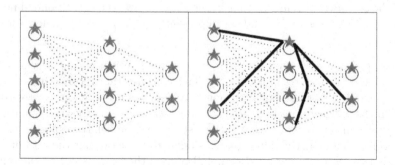

Fig. 3. Glia-astrocytes are shown with stars. The left image depicts a neuron-glia network (adapted from Figure 3 in [23]) and the image on the right is a neuron-glia network with artificial astrocyte network, the solid lines in the image shows one possible astrocyte network.

network. Having a complete network is inspired by the work of Pereira and Furlan [20]. Each astrocyte network may contain two to n astrocytes[1], where the maximum value for n is the summation of the number of neurons in all layers. The efficient number of astrocytes participating in an AAN can be determined by experiments. Figure 3 presents an ANGN and a possible structure for its corresponding AAN.

3.2   Learning Algorithm of Artificial Astrocytes Networks

Artificial astrocyte networks can be defined as a set of nodes, parameters and functions. All astrocytes run the same algorithm, and the behavior of an astrocyte can be divided into two phases. In the first phase, if the activation conditions of the astrocyte are satisfied, it will become activated and sends an activation signal to all the connected astrocytes. The second phase is responsible for modifying the weights of the active astrocyte.

In the first phase, the functions and parameters are analogous to the former algorithms of neuro-glia networks [22] explained in section two, where a single astrocyte is defined as $k \in \mathbb{N}\backslash 0$, $\theta \in [1, k]$, $a, b \in [0, 1]$ and $ft \in \mathbb{R}$. The activity of the corresponding astrocyte to each neuron will be represented by the following functions:

- $u : \mathbb{R} \to \mathbb{Z}$, determines whether the corresponded neuron to the astrocyte is fired or not, and is defined as follows:

$$u(x) = \begin{cases} -1 & x \leq ft \\ 1 & x > ft \end{cases}$$

where x is the output of the corresponding neuron, ft is the threshold of firing, and the output of u indicates whether the neurons has fired $(u(x) = 1)$ or not $(u(x) = -1)$.
- $r : \mathbb{N} \to [-\theta, +\theta]$, where r represents how many times the neuron was fired in the k consecutive cycles. The output of $-\theta$ or $+\theta$ results in the activation of the astrocyte. $-\theta$ means that in the the k cycles, the corresponded neuron did not fire for θ times, and $+\theta$ represents the firing of the neuron for $+\theta$ times.

If the output of r is θ then the astrocyte become activated and it will send a "+" connected astrocytes in the AAN. The astrocytes that receive the signal are then activated. The same behavior will be repeated for $-\theta$; if the output of r is $-\theta$, then the astrocyte become activated and sends a "-" activation signal to all astrocytes connect to the current active astrocyte. The behavior of an astrocyte that received a "+" activation signal is similar to the case that the output of its r function is $+\theta$; receiving a "-" signal also gives the same result to the output $-\theta$ for r.

---

[1]   In each portion of the brain, generally more than one astrocyte network is connected to neurons, but for simplicity of the artificial networks, we assume that only one astrocyte network can be implemented on top of an ANN.

In the second phase, the associated weights to active astrocytes[2] will be modified as follows:

$$w(t + \Delta t) = w(t) + \Delta w(t)$$

where $\Delta w(t)$ is defined as

$$\Delta w(t) = |w(t)| z(t)$$

and function $z : \mathbb{N} \backslash 0 \to \mathbb{R}$ indicates the percentage of the change of the weights based on the astrocyte activation.

$$z(t) = \begin{cases} a & r(t) = \theta \\ -b & r(t) = -\theta \end{cases}$$

Figure 4 depicts a flow chart of the AAN algorithm.

4   Artificial Astrocyte Networks and Their Application to a Classification Problem

For testing the performance of AAN, we answer the following question:

> Are there possible connections between astrocytes of a neuron-glia network that produce more accurate classification results?

We implement AAN to solve two classification problems. The first problem is classifying breast cancer cells and the second one is a classification of ionosphere data. The breast cancer and the ionosphere data sets used in this work were the UCI data sets provided based on real world data and has repeatedly appeared in the machine learning literature [30,28,29,31,10]. The breast cancer data set includes 201 instances of one class and 85 instances of another class. The instances are described by nine attributes, some of which are linear and others are nominal. The available 286 breast cancer instances in the data set were organized into 146 training and 146 testing instances. The ionosphere data set consisted of 351 instances, with each instance having 34 attribute classified as either "good" or "bad". The 351 instances of ionosphere data set were divided into 175 training and 176 testing instances; both problems were binary classification tasks. The training and testing of the networks were implemented on a system with a 1.30 GHz processor and 2 GB of RAM using the Windows 8 operating system, Java language source code and the Eclipse compiler.

The experiments aimed to test the performance of the proposed artificial astrocyte networks and to compare them with typical ANNs and ANGNs. The typical ANNs were designed as multi-layer back propagation network, which is composed of three layers. For the breast cancer problem, the input layer consists of nine neurons, each of which receives one feature of the cells. The output layer

---

[2] The associated weights to an astrocyte is defined as the weights connecting the astrocyte's corresponded neuron and the neurons in the next layer.

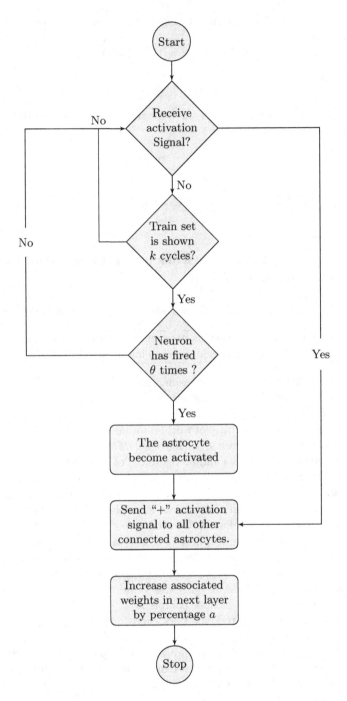

Fig. 4. A flowchart of the AAN algorithm. This algorithm is executed by every single astrocyte in each cycle. For simplicity, -θ is omitted from the algorithm.

Table 1. The first four columns define the ANN. The other columns present the parameters related to astrocytes.

Parameters	Neurons in first Layer	Neurons in 2nd Layer	Neurons in 3rd Layer	α	k	θ	a	b	ft
Breast cancer	9	8	2	0.1	100	40	1.25	0.75	0.75
Ionosphere	9	8	2	0.1	90	27	1.25	0.75	0.6

Table 2. The accuracy of classification on test data for ANN, ANGN and AAN

Network	Test Accuracy (Breast Cancer)	Test Accuracy (Ionosphere)
ANN	0.87	0.80
ANGN	0.91	0.86
AAN	0.93	0.88

consists of two neurons, which represents healthy and unhealthy cells. The hidden layer consists of eight neurons. The number of neurons in the hidden layer was determined by experiments that adjusted the number of neurons in the hidden layer from 1 to 14. For the ionosphere problem, the input layer consisted of 34 neurons, each neuron corresponded to one attribute and the output layer had two neurons, representing "good" and "bad". The number of neurons in the hidden layer was also experimentally determined to be 18.

The neuron-glia network was implemented on top of the networks by including the following astrocyte parameters: k, θ, a,b and $ft \in \mathbb{R}$. The values of these parameters were experimentally determined. Table 1 gives the final parameter values chosen for the training and testing of the networks. The network of interest in this research, the artificial astrocyte network, was implemented by employing the same parameters of the ANGN (Table 1). The astrocyte networks were defined based on the random selection of the astrocytes as explained in section 3. The astrocyte network for breast cancer data set was tested by involving three random astrocytes, and for ionosphere data with 5 astrocytes; The accuracy of classification in these experiments is reported[3] in Table 2. The accuracy value was obtained by executing the trained network on the testing data.

Table 2 shows a comparison between typical neural networks, neuron-glia networks and artificial astrocyte networks. It can be seen that the inclusion of the single astrocytes (ANGNs) improves the performance of the typical neural network(as also discussed in [23]), the performance of ANGNs can also be enhanced by connecting astrocytes and forming astrocyte networks. It should be noted that the common parameters have the same value in all models. Therefore, the variations of the accuracy between ANN and ANGN is solely for the

---

[3] Here, we show that there are random astrocyte networks that provide more accurate results. The impact of the number of astrocytes and their connection in an AAN on the classification results will be discussed in future work.

inclusion of single astrocyte elements and between ANGN and AANs is for the connections established between some astrocytes.

5   Conclusion and Future Work

The higher computing power achieved by the inclusion of the artificial astrocyte networks can be explained in two ways. Firstly, there is some similarity between AANs, liquid state machines, and recurrent neural networks, which results in the reception of time-varying inputs from external astrocyte sources, as well as neurons. In the AAN algorithm, astrocytes are randomly connected to each other. The recurrent nature of the connections turns the time varying input into a spatio-temporal pattern of activation in the network nodes that enables the network to compute a large variety of non-linear functions on the input. In other words, the astrocytes serve as a memory that records information of past k cycles and use this information to shape the network in a way that reduces error. Secondly, from a physiological point of view, astrocyte networks give a simple interpretation of data integration in the brain. Physiologists believe that the neurons' digital processes provide contents of the information, while the calcium waves generated by astrocytes provide integration of the contents [20]. Therefore, having an AAN on top of typical neural networks add the benefit of data integration; this gives us a more realistic model of the human brain that is able to provide a more detailed analysis and yields a more powerful artificial neural network.

Possible future work in this area can be divided into four main directions. The first will focus on designing more accurate models for describing artificial astrocytes and astrocyte networks. Since 2009, when artificial astrocytes were introduced until now, new physiological studies revealed other aspects of the functionality and structure of astrocytes and their networks; a simplified version of these aspects, specifically astrocyte networks with the ability to learn can be added to current astrocyte models. Secondly, the future research in this area needs to address the theoretical issues regarding the computational complexity of the network. Analyzing the network from the computational complexity perspective in general and parametrized complexity in particular, will help us to recognize the aspects that reduce the efficiency and will suggest new restricted models that operate more quickly. The third direction will implement AANs on different neural network architectures and evaluate their performance with and without the added astrocyte networks. Finally, the fourth direction will evaluate possible astrocyte networks. In this work, we only test the performance of one random astrocyte network. It is possible to evaluate the performance by considering all types of astrocyte networks, which are represented in the form of trees, bi-partite or other types of graphs. Then, a delay in transmitting data on astrocyte connections could be considered in these networks.

Acknowledgements. I would like to thank my M.Sc. supervisor, Dr. Todd Wareham, for his support, helpful suggestions on the relation between liquid state machines and AANs, time-delaying astrocyte networks, and his assistance for preparing this paper. My gratitude is also extended to Jenna Flogeras and Aileen Worrall of the Memorial University Writing Center for their help with editing.

References

1. Alvarellos-González, A., Pazos, A., Porto-Pazos, A.B.: Computational models of neuron-astrocyte interactions lead to improved efficacy in the performance of neural networks. Computational and Mathematical Methods in Medicine 2012, 10 (2012)
2. Araque, A., Carmignoto, G., Haydon, P.G.: Dynamic signaling between astrocytes and neurons. Annual Review of Physiology 63(1), 795–813 (2001)
3. Araque, A., Parpura, V., Sanzgiri, R.P., Haydon, P.G.: Tripartite synapses: glia, the unacknowledged partner. Trends in Neurosciences 22(5), 208–215 (1999)
4. Bonansco, C., Couve, A., Perea, G., Ferradas, C.Á., Roncagliolo, M., Fuenzalida, M.: Glutamate released spontaneously from astrocytes sets the threshold for synaptic plasticity. European Journal of Neuroscience 33(8), 1483–1492 (2011)
5. Giaume, C., Koulakoff, A., Roux, L., Holcman, D., Rouach, N.: Astroglial networks: a step further in neuroglial and gliovascular interactions. Nature Reviews Neuroscience 11(2), 87–99 (2010)
6. Hatton, G.I., Parpura, V.: Glial neuronal signaling, vol. 1. Springer (2004)
7. Haydon, P.G.: Glia: listening and talking to the synapse. Nature Reviews Neuroscience 2(3), 185–193 (2001)
8. Ikuta, C., Uwate, Y., Nishio, Y.: Chaos glial network connected to multi-layer perceptron for solving two-spiral problem. In: Proceedings of 2010 IEEE International Symposium on Circuits and Systems (ISCAS), pp. 1360–1363. IEEE (2010)
9. Ikuta, C., Uwate, Y., Nishio, Y.: Performance and features of multi-layer perceptron with impulse glial network. In: The 2011 International Joint Conference on Neural Networks (IJCNN), pp. 2536–2541. IEEE (2011)
10. Kim, H., Park, H.: Data reduction in support vector machines by a kernelized ionic interaction model. In: SDM. SIAM (2004)
11. Konishi, E.: Modeling quantum mechanical observers via neural-glial networks. International Journal of Modern Physics B 26(09) (2012)
12. Lallouette, J., Berry, H.: Topology drives calcium wave propagation in 3d astrocyte networks. In: Proceedings of the European Conference on Complex Systems 2012, pp. 453–463. Springer (2013)
13. Pannasch, U., Vargová, L., Reingruber, J., Ezan, P., Holcman, D., Giaume, C., Syková, E., Rouach, N.: Astroglial networks scale synaptic activity and plasticity. Proceedings of the National Academy of Sciences 108(20), 8467–8472 (2011)
14. Pasti, L., Volterra, A., Pozzan, T., Carmignoto, G.: Intracellular calcium oscillations in astrocytes: a highly plastic, bidirectional form of communication between neurons and astrocytes in situ. The Journal of Neuroscience 17(20), 7817–7830 (1997)
15. Perea, G., Araque, A.: Communication between astrocytes and neurons: a complex language. Journal of Physiology-Paris 96(3), 199–207 (2002)
16. Perea, G., Araque, A.: Properties of synaptically evoked astrocyte calcium signal reveal synaptic information processing by astrocytes. The Journal of Neuroscience 25(9), 2192–2203 (2005)

17. Perea, G., Araque, A.: Astrocytes potentiate transmitter release at single hippocampal synapses. Science 317(5841), 1083–1086 (2007)
18. Perea, G., Araque, A.: Glia modulates synaptic transmission. Brain Research Reviews 63(1), 93–102 (2010)
19. Perea, G., Navarrete, M., Araque, A.: Tripartite synapses: astrocytes process and control synaptic information. Trends in Neurosciences 32(8), 421–431 (2009)
20. Pereira Jr., A., Furlan, F.A.: Astrocytes and human cognition: modeling information integration and modulation of neuronal activity. Progress in Neurobiology 92(3), 405–420 (2010)
21. Pirttimaki, T.M., Parri, H.R.: Astrocyte plasticity implications for synaptic and neuronal activity. The Neuroscientist 19(6), 604–615 (2013)
22. Porto, A.: Computational models for optimizing the learning and the information processing in adaptive systems. Ph. D. Thesis, Faculty of Computer Science, University of A Coruña (2004)
23. Porto-Pazos, A.B., Veiguela, N., Mesejo, P., Navarrete, M., Alvarellos, A., Ibáñez, O., Pazos, A., Araque, A.: Artificial astrocytes improve neural network performance. PLoS One 6(4), e19109 (2011)
24. Robertson, J.M.: The astrocentric hypothesis: proposed role of astrocytes in consciousness and memory formation. Journal of Physiology-Paris 96(3), 251–255 (2002)
25. Rusakov, D.A., Zheng, K., Henneberger, C.: Astrocytes as regulators of synaptic function a quest for the ca2+ master key. The Neuroscientist 17(5), 513–523 (2011)
26. Sajedinia, Z.: Artificial glia astrocytes; a new element in adaptive neuro fuzzy systems. In: Proceedings of the 22th Annual Newfoundland Electrical and Computer Engineering Conference, NECEC 2013 (2013)
27. Wade, J., McDaid, L., Harkin, J., Crunelli, V., Kelso, S.: Self-repair in a bidirectionally coupled astrocyte-neuron (an) system based on retrograde signaling. Frontiers in Computational Neuroscience 6 (2012)
28. Wolberg, W.H., Street, W.N., Heisey, D.M., Mangasarian, O.L.: Computerized breast cancer diagnosis and prognosis from fine-needle aspirates. Archives of Surgery 130(5), 511 (1995)
29. Wolberg, W.H., Street, W.N., Mangasarian, O.: Machine learning techniques to diagnose breast cancer from image-processed nuclear features of fine needle aspirates. Cancer Letters 77(2), 163–171 (1994)
30. Wolberg, W.H., Street, W.N., Mangasarian, O.L.: Image analysis and machine learning applied to breast cancer diagnosis and prognosis. Analytical and Quantitative Cytology and Histology 17(2), 77–87 (1995)
31. Zhou, Z.H., Jiang, Y.: Nec4. 5: neural ensemble based c4. 5. IEEE Transactions on Knowledge and Data Engineering 16(6), 770–773 (2004)

Quantum, Stochastic, and Pseudo Stochastic Languages with Few States*

Arseny M. Shur[1],[**] and Abuzer Yakaryılmaz[2],[3],[***]

[1] Ural Federal University, Ekaterinburg, Russia
[2] National Laboratory for Scientific Computing, Petrópolis, RJ, 25651-075, Brazil
[3] University of Latvia, Faculty of Computing, Raina bulv. 19, Rīga, LV-1586, Latvia
`arseny.shur@usu.ru, abuzer@lncc.br`

Abstract. Stochastic languages are the languages recognized by probabilistic finite automata (PFAs) with cutpoint over the field of real numbers. More general computational models over the same field such as generalized finite automata (GFAs) and quantum finite automata (QFAs) define the same class. In 1963, Rabin proved the set of stochastic languages to be uncountable presenting a single 2-state PFA over the binary alphabet recognizing uncountably many languages depending on the cutpoint. In this paper, we show the same result for unary stochastic languages. Namely, we exhibit a 2-state unary GFA, a 2-state unary QFA, and a family of 4-state unary PFAs recognizing uncountably many languages. After this, we completely characterize the class of languages recognized by 1-state GFAs, which is the only nontrivial class of languages recognized by 1-state automata.

Keywords: stochastic languages, unary languages, quantum finite automata, generalized finite automata, probabilistic finite automata.

1 Introduction

Computation models based on real or complex numbers are much more powerful than conventional Turing machines that define recursively enumerable languages. Since there is a possibility that some of these models, like the quantum model, will become physically available for experiments in the nearest future, it is quite important to know the limitations of the models. In the paper, we focus on the power of very small probabilistic, generalized, and quantum automata. In his seminal paper, Rabin [Rab63] showed that 2-state PFAs define uncountably many binary languages. Since GFAs and QFAs are generalizations of PFAs, the same result holds for them as well. However, to get a complete picture, more restricted cases for these automata, like 1-state automata or unary languages, should be investigated. Two questions addressed in this paper are *how many*

---

* Check arXiv:1405.0055 [SY14] for the full paper.
** Supported under the Agreement 02.A03.21.0006 of 27.08.2013 between the Ministry of Education and Science of the Russian Federation and Ural Federal University.
*** Partially supported by CAPES, ERC Advanced Grant MQC, and FP7 FET project QALGO.

O.H. Ibarra et al. (Eds.): UCNC 2014, LNCS 8553, pp. 327–339, 2014.
DOI: 10.1007/978-3-319-08123-6_27, © Springer International Publishing Switzerland 2014

states are sufficient to recognize uncountably many unary languages? which languages can be recognized by one state?

Our results are as follows. We show that a rotation operator implemented by a 2-state unary GFA or QFA generates uncountably many languages depending on the choice of cutpoint. For QFAs, the result holds even for the most restricted model of such an automaton, described in [MC00]. This fact also allows us to answer an open question stated in [YS10]. Then we use a different technique to prove that there are uncountably many 4-state unary PFAs recognizing different languages with the same cutpoint $\frac{1}{4}$. We left open the question whether this bound can be lowered to 3 states, but we guess that the answer is no. Note that 2-state unary PFAs recognize only regular languages [Paz71].

1-state PFAs and QFAs define trivial languages but the situation is completely different for GFAs. In the unary case, 1-state GFAs recognize a proper subclass of regular languages, while the set of binary languages recognized by 1-state GFAs is uncountable. In the last part of the paper we introduce three classes of languages (solution, parity, and indicator languages) and fully characterize the languages recognized by 1-state GFAs in terms of these classes.

2   Background

Let Σ be a finite alphabet, Σ^* be the set of all words over Σ, and $\Sigma^+ = \Sigma^* \backslash \{\varepsilon\}$, where ε denotes the empty word. The end-markers ¢ (left) and $ (right) do not belong to Σ.

Let us recall different models of finite automata. All models in the paper read inputs from the left to the right symbol by symbol. A *deterministic finite automaton* (DFA) is a quintuple $\mathcal{A} = (Q, \Sigma, \delta, s, F)$ containing a set of states $Q = \{q_1, \ldots, q_n\}$, a transition function $\delta : Q \times \Sigma \to Q$, an initial state s, and a set F of final states. The transition function can be naturally extended to $Q \times \Sigma^*$ and the acceptance condition for a word w is $\delta(s, w) \in F$. *Nondeterministic* and *ε-nondeterministic automata* [resp., NFA and ε-NFA] are obtained by replacing the initial state by a set S and the transition function by an arbitrary relation $\delta \subseteq Q \times \Sigma \times Q$ [resp., $\delta \subseteq Q \times (\Sigma \cup \{\varepsilon\}) \times Q$]. The acceptance condition is $(s, w, f) \in \delta$ for some $s \in S$, $f \in F$. These three models are equivalent in the sense that they recognize the same class of regular languages.

The acceptance conditions above can be easily restated in terms of matrix multiplication, making DFA's and NFA's particular cases of a general model called *generalized finite automaton* (GFA) [Tur69, Paz71]. A GFA is a quintuple $\mathcal{G} = (Q, \Sigma, \{A_\sigma \mid \sigma \in \Sigma\}, v_0, f)$, where $A_\sigma \in \mathbb{R}_{|Q| \times |Q|}$ is the *transition matrix* for the symbol $\sigma \in \Sigma$, $v_0 \in \mathbb{R}_{|Q| \times 1}$ is the *initial vector*, and $f \in \mathbb{R}_{1 \times |Q|}$ is the *final vector*. For an input word $w \in \Sigma^*$, the computation of $\mathcal{G}$ is traced by a $|Q|$-dimensional column vector $v_i = A_{w_i} v_{i-1}$, where $1 \le i \le |w|$ and the accepting value of $\mathcal{G}$ on w is calculated as

$$f_{\mathcal{G}}(w) = f v_{|w|} = f A_{w_{|w|}} A_{w_{|w|-1}} \cdots A_{w_2} A_{w_1} v_0.$$

A probabilistic finite automaton (PFA) [Rab63] is a special case of GFA where each transition matrix is (left) stochastic, v_0 is a 0-1 stochastic vector, and f is a 0-1 vector. Note that the entry of 1 in v_0 corresponds to the initial state and the entries of 1's in f correspond to final states.

A PFA can be defined to start its computation in a distribution of states instead of a single state. Then any stochastic vector can serve as the initial vector. Similarly, instead of fixed accepting states, each state contributes to the accepting probability with some weight from $[0, 1]$. Formally, one can assume that a PFA (i) reads the end-marker ¢ for preprocessing before reading the input (and so the new initial vector is $A_¢ v_0$ for a stochastic matrix $A_¢$) and (ii) reads the end-marker \$ for post-processing after finishing the whole input (and so the new final vector is $f A_\$$ for a stochastic matrix $A_\$$).

In the literature, there are different models of quantum finite automata (QFAs). The most general one [Hir10, YS11] can, in particular, simulate PFAs exactly. In this paper, we use a more restrictive model which is sufficient to follow our results. It is due to Moore and Crutchfield [MC00] and is called MCQFA.

We begin with a concise review of quantum computation. We refer the reader to [SY14] for further details. Conventionally, any vector is represented in "ket" notation, e.g. $|v\rangle$. Its conjugate transpose is denoted by $\langle v|$ and the inner product of $\langle u|$ and $|v\rangle$ is denoted by $\langle u|v\rangle$. A *quantum state* of a *quantum system* $\mathcal{M}$ *with the set of states* $Q = \{q_1, \ldots, q_n\}$ is a norm-1 (column) vector in the n-dimensional Hilbert space $\mathcal{H}_n$:

$$|v\rangle = \begin{pmatrix} \alpha_1 \\ \vdots \\ \alpha_n \end{pmatrix}, \quad \text{where } \sum_{j=1}^{n} |\alpha_j|^2 = 1.$$

The entries $\alpha_1, \ldots, \alpha_n$ are called *amplitudes* of the states $q_1, \ldots, q_n$, respectively, while $|\alpha_j|^2$ is viewed as the probability of the system being in the state q_j. The quantum state containing 1 in the jth entry (and hence zeroes in the other entries) is denoted by $|q_j\rangle$. Clearly, $|q_1\rangle, \ldots, |q_n\rangle$ form a basis of $\mathcal{H}_n$.

There are two fundamental quantum operations: *unitary* and *measurement* operators. A unitary operator U applicable to $\mathcal{M}$ is an $n \times n$ complex-valued matrix preserving the norm. Such an operator transforms a quantum state $|v\rangle$ to a new state $|v'\rangle = U|v\rangle$. Measurement operators are used to retrieve information from quantum systems. We use simple measurement operators defined as follows. The set of states Q is partitioned into sets $Q_1, \ldots, Q_k$ ($k > 1$) inducing the decomposition of $\mathcal{H}_n$ into the sum $\mathcal{H} = \mathcal{H}_1 \oplus \cdots \oplus \mathcal{H}_k$ of orthogonal subspaces $\mathcal{H}_l = \text{span}\{|q\rangle \mid q \in Q_l\}$. A measurement operator P has k operation elements $P_l = \sum_{q \in Q_l} |q\rangle\langle q|$ and forces the system to collapse into one of k quantum subsystems corresponding to the subspaces $\mathcal{H}_l$. We denote the outcomes of P with the indices "1", ..., "k". The probability of getting the outcome "l" is

$$p_l = \langle \tilde{v}_l | \tilde{v}_l \rangle = \sum_{q_j \in Q_l} |\alpha_j|^2, \quad \text{where } |\tilde{v}_l\rangle = P_l|v\rangle.$$

If $\mathcal{M}$ collapses to this subsystem ($p_l > 0$), the new quantum state is obtained by normalizing $|\tilde{v}_l\rangle$:

$$|v_l\rangle = \frac{1}{\sqrt{p_l}}|\tilde{v}_l\rangle.$$

A MCQFA is a quintuple $\mathcal{M} = (Q, \Sigma, \{U_\sigma \mid \sigma \in \Sigma\}, |v_0\rangle, P)$, where $Q = \{q_1, \ldots, q_n\}$, $U_\sigma \in \mathbb{C}_{|Q| \times |Q|}$ is the unitary transition matrix for the symbol $\sigma \in \Sigma$, $|v_0\rangle \in \{|q_1\rangle, \ldots, |q_n\rangle\}$ is the initial state, and $P = \{P_a, P_r\}$ is the measurement operator applied after reading the whole input. An input is accepted if the outcome "a" of P is observed. For any given input $w \in \Sigma^*$, the computation of $\mathcal{M}$ can be traced by a $|Q|$-dimensional quantum state:

$$|v_i\rangle = U_{w_i}|v_{i-1}\rangle,$$

where $1 \leq i \leq |w|$. The accepting probability of $\mathcal{M}$ on w is

$$f_\mathcal{M}(w) = \langle \tilde{v}_a | \tilde{v}_a \rangle, \text{ where } |\tilde{v}_a\rangle = P_a |v_{|w|}\rangle.$$

MCQFAs can also be defined with the end-markers to perform pre- and post-processing of the input. Then the initial state can be an arbitrary quantum state $U_\mathcal{¢}|v_0\rangle$ for a unitary operator $U_¢$, and the measurement turns out to be a general one with two outcomes, $\{P_a U_\$, P_r U_\$\}$, for a unitary $U_\$$.

The language recognized by a GFA/PFA/QFA $\mathcal{M}$ with *cutpoint* λ is defined by

$$L(\mathcal{M}, \lambda) = \{w \in \Sigma^* \mid f_\mathcal{M}(w) > \lambda\},$$

where $\lambda \in \mathbb{R}$ for GFAs and $\lambda \in [0, 1)$ for PFAs and QFAs. Any such language recognized by an n-state GFA [PFA, QFA] is called (n-state) pseudo stochastic [resp., stochastic, quantum automaton] language. The class names are given in Table 1. For class C, one can define a new class using up to three parameters in brackets C[¢n\$], where ¢ (\$) means the automaton reads the left (resp., the right) end-marker and n means that the class is defined by the automata with $\leq n$ states.

Table 1. The models and their class names

model	general alphabet	unary alphabet
GFA	PseudoS	UnaryPseudoS
PFA	S	UnaryS
QFA	QAL	UnaryQAL
MCQFA	MCL	UnaryMCL

3   Cardinality of Classes of Unary Languages

GFAs, PFAs, and QFAs define the same class [Tur69, YS09, YS11]:

$$\text{S} = \text{PseudoS} = \text{QAL} \quad \text{and} \quad \text{UnaryS} = \text{UnaryPseudoS} = \text{UnaryQAL}. \tag{3.1}$$

In other words, any pseudo stochastic or any quantum language is a stochastic language. Note that using end-markers does not change the classes. On the other hand, MCL[¢$] $\subsetneq$ S and UnaryMCL[¢$] $\subsetneq$ UnaryS because MCQFA's cannot recognize non-empty finite languages [BC01].

In [Rab63], Rabin proved that the cardinality of S[2] (and then of S) is uncountable for any non-unary alphabet. To the best of our knowledge, such a cardinality problem for unary languages has been open up to now. In this section, we solve this problem and provide state bounds for all considered models of automata. We use rotations of the unit circle as transition matrices. Let $\theta \in [0, 2\pi)$; the *rotation automaton* $\mathcal{R}_\theta$ is the 2-state GFA on the alphabet $\Sigma = \{a\}$ with the initial vector $\left(\begin{smallmatrix} 1 \\ 0 \end{smallmatrix}\right)$, the transition matrix $R_\theta = \left(\begin{smallmatrix} \cos\theta & -\sin\theta \\ \sin\theta & \cos\theta \end{smallmatrix}\right)$ of the operator of the counter-clockwise rotation of the plane by the angle θ, and the final vector $(1\ 0)$. The accepting value of $\mathcal{R}_\theta$ on the input a^k ($k \geq 0$) is then equal to $\cos(k\theta)$. Let α be an irrational number. Note the following simple fact.

Fact 1. *The set* $\{\cos(k\alpha\pi) \mid k \in \mathbb{N} \cup \{0\}\}$ *is dense in* $[-1, 1]$.

By Fact 1, for any given $\lambda_1 < \lambda_2 \in (-1, 1)$ there is an integer $k > 0$ such that $\lambda_1 < \cos(k\alpha\pi) < \lambda_2$. Hence $a^k \in L(\mathcal{R}_{\alpha\pi}, \lambda_1) \backslash L(\mathcal{R}_{\alpha\pi}, \lambda_2)$ and

$$L(\mathcal{R}_{\alpha\pi}, \lambda_2) \subsetneq L(\mathcal{R}_{\alpha\pi}, \lambda_1)$$

Thus, any $\lambda \in (-1, 1)$ produces a different language $L(\mathcal{R}_{\alpha\pi}, \lambda)$. We have proved

Theorem 1. *The cardinality of* UnaryPseudoS[2] *is uncountable.*

Remark 1. Since the sequence $\{\cos(k\alpha\pi)\}_{k=0}^\infty$ is aperiodic for irrational α, the language $L(\mathcal{R}_{\alpha\pi}, \lambda)$ is nonregular for any $\lambda \in (-1, 1)$.

By (3.1), UnaryS and UnaryQAL also have uncountable cardinality. Moreover, the automaton $\mathcal{R}_\theta$ is also a MCQFA with the accepting probability $\cos^2(k\theta)$ on the input a^k. So, for any given $\lambda_1 < \lambda_2 \in [0, 1)$, there is some $k > 0$ such that $\lambda_1^2 < \cos^2(k\theta) < \lambda_2^2$. Repeating the rest of the proof of Theorem 1, we get

Theorem 2. *The cardinality of* UnaryMCL[2] *(and hence of* UnaryMCL *and of* UnaryQAL[2]*) is uncountable.*

The classes S and QAL remain the same when the cutpoint is fixed to a value between 0 and 1. But with cutpoint 0, PFAs recognize only regular languages [Paz71] and QFAs recognize "exclusive" stochastic languages but not all stochastic languages [YS10]. Note that unary "exclusive" stochastic languages are regular [SS78].

It was an open question whether with cutpoint 0 MCQFAs recognize a proper subset of MCL [YS10]. Now we answer this question in the affirmative. All unary languages recognized by MCQFAs with cutpoint 0 are regular as mentioned above, while UnaryMCL contains uncountably many unary nonregular languages.

We continue with unary PFAs with few states. Contrary to GFAs and QFAs, 2-state unary PFAs recognize only regular languages [Paz71, Exercise 15, P. 170].

Another deep distinction of PFAs is the following. A single unary GFA or QFA can define uncountably many languages by selecting different cutpoints. On the other hand, a unary n-state PFA can define at most n nonregular languages, and hence, countably many languages at all [Paz71, Exercise 11, P. 170]. Thus, in order to prove that the cardinality of UnaryS$[n]$ is uncountable for some n, we need a different argument.

Unary PFAs with three states recognize some nonregular languages [Paz71]. But it is still unknown whether the cardinality of UnaryS$[3]$ (or UnaryS$[¢3\$]$) is countable or not. Using a result by Turakainen [Tur75, Theorem 1(i)], we show that the cardinality of UnaryS$[4]$ is uncountable. Adopting Turakainen's proof for unary automata, we get

Fact 2. *For any n-state unary GFA $\mathcal{G} = (Q, \{a\}, A, (1,0,\ldots,0)^t, (1,0,\ldots,0))$, there exists an $(n+2)$-state unary PFA $\mathcal{P}$ such that $f_{\mathcal{P}}(\varepsilon) = 1$ and*

$$f_{\mathcal{P}}(w) = \frac{f_{\mathcal{G}}(w)}{b^{|w|}} + \frac{1}{n+2} \tag{3.2}$$

for some positive constant b and any word $w \in \Sigma^+$.

Let $\mathcal{G}$ and $\mathcal{P}$ be the automata given in Fact 2. By (3.2) we have $f_{\mathcal{G}}(w) > 0$ if and only if $f_{\mathcal{P}}(w) > \frac{1}{n+2}$ for any $w \in \Sigma^+$. Since $f_{\mathcal{G}}(\varepsilon) = 1 > 0$ and $f_{\mathcal{P}}(\varepsilon) = 1 > \frac{1}{n+2}$, we obtain $L(\mathcal{G}, 0) = L(\mathcal{P}, \frac{1}{n+2})$.

Now we fix the cutpoint to 0 and present an uncountable family of languages recognized by 2-state GFAs. For any $\theta \in (0, \pi)$, we can build the rotation automaton $\mathcal{R}_\theta$ as described before. It is straightforward that $a^k \in L(\mathcal{R}_\theta, 0)$ if and only if the corresponding state vector ends in the right hemisphere of the unit circle, i.e., if $\cos(k\theta) > 0$. Let θ_1 and θ_2 be two irrational multiples of π such that $0 < \theta_1 < \theta_2 = \theta_1 + \Delta < \pi$. Consider the rotational automata $\mathcal{R}_{\theta_1}$ and $\mathcal{R}_{\theta_2}$.

Let $m < \frac{\min(\theta_1, \Delta)}{2}$ be a positive number. Suppose that $\Delta = \theta_2 - \theta_1$ is an irrational multiple of π. Then, there is an integer $k > 1$ such that

$$k\Delta \bmod 2\pi \in [\pi - m, \pi + m].$$

Denote the state vectors of $\mathcal{R}_{\theta_1}$ and $\mathcal{R}_{\theta_2}$ after reading a^k by v_k^1 and v_k^2, respectively. The minimum angle between these vectors is at least $\pi - m$. If exactly one of these vectors lies in the right hemisphere of the unit circle, then a^k separates the languages $L(\mathcal{R}_{\theta_1}, 0)$ and $L(\mathcal{R}_{\theta_2}, 0)$. (One of the accepting probabilities is positive and the other is negative and so the languages are different.)

If both v_k^1 and v_k^2 lie in the right hemisphere, then we have one of the pictures drawn in Fig. 1. (The case of two vectors in the left hemisphere is symmetric.) Note that in both pictures $\beta_1 + \beta_2 \leq m$. In the left picture, v_{k-1}^2 must be in the left hemisphere since $m \leq \theta_2 \leq \pi$. On the other hand, v_{k-1}^1 must be in the right hemisphere since $\theta_1 \leq \pi - 2m$. So, a^{k-1} separates $L(\mathcal{R}_{\theta_1}, 0)$ and $L(\mathcal{R}_{\theta_2}, 0)$. In a similar way, the situation in the right picture provides us with the separator string a^{k+1}: we rotate both vectors counterclockwise, and the vector v_k^1 stays in the right hemisphere while v_k^2 moves to the left one.

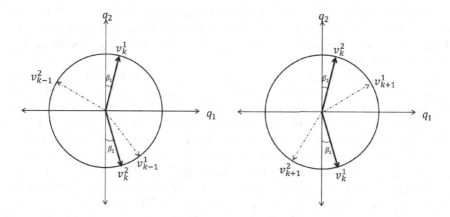

Fig. 1. State vectors in the same hemisphere: two possibilities

Since any language $L(\mathcal{R}_\theta, 0)$ satisfies the condition $fv_0 = 1$, from Fact 2 we know that $L(\mathcal{R}_\theta, 0)$ can be recognized by some 4-state unary PFA $\mathcal{P}_\theta$ with cutpoint $\frac{1}{4}$.

Lemma 1. *There is an uncountable set I of irrational numbers between 0 and 1 such that all their pairwise differences are irrational, i.e., for any $\alpha_1 \neq \alpha_2 \in I$, $\alpha_1 - \alpha_2 \notin \mathbb{Q}$.*

Proof. Let ρ be a binary relation on $(0, 1)$ such that $(\alpha_1, \alpha_2) \in \rho$ means $\alpha_1 - \alpha_2$ is rational. Then ρ is an equivalence relation, and each class of the corresponding partition is countable. Hence, the number of classes is uncountable. Taking one representative from each class, one gets the required set.   □

Let I be the set described in Lemma 1. Then the cardinality of the set

$$\{L(\mathcal{R}_{\alpha\pi}, 0) \mid \alpha \in I\} = \{L(\mathcal{P}_{\alpha\pi}, \tfrac{1}{4}) \mid \alpha \in I\}$$

is uncountable. So we have proved

Theorem 3. *The cardinality of* UnaryS[4] *is uncountable.*

4   One-State Pseudo Stochastic Languages

In the previous section, we have shown that 2-state GFAs and QFAs can define uncountably many languages. So, it can be interesting to consider the case of 1-state automata. But the languages defined by 1-state QFAs (and so PFAs) are trivial. Indeed, the transition matrix of a 1-state QFA is $(e^{i\theta})$ for some real number θ and then all words have the same accepting probability. On the other hand, 1-state GFAs recognize many nontrivial languages. For example, the GFA $(\{q\}, \{a, b\}, \{A_a = (\frac{1}{2}), A_b = (2)\}, v_0 = 1, f = 1)$ recognizes the language of all words containing more b's than a's with cutpoint 1.

In this section, we completely describe the languages contained in PseudoS[1] and relate them to regular and context-free languages. As a corollary, we get a characterization of UnaryPseudoS[1]. For convenience, we write PseudoS[1, Σ] if the alphabet Σ is fixed.

Suppose $\Sigma = \{a_1, \ldots, a_n\}$, $w \in \Sigma^*$, and $|w|_{a_i}$ denotes the number of occurrences of the letter a_i in w. The vector $\pi(w) = (|w|_{a_1}, \ldots, |w|_{a_n})$ is called the *Parikh vector* of w. For a language L, $\pi(L) = \{\pi(w) \mid w \in L\}$ is the *Parikh set* of L. A language L is *Parikh closed* if $\pi^{-1}(\pi(L)) = L$. In other words, a Parikh closed language contains a word w if and only if it contains all anagrams of w.

Let us introduce three types of Parikh closed languages. For arbitrary $\alpha \in \mathbb{R} \cup \{+\infty\}$, $b_1, \ldots, b_n \in \mathbb{R}$, the *solution language* $\mathsf{Sol}(\Sigma, b_1, \ldots, b_n, \alpha)$ is the language whose Parikh set coincides with the set of all nonnegative integer solutions to the linear inequality $(\boldsymbol{b}, \boldsymbol{x}) = b_1 x_1 + \cdots + b_n x_n < \alpha$. The numbers $b_1, \ldots, b_n$ are *coefficients* of the language. For a given $Y \subseteq \Sigma$, the *parity language* $\mathsf{Par}(\Sigma, Y, 0)$ [resp., $\mathsf{Par}(\Sigma, Y, 1)$] consists of all words from Σ^* having even [resp., odd] number of occurrences of letters from Y. Finally, the *indicator language* $\mathsf{Ind}(\Sigma, Y)$ consists of all words containing at least one letter from Y. In particular, one has $\mathsf{Par}(\Sigma, \varnothing, 0) = \Sigma^*$, $\mathsf{Par}(\Sigma, \varnothing, 1) = \mathsf{Ind}(\Sigma, \varnothing) = \varnothing$. It is easy to see that all parity languages and indicator languages are regular. On the other hand, most of the solution languages are not regular. For example, the inequality $x_1 - x_2 < 0$ generates the above mentioned binary language $\{w \in \{a, b\}^* \mid |w|_a < |w|_b\}$.

Theorem 4. *For a fixed finite alphabet Σ, let $\boldsymbol{\Lambda}$ be the set of all languages of the form*

$$\mathsf{Sol}(X, b_1, \ldots, b_{|X|}, \alpha) \cap \mathsf{Par}(X, Y, i), \tag{4.1}$$

where $Y \subseteq X \subseteq \Sigma$, $i \in \{0, 1\}$. Further, let $\boldsymbol{V}$ be set of all languages of the form

$$\mathsf{Sol}(X, b_1, \ldots, b_{|X|}, \alpha) \cup \mathsf{Par}(X, Y, i) \cup \mathsf{Ind}(\Sigma, \Sigma \backslash X), \tag{4.2}$$

where $Y \subseteq X \subseteq \Sigma$, $i \in \{0, 1\}$, and $\alpha \neq +\infty$. Then

$$\mathsf{PseudoS}[1, \boldsymbol{\Sigma}] = \boldsymbol{\Lambda} \cup \boldsymbol{V}. \tag{4.3}$$

Proof. The 1×1 matrices are just real numbers, so we replace "transition matrices" with "transition numbers" in our terminology. The multiplication of transition numbers is commutative, and this fact has two consequences. First, any $L \in \mathsf{PseudoS}[1]$ is Parikh closed. Second, the individual values of v_0, f, and λ do not matter; namely, one can put $\lambda' = \frac{\lambda}{f v_0}$ and consider two possible acceptance conditions[1]:

$$A_{a_1}^{|w|_{a_1}} A_{a_2}^{|w|_{a_2}} \cdots A_{a_n}^{|w|_{a_n}} < \lambda' \text{ and } A_{a_1}^{|w|_{a_1}} A_{a_2}^{|w|_{a_2}} \cdots A_{a_n}^{|w|_{a_n}} > \lambda'. \tag{4.4}$$

So, below we assume that a 1-state GFA over an n-letter alphabet Σ is given by an n-tuple $\boldsymbol{A} = (A_1 = A_{a_1}, \ldots, A_n = A_{a_n})$ of real numbers. The cutpoint $\lambda = \lambda'$ and an additional bit to choose among the conditions (4.4) are given separately.

---

[1] A GFA with $v_0 = 0$ or $f = 0$ recognizes either $\varnothing$ or Σ^*. The same effect can be achieved by setting all transition numbers to 0. Hence we assume without loss of generality $v_0, f \neq 0$.

We say that a 1-state GFA $\mathcal{G}$ is *positive* if all numbers A_i and λ are positive. If $\pi(w) = (x_1, \ldots, x_n)$, then the acceptance condition

$$A_1^{x_1} \cdots A_n^{x_n} < (>)\lambda \tag{4.5}$$

for a positive GFA can be rewritten as

$$x_1 \log A_1 + \cdots + x_n \log A_n < (>) \log \lambda, \tag{4.6}$$

where the logarithms are taken at any base greater than 1. But this linear inequality defines either the language $\mathsf{Sol}(\Sigma, \log A_1, \ldots, \log A_n, \log \lambda)$ (for the "<" sign in (4.6)) or the language $\mathsf{Sol}(\Sigma, -\log A_1, \ldots, -\log A_n, -\log \lambda)$ (for the ">" sign)[2].

Now we proceed with the general case. We assume the "<" sign in (4.5); the case of the ">" sign admits a completely similar proof, so we omit it. For convenience, we reorder the alphabet such that the numbers $A_1, \ldots, A_k$ are nonzero, while the other transition numbers, if any, are zero. We also put $X = \{a_1, \ldots, a_k\}$ and denote by the set of letters with negative transition numbers by Y. There are two possibilities. If $\lambda \leq 0$, the inequality (4.5) for the Parikh vector $(x_1, \ldots, x_n)$ of a word w is equivalent to the conjunction of the following conditions:

- w contains no letters from outside X;
- the number of letters from Y in w is odd;
- $|A_1|^{x_1} \cdots |A_k|^{x_k} > |\lambda|$.

The first two conditions define the language $\mathsf{Par}(X, Y, 1)$, and the first and the third conditions define $\mathsf{Sol}(X, -\log|A_1|, \ldots, -\log|A_k|, -\log|\lambda|)$ (assuming $\log 0 = -\infty$). Thus, we get a language from $\boldsymbol{\Lambda}$.

The second possibility is $\lambda > 0$. Here (4.5) is equivalent to the disjunction of the conditions

- w contains a letter from outside X;
- the number of letters from Y in w is odd;
- $|A_1|^{x_1} \cdots |A_k|^{x_k} < \lambda$.

Similar to the above, these conditions define a language in $\mathbf{V}$ (note that α is finite because $\lambda > 0$). Hence we obtain $\mathsf{PseudoS}[1, \Sigma] \subseteq \boldsymbol{\Lambda} \cup \mathbf{V}$.

In order to show the reverse inclusion, we use the above considerations to build 1-state GFAs with appropriate acceptance conditions from the elements of $\boldsymbol{\Lambda} \cup \mathbf{V}$. Let us first take a language $\mathsf{Sol}(X, b_1, \ldots, b_k, \alpha) \cap \mathsf{Par}(X, Y, i)$ (as above, we assume $X = \{a_1, \ldots, a_k\}$). We put

$$A_j = \begin{cases} 0, & \text{if } j > k, \\ 2^{b_j}, & \text{if } a_j \in X \backslash Y, \\ -2^{b_j}, & \text{if } a_j \in Y. \end{cases} \tag{4.7}$$

---

[2] From the geometric point of view, a 1-state positive GFA defines a hyperplane in $\mathbb{R}^n$ and accepts exactly the words having the ends of their Parikh vectors on the prescribed side of this hyperplane.

If $i = 1$, then we use the acceptance condition "$<-2^{-\alpha}$". For $i = 0$, the condition is "$>2^{-\alpha}$". In the case of a language $\mathsf{Sol}(X, b_1, \ldots, b_k, \alpha) \cup \mathsf{Par}(X, Y, i) \cup \mathsf{Ind}(\Sigma, \Sigma\backslash X)$ we also use (4.7) to define a GFA, but the acceptance conditions are different: "$>2^{\alpha}$" for $i = 1$ and "$<-2^{\alpha}$" for $i = 0$. Thus we have $\mathsf{PseudoS}[1, \Sigma] \supseteq \mathbf{\Lambda} \cup \mathbf{V}$. The theorem is proved. $\qquad\square$

Corollary 1. *All languages in* $\mathsf{UnaryPseudoS}[1]$ *are regular. Moreover, the class* $\mathsf{UnaryPseudoS}[1]$ *consists of* $\varnothing$, a^*, $E = \{a^n \mid n \text{ is even}\}$, $\bar{E} = a^*\backslash E$, *and all languages of the forms*

$$S_i = \{a^n \mid n \leq i\}, \ \bar{S}_i = a^*\backslash S_i, \ (S_i \text{ or } \bar{S}_i) \cup (E \text{ or } \bar{E}), \ (S_i \text{ or } \bar{S}_i) \cap (E \text{ or } \bar{E}).$$

Proof. The possible cases are $X = \varnothing$, $X = Y = \{a\}$, and $(X = \{a\} \wedge Y = \varnothing)$. The required list of languages can be obtained directly from (4.1)–(4.3). $\qquad\square$

Corollary 2. *The cardinality of* $\mathsf{PseudoS}[1, \{a, b\}]$ *is uncountable.*

Proof. On a plane, there are uncountably many pairwise non-parallel lines, and each of them defines a different binary solution language. $\qquad\square$

Now we are going to relate the 1-state pseudo stochastic languages to the classes of the Chomsky hierarchy. We need some additional notions. Real numbers $b_1, \ldots, b_n$ are called *rationally equivalent* if there exist $\gamma \in \mathbb{R}$, $q_1, \ldots, q_n \in \mathbb{Q}$ such that $b_i = q_i\gamma$ for all i. Let $L = \mathsf{Sol}(\Sigma, b_1, \ldots, b_n, \alpha)$, $N \subseteq \Sigma$ be the set of letters corresponding to zero coefficients b_i. By *decimation* $\mathsf{dec}(L)$ of L we mean the language over $\Sigma\backslash N$ obtained from L by deleting all letters of N from all words (if $N = \varnothing$, then $\mathsf{dec}(L) = L$). The following lemma is crucial.

Lemma 2. *1) A solution language is regular if and only if all its nonzero coefficients have the same sign.*
2) A nonregular solution language is context-free if and only if its coefficients are rationally equivalent.

Proof. First we note that the decimation of a solution language is a solution language defined by the same linear inequality in a vector space of a smaller dimension.

Next, a solution language L is regular if and only if $\mathsf{dec}(L)$ is regular. Indeed, if L is regular, one can take its recognizing DFA and replace all labels from N by ε, getting a ε-NFA recognizing $\mathsf{dec}(L)$. For the converse, note that

$$L = \bigcup_{w = c_1 \cdots c_k \in \mathsf{dec}(L)} N^* c_1 N^* c_2 \cdots N^* c_k N^*.$$

So, one can take a DFA recognizing $\mathsf{dec}(L)$ and add loops labeled by all letters from N to each its state. The resulting automaton will recognize L.

Let D be the decimation of some solution language. The Parikh vectors of its words satisfy an inequality $b_1 x_1 + \cdots + b_k x_k < \alpha$, where all coefficients b_i are nonzero. If all these coefficients are positive [resp. negative], then D is finite [resp., cofinite]. As was proved above, in this case any solution language with the decimation D is regular. Now assume that some coefficients have different signs; without loss of generality, $b_1 > 0 > b_2$. Let the letters a_1 and a_2 correspond to b_1 and b_2, respectively. If D is regular, then it is recognized by a DFA $\mathcal{A}$ with, say, t states. This DFA accepts all words from D including all words $a_1^{x_1} a_2^{x_2}$ such that $b_1 x_1 + b_2 x_2 < \alpha$. Such words exist for any x_1, in particular, for $x_1 > t$. Then $\mathcal{A}$ has a cycle labelled by some a_1^i, $i \le t$. Iterating this cycle appropriate numbers of times, we will get a word of the form $a_1^{x_1 + ri} a_2^{x_2}$ which is recognized by $\mathcal{A}$ but does not belong to D. Thus, D is not regular, and we finished the proof of statement 1.

Now we turn to the proof of statement 2. Take a solution language L with the decimation $D = \mathsf{Sol}(\Sigma, b_1, \ldots, b_k, \alpha)$. Since L is not regular, we know from above that some b_i's have different signs; without loss of generality, $b_1 > 0 > b_2$.

Both L and D are determined by the inequality $b_1 x_1 + \cdots + b_k x_k < \alpha$. If the coefficients are rationally equivalent, we transform this inequality, dividing both sides by the common irrational factor of all coefficients and than multiplying both sides by the least common multiple of denominators of the obtained rational coefficients. As a result, we get a linear inequality

$$\hat{b}_1 x_1 + \cdots + \hat{b}_k x_k < \hat{\alpha}$$

with integer coefficients and the same set of solutions. Finally, we replace $\hat{\alpha}$ by $\lceil \hat{\alpha} \rceil$ preserving the set of *integer* solutions of the inequality. To check whether the Parikh vector of a word satisfies the resulting diophantine inequality, one can implement a counter in the stack of a pushdown automaton. Hence, the solution languages with rationally equivalent coefficients are context-free.

Now consider a solution language L having rationally non-equivalent coefficients. If any positive coefficient is equivalent to any negative one, then all coefficients are equivalent; so, L has a pair of rationally non-equivalent coefficients of different signs, say, b_1 and b_2. Then the value of the expression $b_1 x_1 + b_2 x_2$ for the word $a_1^{x_1} a_2^{x_2} \in L$ can be arbitrarily close from below to α. Thus, $(\boldsymbol{b}, \pi(w))$ for $w \in L$ can be arbitrarily close from below to α (and the supremum cannot be reached by the definition of solution language). Let us show that this is impossible for context-free languages. Aiming at a comtradiction, assume that L is context-free. By Parikh's Theorem [Par66] there exists a regular language L' such that $\pi(L') = \pi(L)$. Since L is infinite, $\pi(L)$ and L' are infinite as well. Consider the minimal DFA $\mathcal{A}$ with partial transition function, recognizing L'. This DFA must contain cycles; let z be the label of some cyclic walk in the graph of $\mathcal{A}$. Then for some $u, v \in \Sigma^*$ the language L' contains the words $uz^t v$ for all nonnegative integers t. Hence we have

$$(\boldsymbol{b}, \pi(uz^t v)) = (\boldsymbol{b}, \pi(uv)) + t(\boldsymbol{b}, \pi(z)) < \alpha,$$

implying $(\boldsymbol{b}, \pi(z)) \le 0$. Since this inequality holds for the label of any cyclic walk, the function $(\boldsymbol{b}, \pi(w))$ reaches its maximum for $w \in L'$ on some short word w. Thus, the maximum of $(\boldsymbol{b}, \pi(w))$ for $w \in L$ is also reachable, a contradiction. Hence, L is not context-free. $\qquad\square$

Now we are able to relate PseudoS[1] to the classes of the Chomsky hierarchy.

Theorem 5. *1) A 1-state pseudo stochastic language is regular if and only if the logarithms of absolute values of all nonzero transition numbers of the generating 1-state GFA have the same sign.*
2) A nonregular 1-state pseudo stochastic language is context-free if and only if the logarithms of absolute values of all nonzero transition numbers of the generating 1-state GFA are rationally equivalent.

Remark 2. It is easy to check that the properties "to have the same sign" and "to be rationally equivalent" for logarithms are independent of the base of the logarithm.

Proof. By (4.3), a language $L \in$ PseudoS[1] is given either by (4.1) or by (4.2). In both cases, L is regular [context-free] if and only if the corresponding solution language is regular [resp., context-free]. As was shown in the proof of Theorem 4, the coefficients of this solution language are logarithms of absolute values of the transition numbers of the GFA recognizing L. The result now follows from Lemma 2. □

Remark 3. The proof of Lemma 2 shows, in fact, that solution languages can be recognized by deterministic pushdown automata. Hence, if a 1-state pseudo stochastic language is context-free, it is deterministic context-free.

5   Concluding Remarks

In this paper, we show that 2-state GFAs, 2-state QFAs (even restricted ones), and 4-state PFAs define uncountably many unary languages. In addition, we completely characterize the class of languages recognized by 1-state GFAs.

Our results were stated for languages without end-markers; however, the only case where end-markers can, in principle, improve the result, in the case of 3-state unary PFAs. Nevertheless, it is interesting to study the general problem whether C[n] and C[¢k$] are incomparable for some $k < n$, where C is one of the (probabilistic or quantum) classes from Table 1. Another related problem is whether the inclusion C[n] ⊆ C[n+1] is always strict.

As aforementioned before, QFAs with cutpoint 0 define exclusive stochastic languages, a superset of regular languages, and it is still open whether the cardinality of this class is uncountable or not [YS10].

Acknowledgements. We are grateful to anonymous referees for their constructive comments.

References

[BC01]   Bertoni, A., Carpentieri, M.: Analogies and differences between quantum and stochastic automata. Theoretical Computer Science 262(1-2), 69–81 (2001)
[Hir10]   Hirvensalo, M.: Quantum automata with open time evolution. International Journal of Natural Computing 1(1), 70–85 (2010)

[MC00]   Moore, C., Crutchfield, J.P.: Quantum automata and quantum grammars. Theoretical Computer Science 237(1-2), 275–306 (2000)

[Par66]   Parikh, R.J.: On context-free languages. Journal of the ACM 13(4), 570–581 (1966)

[Paz71]   Paz, A.: Introduction to Probabilistic Automata. Academic Press, New York (1971)

[Rab63]   Rabin, M.O.: Probabilistic automata. Information and Control 6, 230–243 (1963)

[SS78]   Salomaa, A., Soittola, M.: Automata-Theoretic Aspects of Formal Power Series. Texts and monographs in computer science. Springer, New York (1978)

[SY14]   Shur, A.M., Yakaryılmaz, A.: Quantum, stochastic, and pseudo stochastic languages with few states. Technical Report arXiv:1405.0055 (2014)

[Tur69]   Turakainen, P.: Generalized automata and stochastic languages. Proceedings of the American Mathematical Society 21, 303–309 (1969)

[Tur75]   Turakainen, P.: Word-functions of stochastic and pseudo stochastic automata. Annales Academiae Scientiarum Fennicae, Series A. I, Mathematica 1, 27–37 (1975)

[YS09]   Yakaryilmaz, A., Say, A.C.C.: Languages recognized with unbounded error by quantum finite automata. In: Frid, A., Morozov, A., Rybalchenko, A., Wagner, K.W. (eds.) CSR 2009. LNCS, vol. 5675, pp. 356–367. Springer, Heidelberg (2009)

[YS10]   Yakaryılmaz, A., Say, A.C.C.: Languages recognized by nondeterministic quantum finite automata. Quantum Information and Computation 10(9&10), 747–770 (2010)

[YS11]   Yakaryılmaz, A., Say, A.C.C.: Unbounded-error quantum computation with small space bounds. Information and Computation 279(6), 873–892 (2011)

Phase Transition and Strong Predictability

Kohtaro Tadaki

Research and Development Initiative, Chuo University
1–13–27 Kasuga, Bunkyo-ku, Tokyo 112-8551, Japan
tadaki@kc.chuo-u.ac.jp
http://www2.odn.ne.jp/tadaki/

Abstract. The statistical mechanical interpretation of algorithmic information theory (AIT, for short) was introduced and developed in our former work [K. Tadaki, Local Proceedings of CiE 2008, pp.425–434, 2008], where we introduced the notion of thermodynamic quantities into AIT. These quantities are real functions of temperature $T > 0$. The values of all the thermodynamic quantities diverge when T exceeds 1. This phenomenon corresponds to phase transition in statistical mechanics. In this paper we introduce the notion of strong predictability for an infinite binary sequence and then apply it to the partition function $Z(T)$, which is one of the thermodynamic quantities in AIT. We then reveal a new computational aspect of the phase transition in AIT by showing the critical difference of the behavior of $Z(T)$ between $T = 1$ and $T < 1$ in terms of the strong predictability for the base-two expansion of $Z(T)$.

Keywords: Algotithmic information theory, statistical mechanics, temperature, phase transition, predictability, partition function.

1 Introduction

Algorithmic information theory (AIT, for short) is a framework for applying information-theoretic and probabilistic ideas to computability theory. One of the primary concepts of AIT is the *program-size complexity* (or *Kolmogorov complexity*) $H(x)$ of a finite binary string x, which is defined as the length of the shortest binary program for a universal decoding algorithm U, called an *optimal prefix-free machine*, to output x. By the definition, $H(x)$ is thought to represent the amount of randomness contained in a finite binary string x. In particular, the notion of program-size complexity plays a crucial role in characterizing the *randomness* of an infinite binary sequence, or equivalently, a real. In [3] Chaitin introduced the Ω number as a concrete example of random real. The first n bits of the base-two expansion of Ω solve the halting problem of U for inputs of length at most n. By this property, Ω is shown to be a random real, and plays a central role in the development of AIT.

In this paper, we study the *statistical mechanical interpretation* of AIT. In a series of works [14–19], we introduced and developed this particular subject of AIT. First, in [14] we introduced the *thermodynamic quantities* at temperature

O.H. Ibarra et al. (Eds.): UCNC 2014, LNCS 8553, pp. 340–352, 2014.
DOI: 10.1007/978-3-319-08123-6_28, © Springer International Publishing Switzerland 2014

T, such as partition function $Z(T)$, free energy $F(T)$, energy $E(T)$, statistical mechanical entropy $S(T)$, and specific heat $C(T)$, into AIT. These quantities are real functions of a real argument $T > 0$, and are introduced in the following manner: Let X be a complete set of energy eigenstates of a quantum system and E_x the energy of an energy eigenstate x of the quantum system. In [14] we introduced thermodynamic quantities into AIT by performing Replacements 1 below for the corresponding thermodynamic quantities in statistical mechanics.

Replacements 1

(i) *Replace the complete set X of energy eigenstates x by the set* $\operatorname{dom} U$ *of all programs p for U.*

(ii) *Replace the energy E_x of an energy eigenstate x by the length $|p|$ of a program p.*

(iii) *Set the Boltzmann Constant k_B to $1/\ln 2$.*   □

For example, in statistical mechanics, the partition function $Z_{sm}(T)$ at temperature T is given by

$$Z_{sm}(T) = \sum_{x \in X} e^{-\frac{E_x}{k_B T}}.$$

Thus, based on Replacements 1, the partition function $Z(T)$ in AIT is defined as

$$Z(T) = \sum_{p \in \operatorname{dom} U} 2^{-\frac{|p|}{T}}. \tag{1}$$

In general, the thermodynamic quantities in AIT are variants of Chaitin Ω number. In fact, in the case of $T = 1$, $Z(1)$ is precisely Chaitin Ω number.[1]

In [14] we then proved that if the temperature T is a computable real with $0 < T < 1$ then, for each of the thermodynamic quantities $Z(T)$, $F(T)$, $E(T)$, $S(T)$, and $C(T)$ in AIT, the partial randomness of its value equals to T, where the notion of *partial randomness* is a stronger representation of the compression rate by means of program-size complexity. Thus, the temperature T plays a role as the partial randomness (and therefore the compression rate) of all the thermodynamic quantities in the statistical mechanical interpretation of AIT. In [14] we further showed that the temperature T plays a role as the partial randomness of the temperature T itself, which is a thermodynamic quantity of itself in thermodynamics or statistical mechanics. Namely, we proved the *fixed point theorem on partial randomness*,[2] which states that, for every $T \in (0, 1)$, if the value of partition function $Z(T)$ at temperature T is a computable real, then the partial randomness of T equals to T, and therefore the compression rate of T equals to T, i.e.,

$$\lim_{n \to \infty} \frac{H(T{\restriction}n)}{n} = T,$$

where $T{\restriction}n$ is the first n bits of the base-two expansion of the real T.

---

[1] To be precise, the partition function is not a thermodynamic quantity but a statistical mechanical quantity.

[2] The fixed point theorem on partial randomness is called a fixed point theorem on compression rate in [14].

In our second work [15] on the statistical mechanical interpretation of AIT, we showed that a fixed point theorem of the same form as for $Z(T)$ holds also for each of $F(T)$, $E(T)$, and $S(T)$. In the third work [16], we further unlocked the properties of the fixed points on partial randomness by introducing the notion of composition of prefix-free machines into AIT, which corresponds to the notion of composition of systems in normal statistical mechanics. In the work [17] we developed a total statistical mechanical interpretation of AIT which attains a perfect correspondence to normal statistical mechanics, by making an argument on the same level of mathematical strictness as normal statistical mechanics in physics. We did this by identifying a *microcanonical ensemble* in AIT. This identification clarifies the meaning of the thermodynamic quantities of AIT.

Our first work [14] showed that the values of all the thermodynamic quantities in AIT diverge when the temperature T exceeds 1. This phenomenon might be regarded as some sort of *phase transition* in statistical mechanics. In the work [19] we revealed a computational aspect of the phase transition in AIT. The notion of *weak truth-table reducibility* plays an important role in recursion theory [5, 9]. In the work [19] we introduced an elaboration of this notion, called *reducibility in query size f*. This elaboration enables us to deal with the notion of asymptotic behavior of computation in a manner like in computational complexity theory, while staying in computability theory. We applied the elaboration to the relation between $Z(T)$ and dom U, where the latter is the set of all halting inputs for the optimal prefix-free machine U, i.e., the *halting problem*. We then revealed the critical difference of the behavior of $Z(T)$ between $T = 1$ and $T < 1$ in relation to dom U. Namely, we revealed the phase transition between the *unidirectionality* at $T = 1$ and the *bidirectionality* at $T < 1$ in the reduction between $Z(T)$ and dom U. This critical phenomenon cannot be captured by the original notion of weak truth-table reducibility.

In this paper, we reveal another computational aspect of the phase transition in AIT between $T = 1$ and $T < 1$. We introduce the notion of *strong predictability* for an infinite binary sequence. Let $X = b_1 b_2 b_3 \ldots$ be an infinite binary sequence with each $b_i \in \{0, 1\}$. The strong predictability of X is the existence of the computational procedure which, given any prefix $b_1 \ldots b_n$ of X, can predict the next bit b_{n+1} in X with unfailing accuracy, where the suspension of an individual prediction for the next bit is allowed to make sure that the whole predictions are error-free. We introduce three types of strong predictability, *finite-state strong predictability*, *total strong predictability*, and *strong predictability*, which differ with respect to computational ability. We apply them to the base-two expansion of $Z(T)$. On the one hand, we show that the base-two expansion of $Z(T)$ is not strongly predictable at $T = 1$ in the sense of any of these three types of strong predictability. On the other hand, we show that it is strongly predictable in the sense of all of the three types in the case where T is computable real with $T < 1$. In this manner, we reveal a new aspect of the phase transition in AIT between $T = 1$ and $T < 1$.

Note that the notion of *pseudorandomness* plays an essential role in modern cryptography and computational complexity theory. One of the equivalent characterizations of pseudorandomness is the notion of *unpredictability in polynomial-time* (see Goldreich [7, Chapter 3] for these notions and their historical detail). As we explained above, our three types of notions of strong predictability are all applied to an infinite binary sequence. By contrast, the notion of unpredictability in polynomial-time is applied not to such a sequence but to an infinite sequence $\{V_n\}_{n\in\mathbb{N}}$ of random variables such that V_n is distributed over the set of finite binary strings of length $\ell(n)$ for every $n \in \mathbb{N}$, where ℓ is some fixed polynomial. Moreover, the notion of unpredictability in polynomial-time is defined using probabilistic polynomial-time Turing machines whose computations are allowed to make an error. On the other hand, our notions of strong predictability are defined based on exact computations by two extremes of computational models: The one extreme is a general deterministic Turing machine without restriction on its computational resource, and the other is a deterministic finite automaton. Thus, the notions of strong predictability which we investigate in this paper are not considered to have an explicit relationship to the notion of unpredictability in polynomial-time.

2   Preliminaries

We start with some notation and definitions which will be used in this paper. For any set S we denote by $\#S$ the cardinality of S. $\mathbb{N} = \{0, 1, 2, 3, \ldots\}$ is the set of natural numbers, and $\mathbb{N}^+$ is the set of positive integers. $\mathbb{Q}$ is the set of rationals, and $\mathbb{R}$ is the set of reals. $\{0, 1\}^* = \{\lambda, 0, 1, 00, 01, 10, 11, 000, \ldots\}$ is the set of finite binary strings, where λ denotes the *empty string*, and $\{0, 1\}^*$ is ordered as indicated. We identify any string in $\{0, 1\}^*$ with a natural number in this order. For any $x \in \{0, 1\}^*$, $|x|$ is the *length* of x. A subset S of $\{0, 1\}^*$ is called *prefix-free* if no string in S is a prefix of another string in S.

We denote by $\{0, 1\}^\infty$ the set of infinite binary sequences, where an infinite binary sequence is infinite to the right but finite to the left. Let $X \in \{0, 1\}^\infty$. For any $n \in \mathbb{N}^+$, we denote the nth bit of X by $X(n)$. For any $n \in \mathbb{N}$, we denote the first n bits of X by $X{\restriction}_n \in \{0, 1\}^*$. Namely, $X{\restriction}_0 = \lambda$, and $X{\restriction}_n = X(1)X(2)\ldots X(n)$ for every $n \in \mathbb{N}^+$.

For any real α, we denote by $\lfloor \alpha \rfloor$ the greatest integer less than or equal to α. When we mention a real α as an infinite binary sequence, we are considering the base-two expansion of the fractional part $\alpha - \lfloor \alpha \rfloor$ of the real α with infinitely many zeros. Thus, for any real α, $\alpha{\restriction}_n$ and $\alpha(n)$ denote $X{\restriction}_n$ and $X(n)$, respectively, where X is the unique infinite binary sequence such that $\alpha - \lfloor \alpha \rfloor = 0.X$ and X contains infinitely many zeros.

A function $f\colon \mathbb{N} \to \{0, 1\}^*$ or $f\colon \mathbb{N} \to \mathbb{Q}$ is called *computable* if there exists a deterministic Turing machine which on every input $n \in \mathbb{N}$ halts and outputs $f(n)$. A real α is called *computable* if there exists a computable function $f\colon \mathbb{N} \to \mathbb{Q}$ such that $|\alpha - f(n)| < 2^{-n}$ for all $n \in \mathbb{N}$. We say that $X \in \{0, 1\}^\infty$ is *computable* if the mapping $\mathbb{N} \ni n \mapsto X\!\restriction_n$ is a computable function, which is equivalent to that the real $0.X$ in base-two notation is computable.

Let S and T be any sets. We say that $f\colon S \to T$ is a *partial function* if f is a function whose domain is a subset of S and whose range is T. The domain of a partial function $f\colon S \to T$ is denoted by $\operatorname{dom} f$. A *partial computable function* $f\colon \{0,1\}^* \to \{0,1\}^*$ is a partial function $f\colon \{0,1\}^* \to \{0,1\}^*$ for which there exits a deterministic Turing machine M such that (i) on every input $x \in \{0,1\}^*$, M halts if and only of $x \in \operatorname{dom} f$, and (ii) on every input $x \in \operatorname{dom}$, M outputs $f(x)$. We write "c.e." instead of "computably enumerable."

2.1 Algorithmic Information Theory

In the following we concisely review some definitions and results of algorithmic information theory (AIT, for short) [3–5, 9]. A *prefix-free machine* is a partial computable function $M\colon \{0,1\}^* \to \{0,1\}^*$ such that $\operatorname{dom} M$ is prefix-free. For each prefix-free machine M and each $x \in \{0,1\}^*$, $H_M(x)$ is defined by $H_M(x) = \min\{\, |p| \mid p \in \{0,1\}^* \,\&\, M(p) = x \,\}$ (may be ∞). A prefix-free machine U is called *optimal* if for each prefix-free machine M there exists $d \in \mathbb{N}$ with the following property; if $p \in \operatorname{dom} M$, then there is $q \in \operatorname{dom} U$ for which $U(q) = M(p)$ and $|q| \le |p| + d$. It is then easy to see that there exists an optimal prefix-free machine. We choose a particular optimal prefix-free machine U as the standard one for use, and define $H(x)$ as $H_U(x)$, which is referred to as the *program-size complexity* of x or the *Kolmogorov complexity* of x [3, 6, 8].

Chaitin [3] introduced Ω number by

$$\Omega = \sum_{p \in \operatorname{dom} U} 2^{-|p|}.$$

Since $\operatorname{dom} U$ is prefix-free, Ω converges and $0 < \Omega \le 1$. For any $X \in \{0,1\}^\infty$, we say that X is *weakly Chaitin random* if there exists $c \in \mathbb{N}$ such that $n - c \le H(X\!\restriction_n)$ for all $n \in \mathbb{N}^+$ [3, 4]. Chaitin [3] showed that Ω is weakly Chaitin random. Therefore $0 < \Omega < 1$.

2.2 Partial Randomness

In the work [12], we generalized the notion of the randomness of a real so that the *partial randomness* of a real can be characterized by a real T with $0 \le T \le 1$ as follows.

Definition 1 (Tadaki [12]). *Let $T \in [0,1]$ and let $X \in \{0,1\}^\infty$. We say that X is* weakly Chaitin T-random *if there exists $c \in \mathbb{N}$ such that, for all $n \in \mathbb{N}^+$, $Tn - c \le H(X\!\restriction_n)$.* □

In the case of $T = 1$, the weak Chaitin T-randomness results in the weak Chaitin randomness.

Definition 2 (Tadaki [19]). *Let $T \in [0,1]$ and let $X \in \{0,1\}^\infty$. We say that X is strictly T-compressible if there exists $d \in \mathbb{N}$ such that, for all $n \in \mathbb{N}^+$, $H(X\lceil_n) \leq Tn + d$. We say that X is strictly Chaitin T-random if X is both weakly Chaitin T-random and strictly T-compressible.* □

In the work [12], we generalized Chaitin Ω number to $Z(T)$ as follows. For each real $T > 0$, the *partition function* $Z(T)$ at temperature T is defined by the equation (1). Thus, $Z(1) = \Omega$. If $0 < T \leq 1$, then $Z(T)$ converges and $0 < Z(T) < 1$, since $Z(T) \leq \Omega < 1$. The following theorem holds for $Z(T)$.

Theorem 1 (Tadaki [12, 19]). *Let $T \in \mathbb{R}$.*

(i) If $0 < T < 1$ and T is computable, then $Z(T)$ is strictly Chaitin T-random.
(ii) If $1 < T$, then $Z(T)$ diverges to ∞. □

This theorem shows some aspect of the phase transition of the behavior of $Z(T)$ when the temperature T exceeds 1.

2.3 Martingales

In this subsection we review the notion of *martingale*. Compared with the notion of strong predictability which is introduced in this paper, the predictability based on martingale is weak one. We refer the reader to Nies [9, Chapter 7] for the notions and results of this subsection.

A martingale B is a betting strategy. Imagine a gambler in a casino is presented with prefixes of an infinite binary sequence X in ascending order. So far she has been seen a prefix x of X, and her current capital is $B(x) \geq 0$. She bets an amount α with $0 \leq \alpha \leq B(x)$ on her prediction that the next bit will be 0, say. Then the bit is revealed. If she was right, she wins α, else she loses α. Thus, $B(x0) = B(x) + \alpha$ and $B(x1) = B(x) - \alpha$, and hence $B(x0) + B(x1) = 2B(x)$. The same considerations apply if she bets that the next bit will be 1. These considerations result in the following definition.

Definition 3 (Martingale). *A martingale is a function $B\colon \{0,1\}^* \to [0,\infty)$ such that $B(x0) + B(x1) = 2B(x)$ for every $x \in \{0,1\}^*$. For any $X \in \{0,1\}^\infty$, we say that the martingale B succeeds on X if the capital it reaches along X is unbounded, i.e., $\sup\{B(X\lceil_n) \mid n \in \mathbb{N}\} = \infty$.* □

For any subset S of $\{0,1\}^* \times \mathbb{Q}$, we say that S is *computably enumerable* (*c.e.*, for short) if there exists a deterministic Turing machine M such that, on every input $s \in \{0,1\}^* \times \mathbb{Q}$, M halts if and only if $s \in S$.

Definition 4 (C.E. Martingale). *A martingale B is called computably enumerable if the set $\{(x,q) \in \{0,1\}^* \times \mathbb{Q} \mid q < B(x)\}$ is c.e.* □

Theorem 2. *For every $X \in \{0,1\}^\infty$, no c.e. martingale succeeds on X if and only if X is weakly Chaitin random.* □

For any subset S of $\{0,1\}^* \times \mathbb{Q}$, we say that S is *computable* if there exists a deterministic Turing machine M such that, on every input $s \in \{0,1\}^* \times \mathbb{Q}$, (i) M halts and (ii) M outputs 1 if $s \in S$ and 0 otherwise.

Definition 5 (Computable Randomness). *A martingale B is called computable if the set $\{(x,q) \in \{0,1\}^* \times \mathbb{Q} \mid q < B(x)\}$ is computable. For any $X \in \{0,1\}^\infty$, we say that X is computably random if no computable martingale succeeds on X.* □

Definition 6 (Partial Computable Martingale). *A partial computable martingale is a partial computable function $B\colon \{0,1\}^* \to \mathbb{Q} \cap [0,\infty)$ such that $\mathrm{dom}\,B$ is closed under prefixes, and for each $x \in \mathrm{dom}\,B$, $B(x0)$ is defined iff $B(x1)$ is defined, in which case $B(x0) + B(x1) = 2B(x)$ holds.* □

Definition 7 (Partial Computable Randomness). *Let B be a partial computable martingale and $X \in \{0,1\}^\infty$. We say that B succeeds on X if $B(X{\restriction_n})$ is defined for all $n \in \mathbb{N}$ and $\sup\{B(X{\restriction_n}) \mid n \in \mathbb{N}\} = \infty$. We say that X is partial computably random if no partial computable martingale succeeds on X.* □

Theorem 3. *Let $X \in \{0,1\}^\infty$.*

(i) If X is weakly Chaitin random then X is partial computably random.
(ii) If X is partial computably random then X is computably random. □

The converse direction of each of the implications (i) and (ii) of Theorem 3 fails.

3   Non Strong Predictability at $T = 1$

The main result in this section is Theorem 5, which shows that partial computable randomness implies non strong predictability. For intelligibility we first show an easier result, Theorem 4, which says that computable randomness implies non total strong predictability.

Definition 8 (Total Strong Predictability). *For any $X \in \{0,1\}^\infty$, we say that X is total strongly predictable if there exists a computable function $F\colon \{0,1\}^* \to \{0,1,N\}$ for which the following two conditions hold:*

(i) For every $n \in \mathbb{N}$, if $F(X{\restriction_n}) \neq N$ then $F(X{\restriction_n}) = X(n+1)$.
(ii) The set $\{n \in \mathbb{N} \mid F(X{\restriction_n}) \neq N\}$ is infinite. □

In the above definition, the letter N outputted by F on the input $X{\restriction_n}$ means that the prediction of the next bit $X(n+1)$ is suspended.

Theorem 4. *For every $X \in \{0,1\}^\infty$, if X is computably random then X is not total strongly predictable.*

Proof. We show the contraposition of Theorem 4. For that purpose, suppose that X is total strongly predictable. Then there exists a computable function $F\colon \{0,1\}^* \to \{0,1,N\}$ which satisfies the conditions (i) and (ii) of Definition 8. We define a function $B\colon \{0,1\}^* \to \mathbb{N}$ recursively as follows: First $B(\lambda)$ is defined as 1. Then, for any $x \in \{0,1\}^*$, $B(x0)$ is defined by

$$B(x0) = \begin{cases} B(x) & \text{if } F(x) = N, \\ 2B(x) & \text{if } F(x) = 0, \\ 0 & \text{otherwise,} \end{cases}$$

and then $B(x1)$ is defined by $B(x1) = 2B(x) - B(x0)$. It follows that $B\colon \{0,1\}^* \to \mathbb{N}$ is a computable function and

$$B(x0) + B(x1) = 2B(x)$$

for every $x \in \{0,1\}^*$. Thus B is a computable martingale. On the other hand, it is easy to see that

$$B(X{\upharpoonright}n) = 2^{\#\{m \in \mathbb{N} \mid m < n \ \& \ F(X{\upharpoonright}m) \neq N\}}$$

for every $n \in \mathbb{N}$. Since the set $\{n \in \mathbb{N} \mid F(X{\upharpoonright}n) \neq N\}$ is infinite, it follows that $\lim_{n \to \infty} B(X{\upharpoonright}n) = \infty$. Therefore, X is not computably random, as desired. $\square$

Definition 9 (Strong Predictability). *For any $X \in \{0,1\}^\infty$, we say that X is strongly predictable if there exists a partial computable function $F\colon \{0,1\}^* \to \{0,1,N\}$ for which the following three conditions hold:*

(i) For every $n \in \mathbb{N}$, $F(X{\upharpoonright}n)$ is defined.
(ii) For every $n \in \mathbb{N}$, if $F(X{\upharpoonright}n) \neq N$ then $F(X{\upharpoonright}n) = X(n+1)$.
(iii) The set $\{n \in \mathbb{N} \mid F(X{\upharpoonright}n) \neq N\}$ is infinite. $\square$

Obviously, the following holds.

Proposition 1. *For every $X \in \{0,1\}^\infty$, if X is total strongly predictable then X is strongly predictable.* $\square$

Theorem 5. *For every $X \in \{0,1\}^\infty$, if X is partial computably random then X is not strongly predictable.*

Proof. We show the contraposition of Theorem 5. For that purpose, suppose that X is strongly predictable. Then there exists a partial computable function $F\colon \{0,1\}^* \to \{0,1,N\}$ which satisfies the conditions (i), (ii), and (iii) of Definition 9. We define a partial function $B\colon \{0,1\}^* \to \mathbb{N}$ recursively as follows: First $B(\lambda)$ is defined as 1. Then, for any $x \in \{0,1\}^*$, $B(x0)$ is defined by

$$B(x0) = \begin{cases} B(x) & \text{if } F(x) = N, \\ 2B(x) & \text{if } F(x) = 0, \\ 0 & \text{if } F(x) = 1, \\ \text{undefined} & \text{if } F(x) \text{ is undefined,} \end{cases}$$

and then $B(x1)$ is defined by

$$B(x1) = \begin{cases} 2B(x) - B(x0) & \text{if } B(x0) \text{ is defined,} \\ \text{undefined} & \text{otherwise.} \end{cases}$$

It follows that $B\colon \{0,1\}^* \to \mathbb{N}$ is a partial recursive function such that

(i) $\operatorname{dom} B$ is closed under prefixes,
(ii) for every $x \in \operatorname{dom} B$, $x0 \in \operatorname{dom} B$ if and only if $x1 \in \operatorname{dom} B$, and
(iii) for every $x \in \{0,1\}^*$, if $x, x0, x1 \in \operatorname{dom} B$ then $B(x0) + B(x1) = 2B(x)$.

Thus B is a partial computable martingale. On the other hand, it is easy to see that, for every $n \in \mathbb{N}$, $B(X{\restriction}n)$ is defined and

$$B(X{\restriction}n) = 2^{\#\{m\in\mathbb{N}\,|\,m<n\ \&\ F(X{\restriction}m)\neq N\}}.$$

Since the set $\{n \in \mathbb{N} \mid F(X{\restriction}n) \neq N\}$ is infinite, it follows that

$$\lim_{n\to\infty} B(X{\restriction}n) = \infty.$$

Therefore, X is not partial computably random, as desired.   □

Theorem 6. *For every $X \in \{0,1\}^\infty$, if X is weakly Chaitin random then X is not strongly predictable.*

Proof. The result follows immediately from (i) of Theorem 3 and Theorem 5.   □

Thus, since $Z(1)$, i.e., Ω, is weakly Chaitin random, we have the following.

Theorem 7. $Z(1)$ *is not strongly predictable.*   □

4   Strong Predictability on $T < 1$

In this section, we introduce the notion of *finite-state strong predictability*. For that purpose, we first introduce the notion of *finite automaton with outputs*. This is just a deterministic finite automaton whose output is determined, depending only on its final state. The formal definitions are as follows.

Definition 10 (Finite Automaton with Outputs). *A finite automaton with outputs is a 6-tuple $(Q, \Sigma, \delta, q_0, \Gamma, f)$, where*

(i) Q is a finite set called the states,
(ii) Σ is a finite set called the input alphabet,
(iii) $\delta\colon Q \times \Sigma \to Q$ is the transition function,
(iv) $q_0 \in Q$ is the initial state,
(v) Γ is a finite set called the output alphabet, *and*
(vi) $f\colon Q \to \Gamma$ is the output function from final states.   □

A finite automaton with outputs computes as follows.

Definition 11. *Let $M = (Q, \Sigma, \delta, q_0, \Gamma, f)$ be a finite automaton with outputs. For every $x = x_1 x_2 \ldots x_n \in \Sigma^*$ with each $x_i \in \Sigma$, the output of M on the input x, denoted $M(x)$, is $y \in \Gamma$ for which there exist $q_1, q_2, \ldots, q_n \in Q$ such that*

(i) $q_i = \delta(q_{i-1}, x_i)$ for every $i \in \{1, 2, \ldots, n\}$, and
(ii) $y = f(q_n)$. □

In Definitions 10 and 11, if we set $\Gamma = \{0, 1\}$, the definitions result in those of a normal deterministic finite automaton and its computation, where $M(x) = 1$ means that M accepts x and $M(x) = 0$ means that M rejects x.

Definition 12 (Finite-State Strong Predictability). *For any $X \in \{0, 1\}^\infty$, we say that X is finite-state strongly predictable if there exists a finite automaton with outputs $M = (Q, \{0, 1\}^*, \delta, q_0, \{0, 1, N\}, f)$ for which the following two conditions hold:*

(i) For every $n \in \mathbb{N}$, if $M(X\!\restriction_n) \neq N$ then $M(X\!\restriction_n) = X(n+1)$.
(ii) The set $\{n \in \mathbb{N} \mid M(X\!\restriction_n) \neq N\}$ is infinite. □

Since the computation of every finite automaton can be simulated by some deterministic Turing machine which always halts, the following holds, obviously.

Proposition 2. *For every $X \in \{0, 1\}^\infty$, if X is finite-state strongly predictable then X is total strongly predictable.* □

Theorem 8. *Let T be a real with $0 < T < 1$. For every $X \in \{0, 1\}^\infty$, if X is strictly Chaitin T-random, then X is finite-state strongly predictable.* □

In order to prove Theorem 8 we need the following theorem. For completeness, we include its proof.

Theorem 9 (Calude, Hay, and Stephan [1]). *Let T be a real with $0 < T < 1$. For every $X \in \{0, 1\}^\infty$, if X is strictly Chaitin T-random, then there exists $L \geq 2$ such that X does not have a run of L consecutive zeros.*

Proof. Based on the optimality of U used in the definition of $H(x)$, it is easy to show that there exists $d \in \mathbb{N}$ such that, for every $x \in \{0, 1\}^*$ and every $n \in \mathbb{N}$,

$$H(x0^n) \leq H(x) + H(n) + d. \tag{2}$$

Since $T > 0$, it follows also from the optimality of U that there exists $c \in \mathbb{N}^+$ such that $H(c) + d \leq Tc - 1$. Hence, by (2) we see that, for every $x \in \{0, 1\}^*$,

$$H(x0^c) \leq H(x) + Tc - 1. \tag{3}$$

Now, suppose that $X \in \{0, 1\}^\infty$ is strictly Chaitin T-random. Then there exists $d_0 \in \mathbb{N}$ such that, for every $n \in \mathbb{N}$,

$$|H(X\!\restriction_n) - Tn| \leq d_0. \tag{4}$$

We choose a particular $k_0 \in \mathbb{N}^+$ with $k_0 > 2d_0$.

Assume that X has a run of ck_0 consecutive zeros. Then $X\!\restriction_{n_0} 0^{ck_0} = X\!\restriction_{n_0+ck_0}$ for some $n_0 \in \mathbb{N}$. It follows from (3) that

$$H(X\!\restriction_{n_0+ck_0}) - T(n_0 + ck_0) + k_0 \le H(X\!\restriction_{n_0}) - Tn_0.$$

Thus, using (4) we have $-d_0 + k_0 \le d_0$, which contradicts the fact that $k_0 > 2d$. Hence, X does not have a run of ck_0 consecutive zeros, as desired.   □

Proof (of Theorem 8). Suppose that $X \in \{0,1\}^\infty$ is strictly Chaitin T-random. Then, by Theorem 9, there exists $d \ge 2$ such that X does not have a run of d consecutive zeros. For each $n \in \mathbb{N}^+$, let $a(n)$ be the length of the nth block of consecutive zeros in X from the left. Namely, assume that X has the form

$$X = 1^{b(0)}0^{a(1)}1^{b(1)}0^{a(2)}1^{b(2)}0^{a(3)}1^{b(3)}\cdots\cdots$$

for some natural number $b(0)$ and some infinite sequence $b(1), b(2), b(3), \ldots$ of positive integers. Let $L = \limsup_{n \to \infty} a(n)$. Since $1 \le a(n) < d$ for all $n \in \mathbb{N}^+$, we have $L \in \mathbb{N}^+$. Moreover, since $\{a(n)\}$ is a sequence of positive integers, there exists $n_0 \in \mathbb{N}^+$ such that

$$a(n) \le L \tag{5}$$

for every $n \ge n_0$, and

$$a(n) = L \tag{6}$$

for infinitely many $n \ge n_0$. Let m be the length of the prefix of X which lies immediately to the left of the n_0th block of consecutive zeros in X. Namely, $m = \sum_{k=0}^{n_0-1} b(k) + \sum_{k=1}^{n_0-1} a(k)$.

Now, we define a finite automaton with outputs $M = (Q, \{0,1\}^*, \delta, q_0, \{0, 1, N\}, f)$ as follows: First, Q is defined as $\{q_0, q_1, \ldots, q_{m+L}\}$. The transition function δ is then defined by

$$\delta(0, q_i) = \delta(1, q_i) = q_{i+1} \quad \text{if } i = 0, \ldots, m-1,$$
$$\delta(0, q_i) = q_{i+1} \quad \text{if } i = m, \ldots, m+L-1,$$
$$\delta(1, q_i) = q_m \quad \text{if } i = m, \ldots, m+L,$$

where $\delta(0, q_{m+L})$ is arbitrary. Finally, the output function $f: Q \to \{0, 1, N\}$ is defined by $f(q) = 1$ if $q = q_{m+L}$ and N otherwise.

Then, it is easy to see that, for every $x \in \{0,1\}^*$,

(i) $M(x) = 1$ if and only if there exists $y \in \{0,1\}^*$ such that $|y| \ge m$ and $x = y0^L$, and
(ii) $M(x) \ne 0$.

Now, for an arbitrary $n \in \mathbb{N}$, assume that $M(X\!\restriction_n) \ne N$. Then, by the condition (ii) above, we have $M(X\!\restriction_n) = 1$. Therefore, by the condition (i) above, there exists $y \in \{0,1\}^*$ such that $|y| \ge m$ and $X\!\restriction_n = y0^L$. It follows from (5) that $X(n + 1) = 1$ and therefore $M(X\!\restriction_n) = X(n + 1)$. Thus the condition (i) of Definition 12 holds for M and X. On the other hand, using (6) and the condition (i) above, it is easy to see that the set $\{n \in \mathbb{N} \mid M(X \upharpoonright_n) = 1\}$ is infinite. Thus the condition (ii) of Definition 12 holds for M and X. Hence, X is finite-state strongly predictable.   □

Theorem 10. *Let T be a computable real with $0 < T < 1$. Then $Z(T)$ is finite-state strongly predictable.*

Proof. The result follows immediately from (i) of Theorem 1 and Theorem 8.   □

In the case where T is a computable real with $0 < T < 1$, $Z(T)$ is not computable despite Theorem 10. This is because, in such a case, $Z(T)$ is weakly Chaitin T-random by (i) of Theorem 1, and therefore $Z(T)$ cannot be computable.

It is worthwhile to investigate the behavior of $Z(T)$ in the case where T is not computable but $0 < T < 1$. On the one hand, note that $Z(T)$ is of class C^∞ as a function of $T \in (0,1)$ [12] and $\frac{d}{dT}Z(T) > 0$ for every $T \in (0,1)$. On the other hand, recall that a real is weakly Chaitin random almost everywhere. Thus, by Theorem 6, we have $\mathcal{L}(S) = 1$, where S is the set of all $T \in (0,1)$ such that T is not computable and $Z(T)$ is not strongly predictable, and $\mathcal{L}$ is Lebesgue measure on $\mathbb{R}$.

Acknowledgment. This work was supported by JSPS KAKENHI Grant Number 23340020.

References

1. Calude, C.S., Hay, N.J., Stephan, F.C.: Representation of left-computable ε-random reals. J. Comput. Syst. Sci. 77, 812–819 (2011)
2. Calude, C.S., Stay, M.A.: Natural halting probabilities, partial randomness, and zeta functions. Inform. and Comput. 204, 1718–1739 (2006)
3. Chaitin, G.J.: A theory of program size formally identical to information theory. J. Assoc. Comput. Mach. 22, 329–340 (1975)
4. Chaitin, G.J.: Algorithmic Information Theory. Cambridge University Press, Cambridge (1987)
5. Downey, R.G., Hirschfeldt, D.R.: Algorithmic Randomness and Complexity. Springer, New York (2010)
6. Gács, P.: On the symmetry of algorithmic information. Soviet Math. Dokl. 15, 1477–1480 (1974); correction, ibid. 15, 1480 (1974)
7. Goldreich, O.: Foundations of Cryptography: Basic Tools, vol. 1. Cambridge University Press, New York (2001)
8. Levin, L.A.: Laws of information conservation (non-growth) and aspects of the foundations of probability theory. Problems of Inform. Transmission 10, 206–210 (1974)
9. Nies, A.: Computability and Randomness. Oxford University Press, Inc., New York (2009)
10. Ruelle, D.: Statistical Mechanics. In: Rigorous Results, 3rd edn. Imperial College Press and World Scientific Publishing Co., Pte. Ltd, Singapore (1999)

11. Schnorr, C.P.: Zufälligkeit und Wahrscheinlichkeit. Eine algorithmische Begründung der Wahrscheinlichkeitstheorie. Lecture Notes in Mathematics, vol. 218. Springer (1971)

12. Tadaki, K.: A generalization of Chaitin's halting probability Ω and halting self-similar sets. Hokkaido Math. J. 31, 219–253 (2002)

13. Tadaki, K.: A statistical mechanical interpretation of instantaneous codes. In: Proceedings of 2007 IEEE International Symposium on Information Theory (ISIT 2007), Nice, France, June 24-29, pp. 1906–1910 (2007)

14. Tadaki, K.: A statistical mechanical interpretation of algorithmic information theory. In: Local Proceedings of Computability in Europe 2008 (CiE 2008), June 15-20, pp. 425–434. University of Athens, Greece (2008), Electronic Version Available at, http://www.cs.swan.ac.uk/cie08/cie2008-local.pdf, Extended Version also Available from: arXiv:0801.4194v1

15. Tadaki, K.: Fixed point theorems on partial randomness. Annals of Pure and Applied Logic 163, 763–774 (2012); Special Issue of the Symposium on Logical Foundations of Computer Science (2009)

16. Tadaki, K.: A statistical mechanical interpretation of algorithmic information theory III: Composite systems and fixed points. In: Special Issue of the CiE 2010 Special Session on Computability of the Physical. Mathematical Structures in Computer Science, vol. 22, pp. 752–770 (2012)

17. Tadaki, K.: A statistical mechanical interpretation of algorithmic information theory: Total statistical mechanical interpretation based on physical argument. Journal of Physics: Conference Series (JPCS) 201, 012006, 10 (2010)

18. Tadaki, K.: Robustness of statistical mechanical interpretation of algorithmic information theory. In: Proceedings of the 2011 IEEE Information Theory Workshop (ITW 2011), Paraty, Brazil, October 16-20, pp. 237–241 (2011)

19. Tadaki, K.: Phase transition between unidirectionality and bidirectionality. In: Dinneen, M.J., Khoussainov, B., Nies, A. (eds.) WTCS 2012 (Calude Festschrift). LNCS, vol. 7160, pp. 203–223. Springer, Heidelberg (2012)

20. Toda, M., Kubo, R., Saitô, N.: Statistical Physics I. Equilibrium Statistical Mechanics, 2nd edn. Springer, Berlin (1992)

PHLOGON: PHase-based LOGic
using Oscillatory Nano-systems

Tianshi Wang and Jaijeet Roychowdhury

Department of EECS, The University of California, Berkeley, CA, USA
{tianshi,jr}@berkeley.edu

Abstract. In this paper we take a fresh look at Goto and von Neumann's phase-based logic ideas, provide enhancements that can overcome major limitations of their previous implementations. We show that with injection locking serving as the central mechanism, almost any DC-powered, self-sustaining nonlinear oscillator — including electronic, spintronic, biological, optical and mechanical ones — can be used to build fundamental components — including latches and combinatorial elements in a phase logic based computing architecture. We also discuss noise immunity and potential power dissipation advantages that can be achieved under this scheme.

Keywords: Phase-based logic, nonlinear oscillators, injection locking.

1   Introduction

In the 1950s, Eiichi Goto and John von Neumann invented a new paradigm for computing: *temporal encoding* of logical states *using phases of oscillatory signals* [39,36,41,9]. Phase logic schemes corresponding to it have been implemented physically [13,28,27,35,25], indeed were popular in Japan in the 1950s due to their simplicity and reliability. However, the advent of transistors and integrated circuits led to their demise, since the devices and circuits they were based on could not compete with level-based logic using transistors.

A key reason for their lack of competitiveness was *size and miniaturizability*. Specifically, they normally require inductors and large capacitors, which are bulky compared to semiconductor transistors, particularly today's nano-scale MOS devices. Another related reason was *lower operating speed*, stemming not only from larger component sizes, but also from inherent features of von Neumann's scheme (*e.g.*, periodic turn-on transients and delays in logic gates) that made phase-based logic slower than transistorized level-based logic. Later attempts (from the 1980s to the present) used superconducting Josephson-junction devices [15], which are fast, but still limited in terms of miniaturizability and practical deployment at room temperature. Therefore, these implementations were quickly overshadowed by the rise of transistorized level-based logic, which has dominated logical computing for decades.

With power dissipation, variability and noise having emerged as serious barriers to semiconductor scaling and Moore's law — both synonymous with progress

O.H. Ibarra et al. (Eds.): UCNC 2014, LNCS 8553, pp. 353–366, 2014.
DOI: 10.1007/978-3-319-08123-6_29, © Springer International Publishing Switzerland 2014

in computing — there has been renewed interest in Goto and von Neumann's phase-based logic ideas. Recently MEMS-based replacement for von Neumann's circuit has been proposed [21]. It could perform bit storage and bit flip operations under AC power and its success in implementing computation and large-scale integration is yet to be seen. In this paper, we propose enhancements (collectively termed **PHLOGON**) to Goto and von Neumann's schemes that employ *self-sustaining oscillators as basic phase logic elements* to eliminate the size and integrability limitations of the previous implementations, opening possibilities for robust, general-purpose computing substrates that offer *significant noise immunity and potential power dissipation advantages* over level-based CMOS computing.

We describe how the core computational block — a finite-state machine (FSM) can be built using phase-based logic. As an example, we show how it can be realized using *CMOS ring oscillators in standard existing technologies*. However, PHLOGON is not limited to electronic oscillators. Indeed, it can use almost any self-sustaining nonlinear oscillator — including spintronic, biological, optical and mechanical ones – as the underlying logical element, expanding the implementation scope of Goto and von Neumann's phase logic ideas greatly.

To better explain our ideas, we provide background on Goto and von Neumann's phase-based computing scheme by summarizing von Neumann's related works in Sec. 2. In Sec. 3.1 we illustrate how sub-harmonic injection locking leads to multiple stable phase states, serving as the key mechanism for encoding phase logic. We show that phase logic offers inherently greater immunity to noise, interference and variability (Sec. 3.2). We then describe our implementation of phase-based computing architecture using self-sustaining nonlinear oscillators (Sec. 3.3) and discuss its potentially lower power/energy operation compared with traditional level-based CMOS computing scheme (Sec. 3.4). Conclusions are provided in Sec. 4.

2   John von Neumann's Phase Logic Scheme

In his patent [39,36,41], von Neumann outlined fundamental ideas and a complete scheme for phase-based computing. We provide a brief sketch of the main ideas here.

von Neumann started with a key observation: the circuit in Fig. 1(a) can feature *two (or more) distinct oscillating steady states*, which can be used to *store two (or more) logical states* stably. The circuit features a *lossless, nonlinear, charge-controlled capacitor* (shown towards the left of Fig. 1(a)), together with bandpass filters used to isolate an AC power source or *pump* (V_g), and an output load (R_L), from the several frequencies simultaneously present in the capacitor's terminal voltage. When the amplitude of the AC pump voltage waveform, assumed sinusoidal at frequency f_0, is larger than a critical threshold V_c (Fig. 1(b)), the voltage waveform across the capacitor can feature components that are *integer sub-multiples* of f_0, *i.e.*, *sub-harmonics of f_0*. Furthermore, as depicted in Fig. 1(c), a generated sub-harmonic can be in *one of several distinct*

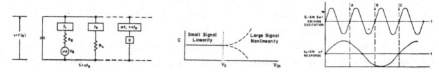

(a) AC-powered subharmonic gener- (b) Multistability beyond (c) Example: discriminating be-
ator features multiple phase-shifted a critical pump amplitude, tween subharmonic steady states
stable states [41, Fig. 2]. V_c [41, Fig. 4].   [41, Fig. 6].

Fig. 1. von Neumann's basic phase-based latch: a nonlinear AC-pumped circuit with
multiple subharmonic steady states

phase relationships with respect to the waveform of the AC pump. Each distinct
phase relationship can be used to encode a logic state. The circuit functions,
effectively, as a *latch* that can store a logic value. The sub-harmonic and multi-
stability properties of the circuit in Fig. 1(a) can be inferred from an elegant
formula, the *Manley-Rowe relationships* [39,23,41].

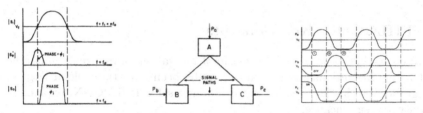

(a) Amplitude modulation of (b) A ring of latches can retain (c) Phase-shifted amplitude
the AC pump to capture an in- a phase-logic state permanently modulation waveforms driving
put logic value [41, Fig. 7].   [41, Fig. 11].   the ring of latches [41, Fig. 11].

Fig. 2. von Neumann's scheme for setting a latch to an input state and retaining it

Setting a phase-encoded latch to an input logic state: Having devised a latch circuit capable of storing logical values encoded in phase, von Neumann considered
the question of setting a latch to a desired logic state supplied as input. He proposed a scheme based on modulating the amplitude of the AC pump slowly with
a waveform similar to the uppermost graph of Fig. 2(a). When this modulation
waveform is low, the latch is, effectively, turned off; as the modulation increases
and magnitude of the AC pump crosses the critical threshold V_c, the latch turns
on and settles to one of the possible logic states. von Neumann suggested that
if a desired logic value (encoded in phase) were to be introduced as an input to
the latch just as it was turning on, the latch would settle to (the sub-harmonic
phase corresponding to) the same logic value. This is depicted in the middle and
bottom graphs of Fig. 2(a).

Holding on to the logic state: A problem with the above input-latching scheme
is, of course, that the latch is turned off periodically, thereby losing its stored

state. von Neumann's solution was a ring of latches (Fig. 2(b)), with each latch's AC pump modulated by a phase shifted version of its predecessor's AC modulation (Fig. 2(c)). The ring operates in merry-go-round fashion, with each succeeding latch turning on, capturing its predecessor's logic state and retaining it as the predecessor subsequently turns off. At any given time, one latch is always on, hence the logic state is never lost.

Combinatorial operations for phase-encoded logic: Next, von Neumann turned to the problem of realizing arbitrary Boolean operations using phase-encoded logic. Noting that two operations, NOT and MAJORITY, constitute a logically complete set [1], he provided especially elegant means of realizing them [41]. NOT is obtained simply by a through connection between latches with different pump modulation phases while MAJORITY is obtained simply by adding the waveforms of the three inputs together.

Having devised phase-based realizations of the latch-ring and the logically complete combinatorial function set NOT and MAJORITY, together with a consistent timing scheme provided by the phase shifted pump modulation waveforms, von Neumann had developed all the basic components needed to make state machines and general computing architectures.

3   PHLOGON: Key Concepts

As discussed before in Sec. 1, previous implementations of von Neumann's scheme suffer from limitations and have not, to date, been miniaturisable or large-scale integrable. In this section, we detail our ideas for PHLOGON, explain their novelty and significance.

3.1   Sub-harmonic Injection Locking (SHIL) Enables Phase Logic

A central paradigm in PHLOGON is that DC-powered nonlinear self-sustaining oscillators can be used as phase logic elements. This paradigm relies on the fact that such oscillators inherently feature a property known as *injection locking* [16,2,19], which enables the oscillator's waveforms to move in lock-step with – *i.e.*, become *phase locked* to – a small external signal injected into it[2]. Injection locking is responsible for many *sychronization phenomena* in nature (*e.g.*, the synchronized flashing of fireflies [4,34,33]) and is exploited in engineering (*e.g.*, injection locked frequency dividers [30]).

A specific type of injection locking, known as sub-harmonic injection locking (SHIL), is the key mechanism involved in phase logic encoding. We have developed theory that shows how SHIL leads to multiple stable phase states[1], as depicted in Fig. 3(b). We have also been able to distill the essential properties needed in an oscillator for it to be an effective sub-harmonically locked oscillator-latch. We provide a sketch of our ideas and results here.

---

[1] *i.e.*, any Boolean function can be realized using compositions of functions in this set.

[2] Phase locking also ensures that the frequency of the oscillator becomes identical to that of the input.

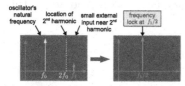

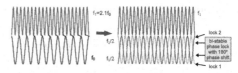

(a) When SHIL happens, the oscillator's frequency locks to the sub-harmonic of the input.

(b) When SHIL happens, phase lock features multi-stability. In this case where $f_1 \approx 2f_0$, there are two stable states with $180°$ phase difference.

Fig. 3. Illustration of frequency and phase lock of sub-harmonic injection locking

The phase response of any amplitude-stable nonlinear oscillator to small external inputs can be captured via a so-called Phase Response Curve (PRC) [22,42,17] or Perturbation Projection Vector (PPV) [7] equation as in (1).

$$\frac{d}{dt}\alpha(t) = v_1^T(t + \alpha(t)) \cdot b(t). \tag{1}$$

In (1), $\alpha(t)$ is a changing *time shift* or *jitter* in the oscillator's waveform caused by $b(t)$, containing small inputs to the oscillator. $\alpha(t)$ is related very simply to the phase shift to the oscillator's response.

The importance of the PPV equation[3] (1) for oscillator-latches lies in that it can model and predict injection locking effectively [20]; however, though easily solved using numerical methods, analytical solution of (1) is usually not possible. To obtain insights into injection-locking properties, and for visualisation and design, we have developed a simplified approximation of (1) known as the *Generalized Adler Equation* (GAE) [3,2]. Given specific periodic inputs to the oscillator, the GAE governs the dynamics of the oscillator's phase as it evolves; in particular, the equilibrium states of the GAE provide good approximations to injection-locked solutions of the PPV equation (1).

Suppose that the PPV of an oscillator-latch consists of a fundamental sinusoidal component (at the oscillator's natural frequency, f_0) of strength k_1, plus a second harmonic component of strength k_2. For the oscillator to develop multi stable phase states, we apply a small input SYNC of amplitude A_1 at frequency $f_1 \simeq 2f_0$[4]. With SHIL, the oscillator changes its frequency to $f_2 \triangleq \frac{f_1}{2}$ (Fig. 3(a)) and its phase becomes bi-stable (Fig. 3(b)). To control which stable phase the oscillator will latch, we apply another input of amplitude A_2 at frequency f_2, with phase shift (relative to SYNC) θ[5]. This input corresponds to one of the stable states thus can be encoded to have a logic value (0 or 1 in binary

---

[3] Well-established computational techniques are available [8,7] to obtain the quantity $v_1^T(\cdot)$, known as the PPV or PRC, of any nonlinear oscillator described in differential equations.

[4] We have shown that when SYNC is at $f_1 \simeq mf_0$, the phase of the oscillator may feature m distinct stable states and the analysis performed here is still applicable[3,1]. We will henceforth take $m = 2$ (binary encoding) to illustrate all the main ideas.

[5] $\theta = 0$ and $\theta = \pi$ correspond to the two logic states for binary phase logic.

logic). We have shown that the GAE equilibrium equation corresponding to this situation is (2).

$$\frac{f_1 - 2f_0}{2f_0} = k_1 A_2 \sin(\phi - \theta) + k_2 A_1 \sin(2\phi).$$
(2)

Solutions ϕ of (2) are the possible phase shifts of the oscillator-latch's waveforms when it is sub-harmonically injection locked. Considerable insight into the number, nature and behaviour of these solutions can be obtained graphically, by plotting its left- and right-hand-sides separately and looking for intersection points.

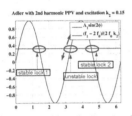

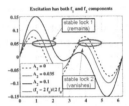

(a) (2) has 2 stable solutions in the absence of a (logic) input.

(b) Acquisition of input phase: phase bistability of (2) vanishes.

Fig. 4. GAE equilibrium equation (2) establishes multi-stability and input phase acquisition properties of oscillator-latches

Fig. 4(a) plots the left- and right-hand-sides (flat red and sinusoidal blue traces, respectively) of (2) when $A_2 = 0$ and no logic input is present at the oscillator-latch. There are 4 intersections between the two traces, corresponding to 4 solutions of (2). Of these, the first and third intersections (from the left) can be shown to be dynamically unstable[6]; but the second and fourth intersections correspond to *two distinct stable oscillations, sub-harmonically locked to* SYNC *with phases separated by* π *radians*. Thus, in the presence of SYNC, the oscillator-latch features bi-stability.

Fig. 4(b) plots the same left-hand-side (flat red trace), but overlays several traces for the right-hand-side of (2), corresponding to A_2 values 0, 0.035 and 0.1, with the latter two values representing two different strengths of an incoming logical signal at f_2 with $\theta = 0$. As can be seen, the first stable intersection remains relatively unaffected as the strength of the incoming input changes, but the second intersection vanishes, structurally, for A_2 value 0.1. This implies that the oscillator acquires the input's logic state. After acquisition, as A_2 is reduced to zero, the GAE can be used to analyze the dynamics of ϕ and show that the acquired logic state is held, even though the second stable intersection is restored.

In summary, the SHIL phenomenon enables the oscillator to develop multiple, well-defined, stable states that can be used to encode logic. It also shows how

---

[6] *i.e.*, they are physically unrealizable in the presence of perturbations, noise or variability.

the oscillator-latch can acquire phase and switch between logic states according to external logic inputs.

3.2   Inherent Noise Immunity of Phase-Based Logic

One of the key attractions of encoding logic in the phase of oscillatory signals is that, compared to level-based schemes, phase encoding provides inherent resistance to errors caused by additive noise and interference. There are two aspects to phase encoding that provide intrinsic resistance to additive noise/interference: 1) the effective SNR[7] for phase is increased by a factor of $\frac{\pi}{2}$ over SNR for level-based encodings, and 2) the oscillatory nature of the signal whose phase encodes the information makes much of the additive noise/interference average out, leading to smaller bit error rates than for the level-based case. These mechanisms are explained below.

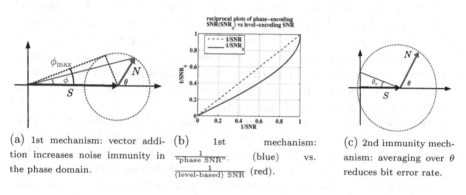

(a) 1st mechanism: vector addition increases noise immunity in the phase domain.

(b)   1st   mechanism: $\frac{1}{\text{"phase SNR"}}$ (blue) vs. $\frac{1}{\text{(level-based) SNR}}$ (red).

(c) 2nd immunity mechanism: averaging over θ reduces bit error rate.

Fig. 5. Mechanisms enhancing the noise resistance of phase-encoded logic

Fig. 5(a) depicts an oscillatory signal as a phasor [12] $\boldsymbol{S}$, superimposed upon which is a noise (or interference) component, $\boldsymbol{N}$. The impact of this noise on the phase of the signal is shown by the phase error $\phi = \angle(\boldsymbol{S} + \boldsymbol{N})$. Given fixed amplitudes[8] $S = |\boldsymbol{S}|$ and $N = |\boldsymbol{N}|$, ϕ depends on the relative angle θ between $\boldsymbol{S}$ and $\boldsymbol{N}$, i.e., $\phi = g(\theta, \frac{N}{S})$[9]. For $N < S$ and fixed N/S, there is a maximum phase error over all θ, i.e., $\phi_{\max} = \sin^{-1}(N/S)$, as depicted in Fig. 5(a). The "phase SNR" is given by $\text{SNR}_\phi = \frac{\frac{\pi}{2}}{\phi_{\max}}$; it is the fraction, in angular terms, of the first quadrant taken up by the maximum phase error. This is to be compared against S/N, the SNR for level-based logic (for which, in Fig. 5(a), $\boldsymbol{N}$ is collinear with $\boldsymbol{S}$). As can be seen from Fig. 5(b), $\frac{1}{\text{SNR}_\phi}$ is always smaller than $\frac{1}{\text{SNR}}$, i.e., the "phase SNR" is always improved over the standard level-based SNR. For small S/N (i.e., a large level-based SNR), this improvement is a factor of $\frac{\pi}{2} \simeq 1.6$. This is the first mechanism by which phase encoding improves noise immunity.

---

[7] Signal to noise ratio.

[8] For illustrative simplicity, we consider noise of only a fixed magnitude. In reality, of course, the magnitude of $\boldsymbol{N}$ has a probability distribution, e.g., a Gaussian one.

[9] For example, $g(0, \cdot) = g(\pi \cdot) = 0$ and $g(\frac{pi}{2}, \frac{N}{S}) = \tan^{-1}(\frac{N}{S})$.

A second mechanism, conferring additional noise immunity, stems from that the phasors S and N are not necessarily always at the same frequency (as assumed implicitly in the analysis of the first mechanism, above), but can rotate at different speeds[10]. Consider now the case where the rotation speeds are very different. The rapid relative change in the angle θ between S and N suggests that the worst-case phase error $\phi_{\max}$, from the first mechanism above, is unduly pessimistic; and that, instead, the phase error *averaged over all values of θ* is the appropriate measure. More precisely, the standard deviation σ_ϕ that results from, *e.g.*, uniformly distributed θ, is an appropriate measure of the phase error. This quantity can be substantially smaller than the worst-case phase error $\phi_{\max}$, implying considerable additional immunity to noise.

Indeed, this second mechanism makes phase encoding useful even when the noise magnitude is *greater* than that of the signal, a situation where level-based logic encoding becomes largely useless. This situation is illustrated in Fig. 5(c). Observe that for most values of θ, the phase error is less than $\frac{\pi}{2}$, the threshold for a bit error. The probability of logical error in the case of phase encoding is $\frac{\theta_c}{\pi} = \frac{\cos^{-1}(S/N)}{\pi}$, which can be very small if N is only slightly greater than S (as depicted); and reaches its maximum, 50%, only as the noise increases to infinity. In contrast, the probability of logical error for level-based encoding is always 50% when $N > S$, since a logical error *always* results when the noise subtracts from the signal (rather than adding to it).

These noise immunity features of phase encoding do not come as a surprise; the superior noise properties of phase and frequency modulation (PM and FM), over those of amplitude modulation (AM), have long been known [24] and exploited in practice, *e.g.*, in radio communications. However, the authors are not aware of their prior realization, or application, in the context of logic encoding for general-purpose computing.

3.3   Computation with Phase Logic

With phase-based logic encoding, we describe ideas on the implementation of phase-based computing in this section.

The central unit of a computer is a finite-state machine (FSM) [36]. As is shown in Fig. 6, latches and combinational logic blocks are the key components of an FSM. We first describe how to build combinational logic blocks using phase logic.

We realize combinatorial operations in a manner almost identical to von Neumann's technique,

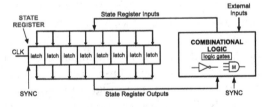

Fig. 6. A general FSM. SYNC is used to develop multi-stability for encoding phase logic; NOT/MAJORITY gates are for combinatorial operations.

---

[10] The phasor N can be thought of as one component, at frequency f, of a spectral expansion [14] of a stochastic process.

using NOT and MAJORITY operations. Phase logic enables elegant implementation of these two operations: NOT is simply inversion and MAJORITY can be implemented by addition. These can be explained using phasors, as is demonstrated in Fig. 7.

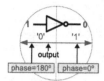 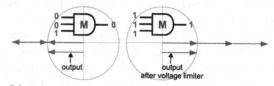

(a) Inverting input signal performs NOT operation in phase logic.

(b) A three-input MAJORITY gate uses addition to perform MAJORITY operation of input signals in phase logic.

Fig. 7. Phase-domain plots illustrating NOT and MAJORITY operations

With oscillator-latches to store phase-based bits and logic gates to perform combinatorial operations, we now have all the components to build general-purpose computing systems using phase logic. Without loss of generality, here we use CMOS ring oscillators as an example to show how such computing systems can be built.

Fig. 8(b) shows a diagram of a D latch implemented using phase logic. The design is analogous to that of a level-based D latch (Fig. 8(a)) except that information is latched in phase. Fig. 8(c) shows waveforms from SPICE-level simulation of the implementation of phase-based D latch with ring oscillators. By aligning the waveforms of Q, D, EN with REF, we see that it achieves the functionality of a transparent D latch in phase logic.

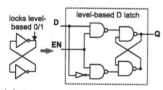 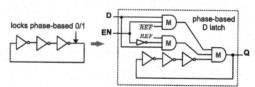

(a) Level-based D latch derives from bi-stable level-latching device.

(b) Phase-based D latch derives from bi-stable phase-based bit storage device (*e.g.* CMOS ring oscillator).

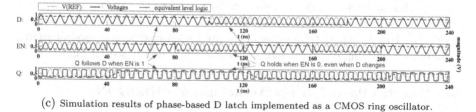

(c) Simulation results of phase-based D latch implemented as a CMOS ring oscillator.

Fig. 8. Design and implementation of phase-based D latch

Tying two such transparent D latches together results in an edge-triggered master-slave D flip-flop. With this we build a simplest FSM just to show a flavour of how computation systems operate in phase logic.

Fig. 9 shows a serial adder made of the D flip-flop and a full adder. Just as in the D latch, here we use only MAJORITY and NOT operations in the design for their simplicity of implementation using phase logic. We emphasize again that such a system can be realized using oscillators from various domains. Here we demonstrate its viability using CMOS ring oscillators only as an example and provide simulation results in Fig. 10. We add $a = 101$ with $b = 101$ sequentially during three clock cycles. From Fig. 10 we can see cin is held stable everytime CLK level is low (translates to having opposite phase as REF). During this time

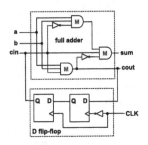

Fig. 9. Serial adder

$cout = 101$ and $sum = 010$ can be read out sequentially. In the full system design their values can then be latched using other registers and connected to following stages in the system, or transformed to level-based logic if connected to other computation or display blocks.

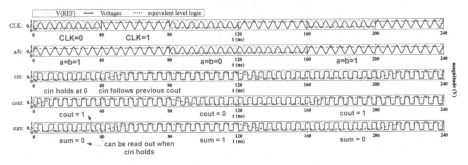

Fig. 10. Waveforms from adding $a = b = 101$ with serial adder in Fig. 9 implemented using ring oscillator

Even though our scheme is fundamentally different from the conventional computation framework in the way logic is encoded, as we have seen in the examples, the system-level design (FSM design) can be quite analogous to that of level-based logic systems. In this way, all the logic synthesis and timing analysis theories and tools can potentially still be used with only minor modifications, immediately enabling complex, large-scale system design based on phase logic.

3.4   Potential Power/Energy Advantages of PHLOGON

PHLOGON offers significant energy-efficiency benefits over von Neumann's original scheme. It uses continuously-running oscillators, which can be much more energy-efficient than von Neumann's latch-rings. Moreover, neither distribution nor modulation of AC power is involved for running a PHLOGON architecture[11]. This reduces parasitic-related losses especially for large, intricately-routed systems, resulting in significant power savings over von Neumann's scheme.

Compared with level-based CMOS computation architecture, the circuits and nanodevice embodiments of PHLOGON can potentially still be considerably more energy efficient. Dynamic (capacitive charging/discharging) and continuous (sub-threshold leakage) power consumption in level-based CMOS are both strongly determined by the supply voltage. The lowest practical supply voltage today for level-based CMOS is about 0.8V; this number is unlikely to drop significantly in future years, due to threshold voltage, variability and noise barriers [37,38]. In contrast, ring oscillators in standard CMOS technologies operate in sub-threshold mode at supply voltages as low as 80mV [6,10,5]; while in III-V technologies, ring oscillators running at 0.23V were demonstrated almost 30 years ago [11]. 10× lower supply voltage translates to 100× lower dynamic (CV^2) power, and more than $20,000×$ lower leakage power (exponential in supply voltage). We emphasize that these power savings result simply by moving from level-based to phase-based logic architectures, without any change in the underlying CMOS technology.

Such large power savings can result even with ring oscillators, which dissipate most or all of their energy every cycle. When harmonic oscillators, with Q factors appreciably greater than 1, are used, further energy savings[12] can be realized. On-chip CMOS LC oscillators with spiral inductors, though considerably larger in area than ring oscillators, are available today with Q factors greater than 10, making them an interesting candidate to explore for additional power efficiency. Integrated MEMS resonators, though even larger in area, feature Q factors of 10^4-10^5 [26], potentially making them extremely attractive for low power computation with easily available and well-developed conventional technologies. Resonant Body Transistor (RBT), a silicon-based resonator compatible with standard CMOS process, has been demonstrated to achieve >10GHz frequency with Q factor of 1830 [40], making it another promising candidate. Spin-torque nano-oscillators (STNOs) feature Q factors of more than 10^4 at frequencies of 25GHz [31,18,32]; as such, they offer very exciting power, as well as speed, possibilities.

4   Conclusions

In this paper we re-examined Goto and von Neumann's phase-based logic ideas and limitations of their previous implementations. We proposed enhancements to them, showing that almost any DC-powered, self-sustaining nonlinear oscillator can be used to build latches and combinatorial elements, enabling phase-based computing. We provided mathematical tools for analysing SHIL as the

---

[11] Note that SYNC and CLK can be weak, dissipating negligible power.

[12] *i.e.*, an energy advantage of roughly Q over ring oscillators using the same technology and supply voltage.

mechanism for phase-based logic encoding. We showed that phase logic offers inherent resistance to noise and variability and also discussed the potential energy-efficiency our scheme may achieve. These features have made PHLOGON an interesting and promising alternative to the conventional level-based computation architecture. We are currently exploring design details and tradeoffs involved in the practical manifestation of PHLOGON in post-CMOS and standard digital CMOS technologies.

Acknowledgements. The authors would like to thank Rajiv Mathur, FCRP liaison in Intel, for pointing us to von Neumann's original works. We would also like to thank the reviewers for the useful comments and in particular anonymous reviewer No.2 for pointing us to Goto's patent on resonator circuits.

References

[1] Neogy, A., Roychowdhury, J.: Analysis and Design of Sub-harmonically Injection Locked Oscillators. In: Proc. IEEE DATE (March 2012)

[2] Adler, R.: A study of locking phenomena in oscillators. Proceedings of the I.R.E. and Waves and Electrons 34, 351–357 (1946)

[3] Bhansali, P., Roychowdhury, J.: Gen-Adler: The generalized Adler's equation for injection locking analysis in oscillators. In: Proc. IEEE ASP-DAC, pp. 522–227 (January 2009)

[4] Buck, J., Buck, E.: Synchronous fireflies. Scientific American (1976)

[5] Cilek, F., Seemann, K., Brenk, D., Essel, J., Heidrich, J., Weigel, R., Holweg, G.: Ultra low power oscillator for UHF RFID transponder. In: Proc. IEEE Freq. Contr. Symp., pp. 418–421 (May 2008)

[6] Deen, M.J., Kazemeini, M.H., Naseh, S.: Performance characteristics of an ultra-low power VCO. In: Proc. IEEE ISCAS (May 2003)

[7] Demir, A., Mehrotra, A., Roychowdhury, J.: Phase Noise in Oscillators: a Unifying Theory and Numerical Methods for Characterization. IEEE Trans. Ckts. Syst. – I: Fund. Th. Appl. 47, 655–674 (2000)

[8] Demir, A., Roychowdhury, J.: A Reliable and Efficient Procedure for Oscillator PPV Computation, with Phase Noise Macromodelling Applications. IEEE Trans. on Computer-Aided Design, 188–197 (2003)

[9] Eiichi, G.: Resonator circuits, US Patent 2,948,818 (August 9, 1960)

[10] Farzeen, S., Ren, G., Chen, C.: An ultra-low power ring oscillator for passive UHF RFID transponders. In: Proc. IEEE MWSCAS, pp. 558–561 (August 2010)

[11] Feuer, M.D., Hendel, R.H., Kiehl, R.A., Hwang, J.C.M., Keramidas, V.G., Allyn, C.L., Dingle, R.: High-speed low-voltage ring oscillators based on selectively doped heterojunction transistors. IEEE Electron Device Letters EDL-4, 306–307 (1983)

[12] Giancoli, D.C.: Physics for Scientists and Engineers. Prentice-Hall, Englewood Cliff (1989)

[13] Goto, E.: New Parametron circuit element using nonlinear reactance, KDD Kenyku Shiryo (1954)

[14] Grigoriu, M.: Stochastic Calculus: Applications in Science and Engineering. Birkhäuser, Boston (2002)

[15] Hoe, W., Goto, E.: Quantum Flux Parametron: A Single Quantum Flux Super-conducting Logic Device. Studies in Josephson Supercomputers, vol. 2. World Scientific (1991)

[16] Huygens, C.: Horologium Oscillatorium. Apud F. Muget, Paris (1672); Observations of injection locking between grandfather clocks

[17] Izhikevich, E.M.: Dynamical Systems in Neuroscience: The Geometry of Excitability and Bursting (Computational Neuroscience), 1st edn. The MIT Press (November 2006)

[18] Kaka, S., Pufall, M.R., Rippard, W.H., Silva, T.J., Russek, S.E., Katine, J.A.: Mutual phase-locking of microwave spin torque nano-oscillators. Nature 437, 389–392 (2005)

[19] Kurokawa, K.: Injection locking of microwave solid-state oscillators. Proceedings of the IEEE 61, 1336–1410, 1386–1410 (1973)

[20] Lai, X., Roychowdhury, J.: Capturing injection locking via nonlinear phase domain macromodels. IEEE Trans. Microwave Theory Tech. 52, 2251–2261 (2004)

[21] Mahboob, I., Yamaguchi, H.: Bit storage and bit flip operations in an electrome-chanical oscillator. Nature Nanotechnology 3, 275–279 (2008)

[22] Malkin, I.G.: Some Problems in Nonlinear Oscillation Theory, Gostexizdat, Moscow (1956)

[23] Manley, J.M., Rowe, R.E.: Some general properties of nonlinear elements – Part I. General energy relations. Proceedings of the Institute of Radio Engineers 44, 904–913 (1956)

[24] Middleton, D.: An Introduction to Statistical Communication Theory. Wiley-IEEE, New York (1996)

[25] Muroga, S.: Elementary principle of Parametron and its application to digital computers. Datamation 4, 31–34 (1958)

[26] Nguyen, C.T.-C.: Vibrating RF MEMS for Next Generation Wireless Applications. In: Proc. IEEE CICC (May 2004)

[27] Oshima, Enemoto, Watanabe: Oscillation theory of Parametron and method of measuring nonlinear elements, KDD Kenkyu Shiryo (1955)

[28] Oshima, S.: Introduction to Parametron. Denshi Kogyo 4, 4 (1955)

[29] Bhansali, P., Srivastava, S., Lai, X., Roychowdhury, J.: Comprehensive Procedure for Fast and Accurate Coupled Oscillator Network Simulation. In: Proc. ICCAD, pp. 815–820 (November 2008)

[30] Kinget, P., Melville, R., Long, D., Gopinathan, V.: An injection-locking scheme for precision quadrature generation. IEEE J. Solid-State Ckts. 37, 845–851 (2002)

[31] Pufall, M.R., Rippard, W.H., Kaka, S., Silva, T.J., Russek, S.E.: Frequency mod-ulation of spin-transfer oscillators. Applied Physics Letters 86, 82506 (2005)

[32] Rippard, W.H., Pufall, M.R., Kaka, S., Silva, T.J., Russek, S.E., Katine, J.A.: Injection locking and phase control of spin transfer nano-oscillators. Phys. Rev. Lett. 95, 067203 (2005)

[33] Strogatz, S.: Sync: The Emerging Science of Spontaneous Order, Theia (March 2003)

[34] Strogatz, S.H., Stewart, I.: Coupled oscillators and biological synchronization. Scientific American 269, 102–109 (1993)

[35] Takahashi, H.: The Parametron. Tsugakkat Shi 39, 56 (1956)

[36] Taub, A.H. (ed.): John von Neumann: Collected Works. Design of Computers, Theory of Automata and Numerical Analysis, vol. V. Pergamon Press, New York (1963)

[37] Toh, S., Tsukamoto, Y., Guo, Z., Jones, L., Liu, T., Nikolic, B.: Impact of random telegraph signals on Vmin in 45nm SRAM. In: Proceedings of the IEEE International Electron Devices Meeting, pp. 767–770 (2009)

[38] Tsukamoto, Y., Toh, S., Shin, C., Mairena, A., Liu, T., Nikolic, B.: Analysis of the relationship between random telegraph signal and negative bias temperature instability. In: Proceedings of the IEEE International Reliability Physics Symposium, pp. 1117–1121 (2010)

[39] von Neumann, J.: Non-linear capacitance or inductance switching, amplifying and memory devices (1954)

[40] Weinstein, D., Bhave, S.A.: The resonant body transistor. Nano Letters 10, 1234–1237 (2010)

[41] Wigington, R.L.: A New Concept in Computing. Proceedings of the Institute of Radio Engineers 47, 516–523 (1959)

[42] Winfree, A.: Biological Rhythms and the Behavior of Populations of Coupled Oscillators. Theoretical Biology 16, 15–42 (1967)

Size-Separable Tile Self-assembly:
A Tight Bound for Temperature-1
Mismatch-Free Systems*

Andrew Winslow

Tufts University, Medford, MA 02155, USA
awinslow@cs.tufts.edu

Abstract. We introduce a new property of tile self-assembly systems that we call *size-separability*. A system is size-separable if every terminal assembly is a constant factor larger than any intermediate assembly. Size-separability is motivated by the practical problem of filtering completed assemblies from a variety of incomplete "garbage" assemblies using gel electrophoresis or other mass-based filtering techniques.

Here we prove that any system without cooperative bonding assembling a unique mismatch-free terminal assembly can be used to construct a size-separable system uniquely assembling the same shape. The proof achieves optimal scale factor, temperature, and tile types (within a factor of 2) for the size-separable system. As part of the proof, we obtain two results of independent interest on mismatch-free temperature-1 two-handed systems.

Keywords: 2HAM, hierarchical, aTAM, glues, gel electrophoresis.

1 Introduction

The study of theoretical tile self-assembly was initiated by the Ph.D. thesis of Erik Winfree [18]. He proved that systems of passive square particles (called *tiles*) that attach according to matching bonds (called *glues*) are capable of universal computation and efficient assembly of shapes such as squares. Soloveichik and Winfree [16] later proved that these systems are capable of efficient assembly of any shape, allowing for an arbitrary scaling of the shape, used to embed a roving Turing machine. In this original *abstract Tile Assembly Model (aTAM)*, tiles attach singly to a growing seed assembly.

An alternative model, called the *two-handed assembly model (2HAM)* [1,2,4,5], *hierarchical tile assembly model* [3,13], or *polyomino tile assembly model* [8,9], allows "seedless" assembly, where tiles can attach spontaneously to form large assemblies that may attach to each other. This seedless assembly was proved by Cannon et al. [2] to be capable of simulating any seeded assembly process, while also achieving more efficient assembly of some classes of shapes.

---

* A full version of this paper can be found at http://arxiv.org/abs/1404.7410

O.H. Ibarra et al. (Eds.): UCNC 2014, LNCS 8553, pp. 367–378, 2014.
DOI: 10.1007/978-3-319-08123-6_30, © Springer International Publishing Switzerland 2014

A generalization of the 2HAM called the *staged tile assembly model* introduced by Demaine et al. [4] utilizes sequences of *mixings*, where each mixing combines a set of *input assemblies* using a 2HAM assembly process. The products of the mixing are the *terminal assemblies* that cannot combine with any other assembly produced during the assembly process (called a *producible assembly*). This set of terminal assemblies can then be used as input assemblies in another mixing, combined with the sets of terminal assemblies from other mixings.

After a presentation by the author of work [19] on the staged self-assembly model at DNA 19, Erik Winfree commented that the staged tile assembly model has a unrealistic assumption: at the end of each mixing process, all producible but non-terminal assemblies are removed from the mixing. A similar assumption is made in the 2HAM model, where only the terminal assemblies are considered to be "produced" by the system.

Ignoring large producible assemblies is done to simplify the model definition, but allows unrealistic scenarios where "nearly terminal" systems differing from some terminal assembly by a small number of tiles are presumed to be eliminated or otherwise removed at the end of the assembly process. While filtering techniques, including well-known gel electrophoresis, may be employed to obtain filtering of particles at the nanoscale, such techniques generally lack the resolution to distinguish between macromolecules that differ in size by only a small amount.

Our Results. In this work, we consider efficient assembly of shapes in the 2HAM model under the restriction that terminal assemblies are significantly larger than all non-terminal producible assemblies. We call a system *factor-c size-separable* if the ratio between the smallest terminal assembly and largest non-terminal producible assembly is at least c. Thus, high-factor size-separable systems lack large but non-terminal assemblies, allowing robust filtering of terminal from non-terminal assemblies in these systems.

Our main result is an algorithm for converting 2HAM systems of a special class into size-separable 2HAM systems. A 2HAM system $\mathcal{S} = (T, f, \tau)$ consists of a set of *tiles* T that attach by forming bonds according to their *glues* and a *glue-strength function* f, and two assemblies can attach if the total strength of the bonds formed meets or exceeds the temperature τ of the system. If a system is temperature-1 ($\tau = 1$), then any two assemblies can attach if they have a single matching glue. An assembly is said to be *mismatch-free* if no two coincident tile sides in the assembly or any assembly in the system have different glues. We prove the following:

Theorem 1. *Let $\mathcal{S} = (T, f, 1)$ be a 2HAM system with a mismatch-free unique terminal assembly A. Then there exists a factor-2 size-separable 2HAM system $\mathcal{S}' = (T', f', 2)$ with a unique mismatch-free finite terminal assembly A' such that $|\mathcal{S}'| \leq 8|\mathcal{S}|$ and A' has the shape of A scaled by a factor of 2.*

Along the way, we prove two results of independent interest on temperature-1 mismatch-free systems. The *bond graph* of an assembly A, denoted $G(A)$, is the dual graph of A formed by a node for each tile, and an edge between two tiles if they form a bond. We show that any system with a unique mismatch-free finite terminal assembly whose bond graph is not a tree can be made so without increasing the number of tile types in the system:

Lemma 7 (Tree-ification Lemma). *Let $S = (T, f, 1)$ be a 2HAM system with unique mismatch-free finite terminal assembly A. Then there exists a 2HAM system $S' = (T', f', 1)$ with unique mismatch-free finite terminal assembly A' and $|S'| \leq |S|$, where A' has the shape of A and $G(A')$ is a tree.*

The proof of the Tree-ification Lemma yields a simple algorithm for obtaining S': while a cycle in $G(A)$ remains, remove a glue on this cycle from the tile type containing it. The challenge is in proving such a process does not disconnect $G(A)$, regardless of the glue and cycle chosen.

We also prove that the tile types used only once in a unique terminal assembly, called *1-occurrence tiles*, form a connected subgraph of $G(A)$. That is, these tiles taken alone form a valid assembly.

Lemma 9. *Let $S = (T, f, 1)$ be a 2HAM system with unique mismatch-free finite terminal assembly A. Then the 1-occurrence tiles in A form a 1-stable subassembly of A.*

For some questions about temperature-1 systems, results have been far easier to obtain for mismatch-free systems than for general systems allowing mismatches. For instance, a lower bound of $2n - 1$ for the assembly of a $n \times n$ square by any temperature 1 aTAM system was conjectured by Rothemund and Winfree [15], and proved for mismatch-free systems by Maňuch, Stacho, and Stoll [10]. Meunier [11] was able to show the same lower bound for systems permitted to have mismatches under the assumption that the seed tile starts in the lower left of the assembly, and removing this restriction remains open. In a similar vein, Reif and Song [14] have shown that temperature-1 mismatch-free aTAM systems are not computationally universal, while the same problem for systems with mismatches permitted is a notoriously difficult problem that remains open, despite significant efforts [7,6,17,12].

In spite of such results, constructing high-factor size-separable versions of temperature-1 mismatch-free systems remains challenging. One difficulty lies in the partitioning the assembly into two equal-sized halves that will come together for the final assembly step. Note that for many assemblies, such a cutting is impossible (e.g. the right assembly in Figure 1). Even if such a cutting is possible, removing the bonds connecting the two halves by modifying the tiles along the boundary may require a large increase in the number of tile types of the system.

Another challenge lies in coping with cycles in the bond graph. Factor-2 size-separability requires that the last assembly step consists of two completely assembled halves of the unique terminal assembly attaching. Cycles in the bond graph (e.g. the left assembly in Figure 1) prevent communication between the tiles inside and outside of the cycles, risking the possibility that the portion of

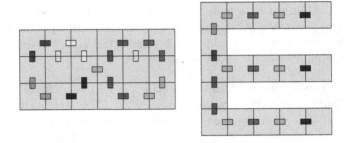

Fig. 1. Unique mismatch-free terminal assemblies of two different temperature-1 2HAM systems. Constructing high-factor size-separable versions of these systems is challenging due to the existence of cycles (left) and lack of equal-sized halves (right).

the assembly inside a cycle still has missing tiles as the exterior takes part in the supposed final assembly step.

Loosely speaking, our approach is to first construct a version of A where the bond graph is a tree and a vertex cut of $G(A)$ consisting of a path of 1-occurrence tiles exists. This modified version of A is then scaled in size and temperature by a factor of 2, using special 2×2 macrotiles that only assemble along the boundary of the scaled assembly via mixed-strength bonds. Finally, the 1-occurrence tiles forming a vertex cut are given weakened glues such that only completely formed subassemblies on both sides of the cut can attach across the weak-glue cut.

2   Definitions

Here we give a complete set of formal definitions of tile self-assembly used throughout the paper. All of the definitions used are equivalent to those found in prior work on the two-handed tile assembly model, e.g. [1,2,3,13].

Assembly Systems. In this work we study the *two-handed tile assembly model (2HAM)*, and instances of the model called *systems*. A 2HAM system $\mathcal{S} = (T, f, \tau)$ is specified by three parts: a *tile set* T, a *glue-strength function* f, and a *temperature* $\tau \in \mathbb{N}$.

The tile set T is a set of unit square *tiles*. Each tile $t \in T$ is defined by 4-tuple $t = (g_n, g_e, g_s, g_w)$ consisting of four *glues* from a set Σ of *glue types*, i.e. $g_n, g_e, g_s, g_w \in \Sigma$. The four glues g_n, g_e, g_s, g_w specify the glue types in Σ found on the north (N), east (E), south (S), and west (W) sides of t, respectively. Each glue also defines a *glue-side*, e.g. (g_n, N). Define $g_D(t)$ to be the glue on the side D of t, e.g. $g_N(t) = g_n$.

The glue function $f : \Sigma^2 \to \mathbb{N}$ determines the strength of the *bond* formed by two coincident glue-sides. For any two glues $g, g' \in \Sigma$, $f(g, g') = f(g', g)$. A unique *null glue* $\varnothing \in \Sigma$ has the property that $f(\varnothing, g) = 0$ for all $g \in \Sigma$. In this work we only consider glue functions such that for all $g, g' \in \Sigma$, $f(g, g') = 0$ and if $g \neq \varnothing, f(g, g) > 0$. For convenience, we sometimes refer to a glue-side with the null glue as a side *without a glue*.

Configurations and Assemblies. A *configuration* is a partial function $C : \mathbb{Z}^2 \to T$ mapping locations on the integer lattice to tiles. Define $L_D(x,y)$ to be the location in $\mathbb{Z}^2$ one unit in direction D from (x,y), e.g. $L_N(0,0) = (0,1)$. For any pair of locations $(x,y), L_D(x,y) \in C$, the *bond strength* between the these tiles is $f(g_D(C(x,y)), g_{D^{-1}}(C(L_D(x,y))))$. If $g_D(C(x,y)) \neq g_{D^{-1}}(C(L_D(x,y)))$, then the pair of tiles is said to form a *mismatch*, and a configuration with no mismatches is *mismatch-free*. If $g_D(C(x,y)) = g_{D^{-1}}(C(L_D(x,y)))$, then the common glue and pair of directions define a *glue-side pair* $(g_D(C(x,y)), \{D, D^{-1}\})$.

The *bond graph of* C, denoted $G(C)$, is defined as the graph with vertices $\mathrm{dom}(C)$ and edges $\{((x,y), L_D(x,y)) : f(g_D(C(x,y)), g_{D^{-1}}(C(L_D(x,y)))) > 0\}$. That is, the graph induced by the neighboring tiles of C forming positive-strength bonds.

A configuration C is a τ-*stable assembly* or an *assembly at temperature* τ if $\mathrm{dom}(C)$ is connected on the lattice and, for any partition of $\mathrm{dom}(C)$ into two subconfigurations C_1 and C_2, the sum of the bond strengths between tiles at pairs of locations $p_1 \in \mathrm{dom}(C_1)$, $p_2 \in \mathrm{dom}(C_2)$ is at least τ, the temperature of the system. Any pair of assemblies A_1, A_2 are equivalent if they are identical up to a translation by $\langle x,y \rangle$ with $x, y \in \mathbb{Z}$. The *size* of an assembly A is $|\mathrm{dom}(A)|$, and $t \in T$ is a k-*occurrence* tile in A if $|\{(x,y) \in \mathrm{dom}(A) : A(x,y) = t\}| = k$. The *shape* of an assembly is the polyomino induced by $\mathrm{dom}(A)$, and a shape is *scaled by a factor* k by replacing each cell of the polyomino with a $k \times k$ block of cells.

Two τ-stable assemblies A_1, A_2 are said to *assemble* into a *superassembly* A_3 if A_2 is equivalent to an assembly A_2' such that $\mathrm{dom}(A_1) \cap \mathrm{dom}(A_2') = \emptyset$ and A_3 defined by the union of the partial functions A_1 and A_2' is a τ-stable assembly. Similarly, an assembly A_1 is a *subassembly* of A_2, denoted $A_1 \subseteq A_2$, if A_2 is equivalent to an assembly A_2' such that $\mathrm{dom}(A_1) \subseteq \mathrm{dom}(A_2')$.

Producible and Terminal Assemblies. An assembly A is a *producible assembly* of a 2HAM system $\mathcal{S}$ if A can be assembled from two other producible assemblies or A is a single tile in T. A producible assembly A is a *terminal assembly* of $\mathcal{S}$ if A is producible and A does not assemble with any other producible assembly of $\mathcal{S}$.

We also consider *seeded* versions of some 2HAM systems, where an assembly is producible if it can be assembled from another producible assembly and a single tile of T. Note that for any temperature-1 2HAM system $\mathcal{S}$, the seeded version of $\mathcal{S}$ has the same set of terminal assemblies as $\mathcal{S}$.

If $\mathcal{S}$ has a single terminal assembly A, we call A the *unique terminal assembly* *(UTA)* of $\mathcal{S}$. In the case that $|A|$ is finite and mismatch-free, we further call A the *unique mismatch-free finite terminal assembly (UMFTA)* of $\mathcal{S}$.

Size-Separability. A 2HAM system $\mathcal{S} = (T, f, \tau)$ is a *factor-c size-separable* if for any pair of producible assemblies A, B of $\mathcal{S}$ with A terminal and B not terminal, $|A|/|B| \geq c$. Since this ratio is undefined when $\mathcal{S}$ has infinite producible assemblies, we define such a system to have undefined size-separability. Every system with defined size-separability has factor-c size-separability for some $1 \leq c \leq 2$.

3   Tree-ification

First, we prove that any $\tau = 1$ system producing a unique terminal assembly can be converted into a system with another unique terminal assembly with the same shape but whose bond graph is a tree.

Lemma 1. *Let $\mathcal{S} = (T, f, 1)$ be a 2HAM system. Every 1-stable assembly consisting of tiles in T is a producible assembly of $\mathcal{S}$.*

Lemma 2. *Let $\mathcal{S} = (T, f, 1)$ be a 2HAM system with UTA A. Let a glue-side pair appear twice on a simple cycle of $G(A)$ between tiles t_1 and t_2, and t_3 and t_4. Then $|\{t_1, t_2, t_3, t_4\}| \neq 4$.*

Lemma 3. *Let $\mathcal{S} = (T, f, 1)$ be a 2HAM system with UMFTA A. Let a glue-side pair appear twice on a simple cycle of $G(A)$ between tiles t_1 and t_2, and t_3 and t_4. Then $|\{t_1, t_2, t_3, t_4\}| \neq 2$.*

Lemma 4. *Let $\mathcal{S} = (T, f, 1)$ be a 2HAM system with UTA A. Let a glue-side pair appear twice on a simple cycle of $G(A)$ between tiles t_1 and t_2, and t_3 and t_4. Then $|\{t_1, t_2, t_3, t_4\}| \neq 3$.*

Lemma 5. *Let $\mathcal{S} = (T, f, 1)$ be a 2HAM system with UMFTA A. Then no glue-side pair appears twice on a simple cycle of $G(A)$.*

Lemma 6. *Let $\mathcal{S} = (T, f, 1)$ be a 2HAM system with UMFTA A. Let (g, p) be the glue-side pair of an edge e in $G(A)$. Then if e lies on a simple cycle in $G(A)$, all edges with glue-side pair (g, p) lie on simple cycles of $G(A)$.*

Lemma 7 (Tree-ification Lemma). *Let $\mathcal{S} = (T, f, 1)$ be a 2HAM system with UMFTA A. Then there exists a 2HAM system $\mathcal{S}' = (T', f', 1)$ with UMFTA A' and $|\mathcal{S}'| \leq |\mathcal{S}|$, where A' has the shape of A and $G(A')$ is a tree.*

4   1-Occurrence Tile Types

In addition to tree-ification, we also make use of the existence of *1-occurrence tile types*: tile types that appear only once in the terminal assembly of the system.

Lemma 8. *Let $\mathcal{S} = (T, f, 1)$ be a 2HAM system with UMFTA A with $G(A)$ a tree and $|A| \geq 2$. Then A has at least two 1-occurrence tiles.*

Lemma 9. *Let $\mathcal{S} = (T, f, 1)$ be a 2HAM system with UMFTA A. Then the 1-occurrence tiles in A form a 1-stable subassembly of A.*

Lemma 10. *Let $\mathcal{S} = (T, f, 1)$ be a 2HAM system with UTA A. For any glue-side pair (g, p) occurring between a pair of 1-occurrence tiles in A, (g, p) occurs only once in A.*

Lemma 11. *Let* $\mathcal{S} = (T, f, 1)$ *be a 2HAM system with UMFTA* A *with* $G(A)$ *a tree. For any tile* $t \in T$, *the simple path in* $G(A)$ *between any two occurrences of* t *uses the same glue-side of* t *on both occurrences.*

Lemma 12. *Let* $\mathcal{S} = (T, f, 1)$ *be a 2HAM system with UMFTA* A *with* $G(A)$ *a tree. Let edges* $e, e' \in G(A)$, *with* e' *between a pair of 1-occurrence tiles. Then there exists a second 2HAM system* $\mathcal{S}' = (T', f', 1)$ *with* $|T'| \leq 2|T|$ *and UMFTA* A' *with* $G(A') = G(A)$ *and the unique path from* e' *to* e *in* $G(A')$ *consisting entirely of 1-occurrence tiles in* A'.

5   A Size-Separable Macrotile Construction

A simple barrier to general high-factor size-separability is the fact that any system with a tree-shaped unique terminal assembly A cannot be factor-c size-separable for any $c > 1 + 1/|A|$. A more subtle challenge is how to partition assemblies into equal-sized 1-stable halves that will come together in the final assembly step. We resolve both of these issues by creating a temperature-2 2HAM system with a unique terminal assembly whose shape is the shape of A scaled by a factor of 2, and whose bond graph has an edge cut of two temperature-1 bonds that partitions $G(A)$ into two subgraphs of equal size.

Lemma 13. *Let* $\mathcal{S} = (T, f, \tau)$ *be a 2HAM system with* P *and* P' *producible assemblies of* $\mathcal{S}$ *with* P *a proper subassembly of* P'. *Then* P *is not a terminal assembly.*

Lemma 14. *Let* $\mathcal{S} = (T, f, 1)$ *be a 2HAM system with UMFTA* A *with* $G(A)$ *a tree. Then there exists a 2HAM system* $\mathcal{S}' = (T', f', 2)$ *with UMFTA* A' *and* $|\mathcal{S}'| \leq 4|\mathcal{S}|$ *such that* A' *has the shape of* A *scaled by a factor of 2.*

Proof. We start by describing common properties of all occurrences of each tile type $t \in T$. Since $G(A)$ is a tree, Lemmas 8 and 9 imply that there exists an edge e' in $G(A)$ between two 1-occurrence tiles and Lemma 11 implies that any path between two occurrences of t use the same glue-side pair. So any breadth-first search $G(A)$ starting at a 1-occurrence tile incident to e' visits all occurrences of t exactly once, and all via incoming edges from the same side of t. Then since A is mismatch-free, if a direction is applied to each edge of $G(A)$ according to the direction of traversal during the breadth-first search, all occurrences of t have the same set of incoming and outgoing edges. So all occurrences of t have their corners visited in the same order during a traversal of the boundary of A.

We use these conditions to construct unique macrotile versions of each tile type according to their incoming and outgoing edges induced by the breadth-first search starting at e'. All possible macrotile constructions (up to symmetry) are shown in Figure 2. For each glue-side pair in the original system, we use two glue-side pairs in the scaled system, one with strength-2 and the other with strength-1. The glue-side pair visited first in the counterclockwise traversal of the boundary starting at e' has strength 2, while the other pair has strength 1.

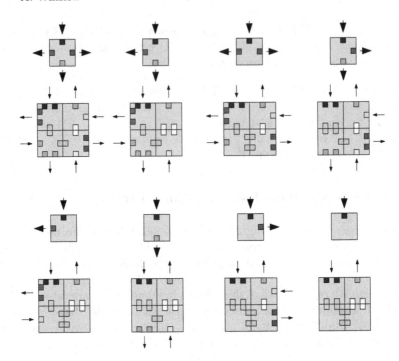

Fig. 2. The individual tiles enumerate (up to symmetry) all combinations of incoming and outgoing edges (large arrows) induced by a breath-first search of $G(A)$. The corresponding 2×2 macrotiles are used in the proof of Theorem 1 to construct a temperature-2 system that carries out the assembly of A at scale 2 in the order that the tiles appear along the boundary (small arrows). All internal macrotile glues are unique to the tile type, while all external macrotile glues correspond to the glues found on the surface of the inducing tile.

There are also three glues internal to each macrotile attaching each pair of adjacent tiles forming a macroedge whose corresponding edge of the tile either has an outgoing edge induced by the breadth-first search, or has no edge. These glues are unique to the macrotile type. The strengths of each of these glues is determined by whether the closest macroside has glues. If not, then the glue is strength-2, otherwise the glue is strength-1.

If the closest macroside does not contain a glue, then the strength-2 internal glue is necessary to allow assembly to continue along the boundary of the assembly in the counterclockwise direction (e.g. from the northwest to the southwest tile). If the closest macroside does contain a glue, then the strength-1 internal glue prevents the placement of the next tile in the macrotile (e.g. the southwest tile after the northwest tile) until a second tile from an adjacent macrotile (e.g. the southeast tile of the macrotile to the west) has been placed. As a result, no pair of tiles in a macrotile can be present in a common assembly unless all tiles between them along a counterclockwise traversal of the boundary of the macrotile assembly are also present.

SCALED ASSEMBLY OF A. We claim that this scaled version of the system has a unique terminal assembly A' obtained by replacing each tile in the original unique terminal assembly with the corresponding 2×2 macrotile. First we prove that any subassembly of A' corresponding to a subtree of $G(A)$ is producible. A subtree of size 1 corresponds to a leaf node, the lower-rightmost case in Figure 2, and is clearly producible. For larger subtrees, the assembly can be formed by combining the 4 tiles of the root macrotile to the (up to) three subtrees assemblies. Grow the assembly in counterclockwise order around the boundary, attaching either a subtree assembly (if the macroside has a glue) or the next tile of the root macrotile. In both cases, placing the second root tile along the macroedge is possible, as either the internal glue shared with the previous root tile is strength-2 or a second glue is provided by the subtree assembly. Then by induction, the assembly A' corresponding to the subtree rooted at the root of the breadth-first search is producible.

By construction, A' is terminal because it corresponds to a mismatch-free terminal assembly in the original system that necessarily has no exposed glues. So A' is a terminal assembly of the scaled system. Next, we prove that A' is the unique terminal assembly of the system.

TERMINAL ASSEMBLY UNIQUENESS. We start by proving that every producible assembly can positioned on a 2×2 macrotile *grid*, where every tile in the south-west corner is a southwest tile of some macrotile, every tile in the northwest corner is the northwest tile of some macrotile, etc. Start by noticing that each glue type appears coincident to only one of 12 edges of the grid: the 4 internal edges of each macrotile, and the 8 external edges. Suppose there is some smallest producible assembly that does not lie on a grid. Then this assembly must be formed by the attachment of two smaller assemblies that do lie on grids, and whose glues utilized in the attachment are coincident to only one of 12 edges of the grid. So if these assemblies are translated to have coincident matching glue sides, then their grids must also be aligned and the assembly resulting from their attachment also lies on the grid, a contradiction.

Let A'_p be a producible assembly of the macrotile system that is not A'. Construct an assembly A_p of the original input system S in the following way: replace each macrotile region with a single tile corresponding to one of the tiles in the macrotile region. If such a replacement is unambiguous, meaning that all tiles in each macrotile region belong to a common macrotile, then the resulting assembly is a 1-stable (and thus producible) assembly of S.

We also claim that such a replacement is always unambiguous. Suppose, for the sake of contradiction, that there is some A'_p such that replacement is ambiguous. The ambiguity must be due to two tiles in the same macrotile region bonded via external strength-2 glues on *different* macrosides to tiles in adjacent macrotiles, since no macroside has two strength-2 glues (see Figure 2). So there is some path in $G(A'_p)$ from the external glue of one of of these tiles to the external glue to the other consisting of length-2 and length-3 subpaths through other macrotile regions, each consisting of tiles of a common macrotile. So this path can be unambiguously replaced with a path from tiles in S from one side of a tile location to the other side, with some tile of S able to attach at this location. But this yields a producible assembly of S (and thus a subassembly of A) with a cycle, a contradiction. Since constructing A_p from A'_p is always unambiguous, and A_p is a subassembly of A, A'_p is a subassembly of A'. Then by Lemma 13, A'_p is not terminal.   □

Theorem 1. *Let $S = (T, f, 1)$ be a 2HAM system with UMFTA A. Then there exists a factor-2 size-separable 2HAM system $S' = (T', f', 2)$ with UMFTA A' and $|S'| \leq 8|S|$. Furthermore, A' has the shape of A scaled by a factor of 2.*

Proof (Sketch). We modify the construction used in the proof of Lemma 14 in two ways. First, we use Lemma 12 to create a path of 1-occurrence tiles in A that partitions A into two 1-stable subassemblies, each containing a contiguous, equal-sized half of the boundary of A. This is done to the original system S, before the macrotile conversion is performed. Second, after constructing the macrotile system S', we modify some of the glues of the macrotiles corresponding to this path of 1-occurrence tiles to give the unique terminal assembly A' of the macrotile system a 2-edge cut. These two edges occur at opposite ends of the path of 1-occurrence tiles, and reducing their strength to 1 enforces that A' can only assemble from two equal-sized halves.   □

6   Open Problems

For temperature-1 systems with mismatch-free unique terminal assemblies, our result is nearly as tight as possible. Scaling to at least a factor of 2 and using temperature of at least 2 are both necessary, since any temperature-1 system or system with a tree-shaped assembly is at most factor-$(1 + 1/|A|)$ size-separable. The only remaining opportunity for improvement is to reduce the number of tile types used to less than $8|S|$.

We contend that our result is a first step in understanding what is possible in size-separable systems, and a large number of open problems remain. Perhaps the most natural problem is to extend this result to the same set of systems, except permitting mismatches. We conjecture that a similar result is possible there:

Conjecture 1. Let $S = (T, f, 1)$ be a 2HAM system with unique finite terminal assembly A. Then there exists factor-2 size-separable system $S' = (T', f', 2)$ with a unique finite terminal assembly A' and $|S'| = O(S)$. Furthermore, A' has the shape A scaled by a factor of $O(1)$.

Extending the result to mismatch-free systems at higher temperatures also is of interest because these systems are generally capable of much more efficient assembly. Soloveichik and Winfree [16] prove that one can construct a temperature-2 system that uses an optimal number of tiles (within a constant factor) to construct any shape, provided one is allowed to scale the shape by an arbitrary amount, and it is likely their construction can be modified to be factor-2 size-separable. However, it remains open to achieve high-factor size-separable systems at temperature 2 using only a small scale factor.

Conjecture 2. Let $\mathcal{S} = (T, f, 1)$ be a 2HAM system with UMFTA A. Then there exists factor-2 size-separable system $\mathcal{S}' = (T', f', 2)$ with a unique terminal assembly A' and $|\mathcal{S}'| = O(\mathcal{S})$. Furthermore, A' has the shape A scaled by a factor of $O(1)$.

In the interest of applying size-separability to system in the staged model of tile self-assembly, we pose the problem of developing size-separable systems with multiple terminal assemblies. Of course, one can construct systems where the smallest terminal assembly is less than half the size of the largest terminal assembly, ensuring that the system cannot even be factor-1 size-separable. But given a system whose ratio of smallest to largest terminal assembly is c, is a size-separable system with optimal factor $\frac{2}{c}$ always possible?

Conjecture 3. Let $\mathcal{S} = (T, f, 1)$ be a 2HAM system with finite terminal assemblies $A_1, A_2, \ldots, A_k$ with A_1 and A_k the smallest and largest terminal assemblies. Then there exists factor-$|A_k|/|A_1|$ size-separable system $\mathcal{S}' = (T', f', 2)$ with $|\mathcal{S}'| = O(\mathcal{S})$ and mismatch-free terminal assemblies $A_1', A_2', \ldots, A_k'$ where A_i' has the shape of A_i scaled by a factor of $O(1)$.

We close by conjecturing that not every system can be made size-separable by paying only a constant factor in scale and tile types. We ask for an example of such a system:

Conjecture 4. There exists a 2HAM system $\mathcal{S} = (T, f, \tau)$ with a unique finite terminal assembly A such that any factor-2 size-separable system $\mathcal{S}' = (T', f', \tau')$ with unique finite terminal assembly A' with the shape of A either has $|\mathcal{S}'| \geq 100|\mathcal{S}|$ or the scale of A' is at least 100.

Acknowledgments. We thank the anonymous UCNC reviews for their comments that improved the presentation and correctness of the paper.

References

1. Abel, Z., Benbernou, N., Damian, M., Demaine, E.D., Demaine, M.L., Flatland, R., Kominers, S.D., Schweller, R.: Shape replication through self-assembly and RNase enzymes. In: Proceedings of the 21st ACM-SIAM Symposium on Discrete Algorithms (SODA), pp. 1045–1064 (2010)
2. Cannon, S., Demaine, E.D., Demaine, M.L., Eisenstat, S., Patitz, M.J., Schweller, R.T., Summers, S.M., Winslow, A.: Two hands are better than one (up to constant factors): Self-assembly in the 2HAM vs. aTAM. In: STACS 2013. LIPIcs, vol. 20, pp. 172–184. Schloss Dagstuhl–Leibniz-Zentrum fuer Informatik (2013)
3. Chen, H., Doty, D.: Parallelism and time in hierarchical self-assembly. In: Proceedings of the 23rd Annual ACM-SIAM Symposium on Discrete Algorithms (SODA), pp. 1163–1182 (2012)
4. Demaine, E.D., Demaine, M.L., Fekete, S.P., Ishaque, M., Rafalin, E., Schweller, R.T., Souvaine, D.L.: Staged self-assembly: nanomanufacture of arbitrary shapes with $O(1)$ glues. Natural Computing 7(3), 347–370 (2008)

5. Doty, D., Patitz, M.J., Reishus, D., Schweller, R.T., Summers, S.M.: Strong fault-tolerance for self-assembly with fuzzy temperature. In: Foundations of Computer Science (FOCS), pp. 417–426 (2010)
6. Doty, D., Patitz, M.J., Summers, S.M.: Limitations of self-assembly at temperature one. In: Deaton, R., Suyama, A. (eds.) DNA 15. LNCS, vol. 5877, pp. 35–44. Springer, Heidelberg (2009)
7. Lathrop, J.I., Lutz, J.H., Patitz, M.J., Summers, S.M.: Computability and complexity in self-assembly. In: Beckmann, A., Dimitracopoulos, C., Löwe, B. (eds.) CiE 2008. LNCS, vol. 5028, pp. 349–358. Springer, Heidelberg (2008)
8. Luhrs, C.: Polyomino-safe DNA self-assembly via block replacement. In: Goel, A., Simmel, F.C., Sosík, P. (eds.) DNA 14. LNCS, vol. 5347, pp. 112–126. Springer, Heidelberg (2009)
9. Luhrs, C.: Polyomino-safe DNA self-assembly via block replacement. Natural Computing 9(1), 97–109 (2010)
10. Mañuch, J., Stacho, L., Stoll, C.: Journal of Computational Biology 16(6), 841–852 (2010)
11. Meunier, P.-E.: The self-assembly of paths and squares at temperature 1. Technical report, arXiv (2014), http://arxiv.org/abs/1312.1299
12. Meunier, P.-E., Patitz, M.J., Summers, S.M., Theyssier, G., Winslow, A., Woods, D.: Intrinsic universality in tile self-assembly requires cooperation. In: Proceedings of the 25th Annual ACM-SIAM Symposium on Discrete Algorithms (SODA), pp. 752–771 (2014)
13. Padilla, J.E., Patitz, M.J., Pena, R., Schweller, R.T., Seeman, N.C., Sheline, R., Summers, S.M., Zhong, X.: Asynchronous signal passing for tile self-assembly: fuel efficient computation and efficient assembly of shapes. In: Mauri, G., Dennunzio, A., Manzoni, L., Porreca, A.E. (eds.) UCNC 2013. LNCS, vol. 7956, pp. 174–185. Springer, Heidelberg (2013)
14. Reif, J., Song, T.: The computation complexity of temperature-1 tilings. Technical report, Duke University (2014)
15. Rothemund, P.W.K., Winfree, E.: The program-size complexity of self-assembled squares (extended abstract). In: Proceedings of ACM Symposium on Theory of Computing (STOC), pp. 459–468 (2000)
16. Soloveichik, D., Winfree, E.: Complexity of self-assembled shapes. SIAM Journal on Computing 36(6), 1544–1569 (2007)
17. Summers, S.M.: Universality in algorithm self-assembly. PhD thesis, Iowa State University (2010)
18. Winfree, E.: Algorithmic Self-Assembly of DNA. PhD thesis, Caltech (1998)
19. Winslow, A.: Staged self-assembly and polyomino context-free grammars. In: Soloveichik, D., Yurke, B. (eds.) DNA 2013. LNCS, vol. 8141, pp. 174–188. Springer, Heidelberg (2013)

Development of Physical Super-Turing Analog Hardware

A. Steven Younger[1], Emmett Redd[1], and Hava Siegelmann[2]

[1] Missouri State University, Springfield, MO, USA
{steveyounger,emmettredd}@missouristate.edu
[2] University of Massachusetts-Amherst, Amherst, MA, USA
hava@cs.umass.edu

Abstract. In the 1930s, mathematician Alan Turing proposed a mathematical model of computation now called a Turing Machine to describe how people follow repetitive procedures given to them in order to come up with final calculation result. This extraordinary computational model has been the foundation of all modern digital computers since the World War II. Turing also speculated that this model had some limits and that more powerful computing machines should exist. In 1993, Siegelmann and colleagues introduced a Super-Turing Computational Model that may be an answer to Turing's call. Super-Turing computation models have no inherent problem to be realizable physically and biologically. This is unlike the general class of hyper-computer as introduced in 1999 to include the Super-Turing model and some others. This report is on research to design, develop and physically realize two prototypes of analog recurrent neural networks that are capable of solving problems in the Super-Turing complexity hierarchy, similar to the class BPP/log*. We present plans to test and characterize these prototypes on problems that demonstrate anticipated Super-Turing capabilities in modeling Chaotic Systems.

Keywords: Neural Networks · Analog Computing · Super-Turing Computation · Hypercomputing

1 Introduction

This paper describes a project to design, physically realize, and test Super-Turing Machines that are Analog Recurrent Neural Networks (ARNNs). After introducing the Theoretical Foundation, we discuss the design of two ARNN machines—a larger, optical, analog/digital hybrid machine and a smaller, fully analog electronic device. Next, we propose a method to test the Super-Turing characteristics of these machines. Finally, we discuss future research of Super-Turing computers.

2 Theoretical Foundation

In mid-20th Century, Mathematician and World War II Code Breaker, Alan Turing created a mathematical model of 'computers' - the human clerks of his time, who performed repetitive calculations; his model provides the theoretical basis for modern

O.H. Ibarra et al. (Eds.): UCNC 2014, LNCS 8553, pp. 379–391, 2014.
DOI: 10.1007/978-3-319-08123-6_31, © Springer International Publishing Switzerland 2014

computers. This model, known as the Turing Machine, has guided the development of virtually all computer hardware and software for the last seventy years.

However, Turing himself recognized that his model had limitations. For instance, the famous halting problem [1] cannot be solved by a Turing Machine. Turing suggested that the brain works in an analog manner [2] and while he was looking for superior implementations, the technology of his time did not allow for it. In a series of publications [3-5], Siegelmann and colleagues introduced a Super-Turing Computational Model based on Analog Recurrent Neural Networks.

- Recurrent Neural Networks with Rational Numbered Synaptic Weights (RNN [Q]) are equivalent to Turing Machines and can solve problems of complexity class P.
- Recurrent Neural Networks with Real Numbered Synaptic Weights (RNN[R]) can compute beyond the Turing Limit, and can efficiently solve problems of complexity class P/Poly, a strict super-set of P, which also includes non-recursive functions.
- In [5], the computational model was extended to RNNs with rational-valued weights and signals with real-valued probability binary noise. These networks can solve problems of complexity class BPP/log*, where BPP/log* is strictly stronger than P and strictly weaker than P/poly.
- Finally, plastic ARNNs (where the synaptic weights change over time) with adaptability and flexibility – can best model systems with more Brain-Like Intelligence (BLI), even when constrained to rational values throughout.

It is perhaps surprising that Recurrent Neural Networks with rational synaptic weights and signals, and with real-valued probability noise are mathematically stronger than a Turing Machine, given that any physically realizable system can read the noise signals only as binary. However, a long sequence of measurements allows indirect access to the real-valued (continuous) stochastic process. More accurately, the stochastic nature of the noise facilitates the approximation of the real value to high precision. This is in contrast to a hypercomputing machine with real-numbered signals, where access to the real values is direct and immediate. Thus, the computation class (BPP/log*) is of intermediate power. It contains some non-recursive functions.

The noise benefits in Digital Neural Networks have been studied by several researchers. A recent example is [6], where the effects of different types of noise on various learning algorithms and problem sets are presented. We expect similar benefits in our Analog Neural Networks.

We take our inspiration from networks of the BPP/log* complexity class and the plastic network. We have no formal proof our hardware is exactly simulating these, but their noise and plasticity support the similarity. It is our conjecture that physical devices inspired by this model can exhibit some Super-Turing computational abilities.

3   Design of Physically Realizable ARNN Prototypes

We have designed and constructed two different prototype systems based on the above Computational Model. At the time of this writing, both prototypes are nearing completion of development. Experimental validation, testing and characterization phases are expected to start soon. Both prototypes are continuous in signal intensity but discrete-in-time. That is, they are clocked devices. Going to continuous-in-time devices is very difficult, and not required by the ARNN model. Discrete time steps also allows for the control of the systems by conventional digital means.

For both prototypes, a "real noise generator" component will not be required. Noise will be generated by the physics of the devices, and will be naturally present in the neural signals. This mimics biological neural systems, where noise is inherent in the physical and chemical processes of life.

Backpropagation is a supervised learning method used by both prototypes. The recurrent system will be providing its output to chaos calculating circuitry to provide the training data. The circuitry is switchable in real time between providing training data for either the Logistic or Hénon map. A single-input, single-output feedforward network should be able to learn the Logistic map, but an Elman-type network would be required to remember the previous input for learning the Hénon map. Having the network switch its learning back and forth between the two supervising functions will show its plasticity. Recording its output for many iterations will allow for testing its chaotic nature. As discussed below, we have already shown that limited-precision, digital simulations repeat, thereby, negating any claim they mimic chaos. We expect neural networks trained to mimic chaos will not repeat and, therefore, show they are calculating at a super-Turing level.

3.1   OpticARNN

The first prototype, called OpticARNN, is based on an opto-electronic computing hardware platform. It is a hybrid system; while its main computing operations are analog, it does have some digital components. While it is possible to implement all of the computing operations in analog optical hardware, the cost in money, speed, size, and complexity would be large.

We believe that the analog computational part of our machine is sufficient to demonstrate Super-Turing capabilities. It is designed to be able to move additional computations into the "analog path" as necessary. For example, the neural squashing function is currently done in by digital hardware on a Field Programmable Gate Array (FPGA) device. It could be done by analog electronics (as we do on the e-ARNN below), or even by an optical non-linear threshold device.

The noise presented in this prototype stems from primarily from optical photon count statistics and exhibits a Poisson distribution. It is also called "shot noise." For large numbers of photon counts (such as we have in our device) the Poisson distribution becomes identical to a Gaussian distribution. The standard deviation of the mean (standard error) is reduced by the square root of the number of photons counted.

The current optical prototype can implement a moderate-sized ARNN of about 30 neurons and 1000 synapses and is described below.

Stanford Matrix Multiplier. Our first prototype is based on an Opto-Electronic Stanford Matrix-Vector Multiplier [7]. The main matrix multiplication operation of the device is an analog process. However, there are some digital electronic components in the data pathway, namely the neuron squashing function and recurrent signal pathways. The neural network input and output are also digital signals. We believe that these limited digital operations will not interfere with the Super-Turing capabilities of the device. Future versions of the OpticARNN may move these digital operations into the analog pathway.

The principle of the Stanford Matrix Multiplier is that light from each of the intensity-modulated horizontal lasers (x_i) is expanded by optics to project onto a Spatial Light Modulator (SLM) as a vertical bar. The SLM attenuates the light according to the pattern of the Matrix Elements (W_{ji}), performing the (analog) $W_{ji}*x_i$ computation. After the attenuation, the light is focused onto a vertical linear array of photodetectors. This performs an analog summation of the attenuated signals, with each $s_j = \Sigma_i W_{ji}*x_i$ corresponding to a region of interest along the linear photodetector array.

Inhibitory and Excitatory Synapses. One issue is that this process can only compute positive signals and matrix elements, since light intensities cannot be easily subtracted. Neural network computations require that some matrix elements be inhibitory: that is negative synaptic weights. We solve this problem by locating positive and negative matrix elements on alternating rows, and performing the final subtraction after the light signals have been converted to electronic ones. Currently, this is done by digital hardware, but may be done with analog electronics (op-amps, etc.) in future versions of the prototype device.

Figure 1 is a schematic of the prototype. Input data to the device is sent from a Host Computer to a Xilinx ML605 Field Programmable Gate Array (FPGA) board. The board, programmed with VHDL Hardware Description Language, generates (in parallel hardware) intensity modulated signals for a linear horizontal array of 60 neural signal source lasers. This laser array consists of five Finisar V850-2092 ICs, each having 12 Vertical Cavity Surface Emitting Lasers (VCSELs). The entire array is only 15 mm in length, and each laser can be independently modulated at high frequencies (~ 1GHz). The laser light is 850mn, which is in the near–infrared region of the spectrum. While not visible to the naked eye, it can be easily detected by photodetectors and also behaves like visible light when interacting with optical components.

Internally, the VHDL architecture is mostly in the form of several Finite State Machines (FSM). One FSM controls the operation and calibration modes. Another FSM controls the communication between the FPGA and the LC1 CCD light sensor array.

Neural Signal Encoding. The OpticARNN can be configured to use a variety of neural signal encoding schemes. Currently, we have implemented Pulse-Width-Modulation (PMW) and Stochastic Pulse Encoding [8], PWM encodes intensities by varying the proportion of 'on' time of the laser during a forward propagation cycle. This should create a very linear response of the CCD-based analog light detector. The time accuracy of the system can be increased by increasing the total number of clock cycles that form a forward propagation cycle.

The second method, Stochastic Pulse encoding, is more similar to the method used by biological neural networks. Neural activations are encoded in a train of ON and OFF pulses. The probability that a given pulse is ON is proportional to the neural activation value. The precision of the signal depends on the length of the pulse train, which is easily adjustable. Pulse based encoding allows for easy extension of the intensity resolution to almost any number of significant bits by changing the length of the pulse trains.

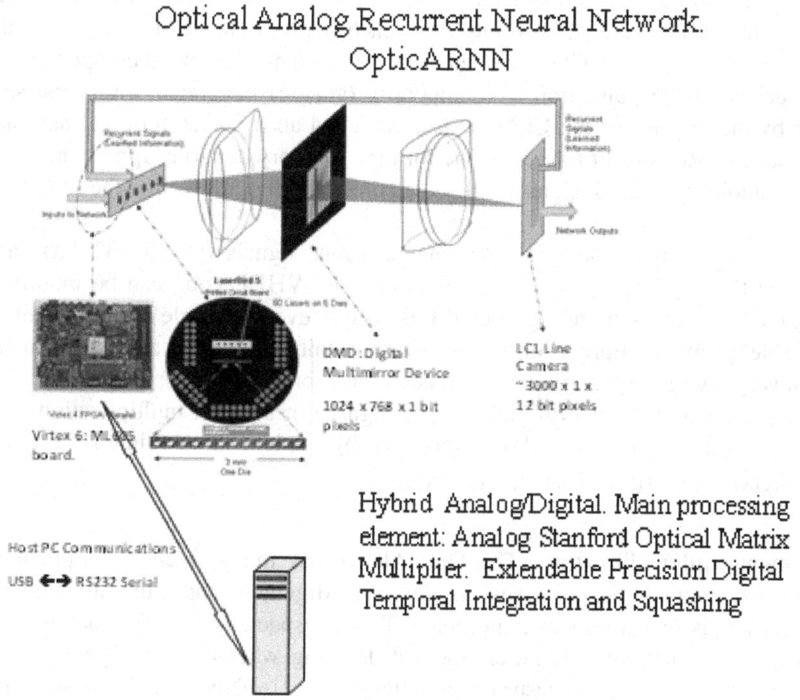

Optical Analog Recurrent Neural Network. OpticARNN

Fig. 1. Schematic of Prototype 1: Optical Analog Recurrent Neural Network (OpticARNN)

Currently, the OpticARNN uses a Linear-Feedback Shift Register based deterministic pseudo-random number generator to produce the pulse train. Note that this encoding method is preferred when one wants a more biologically plausible pulse-based encoding scheme. It is not meant to be the source of the stochastic enhancement required by the BPP/log* Super-Turing properties of the prototype.

The pulses are attenuated (reduced in intensity) by the Spatial Light Modulator (SLM), which encodes the synaptic weight matrix as a 2-Dimensional geometric pattern of pixels that resolve to gray intensity values. Each synaptic weight has a prescribed region of interest at the intersection of the source laser vertical bar and the terminal neuron receptive region on the terminal linear neuron sensor array.

Component Hardware. The SLM used in the prototype is a reflective-mode Digital Micro-Mirror Device (DMD), the same technology used in DLP projectors. It consists of an array of 1024 x 738 tiny mirrors. The mirrors can rapidly and independently flip between ON and OFF positions under software control from the Host Computer. Since each synaptic region of interest consists of more than 256 pixels, several significant bits of attenuation can be devoted per synaptic weight. Future versions may replace the DMD with continuous grey scale devices, such as photographic film or an analog SLM.

The terminal neuron photodetectors are a 2048 x 1 linear array of photodetectors. The (attenuated) optical pulse trains from each appropriate SLM synaptic area are focused onto a range of CCD photodetectors by postsynaptic optical components. The net intensity of the pulse trains is temporally (analog) integrated within the sensor pixels by the physics of the CCD device. As noted above, each terminal neuron actually has two Regions of Interest—one for the excitatory dendrite signals and another for the inhibitory dendrite signals. They are combined digitally within the FPGA Controller.

The internal digital pathways for the recurrent signals (usually 32 bit) can be increased to very large precision as required. The VHDL code can be modified to accommodate 128 or more significant bits. It can even be made to be dynamically adjustable, growing in precision as the system requires it. This is a feature which exists on very few (if any) software-based neural networks.

The prototype can perform higher-order signal-times-signal multiplications by either using a Σ-$\wedge$ (SIGMA-AND) method [9], by implementing (digital) product, or Σ-Π (SIGMA-PI) [10] neurons in the FPGA.

Alignment and Calibration. The OpticARNN has many free-space optical light signals, each interacting with several devices. Alignment and calibration of all of these signals is of paramount importance. This is especially true for analog signals, where proper functioning requires not just deciding whether each signal is ON or OFF, but also accurately measuring the intensity level of the signal. Substantial development effort was spent in developing alignment and calibration procedures. We believe that these procedures insure the proper accuracy and functioning of the prototype.

3.2   Electronic Analog Recurrent Neural Networks (e-ARNN)

The second prototype, called e-ARNN, is based on analog electronics. All of its computing operations are analog with no digital components except for interfacing to a host computer system. It implements a fully analog recurrent neural network and a Backpropagation of Errors learning algorithm. Although not the normal mode of operation, external learning algorithms can provide the e-ARNN synaptic weights. These weights will be rational if provided by a digital-to-analog converter. The Backpropagation synaptic weights will be fully analog. However, we can only implement a small ARNN in its current configuration—3 neurons and 11 synapses. It uses analog multipliers, summers, op amps, and other components to perform both neural network forward propagation and the Backpropagation learning algorithm.

This device will have stochastic noise via Johnson–Nyquist noise, which stems from the thermal agitation of the electrons inside the wires and components of the system. This noise, like shot noise, also tends to have a Gaussian distribution.

Siegelmann's theoretical results [3-5] depend on an Analog Recurrent Neural Network. Her example theoretical network to construct circuits implements a specific algorithm; it cannot learn as does other neural network implementations. It also quickly consumes resolving power which cannot be accommodated in real circuitry.

Integrated circuit (IC), analog voltage multipliers coupled with Younger's analysis [11] of the back propagation learning algorithm allows a fully analog, learning neural network to be designed. Regardless of the layer (input, hidden, or output), the back propagation learning algorithm has similar equations for neurons or synapses. Following Fiesler's notation [10], a 3-layer network has H input neurons, R hidden neurons, and K output neurons.

Back Propagation Synapses. In a three-layer network, between the input and hidden layers are H*R synapses of which one is denoted with 1,h;2,r. Between the hidden and output layers are R*K synapses of which one is denoted 2,r;3,k. Figure 2 shows these in the two colored boxes on the left. In both cases, the forward propagated signal is input at the upper left, multiplied by the synaptic weight, and output at the upper right. The learning algorithm combines specific signals to change the weight depending on how close the network's previous output and its true value are. The synapse's weight is updated by multiplying a signal backpropagating from the downstream neuron (input at lower right) and a one-step-delayed input and, then, adding the previous weight. While the 1,h;2,r synapse needs do nothing else, the 2,r;3,k synapse also has to multiply the signal back-propagating from its downstream neuron and its weight. This signal is output at the lower left and is connected to its upstream (hidden) neuron. In practice, more complex networks (i.e. those with synapses that skip around layers or that recur to their own layer) can be built with these synapses, but the discussion above does not need those complications. Such a network will be illustrated later.

Back Propagation Neurons. A hidden layer neuron (denoted by 2,r) and an output layer neuron (denoted by 3,k) are in the colored boxes on the right of Fig. 3. Both collect outputs from their upstream synapses at their upper left input, sum them, and squash the output that is then presented at the upper right. Both supply a delayed output signal to multiplying and summing circuitry that combines a signal input on the lower right with it. This lower-right (input) signal contains external, error-correcting information. The circuitry uses the external and delayed internal signals to generate the output at lower left. This output is connected to all upstream synapses for their weight-updating calculations discussed above. Except for two items, an output neuron is the same as a hidden neuron; the output neuron must supply the learning rate, η, and proper delay and processing of the previous true value.

For simple summing and squashing operations in the neurons, an AD711 operational amplifier with a specific Zener diode/resistor feedback network is used. Hidden neurons use an op amp to sum the error signals from their downstream synapses.

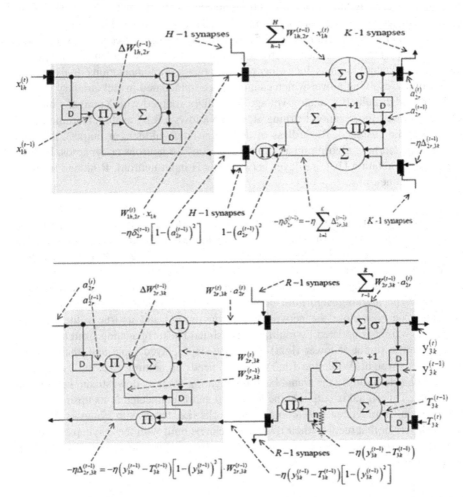

Fig. 2. Functional Schematic of Prototype 2: Electronic Analog Recurrent Neural Network (e-ARNN). Blocks: Upper Left: Input<=>Hidden Synapse, Upper Right: Hidden Neuron, Lower Left: Hidden<=>Output Synapse. Lower Right: Output Neuron.

Analog Elman Network. Figure 4 shows three neurons and eleven synapses implementing a single-input (not counting the bias), two hidden-neuron, single-output Elman neural network[12].

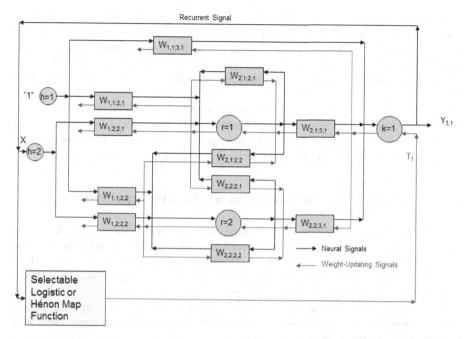

Fig. 3. e-ARNN configured as an Elman Neural Network with Backpropagating Neurons and Synapses. It has recurrence from the output to the input to determine successive points of a chaotic system. It implements supervised learning. The system will be operated to learn either the Logistic [13] or the Hénon [14] map on-the-fly and to switch from learning one to the other.

Fig. 4. Wire Wrap implementation of e-ARNN on Prototyping Board. Left: Component Side (partially populated). Right: Pin Side showing multicolored wiring.

Its output recurs back to the single input. The output is also connected to circuitry which calculates the non-recurring Logistic [13] or Hénon [14] map function. The function provides its output to the T input of the Backpropagation electronics and implements supervised learning. The chaos calculating circuitry will switch between the two maps on external command. The Y output will be tested for consistency with chaos.

The circuitry fills up the circa 1975 computer prototyping board (Fig. 5). The wiring is near completion. Several components in each neuron and synapse must be tuned before training. Part of the Selectable Logistic or Hénon Map Function circuitry is shown in the lower left of the component side of figure.

4   Validation and Measuring Super-Turing Capabilities

Validating and measuring any Super-Turing capability is problematic, similar to the problem of estimating a Turing power (over finite automata), since any data set has is finite precision, while the proofs require infinite precision. The best that can be done are approximation statements of the kind: this data set can be generated by a super-Turing of size X or else by a Turing machine of size Y, or by automata of size Z.

Super-Turing test problems have been suggested, such as the Halting Problem [1] and non-recurrent functions. However, it was not clear to us how to apply these tests to a physically realized machine.

We decided to focus on an area where ARNNs Super-Turing capabilities are expected to manifest: the improved modeling of certain Chaotic systems. The prototype machines' behaviors will be compared with the behaviors of similar Digital Recurrent Neural Networks (DRNN).

4.1   Initial Digital Simulations and DRNN Learning of Chaotic Systems

Much work has been done on simulating Chaotic Systems, mostly on Digital Computers (Turing Machines). One characteristic of Chaotic Systems is that their behavior is sensitive to small perturbations of system's parameters. Because these are physical parameters, the system dynamics are defined on a continuous space rather than discrete phase space, and cannot be fully described in the Turing Model [3, p. 155]. The continuous nature (ignoring quantum effects) of the ARNN neural signals should remove this problem. We have developed digital simulations of the ARNNs learning the chaotic Hénon Map [14]. A Turing machine will not exhibit 'sensitive dependence on initial conditions'-- with the same starting point, it identically reproduces the exact same time series.

Figure 5 shows the results from some of these digital simulations. Figure 5(a) is the plot of the Hénon Map as generated by the formula in Eq. (1). All calculations are done in single precision floating point arithmetic in MATLAB to make digital effects observable. The map is also scaled so it fits in the neural network output signal range of [-1,+1]. Figure 5(b) is the map as learned by a digital neural network with 2 input-layer neurons, 2 hidden-layer neurons, and 2 output-layer neurons; and Fig. 5(c) is the map as learned by a neural network with 2 input-layer neurons, 14 hidden-layer neurons, and 2 output-layer neurons.

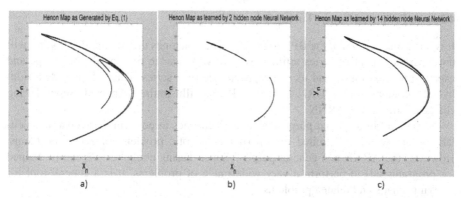

Fig. 5. Results of Digital Neural Networks learning Hénon Map. (a) is the scaled Hénon Map as presented in Eq. (1), (b) is the map as learned by a 2 hidden-neuron neural network, (c) the map as learned by a 14 hidden-neuron neural network.

$$x_{n+1} = 1.31 + 0.3y_n - x_n^2, \qquad y_{n+1} = x_n \qquad (1)$$

These networks were trained in feed-forward mode; the training input data (x_n, y_n) was generated by selecting random pairs from the basin of attraction of the scaled map with absolute values < 2; training target data pairs (x_{n+1}, y_{n+1}) were calculated by Eq. (1). Training data was scaled into the $[-1, +1]$ range of the network. After training, the feed-forward networks were tested by connecting the network outputs back to the inputs, producing inputs for step n+1 from the results of step n.

As one may expect, the larger network produced a more complete and accurate learning of the Hénon Map but was not a big improvement over results from seven hidden nodes. However, the small network did (perhaps unexpectedly) well over the part of the map that it learned.

When we tried to train the networks just on data from the curve (vs. the entire basin of attraction) both networks failed to learn the mapping. This underscores the importance of using training data that is fully representative of the domain of interest. Even though the Eq. (1) recurrently generates data which rapidly converges and stays on the curve, a neural network trained on just the curve data does not learn how to converge onto the curve and will not return to the curve if it gets off.

Autocorrelation analysis of the Fig. 5 data shows an important property not revealed by the plots. All of the data sets repeat exactly after they run long enough. Eq. (1) repeats after 9099 iterations, the 2 hidden-neuron network repeats after 1342 iterations, and the 14 hidden-neuron network repeats after 4631 iterations. We believe this is due to the limited-precision nature of the digital simulation of neural networks. This is an artifact and limitation of the Turing nature of the digital computer. This artifact would be negligible in a real-valued computation of Eq. (1) and in physical systems that it models (neglecting thermodynamic and quantum effects). Increasing the number of significant bits of the computation can increase the length of the limit cycle, but not eliminate it. Single precision makes repeat lengths manageable and represent noise at -145 dB. This is still more precise than the available analog circuitry, which represent noise at about -90 dB.

4.2 A Proposed Super-Turing Test

It is our expectation that the BPP/log* prototype machines that we are developing will not have the repeating series artifact. We are very near to training the prototype and expect it to learn chaos and its non-reproducible time series. This will provide a side-by-side comparison of DRNNs with ARNNs, illustrating expected Super-Turing characteristics of the ARNN.

One could build special-purpose analog electronics to perform these chaotic calculations that would be limited to a particular chaotic problem, or set of problems. However, the ARNN is a general-purpose Super-Turing computer – it can be trained (or programmed) to perform a very wide range of problems. It is a general tool for studying Chaos and related problems.

5   Discussion and Future Work

We reported on the design and development of computing machines based on Siegelmann's Analog Recurrent Neural Network Super-Turing Computational Model. We are physically realizing two prototype machines to measure and characterize the properties of such machines. We developed a plan to test these machines on problems which illuminate their expected Super-Turing characteristics in the Modeling of Chaotic Systems.

Future work will be to experimentally characterize the prototypes, and to design and develop larger and more capable ARNN systems. We plan to use these systems to further explore Super-Turing computation and apply the increased computer power to a variety of problems.

Acknowledgements. This work is supported by U.S. National Science Foundation Grant ECCS-1201790. We thank student Meghan Burkhart for work on the chaotic neural network simulations.

References

1. Turing, A.: On computable numbers, with an application to the Entscheidungsproblem. Proceedings of the London Mathematical Society, Series 2, 42, 230–265 (1936)
2. Turing, A.M.: Intelligent Machinery, report for National Physical Laboratory. In: Meltzer, B., Michie, D. (eds.) Machine Intelligence 7 (1969)
3. Siegelmann, H.T.: Computation Beyond the Turing Limit. Science 238(28), 632–637 (1995)
4. Siegelmann, H.T.: Neural Networks and Analog Computation: Beyond the Turing Limit, Birkhauser, Boston (December 1998)
5. Siegelmann, H.T.: Stochastic Analog Networks and Computational Complexity. Journal of Complexity 15(4), 451–475 (1999)
6. Audhkhasi, K., Osoba, O., Kosko, B.: Noise Benefits in Backpropagaton and Deep Bidirectional Pre-training. In: Procedings of the International Joint Conference on Neural Networks, Dallas Texas, USA, pp. 2254–2261 (2013)

7. Goodman, J.W., Dias, A.R., Woody, L.M., Erickson, J.: Parallel Optical Incoherent Matrix-Vector Multiplier, Technical Report L-723-1, Department of Electrical Engineering. Stanford University (February 15, 1979)

8. Bade, S.L., Hutchings, B.L.: FPGA-Based Stochastic Neural Networks – Implementation. In: IEEE FPGAs for Custom Computing Machines Workshop, Napa, CA, pp. 189–198 (1994)

9. Younger, A.S., Redd, E.: Computing by Means of Physics-Based Optical Neural Networks. In: Developments in Computational Modeling 2010. EPTCS 26, pp. 159–167 (2010) arXiv:1006.1434v1

10. Fiesler, E.: Neural Network Classification and Formalization. Computer Standards & Interfaces 16(03), 231–239 (1994)

11. Younger, A.S.: Learning in Fixed-Weight Recurrent Neural Networks, Ph.D. Dissertation. University of Utah (1996)

12. Elman, J.L.: Finding Structure in Time. Cognitive Science 14, 179–211 (1990)

13. May, R.M.: Simple mathematical models with very complicated dynamics. Nature 261(5560), 459–467 (1976)

14. Hénon, M.: A two-dimensional mapping with a strange attractor. Communications in Mathematical Physics 50(1), 69–77 (1976)

Author Index

Printed in the United States
By Bookmasters